Author's Note

This book is a *critical* biography. Inevitably it contains a certain amount of information about Elia Kazan's personal life because it often intersected, to palpable effect, with his public life. But the emphasis in my research and in my thinking was always on his professional activities.

At the outset I thought—and continue to think—that the details and the significance of Kazan's singular career (no one has ever been such a dominant directorial force simultaneously in film and theater) were in danger of being lost in recent years, blotted out in particular by the near-frenzy of argument that surrounded the presentation to him of an honorary Academy Award in 1999. In the two months of media coverage leading up to that event there was not a single article that went into any detail about the work for which he was (ostensibly) being honored. It was all politics all the time. And hugely unsophisticated politics at that. A few op-ed essayists aside, there was no attempt to re-create the quite complex circumstances in which Kazan, and many others, "named names" to the House Committee on Un-American Activities, no attempt to identify show business's Stalinists as anything other than victimized liberals, when I believed they fitted only the first part of that description; they *were* victimized, but they were never liberals, as I, a lifelong liberal, understand the term.

So, inevitably, this book also became a study of twentieth-century American politics, with particular emphasis on its left wing, with particular emphasis on the period between, roughly, 1930 and 1960, when

Kazan's directorial career rose and fell. Since I had conducted a long interview with Kazan, largely focused on his films—it was the last of such wide range that he granted—and because, subsequently, we became friends, I thought I was as well placed as anyone to undertake this task.

In pursuing this activity I was particularly fortunate that Kazan granted me access to his papers at the Wesleyan University Cinema Archives. There I read the extensive production notes he made for virtually every play and movie he directed. These jottings were raw, unmediated collections of sudden thoughts, ideas, memories and experiences he thought he might draw on for whatever work was at hand. Elia Kazan was a talkative man. In addition to *A Life,* his long and richly detailed autobiography, he gave two book-length interviews about his movie career and was ever available to the press for interviews and profiles. But these notes were different, not just because of their frankness, but because they related so directly to the practical production problems he was trying to solve.

It's odd to me that Kazan did not draw more heavily on this material for *A Life,* which he published in 1988, though I'm told he intended someday to revisit it and publish some of it in another book. I'm sorry he did not. But, of course, as a writer, I am grateful that I was the first to have extensive access to it. These notes somewhat changed the shape—and length—of this book. In particular, I think, they grant a unique insight into that most enigmatic of topics—the workings of a first-class directorial mind.

To offer just one example, the way actors act and the ways by which we judge their performances have totally changed in large part because of Kazan's work. Which means, in turn, that the ways we perceive reality, and perceive ourselves, have also changed. And that says nothing of the specific films—some of them masterpieces—Kazan left behind. Or some of the theatrical productions that continue to condition our memories of what great theater can be.

What directors do is, in its nature, ephemeral, hard to specify. But a few of them—Kazan among them—stamp their works with something of their own personalities and preoccupations. You need see only a few seconds of these works to recognize their authorship. At the least, I hope this book restores Kazan to the sort of critical and historical consciousness—and, for that matter, to the kind of *useful* controversy that figures of his significance should always stir.

That's what I mean when I insist on my description of this book as a critical biography. It offers no more insight into Elia Kazan's personal life than he himself offered in his own autobiography, on which I have relied for many details of his day-to-day existence. It is a wonderful work—one of the few truly great theatrical autobiographies. Nonetheless, I think my book supplies a historical, critical and, yes, political positioning—that he did not address in that work. If it does, then I feel I have accomplished what I set out to do.

I have emerged from this book with my affection for its subject undimmed—a fairly rare state for writers who spend a long time trying to understand a figure as complex and contradictory as Kazan. I have not attempted fully to resolve all those contradictions. I have, I hope, allowed Elia Kazan at least some of his enigmas, which is a courtesy we extend to our friends.

But time past, as the poet hints, should remain a part of time present and time future. It is why some of us write and more of us read—to make those sometimes tenuous links that allow us to believe that our thoughts and the world we inhabit are not arrived at entirely by accident. I hope I have supplied at least some of that logic to this life.

I wish to thank all the people whose time, patience and good nature made this book possible. First among them, of course, is Elia Kazan, whose interview with me and whose notebooks are such an important source for this book. At the Wesleyan archive my friend Jeanine Basinger was, as always, the most gracious and delightful of hosts, and her associates, Leith Johnson, Joan Miller and Lea Carlson, were unfailingly helpful and kind. I interviewed many of Elia Kazan's friends, family and associates and was always given more help and information than I asked for. I herewith thank all of them: Dede Allen, Jeanine Basinger, Warren Beatty, Patricia Bosworth, Corinne Chateau, Frances Fisher, Hal Holbrook, Anne Jackson, Frances Kazan, Katherine Kazan, Nicholas Kazan, Arthur Laurents,

Cathleen Leslie, Norman Lloyd, Karl Malden, Judy (Kazan) Morris, Austin Pendleton, Arthur Penn, Nick Proferes, Carol Rossen, Eva Marie Saint, Budd Schulberg, Martin Scorsese, Paul Sylbert, Eli Wallach, Haskell Wexler, Michael Wilson. Three scholars—Leo Braudy, Ronald Radosh and Stephen Schwartz—shared with me research material they had gathered for projects of their own, and I'm grateful for their generosity. Two researchers, Daniella Romano and Jode Ryskiewicz, combed the New York Public Library's Performing Arts Collection and the Academy of Motion Picture Arts and Sciences' Margaret Herrick Library, turning up literally hundreds of reviews of Kazan's work as well as dozens of articles about him. Their work was invaluable to this book, and I'm sure they would like me to thank, as well, the librarians who aided them.

Also, I wish to thank my agents. Don Congdon believed in this book perhaps before I did and oversaw the contract for it. His associate, Susan Ramer, has patiently stayed with it, and me, through a much longer period of writing than any of us anticipated. The same is true of Gail Winston, my editor at HarperCollins, whose forbearance has been as exemplary as her editorial skill. She has made this a better book than it would otherwise have been. Finally, as always, I thank Barbara Isenberg for her loving patience with the author and his sometimes obsessive, always distracting work.

I am, of course, entirely responsible for any errors of commission and omission contained in this volume.

Richard Schickel

Contents

We All Make Mistakes

On the evening of January 7, 1999, most of the thirty-nine-member Board of Governors of the Academy of Motion Picture Arts and Sciences assembled at the academy's headquarters on Wilshire Boulevard in Beverly Hills. Their task was to choose the recipients for the various honorary awards to be bestowed at its annual Oscar ceremonies, scheduled that year for Sunday, March 21.

In recent years honorary Oscars had tended to go to distinguished foreign filmmakers—Akira Kurosawa, Federico Fellini, Satyajit Ray, Michelangelo Antonioni—auteurs not only of great bodies of work, but authors, as well, of the surge of American interest in foreign films that began in the 1950s. It was hard to think of an internationally celebrated director the academy had, by now, failed to honor. The same could be said for older American directors and stars, products and creators of the so-called Classic Age of the American cinema (the 1930s and '40s).

Karl Malden, however, thought there was one notable omission among the Americans. That was the friend of his youth, as well as the director of some of his own best performances: Elia Kazan, then eighty-nine years old. Malden, who was himself eighty-five at the time, was an academy elder statesman. Winner of the 1951 supporting actor Oscar (for his performance in Kazan's *A Streetcar Named Desire*), he was also one of its former presidents—still an active, respected figure on its governing board, not given to radical statements or quixotic gestures.

He expected to encounter difficulties making his case for Kazan. For one thing, the honorary Oscar had also become something of a consolation prize for American moviemakers, awarded to people like Cary Grant, Alfred Hitchcock and Howard Hawks, who, despite great bodies of work, had somehow not won the prize for a specific film. Kazan, however, had two such Oscars—for directing *Gentleman's Agreement* (1947) and *On the Waterfront* (1954)—and that might weigh against him.

Infinitely more important was the fact that in 1952 Kazan had "named names" to the notorious House Committee on Un-American Activities (hereinafter referred to by the common, if slightly inaccurate, acronym HUAC) during the course of its intermittent investigations (between 1947 and 1958) of alleged Communist infiltration in the entertainment industry. Kazan had not been alone in naming past party associates; close to one-third of the show folks called before the committee had done the same. Nor had he been a particularly voluble witness. He had joined the fractious, influential Group Theatre in 1932 and in 1935 joined The Group's Communist "unit," which he left (in considerable disgust) some nineteen months later. In his account, the party had ordered its members to "take over" The Group Theatre, setting a new, more narrowly leftist political agenda for it. This Kazan, fiercely loyal to an institution that had offered him his first artistic home, refused to do.

When he testified before HUAC, he named eight Group Theatre members who were also Communists, one of whom was dead, and two of whom had long since left the party. He also named two open members of the party; a non-Group actor, also deceased, a stagestruck Group hanger-on, and four individuals who had been noncreative members of another organization, the League of Workers Theatre, where Kazan had taught and directed.

The transcript of his testimony shows him refusing to speculate about the political beliefs of other leftists he had known in those years. He spoke only of what he knew from direct personal experience. He could not, and did not, speak of their present political beliefs. It appears to me certain that the names of all members of the Group's Communist "unit" were known to the committee, though it may be that Kazan was the first to openly identify one or two of them. Only one of them, however, a man who had become a television executive, was interesting enough for the committee to subpoena. Another man, still an actor, was immediately blacklisted and prevented from pursuing his modest career as a movie character player.

The largest harm Kazan did was to himself. More than any of the other "friendly" HUAC witnesses, he became a symbol of collaboration with the enemies of, as it were, liberal belief. In part that was because he truculently defended his actions in a paid advertisement in the *New York Times,* outraging what remained of the Communist left and its allies. Though he later demonstrated considerable remorse over his actions, he had never seemed sufficiently contrite to his enemies. You had to ferret his regrets out of a book-length interview he had granted the French critic Michel Ciment in 1974 and out of his 1988 autobiography.

A large part of the condemnation of Kazan derived from the widely held belief that he had been in the most secure position to defy the committee. In the forties and fifties he was unquestionably the most important director in the American theater as well as the most significant of the younger movie directors. It was thought—and people have continued to believe—that Kazan might have gone on working untrammeled in the theater (where the blacklist had less influence) while awaiting its inevitable demise in the movies. So his choice became an ineradicable black mark against him, even though others who testified as he did were, if not entirely forgiven, then reaccepted, without undue rancor, within the show business community.

Kazan, too, went on working. He was too gifted not to, and, besides, in the 1950s, with the cold war at its height, there were many who accepted his testimony as an intelligible and realistic action. It was only later, beginning in the 1960s, with its vast sea change in American political attitudes—which included ending the Hollywood blacklist—that his testimony began to be more generally abhorred.

There is no doubt that his political position cost him some honors that normally accrue to men and women of his accomplishment in their later years. He had, to be sure, received, without incident, one of the Kennedy Center Honors in 1983. But as early as 1989 Malden had proposed him for the American Film Institute's Life Achievement Award, which was refused him after an acrimonious boardroom debate, some details of which eventually leaked to the press. Other awards from the San Francisco Film Festival and the Los Angeles Film Critics had also been hotly discussed and denied.

So Malden's guess that he had his work cut out for him when he entered the academy's boardroom was not unreasonable. In his presentation Malden admitted what everyone knew, that he was asking them to "honor a friend—a dear friend," who, he observed, had been more frequently honored abroad than in the United States. He also stressed "how many people he had made stars of, from nothing. How many people he had found." To that thought he added another: "I've sat on this board for over nine years and I can't tell you how many times we have heard, we are not interested, we have nothing to do with politics, only with art. And that's why I'm telling you, if you're picking on art, you couldn't have picked a better person." He told me later, "I think that's what sold it."

Something surely did. By all accounts, his proposal encountered no opposition, even though the governors included many individuals who continued to deplore Kazan's testimony. The motion to award an honorary Academy Award to Elia Kazan was seconded by several board members and passed unanimously.

An element of calculation may be imputed to the board. Kazan was by now a very old man—he would turn ninety the following September—and he had been ill. They may have thought that age and infirmity would engender a certain sympathy for the man, as it had for others on similar occasions. They may also have reasoned that his apostasy had, after all, occurred a very long time ago; forty-seven years had passed since his testimony and no one he named was still alive. In fact, of show business's most famous Communist martyrs, the Hollywood Ten, only two were still living—and one of them, Edward Dmytryk, had reappeared before the committee in 1951, this time as a friendly witness, earning him calumny from the left comparable to that visited on Kazan.

The passing years had taken their toll on other, less prominent Communists and former Communists as well. They were never many—HUAC once listed 222 Hollywood Communists, a cumulative total, since not all of them were party members at the same moment. We may suppose that a similar number of non-Communists—one estimate puts it at 250 individuals—also suffered some form of blacklisting in movies, radio and television because they had signed a petition on behalf of some "radical" cause or given a few dollars to some politically dubious organization. But many of them had died or repented their former beliefs or had simply fallen silent about battles long past.

Moreover, Communism itself had collapsed in the Soviet Union and there was virtually no one remaining on the left who had anything good to say about it. There was even an emerging agreement that some of its former martyrs—Alger Hiss, for example, or Julius Rosenberg—were, in fact, guilty as charged of espionage against the United States. What one tended to encounter, among the old leftists, was a sort of nostalgia for the idealism of their youth—"The Romance of American Communism," as Vivian Gornick had called it in the title of her excellent book on the subject. This vision was shared by members of the New Left, who idealized the sacrifices their elders had made to a set of beliefs, the totalitarian component of which was unclear to them.

This obvious context was almost entirely missing from the Kazan controversy. Its terms were almost entirely set by the aged remnants of Stalinism, by their younger allies from the New Left and by good-hearted, liberal-minded show folks who had no understanding of the left-sectarian battles that had long ago shaped the politics of their trade. They simply identified with the Stalinists as innocent liberals not unlike themselves and had neither the experience nor the capacity to recognize, in the campaign that developed against Kazan, a typical Stalinist tactic—seize the high, easy-to-understand moral ground, then try to crush nuanced opposition to that position through simplifying sloganeering.

Malden was himself unprepared for this controversy. He had thought the academy's governors might receive a few angry phone calls from the remaining members of the old left. He was prepared, as well, to hear from some of their younger allies. No one expected the perfect storm of protest that soon broke around them.

———————

Normally, my own position about the Academy Awards is benignly cynical. Oscars only rarely go to the movie I think is the year's best, and the acting awards typically go to the showiest performances, not the most subtle ones. But that's all right with me. I'm comfortable with the patient workings of history, which ultimately, inevitably discounts the frenzied hype, the obsessive buzz, that surrounds the Academy Awards. Eventually the great movies conquer. For example, we go on delightedly watching *Double Indemnity*; we pay not the slightest heed to *Going My Way*, which beat it out for the 1944 Oscar. Who, nowadays, has even seen such past winners as *Cimarron* or *Cavalcade*?

But the Kazan controversy was different for me—because I was personally invested in him. I had admired his work since childhood, when his first film, *A Tree Grows in Brooklyn*, in 1945, made a curiously indelible impression on me. Later, his movies and theatrical productions spoke to me and many of my generation with singular vividness. Emerging into a postwar world in which the old, bold political verities seemed largely irrelevant, the issues that riveted us were often private discontents, difficult to articulate in the bland fifties, but somehow crystallized for us by his productions, his actors.

The publication of his autobiography in 1988, which is one of the few truly great accounts of a show business life—brutally frank, self-lacerating, hypnotically readable—renewed my interest in him, and in the course of making a television program about him I came to like Kazan enormously—for, among other reasons, his energy, his passionately engaged intelligence, the seductively unpretentious way he talked about his life and work.

So when I heard about the academy's decision, I called Gilbert Cates, producer of the awards broadcast, and volunteered to produce the film tribute that would precede the presentation of Kazan's Oscar. We were old friends, and since I had done several similar chores for him on earlier Oscar telecasts, he accepted my offer.

To be honest, Kazan's HUAC testimony did not loom large in my mind at that moment, because no organized opposition to his award had yet developed. But the silence did not last long. Jeff Young, author of a long-delayed book of interviews with Kazan, due to be published that very spring, noted wryly that at least the press had a worthwhile Oscar story for a change, something more meaningful to chew on than what dresses the actresses attending the ceremony would be wearing. Quite quickly, however, wryness disappeared from the discussion as the media rode the Kazan story both obsessively and with their customary carelessness about historical nuance.

This became clear less than a week after the academy announced Kazan's award. In a January 13 story, Bernard Weinraub, the *New York Times* movie reporter, stressed, in his lead, that it was "in some ways, a direct rebuke to the American Film Institute, which has gone out of its way to ignore Mr. Kazan in its yearly awards." This, perhaps, imputed a false intentionality to the governors' actions; one doubts that the AFI's rejection of Kazan weighed heavily with them. Otherwise the story reported that up to then public response to the academy's action had been muted.

The *Los Angeles Times*'s story, by Patrick Goldstein, ran under a rather bland and, as it turned out, entirely erroneous headline ("Film Director Elia Kazan to Receive Oscar, Forgiveness"), but it reported the first rumblings of discontent. In it Kazan was blandly quoted as saying that "above all" he intended to share the award with all who had worked with him on his films; "it's their achievement as well as mine." On the other hand, Abraham Polonsky, the blacklisted writer and director, was colorful in his contempt. He told Goldstein: "I don't like Kazan, but I try not to confuse my moral hatreds with my aesthetic hatreds. He made a lot of good pictures, so you could say he deserves an award for his work—I just wouldn't want to give it to him. He was a creep. I wouldn't want to be wrecked on a desert island with him because if he was hungry, he would eat me alive."

This was a fair sample of the carelessly heated rhetoric that would issue from Polonsky over the next few weeks, as he (along with another leftist screenwriter-producer, Burt Gordon, whose credits were more modest, if more extensive) assumed *de facto* leadership of the anti-Kazan campaign. This would shortly take the form of asking the audience in the Dorothy Chandler Pavilion not to accord Kazan the customary standing ovation—or for that matter applause—when the honorary Oscar was bestowed on him.

Gordon told Weinraub, in a story that ran February 23: "We do not wish to disrupt the awards ceremony, which is important for the industry and for many of our fellow workers. But we do ask for some minimal evidence of disapproval for the academy's insensitive and unconscionable act. Do not stand and applaud Mr. Kazan. Sit on your hands. Let audiences around the world see that there are some in Hollywood, some Americans who do not support blacklisting, who do not support informers."

Gordon (and according to Weinraub, "several other screenwriters") offered Kazan this out: If he would apologize for naming names it would, in Weinraub's phrase, "defuse much of the opposition to him." But what Kazan had done was not something he could make right with an apology. It was not a social gaffe—a tasteless joke that had fallen flat, for example—for which you could say "Sorry" and move on. He had always said that his was a principled political act and that he had not abandoned those principles.

Kazan's opponents assumed—and made others assume—that his testimony had been purely opportunistic, therefore something he could beg forgiveness for—which they might, in turn, magnanimously grant. But in this same article, Kazan's longtime attorney, Floria V. Lasky, was heard to snort: "Apologize? Recant? That's a good Stalinist word." She instead called on them to apologize for supporting brutish Stalinist Russia.

The lines were now narrowly drawn and the story's implicitly agreed upon meta-narrative, was as follows: For unexplained, but probably base, reasons Kazan had behaved badly in 1952; nevertheless, he had previously made, and would go on to make, excellent movies. Therefore, in 1999, one was confronted with this choice: implacable lack of forgiveness for a political sin or forgiveness based on the notion that artistic accomplishment trumped politics. The idea that Kazan might have had legitimate reasons for testifying as he did entered this discussion only occasionally and without discernible impact.

Kazan himself was no longer able to re-create the complex historical circumstances that had influenced his decision. His physical and mental condition was accurately described, by a family member, as "alternately vigorous and frail." What one observed about him was that he was unable to sustain a coherent conversation on any topic.

He would offer a sentence or two, then veer off on some new subject. Still, he warmly welcomed friends, clinging to them with fierce hugs and smiling gratitude when they dropped by his New York brownstone to say hello.

It was clear that where once his general refusal to discuss his testimony, had been based on conscious acknowledgment that the discussion was feckless, that everyone's positions were fixed and therefore inarguable, the element of infirmity had now entered the picture. So he contented himself with bland expressions of gratitude. "I feel very happy about this," he said to Weinraub. "I'm flattered to death. I'm pleased with it. What more can I say?"

Typically, there was no discussion of his sending a surrogate to pick up his Oscar. He had never hidden from the consequences of his act. He would not, in public, appear to bend to opinion that ran against him. He would put on a stoic's mask (or, perhaps more appropriate to his case, the famously enigmatic "Anatolian smile"). He was, after all, Greek by birth; he had imbibed fatalism with his mother's milk.

In late February and early March, the papers were full of largely unilluminating discussion of the academy's decision and simplistic moralizing about Kazan's behavior. Early on, actors Allen Garfield and Robin Bartlett contributed pieces to "Counterpunch," a sort of weekly op-ed section of the *Los Angeles Times* calendar section, which reports show business doings. Garfield, claiming to "personally love the man, even idolize him," and saying that he "would be there in a heartbeat for him as an actor," nevertheless went into Uriah Heep mode: "There is no honor—there can never *be* an honor—much less an honorary Oscar, for one who sells the lives and futures of his fellow man in order to advance his own special interests and ambitions . . ." Bartlett was less self-serving in her condemnation, but felt deeply deprived as an artist by the work blacklisted creators were prevented from doing. This had long been a common comment on blacklisting, though what loss to film history the silencing of John Howard Lawson or Lester Cole entailed has never been adequately explained. "Two of them were talented," Billy Wilder had famously wisecracked about the Hollywood Ten, "the rest were just unfriendly."

These little essays elicited a hot letters-column discussion, with a surprising number of writers citing Stalinist crimes as a justification for naming names or noting that if he had blown the whistle on a Nazi conspiracy Kazan might now be regarded as a hero. The same was true of letters responding to Weinraub's reporting in the *New York Times*. Debate at this unrewarding level would persist until the Oscar show. Indeed, in its February 5 issue, *Entertainment Weekly* published a rather alarming quotation from Abe Polonsky. "I'll be watching, hoping someone shoots him. It would no doubt be a thrill in an otherwise dull evening."

Everyone understood that Polonsky had been one of the blacklist's more grievously afflicted victims. He had written a solid, Oscar-nominated screenplay for Robert Rossen's *Body and Soul* in 1947 and a year later wrote and directed *Force of Evil,* a good film noir, then had been silenced by the blacklist (though he kept writing under pseudonyms) for more than two decades. He never really reestablished the career many thought he deserved.

But still . . . assassination? It was either a badly failed joke or evidence of octogenarian dottiness (he was eighty-nine, the same age as Kazan).

As odd, in a different way, was Rod Steiger's response. He had, of course, given one of his most memorable performances for Kazan in *On the Waterfront,* but he had not been particularly voluble about his director. Now, suddenly, he was everywhere, violently criticizing Kazan. Typically, he said to *Time* magazine's Jeff Resner: "If a person's a good director, he's almost the father of a family and must know how to handle his children. He had done wonderful work and we all idolized him, and then found out that in a way he had destroyed the lives of his children. He was my father and he double-crossed my family. We were shattered. One person died of a heart attack. There were suicides. Time does not forgive a crime. The crime still exists. There is no forgiveness. He was our father and he fucked us."

This remarkable statement deserves a bit of parsing. The person who died of a heart attack, J. Edward Bromberg, was named by

Kazan, but posthumously. The suicide, Philip Loeb, was not mentioned by Kazan. More curious is the implication that Steiger and the rest of the *Waterfront* cast had been hired not knowing of Kazan's testimony, then, while making the film, had learned of his betrayal. But Kazan's widely reported HUAC testimony occurred on April 10, 1952. Shooting on *Waterfront* did not begin until the early fall of 1953, with Brando almost absenting himself from the production precisely because of Kazan's testimony. In other words, if Steiger and the rest of the cast had been "fucked" by Kazan, the deed had occurred almost a year and a half before they went to work on the picture—plenty of time to make a principled decision not to do so if one so chose.

What can one say? Only, perhaps, that Steiger was an actor. And actors find showy scenes—even if they are self-invented—difficult to resist. That proved to be the case with Marlon Brando. One day in early March, he got in touch with me and I found myself engaged in a rambling, sometimes humorous, sometimes steely, conversation. He began disarmingly, with praise for Kazan as "the best director of actors" he had ever encountered. But he soon followed with the assertion that he was going to refuse permission to use clips from the movies he had made with Kazan on the Oscar show.

This is something of a gray area. Actors have an absolute right of clip refusal in films made after 1960. A few—and I had heard that Brando was one of them—had that right written into their contracts on pre-sixties movies. I argued with him, pointing out that his collaboration with Kazan on three movies was an undeniable part of film history. What was the point of refusing to acknowledge that fact at this late date?

Brando, however, remained adamant and our talk naturally troubled me. There was no way to make a tribute to Kazan without using his greatest actor in scenes from two of the best movies either had ever made (*A Streetcar Named Desire* and *On the Waterfront*). I reported this conversation to Cates and was advised that the academy would handle negotiations for the clips with the studios at a level well beyond my own. In the end, for whatever reasons, permission to use the clips was granted and, for better or worse, my little film eventually went on the air as I had edited it.

Meantime, the campaign to deny Kazan a standing ovation proceeded apace. In late February, at the Writers Guild Awards banquet, people were soliciting funds for an anti-Kazan ad that eventually ran in *Daily Variety* a few days before the Academy Awards broadcast. On that occasion some academy governors, who were also WGA members, rued their action to the *Variety* gossip columnist, Army Archerd.

Even so, some Kazan defenders made their voices heard. On February 28, Arthur Schlesinger, Jr., defended Kazan in a *New York Times* op-ed piece entitled "Hollywood Hypocrisy." Schlesinger had been one of the founders of Americans for Democratic Action, an attempt in the 1950s to create a sort of third force between Stalinism and the know-nothing right, into whose clumsy hands anti-Communism had fallen. His contempt for HUAC was as potent as ever. He termed its Hollywood investigation "among the most indefensible, scandalous and cruel episodes in the entire history of legislative investigations." Collaboration with these "clowns" had, he said, "its elements of disgust and shame," which, as he wrote, Kazan had acknowledged.

But he raised the unexceptionable point that informing is not always considered a bad thing. He cited, as instances, those who might, at different times, have informed on the German-American Bund, the Ku Klux Klan, Mafia thugs or the Nixon White House during Watergate. Kazan's "true offense in the minds of the Hollywood protesters is *that he informed on the Communist Party* [italics his]."

He added: "Mr. Kazan's critics are those—or latter-day admirers of those—who continued to defend Stalin after the Moscow trials, after the pact with Hitler, through the age of the Gulag. One wonders at their presumption in condemning others for recognizing the horrors of Stalinism—horrors that the entire world, including Russia, acknowledge today." He insisted that informing on the Communist Party was neither more nor less heinous than collaborating with it.

Schlesinger here elucidated what was, I believe, the central disconnect of this ugly conflict. On the one hand, virtually the entire political continuum, from radical left to radical right, now vied with one another to heap contempt on the failed Soviet "experiment." On the other, Stalin's American apologists were treated as if they were entirely innocent victims—mere "liberals in a hurry" (to borrow an old phrase), mindlessly harassed by a terror scarcely less Draconian than that unleashed by Stalin himself.

In the historical literature of the left an argument is sometimes made that there was, in the 1930s, no alternative other than Communist Party membership for decent-minded American radicals. No other party or program offered them an agenda suitable to their passion for economic, racial and political justice in a country they judged to be in a prerevolutionary condition. But that was untrue. Communism had ever been a distinctly minority party in the United States, as opposed to Europe and elsewhere. And in the America of the 1930s other left wing alternatives—democratic socialism or the New Deal, for that matter—attracted far greater support.

Public protests against the Gulag had been mounted as early as 1931. After that came the events Schlesinger cited, as well as the post-Stalinist crushing of revolts in Hungary (1956) and Czechoslovakia (1968). There had been, moreover, no lack of testimony from former Communists about "The God That Failed"—to borrow the title of a famous book by former Communists (among them Richard Wright, André Gide, Arthur Koestler and Stephen Spender), in which they laid out the terms of their disenchantment. This says nothing about the almost sainted George Orwell, whose opposition to Stalinism was as powerful as his commitment to democratic socialism, and was the basis for his best-selling books *Animal Farm* and *1984*, embraced by readers of every political stripe.

All these excoriations of Stalin's crimes were public acts; it was impossible to ignore them. Yet America's radical left, even when it belatedly admitted Stalin's crimes, clung to its reverence for the martyrs to "McCarthyism" (though the Wisconsin senator, whose name will always be associated with the hysterical effort to uproot "subversives," never said a word about Communism in show business). They became the great victims of reaction, heroes of free speech whose tongues (and pens) had been cruelly silenced.

The screenwriters, actors and directors, persecuted in the late forties and early fifties by HUAC, held the central position in this peculiar pantheon. It occurred to few that in supporting Communism, they were supporting a doctrine that was, in all other respects,

noxious. It seemed odd to me that the Hollywood Ten and the rest
of showbiz Communism had not only generally escaped criticism,
but were now being honored on every hand—at public forums, in
television documentaries. The Writers Guild was ostentatiously
restoring their names to films they had worked on anonymously or
under pseudonyms when they were blacklisted. There is even a garden honoring the Hollywood Ten on the University of Southern California campus.

To me, this celebratory logic simply did not track. The failure of
the Communist left to own up to Stalin's crimes against humanity in
a timely fashion was—let's put this as mildly as possible—illiberal
behavior. The failure of much of the American left to acknowledge
this fact is illiberal behavior. And the failure of most of the American
press to allude to it during the course of the Kazan controversy is
also, in an admittedly more minor way, illiberal behavior—or, at any
rate, historically careless behavior.

The day after Schlesinger's article appeared, *Time* published a
defense of Kazan that I wrote. I argued pretty much what I have argued here: that Kazan's decision to testify was, in the context of its
cold war moment, not quite as black and white as it now seemed to
many, that it was largely symbolic, that his best films and plays had a
significant impact on what would henceforth be deemed acceptable
subject matter in both mediums.

Beyond that, I raised a point I had not seen elsewhere; it had to do
with loyalty and the passage of time. In the current, deliberately mud-
dled argument, Kazan's action was presented as if he had betrayed current associates. The Communists liked to impose retroactive loyalty on
apostates. Several among the Hollywood Nineteen—later reduced to
the Hollywood Ten—were no longer, at the time they were subpoe-
naed, party members, but were induced to stand with those who were
still in the party, to their ultimate sorrow.

This same demand had been implicitly applied to Kazan, despite
the fact that, when he testified, seventeen years had passed since he
had been a party member. How, I asked, could anyone expect people like Kazan to "assert blind, retrospective loyalty to a cause they
had abandoned for good principled reasons. By that time [1952]
Kazan, like many others, had acquired new, better and more press-

ing obligations—to the hard-learned truth about a secretive party controlled on virtually a day-to-day basis by Moscow, to the art that defined him more accurately than any politics" and, above all, to new relationships. Changing times quite legitimately beget changing friends, changing loyalties, changing principles. That, I was trying to say, is the way people who are not ideologues live their lives.

The response to this piece was generally predictable. Kazan's wife, Frances, called to say that she had returned home from some errands to find her husband sitting with *Time* opened to my article, in a state close to tears. A few minutes later, she placed a second call, putting Kazan on the phone for a few words of thanks. What was more interesting to me was a letter to *Time*'s editor from a man claiming that his father, a cameraman, had been ruined by Kazan, though, in fact, Kazan had not named him. Later, a woman I know claimed similar personal hurt. Her father, she insisted, had been one of those fingered by Kazan. But, again, that was not the case. I began to sense the celebrity system doing its weird work. It seemed that it was not enough to have been called a Communist by some virtually anonymous informant. If you were going to be named, it was apparently better to have been named by the most famous of the friendly witnesses.

Of course, nothing I or anyone wrote changed any minds. But still people went on trying. For instance, on March 12, in his "At the Movies" column in the *New York Times*, Weinraub ran an interview with Warren Beatty about Kazan. For some years the actor had been devoting as much of his time to liberal politics as he had to moviemaking, and one might have thought he would have taken a negative position about him. But Kazan had given him his first starring role in 1961, and Beatty felt that Kazan had been his most important early mentor: "I can only say he is a person for whom I have tremendous respect and affection and whose work in movies speaks for itself. He was my first teacher. I learned more about movies from Kazan than anyone else. . . . I love the guy."

Beatty took this sensible view of Kazan's behavior: "I don't want to be reductive about his politics," he said. "Although you and I might feel he made a mistake, neither you nor I was around in that period. And although you and I might think we would not have made that mistake, we didn't have to make that choice. We all make mistakes. Some of them are mistakes everyone knows about. Some of them aren't."

Beatty participated in a pre-Oscar Writers Guild ceremony, reading the names of blacklisted screenwriters now being restored to movies from which they had once been elided. But after the Oscars he also hosted a dinner party for Kazan and a number of his old friends and colleagues. One could say he qualified for F. Scott Fitzgerald's test of a good mind—the ability to simultaneously hold contradictory ideas.

Another historian, Allen Weinstein, added an interesting point to the debate in the *Los Angeles Times* op-ed page five days before the Academy Awards telecast. He had gone back to Kazan's *A Life*, to see if, perhaps, he might already have made the apology he was being called on to make and found this passage: "I thought what a terrible thing I had done; not the political aspect of it, because maybe that was correct; but it didn't matter now, correct or not; all that mattered was the human side of the thing; . . . I felt no political cause was worth hurting any other human for. What good deeds were stimulated by what I'd done? What villains exposed? How is the world better for what I did? It had just been a game of power and influence, and I'd been taken in and twisted from my true self."

To this Weinstein added this gloss: "What more do those who plan to picket or not applaud wish? And do they demand similar accountability from those who, in an earlier day, served for a time the Stalinist 'god that failed'? From neither side would formal apologies at this point seem useful."

———

There the debate pretty much rested. Kazan and his third wife, Frances—a pretty blonde Englishwoman whom he had married in 1982—arrived in Los Angeles in the middle of the week prior to the Oscar telecast. They were later joined by his youngest daughter, Kate. The Kazans stayed at the home of his son Nicholas, a widely respected screenwriter.

By this time it had been decided that his award would be presented jointly by Martin Scorsese, the director, and Robert De Niro, the actor, who had worked for Kazan in his last film, the unfortunate adaptation of F. Scott Fitzgerald's *The Last Tycoon*. They were a shrewd choice—a director in the psychologically intense Kazan tradition, an actor who worked in the Stanislavskian manner Kazan had championed. Scorsese, in particular, had long been a voluble admirer of Kazan's work; in a conversation with me he once called Kazan "the head of the family"—meaning the New York filmmaking family. His presence, together with De Niro's, would remind people, if anything could, not of Kazan's past politics, but of his past work and its formative influence on one of American filmmaking's best—most realistic—strains.

On the morning of March 19 the long promised ad, urging academy members not to stand and applaud Kazan when he received his award, appeared in *Daily Variety*. The text made the usual erroneous assertions that Kazan had acted to "further his own career" and had betrayed "close friends." Though several hundred people signed it, it was notably lacking in star names.

That morning, I journeyed to the Dorothy Chandler Pavilion, in the Music Center complex in downtown Los Angeles, for a rehearsal of Kazan's portion of the program. Scorsese and De Niro would be represented by stand-ins, but Kazan was present, though not in the greenroom where I expected to find him. Instead, he was in the wings, watching the dancers and other presenter stand-ins (stars rarely appear for early rehearsals of the show) going through their paces.

He was beaming happily. It had been years since he had been backstage at a theatrical presentation, and he was reveling in the bustle and stir, back in an element he had obviously missed. We exchanged greetings, we watched my film and I departed. That night, Karl Malden hosted a small dinner party at the Peninsula Hotel for Kazan, his family and a few friends. The mood was distinctly upbeat and nostalgic. Kazan and Malden reminisced about their days together in the theater sixty years earlier. The next day I returned to the Dorothy Chandler, where Scorsese rehearsed without Kazan or De Niro. The introduction I had written for him contained an awkward phrase that he stumbled over. I offered to change it. He said he would nail it. I knew he would not and, sure enough, he muffed it again on the broadcast—and no matter.

By now the Oscar broadcast had taken on—as it always does—a life of its own. Like all live awards shows, it is something of a dinosaur. They are the last real-time nonsports broadcasts on television, and this big, awkward but entirely implacable machine was rumbling toward its airtime. Whatever protest took place in the Dorothy Chandler Pavilion on Sunday night would simply be absorbed—and minimized—as the program ground forward.

I detected, among academy functionaries, only a little more tension than usual. They feared, I thought, some visible or audible outburst that Cates's sure-to-be-discreet cameras could not hide. Basically, however, they knew the show would go on as usual—too long, too vulgar in this or that response of this or that award winner, yet also possibly offering a surprisingly human, even touching, moment or two. It would, of course, be a ratings triumph.

I, naturally, was more than usually tense on the day of the broadcast—concerned about my friend, concerned about the reception of my tribute film. On the other hand, I had by this time decided that this story was not going to end, for me, with this broadcast. I had decided to write a book—this book—about Kazan, something that, after all the braying and posturing of recent weeks, would restore complexity to the life and work of one of the most complicated men I have ever known, something that would restore the best of his work to some sort of living consciousness—for its own sake, of course, but also as significant cultural signposts erected at the very center of their times.

Kazan's best films, I firmly believe, are far more effective criticism (and much more enjoyable products) than any works that emanated from the more ideologically rigid Communist left, which, culturally speaking, remained irrelevant to the American "masses." There are moments in Kazan's work that are, quite simply, touchstones of the modern conscience, constantly quoted, referred to, treasured by civilized people.

Thinking in this way about Kazan, I frankly began to discern in his struggles, in his failures and in his successes, something exemplary about our culture and our country in the century he inhabited, in a small corner of which he was, for a time, a dominant figure. Read his nature and his accomplishments with some degree of sensitivity, I felt, and you might read more about America and its halting, anguished, still incomplete, progress toward maturity than you might imagine it possible to do.

Yes, he had stood at the "bloody crossroad" where, in Lionel Trilling's memorable phrase, art and politics meet. But there was more to this life than that crucial moment, though that's what it was reduced to in 1999—as if it were the subject of a bad play or novel. That's the way ideologues of both the left and the right view history—simplifying it, rendering its leading performers one-dimensional, less than fully human. I hoped to do better than that.

Elia Kazan

1

The Anatolian Smile

He wanted to be something—somebody—long before he knew what, exactly, he wanted to be. In that sense, Elia Kazan's story is a typical immigrant's story. There is something fierce and needy about this young man that chimes with the tales of thousands upon thousands of American newcomers in the first decades of the twentieth century. For these young strangers, living, often precariously, in families where English was forever the second language, the simple desire to make something of themselves—they didn't much care what, as long as it entailed rising out of a class treated contemptuously by America's ruling WASPs—was their ruling passion.

But making something of yourself implies a remaking of that self—either by aping the manner, dress, speech, attitudes of the elite or by becoming a determined rebel, if not a full-scale revolutionary. The annals of the radical left (and, more recently, the radical right) are rich in figures from bourgeois families (as Kazan's briefly was) who became cultural and political subversives (as Kazan did, in his early years).

He could not, however, long maintain the dedicated political or cultural radical's vow of poverty. The pull of his family's values and ambitions was too strong. They had come to America for the simplest reasons—to escape tyranny in their native land (they were Anatolian Greeks, ruled for centuries by Turks)—and to make good, which they defined simply as making as much money as possible as quickly as possible. Kazan might insist that he remained a lifelong "man of the left."

But he also remained his father's son and his uncle's nephew, inheriting their Depression-dashed dreams of riches.

So there was always in Elia Kazan a conflict between his ideals and his ambitions. It was a conflict he tried to ameliorate—though he never succeeded in fully settling it—by burying a profound anger under an air of eager accommodation, of ostensible good nature. It was a conflict that shaped the potent realism of his plays and movies, imparting to them a passion, a psychological intensity, particularly in the performances of his actors, that was largely without precedent in the theatrical arts, and hugely influential on their later history.

Kazan's autobiography, *A Life,* published in 1988, when he was seventy-nine years old, begins with a reflection on his seemingly perpetual outrage, and his lifelong need to cover it with his "Anatolian smile," an expression, much remarked upon by Greeks of his and previous generations, betokening a sort of noncommittal agreeability, at once distant and obliging—but masking one's deepest feelings. Looking back Kazan wrote simply, "I used to spend most of my time straining to be a nice guy so people would like me."

The Anatolian smile may be a sort of racial tic, but after his arrival in the United States (at age four), it became a major tool of survival. His father, George—full name Kazanjioglou—was an old-world *paterfamilias*, demanding absolute obedience to his will in matters both great and small. One of George's brothers, whose story his nephew would eventually tell with candor, sympathy and irony in *America, America,* as well as in two novels, had preceded them and set up a carpet business, in which George joined him. By the 1920s, that business was prospering—though "Uncle Joe" had left it—and George and his family had moved to a fine suburban house. His father expected Elia and his brother to join him in the business—no questions asked or, for that matter, permitted.

But Kazan's mother, Athena, strong-minded and stubborn, had other ideas for him. She entered into a "conspiracy" (Kazan's word) with one of his high school teachers in New Rochelle to see if her bright lad could gain admission to a good college. They settled on

Williams College, for no other reason, so far as Kazan could remember, except that its WASPy name appealed to them. He enthusiastically joined the conspiracy, working after school and on summer vacation to earn money for his tuition. When his father was informed of Elia's college acceptance, he struck his wife so hard that she was knocked to the floor. Shortly thereafter, they began sleeping in separate bedrooms.

The old man was—and remained—a frightening figure to Kazan. Many years later, Kazan's son Nicholas would recall that the only man he had ever seen his father fear was George Kazan, which Kazan himself admitted in his book. By the time Nick could observe the two men together his grandfather was a shrunken, silent figure, but still capable of making his famous son tremble.

It is worth observing that such characters, confident and bullying (until, generally, they got their comeuppance), became staples in all Kazan's work. They are, symbolically, fascist tyrants ruling the little nations—fractious, rebellious, struggling for democratic emergence—that is the family in so many of his dramas.

That someday he would make such use of his own family's drama had not entered Kazan's mind when his parents deposited him, wearing a boxy, itchy blue serge suit, on the idyllic Williams campus in the fall of 1926. It did not occur to him at any time in the four subsequent years, which were anything but idyllic to Kazan. He was obliged to supplement his savings by waiting tables at fraternity houses where, amid the well-born and well-favored, he was patronized when he was noticed at all. He yearned for the frat boys' dates, the lithe, blond girls he served meals, but he was only comfortable with small, dark, intense young women. He also wanted to be smooth and articulate like their handsome swains.

But often he would go days without speaking—a swarthy, runty, big-nosed outsider, nursing a new set of resentments. "It . . . made me rebellious. It also made me join the Communist Party at a certain time because I got resentful of being excluded. I was an outsider . . . but I also was sympathetic with people that were struggling to get up, because I struggled to get up."

Does this sound almost preposterously simple-minded? Possibly. But you have to remember that Kazan, the director, though good at showing the anguish of conflicting emotions, was always looking for a drama's "spine" (a word much used in Stanislavskian analyses of plays)—those simple, direct emotions that power the action—and this was the "spine" of his early life.

For a long time at Williams he was merely a resentful observer of the life flowing past him. He was not chosen for a fraternity or for the honor society. At first he went out for no extracurricular activities—not even the dramatic club—but, in time, he began palling around with a few other contemptibles and even enjoyed some success as an intramural athlete. And he did well enough in his studies—he was particularly fond of an English class taught by a Mr. Dutton—and loved best the hours he spent by himself in the library. Still, when he was graduated from Williams in 1930, he had no particular purpose in mind.

The Depression had not yet reached its depths, but times were already hard in the early summer of 1930. His father was now "eating capital," as Kazan would later put it and had stopped his almost daily excursions to the racetrack because he could no longer afford to lose a bet. Kazan himself drifted off to the Yale Drama School, mainly, it seems, because his best college friend, Alan Baxter, later to become an undistinguished movie actor, was headed there.

He didn't much care for Yale. The acting classes focused on externals, on well-spoken imitations of life instead of its core emotions. A failed effort was made to erase Kazan's New York accent and to turn him into an emotionally remote actor in the traditional mode. The directing classes weren't much better. He learned something about creating effective stage pictures, but nothing about focusing the actors on a play's salient emotions. He liked best the scene shop and the people who created the sets and the light plots for plays. They were hardworking, practical and, in his view, much more emotionally stable than the more visibly "creative" theater people.

He also gravitated toward Molly Day Thatcher, Baxter's girlfriend. She was tall and slender, but "voluptuous" in Kazan's description, and, above all, impeccably WASP in heritage. Her grandfather, indeed, had been president of Yale. She, of course, was attracted to her opposite—dark, intense Elia Kazan, though she was some three years older than he was, perhaps more. They became lovers, with the amiable Baxter more or less graciously backing away.

Here, at last, was the shiksa of Elia Kazan's dreams. And best of all she was as intellectually intense as any of the darker beauties he had previously communed with. In the early days of the Depression, she was drawn toward good works among the needy and was an outspoken New Dealer. But she was also a theater intellectual and would remain, through all the years of their marriage more abstract in her approach to the theater—to literature and politics in general—than Kazan. She wanted to be a playwright, but she was always more dramaturge than dramatist, and she became influential as a play reader, a spotter of talent, an editor of theatrical journals, an occasional critic—and someone whose opinion her husband always sought when he was considering a play or film to direct or when one of his productions was in trouble.

She was also a source of some anguish for him. Some of this was sexual; he could not and would not remain faithful to her for any length of time—the record of his epic strayings spreads through many pages of his autobiography. But she was also—and this was the more important challenge and frustration to him—the "intellectual" and the "writer" in the family, while he was, at best, the servant of writers. These eventually included the best American dramatists of his time, men who valued, sometimes publicly acknowledged, his contributions, though that was never quite enough for him. Not until his wife died, more than thirty years after they met, did he become an openly proclaimed author.

Molly's presence, like his father's, is all over his work, which is full of smart, spirited WASP women, who, like Alfred Hitchcock's more famous blonds, hint at a sexuality that needs to be—ultimately will be—unlocked. The difference between Hitch's blonds and Kazan's is that the former's troubles tend to arise from whatever issues the narrative imposes on them, not from their own inner conflicts.

By the time he left Yale in 1932—a year before he was due to receive his graduate degree—Kazan was committed to Molly and commited, in his own mind, at least, to becoming, of all things, a movie director. He had fallen under the sway of the great Russian masters of the silent epic, especially the works of Alexander Dovzhenko, the most lyrical and poetic of them. But "I watched them all, and I said, 'God, that's it. That's life doing something like that' . . . That's adventure . . . not just some friends of yours on the stage yelling at each other." He added: "I think I got interested in Russia mostly not for their politics, but for their films."

This was all well and good, but "How do you get a start as a film director in 1932. I mean, there's no way . . . to do it. Now you can get into TV and one thing and another. But then, nothing."

———————

Nothing except the fledgling Group Theatre, to which he and Alan Baxter had introductions from a Yale faculty member who was consulting to this radically new theatrical entity. It is not too much to say that the unpromising meeting of this unformed young man and this still-forming organization changed the former's life and eventually had a not inconsiderable influence on the latter's.

You cannot understand Kazan's life without understanding "the dream of passion" that was The Group—possibly the single most important theatrical enterprise in American history. It was not that its "business model" had any lasting effect on the way theater was organized economically, not that many of the plays it produced during its ten seasons have had much lasting influence, not that many great stars emerged from its acting company. It was not even unique in producing left-wing drama during its time. In the decade of its existence, despised Broadway produced all sorts of socially conscious plays, ranging from the Communist John Wexley's *They Shall Not Die* (about the Scottsboro Boys) to Maxwell Anderson's *Winterset* (Sacco and Vanzetti), to Irwin Shaw's *Bury the Dead* (antiwar), which says nothing about such Federal Theatre productions as *The Cradle Will Rock* and *One Third of a Nation*.

No, it was something else. The Group had, among its aims, the goal of creating a revolution in performance—in the way actors perceive their task and go about achieving it and in the way the audience understands and appreciates their work. It wanted to achieve a codification of the rules by which performers could "correctly" achieve their effects. Implicit in this activity was that these rules would be teachable. Implicit in that was the notion that acting could, at last, become a profession, like all the others, in which students, after a demanding apprenticeship, would make a lifelong commitment to the highly disciplined practice of an austere and difficult art, as worthy of respect as painting or poetry. Finally, implicit in all of the above was a full-scale reformation of flighty, hit-or-flop American showbiz, dominated by stars and measuring success—whether on Broadway or in the movies—solely by box office takings.

Reformation on that grand scale The Group never achieved. But it—and its post–World War II offshoot, the Actors Studio, of which Kazan was a cofounder—did achieve the revolution it desired in acting. Almost every American appearing today on the stage or screen is, in some sense, a "method" actor, trained in the studio or lab of some guru offering this or that variation on the Stanislavskian system, which The Group practiced. And, it must be said, all exceptions duly noted, that the general standard to which performers aspire and by which we judge their work is higher now than it was seventy years ago. That this spirit was born when and where it was must seem to us, looking back, the unlikeliest of occurrences.

For The Group was the lengthened shadow of three (at that time) rather troubled and marginal theatrical idealists—Harold Clurman, Lee Strasberg and Cheryl Crawford, all of whom had found intermittent work but little personal satisfaction in 1920s commercial theater. It was, they believed, in desperate need of reform, though when they began groping toward a statement of their ideals, that need was by no means clear to the theatergoing public. It was among the theater's working stiffs—its actors and designers in particular—that they found an enthusiastic response.

Superficially, it is hard to see what they were complaining about. As late as the 1929–30 season, the very year of the stock market crash (and the year before The Group's official founding), Broadway seemed healthy and prosperous; it mounted 249 productions that season. Moreover, many of its works in the 1920s had been far from negligible. Eugene O'Neill had, after all, emerged from the little theaters of Greenwich Village as the American theater's most dominant and critically worshipped figure. Nor was he alone: Elmer Rice

(*The Adding Machine*), Maxwell Anderson (*What Price Glory?* written with Laurence Stallings), George Kelly (*The Show Off*), Philip Barry (*Holiday*), S. N. Behrman (*The Second Man*), Sidney Howard (*They Knew What They Wanted*, best known now as the basis for the musical *The Most Happy Fella*), Robert E. Sherwood (who had the first of his many successes with *The Road to Rome* in 1927), all began their careers at this time. There was even among them a promising Marxist, John Howard Lawson, in those days as much an expressionist as a social realist, deploying music, vaudeville turns and direct address to the audience in *Processional,* his 1925 "jazz symphony of American life," about strikers and strikebreakers in West Virginia.

Beyond that, the Theatre Guild, which had emerged with O'Neill from the theatrically experimental Village, was at the height of its influence. Over the decade it presented no fewer than forty-seven plays by distinguished modernist playwrights—Shaw, Ibsen, Strindberg, the Capeks, Molnar, Claudel, Franz Werfel. Meanwhile, Eva Le Gallienne had established her Civic Repertory Theatre, the longest-lived and most ambitious attempt to establish a repertory company in the United States. Moreover, in this period there was no dearth of comic voices— George S. Kaufman, Hecht and MacArthur—or legendary stars— Jeanne Eagels, Katharine Cornell, Lunt and Fontanne. Strasberg himself had been hugely impressed by Eleonora Duse. Awash with talent, with film still silent until the end of this period, radio in its brash infancy, and television nonexistent, Broadway's great figures achieved in the 1920s an admiring national attention they would never again enjoy.

Clurman, Strasberg and Crawford somewhat grudgingly admitted as much. But it was all terribly catch-as-catch-can. What was needed, they believed, was a theater that permanently offered an integrated approach to playmaking, with directors, actors, designers and writers working from the same artistic principles, a theater that eschewed the star system, with all the actors instead working as members of an ensemble that could achieve deeper, more harmonious productions than the hastily assembled, hastily rehearsed commercial companies could.

Of The Group's founders, Cheryl Crawford was and remains the least well known. A midwesterner, a graduate of Smith, a lesbian, something of a bohemian in her private life, something of an avant-gardist in her professional one, she was less interested than Strasberg and Clurman in directing (or possibly she was thwarted by them in that ambition). As The Group evolved, she became its de facto producer, overseeing fund-raising, publicity, subscriptions. She was also something of a den mother to a company that was always emotionally roiled in one way or another. Kazan, among others, always found her willing to listen sympathetically to his frustrations.

Clurman was the most colorful of The Group's founders. The son of a prosperous Lower East Side doctor, he was a graduate of Columbia University, with enough money to indulge his intellectual pursuits. He had loved the theater since childhood, particularly the boisterous and thriving Yiddish theater, but after college he had taken up expatriate life in Paris with his friend Aaron Copland. In its world capital he was exposed to every aspect of modernism—in painting, music, literature. And theater; he was much taken with Stanislavsky's Moscow Art Theatre when it trouped through on its way to America. He was also impressed with Jacques Copeau, who had established a unified theater, which schooled actors specifically to the needs of his productions. Returning to New York in 1924, Clurman flirted briefly with publishing, worked as a small-parts actor, eventually attached himself to the Theatre Guild as a stage manager, play reader, sometimes annoying gadfly.

He had been a rather shy young man, with a slight lisp, but when he was talking theater the shyness disappeared and, finally, in fall 1930, he began spellbinding potential acolytes with his lectures on theater—first in his hotel room, then in Cheryl Crawford's larger apartment, finally in a rent-free room at Steinway Hall, on West Fifty-seventh Street, where as many as two hundred people would gather to hear his endless, eagerly stammering spiels.

The texts of these talks do not survive, but Wendy Smith, in her masterful history of The Group, *Real Life Drama,* has found enough contemporary documentation, articles and proposals, to give us his gist. Basically, Clurman was railing against the incoherence of theatrical life. "We have, on the American stage," he said, "all the separate elements for a Theatre, but no Theatre. We have playwrights without their theatre-groups, directors without their actors, actors without plays and directors, scene-designers without anything. Our theatre is an anarchy of individual talents."

Clurman's antidote to anarchy was a theater whose members *"give their group feeling an adequate theatrical expression* [italics his]." He was aiming, most significantly, for a theater not as an expression of "art," but as an expression of life itself. This was a strong talking point. For all its ambitions and occasional felicities, the American theater of the 1920s had not given voice to the experiences of what amounted to a new class: urban, immigrant and first-generation immigrant, poor but culturally aspiring—the class, quite simply, that had given birth to Harold Clurman (and Elia Kazan).

The lives of actors emerging from this class were depressingly ad hoc—the endless search for work, the occasional, often short-lived job, usually in shows that did not satisfy any need beyond a paycheck. Even fairly well-established actors, people like Luther Adler, Morris Carnovsky and the dashing young leading man Franchot Tone, more or less steadily employed and well-received on Broadway, shared these dissatisfactions. A company of the kind Clurman was proposing—a cooperative in which everyone received some sort of steady paycheck, had some say about the plays performed and the style in which they were presented, a company that stood outside Broadway's hit-or-flop syndrome—had vast appeal for young theater people. It does not detract from Clurman's spiraling idealism to say that such a company was very likely the only one in which he could himself find a comfortable home.

It must be said that in The Group's earliest years Lee Strasberg was, despite his abrupt manner, one of its great strengths. The man didn't give a hoot about hits or flops. One almost gets the feeling that he didn't care all that much about the content of the plays he directed—except insofar as they were showcases for the thing he narrowly, passionately and forever cared about, which was his "method."

He was a Jewish immigrant, born Israel Strassberg in Galicia, brought to this country when he was nine and also raised on the Lower East Side. He dropped out of high school, worked in a shop that made hairpieces, drifted into the theater via a settlement house company and, like Clurman, had his life-shaping revelation when Stanislavsky brought his Moscow Art Theatre to the United States in

1923. He had seen good acting before, of course, but never an ensemble like this with actors completely surrendering their egos to the work.

He observed, first of all, that all the actors, whether they were playing leads or small parts, worked with the same commitment and intensity. No actors idled about posing and preening (or thinking about where they might dine after the performance). More important, every actor seemed to project some sort of unspoken, yet palpable, inner life for his or her character. This was acting of a sort that one rarely saw on the American stage, the performance values of which were very much in the English tradition, with its emphasis on well-spoken line readings, but with little stress on the psychology of the characters or their interactions.

Strasberg was galvanized. He knew that his own future as an actor—he was a slight and unhandsome man—was limited. But he soon perceived that as a theoretician and teacher of this new "system" he might become a major force in American theater. He also saw that his passion for a new style of acting could easily be blended with Clurman's passion for a new kind of theater.

They were further inspired by the Actor's Laboratory Theatre. This half-forgotten, but historically significant organization had been founded by two members of Stanislavsky's company who stayed on in the United States after the Muscovites returned home. One of them was Madame Maria Ouspenskaya, once a Chekhovian leading lady, latterly one of Hollywood's more amusing (if occasionally incomprehensible) character women. The other was Richard Boleslavsky, a figure who continues to deserve more study. A onetime Polish cavalry officer (his autobiography is entitled *Lances Down*), he had become a stalwart of the Moscow Art Theatre. In New York he wrote an invaluable little book, *Acting—The First Six Lessons*, which remains in print. He, too, would go to Hollywood, where he had one of the most eclectic directorial careers of the 1930s (his filmography includes *Rasputin and the Empress, Hollywood Party, Theodora Goes Wild* and *The Garden of Allah*), cut short by his premature death at age forty-eight in 1937.

What Strasberg and Clurman took away from the Actor's Lab was a belief that just as an actor could be prepared physically for his work with dance, movement and fencing classes, he could be mentally prepared by resort to analogous mental exercises. They worked on relaxation as well as concentration. They worked with nonexistent objects that helped prepare them for the exploration of equally ephemeral emotions. They learned to use "affective memory," as Strasberg called the most controversial aspect of his teaching—summoning emotions from their own lives to illuminate their stage roles.

Not every actor Strasberg later directed bought into all this. "Hocus-pocus," Morris Carnovsky called it. It must also be said that many an actor instinctively worked in this manner, without coaching. But Strasberg believed he could codify this system, a necessary precursor to teaching it to anyone who wanted to learn it.

He was, as a director, more preoccupied with getting his actors to work in the "correct" way than he was in shaping the overall presentation. In the latter realm he was erratic. Sometimes the way he moved and grouped the company on stage was awesome; sometimes it was awkward and unfinished, and he was always notorious for strange casting choices, in which the physical "rightness" of the performer for his or her role was discounted, often with disastrous results.

There was about him no small measure of the intellectual dictator. There is a famous story, told in many variations, of Strasberg preparing an early Group production. With its first performance looming over the company, and much work still to be done, an actress made a "mistake" in the way she played some moment. She immediately admitted it, but that was insufficient for Strasberg. He insisted on going over and over the moment. Finally one of the play's authors protested; they needed to move on, he said, to more important matters. Strasberg turned coldly on him and said, according to Bobby Lewis, "Mr. Sifton, we are not here to rehearse your play." This attitude would finally be his undoing in The Group, but at first his idealism, narrow though it might be, was inspiring.

In the winter of 1930–31 Clurman and Crawford inched The Group Theatre toward reality, raising what money they could for a first season (Strasberg was touring as the Jewish peddler in *Green Grow the Lilacs,* on which *Oklahoma!* would ultimately be based) while cadging a promising script—Paul Green's *The House of Connelly*—and some financial support from the Theatre Guild, which promised at least to consider a Broadway production of Green's play.

No salaries would be paid for the ten weeks of rehearsal and study that preceded that event. This retreat would occur over the summer on an abandoned farm near Brookfield Center, Connecticut. To which the company set forth on June 8, 1931, with high and happy hearts. Prominent among its twenty-seven acting members were Stella Adler, who would become Strasberg's chief rival as an acting teacher, and Franchot Tone, the first movie star to come out of the group. Also present were Sanford Meisner, soon to become a respected acting teacher, and Bobby Lewis, latterly also a well-known teacher and director. Clifford Odets, not a good actor, not yet a produced playwright, was also present. ("Let's take Odets," Clurman said. "That fellow has something—not as an actor: humanly.")

The company also included people who would become famously reliable character actors, including the likes of Phoebe Brand, J. Edward Bromberg, Morris Carnovsky and the beautiful Ruth Nelson. As Wendy Smith says, a substantial portion of this company were New York Jews, to whom the urban accents in which The Group most wanted to speak came naturally. But she also notes that the company drew actors from virtually every American class and region—former debutantes and former merchant sailors among them.

The pioneers of The Group's first summer at Brookfield Farm needed all their idealism to sustain them. Room and board were provided, but the food was terrible, the accommodations rude, the work demanding. There were, of course, love affairs that caused teapot tempests—most notably Clurman's endlessly tormented relationship with Stella Adler, the ups and downs of which would distract him and trouble The Group throughout its history.

Yet a brave beginning on something unprecedented was made. Clurman lectured inspirationally on Stanislavsky's system, and, though he was cruelly demanding, Strasberg commanded The Group's awe. As they worked on *The House of Connelly*, the actors "took an exercise" in affective memory on almost every line. This was fine with most of them. They liked having the time to delve into their roles and into the nuances of Green's play, which was a brooding study of the Old South, represented by the Connellys of its title, confronting a sharecropper's revolt against their rule.

The play ended tragically, a conclusion that troubled many in

The Group. Throughout the 1930s, the preferred way of left-wing theater—not just The Group—was optimism. They wanted honestly to show the problems confronting a nation in dire economic crisis, but still bring their dramas to a hopeful conclusion. So they asked Green for something a little more upbeat.

He was a somewhat unworldly figure, a philosophy professor at the University of North Carolina who, though he had earlier won a Pulitzer Prize (for *In Abraham's Bosom*), was quite content to have his plays done by his university's dramatic club. (At least one of the outdoor historical pageants he wrote, *The Lost Colony,* is still mounted every summer in Roanoke, Virginia.) Approving The Group's new approach to theater, Green amiably rewrote *The House of Connelly* more or less to its specifications—thereby outraging his original sponsors at the Theatre Guild. It may have been commercially oriented, but it still believed tragedy was the theater's highest calling, and it wanted this new company to uphold its ideals. It also objected to a couple of performances in The Group's production. The Group was told to restore the original ending and recast the offending actors. If it did not, the Guild said it would withdraw half its promised Broadway funding. Outraged, The Group clung to its principles (and performers), and *Connelly* opened on Broadway on September 29, 1931—to reviews that were just short of raves.

But despite the new ending, in which the scion of the Connelly family is rejuvenated by marriage to a sharecropper's daughter, *The House of Connelly* ran for only ninety-one performances, making no profit. This did not daunt The Group. It had done what it meant to do; it had offered a sober, well-received play to serious theatergoers.

And it found another play the Guild had under option—*1931* by Paul and Claire Sifton. Recounting the story of a warehouse worker who loses his job and is then swept up in the apocalyptic revolutionary fervor generated by mass unemployment, it offered The Group (and Strasberg) an opportunity to strut their stuff with epic scenes of mass protest. It was, in a sense, everything that *The House of Connelly* was not. But it was by all accounts crudely written and the critics excoriated it. It closed after nine performances.

The Group next turned to one of its most enthusiastic supporters, Maxwell Anderson. He had abandoned the realistic manner of his early hits to embrace verse drama, a choice that brought him prizes at the time but largely doomed these leaden works for posterity. Written specifically for The Group, *Night over Taos* was about the overthrow of a feudal way of life in nineteenth-century Mexico— verse drama, a historical subject, the opportunity to demonstrate the company's range. But it, too, flopped, closing after a ten-day run, which ended The Group's first season.

Thus, in its first season the company to which Kazan and Baxter presented themselves in the spring of 1932 as potential apprentices had experienced virtually all the problems that would plague it for the rest of its existence: Its inability to subvert Broadway's economic model while still working within it; the inability to find reliable sources of good new plays on the open market or, alternatively, to develop its own playwrights (only Odets would fulfill that hope and he was still three years away from his first success); Strasberg's unyielding and ultimately destructive arrogance—which, as it happened, strongly colored Kazan's introduction to The Group.

Strasberg and Clurman conducted the apprentice interviews, and it's possible they felt Kazan was not exactly the kind of young man who would fit easily into their collective. Applying for funding from the Theatre Guild, Clurman had written: "We believe that the individual can achieve his fullest stature only through the identification of his own good with the good of the group, a group which he himself must help to create." So far in his twenty-two years Elia Kazan had not achieved identification with any group—rather the opposite.

At this first meeting Clurman was distracted and Strasberg was preoccupied with a newspaper sports page. He did finally bestir himself to ask what it was Kazan wanted—from the group, from life, he did not say. Kazan's blurted reply: "What I want is your job."

What he got was the chance to pay $20 a week to spend the summer with the company, doing whatever odd jobs needed doing. He only had enough money to pay for six weeks, but unhesitatingly signed on. Even if you had to pay for the privilege it was still a job— in a year when twenty-five million Americans were without work.

It is perhaps worth pausing over Kazan's cheeky reply to Strasberg's *de rigueur* question. Already preternaturally alert to other
people's strengths and weaknesses, Kazan perhaps immediately, instinctively understood that Strasberg was The Group's weak link.
For his cold and sneering manner on this occasion was typical of
him. Positive reinforcement was never part of his lexicon. You could
never tell where one of his tantrums would alight, and he was constantly reducing actors of both sexes to tears. Kazan, when he became a director, would prove to be his opposite—a seducer, not a
dictator. He tended to get what he wanted by sly manipulation—
some of it quite comical in the retelling—not by direct force of will
and intellect. Possibly it's giving the kid too much credit, but he was
already something of an expert on defective father figures.

In any case, Kazan was resoundingly right about one thing: He
would one day get Strasberg's "job." Or, anyway, the job he aspired
to, which was as the American theater's leading director. To give him
his due, Strasberg was capable of sharing, in a kindly way, some of
his intellectual enthusiasms. That summer he was having translated,
and was hoping to publish, theoretical works by two of Europe's
leading avant-garde directors, Vakhtangov and Meyerhold, and
sometimes he would show Kazan drawings and photographs of their
productions, which he aspired to emulate. As Kazan comments, he
would become famous enough and prosperous enough as a peda-
gogue, but this "was not the way of his dearest dreams." What's
worse, he had to witness the once despised kid, so much his opposite
in every way, so patronizingly treated in his first Group years, gain
the success he coveted.

In the summer of 1932, there was, on balance, some reason for
guarded optimism about the forthcoming season. Money was, as always, short. Crawford's attempt to sell season subscription tickets
and an effort to sell stock in the company had both failed. But some
donations drifted in and the actors put on some little one-night
shows around New York, raising a bit more operating capital. The
company had also generated a certain amount of goodwill in the theater community. Maybe the critics had been unkind to its last two
productions, but they always paused to praise this or that perform-

ance or Mordecai Gorelik's or Robert Edmund Jones's scenery. One gets the sense that they were pulling for The Group, especially now, when every aspect of the American status quo was under question.

The Group's new quarters, at Dover Furnace, New York, were more comfortable than the ones at Brookfield Farm had been, but, reserved and watchful, Kazan did not fit in very well. Aside from Clifford Odets, also something of an outsider, patronized for his bumptious and sometimes disruptive manner, he made few friends. Odets (also deeply scarred by his father) was, by all accounts, a terrible actor—though he was always outraged when The Group refused him good roles. He was also serially, noisily, self-pityingly pursuing all The Group's unattached actresses (and some who were attached). People heard his typewriter chattering at all hours of the night as he worked on stories, novels, plays that they didn't quite believe they would ever see.

Kazan's typewriter was busy, too—churning out copies of playscripts to earn the balance of the money he needed to pay his way. But he also worked hard in all The Group's classes—diction, movement, formal acting exercises. He did any job anyone asked him to do, but by the end of the summer he was back to his Williams occupation—waiting on tables.

Most of The Group's attention that summer was focused on John Howard Lawson's *Success Story*. They hoped perhaps he might become their first house playwright. Like its other property for the 1932–33 season, Dawn Powell's generally disliked *Big Night,* it dealt with people using sex to advance themselves in business. Apparently unknown to The Group, they were written by a man and a woman who were, according to Powell's biographer, Tim Page, almost certainly lovers.

Kazan attended every rehearsal he could of the Lawson play and had an ambivalent response to Strasberg's work. He thought his harsh methods were turning the company into a group of masochists, demeaning themselves to please their master. He heard members of the company comparing this summer's work unfavorably to that of the previous one and saw them skulking off to New York to look for other jobs. He was sympathetic with the hard-drinking Tone and, of course, envious of his inherited wealth, his Hollywood offers and his smart red roadster in which he could escape the grinding seriousness of Dover Furnace.

Kazan was also ambivalent about The Group's more general principles and practices. On the one hand, he desperately wanted its acceptance. It was the only way into the professional theater that he could then imagine. On the other, he was not certain that The Group was a fully professional organization. He was still somewhat starry-eyed about Broadway, not as convinced as they were of its decadence.

But he was devastated when neither he nor Baxter was made a Group member at the end of the summer. He always remembered what Clurman said when he gave him the news: "You may have talent for the theater, but it's certainly not for acting." He did not know how he would make a living when he returned to New York.

Sympathetic Cheryl Crawford to the rescue. She talked her friend Theresa Helburn, the Theatre Guild's executive director, into giving Kazan a job as an assistant stage manager in her production of another Lawson play, *The Pure in Heart*, starring Osgood Perkins. It closed out of town, partly, Kazan would insist, because Helburn's production was clueless. Still, later in the season Helburn would give him another job, assistant stage managing and playing a small role, in another short-lived production. This was *Chrysalis,* also starring Perkins, and including in its cast Humphrey Bogart and Margaret Sullavan, with Elisha Cook, Jr., in a supporting role. Describing it as "a cinematic" production, contrasting love among the New York rich and poor, the *Times* critic, Brooks Atkinson, dismissed it as "astonishingly insignificant."

In that winter of 1932–33 Kazan also did some stints at the Kazan Carpet Company. And he married Molly Thatcher. His new friend Clifford Odets thought it was a mistake. So, predictably, did his father. They thought he should marry a peasant girl, not a high-spirited blueblood. But she brought flatware and china and a small trust fund to their marriage. And a ferocious love, which may later have wavered under the impress of Kazan's philanderings, but never fully flagged. In that first winter she took a job demonstrating puppets in a New Jersey department store while he dragged himself to the carpet store. He writes that the sight of her making her foggy way homeward after a hard day's work helped him, much later, to visualize Stella—another wellborn lady in thrall to a low-life stud—in *A Streetcar Named Desire.*

Meantime, he kept up his ties with The Group, even, before his marriage, living for a time in a kind of cooperative crash pad several of its members—Odets, Strasberg and his wife, Paula, a Group actress, among them—had set up. They called it "Groupstroy," reveling in the Russianate name.

There was little else to revel in for The Group that year. *Success Story* was not well received by the critics. It is a lugubrious narrative in which Sol (Luther Adler, Stella's brother and a newcomer to the company) a young Jew, abandons both the radicalism of his youth and his radical girlfriend, Sarah (Stella Adler), to take over an ad agency run by Raymond Merritt (Franchot Tone). Sol takes over his mistress as well. Sarah accidentally-on-purpose shoots him but, dying, he grabs the gun and turns it toward himself, so that his death will look like a suicide. The Group thought it a searing indictment of American materialism. Lawson thought it more an indictment of America's ideological immaturity. The critics thought it a load of hooey.

This was a problem that would recur again and again in the The Group's history. The reviewers were open to innovations in stagecraft and style of presentation, and were often generous with actors (as they were in this case). But they were essentially bourgeois gentlemen when it came to ideology. Direct critiques of contemporary American culture, even in these parlous times, were mostly unacceptable to them. They refused to come to grips with Lawson's social criticisms; it was easier for them to give him low marks for style and leave the heavy thinking to their editorial pages.

The Group, however, decided to make a fight for *Success Story.* They even embraced the despised star system, taking out quote ads in which Tone and Adler were praised for their performances. By taking pay cuts as well, they were able to keep Lawson's play running until the first of the year, while they rehearsed Powell's play.

Big Night was another Theatre Guild castoff, about a businessman offering his wife's sexual favors to a client. Powell thought it was a comedy. The Group thought it a waste of its idealism, while Tone thought it just plain awful. He told The Group that he would leave for Hollywood as soon as his run in Lawson's play was finished. Crawford, who started directing it, and Clurman, who finished it, kept sobering it up, thus betraying what merits the play had. As Powell, a merry and shrewd social observer, put it, "The Group has put on a careful production with no knowledge whatever of the characters—as they might put on a picture of Siberian home life—made up bit by bit of exact details but [with] the actual realism of the whole missing." Years later Clurman conceded that they should have lightened up: "The play was one we should have done in four swift weeks—or not at all. We had worried and harried our actors with it for months."

The critics were vicious. "Immoral . . . debauched . . . sordid," one of them wrote. "Odious" said another. Only the *New Yorker's* Robert Benchley perceived some merits in the production which closed after nine days, in late January, just weeks before the incoming Roosevelt administration declared a bank holiday, signifying that the depths of the Depression had been reached. It was going to be a long time until summer camp—if, indeed, The Group would actually be able to make its annual retreat. In his memoir, *The Fervent Years,* Clurman called this period "one of the most painful and one of the most pregnant periods of our Group life . . . we were in a state of complete rout."

Elia Kazan was not routed. He was thinking. And feeling he had learned more from his short stints in the commercial theater than he had in the whole previous summer at Dover Furnace. It was Osgood Perkins, father of Anthony Perkins and a beloved and respected theatrical leading man who died prematurely, who most influenced him. One of Kazan's tasks on *The Pure in Heart* was to lay out Perkins's props and make sure they were in working order. But every night before the curtain went up, Perkins would appear, and despite Kazan's reassurances, check them out. He was, Kazan would later write, the only "real pro" he met in the course of his two Theatre Guild outings, and he began, as well, to respond to Perkins's acting manner. Kazan thought he might take the directness and simplicity of Perkins's style—"externally clear action, controlled every minute at every turn, with gestures spare yet eloquent"—and somehow blend that with the kind of acting The Group was built on: "intense and truly emotional, rooted in the subconscious, therefore often surprising and shocking in its revelations."

Direction, he reflected, was not "what the Group directors seem to think it is, a matter of coaching actors. It is turning psychological events into behavior, inner events into visible, external patterns of life on stage." It is as good a short definition of Kazan's working method as anyone has ever written, and it came to him in a sudden flash, "as if it had been born in me."

Implicit in these few words was a belief in the kind of typecasting Strasberg rejected. There had been trouble in *Success Story,* with an actress who was supposed to be a sex symbol, and was neither physically nor emotionally right for the role. Everyone in the company knew it, but Strasberg remained convinced that any actor working correctly could play anything, and he had simply redoubled his efforts with the young woman, convinced that she could, by some magical power of thought, attain the requisite spirit. The result remained a disaster.

Kazan rarely made such mistakes. He often cast nonactors in his films. But only if the part drew on their real-life experiences. A cop, he said, could usually play a cop, though no amount of coaching could turn him into, say, a literary intellectual. This, too, would become a significant distinction between his work and Strasberg's.

More immediately, it was this bias toward the practical that finally won him his place within The Group. He was asked to return for its third summer outing, this time as a nonpaying apprentice. Headquarters for 1933 would be at Green Mansions, near Lake George in upstate New York. It was a Borscht Belt resort, and in return for food and lodging The Group was to provide entertainment for the paying guests—short plays, skits, musical evenings. This proved a godsend for Kazan. He could—and did—build (or at least supervise) the scenery for these events. He also played small parts in them—and no part was too small for him.

He proved to be just what The Group had long needed—someone willing to do the scut work the rest of the company disdained. People started calling him by his Yale nickname, "Gadget," because he was such a handy little human tool to have around. It was a name he came to detest—even in its shortened form, "Gadge," by which only his old-est and closest friends dared address him in his later years.

But the best news for Gadget that summer was the play The Group was rehearsing. It was Sidney Kingsley's *Crisis*, later renamed *Men in White*. Crawford had rescued it from the slush pile in Lee Shubert's office, made a coproduction deal with the producers who held an option on this well-traveled property, and imposed it on The Group, which, on the whole, thought it rather beneath them. The thirties were a period during which showbiz was for some reason awash in plays and films about medicine—*Yellow Jack, Arrowsmith,* the beginnings of the Dr. Kildare series—possibly because doctors were familiar figures to the middle-class audience yet also men for-ever obliged to make morally conscientious (and dramatic) choices on matters involving life and death, materialism and idealism.

Men in White was just such a play. It had no particular political message, but since they literally had nothing better to work on that summer and since Strasberg thought he could do something with it, The Group reluctantly took it on.

Watching Strasberg get the show on its feet, Kazan came to agree with his judgment. Always willing to throw himself into a good gutsy show, political correctness be damned, Kazan was delighted when he was asked to assistant stage manage, and later stage manage, *Men in White,* in which he also had a one-line role. He came to think that with this production Strasberg reached his apotheosis with The Group. He sent his actors out to hospitals to observe medical professionals at work, and this gave the production a solid air of felt reality. As Kazan later wrote: "Lee and the actors were doing a brilliant job, and I learned a great deal about the technique of improvisation, what and where its value was. Lee's production, at moments, seemed like a modern ballet; it relied not on words, but on movement, activity, and behavior. In the theatre of the time, this was new."

The play was episodic, rich in minor characters and moral dilem-mas. Its "spine" concerned a young nurse having an affair with a doctor, becoming pregnant and then dying as a result of a botched abortion. The play's famous last scene, brilliantly choreographed by Strasberg (and also lit in a striking way) has her on the operating table, with the head surgeon (J. Edward Bromberg) performing a desperate operation to save her life.

He fails. But the play became an instant and huge success when it opened in New York on September 26, 1933, running for almost a year and eventually winning the Pulitzer Prize. Typically, this success caused consternation in The Group. Hit or not, many in the company continued to think of the piece as no more than a bourgeois problem play, somehow a sellout to the very Broadway values The Group had been born to fight.

On the other hand a hit was a hit, and if they did not quite revel in it, they at least found relief in it; rent could be paid, food placed on the table. But, typically, after the first of the year, they plunged into rehearsals with a play that was much more to their ideological liking—John Howard Lawson's *Gentlewoman*. It starred the ever-fractious Stella Adler, whose imperious ways never quite fit The Group spirit, as a wellborn, well-to-do woman who takes as a lover a sort of hobo intellectual (Lloyd Nolan). The play reflected Lawson's own confusions of the time, as he made his way from a more generalized radicalism toward hard-line Stalinism, and the left-wing hacks were particularly hard on it, largely because Nolan's character was not more definitively a working-class figure. Lawson accepted this criticism with apologetic passivity. "I have not demonstrated my ability to serve the revolutionary working class either in my writing or in practical activity," he sniveled in a reply to the harsh assault critic and sometime novelist Mike Gold launched on *Gentlewoman* in *New Masses*. The middle-class critics didn't like it any better, and the play ran for only a couple of weeks. It was Lawson's third failure in two years, and he decamped for the South to do some radical journalism. Only one more play of his was produced in New York and soon he was in Hollywood, writing dreadful screenplays, on his way to becoming the Communist Party's commissar to the industry.

―――――――

Kazan, too, was making his way further left in this period. The Group decided that, based on the success of *Men in White*, everyone was entitled to a two-week vacation with pay. When his turn came, Kazan, accompanied part of the time by Nick Ray, then a young actor, later to become a gifted, troubled film director, set forth for Tennessee and, later, Texas. In Tennessee Kazan met a Communist Party organizer whose thoughtfulness and manliness impressed him. In Texas he helped an impoverished rancher to dig a well. Along the way he managed to meet Leadbelly, the famous folksinger, whose work, along with that of many similar singers was at this time recorded by leftist folklorists (like Alan Lomax) searching for such "authentic," but previously unheard, voices of the toiling masses.

Did the trip "radicalize" Kazan? No, not exactly. He had already joined the Communist Party, recruited to The Group's small "unit" (they were not called "cells") by his friend and tennis partner Tony Kraber, who acted small roles in the company. But the trip did color Kazan's beliefs with a romantic aura.

During Kazan's time in the party The Group's CP unit never grew beyond the eight members he later named in his HUAC testimony, though a few other Group members may have wandered in after Kazan left it—just as a few others wandered out. Wendy Smith reports a dispute as to the unit's influence. Some Group members thought they played a significant role in undermining the authority of The Group's three leaders. Others agreed with Clurman that they were no more than "romantic idealists" whose influence was negligible.

But it was not within The Group that Kazan's newfound ideological commitment had the most effect. Besides giving him a vacation, the success of *Men in White* put money in his pocket—he was making $60 a week, plenty to indulge himself in a gym membership, speech, movement and even fencing classes—and gave him time to find other outlets for an energy that, by all accounts, was close to demonic in those days.

He was drawn to the burgeoning left-wing theater movement centered in downtown New York—notably the League of Workers Theatre and the Workers Laboratory Theatre, which had as its slogan, "Theatre Is a Weapon." It is difficult to determine when, precisely, Kazan began working with these Communist fronts, but one student of his life, Thomas H. Pauly, says that as early as 1933 he wrote two unproduced plays for the WLT. He began, in the winter of 1934, to teach directing classes at the New Theatre League, as the League of Workers Theatre renamed itself.

Without questioning Kazan's ideological commitments of the time, one can't help but observe that he was using these organizations as determinedly as they were using him, for these radical groups would give him the chance to direct that The Group would not.

As important, the New Theatre League also produced a play he had written with Art Smith, The Group actor with the strongest working-class credentials. Called *Dimitroff*, it was about the Bulgarian Communist falsely accused by the Nazis of setting the Reichstag fire in 1933. It was staged on a couple of Sunday nights, proceeds going to the organization's perpetually hard-pressed magazine, *New Theatre*, with which Molly was connected.

Dimitroff was short—just eleven scenes—and punchily expressionistic in the agitprop manner—bare stage, bold, simple lighting, bustling crowd scenes, characters more representative of "ideas" (both idealistic and evil) than of human complexity. Cast with Group Theatre colleagues and directed by its coauthors, it was subtitled "A Play of Mass Pressure." Its message, very simply, was that the Communists falsely imprisoned for arson by the Nazis (whose agents actually set the fire) could be freed only by the collective protests of the world's masses. In making this point the play brings on Hitler, Goering and Goebbels, as well as the Nazi stooge who set the fire and Dimitroff himself, as noble and intelligent a working-class hero as anyone has ever placed on a stage.

As such things go, *Dimitroff* was a fairly lively little piece. On the page (*New Theatre* published it and offered it, royalty-free, to like-minded theatrical groups), it is bold and crude, its arguments scarcely subtle, but passionately stated. It is not hard to see in it a model for the production—still a half-year in the future—that would become The Group's signature piece, *Waiting for Lefty*. More immediately, it made some in The Group sit up and take notice of Smith and Kazan. The month *Dimitroff* premiered, The Group, once again reorganizing, placed the pair on the committee charged with finding new (and better) plays for them to mount.

This effort did not bear immediate fruit. Indeed, as The Group decamped for its summer retreat—this time at Ellenville, New

York—its cupboard was bare. They would be rehearsing the only script they had, something entitled *Gold Eagle Guy,* by a left-wing novelist named Melvin Levy. It was an epic drama portraying the rise, over a forty-year span, of a San Francisco shipping magnate, climaxing with the earthquake and fire of 1906. This figure, Joe Button, was supposed to symbolize greed and ruthlessness, but many in The Group thought the play instead romanticized him. And, as the summer wore on, some began to feel that the play was being mishandled by Strasberg. Unlike his staging of *Men in White,* it lacked color, passion, movement.

These doubts were exacerbated by Stella Adler. With Clurman and Strasberg she had toured Europe in the early summer, where they were disappointed by the work they saw the Moscow Art Theatre now doing. No longer in day-to-day charge of the company, Stanislavsky was in Paris, where Adler sought him out, melodramatically accusing him of ruining her life by robbing it of her former joy in performance. They settled down to some long talks, in the course of which it emerged that the old director had pretty much abandoned affective memory as the touchstone of his "system." Vastly oversimplifying his argument, he now thought it unnecessary for the actor to consult his own feelings and recollections to animate his performance. What he should do instead was consult the script and take his feelings from the work itself.

This was a revelation to Adler—the basis for her long and revered career as a teacher, her long and toxic controversy with Strasberg, who, of course, found Stanislavsky's new idea an anathema; he would cling to affective memory until his dying day.

Adler gave lectures on what she had learned from Stanislavsky when she reached Ellenville, and some of the younger members of the company gravitated to her, Kazan among them. He never much cared for her personally, but in his later directorial practice, he would be more an Adlerian than a Strasbergian, with actors taking their emotional cues anywhere they found them—from memory if they wanted, but also from the text, from observed behavioral reality, even from their props. Strasberg grandly countered this would-be revolution by declaring that Stanislavsky was wrong, that he was

right and that The Group would continue on the path he had laid
out for them.

Adler's camp thought Strasberg's production of *Gold Eagle Guy*
offered good arguments for their case. As the actors stood about,
groping for their feelings, the play essentially ground to a halt. Now,
as Kazan later admitted, the play wasn't much (and it got worse
when Donald Oenslager's scenery began to overwhelm it), so Strasberg was perhaps burdened with too much blame for the failure
many saw coming. ("Boys, I think we're working on a stiff," Luther
Adler famously wisecracked.) But still . . .

For Kazan, the moment of truth in his relationship with Strasberg occurred during the Boston tryout of *Gold Eagle Guy*. He was
stage managing, and his biggest problem was the play's climactic
earthquake. He claimed that Strasberg never orchestrated the complex succession of effects the scene required in a manner he could
comprehend and execute properly. One night the sequence disastrously misfired and Strasberg dressed Kazan down so violently, in
front of the entire company, that that tough little nut retreated to the
theater basement sobbing.

"He was not a man, then or later, able to take his share of the blame
for any failure," Kazan would write in his autobiography; "he relieved
himself of guilt by chastising those who couldn't fight back." It was the
end of Kazan's always shaky trust in the man: "It's amazing how a humiliation, so small, so passing, remained in my memory—'like a knife,'
Greeks say . . ." Despite admiration for some of his insights—and
much public praise of him—over the decades ahead, he remained always on guard against Strasberg. "I felt—and I often felt again—that in
order to be close to this tight knot of a man, one had to knuckle under.
Others did; I did not."

A latter day Strasberg observer, Arthur Penn, the distinguished
director, put this point differently and more accurately. They worked
together at the Actors Studio (of which Penn eventually became
president), and he saw that what Strasberg was aiming at was "transference" in the full psychoanalytical sense of the term, with his "pa-
tients" (the actors) redirecting all the feelings they brought to their
work to the director (Strasberg), which, of course, gave him dictato-

rial power over them. Moreover, he was aiming at "mass transference," bringing an entire company under his sway—no laggards allowed—in which "they enraptured one another." It was, Penn said, "an awkward, wasteful way of getting to a certain place"—especially for those who resisted his "method."

No one who has written about The Group mentions the fact that Strasberg's method was often antithetical to the plays he directed. They were full of mass actions, expressionistic moments, historical generalizations, calling for a presentational style of acting, antithetical to the method. Given this conflict, it's perhaps no wonder he could not come to grips with the earthquake effect Kazan was supposed to provide; it was the kind of spectacularly realistic Belasco-like moment that was bound to send Strasberg into a tense and angry dither.

Sustained by a few positive notices, *Gold Eagle Guy* limped along the road to oblivion for a couple of months. But The Group had nothing with which to follow it. There was some interest in *I Got the Blues* (latterly *Awake and Sing!*), which Odets had been hammering away at for more than a year, but neither Clurman nor Strasberg was enthusiastic. Once again, the company was stalled.

The Communist Party—of all things—to the rescue. Its front, the New Theatre League, was looking for another short play for another Sunday evening benefit. The Group's Communist "unit" was approached to see if it had any ideas. Odets, with whom Kazan had grown even closer over the last year, was now a member of that unit, and he proposed a short play, the overall structure of which he would supply, with each member of a writing cartel calling itself SKKOB (after its members' initials) supplying one of its scenes. Two of the five would-be writers were not Communists—not that it mattered—but all agreed that the play should somehow deal with a strike.

That was scarcely a novel idea. The "strike play" had, in these years, become one of the left-wing theater's standard subgenres—everyone was doing plays in which downtrodden workers took their fates into their own hands by mounting insurrections against their exploitative bosses. Why the strike in *Waiting for Lefty*, as this little play came to be called, turned out to be a taxi strike is unclear. There had been such a strike in New York a year or so earlier, but Odets later claimed he knew nothing about it except what he read in the newspapers. All we know for certain is that the other members of SKKOB failed to develop their assigned scenes and that Odets finally retreated to his room and, in three days, knocked out a script.

He also took over such direction as the production had, which was minimal. In Kazan's recollection the piece "moved without the burden of analysis; it was energetic, light-hearted, bold, and sassy. And felt." In purely Group terms, everyone felt liberated by Strasberg's absence. "The lines didn't sound learned; they leaped out of the mouth at the moment. Still the total effect was sure-footed and confident."

Kazan does not mention, though we should, the play's fairly novel dramaturgy, which contributed greatly to its success. In effect, it broke through the so-called fourth wall, separating audience from players. Actors from the company—most notably Kazan—were in the house, responding to events as they unfolded on stage. From time to time the onstage actors spoke directly to the audience, as if they were part of the union meeting deliberating whether to call a strike.

The play was mounted on Sunday night, January 6, 1935, to a packed fourteen-hundred-seat house at Le Gallienne's Civic Rep theater on Fourteenth Street, where *Dimitroff* had been staged. But this time the response was electrifying. Kazan always called it the most exciting night he ever experienced in the theater, and he was not alone in this opinion. Curiously enough, some seventy years later, it remains entirely possible to see why that was so.

The controlling action of the play is simple: The members of a taxi union are, quite literally, waiting for Lefty, their chairman, to return from a mysterious errand, which will determine whether they will go out on strike. Their deliberations are dominated by a corrupt, cigar-chomping goon named Harry Fatt, who is obviously a tool of the bosses. He, of course, is counseling caution. Various anonymous voices from time to time shout out questions and comments from the auditorium. More important, the lights go down on this group and come up on several vignettes, not all of which are directly connected to the question of whether a strike should be called.

In the first of these a cabby comes home from work carrying his pathetic wages—not enough to support his wife and two children.

She passionately urges him to militancy. In the next we meet a scientist, working on developing poison gas in a laboratory. He is tempted by—but ultimately refuses—a huge wage increase, offered him by a cartoonish capitalist, if he will spy on the head scientist. Next we meet a young cabby and his girlfriend, who cannot get married because he does not earn enough money. They are left in despair by their hopeless economic circumstances. We come then to the emotional heart of the play, a scene in which a seemingly earnest union member urges caution on the unionists—only to be denounced by his own brother as a labor spy. It was Elia Kazan, sitting through the opening scenes of the play in the auditorium, wearing a soft cloth cap with a rabbit's foot tucked in the visor for good luck (he'd seen a real cabby wearing such headwear), who charged the stage to identify the fink. And received a storm of applause such as he had never known before.

He would later attribute part of his welcome to the fact that he was such an utterly unknown actor; for a minute it seemed to some that an actual member of the audience had been drawn into the play's action by the strength of his feelings. But no matter—the Communist *New Masses* called him a "proletariat thunderbolt"—an appellation he reveled in.

This crucial sequence is followed by one in which we see a brilliant intern denied the opportunity to practice medicine at its highest levels because he is Jewish. He watches helplessly as a well-connected incompetent botches an operation he should have performed. The original (as opposed to the published) version of the play contains a little sequence in which an out-of-work actor is radicalized by a secretary (Paula Strasberg) in a producer's office ("A dollar buys nine loaves of bread and one copy of the Communist Manifesto," she says, "learn while you eat") and another, also later excised, in which an American aristocrat denounces the American Constitution in terms borrowed from Charles Beard's then famous *An Economic Interpretation of the Constitution,* which held that that sacred American document was an economically determined instrument of class domination.

This brings us to the play's climax, in which it is announced that Lefty has been murdered and Agate Keller, the angriest and most radical of the union members, addresses his fellows. He is not, he says, a Communist, but he has seen them succoring those wounded in class warfare. And he raises his arm in the closed-fist Communist salute (which he analogizes to an uppercut). He calls for a strike in words capitalized in the script:

"HELLO AMERICA! HELLO. WE'RE STORMBIRDS OF THE WORKING-CLASS. WORKERS OF THE WORLD . . . OUR BONES AND BLOOD! And when we die they'll know what we did to make a new world! Christ, cut us up in little pieces. We'll die for what is right! Put fruit trees where our ashes are!"

Whereupon he turns to the audience and asks, "Well, what's the answer?" Elia Kazan was back in the auditorium again, his job now to take up the cry of "Strike" and again rush the stage, his fist also upraised in the Communist salute.

On that January night the audience rose with him, echoing his cry. And they did not leave the theater when the play was over. The curtain did not come down for something like forty-five minutes as fourteen hundred people cheered, applauded, stomped their feet. Cheryl Crawford remembered fearing the uproar might shake the balcony free of its moorings. Odets was brought forward for a tumultuous ovation, which caused him both to weep and (offstage) to throw up. Eventually audience and actors mingled for hours, lost in the rush of revolutionary emotion.

There was no sleep, that night, for The Group actors—and perhaps for many in the agitated audience. And reading the play now one has to say that it somehow retains its uncanny power to link simple emotions and primitive ideas in ways that retain their ability to stir us. Its characters are scarcely characters at all—they are representations of the most familiar class types. The situations they confront, the ideas they present, are crude to the point of banality. But the rush of feelings this play mobilizes, the passions it unleashes, our sense of good American people pressed to the wall by circumstances and fighting back with a desperation unknown in this country before or since, remains heartbreakingly palpable.

Is *Waiting for Lefty* a great play? No, it is hardly a play at all. But it is a wonderful act of conscience, and a great summary of a moment's mood—very likely the defining artistic gesture of its age. Nothing else—no film, no novel, no painting or poem—comes close to its raw power. Reencountering it decades later, we understand the profound sense in which American complacency, American good nature, was shattered by the cataclysm of the Depression, how deeply attractive revolutionary oversimplification was not just for people in a New York theater, but for the nation as a whole.

2

Awake and Sing

Waiting for Lefty quickly became one of the most produced plays in America (like *Dimitroff* it was offered free to working class theater groups). And one of the most banned. In the judgment of authorities everywhere it was an incitement to riot. There was no question that The Group had to produce this signature piece, short as it was, for a regular Broadway run.

Strasberg remained apart from this surprise success. He had been unhelpful when Odets asked for his advice on some questions of staging. And Kazan would recall getting no answer beyond a superior sort of smirk when he asked Strasberg for his opinion of *Lefty*. Worse, he made a colossal blunder in his relationship with the company.

Just prior to the sensational *Lefty* premiere The Group's directorate called a company meeting to say that when *Gold Eagle Guy* closed, their season would end. They had no play to follow it. Outrage, led by Stella Adler, greeted them. Promises of full employment had been made—and repeatedly broken. She contrasted this situation to her experience in the Yiddish theater, where actors in her father's famous company had always enjoyed full employment. Surely there must be something.

Whereupon Odets piped up. He had once again rewritten much of his long-cherished *I've Got the Blues* script to Clurman's specifications. It was now retitled *Awake and Sing!* And he was, he said, prepared to do still more work on it—including perhaps finding financing for it. Even more to the point, hadn't the company liked what they'd heard at readings of this work in progress the previous summer? Here was a sliver of hope and the actors responded optimistically to it.

Then Strasberg spoke: "You don't seem to understand, Cliff. We don't *like* your play." He subsequently repeated his words, as if thinking perhaps he had not been heard. It was a watershed moment in Group history. They were sick of Strasberg's pretense that he spoke for all of them instead of just for himself. They were a collective. Or they were nothing. Many years later, on a television documentary about The Group, Kazan, all passion on this point long since spent, stated the issues that had grown between Strasberg and the company as gently as possible: "They began to doubt his mastery and preeminence and he felt it and he gradually became alienated and hurt."

There was no open rebellion. They simply turned away from him. They agreed to read all the new plays currently on offer. And they agreed to a reading of Odets's revised script. This took place without Strasberg's presence, but with Clurman there—and, at last, openly enthusiastic about the work.

There is reason to believe that Clurman—even though he could not have predicted the success of *Lefty*—had shrewdly managed this scenario; he had always liked the Odets play and felt it was long past time that he assert himself as a director. Here, at last, was material that almost perfectly suited his sensibility.

So the show was placed in rehearsal on an accelerated schedule; it opened in mid-February, more than a month before *Lefty* began its uptown run. *Awake and Sing!* is something less than a perfect play; certainly it has none of *Lefty*'s almost kinesthetic power to stir blunt emotions. It is simply a slice of Bronx Jewish life, in which a fractious, hard-pressed family, the Bergers—middle class, at least in aspirations, but sliding downward because of the Depression—work out their rather dubious fates.

Stella Adler played the matriarch, shrewd and bitter, wearing a gray wig and body padding. Art Smith was her feckless husband. Their daughter, Hennie (Phoebe Brand), strong-willed and independent of mind, is a young mother, unhappily married to a wistful, almost poetic man named Sam (Sandy Meisner), but drawn to a bitter, wisecracking, one-legged war veteran and family friend named Moe (Luther Adler). The family's hopes are focused on Ralph (played by John Garfield then still called Julie, whose first Group role had been in *Lefty*). He's a young man eager for a better life, pursuing a hopeless romance with a woman who cannnot escape her domineering family. He also has a sweet relationship with his grandfather Jacob (Morris Carnovsky), a sympathetic, philosophical observer of the family's petty, yet curiously intense, drama.

At the end of the play, Jacob kills himself, "accidentally" falling from the roof of the Bergers' tenement, his $3,000 life insurance policy meant for Ralph. More shockingly, Hennie actually abandons child and husband to go off with Moe. There is talk of a slow boat to Cuba and a more exotic and adventurous life. Ralph encourages them. He'll give his money to his mother, thus solving their economic problems, and he says:

"I'm twenty-two and kickin'! I'll get along. Did Jake die for us to fight about nickels? No! 'Awake and Sing,' he said. Right here he stood and said it. The night he died, I saw it like a thunderbolt! I saw he was dead and I was born. I swear to God, I'm one week old! I want the whole city to hear it—fresh blood, arms. We got 'em. We're glad we're living."

There is, perhaps, something slightly desperate in this conclusion, something willed into existence by Odets, inspired by The Group's standard request for an upbeat ending. But plotting was, perhaps, beside the point. What Odets had given The Group was what it had been looking for since its founding—an authentic and singular voice, unlike almost anything previously heard on Broadway. These people spoke in the true vernacular of the city—tough, often street-smart, occasionally cliched, occasionally poetic in a rough sort of way. People who rarely went to the theater found their way to the Belasco from *their* tenements in the Bronx and Queens to see versions of themselves where they had never expected to find them—in a Broadway theater.

People spoke occasionally of Odets being the American Chekhov, which overstated the case and his talent. His people were scarcely declassed nobility, their thwarted ambitions were not so high or fine as those Chekhov examined. And there was, clearly, an awkward melodramatic edge to Odets's writing that is not present in the great Russian's work.

That said, it must also be acknowledged that Odets's work very much suited the Stanislavskian principles of The Group. They could feel the psychology of his characters in their bones, and deliver it in naturalistic performances. Clurman demanded little of them in the way of affective memory exercises; they were free to use the technique or not. Instead, the production was suffused with his own affection for characters he understood from his Lower East Side past, and by his affection for the playwright, for whom he was perhaps the benign father figure Odets had long sought. There was an easy warmth to the production that had been missing from Strasberg's work.

By and large, the critics noticed this quality, as did Kazan, stage managing it. It did not have the spectacular reach of Strasberg's big productions, but it was not tense with his vaulting ambitions, either. Clurman's direction was, apparently, patchy. To borrow a metaphor from Kazan, Clurman was much more an architect than a carpenter. Some critics faulted Clurman's production as "shrill" and "brittle." Some found it rather messily "Jewish," that is, too edgy and confrontational. Unlike modern auditors, they were unused to so open a portrayal of ethnicity.

In any case, *Awake and Sing!* had heart and soul, and its audience didn't give a damn about its defects; they simply loved seeing people they recognized, could identify with—was Stella Adler perhaps the first full-scale Jewish mother, dangerous yet somehow affecting, in theater history? As Wendy Smith says, *Awake and Sing!* was in its way as radical a gesture as *Lefty* had been.

And it was a success, though not quite a smash hit. It would run for something like a half-year, returning modest profits to The Group—and to Franchot Tone, who had used some of his Hollywood money to underwrite the production.

But this was not the end of what was surely the most astounding year of Odets's life. He had an immediate task before him. In order to place *Waiting for Lefty* on Broadway, another short play had to be added to the bill; so Odets wrote a one-act play, *Till the Day I Died*—this time taking four days to knock it out. The result was negligible, a play about the German resistance to Hitler, based on a letter from Germany that had appeared in *New Masses*. In essence, it tells the story of a onetime violinist, a Communist, named Tausig, who is arrested by the Nazis, but under torture refuses to betray his comrades. The Nazis, however, make it seem as if he did. Released, a broken man, he tries to convince his wife and brother of his steadfastness, but only she believes him, and he then commits suicide, convinced that no one else in the movement will ever again trust him.

The play will remind the modern reader of the kind of movies about life in the underground, some of them written by Communists, that in less than a decade Hollywood would be turning out as one of its contributions to the war effort. The difference is that Odets's play openly identifies the resistance leadership as Communist (which was largely true historically, but unmentioned in Hollywood) and that it offers a certain complexity of characterization—one Nazi is less than certain of his party's correctness, and both Tausig and Tilly, his wife, are rather appealing figures; in a couple of scenes their romance has a texture not generally found in agitprop works.

In short, the play was serviceable (and, like *Dimitroff,* a warning cry against Nazism, a rarity in the theater of its moment). For the most part it was patiently received and it had the practical virtue of granting a large cast of Group actors onstage employment. But no one went to the Longacre to see it. They sat through it literally waiting for *Lefty.*

Kazan gave up stage managing *Awake and Sing!* to play two roles in *Till the Day I Die* as well as the part of Agate (originated by the normally more comical J. Edward Bromberg) in *Lefty,* because Bromberg had taken a role in the longer Odets play. This was one of eight cast changes in this new *Lefty*—and at one point Kazan actually replaced an ailing Sandy Meisner for a week in his smallish role in *Awake and Sing!* (Kazan would change his costume in the taxi that ferried him from the Longacre to the Belasco every night.)

———

And still this breathless year was not over for Odets or for Kazan. The former had another play to polish—*Paradise Lost*—which The Group planned to produce in December with Kazan acting a strong supporting role in it. The young man who had so recently been told he would never be a successful performer was, in fact, beginning to build a career as an effective character actor.

But he was living more intensely elsewhere. He appeared in his first film in May 1935—a short, amateurish production called *Pie in the Sky,* about two bums in a garbage dump, spouting an essentially atheistic message. People who remembered it later thought it had something of the spirit of the 1960s about it, though it never had a theatrical release.

More important to him, just now, was the New Theatre League, where he taught a course in direction, preparing for each session by making hasty notes on the twenty-minute subway ride downtown. Even more significant to him was his work at the Theatre of Action, directing a company of fifteen actors and actresses who all seemed to him pretty much his own shape and size—small in stature, thin and wiry in build, with quick reflexes and politically contentious spirits. As the Workers Laboratory Theatre they had enjoyed an early success with a expressionistic play called *Newsboy,* based on a piece by V. J. Jerome, infamous as the Communist Party's chief aesthetic theoretician and commissar. Now, as the Theatre of Action, they were struggling desperately for audiences. Kazan recalled them working for contributions from labor unions and other leftist groups that turned out audiences not much larger than their acting company. One night their pay consisted of a large number of pumpkin pies, on which they gorged.

He became, he said, a temporary "hero" of this company. A nonmember, Norman Lloyd, who worked in one of their shows, remembered that their rehearsals "were like top-speed basketball games." More important, perhaps, he recalled Kazan believing that the director should "preserve the ego of the actor," instead of trying to tear it down as Strasberg often did. "He would persist with actors—he was with you, on you, all the time. You always felt that the two of you were together."

This approach brought him tremendous loyalty. Perry Bruskin, an actor in the company, would say that this respect derived from the way Kazan presented himself as a "professional theater *worker*" (italics his) and as "a man of iron. His muscularity, his macho was all there, and genuinely there." He and Nick Ray (among others) idolized him. "My version is that if we were on the second floor . . . if Kazan had said 'Nick, Perry, jump out that window!' we'd have done it. Or we'd have got awfully close to opening that window." Kazan himself would remember that the rehearsals were so intense that staged fights often became real ones, that staged romantic interludes sometimes threatened to deteriorate into public lovemaking.

In the spring of 1935, a little more than four months after the wild *Lefty* premiere, three months after *Awake and Sing!* opened, Kazan, codirecting with a man named Alfred Saxe, staged a play called *The Young Go First* about the CCC (Civilian Conservation Corps), a New Deal program designed to get young men doing useful public works. Middle-class America was always ironic and dubious about the CCC. It had seen too many of its members leaning on their shovels instead of digging ditches. *The Young Go First* was dubious about the program in a more ideological and melodramatic way.

Written by a consortium of three writers, it lacked, when Kazan took it on, a coherent third act. So he set the actors to improvising one—with a secretary taking notes on the thoughts, the variations on the play's themes, that occurred to them while they were on their feet. Essentially the play argued, rather improbably, that the CCC, which worked to improve the more bucolic portions of the American infrastructure, had an uglier agenda than providing healthy, outdoor jobs for young, jobless Americans. *The Young Go First* proposed that the CCC was a paramilitary training organization, breaking the wills of its innocent "soldiers," preparing them to become the storm troopers of native American fascism. The play was apparently not as rough and confrontational as its rehearsals had promised. The *New York Times* critic, Lewis Nichols, found it "too quiet an evening . . . a cracker barrel discussion where a brawl would be indicated." It managed a run of forty-eight performances in an off-Broadway house near Columbus Circle.

The Theatre of Action did not lose faith in Kazan, but he was beginning to be shadowed by doubts. He lived briefly in a collective apartment the Theatre of Action maintained, and he would remember his discomfort with shabby group living, confirmed by Norman Lloyd's vivid recollection of his unhappiness.

Kazan was disturbed, too, by the Theatre of Action's handling of a little play about New York's popular mayor, Fiorello La Guardia, then presiding over a government that fused a number of leftist political parties into an effective municipal regime. In its first version the play had offered a benign take on the mayor—at worst affectionately satirical about him. Then the Communists spoke and, according to Kazan, the play was revised and turned into an assault on La Guardia.

Even worse for Kazan was the atmosphere in what he had begun to think of as "his" company. There was, for example, the matter of self-criticism. This was a standard Communist procedure, in which the unit would confront an individual suspected of not following some aspect of the current party line and viciously assault him or her until an apology and a promise not to err in the future was made. It accounts, of course, for Jack Lawson's abject behavior in the matter of *Gentlewoman.* For the moment, in the case of the Theatre of Action, it took the form of actors vociferously criticizing other actors with whom they shared scenes. This was, of course, antithetical to Kazan's way of working—negative as opposed to positive reinforcement—but it was also a way in which performers could ideologically justify standard professional complaints: He upstaged me, he stepped on my line, he broke my concentration.

There is something comical about these sessions—acting egos and political ideology all mixed up—but only to us, looking back. At the time they were deeply wounding to individuals and, of course, harmful to company morale. Combine that with the fact that many in this group were attempting to live together in the cozy collective that Kazan also deplored, and one begins to see why, in his heart, doubt began to grow. "I was not a collective person or a bohemian; I was an elitist," he later wrote. He found the Theatre of Action's shared apartment "rather squalid." He did not, for example, like the idea of sleeping three to a room; "Where did they fuck? I wondered." And he did not like the notion of "a meeting every night. I hate meetings—hated them then, hated them now."

Yet he maintained his allegiance to the Communist Party—because for the moment it seemed part of the happiness he had found. It began with the success of *Lefty,* but that was only a beginning: "Whereas up until so recently—three years before—I'd been out of things, hostile, secretive, frightened, uncertain, adrift, a boy without confidence and with no direction, anxious about my future and living outside the course of the rest of humankind, I now felt proud, positive, busy, certain, confident, not only 'in' but in front, convinced of my worth, even a potential leader." His lonely alienation, had been collectivized; he felt a oneness with the millions, the prisoners of starvation that the *Internationale* assured him were in the process of arising.

So, for at least another year, Elia Kazan buried his doubts. As far as he could see he owed his newfound sense of himself—"Admired, respected, needed, acclaimed!"—entirely to his Communist connections. Some twenty years later, struggling (unsuccessfully, as it turned out) to write his first screenplay (for the film eventually entitled *Wild River*), he reflected on his sense of himself in 1935 in these scribbled notes: "I was the hero of the young insurgent working class art movement. I spoke without fear of contradiction. I had done nothing to prove my position. But I simply did not suffer self-doubt. The world was like a huge red carpet out ahead of me to be walked on. And it stretched on and on, no end."

He thought he was a hero because "A hero's an original. The only one of a kind. I was that rare thing, the first of the Communist intellectuals in the dramatic arts." He conceded, of course, that there were other party members in the theater, but they were pretty much confined to off-Broadway. He, thanks to The Group, was appearing on Broadway. And that, to him, made all the difference. It did not hurt, either, that he was fit from his workout and his strenuous theatrical classes—and attractive to women. Yes, he was married to Molly, but that did not stop his pursuit of others. Or stay his arrogance with them (in his "narcissism" he "wasn't interested in their problems").

Womanizing is, among other things, one of celebrity's prerogatives, and his friend Clifford Odets, whose fame was, in this moment, much larger than Kazan's, fully partook of that privilege as well. Since what Kazan was thinking about when he wrote these notes was a character meant to be a supremely confident New Dealer (sent to Tennessee to buy the land and relocate its owners so the TVA could build its dams and flood a river valley to create its great hydroelectric scheme), he considered making this figure a combination of himself and Odets.

He was to be a Jew and, yes, "pushy"—driven by a powerful need to improve on his parents' status, and perhaps most important, assert something like the same cocksure sense of entitlement that Kazan and Odets manifested in the first flush of their fame. One idea he had was to have a scene in which Dave tells the Tennessee woman he falls in love with to wear clothes emphasizing instead of suppressing her breasts, which he thought too small in the first place.

That notion went—wisely—undeveloped, but the controlling idea of Kazan's script remained. "I AM DAVE" (caps and underlining his), he wrote in his notes. Except, of course, there was to be a powerful admixture of Odets as well. "He was a different kind of glamour boy than we have today," Kazan wrote, remembering Odets carrying his recordings of Beethoven quartets around with him wherever he went "and planning to write music Horowitz, he was told, was interested in." In his hubris he thought he could have it all, and he had, according to Kazan "notes and plans that stretched twenty years ahead," some of which he realized, many of which he did not.

For his energies were scattered. When we think of Odets today, we think of a hugely talented man who never quite fulfilled his early promise, a man who, trying to embrace too much, lost his grip on the best that was in him and, finally as a man who died too young and burned out. Kazan was obviously no less ambitious and energetic. But he was focused in a way that was not only unique in his time and place, but rare enough in any time or any place.

By the summer of 1935 Odets had another play ready. Or, since this was the ever-distracted Odets, almost ready. It was called *Paradise Lost* and it was, once again, about middle-class New York life, though its principal figures, the Gordon family, were socially and economically a cut above the Bergers of *Awake and Sing!* The father, Leo (Morris Carnovsky), co-owns with Sam Katz (Luther Adler) a company that manufactures ladies' purses. It has, because of the Depression, fallen on bad times. The Gordons have a son, Ben (Walter Coy), whom they idolize, because he has been an Olympic track star, though he is now sidelined by a heart condition, another son, Julie (Sanford Meisner), who works in a bank and is frustrated by the lack of attention it pays his ideas, and a daughter, Pearl, who is a pianist.

The essential action of the play is to destroy the Gordons' social pretensions. It turns out that Katz has been cheating his partner—and exploiting their workers. Even worse, Ben is led into a life of crime by his friend Kewpie, and is killed in a shootout. At the end of the play they are evicted from their house, with their furniture piled on the street outside. About all they have to cling to—and it isn't much—is another of Odets's soaring, hopeful speeches, which the father declaims.

The play closely followed another of those hopeless Group flops, *Weep for the Virgins,* a piece about three sisters working in a cannery and fed futile dreams about movie stardom by their crazily ambitious mother, which closed after nine performances. Directed rather staidly by Cheryl Crawford and produced almost simultaneously with the Odets play, it had had the effect of draining some of The Group's best acting talent—notably J. Edward Bromberg—away from *Paradise Lost.* The failure of *Virgin,* naturally, put heavy pressure to succeed on *Paradise Lost* (though the production had been financed, curiously enough, by MGM, in return for its never-exercised film rights).

Paradise's chances were further diminished by Stella Adler's voluble dislike of yet another matriarchal role. She was an extremely attractive woman, and hated wearing gray wigs and body padding to play an older woman (at the *Awake and Sing!* curtain calls, she had always ripped the wig from her head so the audience could see her true age). But what probably doomed the work commercially was a letter Odets addressed to the drama critics before opening night, pointing out comparisons between his work and Chekhov's. Many critics noted this act of self-aggrandizement in their unfavorable, but not scathing, notices after the play opened on December 9. In particular, according to Wendy Smith, many of them were at pains to point out that middle-class life, as they lived and observed it, was not as desperate and melodramatic as Odets portrayed it.

With something like twenty-eight million Americans still on

some form of relief, there is something disingenuous about that critical stance. Not all of those millions, surely, were of the proletariat. Indeed, one gets a sense that after two hits in one year, it was time for the reviewers to bring Odets down a peg or two. It is a familiar pattern among critics. And it may also have reflected the fact that they had good seats in the orchestra on opening night. More than one Group actor observed that section of the audience receiving the play distantly, stonily.

This was an opinion not shared by the balcony. Its denizens had discovered Odets in his previous play, and their loyalty remained steadfast and, on opening night, vociferous. It was by no means misplaced. The Group acting company had always liked this play, if for no other reason than that it offered them some rich roles. One of them was a character called Mr. May, an arsonist who offers his services to Leo Gordon and Sam Katz as a last chance to save their business—burn it down and collect the fire insurance. Bobby Lewis, the company member least attuned to the method, played him as written—with a weird accent and a flamboyant manner. Another such figure—they were both seemingly dredged out of a bourgeois nightmare—was Kewpie, played by none other than Elia Kazan. He wasn't a mobbed-up gangster; he was more of a freelance delinquent, to whom Ben, tormented by the illness that had destroyed his running career, thus his pride, is fatally drawn.

It was said that Odets wrote the character with Kazan in mind. And it must be said that Kewpie's heedless ambition did square with everyone's impression of Kazan's hustling, bustling, try-anything spirit. But he is, as well, a challenging figure, because of the way he attacks the middle-class morality of the Gordons, their failure more actively to struggle against the fate crashing down on them. He is not, as we read him today, a completely dislikable figure—he has the energy of his amorality and he does truly love their son, whose death, he implies, may have had an element of suicide in it—he refused to run from a police ambush—a possibility his family will not entertain, but which the audience does.

That's the way it is with this play. It is not, by any stretch of the imagination, Chekhovian. But it is not entirely improbable, either.

Its language seems to me on the whole somewhat less strained than that of *Awake and Sing!*, its people in some sense more entertaining, or at least more theatrically satisfying, despite its glum conclusion.

Once again, The Group made a fight for it. There were letters to the drama editors, they took salary cuts, they addressed groups they thought might be sympathetic to the play. They derived consolation from the fact that people like Elmer Rice—a playwright with a taste for innovation—kept returning to the play. In *The Fervent Years,* Clurman, who had once again directed, quoted from something Clifton Fadiman, then a respected *New Yorker* book reviewer and a man of populist spirit, wrote: "As it is practically impossible to make oneself heard amidst the hurly-burly of the Odets controversy, this department wishes merely to mutter doggedly that with all its faults . . . *Paradise Lost* is a pivotal American drama."

That seems to me right. Flawed, yet spirited, it says more about the anxious edge a majority of Americans were living on at that time than, let us say, a typical strike play did. And it does so in a unique and compelling voice.

In the end, though, it was no use. The play closed after a run of just two months. Once again a Group season had come to an abrupt end. Once again its leading figures—the two Adlers, Morris Carnovsky— had proved their mettle. And the younger performers, Lewis and Kazan, had actually advanced their careers. This was the first "gangster" Kazan played, but not his last. He would over the next few years develop quite a nice little line in this type of role, with eventually no less an authority than J. Edgar Hoover pronouncing him perhaps the most authentic hood he had seen.

It was now 1936, and Kazan retreated to the Theatre of Action to stage his last play for the company. Called *The Crime*, it was written by Michael Blankfort, later to be a successful screenwriter (*Broken Arrow, The Caine Mutiny, Tribute to a Bad Man*) and, yes, a friendly witness before HUAC in the very month Kazan testified. In the thirties he was a left-wing novelist, playwright and drama critic. It's possible—though I think unlikely—that Blankfort was a secret Communist—he had been so named by Louis Budenz—but he was surely a troublemaker. Reviewing for *New Masses*, he had not liked

Awake and Sing! when the party line had favored it. Later, writing for the *Daily Worker,* he found himself admiring *Paradise Lost,* when the line had turned against Odets. Both reviews were spiked, and Blankfort ceased being a reviewer.° Keeping up with the party line as it snaked its way through modern American history could be a full-time—and ultimately maddening—task. It is why so many artists and intellectuals quit the party. It is also one reason that the act of testifying later on was so fraught with emotion. These conflicts may now strike us as ludicrous, but people invested them with high passion at the time, and the choice they presented—apologetic adherence to party discipline or rebellion against it—was stark and deeply troubling.

There is no record of Kazan discussing Blankfort's views as he and Alfred Saxe worked with him on *The Crime.* It was another "strike play," this time based on real incidents in South Dakota and Omaha. The argument is between adherents of the American Federation of Labor, conservative and craft-oriented, and organizers from the more radical Congress of Industrial Organizations, which militantly believed in industrywide labor unions, sweeping all workers into a union that would speak for all of them.

Norman Lloyd had one of the leads as the AFL representative— "I was a good villain," he later recalled, "because I really was closer to being a bourgeois than they were." Nick Ray and another actor who would go on to a major directing career in film, Martin Ritt, were also in the company. The play received lackluster notices and ran for only three nights. It was largely remembered by some in the audience for a rather startling effect—guns (loaded with blank cartridges) being fired over their heads at its climax.

In a sense, everyone was firing blanks that spring. The Group, trying to rally from the *Paradise Lost* failure, mounted a short-lived adaptation of Theodore Dreiser's *An American Tragedy,* which was

---

° One of the curiosities of Blankfort's career was that he helped Evans Carlson, a Marine Corps colonel whose wartime exploits were recorded in the movie *Gung Ho,* write a book. The hard-bitten career officer had served in China, where he became an admirer of Chairman Mao's guerrilla tactics, which he taught—against all current military doctrine—to his troops.

cowritten by Irwin Piscator, a great name in the left-wing avant-garde theater of the time (Marlon Brando would debut in his company a few years later). Called *The Case of Clyde Griffiths*, it was directed by Strasberg, who for once set aside his belief in affective memory. He told his company, "It does not call for psychological progression of acting, but essentially for full, precise actor's energy and the strictest kind of relationship to stage space."

The main defect of the piece, the critics said, was a "Speaker" narrating and commenting on the action. He was played by Carnovsky, who never quite believed in this bloodless, didactic figure, and the play closed after nineteen performances.

The Group now had nothing to do. It mounted a tour of *Awake and Sing!*, which started profitably and ended unprofitably; it looked for a new play, but had nothing in hand other than the Odets script they deemed unready for rehearsal and a musical by Paul Green and Kurt Weill, a version of *The Good Soldier Schweik*, called *Johnny Johnson*, which they would work on over their summer hiatus.

Kazan was not involved in *Clyde Griffiths*, and though he would play a role in *Johnny Johnson* when it opened on Broadway the following fall, he seems to have been in a state of emotional withdrawal from The Group. For one thing, Molly was carrying their first child, and he was heavily preoccupied with his impending fatherhood. He also busied himself in radio to earn extra money. At least as riveting to him was a reexamination of his ties to the Communist Party, in part occasioned by the fact that The Group was, once again, engaged in a reorganization, which the Communists perceived as an opportunity to assert themselves more boldly within its councils.

3

The Drama of Ordinary Life

In his memoir Kazan implies that its success with *Waiting for Lefty* and *Awake and Sing!* emboldened the Communist Party, led by V. J. Jerome, to try to take over The Group. Rather the opposite is true; it was the failure of *Paradise Lost* and *The Case of Clyde Griffiths* that more likely moved the party to action. The growing revolt against Strasberg's high-handedness, coupled with the sense that Harold Clurman lacked the organizational skills to make the company into a steadily going concern, was known outside The Group as well as within it and made it seem vulnerable to the more ideologically focused Communists.

Thus it was that Elia Kazan, as de facto leader of The Group's CP unit, found himself sitting opposite Jerome in his Twelfth Street office, receiving instructions. In essence, Kazan was told that The Group's three-person directorate should be removed and it should become more of an actor's cooperative, devoting itself to more overtly propagandistic pieces than it had. That, with the exception of *Waiting for Lefty*, The Group's successes had been with socially conscientious, but ideologically muted, plays—*The House of Connelly, Men in White, Awake and Sing!*—was inconsequential to Jerome.

Kazan was dubious. And his wife was outraged. When Jerome had heavy-handedly intervened in the affairs of the Theatre of Action she had cried, "What the hell does Jerome know about the oper-

ation of a theatre." She had been equally contemptuous of the grov-
eling the party hacks had elicited from John Howard Lawson.

As for Kazan, his first loyalty was to The Group. It was not just
that it had given him a home; it was also on the brink of giving him
influence on its management. Maybe his work on the playwrights
committee was not particularly heeded, but it was obvious that he
increasingly had Clurman's ear and that as it moved toward major
reorganization, he would inevitably have a larger say in the direction
The Group took.

But, for the moment, the most important of The Group's gifts to
him was his first touch of fame, deriving, of course, from his critically well-received roles in Group productions. Recalling this period
in his autobiography, he would say: "Acting . . . was the biggest
charge I ever had. I knew the exuberance of playing before an admiring audience and hearing my secret voice. . . . Every night I was
being reassured by hundreds of beating hands. Who could ask for
anything more. Oh, how that satisfied my soul? What other artist has
it so good? Approval so quick!"

He was being ironic. He expressed his true feelings about performance in other ways at other times. In 1952, for example, with his
directing career at its height, he would say to a newspaperman: "I
wouldn't go up on a stage now if you paid a thousand dollars for one
minute of acting. It's a nasty experience. You're up there all by yourself. You're so damn exposed. I was always a self-conscious person
anyway." He added that he had become an actor because his liberal
arts education had not fitted him for anything else. And besides, "I
didn't like to get up early in the morning or have to keep those regular hours."

Still, he never denied that acting had deeply influenced his directorial practice. "I was not what you'd call a first-class actor," he
said to me, "but I did all right. I was very intense, and I learned a
lot." This consisted of two things. One was to be proud to be an
actor. The other was not to be afraid of them as a director. On the
first point he said, "I think it's a privilege to be an actor. You can't just
sit there and do the lines. You have to do something that's revealing
or unusual. Or you have to remind people of their own struggles. In

other words, it's a responsibility to be a good actor," and, in the light of that belief, he said that he never felt sorry for actors, despite the profession's chancy nature. As for not being afraid of them, he meant simply that "they weren't foreign people to me. . . . A lot of directors . . . flatter them too much, and then, gradually they turn on them." Both thoughts are true as generalizations and true specifically of Kazan's later practice as a director.

But in 1935 Kazan was full of himself, rich in self-confidence, and not about to blindly follow the Communists' lead. So at the Communist unit's regular weekly meeting in the basement of the Belasco Theatre, Kazan set forth Jerome's demands objectively, but without much enthusiasm. If anything, one can safely imagine, he thought The Group was already too much an actors' cooperative; he thought it needed stronger, not necessarily more "democratic," leadership. And he thought it needed to broaden the range of what it was presenting, not narrow it still further.

His statement of the party's ideas for The Group did not satisfy some members of the unit, word of Kazan's failure of "leadership" was communicated to Twelfth Street and a second meeting was scheduled, this time in Lee and Paula Strasberg's living room (he was not a party member, but she was). Lee went out to the movies on the night of the meeting.

In Kazan's account (which has never been challenged), a stranger— "a man from Detroit," almost certainly an organizer for the United Automobile Workers, which had, at the time, a large and vociferous Communist element—took charge. Kazan identifies him, in the common term, as a "leading Communist," that is, someone privy to the party line as laid down by its leadership. His task was to impose "democratic centralism" on the group—get them to endorse the party's predetermined plan unanimously. He accused Kazan of a "foreman's" mentality, by which he meant that he was an intermediary, pretending a certain solidarity with the workers, but actually representing management's views.

That there is something almost laughable in applying this formulation to an extraordinarily fractious theatrical group is obvious. As we've seen, "management" in The Group was scarcely Draconian and its working stiffs were scarcely unified in their opinions. This

was somewhat patronizingly acknowledged by the Man from Detroit. He implied that the "kids"—these wayward children—needed
some "straightening out," needed to become more mature revolutionists. According to Kazan they "simpered" in agreement.

The meeting lasted for hours. Lee Strasberg returned from his
movie, poked his head in the door and was quickly banished. Eventually Kazan was offered a stark choice: between his loyalty to The
Group at large or to its Communist faction. He was also told that
forgiveness was possible. He had but to confess the error of his ways
and resolve to follow the party line in future. A vote was taken on his
behavior and the only one voting for Kazan was, of course, Kazan.

He did not resign on the spot. He took a brooding, circuitous
walk home and the next day delivered what he says was an unambiguous letter of resignation from the party. One has to wonder: If
perhaps even one or two of his Group unit had spoken up for him, if
a real debate about the role of the party in The Group had taken
place, might he have acted differently—at least for the moment?
One also has to wonder: If some of them had come to his defense in
1936, might he have more readily defended them seventeen years
later?

It is impossible to say. He was never much of an ideologue. He
rarely thought in abstract terms. His support of Communism and his
criticisms of it were not sophisticated; he invoked no high, wide or
handsome principles on this occasion. And in his later writings and
in his HUAC testimony Kazan scarcely mentioned any of those
events, like the Hitler-Stalin Pact, that became the way stations at
which many later hopped off the express train of history. Nor did he
mention, for a long time—until he was testifying before HUAC—
the fact that became obvious to many former Communists—that the
American party was very largely financed by funds from Moscow
and that its positions on any given political issue were always rigidly
set by the Kremlin.

Kazan's motive for joining the party was (as he later told HUAC)
"that the Party had at heart the cause of the poor and unemployed
people whom I saw on the streets about me" and that, fighting for
them, he would be "acting for the good of the American people."
this is pretty vague and, at the time, quite unexceptionable stuff.

He was by no means alone in this simple idealism. In *The Romance of American Communism,* Vivian Gornick writes: "It was the Party whose moral authority gave shape and substance to an abstraction, thereby making it a powerful human experience. It was the Party that brought to astonishing life the kind of comradeship that makes swell in men and women the deepest sense of their own humanness, allowing themselves to love themselves through the act of loving each other." She adds, "You were, if you were there, in the presence of one of the most amazing humanizing processes: that process by which one emerges by merging . . ."

But The Group offered something like this, too. And Strasberg's impositions aside, it did so without the often inexplicable demands, rigid in their expression, endlessly changeable in their content, of the party's bureaucracy. It was, for Kazan, a much better fit with his essential nature. He could and would go on vaguely believing in the general principles endorsed by official Communism, but he would quite cheerfully escape party "discipline." Like many another artist and intellectual in this period, he simply would not tolerate this failing god's interference with his work.

Kazan, more than most, was moved by offended pride, for, pleased by his quick rise to theatrical prominence, he thought of himself as "the only one of a kind." As he put it in his *Wild River* notes: "I thought everyone complicated things far, far too much. I was even superior to the Communists and when they didn't go along with me, I quit them, finding all inhibition of party insufferable. . . . I was the true future. I understood Communism better than they did." This is quite a remarkable statement, even if it is obviously colored by hindsight and written well after his HUAC apostasy, for if it is self-aggrandizing, and self-defensive, it is not, one thinks, emotionally false.

There is something else in these notes worth commenting on—the line in which he writes, "I understood Communism better than they did." So, I think, he honestly believed. As he wrote in *A Life,* as he told his son as late as 1999, he did not abandon the basic ideals the party pretended to support. In his book-length interview with Michel Ciment he says, "for years after I resigned, I was still faithful to their way of thinking. I still believed in it. But not in the American

Communists. I used to make a difference and think, 'These people here are damned fools but in Russia they have got the real thing.'" He says it was not until the Hitler-Stalin Pact that he abandoned this distinction. But he never abandoned his working-class sympathies or his belief in the need for some sort of revolutionary reform in America. He remained a sort of free-floating secret sharer of our subversive impulses, a lifelong rebel without a narrowly defined ideological cause.

Kazan would later say that he noticed no great change in his relationship with The Group or anyone else on the theatrical left after his defection. He continued to teach at the Theatre of Action and he even marched in the annual May Day parade in 1936 with other leftist show people. There were then, as there always had been, people in The Group Theatre who distrusted his ambition and his tireless energy. But their suspicion of him had little to do with his politics. Indeed, as far as one can tell, on the surface at least he maintained his former, largely agreeable, relations with members of the Communist unit.

Nonetheless, the rest of that year and the first half of 1937 was a particularly troubled time in Group history—though one is hard-pressed to name a period when its history was untroubled. But still, this passage ended with the resignation of two of its three founding directors (Strasberg and Crawford) and a fundamental change in the way it conducted business.

In brief, what happened was this: In summer 1936 The Group was, as usual, hopefully awaiting a producible script. Odets, in Hollywood, was working on something called *The Silent Partner.* At the same time, John Howard Lawson, the wounds from his previous Broadway failures having more or less healed, had a first draft of a play called *Marching Song* ready. Both were—well, yes—strike plays. The former has been characterized by Wendy Smith, who read the only (incomplete) version of it still extant, as "a mess"; the latter, an ambitious attempt to replace agitprop sloganeering with more elevated and spiritual language, seemed even less promising to Clurman.

Whose word this summer was, more than ever, law. He had proposed and won favor for a reorganization in which he, as "Managing
Director," would be the final arbiter of all significant Group issues,
with a committee of actors (Kazan, Stella Adler, Morris Carnovsky
and good-humored, popular Roman "Bud" Bohnen as his principal
advisers). Strasberg and Crawford would remain with the company,
but not as codirectors, which Strasberg said was fine with him. In a
letter Strasberg said that all three of them had, over the years, more
than once worked themselves to the verge of nervous breakdowns.
He wanted to be free, for a year or two, to do nothing but direct.

It was Clurman, in his new capacity, who formally rejected the
Odets and Lawson plays, which meant that the only script available
for The Group's first fall production was *Johnny Johnson,* which he
among others thought needed more work. An Americanized adaptation of Jaroslav Hasek's immortal satirical novel, *The Good Soldier
Schweik*—book by Paul Green, music by Kurt Weill, whose first
American show it was—it is about an ingenuous (and occasionally
ingenious) simpleton who subverts the military high command during World War I, emerging from his experiences, if not triumphant,
then at least physically, mentally and morally intact. As The Group's
first musical, it presented difficulties—large cast, many mood shifts
and a style of presentation far from its realistic main line.

Cheryl Crawford spent much of the summer in North Carolina
working with Green to improve the book, which neverthless was not
ready for rehearsal until quite late in The Group's annual bucolic retreat. On the other hand, Weill had appeared at their camp and
stirred high excitement among the company with his impassioned
talks about the kind of theater he believed in. He got The Group
working on *Sprechstimme,* the technique of speaking songs in a musical manner, which he had used in his most famous work, *The
Threepenny Opera.* It was something this company, which contained
few actors who could carry a tune professionally, thought they might
master. Beyond that, they simply liked this serious, cultivated but
approachable man.

Slowly, script revisions began to appear. The trouble was that the
show lacked a director. Clurman at first proposed that Stella Adler
and Kazan jointly direct. This was not a good idea. They didn't much

care for each other. Adler was jealous of Kazan's friendship with Clurman—she might or might not want him, but she surely didn't want anyone else to have a major claim on him—and reportedly, if ludicrously, wondered aloud if Kazan might be a homosexual. Kazan, for his part, resented her queenly manner and, in any case, thought he was qualified by now to stage the show on his own; he was miffed by Clurman's careless characterization of him as no more than a technically competent director. Finally, reluctantly, Clurman said he'd do it. But from the outset he felt overmatched by the material, and in late September, with trepidation all around, he yielded to Strasberg.

By now, time was short. The play was supposed to open in less than two months. As usual, there was a typical Group scramble for funding. Then, too, Strasberg appeared to be as much at sea with this show as Clurman had been. In his fine book on Weill's theatrical career, Foster Hirsch quotes Bobby Lewis on the production's "miserable" direction: "How helpless Strasberg was to find musical staging. The show was heavy with the kind of realism he was comfortable with. Lee only knew about the text and about the psychology and its relation to life. But with the music, he was not sure what he was doing. He could not help anyone deal with rhythm or movement . . . He didn't understand the style a musical—*that* musical—needed. And if Lee was the director you couldn't open your mouth."

Strasberg mentioned wanting to make the show a sort of "vaudeville," taking his cues from Weill's score, which satirized a lot of traditional American music. In any case, he wanted a show that was light, glancing, as often as possible amusing. But he couldn't keep this concept firmly in mind and the thing floundered. In his reminiscences of the show's desperate dress rehearsals, Clurman wrote that they were among the most depressing theatrical experiences he had ever endured. Kazan, working in a chorus of eight soldiers, intoning some of Weill's songs, was contemptuous of the whole "banal" enterprise. He took to wandering about looking uncharacteristically glum and withdrawn. He might agree with the play's antiwar sentiments, but its manner—arch, cute, flighty—was the antithesis of the kind of theater he believed in.

Worse was yet to come. Clurman had given Donald Oenslager

rather vague instructions about the sets, and when they arrived they overpowered the show. The same could be said of the house where it was booked, the vast 44th Street Theatre, seating fourteen hundred people. The play was meant to be intimate and insinuating; the sets and the venue suggested to audiences more epic ambitions, which, of course, it failed.

Somehow, though, the production began to come together in a respectable form. It partook of a mood that had been common in film and theater since *What Price Glory?* and is, in only a slightly different form, still familiar to us in film and theatrical representations of later American military efforts. In such productions (King Vidor's *The Big Parade*, Lewis Milestone's *All Quiet on the Western Front*) the ordinary soldier of World War I, whichever side he fought for, was presented as a victim of heedless jingoism and super-patriotism, risking life and limb in a bad cause. Very often, in the 1930s, the individual soldier, now of course a "forgotten man"—see the great, glum musical number in Busby Berkeley's *Golddiggers of 1933* or William A. Wellman's *Heroes for Sale*—was shown to be further victimized by an economy run for the convenience of the American plutocracy.

What the audience saw on the opening night of *Johnny Johnson* was very much in this vein—the story of a reluctant common man (played by Russell Collins) whose doubts about combat were momentarily stifled by Wilsonian idealism, then rekindled by service at the front. There is a sequence in which Johnny, sent out to kill a German sniper, instead befriends him. There is another scene in which, committed to an insane asylum, he is shown to be more sane than his keepers—a trope that, again, would be familiar to audiences in the sixties and later. Eventually, he is restored to normalcy and at the end he is shown playing with his child, but insisting that he have no war toys.

In short, the play veered constantly from sobriety to farce to romance, and in his balanced, intelligent *New York Times* review, Brooks Atkinson wrote that it was "part fantasy, part musical satire, part symbolic poetry in the common interests of peace; and, one is compelled to add, part good and part bad." Despite its "restless emptiness," Atkinson concluded that "people who believe that plays should be written about intelligent themes and who also relish experiments in form have something to be thankful for this morning. The Group Theatre has sponsored the first departure from polite mediocrity of the season. If it is not all buoyant, that merely proves, in this column's opinion, that the aim has been high . . ."

Most of the other reviews were similar in tone, as they so often were for The Group—encouraging of its aspirations, but making the play sound rather medicinal; good for you, but not much fun to swallow. Typically, The Group waged a fight for *Johnny Johnson*, but it ran for only a couple of months. It did, however, establish Weill in America. The notices for his music were uniformly excellent and this work had, for some time, a lively afterlife in college and community productions and, after World War II, in the Iron Curtain countries, which naturally admired its antimilitarist, anticapitalist sentiments.

The Group, though, looked as if it might not have any life at all in the midwinter of 1936–37. For the actors' committee delivered, not long after *Johnny Johnson* opened, a scathing report on the institution. It said some nice things about The Group's founders, but it also rehearsed, in quite brutal terms, all the charges we have seen accumulating against the leadership—Clurman's distractions, Strasberg's coldness and cruelty, Crawford's tendency to get lost in commercial details. The difference here was that these opinions were no longer gossip; they were set forth in cold typescript.

The report also stressed the common complaint that Group actors could not count on salaries or artistic coherence in their lives. The committee wrote: "We must set ourselves up for what we are and WHAT WE WANT TO BE—the Moscow Art Theatre of America." To that end, they proposed that somehow The Group acquire a theater of its own, a place where costumes and sets could be stored, rehearsal rooms were readily available, and, most importantly, a theatrical community grounded in real estate could be established. The savings, over the long run, would be great. But they didn't say how such a theater might be acquired. They did, however, suggest how it might be maintained; by establishing a theatrical school in which the actors could teach, earning modest livings when they weren't cast in a show, with The Group as a whole benefiting from tuitions.

In this idea lay the embryo of the Actors Studio, and the theory was right: The Group was the most admired acting ensemble in the

United States, just as the Studio actors were the most admired young acting talents of the next generation. Aspiring actors would have flocked to a Group school.

The problem, of course, would be a capital drive to establish this theater complex. The Depression, though somewhat alleviated, was still on; the kinds of community organizations that have since funded all sorts of performing arts organizations were unknown, and there was no one among The Group's desperately challenged leadership with the will or skill to lead the kind of funding drive this grand plan would have required.

The actors' committee concluded by offering The Group a stark and novel alternative, a "possibility we have not discussed—DISSOLUTION—to let a new and more fit Group rise from the ashes, to start on a clean slate—reorganize fully, bearing in mind our past mistakes."

This report stopped The Group in its tracks. Desultory rehearsals of Odets's rewritten *The Silent Partner* ceased (it didn't help that the ever-distracted playwright was unavailable to them). With the closing of *Johnny Johnson* in mid-January Clurman wrote a *New York Times* piece hopefully entitled, "The Group Pauses, but Only to Think It Over." A committee composed of the former directors and some actors gathered to plan such future as The Group might have. But mostly the players scurried to find work in the commercial theater, radio, movies and, yes, the Federal Theatre Project, which, subsidized by the Works Progress Administration, briefly had the financial stability The Group had always lacked, and had become, also briefly, the nation's leading left-wing theater. Kazan thought the luckiest member of the company was Julie Garfield, who had gotten good notices in *Johnny Johnson*, which led to a large role in *Having Wonderful Time*, Arthur Kober's comedy of life in a Catskills resort, which made him a Broadway star and soon led to a Hollywood offer.

The Group's hiatus would not be long. It would return in the fall of 1937 with its biggest success since *Men in White*. But it would not be The Group anymore—not really. Strasberg and Crawford resigned in the spring of 1937, never to return. They announced plans for a company of their own, which never came to fruition. Clurman would stay with The Group, but it was now little more than a producing office, not so very different from the Theatre Guild from which it had sprung. The eight plays it produced between 1937 and 1940 would by and large not be in The Group's traditional vein— some, indeed, were indistinguishable from standard Broadway commercial fare—though it would continue to draw frequently on actors who had been stalwarts of the old company. That the new Group would be more to Elia Kazan's practical-minded taste is hard to doubt. That something valuable was lost to the American theater when The Group took its "pause" in 1936 is also indisputable.

Kazan was luckier than most of the other Group actors. During the 1937 Group hiatus, he participated in the making of a film—his first substantial involvement with the movie medium—and he had his first taste of Hollywood living. Both experiences would have a lingering influence on his life.

The film was a documentary, *People of the Cumberland*, about the lives of strip miners in Tennessee. It was the creation of a cooperative organization called Frontier Films, which, when it was founded, was described by *Variety* as "The Group Theatre of Motion Pictures," possibly because two of its leading figures, the photographers Ralph Steiner, who was a particular friend of Kazan's, and Leo Hurwitz, had recently taken a directing course with Strasberg and saw ways of using his techniques in nonfiction film. Others who cast their idealistic lot with Frontier included Paul Strand, eventually to be regarded as one of the great photographers of his era, as well as Jay Leyda and Willard Van Dyke, both scholars and filmmakers with a lifelong interest in documentary.

The 1930s was a great period for documentaries, witnessing the creation of legendary examples of the genre—films like Pare Lorentz's *The Plow That Broke the Plains* and *The River*, and Van Dyke's *The City* . These films were all distinctly left-wing in their political orientation. *Plow,* for example, took up the idea that overfarming had so damaged the land that it caused the Dust Bowl. *The River* supported hydroelectric schemes like TVA, *The City* supported the New Deal's "Greenbelt" idea—the creation of suburban housing developments, which, it was hoped, would relieve the urban pressures causing crime and poverty.

These films later were of high interest to HUAC, in part because some of them had been made with federal money. Kazan, indeed, was questioned by HUAC about *Frontier*, but maintained that Steiner was anti-Stalinist and claimed to know nothing about the beliefs of others in the organization.

On the whole, these films were rather symphonic in manner. They often attracted major composers (Aaron Copland, Virgil Thomson, Marc Blitzstein) and their narrations were quite poetically written (in the mock-simple proletarian style of the day). Cinematically, they embraced Soviet-style montage—big close-ups of honest, economically marginal workers alternating with pastoral and industrial landscapes, insert shots of hands busy at their humble tasks, even, occasionally, speeded up or slow-motion sequences. It is not too much to say that there was more self-conscious striving for art in these pictures than there was in most American fictional films of the time.

People of the Cumberland was in the same vein as the more famous documentaries of its day, though it was not so epic in scope or length. It gives a good, gritty portrait of the miners—plain, simple, dignified folk—and shows how a school in the area promoted unionization among them. Steiner himself did the photography, the narration was written by novelist Erskine Caldwell (already famous for the sensational *Tobacco Road,* but also a writer of documentary-style books about the Southern poor) and the music was composed by Alex North (later to contribute the haunting incidental music to *A Streetcar Named Desire*) and Earl Robinson (later to write the music for the Academy Award–winning short about tolerance, *The House I Live In*).

It is hard to say, exactly, what Kazan contributed to this enterprise. Three other men are listed as codirectors. Thomas Pauly speculates that his "Group training gave him insight into what made a scene or action convincing." Kazan himself would say that he gained from the experience "great confidence in my ability to go into an environment and get drama and color and entertainment out of the most ordinary people"—a hallmark of his later style.

Handsome and moving as these documentaries were (and remain), there was something troubling about them, too. When he reviewed *People of the Cumberland* in the *Nation,* Mark Van Doren was dubious about some of its effects. He was not sure, for example, if some of the film's images were, strictly speaking, truthful, by which he meant items an historian could document and footnote. In any case, he questioned the whole "gravitation of left-wing aesthetics toward 'realism.'"

Others as liberal in temperament as Van Doren have continued to raise that point. Realism as an aesthetic principle is, strictly speaking, impossible to achieve. However lifelike a performance or a painting or a play or a movie is, it can never fully reproduce the situation portrayed; selection, emphasis and, yes, ideological considerations are always basic to the artistic process. So, as the distinguished English critic Terry Eagleton has forcefully argued, realism, in practical terms, "is the artistic word for warm-hearted populist humanism." He adds, "Realism is the artistic form that takes the life of the common people with supreme seriousness, in contrast to an ancient or neo-classical art which is static, hierarchical, dehistoricised, elevated, idealist and socially exclusive."

Using that definition we can see why realism was, artistically, such a dominant force in the 1930s and perhaps begin to understand why Strasberg's epic scale and more abstract productions (*Gold Eagle Guy, The Case of Clyde Griffiths, Johnny Johnson,* et al.) failed. In some ways these productions actually flirted with neo-classicism, which, Eagleton argues, implied a continuity between, for example, Homeric epic and Nazi art, "with its heroic myths, tragic posturing and spurious sublimity."

What I believe Kazan perceived in the "montage tropes" (to borrow a phrase from Eisenstein) of the little film about the Cumberland folk, what he may have more dimly sensed earlier, when the Russian epic caught his eye, was that movies offered him a visual language—close-ups, editing, insert shots—that more efficiently and powerfully permitted the poeticizing of reality than the stage ever could. Even when he staged poetic or expressionistic works, they remained grounded in reality, which always, unquestionably, was central to his aesthetic. What he did not notice, what few, if any, at the time noticed, was that there was a close analogy between left-wing and right-wing movie epics; both were tainted by a totalitarian aesthetic.

Be that as it may, his few weeks in Tennessee were, for him, infinitely more rewarding than his few months in Hollywood later in 1937. Walter Wanger, Dartmouth and Oxford educated, literate and intelligent, but also slick and superficial, well dressed and perfumed (in Kazan's observation), was at the time Hollywood's hottest independent producer. He conceived the notion of using The Group's leading players as a sort of stock company in his films and he screen-tested a number of them, including Luther Adler, Bud Bohnen, Morris Carnovsky, Lee J. Cobb and Kazan. He intended first to cast them in a script Odets had written with help from its potential director, Lewis Milestone. It was to be called *Castles in the Air,* and it was to be about Spanish loyalists in Paris, trying to return to their native country and join the fight against fascism.

The film was most basically to have been a sort of liberal-minded romance (Charles Boyer and Madeleine Carroll were mentioned for the leads), but it was at least an attempt to deal, in however gingerly a fashion, with the Spanish Civil War, at the time a defining and passionately preoccupying matter for the American left.

Years later, Kazan would recall: "Everybody in The Group was . . . jealous of you when you made a film [and] every move away from the Group into the film world, like Franchot Tone, was a betrayal of something everyone was devoting their full heart and their full time to. I mean, it was a mania, The Group Theatre. No one dared leave family, say, and go 'outside.' The word 'outside' was used all the time." He detected something both "very stuffy [and] also very Jewish" in The Group's familial values.

But now The Group was at least temporarily disbanded and here he was, on his own, in a strange new country, which, however often he worked there, he never came to enjoy, making a screen test, apparently directed by Milestone. His screen test seems to have been an improvisation (with his old friend Alan Baxter), in which two hungry soldiers, serving an unnamed country, squabble over a sandwich they must share and a woman they are eyeing. In it, Baxter, affecting something of an upper-crust accent, is much more the comfortable *movie* actor, at ease and ironic in the situation. Kazan is not fully relaxed before the camera. He is very intensely focused on the business at hand—argumentatively, if with due philosophical punctiliousness, splitting up the sandwich. But he's trying too hard to make a good impression.

He did well enough, though; he was among The Group players Wanger granted $150 per week contracts—big money by their humble standards, chump change by Hollywood's. Nothing much came of Wanger's scheme. *Castles in the Air* was never made, though Wanger did, the following year, make his Spanish war picture. *Blockade* was written by John Howard Lawson, and starred Carroll opposite Henry Fonda in a film the Catholic-controlled movie censors insisted not openly identify which side in the war the stars were supporting. Which is why Odets and Milestone dropped out of the project, which was directed by William Dieterle.

Some of the other Group players got jobs in other films. And some of them learned to relax and enjoy their brief season in the sun. Kazan did neither. He recorded an anecdote in which one of Wanger's assistants tried to get him to change his name, to "Cezanne," Kazan pointed out that it was already taken, as it were, by an immortal painter. Never mind, came the reply; after a couple of pictures no one will remember the other guy. The incident was emblematic of Hollywood to him.

The best thing about his stay was the friendship he struck up with Milestone, living off the reputation of *All Quiet on the Western Front,* and deeply respected in Hollywood leftist, intellectual circles. Kazan began working for him as an unpaid assistant, once again employing his typing skills, soaking up, along the way, valuable knowledge about constructing screenplays.

He also found himself, somewhat to his surprise, missing The Group Theatre and worrying about Harold Clurman. The director was enjoying his Hollywood prosperity, dressing smartly, eating in the better restaurants, putting on weight. But in Kazan's view he was drifting, rudderless, in Wanger's wake. He had a job consulting to the producer, but his tasks—like teaching a group of models how to walk gracefully in front of the cameras—were degrading, in Kazan's opinion. Clurman was a man of the theater or he was nothing. And Kazan thought he was in serious danger of becoming the latter.

Here good luck intervened. Odets had given up on *The Silent Partner,* and Hollywood had, for the moment, given up on him. He was doing a little script doctoring and toying with an idea for a new play, which he called *Golden Gloves.* It was about a prizefighter who is also a violinist and must choose between the two careers. He showed a simple outline of it to Clurman and other Group friends, and they began buzzing about it. In his autobiography Kazan makes the same shrewd point about Odets that he later made about Marlon Brando; both men were like fine autos with faulty starters. They needed others to jump-start their motors.

Golden Gloves, even in rough form, was a ballsy piece—like Odets's earlier work in that it portrayed the boxer's immigrant family (they were Italians this time) in warm, yet contentious terms, but unlike the previous plays in that it was not confined to a living room. At least half the action takes place in gyms, in fight arena dressing rooms, in a boxing manager's office, and it was replete with colorful and even criminal characters. It had the kind of clear, hard-hitting melodramatic elements Odets's earlier works had lacked.

Galvanized, Clurman sent Kazan and Luther Adler back to New York to open a new Group office. Kazan told the faithful there that he didn't know who would be cast in the new show, who would not. But at least The Group was up and running again. There were, naturally, money troubles, which the playwright himself helped solve. And there were casting problems. The lead role, Joe Bonaparte, was dangled before both Luther Adler and John (formerly Jules) Garfield, with Kazan, too, briefly under consideration (he would play Joe in the road company). The part went to Adler, who was a touch too old for it, possibly because Clurman sought to placate his ever-instructing wife, Stella, who was, of course, Luther's sister. Garfield, according to one biographer, "never got over" this rejection, but Adler gave a widely admired performance in the show, which opened under the title, *Golden Boy* on November 4, 1937.

Many people noted that it was not in every respect a typical Group production. It had its villains, naturally, but they did not particularly symbolize capitalism turned rancid; they were just ordinary urban lowlifes. It was the same with its heroes; they did not particularly represent upbeat virtue. They were just rough-hewn but instinctively decent folks. Some observers—Kazan among them—noticed that the conflict in which Joe Bonaparte found himself—fame and wealth versus the impulse to art—analogized quite neatly with Odets's own situation.

One sometimes thinks Odets was a man betrayed by his own energy. He could delude himself into thinking he could do everything, including, possibly, imposing his artistic conscience on Hollywood. For all that, he was a lovable guy. His biographer, Margaret Brenman-Gibson, speaks of the tactile, tousling relationship he and Kazan always maintained in those days, with Kazan remaining a sympathetic, compassionate witness to his friend's increasingly hard struggles to remain a force in film and theater in the years ahead.

Odets required no compassion in November 1937. *Golden Boy* was a huge hit, so large that if The Group had not been compelled to sell off large pieces of it in return for backing, it might have provided the kind of subsidy it had always needed. It did, at least, substantially underwrite its next two seasons.

Reread now, *Golden Boy* seems like the model no subsequent boxing fiction could ever fully avoid. It's all here—the clean, hard-hitting protagonist fearful of the potential killing power in his fists (Joe does actually kill an opponent), his fast rise to "contender" status, the abandonment of simple family values and the embrace of heedless materialism, the circling pressure to throw the big fight, the dark ending (in this case a tragic one). Maybe there's something schematically oversimplified in its violin versus squared circle conflict, but there's freshness in much of its language and in Odets's portrayal of minor characters. His material was not yet clichéd and there is, above all, a compelling rush to the play that had not been present in his work since *Lefty*.

The voluble Odets was, once again, his own worst enemy in the interviews he gave and the pieces he wrote about his work, wherein he was inclined to attribute the play's strength to his screenwriting experiences. In an interview with the *Daily Worker*, a few days before the play opened, he was scornful of left-wing playwrights bitten by the "Broadway bug." He couldn't blame them for lusting after "bourgeois glory," though he thought "real theater isn't on Broadway—it's to be played on the back of a wagon and in a union hall." If,

however, there was to be socially conscientious theater on Broadway,
he implied that he and others like him might just be the men to
write it. "Our left wing playwrights can learn a lot from the movies.
It's a training school in technique. I know I'm a better writer now
than when I wrote *Lefty*. The movies teach you how to please people, how to entertain them and—most important—how to change
their minds. That won't do any left wing writer any harm."

Obviously, he was anticipating criticism of *Golden Boy* for being
excessively cinematic. The notion that the theater was inherently pure,
the movies inherently corrupt, was a powerful one for decades. And it
was wildly wrongheaded. Maybe there were more overt idealists in the
former field, more cynics in the latter. And certainly the money was
better in Hollywood. But, in truth, they were both branches of show
business, and both held huge potential dangers for the serious artist. It
is, I think, one of Elia Kazan's salient virtues that he understood the
falseness of this commonly stated dichotomy. You never found him de-
bating it; you only found him working, on stage or screen, his happiness
dependent solely on his immediate circumstances.

In the fall of 1937 we must imagine him happy, in what was unquestionably his richest role to date, as Eddie Fuseli, a gangster who
wants, and eventually gets, a piece of Joe Bonaparte. Brooks Atkinson thought his work, and that of Art Smith, playing Joe's honest,
straightforward trainer, were "the simplest and most effective char-
acterizations in the cast." Maybe Kazan's performance was not as
simple as it seemed. Odets had written, and Kazan consciously
played, the elegantly dressed and rather mannerly mobster as a
predatory (if unacknowledged) homosexual, his eyes fixed, hawklike,
on Adler, but filled with loathing when they turned to his love interest, played by Frances Farmer.

Karl Malden, a Goodman Theatre actor from Chicago (and a former steelworker in his native Gary, Indiana), had been encouraged to
come to New York by another Chicagoan, Robert Ardrey, for a role in
the latter's *Casey Jones*. But Herman Shumlin, the producer, unable to
get the star he wanted—Walter Huston—backed out, stranding
Malden. Ardrey got him an interview with The Group, and, largely
thanks to Kazan—who, as always, looking for working-class authenticity in actors, was visibly impressed by the time the actor had spent in

the mills—he got a small role in *Golden Boy*. Every night he watched Kazan work and thought his manner was not at all that of the other Group actors—not as introspective, more eager for the audience's attention. He played, in Malden's words, "on the slant . . . on the fey side." In both his memoir and in an interview, Malden made much of a moment in which Kazan simply had to take his hat off "in a kind of feminine way and you knew, right away—oh, oh—there's something fishy here." Malden thought, correctly, that Kazan's style didn't work in the movies, but, on the stage, at least in this production, "you couldn't keep your eyes off him."

Their friendship began in those days, and Malden would become the actor Kazan most frequently cast in his plays and films—in part, Malden says, because Molly Kazan took a shine to him, and was always badgering her husband to give him roles. For the moment, along with Martin Ritt, whose knowledge of boxing helped secure him a small part in the play, they worked out together in gyms, played a little handball, shared the odd meal.

Marked as it was by everyone, Fuseli's homosexual yearning for Joe was only one part of a fairly complex character. Odets penetrated, as no one else had, his friend's Anatolian smile. In a long note he gave to Kazan, quoted by Brenman-Gibson, Odets wrote: "His dominant mood is loneliness. [He believes] no one does anything except from fear and a desire for power or gain. He distrusts everyone, even the people he loves. . . . This gives him adjustments of furtiveness, carefulness, watchfulness . . . People don't trust him and he doesn't mind it . . . He is completely shut off from other people."

Odets did not, of course, think his friend was "evil" (a word he applies to Fuseli in the note), or shut off, but he did detect the tough, shrewd core of his nature—and the essential loneliness of the man, often ingratiating but sometimes grating as he tried both to advance himself and to bend others to his will.

In his own estimation, Kazan did neither when, at last, he attained his dream—directing a Broadway show. The play was the very one Herman Shumlin had dropped: Ardrey's *Casey Jones*, now picked up by

The Group and given to Kazan to direct, which he left *Golden Boy* to do. The playwright had an interesting and wide-ranging intelligence. He had studied the natural sciences at the University of Chicago and lectured in anthropology there before turning to the stage. Two previous works had failed on Broadway—one of them just a week or two before *Casey Jones* premiered. But he was undaunted, which was one of his more attractive characteristics. Before he died in 1980 Ardrey would write more plays, two novels and several screenplays and enjoy best selling success in the 1960s with popular, controversial anthropological studies of primitive man, *African Genesis, The Territorial Imperative* and *The Social Contract.* He was a liberal, but with a distinctly non- (if not anti-) Communist cast of mind, and in this play he was trying to write about working-class people without imposing conventional Marxism on them.

Ardrey's narrative was imaginative: The title character, named after the hero of the famous folk song and carrying something of his heroic dutifulness about him, too, is a railroad engineer. He has sacrificed his life to making his express train run on time. By extension, that means he has sacrificed everything to "the line" that employs him. He's a cold, hard-bitten man whose eyes start to fail him—he first stops his train, delaying its on-time arrival at its destination, because he imagines seeing a signalman flagging him down, then runs through a real stop signal, causing an accident. The line finds a job for him as the master of a small station with virtually no traffic, where at the end he flags down an express train—a belated expression of his independence of the rules and regulations by which he has always lived—hops the train and heads off into the night—and an ambiguous ending.

Casey Jones, the critics agreed, was episodic and not well-made. Yet there is something touching, even intermittently powerful, in Casey's bafflement over the way his life has turned out. There's a caged-animal quality about him, and a blindness about his own fate, matching his physical blindness, that is quite arresting.

There is something else in the play that is manifest on the page and must surely have come through even in the blighted production Kazan made of it—a sense of alienation, a lack of true camaraderie among working Americans. "America is the most lonely country in the world," Kazan wrote in his notes for the play. "In Europe, the working man at night gathers with his fellows, sings, carouses, converses, drinks, talks . . . They are wholly what they are. They don't expect to get rich, there's no reason to distrust one another. Contrast this with any large American city . . . all you see is the lonely single male, bitter, outcast, lonely, isolated, distrustful, like a snarling jungle cat. Even the successful people are lonely. Cliff says success isolates you . . ."

These generalizations are dubious, perhaps, but Kazan found in them the play's "spine," which is, as Kazan wrote in capitals, to find a way, in America, "TO LIVE LIKE A MAN." It is possible, judging by the reviews, that these qualities were not made manifest in Kazan's production, though his hero's fierce and misguided isolation possibly was. Among the Marxist ideas that still enthralled Kazan was the alienation of labor. In his notes he wrote: "In Russia today, when a man gives his life to the machine, so to speak, he is fundamentally working for himself, for the machine is his strongest aid in making a better life closer." In short, thanks to ideology—to something like Gornick's idea of "emerging through merging"—he finds a satisfaction in his work that transcends his paycheck.

Kazan personalized this notion: "I gave my life to the Group Theatre, because in it I'm building something for myself. What I build, I am. . . . I don't do it as a means to live, rather THRU it I live." This is, at best, an idea that might have occurred to a politically conscious viewer well after seeing *Casey Jones*. But it is a response to those colleagues who distrusted Kazan's ambition and drive. And in the earnestness of his expression there is, I think, a truth. Or, perhaps by now, only a half-truth. These are the reflections of a man trying a bit desperately to reassert his loyalty to an entity that had permanently formed his sensibility, but that he was now beginning to distrust. Within a year, he would be openly wondering to his wife, in his notes, if he and The Group had not outlived their usefulness to each other.

For the moment there were, in Kazan's own opinion, defects in his direction of *Casey Jones* that he did not solve. For one thing, he perhaps allowed Mordecai Gorelik's set, which featured a huge train chugging and clanging and whistling on the stage of the Fulton Theatre, too much dominance. It was a great effect—most of the critics commented favorably on it—but it rather overwhelmed the play. Perhaps more important, Kazan could not handle his star, the veteran Charles Bickford. He was not an easy man, and though he could play sympathetically, there was sometimes something cold and ungiving in his presence; "warmth" was something he could only "indicate." This quality came to the fore here, where he was "hostile and invariably suspicious" from the start. Kazan, was "afraid" of the actor "and he, like any beast, could smell my fear."

There were other matters distracting Kazan at the time. He was engaged in what was, to date, his most passionate and long-lasting extramarital affair, with a young actress, Constance Dowling. Some in The Group knew of it and disapproved; they were aggrieved on behalf of Molly, who had become their well-liked play reader. Then, too, there was the matter of a young actress named Katherine Bard, whom Kazan had cast as Casey's daughter and the love interest of his happy-go-lucky fireman, played by Van Heflin (who would get the production's best reviews). Clurman brought Stella Adler in to coach Bard, challenging Kazan's authority and causing him to consider quitting. He did not, but Bard was replaced and the show opened to tepid reviews on February 19, 1938.

The critics were particularly reserved about Bickford. One mentioned that he had a cold on opening night and so was not at his best, which may or may not have been true. "Stalwart" was the word another applied to him. Kazan was not present on this glum occasion. He had retreated to Florida for a brief rest. There he got a telegram from Kermit Bloomgarden, later to be a leading Broadway producer, but then The Group's general manager. He said that the piece had failed because Bickford was "scared stiff."

But Kazan knew Bickford's failure was his own failure. Directing, he says in his memoir, "was a complete trial of a man's character," and by not challenging Bickford, by failing to answer bullying with firmness, by failing to stand by the untried Bard, by failing to stand up to Clurman and Adler, he had failed himself, Ardrey and The Group in general.

Typically, Kazan did not mourn long for Casey's passing (after twenty-five performances). The Group finally, actually, had an acting school up and running (it opened ten days after *Golden Boy*, with fifty students, chosen from a thousand applicants, paying $110 for a twenty-week course). Kazan and Bobby Lewis were the principal teachers, and Kazan now returned to classes and to *Golden Boy*.

In June he and many of the Broadway production's leading players mounted *Golden Boy* in London, where their ensemble playing—and their working class accents and style—were a revelation to English critics and audiences. The following fall he played the title character in a touring company that opened in Chicago. Such was his authenticity that the local mobsters took him to heart, offering him "protection" should he require it. Kazan was amused and pleased by their approval. The man loved low-life characters, "real" people, and none in his experience was lower and realer than these gangsters. They got him a better apartment than he was able to afford on his modest salary; they took him to see the silent rooms where once Al Capone had lived; most of all, they reassured him that he had captured their true essence in his performance.

4

Quiet City,
Restless Spirit

For the next three years Kazan was basically a working actor. Between January 1939 and February 1942, he directed only two plays (one of them a two performance Sunday night experiment). But he appeared in five Broadway shows and two movies.

Some of this activity was the result of The Group's regeneration. And some of that was the result of Molly Kazan's devoted work as a play reader. Finally, finally, under her encouragement, new playwrights were gravitating toward The Group. In 1939, for example, Molly, Clurman and Irwin Shaw were the judges in a Group-sponsored playwriting contest. They decided to award a sort of consolation prize (of $100) to a young playwright with the improbable name of Tennessee Williams. It was for an early draft of a cycle of short plays, later produced and published as *American Blues*. The award was the first serious professional recognition Williams received. Moreover, the money came in handy, arriving when, as he so often was in those days, close to destitution. Better still, it brought him into contact with Molly, who became one of his great champions. Best of all, she introduced him to Audrey Wood, who became his devoted agent, the woman who would, eventually, make astonishing deals for him (especially with the movies), while constantly sorting out his messy, footloose life.

As these relationships took root, The Group entered upon a final feverish period. In addition to mounting two new Odets plays (plus a revival of *Awake and Sing!*), The Group in these years also presented two plays by the young Irwin Shaw, one by William Saroyan and another Ardrey work. Unfortunately none of them was a hit and the company finally ceased functioning in late 1940. But in this period it presented a group of plays that reached out beyond realism, sometimes toward the poetic, sometimes toward the purely commercial. All of them acknowledged that times were changing, that social problem plays with an overtly leftist viewpoint no longer particularly stirred audiences.

This is true, for example, of Odets's *Rocket to the Moon,* which was produced while Kazan was still touring in *Golden Boy.* In a way, it is the antithesis of that great success. It tells the story of a wistful, henpecked, economically hard-pressed dentist, who falls in love with his beautiful assistant, and almost loses her to his father-in-law, who is rich, bold and funnily eccentric in his manner. Eventually she leaves both of them, seeking a richer, more fulfilling life than either of them can offer. As the critics noted, the play is the first by Odets that does not revolve around violence, and it profits from that refusal. There is a kind of easy, unforced naturalism in its writing and something sweetly comic and sad in its overall tone. Of Odets's earlier works this is the one that, to the modern reader, seems to require the fewest apologies. It is an attractive, smoothly functioning minor piece. The reviews were mixed but on the favorable side, particularly about the acting and the physical production. Since it required only one set and seven actors, and since by this time The Group had a substantial subscription base, it achieved a decent run and modest profitability.

Something similar was achieved by Irwin Shaw's *The Gentle People* when it opened less than two months later. Shaw would, of course, become a famously popular novelist beginning with *The Young Lions* in 1949, with his works often being adapted to film and television. In these days, however, he was regarded as a highly promising literary figure. His one-act antiwar play, *Bury the Dead,* had been a huge success in 1936 (and a source of frustration to The Group, which just missed the opportunity to produce it). In this period he was back and forth to Hollywood, where he wrote unmemorable screenplays while continuing to write plays that did not match *Bury the Dead*'s power. Perhaps most important, he began writing the pungent *New Yorker* short stories that would eventually include the likes of "The Girls in Their Summer Dresses," "Main Currents of American Thought," and "Sailor Off the Bremen," on which his minor posthumous reputation largely depends.

He was a good-natured, convivial sort of man, a former Brooklyn College football player and radio writer with a heavy New York accent, a sort of Odets without the latter's torment and frenzy. Indeed, their work was often compared. Shaw's first produced play, like Odets's, had been short, expressionistic, crude, powerful. And *The Gentle People* was, like Odets's later work, concerned with humble urban types trying to gain modest measures of happiness in bleak settings.

This play had been commissioned by Clurman in rather odd circumstances. He ran into Shaw on his way to the opening night of Shaw's second produced play, *Siege,* a drama about the Spanish Civil War. The playwright begged him not to attend; he knew his play was going to fail. Whereupon Clurman whipped out his checkbook and wrote him a draft for $500 as an advance on his next play, telling him to go home and start writing.

Actually, Shaw wrote two plays simultaneously, of which *The Gentle People* was the first, and for The Group, the easier to mount (the second, *Quiet City,* is in some ways more interesting and ambitious, though it would present serious production problems). The play tells the story of two fishermen, a Jew and a Greek (Sam Jaffe and Roman Bohnen), angling and schmoozing on a Brooklyn dock. A gangster, played by Franchot Tone, attempts to sell them "protection," then seduces the Jew's daughter (Sylvia Sidney), intending to use the profits from his scam to take the girl on a fancy trip to Cuba. His two would-be victims turn on him and murder him, restoring peace to their little world.

Some of The Group's veterans were dubious about the casting—three movie stars (Tone, of course, and Sidney, who was then a leading Hollywood player and Jaffe, who had just scored a success in Frank Capra's *Lost Horizon*). There might, indeed, have been a fourth movie person had Jules Garfield agreed to take the role of a neighborhood lad that eventually went to Kazan, for once not playing a gangster but a rather simple soul. There were also some doubts about the play itself. Shaw frankly intended it as a parable about fascism (how often, at this time—see Brecht, among others—did thugs stand in for Europe's monsters in our plays and films) and the need for common people to stand up to it. But there were also whimsical and humorous passages in the work and, again, the reviews were mixed-favorable.

Atkinson in the *Times* found the piece "thin and inconsequential," and questioned the awkwardness of some of Clurman's staging. He found Tone's charm "great and decisive," but also thought the actor lacked "something of the menacing hardness that would pull the whole play together and give it bite . . ." Tone, indeed, was unhappy in his return to The Group. He had put some of his own money into the show, but came to feel that he was being exploited because of his movie stardom.

But still, the critics again rewarded The Group for its ambitions and the general excellence of its actors, and they were not yet ready to give up on Shaw. If they did not particularly single out Kazan's work in *The Gentle People,* they certainly did not condemn it. The play—in part because of its star casting—achieved a run roughly as respectable as *Rocket to the Moon* (something over one hundred performances); it also apparently made a small profit and was sold to Warner Bros., which released its version of it as *Out of the Fog,* a minor, and rather dreary, production starring John Garfield.

While the play limped along, Kazan busied himself directing a workshop production of Shaw's other new script. *Quiet City* is a much more presuming work, almost epic in scale. It tells the story of Gabriel Mellon (nee Mellenkoff—"That last syllable's too big a load for a man to carry when he's going up hill in a hurry"), who was born poor, married well, became the president of his wife's family's department store and, as the play opens, is about to become ambassador to Finland. But the "quiet city" surrounding him (he was played by Bobby Lewis), is actually alive with voices, some real, some imagined by Gabriel: his store's employees, threatening to strike; a woman whose husband, a fired employee, has killed himself; the woman he loved and deserted for his advantageous marriage; a younger, idealistic brother, David, who frequently plays a wistful trumpet and at the end of the play joins the Communist Party; most especially his father, Israel, who carries the play's most important message.

This character, played by Morris Carnovsky, is an unacculturated Jew, the proprietor of a hardware store, but alert, as his son is not, to the threat of Nazism. "There are times coming," he says, "when people with the same blood in them will have to hold on to each other to save each other. Who'll save a man who denies his own blood?" That said, Israel acquires a gun, with which he practices. Finally, he assaults an American Nazi (Karl Malden) who has etched the word "Jew" on his store window. At one point in the play he says, "Every Jew should know what a gun feels like in his hand . . . In the beginning the Jews were a stiff-necked people, with swords in their hands. They should be that way, proud, surrounded by the bodies of their enemies." Later, he says to his younger son: "The Jew's agony is his own and he must meet it without hope, by himself." To which the boy replies, "God almighty, even in suffering you insist on being something special."

Read today, long after the Holocaust and the founding of Israel, *Quiet City* has a certain prescient power. This spirit is matched by the uniqueness of its free-form, expressionistic structure. Norman Lloyd, who played the younger brother, remembers it as "one of the most exciting things I did in the theater."

Kazan agreed. He told his cast, "I think Irwin is the most talented young author in the country, since Cliff arrived . . . and I think, and here formally predict that, excluding the possibility of war, you will see him acclaimed . . . one of the most popular and successful authors in the country. . . . This play has weaknesses, but it comes from a great effort, rather than from a meager soul."

Why, then, one wonders, did it receive only two Sunday-night performances, on a stage with *The Gentle People*'s sets very much in evidence? For one thing, it seems not to have elicited universal enthusiasm from The Group players. Clurman, for example, tried to enlist Franchot Tone in the project. The star attended a reading and responded to it with characteristic cynicism; he guessed The Group should be able to "achieve failure" with it. In the event, Kazan could not, he felt, reach Carnovsky, playing the old, militant Jew. It was the Bickford story repeated, but with a long-standing if largely unspoken enmity adding an edge to their conflict. As with Bickford, Kazan tried to ingratiate himself with Carnovksy and this, he thought, was taken as a sign of weakness. One cannot help but feel some of their animosity was political in origin. Carnovsky was, perhaps, the hardest-core Communist in the Group unit, persisting in his beliefs until well after he was blacklisted from the movies in 1951. In this period he would surely have mistrusted Kazan as an apostate. Moreover, Kazan felt deserted; Clurman and Adler decamped for Florida, supposedly to consult with Odets on revisions for the endlessly simmering *Silent Partner,* and Irwin Shaw was not to be found anywhere.

Kazan's frustrations boiled over in his notes on the play. "Very often the Group actor is a critic when he's acting and an actor when he's criticizing . . . Reservations he or she may have about the script or the director or the productions dilute, or completely kill a central creative impulse which is at the heart of every good performance." This is pure Kazan, always looking for the freshness of the heedless, instinctive moment, always dubious about over-thought performances, and these views lie at the heart of his new, passionate lover's quarrel with The Group.

There is evidence that these notes are for a speech he never actually delivered. But this is the challenge he was at least thinking about throwing down to them: "There is only one thing I respect and like in so-called Broadway actors . . . and that is their competitive sense. . . . The young alive ones in the new mould, especially the comedians, are inventive and the necessity of getting, winning, holding and getting more jobs makes them work. For Christsake if despite what I tell you or what Harold might tell you about the play you can't believe in it . . . believe in yourselves, in your own performances."

The great director who would shortly emerge is predicted in that cry. The director who would boldly cast performers from the lighter realms of show business—Zero Mostel, Andy Griffith, Burl Ives—in powerful dramatic roles precisely because those roles would inventively drive them to prove themselves, speaks here. So does the director who was always willing to take a shot with a hungry young performer not yet set in his ways—think Brando, think Dean. He was grateful to The Group and loyal to it, but his belief in good old American commercial competitivness, his sense that good acting could arise in unlikely places—ideas that were never a large part of The Group's ethos—were essential to his expanding sensibility.

But his actors, doubtless taking their cue from Carnovsky, were not, for the most part, "buying in" to Kazan's style, as Norman Lloyd would put it. According to Lloyd (and others), Kazan's refusal to do long, Clurmanesque analyses of the work put off some of the older performers and his "get on with it" manner seems to have offended these more "intellectually developed" members of the company, though, again according to Lloyd, the younger players were "eating it up." Kazan himself thought he was still on trial as a Group director. And failing the test.

Clurman had merely promised Shaw a production of *Quiet City,* and by his lights the two Sunday presentations fulfilled that promise. There just wasn't the will to work harder and longer on the play. This was probably a mistake—there is great, unrealized promise in the unpolished script Kazan and company presented in a relatively unpolished manner. There are also hints in it of some of Kazan's more successful future attempts at expressionism.

Only one person benefited substantially from this abortive production; that was Aaron Copland, who composed a haunting score for *Quiet City* that continues to be a part of the modern symphonic repertory. As for The Group, it moved on to a succession of failures, beginning with its short-lived production of William Saroyan's *My Heart's in the Highlands,* one of those bits of folksy whimsy with which the playwright was simultaneously annoying and exciting the theatrical community at the time.

Kazan had nothing to do with that production, and we must agree with Norman Lloyd that Kazan was not having "much luck" so far with his directorial career. Still, he had found another play, and Clurman placed it on the schedule for the following fall.

———

Initially entitled *Tower of Light,* it was another work by Robert Ardrey, an early draft of which he had shown Kazan when he was working in Chicago in *Golden Boy.* It was much more intellectually ambitious than *Casey Jones* though, ironically its fatal flaw was topicality. In this year, when Madrid had finally fallen to Franco, when

Hitler and Stalin had signed their nonaggression pact and Germany invaded Poland, events were moving too rapidly (and tragically) for a mere play to stay abreast of them.

Eventually retitled *Thunder Rock*, the play was set in a lighthouse in the middle of Lake Michigan. As it opens, a new keeper, a man named Charleston (Luther Adler), is taking over. He's a world-weary journalist whom Kazan, in his notes, identifies as more Vincent Sheehan than André Malraux. Seeking a respite from wars and the other horrors of the world, he begs his supervisor not to leave him even a radio (though one is, in fact, left), not to fly in newspapers or books when he is resupplied once a month. He wants his withdrawal from the world to be total.

The lighthouse is dedicated to the memory of a group of immigrants whose boat, carrying them to new lives in Wisconsin and beyond in 1849, was blown onto a nearby reef where it sank, all hands lost. The ship's log is stored in the lighthouse and, reading it, Charleston begins summoning their ghosts to life. Among them are the ship's captain (Morris Carnovsky), a doctor (Lee J. Cobb) and his daughter (Frances Farmer), to whom Charleston takes a fancy. The appearance of these ghosts in the second act provided a strong theatrical effect—perhaps the thing Clurman liked best about the play—and their conversations with Charleston form the metaphorical heart of the piece.

All the immigrants, it develops, were escaping the old world in despair. The doctor, for example, was hounded out of Vienna because people feared his experiments in anesthesiology. A suffragette is lost in what appears to be the hopelessness of her cause. A pottery worker vaguely hopes to find the wealth and contentment in the new world that eluded him in England, but in the course of the play his wife dies giving birth to their tenth child. Since Charleston knows the ninety years of history that have intervened since they died, knows that, despite its manifest horror, some progress has been achieved, he becomes, despite his own despair, a kind of cheerleader for them, urging them, in effect, to embrace at least a degree of hope.

At the end of the play the sun has risen, the ghosts have been banished and Charleston is packing both his typewriter and a rifle, preparing to the rejoin the contemporary struggle. In the published version of the play he says: "A man who fights for an ideal—a man who fights against poverty or ignorance or the rule of tyrants—he doesn't ask for assurances that he'll win. He wouldn't believe it if he got it. All he asks for is assurance that he has a chance to win."

The sentiments, obviously, are naïve, though they are somewhat redeemed by Ardrey's writing, which is often livelier than his thoughts. But as a liberal non-Communist he was denied the possibilities of the ringing peroration that agitprop so readily supplied more ideologically committed playwrights.

On the other hand, we know that the published play is not exactly the play that opened in New York on November 2. Wendy Smith had access to the prompt books for the production and she reports a concluding speech in which Charleston is advocating neutrality. "America's not going to war. She's got a bigger job than war. Peace in the face of war, that's the job, and she can do it. . . . We've got to show others what freedom means, freedom of speech, freedom of conscience. . . . America's got one high obligation: to preserve the last peace on earth."

She correctly notes that this speech follows the then current Communist Party line, which after the Hitler-Stalin Pact urged America to stay out of the European conflict. It held that it was simply a capitalist squabble—perhaps the system's death throes. She cites a Baltimore review—the show had a brief trial run there—suggesting that this speech replaced one that was more overtly interventionist.

Still, this was the fall of 1939, Ardrey was a midwesterner, thus a product of the region where American isolationism had its deepest roots. And there was at this moment, a flaring, if despairing, hope that the United States might this time avoid a European conflict. Perhaps, putting the best possible light on it, that's what Ardrey was trying to write about in *Thunder Rock*, though he and Kazan were not getting much help from The Group. In his memoir Clurman makes much of his actors' dislike of the play, based perhaps on its fantastic qualities and its lack of political commitment. He urged professionalism on them. Kazan himself, judging from his relatively brief production notes, sees the play as debate between life and death. With the former constituting an embrace of the search for meaning, with the latter occurring when people abandon their "vital belief" in "the living utterance."

The most interesting thing he says in his notes is: "This is not an old tired play. This is a play where the youthful optimism of the author must be met by that of the director and the actors." This is not quite what he got from his company. He got, perhaps, a sort of febrile energy from them. But, he came to think, it was the wrong sort of energy. Later, in his autobiography he wrote that he was coming to believe "The cast of a play should have the same basic quality as its author. If Bob Ardrey justified the nickname some of the Group gave him, 'Cornsilk,' his play should have been performed by actors who had the qualities of people from mid-America—or by English actors; their emotion is understated and generally accompanied by wry humor. Bob's play should not have been performed by our urban-bred and vividly posturing actors. The same goes for the director; I was out of place. . . . We went on playing Odets and it didn't work."

The reviewers agreed with Kazan. Atkinson was particularly hard on Luther Adler, "playing with a nervous tension that hardly blends with the flowing style of Mr. Ardrey's writing." There were other problems, as well. Frances Farmer, for example. Irwin Shaw's biographer, Michael Shnayerson, goes so far as to say that the earlier failure of *Quiet City* began her addiction to pills and alcohol that led her, finally, into a sanitarium. Whether that's the case, it is certain that her behavior in this production, in which she often appeared at rehearsals drunk and disheveled, was highly erratic. Wendy Smith thinks it had more to do with Clifford Odets's ending their affair and returning to his wife, Luise Rainer, a matter he handled with a brutal lack of tact and feeling.

In any case, *Thunder Rock* was a failure. It had its partisans within the theatrical community, and The Group considered making one of its fights for it. But it closed after twenty-three performances when Adler refused to take a pay cut to keep it running, We need, however, to attach an asterisk to our account of this failure. It was mounted in London, where it starred Michael Redgrave, and became a substantial wartime hit. It was also made into a movie in England, with Redgrave again starring—with yet another rewritten ending, this time with a more overtly anti-Nazi message. The ending of the revised version, which Ardrey copyrighted and published in 1950, also contains a nicely put, if rather dispassionate, antifascist statement.

———————

Elia Kazan would not direct another play for more than two years, by which time The Group had folded, the United State had entered the war and he had endured success, failure and critical ambivalence as a performer.

The last was his lot in *Night Music,* the penultimate Group production, rehearsals of which he joined immediately after *Thunder Rock* closed. He would have his first lead in this new Odets play, which both the playwright and Harold Clurman thought was his best work. That seems dubious, but however you evaluate it, the play definitively broke the mold into which Odets had previously poured his gifts.

It was, to begin with, an out-and-out comedy—at least in the playwright's mind. It was also a sprawling, episodic play, which recounts the less than realistic adventures of a young Greek American named Steve Takis (Kazan), in New York from Hollywood on a goofy errand; he's supposed to retrieve two trained monkeys, required for a new movie, and bring them to the West Coast. Of course, he loses his money and tickets and meets a girl, Fay Tucker (Jane Wyatt, also fresh from *Lost Horizon*).

Odets was writing quite close to the bone, for among the amusing and sympathetic New York types the couple encounters is an old, dying New York detective, named A. L. Rosenberg (Morris Carnovsky), who protectively shadows them. He is a father figure who represents, according to Odets's biographer, Brenman-Gibson, Clurman as Odets saw him in those days. In the end, the studio decides to dispense with its East Coast simians, Steve quits pretending to be a promising movie big shot, and decides to settle down in New York with Fay. In the last scene, war planes drone in the skies above.

It does not, admittedly, sound too promising. But in *The Fervent Years* Clurman approvingly quotes Odets, who thought it belonged with his other, non–kitchen sink dramas as "a song cycle on a given theme" (homelessness in this case). The company set out for its Boston tryout with high hearts and the reviews there were promising, even though the city was caught in a cold spell and audiences were small and chilly, and Odets began to worry about the play.

Nevertheless, he and Clurman squabbled about what New York house *Night Music* should lease, Clurman arguing for an intimate venue, Odets holding out successfully for a more spacious one. Maybe that's one of the things that went wrong with the production. But it was not the only one.

Another was overconfidence. At the final dress rehearsal Odets told Clurman, "Harold, I think this is the best play and the finest production in New York," the kind of statement bitter experience usually teaches show business veterans, which Odets by this time was, to avoid. Another problem was—once again—dissension in the ranks. The Group, Clurman reports, generally liked *Night Music*, but it was again embroiled in one of its inner turmoils—the last of them, as it would turn out. The veterans—and a large number of them were in the large cast—thought The Group was now just an extension of Clurman's ego, more or less a director-manager's personal company. It was, they felt, The Group in name only. Molly Kazan felt so strongly on this point that she resigned as literary adviser. Whether this dispute affected the company's performance is hard to say—especially since the reviewing community concentrated its fire on the playwright.

Brooks Atkinson caught its prevailing response with this lead: "Now that Odets writes like Saroyan, Doomsday is near." As with Saroyan, the reviewer found "vivid scenes" and characters full of "fire and daring." But he also thought Odets was "writing entirely without discipline and listening fondly to the sound of his own voice." Saroyan's name came up in other reviews, too, much to Clurman's displeasure. He had always disliked comparisons between writers and he found this one particularly egregious. He would later write that it was almost as if Odets, then only thirty-four years old, was a has-been—the voice of the 1930s—while Saroyan was supposed to be the voice of a new decade, then less than a month old. Since this was a decade that would include the first works of the then unknown Arthur Miller and Tennessee Williams, he had a good point; people should not write history until it has happened.

Kazan received an excellent review from Atkinson, who had always liked his work and here called him "one of the most exciting actors in America." Others were less certain that he had made the right choices—among them, to Kazan's surprise, Clurman and Odets. Until opening night they had been jovially dining together almost every night—cigars all around, and the cafeterias of The Group's beginnings long forgotten. Now, however, word that somehow Kazan, with his performance, had betrayed both the writer's and the director's intent began to leak out. Odets's biographer, Brenman-Gibson, would later write that he had traduced the play's delicacy. Something meant to have been light and airy and full of sweetness had been turned into something heavy and oppressive. Writing specifically, but with a touch of irony, about criticisms of Kazan's performance, Clurman said: "He was oafish, unsympathetic. Had I not told him that the character was a Pierrot? Why had I not persisted on this tack?"

Comments like these, echoed by Odets, hurt Kazan's feelings, though he did not openly break with either man—perhaps because, in some part of his soul, he agreed with them. Eli Wallach, whose long friendship with Kazan began around this time, recalls Kazan telling him, "I'm not a good actor. I'm always angry. I'm always angry on stage." There is probably some truth in that self-judgment, especially in this instance. Some reviewers agreed with Clurman and Odets that he brought too much intensity, too little humor, to his performance.

On the other hand, Wallach has a specific memory of one terrific moment of behavioral truth that stayed with him for more than fifty years. Kazan and Wyatt, having been out on the town, repair to a park bench to rest. "His arm's around her and she's asleep on his arm and he slides the arm out from under her and the arm is asleep. And he took—I don't know—maybe two, three minutes to wake up his arm. And I thought, that's extraordinary, to really investigate what it's like when you're on pins and needles."

It is, as they say, an actor's moment. And one more likely to be appreciated by other actors than by the audience. It is also, of course, the kind of thing Kazan was always looking for as a director. But he took a larger lesson from this flop—*Night Music* closed after twenty performances—which was this: "I'd make sure, in the years to come, that my rehearsals were so conducted that the truth, if it had to be forced out, would be confronted early, when something could be done about it. As for the chumminess which makes frank talk impossible and prevents the kind of contention that is essential during a proper rehearsal. It should be kept in its place. It's friendship that killed *Night Music,* if anything beyond itself did."

Whether Kazan might have done another Group production is a moot point. It would mount only one more play the following fall, *Retreat to Pleasure,* an attempt at a romantic comedy by Irwin Shaw, that some reviewers found reasonably witty, but most found inappropriate to his talent. Reviewing it in *Newsweek,* his fellow *New Yorker* writer, John O'Hara, wrote that Shaw could successfully do Brooklyn or even Greenwich Village characters, but that upper-class swells were beyond him. The most interesting thing about the production was a near-riotous outburst at a benefit matinee for B'nai Brith. The audience mistook a satirical thrust at anti-Semitism as an actual statement of prejudice. Shaw and Clurman, both Jews, thought it best to bring Hume Cronyn, who was a WASP, and playing a sympathetic figure, out to quell the crowd. The Group veterans thought this failed attempt at a commercial comedy a sad comedown for their old idealism, and it closed after a short run. There were some halfhearted discussions about bringing The Group back in some new form—even Strasberg was consulted—but nothing came of them.

Kazan, meantime, was working fairly steadily. Immediately after *Night Music* closed he took a supporting role in a revival of *Liliom,* then got a Hollywood job. Anatole Litvak, a Russian who had scored an international success with his French production of *Mayerling,* had seen Kazan in *Golden Boy* and invited him to play a similar gangster role in *City for Conquest,* which he was making at Warner Bros. The picture starred James Cagney as a prizefighter who fights mainly to further his brother's musical education, is blinded in the ring, but opens a newsstand, where, on a radio he hears his brother's debut composition triumphantly performed at Carnegie Hall.

For some reason, Cagney harbored high hopes for the film—perhaps in part because it was derived from a serious and well-received novel, in the proletarian vein, by Aben Kandel. The actor had always hated the way Warner's kept sticking him in quickie little pictures without literary credentials. This movie promised to be different. But it did not, in the actor's estimation, fulfill that promise.

He—and Kazan—thought that was largely Tola (as everyone called him) Litvak's fault. Basically, he seems to have been making nothing grander than a *Golden Boy* knockoff, with the art-sport conflict divided between two brothers (the composer was played by Arthur Kennedy, later to enjoy a huge stage success under Kazan's direction, making his screen debut) instead of being located in a single figure. In any case, when he saw the final cut of the movie Cagney judged that Litvak (or someone) had cut out the picture's best scenes.

Kazan didn't much liked Tola. The director's manner on the set was arrogant and inattentive, in his view. He would appear impeccably dressed, often with cast and crew well aware, from trade paper reports, which famous star he had escorted to this or that famous watering spot the night before. Being European, he had a liking for complicated dolly and crane shots, so much of his time was spent setting these up and making sure the actors hit their marks once the camera moves had been laid out. It was not Cagney's preferred way nor that of the crew. They also didn't like the arrogant way Litvak spoke to the star, who was much more their kind of guy—unpretentious, street-wise, always looking out for their interests.

Kazan liked Cagney, too. He especially liked the way he'd pull off the scar-tissue makeup he wore late in the film when quitting time approached to avoid unpaid overtime for the crew. Litvak never called him on it. "What's pride when you have to beat a tough schedule. You eat the scorn and wag your tail."

More important, Kazan admired Cagney's acting style. He never saw him preparing and he concealed his own preparations from Cagney. "Jimmy didn't see scenes in great complexity; he saw them in a forthright fashion, played them with savage energy, enjoyed his work. He believed in himself and didn't need to be praised constantly. He was a complete actor." Cagney liked to say that the secret of acting was, "plant your feet and tell the truth." And watching him,

absorbing the friendly little tips the actor gave him about screen acting, Kazan found him raising "many doubts in my mind about the
artistic snobbery of some actors in the Group."

Kazan judged himself no more than "all right" as a screen actor and
that's a fairly sound assessment. He was playing a character called
"Googie," who first appears in the picture looking for a handout from
Cagney. He later does a little time for unspecified crimes, then reap-
pears sharply dressed, obviously now mobbed up, but still supportive
of his old friend. For the rest of the picture—and it is obvious some of
his scenes were among those cut—his is a fairly standard movie portrayal. He's eager, restless, good-natured, but perhaps a little too obviously looking for ways to make his mark in the film.

Which he does in his last scene. Googie loses $50,000 betting on
Cagney when a crooked fighter rubs resin in Cagney's eyes, causing
him to lose his big fight. Googie decides to take the mobsters who
ordered that act for a ride, manages to kill one of them, but then is
himself shot. "Gee, I never figured on that" he says—honestly, almost comically puzzled at his own sudden demise. It may be the
movie's best line, and it is surely Kazan's best moment in it.

But the main thing Kazan got out of the experience was the
sense that Litvak was over-directing, which (a) struck him as a waste
of time and (b) imparted to him a sense that "I sure as hell can direct
better than Anatole Litvak." He returned home with money in his
pocket—enough to make a down payment on a summer place he
and Molly found in Connecticut, which he retained until the day he
died—and to a lead in a new play, which Bobby Lewis was staging.

It was sort of a grouplet enterprise, with the likes of Bud
Bohnen and Curt Conway also in the cast. Written by someone
named Lucille S. Prumbs, it was a farce clearly based on the free-
wheeling life of William Saroyan, so much so that Walter Winchell
reported that the playwright was really Saroyan himself, operating
under a pseudonym. The conceit was that the Saroyanesque figure is
married to a playwright and, after interrupting her creatively, responds to her challenge by writing a play better than her own. Lewis
reported that "The critics and the audience didn't have as much fun
watching it as Gadget and I had rehearsing it." Indeed, Kazan got
the worst reviews of his life, with even Atkinson writing, "he is get-

ting to be a self-conscious actor with purple patches and little curlicues on the side." He praised Kazan's chest hair (he played several scenes in his drawers) but called the performance "studiously spontaneous." The show closed after four performances and was Kazan's last Broadway appearance.

That was in March. He and Lewis spent the remainder of the season planning a theater, "The Dollar Top," that would present new plays with its admission price no higher than the amount specified in its name. It was, so far as one can tell, a last little flaring of Group idealism. But Kazan interrupted their work—nothing ultimately came of it—to take another Hollywood job—again for Warner Bros. and Litvak.

This offer was not entirely coincidental. Kazan had, at some previous point, optioned a play called *Hot Nocturne* by Edwin Gilbert. Unable to set it up on Broadway, Kazan had obviously peddled the script to the studio on his previous visit. Adapted by Robert Rossen, with songs, including the immortal title tune, "Blues in the Night," by Johnny Mercer and Harold Arlen, it offered Kazan a supporting role rather less good than his part in *City for Conquest*. He plays the clarinetist–business manager of a not very good jazz band, which includes Priscilla Lane as the singer, Jack Carson as the trumpeter and Richard Whorf as the pianist.

They hear some authentic blues, sung by a black man, when they are locked up one night in a jail and resolve to play them in their gigs. They are tempted away from this purity by Lloyd Nolan, who attempts to rob them one night when they're hopping a freight. They make friends with him instead and he offers them a job in a New Jersey roadhouse in which he has an interest. The mob shares that interest, and the place becomes the site of some doomy romance as well.

The film has a nice, dark atmosphere, and thanks to Rossen, who was a Communist at the time, it has a certain proletarian pungency about it. The band, despite the romantic cross-currents swirling through it, tries its best to maintain its musical "authenticity," deriving strength from their proletarian values. They are almost like a little Communist cell—indeed, they call themselves a "unit"—traveling about, propagating music derived from the people. In a sense, the film feels like a throwback to, or last gasp from, the 1930s.

On the other hand, the movie is very much some white guys' idea of what black music is about, and clearly Tola Litvak hasn't the slightest idea of what that meant. He's just doing a studio assignment on a picture that was less important than originally intended.

At one time Cagney had been mentioned for the film, and John Garfield, too, but it went forth with essentially a B picture cast, doing, frankly, B picture work. Kazan does his best to pretend to play the clarinet, but he's none too persuasive, and his performance is fussy and aggressive; he wants to be noticed, but succeeds largely in being kind of a minor pest at the edge of the frame, which he later admitted. "The only thing about the production that impressed me was the musical side. Jimmie Lunceford and his band were the best artists on the lot. Close at hand were Johnny Mercer, who wrote the lyrics and with him the man who wrote the music, Harold Arlen, a genius." Everyone else, including himself, he writes, were "second raters."

This was to be his last role as an actor. In his autobiography he makes much of the fact that he returned to New York determined to relaunch his directorial career. He understood that acting offered him mere repetition—and frustration—within a limited, character actor's range. Directing was, one might say, a more "manly art"—offering him the possibility of making his own choices instead of waiting around to see if someone thought him "right" for a part.

More important, he finally felt fully ready to direct. He certainly knew from Strasberg, from Clurman, from Litvak, what not to do. He had also profited from his own previous mistakes. And he knew that he would have to make his way in the commercial theater; it was too late for The Group or anything like it to prosper, too early for nonprofit alternatives to appear. In any case, he liked the desperate energy of the commercial theater. It suited his own personality, as it had developed over the last decade.

That said, he had no directorial prospects when he returned to New York in autumn 1941, and we cannot doubt that if a decent part had presented itself he would have grabbed it; he had a growing family to support. Luckily for Kazan, a directorial prospect—not wildly promising, but not entirely unpromising, either—presented itself.

5

"I'm Still Here"

It was Kazan's friend Martin Gabel, a short, round actor with a notably mellifluous voice, who offered him his opportunity. Gabel had a prospering career in radio and a profitable career as a Broadway producer as well. He was then in partnership with a woman named Carly Wharton, the wife of a prominent New York lawyer, and they had under option a minor, amusing play called *Café Crown* that Gabel thought Kazan might direct.

It was the work of H. S. (Hy) Kraft, who had previously written for the stage and would gain his largest fame as author of the book (and screenplay) for *Top Banana* and would, still later, be blacklisted in Hollywood. It was based on the bustling life of an actual restaurant, the Café Royale, on Second Avenue and Twelfth Street, that had, for decades, been the informal social center of the Yiddish theater. The "spine" of the piece has David Cole—played by Morris Carnovsky (considering how little they liked each other, Kazan certainly worked with the actor a lot)—as a figure quite obviously based on Jacob Adler, father of Luther and Stella, that most legendary of Yiddish theater actors, trying to finance one last Shakespearean production, a modern *Lear*. His largest hopes in this regard center on Hymie (Sam Jaffe), a busboy who is actually the community's informal banker, with more wherewithal than one might imagine, given his humble job.

But that's only a pretext. The bubbling life of the play is in the equally bubbling dialogue and crises of its many subsidiary characters. They constitute a full roster of showbiz types, including (but not limited to) a failed playwright, a drama critic who writes his reviews before seeing the plays, a slick uptown talent agent trying to lure a young actor to Hollywood. Perhaps the most interesting of the lot is Cole's somewhat estranged daughter, Norma, definitely a Stella Adler clone, who sees that ethnic theater of her father's kind will not long survive in an increasingly deracinated America.

When he came to write about *Café Crown* in his autobiography, Kazan noted that Kraft "had the thinnest talent of any playwright I've worked with," but he also acknowledged his one authentic gift, which was "for Jewish anecdote." And, one must add, for the accents and rhythms of Yiddishkeit, fresher and more pungent than they are now, after they have influenced the delivery (and substance) of a thousand stand-up comics. Kazan, who was glumly certain he'd gotten this job because other, better known directors had turned it down, resolved to stress the jokes and let the subtexts fall where they might. He didn't do a Clurmanesque analysis of the play for his actors and he didn't do Strasbergian psychologizing, either. He just moved the actors around in ways that would look "spontaneous and unstudied." And he pretty much let his Broadway actors be Broadway actors. Basically, he got out of their way and let 'em rip. And perhaps riff.

Or so he would later say, doubtless forgetting some notes he had made to himself at the time. In them, he addressed some slightly more profound feelings *Café Crown* stirred in him, notably that the Yiddish theater was "the first art theater in the wilderness of America" and that this was, at heart, "a comedy of decay." He said he wanted the play to have some of the odor of Roquefort cheese, "pungent and rotting," about it.

It is impossible to say whether the play, in performance, had that air. But there are hints, in the text, that a lot of these characters could see the handwriting on the wall. One of its more interesting subplots involves a young actor, played by Sam Wanamaker (also later to be a blacklistee), who has agreed to be in Cole's *Lear*, but then gets a movie offer that obliges him to catch a train west on opening night. Norma urges him to take it: "This theater is dying a slow death and if we don't escape it we'll die with it. That's why you've got to go, Lester. This is your chance, as an actor and a human being."

Later on, her father speaks to the same actor in even more moving—and, indeed, Kazanian—terms: "I may be getting old, but not foolish. How can I deny that Broadway exists, that fine actors play there. How can I close my eyes to Hollywood and say there is no art and greatness. This is *my* theater, *my* language, these are *my* people. What right have I to demand *your* life, your sacrifices . . . take whatever you want. These are my gifts to Broadway and Hollywood. Why not? Goodbye, Freed. You haven't much time and neither have I. Be an honor to your people, be a great American actor."

We can easily believe Kazan saying something similar to the idealistically torn young actor. For the young actor is not so different from Franchot Tone or Julie Garfield (or Elia Kazan), making their painful breaks from The Group, but hoping to carry with them at least a tincture of their youthful idealism.

In his notes Kazan worried that the conflict between the old and new theatrical worlds was "under done" in this play. Indeed, one gets the impression from the reviews (and from the text) that as presented, *Café Crown* was less a play about "decay" than it is about "integration," about people accepting, with a nostalgic, affectionate shrug, the passing of the old order. The first generations of Jewish immigrants were leaving the Lower East Side. But now they lived in the Bronx, in Brooklyn or Queens. And soon enough their children and grandchildren would be suburbanites.

The reviewers were utterly unconcerned with theatrical history or contemporary sociology. Atkinson in the *Times* was typical, calling the play "genial, comic and original" and praising Kazan's direction as "droll and friendly." Which—quite self-consciously—it was. He made sure that the people about to speak a good line were correctly focused for the audience, facing outward, well lit. He spoke plainly to the actors, making sure they stressed what needed to be stressed, and though scarcely a drill sergeant, he did not try particularly to ingratiate himself with his players. Nonetheless, "The tension I had felt directing the Group lifted . . . Relaxed, at last, I enjoyed myself."

And audiences enjoyed his work. Which is quite remarkable, considering that the Pearl Harbor attack occurred while Kazan was casting the play and that it opened only about seven weeks after America entered World War II. It is possible that that was part of *Café Crown*'s modest good luck. It reminded people of the past they had so recently enjoyed, gave them, perhaps, some sense of one of the traditions—albeit, a modest and local one—that we were now called upon to defend. Many plays and movies of the war years did just that, with perhaps more conscious effort. The play was a minor hit; it ran for 141 performances. And it gave Kazan, at last, a foothold in the commercial theater.

A slightly slippery foothold, to be sure. Still, Paul Vincent Carroll was, at the time, a highly regarded Irish playwright—not quite Sean O'Casey or J. M. Synge, perhaps, but yet a figure to be reckoned with in that country's theatrical renaissance. His *Shadow and Substance* had been a success a few years earlier, and now Kazan signed to direct his new work, *The Strings, My Lord, Are False,* while *Café Crown* was still running.

Set in Glasgow, where Carroll himself served for a time as an air raid warden, it recounts the story of a parish priest (Carroll frequently wrote about Catholic clerics) who is using his church as a shelter for victims of the Nazis' bombing raids, with a more or less customary assortment of theatrical types—a Communist, a man who lost an arm at Dunkirk and is the (temporary) voice of despair, a pacifist, a war profiteer, a plucky young woman who falls in love with an air raid warden with noble impulses, another girl who bears an illegitimate child.

The cast, typical of a Kazan production, mixed well-known performers with those who were less famous. Among others, they included Ruth Gordon, then a highly regarded theatrical leading lady (she had done Ibsen and Chekhov) before settling into the slightly grotesque character roles of her later years. Here she played the love interest. Kazan's lover, Constance Dowling, had a featured role and his old pal Art Smith, played the Communist. The lead was Walter Hampden, a romantic Shakespearean leading man for many decades, playing the kindly priest, squabbling with the Church's hidebound hierarchy, and somewhat looking forward to the people's padres of the 1960s and later. He's definitely the kind of man we can imagine favoring masses spoken in English.

And *The Strings, My Lord, Are False* is actually the kind of play we can imagine The Group doing, were it slightly more secular in tone, since it celebrates the plucky common sense of the common people under duress. In his rather perfunctory notes on the play, Kazan stressed the "desperate comradeship" they find in The Blitz, their bonding into oneness under its impress. He wrote:

The people, yes!
They endure
The basic animal
The basic spirit
Which are one
Cannot
Be
Licked!!

But this play could be licked. In her autobiography Ruth Gordon recalls a preview at which an ebullient Kazan, loving most of what he saw and saying that he knew just how to fix what needed to be fixed, was then immediately fired. But he remained the director of record, and Lewis Nichols, filling in for Brooks Atkinson, who had become a war correspondent for the duration, damned it with one of those reviews that offers little more than a description of the occurrences on stage. It was, he said, "played for the most part well" and Kazan had directed "some scenes beautifully, others with a flurry." The play closed after fifteen performances.

With *Café Crown* approaching the end of its run and this play flopping so quickly, Kazan's professional circumstances in the spring of 1942 were unpromising. And his personal situation was desperate. For the constantly meddling Paula Strasberg had written a letter to Molly, informing her of his continuing relationship with Constance Dowling. By this time she and Kazan had rented a small apartment as a trysting place and they were constantly being seen together around Broadway. Molly's response was typical. She first forced Kazan to move out of their bedroom. Then she went home to mother. To *his* mother, taking the children with her. The Kazan's eldest daughter, Judy, thought this perfectly logical. The kids called the older woman "Yaya," and loved her in the uncomplicated way of children with an idolized grandparent. "It was a very, very hard time," Judy says, greatly eased by Yaya, who was fond of saying that "Molly brought us into this country," by which she meant that it was she who finally made them feel they were no longer immigrants, strangers in a strange land. She also did what she could, in letter and conversations, to effect a reconciliation between her son and daughter-in-law.

This was not quickly or easily accomplished, though Kazan found himself in agony once he had moved out. Put simply, he loved Constance and Molly equally, did not fully understand why some sort of "arrangement"—can we doubt that some of his feelings at this time informed the novel of that title that he would one day write—could not be worked out. He comes close to admitting, in his autobiography, that deep in his sexually scheming soul, he saw no reason—other than bourgeois convention—why that outcome could not be realized.

All that anguish aside, he needed a hit—a big, unambiguous Broadway success. That, anyway, was what Martin Gabel whispered to Norman Lloyd one night at Sardi's after Kazan stopped at their table to exchange pleasantries. This quite literally. Lloyd recalls his having in his hands a copy of Thornton Wilder's *The Skin of Our Teeth*.

For some time in the spring of that year Michael Myerberg, a lean, hungry fringe theatrical figure who was producing the show, entrusted Wilder's most ambitious theatrical work to Kazan, who would ever afterward date his arrival as a director, in the fullest sense of the term, to this play—and the epic struggle he endured to bring it forth in all its Pulitzer Prize–winning glory.

Or perhaps one should say, "in all its dubious glory," since nothing dates faster than yesteryear's avant-garde (or *faux* avant-garde) successes. Thornton Wilder was a good natured, scholarly man—he had taught classics in a New England prep school and at the University of Chicago, where he was close to Robert M. Hutchins and his attempts to reform its educational practices. He had won his first Pulitzer for his novel *The Bridge at San Luis Rey* in 1927, and in 1938 had won a second for his play *Our Town*, which has taken its place, of course, in the middle-brow theatrical canon.

That play in some ways predicts the manner of *The Skin of Our Teeth*: radical stagecraft in the service of a conventionally uplifting message. It says that despite the troubles it imposes on the citizens of Grovers Corner, the world is basically a benign place, its citizens good folks, enduring what must be endured (most notably death), with hopeful hearts. It is an interesting trick, which *Skin* repeats in a far showier and more complicated form.

It tells the story of the Antrobus family—the parents, George and Maggie (played in the original production by Fredric March and his wife, Florence Eldridge), their two childen, Gladys and Henry (Frances Heflin and Montgomery Clift) and their saucy maid, Sabina (Tallulah Bankhead). They live middle-class lives in New Jersey and George commutes to work in New York. But . . . they are immortal. They have been married for five thousand years and in each of the play's three acts they endure a vast disaster—in order, the Ice Age, Noah's Flood and, finally, a World War. Along their way Mr. Antrobus invents things—the alphabet, the wheel—and becomes president of the fraternal order of Mammals (Subdivision, Human) as well as a military leader. Sabina, in addition to being a maid, is also a beauty-contest winner at the mammal convention in Atlantic City, a seductress, and a camp follower during the war. Henry, the Antrobus son, is, in actuality, Cain (though Abel is never seen), constantly threatening people with his slingshot, and eventually a "war criminal."

Mr. Antrobus may occasionally become cranky or discouraged, his wife may be ditsily focused on cooking and housekeeping, their son may be a nasty little twerp, but they endure whatever disasters the cosmos throws at them. The play employs slide projections and voice-overs, it has a stage manager (played by a young E. G. Marshall) who is less intrusive than his *Our Town* counterpart, it has scenery that collapses and reassembles itself. It has actors in the audience and every once in a while someone (usually Sabina) interrupts the action of the play because she judges that what is about to be performed may be too shocking for the audience to bear. At one point she even asks the viewers to rip out their theater seats and contribute them to the fire the family needs to ward off its Ice Age chill. For most of the first act the Antrobuses' pet dinosaur and pet mammoth keep them comic company.

From a director's point of view, the play is a three-ring circus, and it has never been quite clear why Myerberg chose the relatively inexperienced Kazan to direct it. Apparently Robert Ardrey, who had been a student of Wilder's at Chicago, spoke highly of him to the writer, which got him a hearing with Myerberg. It's possible that his ability to handle fairly large forces—*Café Crown* had twenty-four parts—and showy stage effects—the *Casey Jones* locomotive, for example—may have been a factor. In any case, at age thirty-four, and hungry, he was not a man to be daunted by this script. Best of all, he was willing to work cheap, which was probably the deciding factor for Myerberg, whose production was under-financed.

What would challenge Kazan—and almost be his undoing—was Tallulah Bankhead. She, too, was a second choice; Myerberg had first approached Helen Hayes with the part. A Southern belle, Alabama born in 1903, Bankhead was the granddaughter of a U.S. senator, and the daughter of Will Bankhead, who was for a time Speaker of the House of Representatives. By this time, she had established herself as her generation's grandest theatrical grande dame. Or perhaps one should say sacred monster. She had worked most of the 1920s in London, had endured a mediocre film career in the early thirties, but had secured her status as a legend when she triumphed as the scheming Regina in Lillian Hellman's *The Little Foxes* in 1939. She came to the Wilder play from *Clash by Night,* a Clifford Odets failure, directed by Lee Strasberg, in which by all accounts she was miscast (she played a lower-class Polish housewife). Her experiences with these Group refugees (the cast also included Lee J. Cobb and Art Smith) made her wary of Kazan and his Group connections.

Hard-drinking, chain-smoking, sexually avaricious, full of almost parodistic star attitudes, she was the model for Margo Channing in *All About Eve* and the antithesis of what Kazan liked and respected among actors. He was a man who resisted star presences in his works. He often discovered stars—Brando, James Dean, Lee Remick—but when they first worked for him they had not yet attained that status. He also often helped working actors to achieve something like stardom—Lee J. Cobb's Willy Loman is a good example—but only rarely did he work with someone like Tallulah, who arrived at *Skin's* first rehearsal trailing entourage and attitude.

She was only six years older than Kazan and she was by no means stupid; her biographer, Brendan Gill, wrote that she had an enviably shrewd judgment about what would and would not be effective theater. She was also in the process of turning herself into a celebrity "character" personifying showbiz excess. With her drawled, signature form of address—"Dahling"—there was not then or later a radio show, magazine or newspaper she refused to favor with her outrageous impersonation of a larger-than-life star. Her self-regard, though humanized by her outspoken liberal politics and her famous (though somewhat suspect) love of baseball, would have taxed any director, and Kazan had his own issues on that point—his failure to speak up to the likes of Bickford and Carnovsky. That was not going to happen again.

He liked and was liked by most of the company. There was, for example, Montgomery Clift, a youthful Broadway veteran. Ardrey had recommended him for the part and he proved to be an agreeable presence. Kazan never warmed to him the way he did to Brando, whom the press and the public later considered his great rival as a method actor. But Molly did; Clift was often at the Kazan home. And for the moment, amid the mess and muddle of getting *Skin* on its feet, Kazan appreciated his hardworking ways and seemly manner. Years later, after Clift had become a notably self-destructive movie star, Kazan took a dangerous, but ultimately rewarding chance on him by casting Clift in *Wild River.*

The disruptive battle lines between Bankhead, the Marches and Kazan were established before rehearsals began. He had, in effect, been obliged to audition for all the stars, who had director approval, and he had to overcome his reputation for being too soft-spoken. Ms. Eldridge was the dominant figure in the March marriage—a genteel, pleasant, but rather steely middle-class person—reducing her husband to a kind of mischievous boy, telling sly jokes and being shushed by her. Kazan got on with them, but found Bankhead—who he says in his autobiography is one of the two people in his life that he completely, uncomplicatedly hated—much more difficult. When Myerberg took him to meet her she scarcely acknowledged his presence, talking over and around him. He would remember her criticizing The Group to him, on the grounds that it did not properly appreciate and accommodate star presences. He implicitly understood that she wanted someone—almost anyone—other than him to direct. Orson Welles was much on her mind.

But Kazan was not replaced. He simply went to work in his best professional manner. And, for a time, enjoyed himself—especially working with the dinosaur and the mammoth. He quickly began to see that the play was going to "work." Whatever it was and was not, it was flamboyantly theatrical. Whereupon Bankhead went to work. Or, rather, didn't come to work. She was sulking because he was, in effect, staging an ensemble piece, not a star vehicle. People were crossing in front of her, Eldridge and March and the veteran Florence Reed, playing a Gypsy fortune-teller (very much in the vein of her famous whorehouse proprietor, Mother Goddam in *Shanghai Gesture*), were, she thought, getting more than their due at her expense. All of these complaints, and more, were aired in a meeting at her apartment, where she eventually collapsed melodramatically on the floor. Myerberg, to Kazan's admiration, calmly told her to take the day off; rehearsals would proceed with her understudy in the role.

Next day, of course, she was back, bullying Eldridge, complaining about the set designs (which Kazan liked), being disruptive in a hundred ways. Her braying discontent was threatening to the entire enterprise. The crisis came at an out-of-town dress rehearsal in New Haven. She missed all her entrances, she talked interruptively offstage, most of all she volubly focused on one element of Albert Johnson's sets which at one point showed the Antrobus house in semi–knocked down condition, which meant the actors could be seen in the wings before making their entrances. She insisted that flats be erected to hide them. Myerberg, by this time ill with a throat infection and lying on a cot in the aisle (Kazan naturally admired his gumption), refused. Like his director he liked the effect.

A dinner break was called and Kazan retreated to a second-tier box to brood. All he could think about was his famous patience, his refusal to be riled, the Anatolian smile that covered his anger. Lee Strasberg and his earthquake outrage recurred to him. And Harold Clurman's insistence that he was no more than a technician. And his pal Odets smugly criticizing his *Night Music* performance without challenge from him. He thought, too, of his wife who had left him when she had found out about his affair with Dowling, of the young actress in this company whom he was going to lovelessly, enjoyably screw before the pre-Broadway tour was over. He descended into self-hatred—he was dirt, an animal. Well, by God, he would assert his animal rights.

The blowout came at three the next morning. The company was leaving through the front of the house, the crew was waiting to hear when the next day's call would be. Bankhead blew by him, complaining at the top of her lungs about his refusal to back up her criticisms of the set. He yelled at her. She yelled back. He pursued her to the lip of the stage, screaming obscenities at her. He would take no more shit from her. "I know you've been trying for a month to have me fired, but I'm still here—see me? I'm still here."

By then she had disappeared into the lobby. But the company was now his. Bankhead, of course, never would be, though Kazan had to admit that some of her criticisms of Eldridge's "goody-good" manner were apt and that he thought the tension between them was good for the show. Thereafter, they communicated only professionally—he giving notes, she taking or not taking them as the spirit moved her. There was one exception. In Baltimore (another tryout town) she knocked on his door, shed her blouse and skirt (she wore no underwear) and headed for his bed. Which was occupied by the young actress Kazan had been eyeing. Bankhead made a hasty exit.

The road notices were good on the whole. And New York smelled a hit in the making. The opening night curtain at the Plymouth Theatre was delayed for an hour and a half, while stagehands finished installing the complex scenery, but audience response was ecstatic. Perhaps the most amusing moment occurred backstage when Kazan's father, finally reconciled to his son's theatrical career, approached Bankhead and, upon being introduced, said, in his broken English, that she must be pleased to have been made a star by his son. The reviews, after the November 18 opening, were enthusiastic. "The best play the Forties have seen in many months, the best pure theatre," Lewis Nichols opined. Like most of his colleagues, he threw most of his praise to Bankhead. Kazan, he wrote rather mysteriously, "directed in the mood meant by Mr. Wilder." Alexander

Woolcott for some inexplicable reason compared Wilder's boldness, impatience and ingenuity to that of Frank Lloyd Wright. Well, they were both modernists of a sort.

But Wilder had not been much of a factor in mounting his work. He had mostly not been present at rehearsals or during the pre-Broadway tour. He had always been a footloose character—he had written this play in a succession of hotel rooms and other rented digs on a couple of continents—and now he had joined the army as an intelligence officer. He had communicated with all concerned through encouraging, placatory wires and letters, refusing to take sides.

Rewarded now with a hit—the play would run for more than a year—he was also rewarded not long after its opening with an accusation of plagiarism. It came from Joseph Campbell, the expert in mythology, and Henry Morton Robinson, later to be the best-selling author of *The Cardinal,* but then a *Reader's Digest* editor. The two were experts in Joyce, the coauthors of *A Skeleton Key to Finnegans Wake.* In a *Saturday Review* article, they accused Wilder of lifting his basic idea and a lot of his wordplay from Joyce's novel.

They must have known that Wilder was, indeed, a Joyce enthusiast, who had spent hundreds of hours studying and annotating *Finnegans Wake*; according to his biographer, Gilbert A. Harrison, he filled 656 pages of his journal with comments on it. He quotes a remark Wilder made to his sister, "Think of all the years I've spent on *Finnegans Wake* when I could have been doing my own work." To which she replied, "But think how much you enjoyed it."

Harrison notes that in his unpublished reply to Campbell and Robinson, Wilder admitted that the idea of "representing mankind's long journey by superimposing different epochs of time simultaneously" was Joycean. The idea that ancient man, placed in close proximity to modern man in a work of art, with the hope of cross-illumination as a result, is also something he took from Joyce. But as the playwright insists, most of Joyce's main themes—original sin, for example, Vico's theory of historical cycles, his playful invention of a language of sleep—were of no use to him.

Defending Wilder, Edmund Wilson notes that he funked certain aspects of Joyce, which might actually have improved his play: He observes, for example, that the Cain character, absent an Abel, is weaker than he might be, that Sabina is nowhere near as powerful a figure as her corresponding Lillith-like character in Joyce, that the Antrobus daughter is, similarly, not as potent dramatically as the Earwicker's daughter is in *Finnegans Wake*. All that aside, however, Wilson found *The Skin of Our Teeth* "an adroit and amusing play on a plane to which we have not been accustomed in the American theater lately, with some passages of Wilder's best. It deserves a good deal of the praise it has had, and all of its success."

Wilson's recently divorced wife, Mary McCarthy, disagreed. Like Wilson, interestingly, she noted the production's indebtedness to Olson and Johnson and the sometimes bracing low-life absurdism of *Hellzapoppin'*. But she thinks its deliberate toying with anachronism is vulgar. "In the first place, it is conservative: it affirms the eternity of capitalism, which it identifies with 'human nature' and it consoles us for the flatness of the present by extending that flatness over the past, so that whatever our sufferings we shall at least not be racked by envy, that most dangerous of human passions. In the second place, it is sacrilegious, for it denies time and history, and this to the modern ear is the equivalent of hubris . . ." Finally, she observes that the middle-brow audience is bound either to find the play either "monstrously profound" or "monstrously bewildering" when, in fact, it is neither. It is, if approached naively, directly, just "a lark . . . a bright children's pantomine."

I think, on balance, she's right. The play won another Pulitzer for Wilder, New York Drama Critics' Awards for Kazan and Bankhead, though not for Wilder, perhaps because the plagiarism charges were more recent than the good reviews. One has to think that it owed some of its success to its appearance in a dark wartime period, when everyone needed bucking up, needed evidence, couched by a highly regarded writer, that middle-class values and virtues would prevail.

The play made Kazan a directorial star, with a play that was philosophically not much different from a Group production. Yes, the mounting was flashier than anything he had been associated with there. But the drift of a typical Odets play also supported the courage and survival skills of ordinary people. All Wilder had done, come right down to it, was extend that celebratory mood upward a little, from Jewish and Italian folks living in the Bronx or Brooklyn to WASPs living in the commuter suburbs.

But for Kazan, the importance of *The Skin of Our Teeth* was not to be found in such matters. "The fact is," Kazan writes in *A Life,* "I owe Bankhead a gift; she made a director of me . . . Patience is a good virtue for a director to have if the threat of violence is waiting underneath. Bankhead taught me, without intending to, that there is nothing as necessary for a director as a tough-handed determination to get the result he wants, get it one way or another, preferably by patient kindness, or gentle, subtle manipulation, but if not by those means, by any the situation calls for—an intimidating voice, or the force of rage, simulated or genuine." Or, as he put it more succinctly to reporter Murray Schmach, "Every fighter has one fight that makes or breaks him. That was my fight."

Would he eventually have had that fight at some other time or place? One has to imagine so. But this one came at just the right moment, when his personal life was in crisis, when he professional life had either to go forward or to fall back. His rage saved him from settling into the routines of theatrical life, jobbing from hit to flop and back again. It began the rise in his reputation that gave him, as much as anyone in show business can have it, control over his own professional destiny.

Kazan was never much of a one, as he admitted, for checking up on his productions once they entered upon a long run. But Bankhead would continue pulling her tricks—combing her hair and distracting the audience's attention during one of Eldridge's big speeches. And March would retaliate—gargling noisily offstage in the midst of a Bankhead speech. This obliged Kazan to intervene and make insecure peace. It is interesting, however, that Bankhead, in her autobiography, perhaps understandably, plays down the conflict between them and quotes a letter Kazan sent her, in response to a Christmas gift she sent him (it was a St. Christopher medal mounted on a money clip), in which he wrote, "Thanks for being right those times when I was completely wrong. . . . And thanks above all for a thing no one can thank you for—for your gift akin to genius."

Considering the depth of Kazan's loathing for Bankhead, this is a fairly amazing document. Was this gamesmanship on Kazan's part, a way of keeping his production up to the mark a couple of months after its opening? Was it just an expression of relief that it had come out all right after all? Or was he, despite his protestations to the contrary, still trying to be liked by his actors? We'll never know. All we know is that Bankhead had presented him with a test of directorial mettle that, in his own mind at least, shaped his subsequent success.

6

Miracle Man

Elia Kazan now entered upon his high tide—a period of roughly fifteen years that are without question the most remarkable era any American director ever experienced. Between March 1943, when he directed Helen Hayes in a long-running, now totally forgotten play called *Harriet*, and the winter of 1953–54, when he directed his common-consent movie masterpiece, *On the Waterfront*, Elia Kazan directed fourteen plays and ten movies. Of the former, nine were long-running hits and two were history-making productions, Arthur Miller's *Death of a Salesman* and Tennessee Williams's *A Streetcar Named Desire*. His movies in that period included, besides *Waterfront*, his very beautiful debut movie, *A Tree Grows in Brooklyn*, and the picture for which he won his first Academy Award, *Gentleman's Agreement*. He, of course, had his Broadway flops, and several of his movies of this period have not worn particularly well. But still . . . there is no track record comparable to this one, either before or since, for no one ever achieved the simultaneous creative success Kazan attained in New York and in Hollywood at this time.

Harriet, based on the life of Harriet Beecher Stowe, author of *Uncle Tom's Cabin*, was written by two long forgotten playwrights, Florence Ryerson and Colin Clements and it was—oh-oh—a vehicle for a beloved Broadway star, Helen Hayes. It came to Kazan accidentally and, again, because he would work on the cheap. The producer—and for the moment, director—was Gilbert Miller, son of Henry Miller, the famous actor. Rotund, Anglophilic and a man who loved a good meal at least as much as he loved a good upper-crust play, he had enjoyed the energy of *Skin* and thought that was just what *Harriet* needed. Having given Kazan an excellent lunch, he brought him back to the theater he controlled—it was named after his father—to observe a rehearsal. At which Miller fell asleep. Whatever else he might bring to this production, afternoon naps were not on Kazan's agenda, so he signed on, reasoning that he couldn't do worse than Miller.

He soon found himself liking Helen Hayes. She was then in her early forties, having been on the Broadway stage since childhood. By now she was regarded as one of its great ladies, ranked with the likes of Katherine Cornell and Lynn Fontanne. Perhaps her most famous role had been as Queen Victoria in *Victoria Regina,* eight years previously. In it, she had perfected the manner that had made her beloved by Broadway audiences, a sort of pert cuteness that masked for a time a steely resolve that all her vehicles eventually revealed.

Kazan didn't much care for that manner and he worked patiently with Hayes to move her beyond it. Acting habit—the perfectly timed pause or gesture, the over-rehearsed intonation—is the enemy of the spontaniety he most valued. Hayes, to her credit, tried earnestly to do his bidding, but in the end resorted to her tried and true tricks. Possibly, as Kazan admitted, to his commercial advantage. Giving the public what it wanted, she made *Harriet* a hit. "It is a portrait that ranks with the best of Miss Hayes's beribboned gallery," said the man from the *Times,* making "an evening at Henry Miller's Theatre one of the best evenings on Broadway."

Kazan was not fooled by the play. In an interview with Lucius Beebe in the *Herald-Tribune*—his first lengthy conversation with a reporter—he called it "a sweet, old-fashioned nosegay of a thing." But he observed that it "reflected favorably on my versatility" taken in conjunction with *Skin.* "I got away with both assignments," he said modestly, "which has the general effect of making me as vain as a 'Follies' girl, and that's all right with me, too."

Beebe was quite taken with Kazan, whom he described as "modestly spoken and mild of appearance" (and obviously playing Beebe's notorious superciliousness cleverly); he devoted much of his space to yet another new Kazan production. This was *It's Up to You,* sponsored by the Department of Agriculture, which was designed to enhance public support of rationing and to rally it against black marketeering.

Beebe correctly described it as "a play in the Living Newspaper vein," written by Arthur Arendt, who had been the chief writer for those productions. Its music was by Earl Robinson of *People of the Cumberland.* To put the point simply, all these old lefties had been united by, of all agencies, the United States Government, and what they created could be described as agitprop. But it also drew on the presentational style of *The Skin of Our Teeth.* And if we are to judge from its script it was quite a lively—if simple-minded—piece. It featured the folksinger Woody Guthrie in its New York cast, used a blaring loudspeaker as a narrator, large-scale photographic projections, and at one point even has an actress talking to herself on a movie screen. Helen Tamaris, the dancer who had taught movement to The Group during its summer retreats, appeared as a dancing steak, much to Kazan's amusement.

Its narrative voice was very much in the 1930s–1940s manner— a sort of knowing folkishness, using a slightly tinny showbiz version of vernacular speech to make its moralizing arguments. It turns its characters from a sort of "people, maybe" group into one that finally shouts "the people, yes." Correct behavior ensues once the facts of the issues at hand are fully presented to them.

Early in the show, we hear this from the loudspeaker:

The man behind the plow is the man behind the gun
Farmer, save democracy.
Farmer, save civilization.
Farmer, save the world
DIG, FARMER, DIG

Developing that theme, the piece is at pains to overcome decades of domestic anti-Soviet propaganda, insisting, for example, that all the food America is shipping to the USSR is going directly to its fighting men, none of it to civilians. When someone asks what the Russian home front is subsisting on, the reply is: "They get along with what they have—black bread, mostly, and soup." They are lumped with the British and the Chinese as hard-pressed, gallant societies, and a nice young married man states that theme thusly: "Uncle Sam is doin' OK. As far as I'm concerned he can crack down on Mary and me and the kids and the rest of us *even more*. If they can take it in England and Russia and China, well, over here in America we can take it, too. Maybe we've been used to a lot of things we ain't goin' to see for awhile. Maybe we've gotten a little soft from this 'highest standard of living in the world' stuff—but when the squeeze is on *we can take it*."

So goes *It's Up to You*. In one of its skits a woman, who's been told by the doctor that her ailing husband must have red meat, tries to buy what he needs in a black-market butcher shop, but then is stricken by her conscience. In another scene a normally law-abiding American couple, people who save on gas for the car, buy war bonds, would never think of hoarding or of buying food illegally are nevertheless chastened for gluttony. Someone goes through their garbage can and finds in it—oh, *scandale*—uneaten veal croquettes. In yet another sequence a farmer's son joins the marines, finds himself pinned down by the Japanese on some Pacific island. His buddy leaves him an orange while he goes out to forage for food and is killed. The loudspeaker intones a letter from a soldier on Bataan: "The lack of food was our undoing."

Kazan had groused to Beebe about how difficult it had been to render in dramatic terms all the facts and statistics the Department of Agriculture had supplied the show. In later years he characterized *It's Up to You* as "A silly thing, really." But in that same interview (with Michel Ciment) he added this interesting thought about how the Living Newspaper tradition had affected the theater in this period: "We suddenly realized how dramatic facts are. Brecht . . . used statistics, technology and information about the operation of things. Steinbeck always did that in his books; he showed how motors were put together and taken apart. That technique, in the theatre, absolutely unrealistic, affected us all." He adds, rather suprisingly, "I think it affected Arthur Miller in *Death of a Salesman*." Many years later, when he turned novelist, factuality would deaden (and lengthen) all his books.

But what lingered longest in his mind were the Department of Agriculture functionaries who supervised *It's Up to You*. Some of them had been involved in the creation of the Tennessee Valley Authority, which offered Kazan common conversational ground with them. He found himself not only in political agreement with them, but enjoying their company as well. In particular he took a shine to his immediate boss—all business in his office, yet after hours, a man who liked to yarn, drink bourbon and listen to his extensive collection of folk music.

He would later say that he began jotting his first notes for *Wild River* around this time. He saw an interesting set of conflicts here: between educated and idealistic bureaucrats and rough plain people, between the forces of social progress and the forces of mute tradition. His early drafts of that screenplay featured a character like his Department of Agriculture boss, whom he imagined Burl Ives playing.

One's impression of Kazan in these days is of ceaseless, relatively thoughtless activity. He was by now an anti-Stalinist. But equally he remained an anticapitalist. Most of his subsequent work would carry some sort of leftist message—about racism, for example, or anti-Semitism. Some of it would be antipatriarchical or anti–middle class. Almost none of it would be entertainment, pure and simple.

But the mood of the country was vastly different than it had been in the 1930s. Washington, still dominated by New Dealers, was officially fighting the war to extend, on a global scale, liberal social values of the kind it had summoned in its fight against the Great Depression. But America was up and doing, constantly on the go—taking new jobs, embracing its vast military necessity—and a sense of conditionality was in the air. People might not be quite able to imagine the postwar future, but instinctively they sensed that it was not going to be exactly like the recent past, either. There was everywhere a sense not just of physical movement, but a feeling that the war might encourage other kinds of movement as well. If you were part of the civilian population, for example, you could think not just of clinging to whatever job you might have, but of striking out in new directions if the spirit (or the government) moved you. You could, more selfishly, think of taking a vacation from your family, from bourgeois staidness, if you liked. Many roads were open, all sure bets were off.

So it was with Kazan. At his age he expected to be drafted momentarily (only the fact that he had two children was briefly delaying that imposition), and this gave him a motivation to swell his savings by taking any job available. More than that, he was hot. His recent theatrial successes had caught Hollywood's eye and though he might tell Beebe that movie actors were overpaid and that a director's opportunities in the movies seemed to him quite limited, he was more than interested in the movies' overtures. Once *It's Up to You* was launched in New York (the script, with extensive staging instructions incorporated, was circulated throughout the country so local groups could duplicate his production) he entrained for the West Coast, mainly to spend time with Constance Dowling, now being built up by Samuel Goldwyn (she starred opposite Danny Kaye in *Up in Arms*), but also to explore his own opportunities. He found himself drawn particularly to Louis "Bud" Lighton, a Fox producer, who gave him *A Tree Grows in Brooklyn,* then high on the best-seller lists, to read. Kazan liked the novel without conceiving a great passion for it. Even so, he returned to New York with the strong impression that a movie career was his for the asking.

What brought him back to Broadway was a musical Cheryl Crawford wanted him to direct. He was ready for it. He had been directing plays with large casts, elaborate sets, complicated movement. All that was missing from them were songs and dances. And the musical theater was perhaps ready for him. The previous spring *Oklahoma!* had opened with its famously revolutionizing effect on musical theater. Essentially it had more closely integrated song, dance and storyline than had generally been the case before (though, of course, the true pioneer of this manner had been *Pal Joey* in 1940).

In any event, Crawford thought she needed a "realist" like Kazan to stage *One Touch of Venus,* and its composer, Kurt Weill, at first agreed with her. After *Johnny Johnson,* Weill had endured two *flops d'estime,* the oratorio-like *The Eternal Road* and *Knickerbocker Holiday* (which contained the haunting "September Song") before having his first American hit, *Lady in the Dark,* a musical on the unlikely subject of psychoanalysis. These productions had inched the art of the musical theater forward. But *One Touch of Venus* was less promising. The problem with it, everyone agreed, was the book by

S. J. Perelman, who was less a realist than a surrealist and, to a lesser extent, with the admittedly clever lyrics by Ogden Nash, whose humorous poetry, always reaching for wildly unexpected rhymes, was not without its own absurdist touches. Their story was, if anything, more nonsensical than pre-*Oklahoma!* musical fables had been—about an imported classical statue that comes to life in New York and falls in love with a barber. The crisis of the play concerns her decision about reverting to statue status or embracing suburban life in Ozone Park, although given the wartime mood, that was not a hard choice; she had to embrace American ordinariness.

In Kazan's judgment the conceit never worked and he fell to wrangling with Perelman in particular, whose book was severely cut in the Boston tryout. Soon Weill turned against Kazan; he told the director to forget about realism and just have his principals move downstage center and belt out his songs. Since they included the pert, pretty, Mary Martin (a Broadway favorite since she had stopped *Leave It to Me!* in 1938 with her famous rendition of "My Heart Belongs to Daddy"), that worked out better than Kazan expected. So did the fact that choreographer Agnes de Mille, fresh from her *Oklahoma!* triumph, insisted that he simply clear the stage to give her dancers, led by Sono Osato, plenty of room to work their enchantment.

Kazan himself was soon similarly shuffled off to the side, more stage manager than director, and the recollections of this production, which Foster Hirsch later collected, make him seem almost oafish in his incompetence. Or perhaps we should say more like Lee Strasberg trying to direct *Johnny Johnson* than he would have liked to admit. "He didn't know what he was doing," de Mille said. "He had no visual sense. Kazan had no eyes at all. He had a wonderful ear, though, not for music, but for speech." Paula Laurence, costarring in the show, recalled, "I never got any direction from him at all . . . I began to wonder how many musicals he had ever seen." Some, anonymously, characterized him as "an arrogant bully," who was also "common and vulgar with women."

Bullying, as we have seen, was not his basic directorial style. Either he must have felt desperately out of his depths, or he was being victimized, *ex post facto,* by the enemies he made on this show. But he did make a contribution, generally acknowledged by eyewitnesses; that was his work with Mary Martin. She was a star who was not unlike Helen Hayes in her no-nonsense professionalism, but not as set in her ways. He focused on her performance, making her, people said, more down-to-earth, less of a soubrette than she had previously been.

But *One Touch of Venus* belonged more to de Mille than to anyone else. She had begun working with her dancers before the rest of the company assembled, and she set a visual tone and a sense of movement that matched Weill's lovely score. And Kazan later acknowledged that fact. In his autobiography he recorded his admiration for de Mille, Osato and the rest of the dancers, whose discipline he thought far exceeded that of most actors. He was glad enough to accept the credit that came his way, undeserved as he saw it, for a show that turned out to be his fourth consecutive hit.

When he was in the process of "saving" *Harriet*, this bit of doggerel, written by the play's authors, was sent to him on opening night: "Kazan, Kazan/The Miracle Man/Call him in/As soon as you can." He doubted that. Excepting his work on *Skin of Our Teeth*, his accounts of his Broadway triumphs in this period are of a man most basically staging commercial products, and pretty much keeping out of their way once the machinery was turning over. The genius pose was never for him. The most he might have said about his ambiguous success with this musical was that it proved, at least to outsiders, that he was a total director, a man Broadway could trust.

To have achieved this status in a matter of three years was no small accomplishment. A "myth" (Kazan's word) had attached itself to him. And whatever doubts he secretly harbored about himself, he was, publicly at least, willing to live within that myth.

———

He quickly found himself drawn to another play, *Jacobowsky and the Colonel*. One of its attractions was the fact that the Theatre Guild had been talking to Jed Harris about directing it. He didn't like Harris, who was, at the time, the theater's reigning mad genius—very likely literally so. Stories of his erratic, not to say certifiable, behavior were legion but he was for a while indulged because his productions (among them, *Our Town*) were successful. He was a star director, of which there were then very few in the theater. The idea that he was now apparently in this league was a big reason Elia Kazan wanted *Jacobowsky* so badly.

The play had a curiously twisted history. Franz Werfel is credited as the author of the play, with an "American play based on same," credit going to S. N. Behrman. This does not quite tell the whole story. Werfel, was, at the time, an internationally famous Austrian-Jewish writer, whose most prominent works (the novel *The Forty Days of Musa Dagh*, for example) reflected his strong religious yearnings and his belief in the brotherhood of man. He was highly respected in literary circles and was married to Alma Mahler Werfel, whose reputation for bedding and marrying world-class artistic figures (who besides Gustav Mahler included Oscar Kokoschka, the painter, and Walter Gropius, the architect) has always been a bemusing footnote among literary and cultural historians. Her last conquest, Werfel, had recently escaped from Nazism, on his journey taking refuge in a shrine to St. Bernadette of Lourdes. He had vowed that if he was spared he would dedicate a book to the Saint and had been as good as his word. His novel *The Song of Bernadette*, published in 1942, became a best seller and the source of a popular, inspirational film, which would bring the young Jennifer Jones an Academy Award.

Sometime in 1943, Werfel, who despite the sobriety of his writing was a merry soul, regaled a dinner party at the house of the great German director Max Reinhardt, which Sam Behrman attended, with humorous tales about his escape from Europe. One of them— at least as it was reshaped by Behrman for the stage—was of a cultivated but practical and clever Polish Jew, who had made his way from Warsaw to Paris, one jump ahead of the Nazis. In Paris he acquired a car—by which he could escape to the South of France, where he hoped to find a ship to take him to America. The trouble was, he didn't know how to drive. Whereupon he meets an anti-Semitic Polish officer who has an aide-de-camp who can drive. In Werfel's telling, the man headed north instead of south, in order to pick up a girlfriend. Comic consternation all around—and the essence of Behrman's play.

Behrman himself was an interesting character. Born into poverty
in Worcester, Massachusetts, he had transformed himself into the elegant author of witty plays about establishment life—a sort of poor
man's Philip Barry. He was also an experienced adapter or "Ameri-
canizer" of European plays, and a likable man (and true to his humble roots, a leftist) who became one of Kazan's best friends. At the
end of the dinner party he had told Werfel he should write a play
about the likable Jew and the stiff-backed officer. In Behrman's account, "Werfel was delighted," but deferred to Behrman's expertise
with light comedy. He suggested it might be something their host,
Reinhardt, could produce and direct.

So Behrman went to work, only to be told a short while later that
Werfel was working on a version of the story with none other than
Clifford Odets. So Behrman bowed out and returned to New York.
Something like a year later he got a call from Theresa Helburn
telling him that, though the Theatre Guild was committed to the
play (it even had tryout theaters booked), the Odets/Werfel collaboration was "unplayable." Would he come back on board? And work
with Kazan, now definitely signed to direct?

In his new version of the story, the whole confusing business about
the travelers' destination is eliminated. They are, from the outset,
heading for the English Channel because the colonel has important
papers to deliver to the Polish government in exile in London, and the
girlfriend is, perhaps, a more appealing and consequential figure.

Somewhere along the line, Kazan was sent back to Los Angeles,
carrying Behrman's work with him. His task was to talk Werfel and
Alma into allowing this version of the play to be produced. Werfel
was, as usual, charming. But evasive. His wife, though once a great
beauty was now something of a Brunhilde and quite disagreeable in
the patronizing manner that European artists and intellectuals often
took to provincial Americans. Finally, it was money, not Kazan's
charm, that won them over. Werfel got top author's billing (and the
lion's share of the royalties) on a play Behrman said, "I had written
every spoken line of."

The play was superbly cast, with the tall and imposing Louis Calhern as the colonel, Annabella (the French movie star whose screen
career in the United States did not amount to much, despite a brief

marriage to Tyrone Power) quite winsome as the girl, J. Edward
Bromberg as the colonel's aide and, most significantly, Oscar Karlweis as Jacobowsky. Both Kazan and Behrman adored him, as did
audiences. He had been a comedy and operetta star in Vienna, had
fled Nazism and was discovered by Behrman in an off-Broadway
production of *Die Fledermaus.* He was a slightly built man, physically a great comic contrast to Calhern. There was something elfin,
perhaps even Chaplinesque, in his shrewd, survivalist manner. The
play ran—for more than a year—largely on the charm and subtle wit
of his performance.

And perhaps on the fact that people could see in him something
of a twentieth-century archetype, literally one of those millions rendered suddenly bereft of country, blown from place to place by the
winds of war and revolution—always on the run, always dreaming of
a place where he can peacefully settle down and take up permanent
citizenship. Our literature, theater and movies would rediscover, and
further develop, this figure time and again in the decades to come,
but Jacobowsky, in Karlweis's performance, was a first. And it is a
minor tragedy of theatrical history that the actor died prematurely of
a heart attack not long after this show closed.

Kazan would later admit that, for a time, he didn't see the
strength of Karlweis's performance. He said he began working on
the play in The Group mode—earnest, realistic, with a lot of subtext.
Theatre Arts magazine assigned a reporter to his rehearsals and she
reported jacket and tie being shed as he warmed to his task, with his
comments always to the practical point—a bit of business here, the
adjustment of an accent there, the odd suggestion accompanied by
the thought that the actor is free to ignore it if it isn't comfortable for
him when he tries to use it in the playing. "I will say nothing to an
actor that cannot be translated into action," he told her. He also,
however, showed her some notes in which he described the play as
"A modern legend of rebirth from death told in comic grotesques."

This does not sound totally wrongheaded, but it does sound a little heavy-handed. And as he watched Karlweis work up his performance he decided the whole piece should be lighter on its feet. Kazan
confessed his conceptual error to the company, which responded
willingly to his frankness, and *Jacobowsky* became more fabulist

than realist in manner. It's hard to doubt that, sooner or later, as he worked on *Jacobowsky*, he began to see it, more or less consciously, as anti-Group in spirit. More than ever, he saw that the theater needed to make room for actors who could enchant simply by deploying skills that were unteachable by exercise or rehearsal or Strasbergian theorizing. His last four shows—*The Skin of Our Teeth, Harriet, One Touch of Venus* and now *Jacobowsky and the Colonel*—had all taken their basic tone from a central performance, a star turn, which Kazan had been smart enough to use to the play's advantage. He would do this over and over again in his career, often shading or softening the playwright's or the screenwriter's intention, when he saw something emerge in rehearsal that gave the audience something to take home and treasure even as the details of the play faded from their minds. It is not too much to say that all his great successes were built around a great performance, that failures occurred when such a performance was lacking.

It was an "impure" way of working, the antithesis of The Group's way, but it was nearly always effective for Kazan. In the particular case of *Jacobowsky and the Colonel,* one suspects a still more personal metaphor was in operation. Was not S. L. Jacobowsky, finally, a handy little "gadget" to have around in difficult circumstances? Was he not someone who—yes—had his own survivalist agenda, but who also just happened incidentally to bring his companions along with him to safety? Was he not someone somewhat like Kazan, as he had been in The Group—busy, benign, too practical to be taken entirely seriously, but yet useful—and was he not a great deal more like Kazan in his maturity—also busy and essentially benign, but now experienced enough to be show business's great enabler? Or, to put it more bluntly, its great fixer.

———————

A fixer of—frankly—ephemera. In interviews Kazan has said that his work on Broadway at this time was largely technical in nature. He was an arranger of scenes, a creator of stage pictures, a mostly seductive and agreeable mentor of actors. Much of what he was doing did not speak to him in powerfully emotional terms; that would come later, in his collaborations with Arthur Miller and Tennessee Williams, particularly.

And most of what he was doing—however successful it was at the time—does not speak to us, either. His plays of this period lie mainly unread in libraries. Movies, treated so contemptuously at the time by haughty Broadway, are different. Because they are physical products, immutable reels of celluloid, they persist. No one saw the means of their cultural ubiquity in the 1940s—late-night television, Turner Classic Movies, the VCR and the DVD, the growth of academic film studies, film archives, film festivals. But, simply put, film history is now a bustling subculture; theatrical history is, in contrast, a backwater.

When he took a train westward in the spring of 1944 to make his first movie, Elia Kazan was, without being aware of it, entering retrievable, permanent history, about to create a body of work that remains intact—something to be reckoned with. Beginning with *A Tree Grows in Brooklyn.*

On the train, committed to making five films in as many years for Twentieth Century–Fox at a salary he considered modest to a fault, Kazan came fully to grips with the book for the first time. Reading and rereading it, he found himself moved to tears by Betty Smith's novel. As well he should have been. For in this tale of first- and second-generation immigrants, clinging desperately to the lower rungs of respectability, trying not to fall into abject poverty, he quite naturally saw points of reference to his own early life.

As many did. From the day it was published in 1943 Smith's novel, written in a serviceably realistic manner, has never been out of print. An immediate best seller (2.5 million copies in its first two years), it became, and to a degree remains, a rite-of-passage experience for many Americans, particularly young women. Turn-of-the-century Brooklyn is a remote environment to them. So is the national mood that made the book such a success on first publication. It is a warm appreciation of the strength of and persistence of good, plain values, heartwarmingly applied to difficult circumstances.

But the book's heroine, Francie Nolan, remains a completely relevant figure to this day. It is hard to know just how much of Smith's own experiences went into her creation, but one can easily see that the writer must have transformed a measure of personal history into a lasting archetype. Francie and her brother, Neeley, are the children of an Irish singing waiter, Johnny Nolan, and his wife, Katie, whose roots are Austrian. Francie's writing has been encouraged at school, and she dreams of going on to high school, then college, then to a career as a professional writer. She is trying to read her way through every book in her neighborhood branch library. Any ambitious young woman can identify with her yearnings.

But there is still richer emotional material in her. There is, for example, her blind adoration of her charming, unreliable father. He has his own frustrated dream—that one night a Broadway producer will wander into a saloon where he's singing, hear his silvery voice and make him a star. But he's also an alcoholic; you can never count on him actually to return home with the pocketful of tips on which his family depends for their subsistence. His wife, Katie, is made of sterner stuff. She's a hard, practical woman who has come to hate (and repress) the romantic side of her nature, which long ago yielded to Johnny's blarney, reducing her and her brood to their anxious and marginal existence. Indeed, in the course of this story she gives in to Johnny one last time, becoming pregnant as a result, thus precipitating the narrative's central crisis.

Thinking about Johnny and Katie at the time, Kazan wrote in his notebook about their "nobility," which, he says, "is fulfilled in spite of themselves." He felt it important that they did not fully understand their own good impulses, but that blindly "they live up to the best in themselves"—through their daughter. In these notes Kazan is more coldly analytical, more schematic in his approach than usual—and more overtly psychologizing as well. When he reviewed the film, James Agee thought it perhaps too easily Freudian in its approach.

But I don't agree. Kazan was right; the way the parents keep losing sight of their better instincts under the impress of their hard lives, but keep rediscovering them, makes them, to me, all the more appealing. It also makes their daughter's endless forgiveness of the romantically perceived father, and her resistance to the harsh practicality of the mother all the more touching. This was, as it continues to be, a common emotional conflict among young women—rendered the more touching in Francie's case because she is so obviously a product of

them both—at once dreamy and striving. Then add to that her relentless, if good-natured, ambition, her willingness to work hard in school,
while picking up, for her family, whatever small advantages that she
can on the streets and in the shops of her neighborhood, and she becomes an exemplary, proto-feminist heroine.

All of this was surely implicit, needing only a little detailed development in the excellent script Kazan was handed, the work of
Tess Slesinger, a leftist novelist and short story writer (*The Unpos-
sessed, Time: The Present*) and her husband, Frank Davis (they had
previously written *The Good Earth*), which was equally touching. It
drew on all the strengths of Smith's work, with their compression
further intensifying it.

In the mysterious way of Hollywood, Kazan never met the writers. But he drew close to Bud Lighton as they prepared the film for
production. As Kazan later recalled, Lighton said he wanted to work
with "a new director whom I can 'help,'" and in Kazan's words, "he
put the word 'help' in quotes, but he did help me." The biggest thing
he learned from Lighton, he said, was to pay meticulous attention to
the script, making sure everything was in near-perfect order before
shooting began. Kazan remembered putting a little more emphasis
on the immigrant elements of the piece, though he also insisted that
this development was quite minor.

In Kazan's account, Lighton became something of a father figure
to him during preproduction. He was a calm, WASPy movie veteran
(he had worked mainly at MGM, mostly with tough old pros like Victor Fleming), a large man, losing his sight (he used a huge magnifying
glass to read the script), rather right wing in his political views, and
given to working off tension by practicing with a bull whip, with which
he was, according to Kazan, quite adept. He also had a small ranch in
Arizona, to which he slipped away whenever he could. Essentially they
seem to have formed a sort of us-against-them bond.

But Lighton was only part of Kazan's good luck on his first Hollywood venture. He found that he liked working at Fox. The studio's
chairman, Spyros Skouras, was, like himself, a Greek immigrant, notorious for his wayward grasp of the English language, not likable or brilliant but tough and sympathetic to Kazan—if only because there were
so few Greeks in the industry. Darryl Zanuck, the chief of production,

was also someone with whom Kazan could identify. They were both small, driven men, whose sexual appetites were as prodigious as the fierce concentration they brought to moviemaking. Zanuck, who tended to work the nights away screening dailies and rough cuts in the basement of the Fox executive building, was famous for his ability to spot the weaknesses in what he saw and to propose corrections for them. Kazan might quarrel with him over details, and generally mistrust him, but he never thought of him as a tyrant or a fool. But the best thing, for Kazan, was the film he was making. He didn't always know what he was doing, but there were plenty of people willing to instruct him. And this was a lucky production, one of those movies in which all the pieces seemed to fall easily into place.

Kazan said to me in 1990 "that every picture that is successful has one little miracle in it, and we had ours—Peggy Ann Garner, the little girl." The daughter of an English-born attorney father and a mother who pushed her into acting, she had made several previous films without quite achieving child stardom. But now at age thirteen, she was luminously right for this role. She was not particularly fond of her ambitious mother, but she adored her father and was "worried as hell about him," as he was overseas, serving as an air force pilot. The analogy between her real life and the fictional role she was playing was perfect. "I could just look at this girl and see the fright on her face," Kazan remembered.

Indeed, he played on that fear. There comes a point in the story where, with his wife pregnant and the family facing utter destitution, Johnny Nolan plunges out into a blizzard, determined to find steady work, and then dies of exposure. Preparing Garner for the scene where she must accept his loss, Kazan "dropped a few words" about the possibility of losing her own father in the war. What, exactly, he said, he claimed not to be able to remember. But he did remember Garner crying "all morning, all afternoon, all night." It was exactly what he needed. "You know," he later reflected, "I think finally a film director has to get a shot, no matter what he does. We're desperate people. And one way or another, no matter what we have to do, we'll do it. And we'll be sweet and nice afterwards. And I hugged her and kissed her and did everything in the world for her. . . . But at that time I had to get it. And I got it."

Is there something chilling in this confession? Yes, there is. But it is by no means unique in movie practice. And it goes to the heart of Kazan's art, setting up emotionally loaded situations on his sets and in his rehearsal halls, hoping the feelings he encouraged would spill over into performance. It is what he did instead of publicly analyzing the script. It is also what he did in casting, hoping his players' offstage relationships would analogize with the ones he was trying to build in performance.

Tree offers a good example of that, too. Garner naturally gravitated to her on-screen father, James Dunn. He had been a minor star in 1930s movies, but his career had been laid low by alcohol, exactly like Johnny Nolan's. This background Kazan judged perfect for his needs. "If you can get the real thing, that's great, and I got Jimmy Dunn. You can't beat that, because he didn't have to act. He just looked like a guy who had boozed too much and also was jolly and lovable at the same time he was also sort of a mess." For the length of the shoot, he and Garner formed a loving bond, and their scenes together are wondrous. It is, for example, he who explains to her the symbolic tree of the title—a tough specimen that sinks down its roots through cracks in the concrete and somehow flourishes, as Francie does, in an unyielding environment. It is he who consoles her when it looks as if she'll have to withdraw from school and go to work to help support the family. It is he, with his impotent dreams, who keeps hers alive.

And it is he, frankly, who annunciates a theme that would be central to Kazan's work for the rest of his career. It is the theme of the damaged male. Johnny was, for all his charm, disastrously wounded by drink, just barely able to navigate life. After him came a deluge of male dysfunction in Kazan's work. Whether we are talking Joe Keller, the cheating manufacturer of *All My Sons* or Willy Loman, driven to suicide by his failure to capture his share of the American Dream, whether we are talking the crypto-homosexuals of *Tea and Sympathy* or *Cat on a Hot Tin Roof*, whether we are talking the rapacious sexual brutality of Stanley Kowalski or Terry Malloy's yearning for tenderness, full human status, in *On the Waterfront,* we are talking of men who somehow fail to match the conventional masculine ideal as it was everywhere presented in popular culture.

Kazan was not alone in questioning the traditional masculine ideal at this time. During the war and its aftermath the whole film noir genre, for example, presented a rich array of damaged males in criminal contexts. It is also fair to note that Kazan himself sometimes skipped the topic in films like *Boomerang* and *Panic in the Streets*. But by and large this was a matter that drew his most avid—and sympathetic—interest. However successful he became, he remained in his own mind the immigrant outsider, ever the imperfect American.

His autobiography lays out his neediness on virtually every page. We understand that it drove almost all his actions—from his marriages to his politics. It is the great given of this life, just as the sympathy he lavished on the likes of Johnny Nolan is one of the the great givens of his work. Along with his predilection for cool blonds.

Kazan makes a joke of this in his best, and most autobiographical, novel, *The Arrangement*. His narrator-protagonist is describing his mistress, whose fine silky hair he adores and he says, simply, "Being Greek blondness is my fetish." To which one almost replies, "No kidding." All three of Kazan's wives were blonds. Almost invariably his leading ladies were, too. Often they were cool blonds, appraising and ironic with his leading men, sometimes angry with them, but almost always wanting them to be better than they are.

Dorothy McGuire's Katie is of the angry variety. Not being Irish, she is more reserved with her emotions than her husband or children are. She had about her a natural, well-bred reserve, but with just a hint of underlying hysteria—a woman guarding her feelings lest they undo her. This held back quality pays off when Francie comes home from school one day and finds her alone, in labor. In her pain, she cries out confessionally. She would have liked to have Francie's gift for expression, Johnny's gift for friendship. She does not wish to be the hard, ungiving woman she has become. In this she is a typical Kazan wife. The more sexualized younger women, often the "other" woman, in his works tend to be more playful, more fun. In other words, Katie was a sort of Molly clone. But, as he often did in his work, Kazan cuts her a break. In that long, beautifully played confessional moment, she wins not only Francie's heart, but the audience's as well.

Curiously, Kazan never claimed for himself great directorial acumen on this picture. He conceded that he knew something of this cut of New York life from his own younger days. In his autobiography he concedes, too, that he was beginning to miss Molly and his children and the comforts they offered him and that his longing infused this film. But he felt himself to be very much the tyro on this project. His director of photography, the veteran Leon Shamroy, sensing his insecurity, particularly with the camera, suggested that perhaps they should codirect the film, and Kazan seriously considered the possibility (it was Lighton who talked him out of it). Almost a half century later he was still saying, "I didn't have that much confidence. . . . Maybe it looks that way. I'm glad it does. But I was essentially a stage director and what I did . . . was I staged the scenes wherever they took place mostly in a room, the way I would on a stage."

There's some truth in that description, but he's being too modest. There's often an instinctive elegance in his framing and a very intelligent movement of figures within those frames. Greatly aided by Shamroy's camera, he creates a very good sense of claustrophobia within the Nolans' tenement and draws a good contrast between it and the streets outside. This may be a backlot Brooklyn, but it has a much stronger authenticity—including a horse-drawn trolley car—than most studio-bound films of the time had. And that says nothing of the bustling life of *Tree*'s subsidiary characters—Joan Blondell's Aunt Cissy with her busy romantic life, Lloyd Nolan's stolidly patient, ultimately rescuing cop are notable—and of the lovely grace notes that the script introduces—Francie and Neeley tricking a prize tree out of a reluctant dealer on Christmas Eve, for example, or the gift of flowers from Johnny, delivered after his death to his daughter when she graduates from primary school, or best of all the fierce immigrant's speech, celebrating the opportunities America offers, coming from Katie's mother and prefiguring themes Kazan would return to again and again.

On the whole *A Tree Grows in Brooklyn* was rapturously received when it opened early in 1945. Only James Agee rendered serious reservations about it. He rather mysteriously thought, for instance, that it might have included a school outing sequence, in order to give viewers a more spacious view of turn-of-the-century urban life. Equally mysteriously, he thought it too self-consciously realistic in its reconstructions of old Brooklyn. What one takes away from his piece—a longer review than he normally gave studio products—is a rather grudging tone; he just doesn't want to concede that a best-seller as mighty as this one could yield up a film as emotionally powerful as this one. Oddly, his hesitant praise of the film matches Kazan's hesitations about it.

Indeed, in his autobiography, Kazan compares the film unfavorably to the book that, at this time, he most admired—Zola's *Germinal,* that brutal saga of a mining community and the way the work reduces the miners almost to the animalistic level. It is an unfair, even absurd, comparison.

But Kazan's mood at the time was very dark, which meant that the success of *A Tree Grows in Brooklyn* appeared to him as a kind of bitter irony. Yet a success it was. One of the top-grossing films of 1945, it brought an Academy Award to James Dunn and a special Oscar for Peggy Ann Garner as the year's best child performer. Moreover, it has had an afterlife that few films enjoy. It became a "family favorite" largely because of its heartwarming aspects, though it is much better than that, especially in its lack of overt sentimentality.

That, however, he could not see at the time. He enjoyed the flattery he received on the Fox lot, rather grudgingly admitting that the atmosphere at the studio was the happiest he had thus far encountered in show business, with Zanuck calling him the greatest directorial discovery of the decade and Skouras inviting Kazan to join him in the steam room, that most exclusive of executive privileges. The studio wanted him to direct another prestigious production, also based on a best-selling book, *Anna and the King of Siam.*

Yet he could not shake his gloom. Partly this was professional. In 1943 he had insisted, in a newspaper interview, that Broadway had more to contribute to the war effort than escapism, which he implicitly understood most of his own work to have been. "It is my opinion that the theatre could and still can contribute much more to the real tone and spirit of our people than it has . . . where the theatre could on the one hand inspire and teach, it has allowed itself to become debased."

But it was the pain and confusion in his personal life that most profoundly colored his mood. Constance Dowling's career was in crisis—Samuel Goldwyn had dropped her option in favor of a more forthrightly sexy blond, Virginia Mayo—while Kazan found himself in increasing conflict over their relationship. He kept telling her that he was moving toward a divorce from Molly and, in fact, they were having some discussions about that.

But on a trip East, he discovered that Molly was seeing (chastely) another man, and he found himself drawn to her stability and missing the wisdom she had always brought to the questions his career constantly raised. He also contrasted the somewhat sybaritic life he enjoyed in Los Angeles with his grittier existence in New York. On the West Coast he had found that he was only happy when he was on the lot, working. In New York there was an intellectual life—a rub and scratch and irritation—that he could not live without. In *A Life* he speaks not merely of the strength of the roots he had sunk there, but of the rootedness in their native soil of artists he admired—Faulkner, Picasso, Flaubert, Proust among them.

So in the end, with considerable ambiguity, he rejoined Molly. And in the comparatively brief interval between completing *A Tree Grows in Brooklyn* and leaving for military service in the South Pacific he involved himself with a musical play. This was *Sing Out, Sweet Land,* a sort of revue of popular American songs with a book that Walter Kerr, soon to be a distinguished drama critic, had worked up.

The piece starred Alfred Drake, fresh from his triumph in *Oklahoma!,* and Burl Ives, the folksinger, a difficult character, given to large angers and a large appetite for drink—just the sort of erratic, dangerous, inexperienced actor Kazan liked. It is obvious that Kazan's connection with this piece, produced by the Theatre Guild, was as a play doctor. The director of record was Leon Leonidoff (later to become the man who staged the Radio City Music Hall revues), with Kerr supposedly staging the book scenes. The songs—all traditional items, ranging from Puritan hymns to "A Bicycle Built for Two"—celebrated American tradition. But the book, which involved Drake as a man wandering the country collecting and encouraging song and a mustachioed villain who wanted to prevent American singing, was lame, and the play closed after a run of about three months. By which time Kazan had left the country, putting both his obligation to Fox and plans for at least one new Broadway show on hold, in order to—not very arduously—serve his country.

7

Eating Fire

Kazan's assignment in the South Pacific was not dangerous. And its contribution to the war effort was negligible. His task was to evaluate the effectiveness of G.I. entertainment. But at this late date, who cared how effective USO shows were in raising morale? Kazan was, as ever, a shrewd observer of whatever scene was playing, and he was close enough to the fighting to observe its effects on men who were risking their lives, and to take what he saw to heart.

To begin with, he quickly became contemptuous of the professional entertainment provided our fighting men. He was not there to observe the visits of major stars, whose celebrity perhaps brought them greater acceptance among the troops. He was looking at small-timers, and the response to them was indifference. The soldiers liked the showgirls well enough—though Kazan thought their presence constituted a sort of institutionalized cock-tease. But he reported that the GI audiences found the comics and specialty acts tiresome and irrelevant. He observed that the army's best recreational program were the craps and poker games that were an endemic feature of every barracks and tent he visited.

More significantly, he saw how the brutal war against the Japanese was affecting the American military. This was a particularly cruel, unforgiving foe, and the Americans had learned how to answer him in kind. Very simply, both sides in the South Pacific relentlessly committed horrendous war crimes, and the sheer brutality of what he saw (and heard about) made a lasting impression on Kazan.

He guessed it would leave a much deeper scar on those who actually endured that kind of combat.

Typically he began thinking that a theater wanting to speak meaningfully to this generation had to be a new sort of theater. He retreated to Manila to write up his report and there was stricken with dengue fever. Its symptoms, intense diarrhea and vomiting, literally forced him to his knees. But crawling from bed to bathroom the idea of an acting school somehow occurred to him—a place where young performers could be trained in a style appropriate to new sorts of plays, plays that were less politically sure of themselves than The Group's had been, more open, perhaps, to the absurdities—the nameless and essentially insoluble terrors—of a new kind of American life.

The difference between the institution he imagined and The Group was that his "studio" (the word occurred to him early on) would not have a performance component; it would aim at infecting a new generation of actors with a radically new performance style, they would then fan out across show business and, in effect, revolutionize it from within.

Kazan did not make this notion public when he wrote about the future of the theater in the October 1945 issue of *Theatre Arts*. Instead, he chastised theater and other media people for following what he called "the law of the least common denominator, only to discover too late that they had misjudged and underestimated" an audience that he felt was "ahead of us." The "makers of entertainment," he said, "must try, in our field, to be as honest and grown up as these kids" who are a "lot tougher, more honest and a lot more progressive" than they were credited with being.

Kazan was not alone in these feelings. In his introduction to the famous disaster, Maxwell Anderson's *Truckline Café,* which Kazan and Harold Clurman would produce early in 1946, the theater historian Thomas H. Pauly cites an article by Rosamond Gilder in *Theatre Arts* in which she observes Broadway preoccupied with "its accustomed toys, finding it all too easy to direct the restless crowds that pour through its streets with the tinsel and gewgaws of its side shows." At the same time, Burns Mantle, introducing his annual col-

lection of Best Plays (the 1944–45 edition), accused the theater of
being "a refugee" from the Second World War. And Lewis Kronenberger, perhaps the most serious and scholarly of the daily reviewers, wrote, "in its trappings and devices, the theater of the moment is
lively, but very little of it is alive . . . we have almost no real seriousness and almost no common ideas."

To some degree this problem was a cyclical one. The interwar
generation of playwrights, which included Anderson and his colleagues in the Playwrights' Company (Sidney Howard, Elmer Rice,
Robert E. Sherwood, S. N. Behrman), were aging and in some cases
distracted from theatrical work. Odets was in the midst of an eight-
year theatrical silence. O'Neill was about to offer a late masterpiece
(*The Iceman Cometh*), that would not, at first, be particularly well
received. It didn't acknowledge it, but Broadway was awaiting a new
crop of playwrights, and had, indeed, already witnessed its first delicate, yet surprisingly strong, tendril, pushing its way up through its
sidewalks.

This was Tennessee Williams's *The Glass Menagerie*, which had
opened the previous spring. At the moment, it seemed too wispy, too
fragile, too singular a play on which to build large hopes for a theatrical
renaissance. But, in its way, it was precisely that. And with Kazan about
to become Williams's great nurturer (and Arthur Miller's as well),
Broadway was about to enjoy its last, brief moment as a major contrib-
utor to the cultural and intellectual life of the country.

It was part of Kazan's good luck that he would become a central
figure in this renaissance. With a couple of exceptions, he would not
in the future direct anything that lacked emotional reality or social
relevance.

Some of this material looks crude to us in retrospect. But there
was at least aspiration in it, a desire to speak truthfully to the social
and psychological issues of the day. *Deep Are the Roots* is a good
case in point. The work of Arnaud d'Usseau and James Gow, who
had enjoyed a wartime success with *Tomorrow the World,* about a
German refugee teenager taken into a suburban American home
who turns out to be a murderous Hitler Youth, it was the first play
Kazan directed after the war. It opened scarcely more than a month
after V-J Day, and it was the first of many plays and movies—in film

it would become virtually a subgenre—to take up the issue of racial prejudice.

The play was, rather surprisingly, a success; the reviews, though aware of its dramatic crudities, were nevertheless indulgent of what we might now call its political correctness, and it ran for well over a year. Its narrative line is old-fashioned, and highly melodramatic: A black man named Brett Charles (Gordon Heath), who was an officer and a hero during the war, returns to the southern mansion, owned by a former U.S. Senator, Ellsworth Langdon (Charles Waldron), where his mother has been a lifelong domestic servant. The atmosphere is, at first, welcoming. But then it becomes clear that his wartime service has made Brett if not "uppity," then ambitious beyond his prewar place; he wants to start a school for black kids, offering a better education than the segregated public schools provide. Worse, it appears that the senator's two daughters have taken an uncommon interest in him. The elder, Alice (Carol Goodner), has a northern liberal boyfriend, Howard (Lloyd Gough), and is herself full of liberal pieties that are sorely tested over the course of the play. The younger sister, Genevra (Barbara Bel Geddes), loves Brett romantically without, at first, being able to acknowledge that inconvenient and, at the time, shocking fact.

Over the course of the play, the senator's true colors become apparent. Underneath his southern graciousness, there lurks a racist heart. He fakes the theft of a watch, accuses the young man of the crime and has him arrested—mainly to teach him a costly lesson in respectful behavior, though the implicit threat of a lynching also hovers in the air. As does the threat of miscegenation. For Genevra finally, openly confesses her love for Brett and actually proposes marriage to him and a move north to a (supposedly) more liberal climate. This he rejects (though she does leave alone in search of such a place).

The twist is that, after much anguish, her sister and her lover decide to stay in the South, as does Brett, doing what they can to conquer racism. Her father has a third act speech in which he cries out hysterically, "They'll return from Europe—this black horde—reeking with rebellion and ready to turn their weapons on us, their masters." In the play's last moment, he declares himself on the side of

those men "armed and awaiting the day" when a violent counterrev-
olution will be required to oppose this "horde."

The play obviously has its contrivances; the reviewers were particularly hard on the stolen watch business, which smacked, to them,
of antique melodrama. Kazan himself didn't much care for it. He
thought it turned the play into a drama of the "falsely accused,"
which he compared unfavorably to Lillian Hellman's *The Children's
Hour*, in which two schoolteachers are falsely charged with lesbian-
ism. On the other hand, in an introduction to the published version
of their work, written almost a decade later, the playwrights quote a
letter to the editor of *PM*, whose critic was among those questioning
this device, from Walter White, leader of the NAACP; he pointed
out that all over the South, for decades, black men had been lynched
for lesser "crimes"—for talking back to a white man or failing to
yield the right of way on a road to a white man.

There were other criticisms that strike one, reading the play
today, as more fatuous. For example, in the *New York Times* Lewis
Nichols, in a Sunday think piece, found "the whole marriage idea is
unnecessary and some of the characters, notably that of the Senator,
are forced into a mold more for the convenience of the playwright
than by the development of personality." But as White also observed, the senator was scarcely an anomalous figure—not in an age
when southern racist politicians—Bilbo, Rankin, Talmadge, East-
land—commanded national attention. It must also be said that the
"whole marriage idea" is far from "unnecessary"; without it, the play
would have no power. For it was always fear of miscegenation that
was the deepest of the prejudicial roots the play was trying to expose.
The problem with the play, which is forcefully, even occasionally bit-
ingly, written, is that it does not follow out its internal logic quite far
enough. It is possible that it needs to go all the way to the tragic—
that is, to a lynching of the innocent Brett. Or conversely, that it
needs to show the white woman and the black man actually hunger-
ing for sex, pawing eagerly, desperately at each other. To put the
point simply, it resolutely stays a "problem" play, neatly resolving the
finite issue—that damn stolen watch—in a way that permits the audience to "discuss" the issues it raises politely, but without the emotional devastation a more shocking conclusion would have enforced.

In the end, it pretty much lets everyone off the hook—except, of course, the irredeemable senator.

A few years later, their friendship and collaboration well established, Tennessee Williams, in a letter to Kazan, confessed that he "hated" the play, but observed that Kazan "liked the orderly marshalling of forces on opposite sides, good and bad, and the message coming out in banner headlines." This was a shrewd thrust. Kazan's natural inclination was to well-made sociopolitical arguments, from which his association with Williams, among other factors, finally led him at least partially away.

But it's foolish to ask more of *Deep Are the Roots* than it could possibly be. It is very much the work of its hopeful, immediate postwar moment. It at least raised a subject—as did *Home of the Brave,* Arthur Laurents's assault on anti-Semitism, which opened (less successfully) at the same time—that had previously been closed to theatrical discussion. And, somewhat willfully, it allowed its audiences to hope for an ameliorative solution to the issues it raises.

As for Kazan, the play itself, and its production generally, contained elements that would haunt both his work and his life.

Important among them was the figure of Senator Langdon, the at first benign, but ultimately corrupt, father figure—basically a family fascist guarding traditions he refuses to examine. There are in him elements of other characters Kazan brought to stage, screen and page—Johnny Friendly and Big Daddy, *East of Eden*'s Adam Trask and *Splendor in the Grass*'s Ace Stamper and, of course, of Kazan's own father.

Figures like Barbara Bel Geddes's Genevra were also favorite Kazan heroines. She got the play's best notices. Based on her subsequent work, one can easily imagine her playing this part in her patented manner, fresh without being dewy, intelligent without being all-knowing, spunky without being domineering, idealistic without being soggy. One sees in her those qualities Kazan admired in his own wife, and which would turn up in so many of his later works.

Kazan, despite his reservations about the play, was content to bask in its success. And to bond both with the playwrights and the show's lead producer, the left-leaning Kermit Bloomgarden, The Group's former company manager. D'Usseau wrote an admiring article about Kazan, which the latter quotes extensively in his autobiography. "James Gow and I believe in writing a play from theme; Kazan believes in directing a play in the same fashion. There have been brilliant directors in our Theatre . . . but these men have lacked a certain moral fibre, a certain ethical base. Their brilliance, after a short while, has been dimmed by a certain irresponsibility in their art. Kazan . . . has a tough-minded seriousness that convinces me everything he has done to date is but a beginning."

That last sentence is demonstrably true. But Kazan quotes this passage mainly for its irony; seven years later d'Usseau would be an unfriendly witness before HUAC. But the more profound point is this: Kazan, though still sympathetic to Communist ideals, was about to move away from politically themed plays. He also wrote later that he never looked forward to having dinner with Bloomgarden, d'Usseau and Gow: "I knew what the talk would be; I'd heard it all. He, Gow and d'Usseau were all fine fellows, but our relationship was cursed by the fact that we agreed on everything." So he turned back to Harold Clurman, who could no longer patronize the demonstrably successful Kazan. They started talking about a producing partnership in which they would take turns directing.

Before they could formalize that arrangement, Kazan had another friendly chore to attend to—directing Sam Behrman's new play, *Dunnigan's Daughter.* Kazan described the playwright as "an endearing man, full of longing and pain, tremulous with uncertainty of every variety, and not a strong man in a crisis." His great gift was for sophisticated dialogue, his great weakness a desire to make serious statements about political issues. Kazan had been working with him on this play before his wartime service and continued to do so after his return. The title character, eventually played by June Havoc, is married to an American capitalist, Clay Rainier (Dennis King), who is living in Mexico where he is exploiting the local population as well as his own wife—who comes to believe that he had been responsible for her own father's false conviction (and death) for a crime Rainier probably perpetrated.

Kazan stressed the analogy between Rainier's exploitation of a third-world country and his wife; if the play was to work there had to be a sort reciprocating action between personal abuse and the more abstract kind. He appears to have felt that if the audience could identify with a woman whose best self was being frustrated by her husband—"she represented what he prized most in life, a warm heart and a civilized mind"—they would also see the larger consequences of his careless cruelty.

It was a tall order, and the play quickly turned into a mess. It was very largely re-cast on the road, with Richard Widmark, less than two years away from his memorable movie debut (*Kiss of Death*), among those coming in. One of the victims of this process was Anne Jackson, later a Broadway star and, as well, a close friend of Kazan's. She agrees that was she was entirely miscast as Rainier's daughter—"I was a virgin playing this nympho"—and thought her replacement, Jan Sterling, was really a much better choice—"she had the kind of thing I didn't have, she was very free on the stage." Kazan, she thought, had done his best to help her overcome her defect—"he was very flirty and darling" trying "to make me feel like this character." She summarized the play's problems (and Kazan's) more succinctly than any of the reviewers: "He was trying to direct this play where you hold a cocktail shaker in one hand and a hammer and sickle in the other—so it wasn't quite working."

It was, in effect, *Deep Are the Roots* as a flop; the play closed after thirty-eight performances. The critics were disappointed, but polite—at least in comparison with their response to Kazan's next enterprise.

This was *Truckline Café*, which to this day remains one of the most famous of Broadway flops, in part because it deserved to be, but more so because Kazan, Clurman (who directed) and its author, Maxwell Anderson, chose to fight its bad reviews with ads and letters to the editors questioning the competence of the critics who had (it must be said) been harsher than necessary with the show. The only thing that made this despised play memorable was that it gave Marlon Brando the role Kazan would remember when he was casting *A Streetcar Named Desire* a year and a half later.

The show was—reluctantly—produced by the Playwrights' Company, many of whose members had urged Anderson to shelve it. But he thought the separations imposed on wives, husbands, lovers of every sort, by war was a poignant and not irrelevant issue. Kazan and Clurman saw something in it, too—wistful and authentic moments of longing and loss. It was, they judged, a little bit different, and therefore worth doing, whatever its flaws.

Were they completely wrong? Was *Truckline Café* really "the worst play I have seen since I have been in the reviewing business" as the *Daily News's* John Chapman called it? Was it, in fact, "downright unbearable" in its more pretentious interludes as Ward Morehouse of the *Sun* insisted? Did Anderson write it "with his left hand and, it is to be feared, in the dark of the moon" as the *Times's* Lewis Nichols speculated? Or was it, just possibly, an honorable attempt to touch crass melodrama with some believably human moments?

The eponymous eatery is located on the Pacific Coast Highway between Los Angeles and San Francisco. It has attracted, as both staff and customers, that population of drifters that is de rigueur in fictions about such establishments—people to whom traumatic things have happened or may happen if they aren't careful. Among them are a waitress named Ann (played by Virginia Gilmore, who, like Anne Jackson, was one of the actors fired from *Dunnigan's Daughter*). She has aborted the child of an idealistic husband named Mort who enlisted in the RAF early in World War II, but was lost and believed killed over Europe. She has also had an affair during his absence.

But Mort has not died. Captured by the Germans, he has escaped a German prison camp, and has been on the run for two years in Europe, where he fell in love with a now deceased Polish refugee, with whom he has fathered a child. Early in the play his prison camp buddy turns up looking for Ann, because she needs to sign off on the sale of a house she still jointly owns with Mort. And, as if deliberately challenging the audience's ability to suspend disbelief, Anderson throws another improbability at them in the form of Sage and Tory McRae (Brando and Ann Shepard). Sage has reason to believe an army buddy of his had an affair with his wife in one of the café's tourist cabins. The interloper is now dead, but Sage has brought the wife here to test her innocence. She fails the test, he pumps her full of bullets from his service automatic, swims out to a nearby pier where the police lay siege to him. Escaping them, he swims back to the restaurant where, meekly, though soaking wet, he surrenders to

Ann and a passing patrolman. Learning some sort of lesson from his desperation, she, in turn, reembraces her estranged husband.

This plot is preposterously over-elaborate and curiously underdeveloped. In a play about the human disruptions caused by the vastest war in human history, the absence of direct reference to the Holocaust is a singular omission. But that said, the play has certain strengths. There is a persuasive naturalism to much of its dialogue, and even some amusing minor characters (including a drunken and libidinous sailor played by Karl Malden). There is often something sweet in the yearning for a return to normalcy expressed by many of the characters. And Brando's success as Sage is not entirely due to the power of his performance. The brooding confusion of this figure, the sense that he is on the edge of terrible destructiveness, followed, once the deed is done, by a return to an essential gentleness, is present in the writing, waiting to be realized on stage.

One has seen and read many worse plays—not a few of them by Anderson, when the blank verse mood was upon him. One understands the impulse that led Clurman and Kazan to mount what was, for the time, a rather expensive production. One also understands the hostile tack they took against the critics in their newspaper ads. It was the argument used by The Group when it was trying to keep one of its less-favored offerings afloat; whatever its flaws, *Truckline Café* merited the attention of people who took drama seriously.

But they went a step further, arguing what everyone knew and no one had previously dared say in public, which was that New York's drama critics lacked the intellect and the knowledge to wield life-and-death power over the theater's offerings. Anyone writing theatrical history has to be struck by their incompetence—opinions unbacked by literary-historical knowledge, total inability to come substantively to grips with the arts of acting, directing and scenic design, the whole rendered in a prose that is near to imbecilic. If they "liked" the "moral" of a play, they would "like" the work. If, on the other hand, they disapproved it, they were quick to render their relentlessly middle-brow discontent.

Or as Kazan and Clurman put it: "Our theater is strangled in a bottleneck . . . made up of a group of men . . . who more and more are acquiring powers which, as a group, they are not qualified to exercise—either by their training or their taste. . . . No opposition point of view is ever expressed. There is a blackout of all taste except the taste of these men." This set off a furor of articles and letters to the editor, which Anderson further inflamed with an ad of his own: "It is an insult to our theater that there should be so many incompetents and irresponsibles among [the reviewers]. . . . Of late years all plays are passed on largely by a sort of Jukes family of journalism."

Reporting this controversy, *Time* magazine asked Wolcott Gibbs, the *New Yorker* reviewer, and a man of a certain snooty literacy, for his opinion. "I'd say offhand that there are only about three newspaper reviewers here who are competent to write about anything," he opined, before delivering this kicker: "But it is absolutely absurd to make an issue out of this play, which has no merit whatsoever." His judgment matched that of the moment—and of history. *Truckline Café* closed after twelve performances. So far as one can tell, it has never been professionally revived anywhere.

Yet the play had unintended consequences far in excess of its ignominious failure. Kazan had been unhappy with the production. As usual, Clurman had given his cast a brilliant analysis of the play at their first rehearsal. As usual, he had been unable to translate that analysis into practical stagecraft that would inspire them or move an audience. Watching the disaster unfold, Kazan began to think about how he would have worked with the playwright to reshape the play, which was also something Clurman did not do.

And Kazan saw, as he had with *Dunnigan's Daughter*, that the actors—Malden and Brando aside—did not have the training to dig meaning out of the play on their own. They required new ways of approaching their roles. He mentioned this to Clurman, together with his idea for starting some sort of actors' school, for which the only requirement for admission would be talent and a willingness to work. Clurman liked the idea—and promised to talk it over with Stella Adler. That, as far as Kazan was concerned, killed the idea; he was not about to share his idea with her.

Instead, Kazan spoke of it with the good-natured and highly practical Bobby Lewis. They spent the better part of a spring day in Central Park, strolling and planning. Others, including Clurman, later claimed the idea, but there is greater congruity between

Lewis's and Kazan's recollections of the founding months than there is in any of the other narratives. They agreed that Clurman would be a frequent guest lecturer on any and all matters of theatrical theory. There was also agreement that Lee Strasberg should not be allowed to teach acting. They thought he might safely be allowed to teach theater history.

But the actual beginnings of the Actors Studio would have to wait for a year. Kazan was heavily committed—he would direct two movies and his most significant theatrical production to date in the year after *Truckline*'s closing. Promising to keep in touch with Lewis, Kazan decamped for Hollywood and his second film, which would turn out to be a less happy experience than his first had been.

Sea of Grass was based on a novel by Conrad Richter that had enjoyed a considerable literary success a decade earlier. He was a novelist of pioneer life, but one who found in the American past something more than nostalgia or epic violence. He developed, in a rather austere manner, themes that a modern reader could relate to without the condescension that so often attends the reading of historical fiction.

The book had been brought to Kazan's attention by Bud Lighton, who had worked on an early version of the script when he was at MGM. And since his Fox contract permitted him to do films for other studios, and since he was coming off a hit version of another sort of historical movie, he got the job. What he dreamed of doing was a sort of thinking man's Western, something without a lot of action, to be sure, but with a certain spaciousness—big skies framing an intense human drama.

In some respects *Sea of Grass* is like a preliminary sketch for *Giant*: A high-spirited woman from back East (in this case St. Louis) marries a cattle baron who is determined to preserve his huge range against those who would diminish it—in this case not with oil wells, but with fences and farms. Herein, Jim Brewton is fighting the "nesters," or small farmers, who enlist the sympathy of his bride, Lutie Cameron. Worse, the lawyer who champions their cause, Bruce Chamberlain

(Melvyn Douglas), enlists her love. Having already had a daughter by Brewton, Lutie also has Chamberlain's son, whom Brewton raises as his own. Lutie leaves Brewton, does her best to keep in touch with the children, and then when her boy, who grows up to be a wild one, is killed in a gunfight, reconciles with Brewton.

One can just barely discern what must have interested Kazan in this tale. There is the potential of something fierce, Kazanian, in the tormented wranglings of Jim and Lutie—his blind passion for the virgin purity of the land clashing with her compassion for the intruders on it, her reluctant straying with the lawyer when her husband will not compromise his vision. Jim is, potentially, another of Kazan's blindly fated patriarchs, waging a doomed struggle against social progress.

But that was not to be—for two reasons. The film was intended as a star vehicle for the beloved Spencer Tracy–Katharine Hepburn team, who were never as effective in drama as they were in comedy and were not, in any case, to be moved beyond their accustomed paces, which were emotionally rather restrained. And it was to be an MGM film, glamorously designed and costumed, but without anything approaching the kind of raw emotions the story presupposed.

Kazan saw trouble the first day he reported to MGM. Until then, he had imagined at least a limited amount of location shooting. Pandro S. Berman, the producer, greeted him with the news that he had some ten thousand feet of stock footage, suitable for rear projection, for Kazan to screen and choose from. Berman was utterly delighted by this trove, and dismayed by his director's lack of enthusiasm. "I admired Jack Ford," Kazan later recalled, "and I even hung around with him for three or four days talking" when he had been at Fox. "I thought if I could get into that, into the sources of America . . ." Not a chance. Not at MGM. Not with these actors.

Next, the wranglers showed Kazan the horses they had chosen for Tracy to ride. They were notably lacking in spirit. And their saddles looked like easy chairs to Kazan. He pointed this out. The wranglers exchanged looks; this, they knew from experience, was what the star wanted. "I found that he did not like horses and horses did not like him," Kazan told Michel Ciment, though he was "supposed to play a man who spends most of his time on a horse." Kazan added: "He was rather plump, not a Western type, a little lazy—only able to do things a few times and then losing interest in them—a little inert, not fierce at all, rather Irish and sly, very funny, very convivial, but not at all, in any way, like the type he was being asked to play."

It was the same with Hepburn, though his complaints about her were different. Take the matter of her costumes: they were elegant, but never looked as if she lived in them before or after the scene in which they were displayed. "[E]very time she went to the bathroom to take a piss in that picture, she came out with a different dress." Hepburn was not, in those days, the sacred monster, close to the grotesque, that she would become in her later years. But she "wanted then above all to be a big Hollywood star." She also wanted to be vocally supportive of Tracy, who was, of course, her lover, but also a volatile (and sometimes abusive) alcoholic. "She'd watch him shoot," Kazan told Jeff Young, "and say, 'Isn't Spence wonderful?' and I'd think, 'He's only giving a tenth of what he's got.'"

But no one cared. This was MGM, a studio that sold star glamour and expensive production values, not deep emotions. For example, the only possible explanation for Lutie marrying Jim and trekking out to the wilderness to make a life with him was irresistible sexual need. But Hepburn and Tracy in real life lived a comfortable, old-shoe sort of relationship (largely in George Cukor's guest house), and whatever the script said, that was the life they almost always appeared to live onscreen.

As a matter of fact, that's what Hepburn essentially plays even when she errs with the Melvyn Douglas character. He was an intelligent, rather slick and sexless actor who, in those days, specialized in playing the essentially unthreatening third leg of romantic triangles. One day they had a scene in which they were obliged to part, and Hepburn, who was proud of her ability to cry copiously on cue, did so effectively. Kazan was, for once, pleased with her effort—until Louis B. Mayer, the head of the studio, looked at the dailies and called Kazan to his office. There, according to Kazan, the following dialogue ensued:

MAYER: She cries too much.
KAZAN: But that is the scene, Mr. Mayer.
MAYER: But the channel of her tears is wrong.

KAZAN: What do you mean?

MAYER: The channel of her tears goes too close to her nostril, it looks like it's coming out of her nose like snot.

KAZAN: Jesus, I can't do anything with the channel of her tears.

MAYER: Young man: you have one thing to learn. We are in the business of making beautiful pictures of beautiful people and anybody who does not acknowledge that should not be in this business.

He was, in a sense, right. And Kazan knew it. He thought he should quit. Or at least insist on doing things his way and get fired. But he was still establishing his foothold in the movies and probably sensed that the movie would not be a disgrace; it would be received as a routine studio product, neither better nor worse than dozens of other star vehicles, with no particular opprobrium attaching to its director. It was only in that director's own mind that the disappointment was bitter. The piece was, even in its bland final form, shadowed by tragedy, but he had not been able to stir and discomfit his principals sufficiently to make its darkness visible.

Most movies featuring major stars are, to some degree, a tug of war between their egos and the director's ego. And it is entirely possible that Kazan's subsequent avoidance of stars was his way of avoiding that battle. But there was, I think, something more going on here. For his struggle with Tracy and Hepburn was not like his fight with Tallulah Bankhead. Those hostilities had been open and moved, very largely, by her lunatic insistence on egomaniac privilege. The battle with movie stars is usually the opposite; it is over their complacencies, their lazy sense of privilege and entitlement.

That attitude, in turn, derives from the stars' relationships with their public. They don't want the stars to play against well-established type. Knowing this, the stars, all protestations to the contrary notwithstanding, tend to work contentedly within the confines of their images.

Finally, one has to think that a certain class resentment arose in Kazan. These people were showbiz royalty and he was still, in his heart, an aspiring immigrant, eager to be understood as a nice, accommodating guy. And, as far as the movies were concerned, he was a tyro. So he stewed in silence. Yet this failure of—shall we say?—manliness remained capable of rankling him even very late in life.

"I question the value of stars," Kazan would say when he and I were discussing *Sea of Grass*. "I think they're overrated. And I think they're over-pumped up . . . They get too much money, too much praise, too much attention. . . . You have to make special considerations for them. They worry about that. And they have their agent hanging out in the dressing room, you know. 'Who's that stranger?' 'That's my agent.' 'Well, keep him off the goddamn set.'" If this attitude did not completely derive from *Sea of Grass*, it—unwaveringly—began there.

Kazan's next film, *Boomerang*, became a different and infinitely more pleasing landmark for him. He moved on to this picture without pause, beginning production on it within a month of completing *Sea of Grass*.

It told a true—or largely true—story, it was shot entirely on location, it used nonactors in most of its minor roles while its leading parts were filled primarily by Broadway actors who were, at that point, not well known to the moviegoing public. Of its many performers, only Dana Andrews, playing the lead, and Jane Wyatt, Kazan's old acting partner from *Night Music*, playing his wife, could even remotely be considered stars.

The story was this: A well-loved priest is murdered in a small Connecticut town, and a man named Waldron (Arthur Kennedy), a war veteran who had lived there for a few months while looking for work, is accused of the crime. He owns a gun that matches the murder weapon's caliber, and several witnesses offer incriminating evidence against him. Eventually, after exhausting interrogation, he signs a confession. But the prosecutor, Henry Harvey (Andrews) does not entirely believe it.

On the other hand, he is under pressure to obtain a quick conviction in what appears to be an open-and-shut case. The local newspaper wants it and the community is in a lynching mood. If, somehow, the case is lost, an election may also be lost, which means disaster for a local realtor (Ed Begley). He has invested heavily in land for a recreation area that will not be built if his party loses. In court, however, Harvey shows that the testimony of the witnesses against Waldron is dubious. Then he loads Waldron's gun with live ammunition and has one of his assistants point it at his head at precisely the angle it would have to have been held in order for it to have been used in the murder. The trigger is pulled—and the gun jams. It has a faulty firing mechanism, which means that it cannot possibly have been the murder weapon. The Begley character then commits suicide and the psychologically troubled man who probably committed the murder is killed as the police pursue him for speeding—though no definitive proof against him is adduced.

This story was not quite as fresh as the movie pretended. It had actually occurred in 1924 in Bridgeport, not Stamford as the movie pretended (the former city had refused permission to shoot in its streets). The "underlying property" was a *Reader's Digest* article entitled "The Perfect Case," which was, in turn, a condensed version of a piece that had appeared in 1945 in the *Rotarian* magazine. Its pseudonymous author was "Anthony Abbot," a pen name employed by Fulton Oursler, a *Digest* staffer who was later the author of *The Greatest Story Ever Told,* a best seller that became a source for George Stevens's excruciating life of Jesus.

It was Louis de Rochement who read the Oursler story and brought it to Kazan. He had created the *March of Time* series, two-reel short subjects, each devoted to a single topic, which had pioneered the use of reconstructions in documentary films. During the war he had concocted what were called "semi-documentary" features like *The House on 92nd Street* (about a Nazi spy ring), which used voice-over narration and, when possible, authentic locations, to recount dramatized accounts of actual events. *Boomerang* was obviously in this vein.

For Kazan, "*Boomerang* meant this: That I went out with a crew into the middle of a city, in Stamford, Connecticut, and we had as many as five thousand people watching. The streets were jammed. It was new then—[location shooting] it wasn't old. . . . And it had a theme. But the theme wasn't the important part of it. The important thing was that I caught something in the background, in the life of a city like that. And I enjoyed that a lot. It gave me a lot of confidence. It made me feel, 'I can go anywhere and make a film.'"

He started talking about the film in these terms almost the minute he finished shooting it. In February 1947, Kazan gave a newspaper interview in which he claimed the film was the "Best fun I've ever had. Not one studio shot. We did it all in Stamford and White Plains—in the streets, the park, a bean wagon, a saloon, a fire station, a detective bureau, a pool room. We did one scene in a jail and there was a murderer in the cell across the way."

On he rolled. "We used real cops—they talked the way they do in real life. Actors talk phony. We wanted a man making love to a girl in the doorway. I stopped a girl in the street and said, 'Want to be in pictures, honey?' She said no, but I persuaded her. She was great." In Kazan's mind, this film was a more important turning point than its significance in film history might suggest.

Henceforth, the majority of his movies were made in similar circumstances, and excepting the film version of A Streetcar Named Desire, all the best ones were. It was the same way with his actors. Most of the leading players of All My Sons—Arthur Kennedy, Ed Begley, Karl Malden—which Kazan would begin rehearsing as soon as this film wrapped, were in Boomerang, as was Lee J. Cobb, two years before his landmark performance in Death of a Salesman. These were, as the director put it to Michel Ciment, "my 'gang' of actors," Indeed, Arthur Miller himself played a small part in the film, as did Kazan's own uncle Joe, the protagonist of America, America, whom Kazan recalled constantly complaining about (and groping) the young actress with whom he had a couple of scenes.

The only actor Kazan was uncomfortable with was Dana Andrews, a man of frozen handsomeness with a resonant voice and a famous drinking problem. There was always something not quite relaxed in his playing. Kazan tried occasionally to shake him up. In his memoir Karl Malden recalls Kazan rewriting one of Andrews's big courtroom speeches, throwing it at the hung-over actor and asking him to memorize it in haste. "Just give me about twenty minutes," the actor responded coolly. He retreated to his dressing room and returned with the speech letter perfect.

Actually, Kazan need not have worried about Andrews. Bad actors are often good in courtroom scenes, since the emotions of lawyers, in the adversary system, are generally false—full of fraudulent outrage and fake moralizing. And, indeed, the film's climax—where the prosecutor appears to risk his life to prove his point—is a marvelously intense coup de théâtre that simply sweeps away disbelief.

This inexpensive, unpretentiously mounted film was a success when it opened the following year—as other films in the semidocumentary subgenre were for a few years. People liked their understated manner, their antimovieness.

Kazan would later say that *Boomerang* represented the beginning of a turning point in his relationship to American institutions. Traditionally the integrity of an authority figure like Andrews's implicitly guaranteed our system's functioning. But here the prosecutor was surrounded by people whose eyes were fixed on the main (or convenient) chance. That he won out in the end seems almost a matter of luck. Kazan said to Ciment: "The belief that the good in American society will finally win out . . . I don't believe any more. I think when we lost faith in the Soviet Union at the end of the thirties a lot of us said: 'Our basic institutions are good but are corrupted by individual people,' but later we realized the corruption is general, throughout."

Faith in man's perfectibility is, of course, central to Marxism, as well as to liberalism. And since Kazan never abandoned his liberal beliefs he was, perhaps, exaggerating this point. But still, many of his future plays and movies would, in one way or another, confront their characters with evils that could not be ameliorated by simple resort to some clearly defined political principle.

———

Such a work was *All My Sons*. I think it is not too much to say that this is the play Elia Kazan had been waiting all his adult life to direct, just as it was the one Arthur Miller had been struggling for a decade to write. Both men would, in the not too distant future, do finer work. But at this particular postwar moment, this was the drama that moved the prewar social problem play away from its Marxist (or quasi-Marxist) roots into a new realm, in which the concrete issue it explores takes on more ambiguous colors.

As of 1945, when he began working on this play—originally known as *The Sign of the Archer* (an astrological reference), Miller was the definition of a struggling playwright. In 1944 he had had one short-lived (four performances) Broadway production of a rather interesting play, *The Man Who Had All the Luck,* and had subsequently published a novel, *Focus,* about anti-Semitism that sold well enough, but was only modestly praised by the reviewers. He had, since leaving college (the University of Michigan) written perhaps a dozen plays, some of them very ambitious, was married, had a young child and was making a living doing writerly odd jobs; he wrote fairly regularly for a radio program, *The Cavalcade of America,* which did historical playlets, and he spent some time working on a movie script about the beloved war correspondent Ernie Pyle, which was eventually made as *The Story of G.I. Joe,* a good, essentially antiheroic war movie, in the final form of which Miller recognized nothing of his.

As he worked on *All My Sons,* Miller often thought of it as a last try; if it failed, he would look for some other sort of work. As it turned out, he need not have worried. One producer promptly rejected the piece, but the Theatre Guild was interested though it dallied over its decision. Impatient, Miller, who had recently left the Leland Hayward office for a new agent, Kay Brown of MCA (who would represent him for forty years), asked her to send it to Kazan and Clurman, who had no hesitations at all. They immediately optioned the play, with Miller shrewdly choosing Kazan as his director. His play did not need Clurman's theories; it needed Kazan's concentrated focus.

Indeed, by the time the play was up and running, the two men had become best friends. In part this derived from a similarity in their backgrounds. Like Kazan, Miller came from a family that had known prosperity (his father had owned a successful garment factory) before the Depression, then lost everything, and like Kazan, he saw his father psychologically destroyed by this reversal. Both had, as well, struggled to establish themselves in a theater that had, at first, denied their gifts. Both had flirted with Communism, Kazan more openly but perhaps less passionately than Miller.

But their main point of reference was this play, the situation of which is this: A man named Joe Keller (Begley) is the proprietor of a small machine shop in Ohio. During the war, operating under a government contract, it shipped a number of cracked cylinder heads, their flaws crudely disguised, to the air force. As a result twenty-one pilots lost their lives. Joe's partner, best friend and next-door neighbor, Steve Deever, was, before the play begins, convicted of this subterfuge. Joe was also charged with the crime, but successfully beat the rap, by claiming he was home sick the day Steve decided to ship the defective parts.

As the play opens, Joe's son Chris (Kennedy) has invited Steve's daughter, Ann (Lois Wheeler), to visit him, with an eye to proposing marriage. She was formerly the girlfriend of his brother, Larry, a fighter pilot who has been lost in the war. "Lost" is the operative word; his body has never been recovered and he is officially still listed as "missing in action." This sets up the most interesting of the play's psychological nexuses; his mother, Kate (Beth Merrill, once a Belasco leading lady and somewhat uncomfortable in this more raffish company), believes he is still alive and will return to her. She insists that the family's history—and future—be placed on hold until that happy day arrives.

This, naturally, places her in conflict with Chris and Ann, and makes her, generally, a pathetic (though not quite tragic) figure to her family and the neighbors who pop in and out of the Kellers' backyard, which is the play's only setting. What gives the play its dramatic impetus is the appearance of Ann's brother, George (Malden), in the second act. His family has shunned his father since his conviction, but now George, a lawyer, has visited him in jail and is stopping by the Kellers, mainly to prevent Ann from marrying Chris, but also to confront Joe, whom he now knows ordered his father to disguise the flawed cylinders. At the end of the second act, Joe finally confesses, leaving Chris in a state of shock—especially since his father insists that he did it for him, so that he would have a prospering business to inherit.

It has often been argued that *All My Sons* is a play about denial and its consequences: the mother refusing to accept her son's death, the father refusing to admit his crime and shifting the blame for it, Chris refusing to listen to the rumors that have long surrounded his father. This being the case, it is the business of the play's very short last act to force everyone to embrace truth. The instrument for this is Ann. She carries with her a last letter from Larry, which she has never shared with anyone. In it, he writes that newspapers have been delivered to his base that contain accounts of Joe and Steve's trial. They are so shattering to him that he tells Ann he plans to take one last flight, from which he does not intend to return. This suicide, of course, ends the mother's fantasies about his return. It also occasions the demise of the father; he says that he will now turn himself in to the authorities, but then commits suicide offstage.

There are two epitaphs to this play, occurring in its last two pages. The first occurs when Joe Keller is preparing to surrender to the law, and his wife—quite oddly—insists that Larry's death does not demand an answering sacrifice from him. He replies, looking at Ann's letter, which he holds in his hand: "Then what is this if it isn't telling me. Sure, he was my son. But I think to him they were all my sons. And I guess they were. I guess they were. . . ."

A moment later, just before we hear Joe's suicidal shot, Chris says to his mother: "Larry didn't kill himself to make you and dad sorry." "What more can we be?" she asks, and he replies: "You can be better! Once and for all you can know there's a universe of people outside and you're responsible to it . . ."

At this time, and certainly after *Death of a Salesman* appeared two years later, there was much talk, in the higher critical circles, about whether plays of this sort could be considered true tragedies. In classical tragedy, it was argued, nobility of birth and station was required for the fall from grace, as a result of some fatal flaw, to induce the purging emotions of pity and terror in an audience. In this view, a machine-shop proprietor, or a salesman, do not quite qualify as tragic figures. On the other hand, it can certainly be argued that the play does indeed contain two elements central to classic tragedy—peripeteia (a great reversal of fortune) and anagnorisis (a climactic recognition of something one had not previously realized).

Still, Miller, as far as one can tell, never made such grand claims for his play. In an interview with the English scholar Christopher Bigsby, quoted in his introduction to the latest edition of the play, Miller says:

> The concept behind it was that Joe Keller was both responsible for and a part of a great web of meaning, of being. He had torn that web; he had ripped apart the structure that supports Life and society . . . And a person who violates it in the way he did has done more than kill a few men. He has killed the possibility of a society having any future, any life. He has destroyed the life-force in that society.

What Miller seems to have been striving for in *All My Sons* is not at all classical tragedy. Rather, it is more or less Ibsenesque in intent and naturalistic language. His people speak in a very good approximation of the way earnest but not very well-educated people speak. Miller doesn't satirize their language, but neither does he poeticize it as Odets sometimes did. In his long first act Miller glides with a certain wry affection for the eccentricities of his characters' rather quotidian preoccupations. Like a good actor holding back, not playing all his subtexts immediately, he lets the Kellers and their friends establish the smooth flow of their little lives well before he jeopardizes it.

The play naturally becomes more Ibsenesque as it develops, but not purely so; the way events of the past condition actions in the present has some Chekhovian undertones. That was particularly so in the case of what is surely the play's most interesting and mysterious character, the mother. She is written by Miller with considerable tenderness, as a cheerful, accommodating woman, ever ready with a glass of fruit juice for anyone in need of refreshment. And she states her dotty conviction that her son is still alive with a serene and unshakable confidence. Miller in *Timebends* and Martin Gottfried in his biography of the playwright both report foreign revival productions of the play in which its center of gravity is shifted to her, with apparently good results.

Indeed, this character was, at the time of the premiere production, the subject of considerable debate among Kazan, Clurman and Miller. Kazan was increasingly at odds with his producing partner.

Clurman had claimed not to be disappointed by Miller's choice of Kazan to direct and was almost too much of a good sport about it at rehearsals. He was full of high spirits, patronizing, as usual, about Kazan's lack of intellectual analysis of the work, and about Kazan's past as "his" stage manager in The Group (which he had been only once). His chief criticism of the play was that the mother must have known of her husband's guilt. Kazan understood that to be Stella Adler's reading of the role and that Clurman was acting as her messenger. He rejected this idea, but could not prevent his partner working on Miller, who tried some revisions along those lines. They did not, according to Kazan, work, although in the published version of the play, we do implicitly understand that she knew more about her husband's crime than she admits.

But, in essence, Kazan insisted on sticking to Miller's guns. They both knew Joe Keller intimately; he was a version of their fathers, a man working obsessively to build and preserve a business for his son(s), a man limited, finally blinded and doomed, by that simple yet all-consuming desire. This—not the mother's tragedy, interesting as it was—was the play's primal material, the gold that would make it a great popular success.

Its appeal for Kazan is obvious. To begin with, it is essentially anticapitalist. All talk of leaving a successful business for his progeny aside, we do not doubt that the profit motive was the main factor moving Joe Keller to criminal action. What makes *All My Sons* a better play than, say, all those "strike plays" of the 1930s, is that it accepts this as a given. No ideological fuss is made about it, because none is necessary in this petit-bourgeois context. Better still, from Kazan's point of view, is the way the father-son conflict is stated in the play. The father—like his own father, like Miller's—represents the old unenlightenment. Yet, helplessly, Chris wants to, tries to, look up to him, wants to, tries to, give him the benefit of his wavering filial devotion.

Finally, the play does say something about America in a moment of transition. A war had been fought and every form of the mass media had insisted it had been fought for liberal ideals. Yet as Miller noted, within his play and elsewhere, those ideals had been tainted by profiteering, and while his play was gestating (and running), corrupt government contractors were being prosecuted for their wartime sins. There was no doubt in his mind (and Kazan's) that justice had to be served in these cases if the nation's wartime idealism was to be extended into the postwar world.

Kazan always threw himself wholeheartedly into his work, but this play seems to have brought out something almost demonic in him. The reason for this seems clear: He was not animating a tired voice from the theatrical past. Or someone's star turn. Or, for that matter, the old Group ideal. In this potent, imperfect play he could hear the fresh voice of the theatrical future he was eager to serve. Far more important, he was beginning to hear his own voice.

Karl Malden, working for the first time under Kazan's direction in a play, noticed this. In The Group Kazan "sensed that he wasn't one of them, that he was an outsider, always an outsider until, goddamnit, he got to be a director and, buddy, he took over. No one was going to tell him what to do, and it sprang from being tied down so long."

Miller, in *Timebends,* draws an unforgettable portrait of his new friend at work. "Kazan was eating fire in those days, working with great certainty and discretion," he writes. And: "Life in a Kazan production had [a] hushed air of conspiracy . . . not only against the existing theatre, but society, capitalism—in fact, everybody who was not part of the production." And: "The audience was an enemy that had to be overwhelmed and dominated like a woman, and only then loved." And: "A theatrical production is, or should be, a slice through the thickness of the culture from which it emerges, and that it is speaking not only to its audience but to other plays, to painting and to dance, to music and to all forms of human expression by which at any moment we read our time." And, finally, though he never mentioned political people or ideas, it was assumed that he "identified himself with the idealism of the left and that his emotional and intellectual loyalties lay with the workers and the simple and the poor."

Mostly, though, his loyalty was to intense and driving realism. All accounts of his previous directorial efforts on Broadway, including his own reminiscences, are shadowed by a sort of tentativeness on Kazan's part, a sense of his own inadequacies; if only he had treated this or that actor more firmly, if only he had insisted on this or that revision from the playwright. There was none of that here. There was only confidence.

For example, Mordecai Gorelik had designed an incongruously sunny and sylvan backyard for the Kellers and their friends to inhabit. At its center there was a perceptible hump, over which the actors occasionally stumbled. Miller asked Kazan about it. He grinned and told the playwright to ask Gorelik what he was thinking of—and to be sure and tell him what Max's answer was. Why, said the rather abrupt, Russian-born designer, it's a grave. Or, at least, it is meant to suggest a grave. For was not this space a cemetery, in which all this family's hope lay buried? The actors thereafter worked with—or at least around—this impediment while Kazan, inhabiting that sublime zone directors sometimes achieve, a zone in which they sense that their every decision is the right one, beamed approval.

Kazan, in Miller's observation, did not so much direct as train emotions, get his actors into a position where, it seemed to them, they discovered their characters' essences on their own. Miller would remember him suggesting they listen to a particular piece of jazz or read a certain novel or see a psychiatrist. Sometimes he would just throw his arm around the player, or give him or her a big kiss. He wanted his actors to bring their discoveries to him, like children finding pretty objects on a beach. He did not want to be caught imposing his ideas on them, as he insatiably rooted out any and all weaknesses that he thought might threaten the work or narrow the margin of victory he wanted to score over disbelief.

He was not, as we've already observed, a man much given to lengthy reflections on a character's motives. His technique was to wait, observe a performance developing, then pounce—with just a word or two of memorable direction. "Avenge," he said one day to Malden, "avenge." "In other words," Malden expounds, "I came in to do what? To avenge my father. Get what's coming to you. Don't let them take that away . . . Boom. That's it. So I go out there . . . and stand center stage—I'm taking over . . . You might say it's . . . not art. But boy, it serves the purpose."

In this instance, Malden has initially appeared as rather a nice fellow, seemingly glad to once again be in the company of people with whom, whatever has happened since, he passed a happy childhood. Now when he reveals the steeliness of his resolve, his hidden need to see justice belatedly done, the moment must have been electrifying—and never mind preparing the audience for it. Impact—the more shattering the better—was everything with Kazan.

All My Sons did well out of town in New Haven and Boston. But there was something grudging about its New York reception— except in one place, the place that counted most, the New York Times, where Brooks Atkinson, back at last from the war, wholeheartedly embraced the play. In his opening night review, he began by saying that, in Miller, "the theatre has acquired a genuine new talent" and that his play was an "honest, forceful drama" and "a pitiless analysis of character that gathers momentum all evening and concludes with both logic and dramatic impact." He praised all the actors and had especially kind words for Kazan. "It is always gratifying to see old hands succeed in the theatre," he wrote. "But there is something uncommonly exhilarating in the spectacle of a new writer bringing unusual gifts to the theatre under the sponsorship of a director with taste and enthusiasm."

A little over a week later, in his Sunday think piece, Atkinson returned to All My Sons in a mood that was even more effusive. He correctly praised Miller's writing—"compact and sinewy prose without flourishes"—and his structure—"There has seldom been a story on the stage so tightly woven as this one." Perhaps most surprisingly, he identified the strengths of Kazan's direction, which he termed "incandescent," keeping the performances "taut and keen and . . . alert to the life swirling around them. It is one thing to cast a play with interesting actors who give the characters flavor and tang. . . . But it is quite another thing to cast a play with creative actors and direct them through a series of transformations that show characters in motion—learning and developing throughout the performance."

Something had been achieved here beyond a hit (All My Sons would run for more than a year and would beat out The Iceman Cometh for the Drama Critics' prize). I think it is not too much to say that with this production Kazan finally achieved what he had long dreamed of doing on Broadway. For this was, at last, a company Kazan completely owned. It had no famous Broadway names in it. It did not even include any of the highly respected Group players—the Carnovskys and Adlers—to whom he had previously felt obligated. Begley, at forty-five, was a show business veteran, but he had debuted on Broadway only three years earlier. Beth Merrill had once been a prominent theatrical figure, but was scarcely a legend and had been rescued from the discard pile by Kazan. Kennedy had been around for a while without making a major impact, and he would become something like Miller's ideal actor, appearing three more times in his plays. Something similar could be said of Malden, who was the only member of the company with (minor) Group experience, but here, like Kennedy, playing his first truly memorable role. In short, all these actors owed their allegiance to no one other than a director encouraging them to state their claim as exemplars of something new—and important—in the theater. Elia Kazan had finally, unambiguously made the statement he had been trying to make on Broadway since 1938.

There are, of course, things wrong about *All My Sons*. We may, for example, wonder whether Joe's suicide is entirely necessary and sufficiently fated by his character's nature. More significantly, many years later Miller was still defending the sudden appearance of Larry's letter in the third act, which is where most of the critical dubiety about his work centered. He would cite similarly improbable manipulations in Greek drama, but still one has to admit that this business felt forced and arbitrary—particularly to Eric Bentley, then the most "intellectual" of drama critics. All right, he argued, Miller did not impose a "happy" ending on his material. But that letter! It was, melodramatically speaking, "the ace of trumps—the time honored stage property . . . in which *all* is revealed. And, true to the tradition of melodrama, he [Miller] asks us not to inquire too closely into the motives of the person who suddenly uses the letter as a lethal weapon."

I think we have to concede Bentley's point. This turning point is placed quite arbitrarily in the drama. It could as well have occurred at several earlier moments. Perhaps more disturbing, Ann, the bearer of this missive, never seems to be particularly burdened by the terrible information it contains. Until she actually presents the letter, she is seen as just a nice, good-natured girl, healthily in love with Chris, by no means deeply shadowed by her past affection for his brother.

We have to believe that Kazan's pounding direction simply drove audiences past these doubts. The fact that Miller dedicated the printed version of *All My Sons* to him reinforces that belief. Maybe it does not quite fulfill its unspoken aspirations toward high tragedy, but that is not to denigrate Miller's achievement. Over a half-century later his play can still be read appreciatively and, one suspects, performed effectively, as there is still no lack of corruptible men and women perp-walking through their business lives, committing crimes that are rich in public consequences, and rich, as well, in their possibilities for criminal humiliation. Joe Keller, one thinks, is no less an American type than Willy Loman—or Stanley Kowalski.

The responses of Miller and Kazan to the success of *All My Sons* were typical of each. Miller was acutely conscious of the fact that one week he was not entirely certain how he was going to feed, clothe and shelter his family, while the next week he was earning $2,000 in royalties. He took a very deep breath and found a job for a few days at forty cents an hour in a Brooklyn box factory—trying to remind himself of how thin the line between poverty and plenty was, perhaps also trying to remind himself how transitory fame might prove to be. Kazan, by now getting used to success, took a train westward, for once bringing his family with him to the land of swimming pools, tennis courts and perpetual sunshine, to begin preproduction on a new movie.

8

A Poetic Tragedy

One has to wonder about Kazan at this moment. He was in these years never out of work and never out of demand. If, officially, he had a few weeks off, they were devoted to planning his next project. He might have been forgiven for believing that nothing could possibly stall or stay his apparently irresistible rise. How could any change in the climate of the larger world afflict him? In particular, how could his brief flirtation with Communism, a decade earlier, rise up to haunt him now? When we're busy and acclaimed and being courted on every hand, we tend not to recall the mistakes of the past. We certainly do not think that they have the capacity to change—or at least deeply shadow—the rest of our lives.

Yet, unacknowledged by him, the general political climate was beginning to change. As early as 1945 employees of *Amerasia* magazine, a small semischolarly magazine devoted to Asian policy, had been found to possess thousands of classified government documents and charged with the intention of passing them on to Moscow. Around the same time, Igor Gouzenko, a Soviet code clerk in the USSR's Ottawa embassy, defected and named a number of high-level agents, employed in the American government, but working secretly for the Russians. In 1946, already suspected in some foreign policy circles of being a Communist agent, Alger Hiss was offered a gentlemanly way of removing himself from the government when he was asked to become president of the Carnegie Endowment for World Peace. That same spring, Winston Churchill gave a commencement address at Fulton College in Missouri, in the process of which he also gave the world a new catchphrase—"the Iron Curtain," which he claimed the Soviet Union had rung down in Europe, separating its eastern reaches from the democratic West. That fall, in the off-year elections, the Republicans gained control of Congress and revived the hunt for Communists in government. In May 1947, as Kazan settled down to work on his new film, HUAC arrived in Los Angeles to hold preliminary hearings on Communist penetration of the movie industry, dress rehearsals for the more notorious hearings that took place in October 1947, at which the Hollywood Ten were named as Communists and began their careers among the most famous of the left's cold war martyrs.

But what did any of that matter to Kazan in the spring of 1947? For the picture he was about to make was, at least by the standards of the motion picture industry, the most "important" one he had ever attempted. *Gentleman's Agreement* was based on the manuscript of what was to become a huge best-seller by Laura Z. Hobson, a clever, if gimmicky, assault on anti-Semitism, which Darryl F. Zanuck intended to make as one of his comparatively rare "personal" productions, busying himself with every detail of its creation. All going well, he expected it to be a contender for more than one Academy Award, and to assure that outcome he involved in the film the best talent at his command. Besides Kazan, his hottest director, it would star his hottest leading man, Gregory Peck, and it would be written by that most sophisticated of Broadway playwrights, Moss Hart. Everything else about the production—from the supporting cast to the technical team—was first-class.

Kazan was excited. As he was to say later, "Being what I was, a *liberal* [italics his], I embraced the project eagerly." And, indeed, it was very much in a long-standing liberal tradition of moviemaking— melodramatically charged attempts to address social problems in such a way that, at the end, audiences were encouraged to believe they could do something about them that was not too arduous or painful. Indeed, this was a tradition that Zanuck, perhaps more than any other production executive, had embraced since the beginning of his career at Warner Bros. in the early thirties. To the degree that *Gentleman's Agreement* was part of a late flowering of that tradition in the late forties, with special emphasis in these films on the issue of racial and religious prejudice, Kazan must have believed that he, and Hollywood, would be able to go on conducting their socially conscientious business pretty much as usual.

Gentleman's Agreement had been serialized in *Cosmopolitan* in late '46 and early '47 and had been acquired by Fox prior to publication in book form, which occurred while the film was still shooting. It became an immediate best-seller—I-can-read moral seriousness presented in slick magazine style, easily translatable to the screen.

The basic story has Phil Green (Peck) as what we would now call an "investigative journalist" coming from California to take a job with a New York newsmagazine where, as a first assignment, he is asked to do something powerful, eye-opening, on anti-Semitism—not about its violent aspects, but about its endemic presence in ordinary American life—the schools and hotels that are closed to Jews, for example, in the ways that decent, polite Americans, people who do not for a moment believe themselves to be anti-Semitic, show themselves actually to be—in their nasty jokes, in their routine refusals, for instance, to allow Jews membership in their country clubs. Or to move in next door to them.

Green finds the topic extremely daunting, suffering a writer's block as he attempts to do a conventional story—full of facts and interviews—about it. He has other problems as well. The transcontinental move is difficult, he is recently widowed and has a young son to raise, with the help of his mother (Anne Revere), who soon suffers a stroke, which adds to his worries. Beyond that, he meets and falls in love with a young woman, Kathy (Dorothy McGuire), a sweet divorcée with a troubling tension about her.

The clouds begin to part for Phil when he finds his "angle": He will pretend to be a Jew himself (he changes his name to Greenberg), opening himself to all the slights and hurts that a Jew of his time was prey to. What particularly (and quickly) becomes clear to him is that he does not have to make any great reportorial effort to find prejudice. The minute he starts calling himself a Jew he finds it close to home—in the office of the magazine (where June Havoc plays an anti-Semitic Jew), in his own apartment building, at his son's school, from a doctor patronizing a Jewish colleague, and particularly in Kathy's heart. The minute he tells her his plan to pretend to be a Jew for purposes of his article, she responds instinctively. "But you're not," she cries, then quickly covers her tracks. "Not that it would make any difference." But, of course, it would. Before the film is over she becomes angrily estranged from Phil, largely (she says) because he becomes so passionately involved with his subject, destroying her hopes for a more placid middle-class existence. "I'm not going to marry into hotheaded shouting and nerves and you might as well know it and know it now."

One suspects that Laura Z. Hobson had endured all the hurts and slights Phil endures in the course of her life. She was herself a Jew who had, thanks to her confident nature, done well in the New York media world, making a career for herself as a writer of advertising and promotional copy, eventually attaining an executive position at Time Inc., where she enjoyed the friendship of the company's founder, Henry Luce and his wife, Clare. Her knowledge of the magazine world contributed to the authenticity of her book. So did the fact that, like Phil Green, she had also been a single parent—in her case of two sons.

Even though the book and film are quite polite in tone, establishment Hollywood was frightened of it—so much so that Harry Warner convened a meeting of studio heads, all of them Jewish, who tried to convince Zanuck not to make it. This, it must be said, was, at the time, a common Jewish response to anti-Semitism, even in its more deadly, or Hitlerian, manifestations. Zanuck, curiously enough, was the only WASP present at this meeting. But he was as tough and willful as any mogul in Hollywood history. No one could ever tell him what he should or should not make and he brushed aside his colleagues' timorousness.

Which still left him with a third act problem—a powerfully stated, dramatically compelling crisis that would command the audience's attention and prepare it for a hopeful climax. There was, however, at least a partial, if not completely satisfactory, solution to the problem lurking in Hobson's story. This lay with a character named Dave Goldman. He is Phil Green's best friend, a Jewish soldier who returns from service in Europe while Phil is working on his story. He has a job offer in New York, but between the housing shortage and the fact that what desirable housing exists is covenanted by the "gentleman's agreement," it looks as if he will not be able to take the job.

Kazan insisted that this role, not really a starring part (Dave does not appear until the movie is half over), go to John Garfield, as opposed to Zanuck's choice, Fox contract player Richard Conte. Garfield was, of course, Jewish, which Conte was not. More important, he had an ingratiating and likable side, which is precisely why Kazan wanted him—"a naïve, pure-hearted, awfully nice boy," with "a natural ebullience . . . life-loving . . . bouncy, playful," a man who could speak his piece forthrightly but in a manner that was far from threatening. Zanuck finally agreed to this casting.

Kazan always credited Moss Hart with discovering the way to use Dave to give the movie its concluding punch. It works this way: Kathy and Phil have had their estranging fight. She has reassured Phil's son that even though the kids at school have called him a "Yid" and a "Kike" he doesn't have to worry; as soon as his father has shown that his "Jewishness" is just a writerly device, the boy will be restored to his natural WASP superiority. Phil objects. She again says she can't live with his bad temper, his endless involvement with great, serious issues.

But then she has a last meeting with Dave and recounts an anecdote in which she remains silent while an anti-Semitic joke is told. Oh, she says, she was burning with rage. "What did you do?" Dave asks. Well, she says, I wanted to speak up, I wanted to leave. He persists: What did she actually do? The answer, of course, is nothing. She abided by the gentleman's agreement. At that moment, her shame is revealed to herself and she offers Dave and his family her house in suburban Darien and, more important, her moral support when, inevitably, they must confront the community's prejudice. This, of course, prepares the way for her reconciliation with Phil.

Kazan's relationship with Moss Hart was always ambivalent. On the one hand Kazan would say, "Moss was a wonderful man, a guy I liked very much." On the other he would sometimes damn him with faint praise—"very gentle and kind and genteel." He had, early on, thought that maybe Lillian Hellman or Paul Osborn might have brought a tougher sensibility to this project. But now here came Hart with this scene between Kathy and Dave. It wasn't an ideal solution—everyone would have preferred this to be a scene between Phil and Kathy—but thanks to the good-natured persistence of

Garfield's playing and the slightly feverish quality of McGuire's, the movie suddenly had a potent climax.

Only it was not actually Hart's scene. In *Dazzler*, his excellent biography of Hart, Steven Bach reveals that it was Hobson herself who came up with this saving moment. They were apparently sitting around a rented house in Palm Springs, mulling over various book-to-film changes, when Hobson recalled a little scene in her novel where Kathy simply endured the awful jokes in silence. What she came up with now was her confession of moral failure to Dave and his insistent response: "There's a funny kind of elation about socking back, Kathy . . ." She wrote this piece out in prose, Hart converted it to screenplay form and into the script it went—with Kazan never the wiser.

There are, however, other problems with the screenplay that remained unsolved. There are hints in it that Phil Green is, or was, a more radical figure than the film permits him to be. In his past, he temporarily became an Okie and a coal miner in order to report accurately on their lives. Given this background, one wonders why it takes him so much time to apply the same technique to his story about anti-Semitism. It ought to be the first thing he thinks of, not the last. But Peck in his suit and his nice little hat can't and won't play that sort of rip-snorting journalist.

Then there's the problem of his mother, or "Maw," as the script insists on calling her. Anne Revere, playing the part, never speaks normally—she intones embarrassingly. Maybe Kazan could do nothing about Peck, but he needed to kick her into naturalism. Something similar occurs with Celeste Holm as Anne, a magazine editor who has her cap set for Peck. She's all "Broadway speak," brittle and smart, but, in her way, as false as Revere is—the kind of creature Hart could write for the stage and possibly get away with, but who cannot stand the camera's close scrutiny. Kazan never quite maneuvers these people into realism.

But the film's central defect is Peck's performance. One of the handsomest movie actors who ever lived, one of Hollywood's most responsibly liberal-minded citizens, he was often the awkward center of his movies—except when stiff rectitude was called for, as it was in *To Kill a Mockingbird*. "Greg's nature was very closed off and rigid," Kazan would later say. Despite the fact that he had studied at the Neighborhood Playhouse with former Group member Sandy Meisner, "He didn't have an artist's nature. He had his own way, and that was always correct. He was logical and listened. He was cooperative. But it was hard to light a fire in a guy like that." Kazan put this point more succinctly to Warren Beatty, who once asked him who was the most difficult actor he ever directed. "Gregory Peck," came the instant reply, "I could never get him off the phone."

Still, the film has its felicities. Dorothy McGuire has her stand-offish moments, but when her desire for serenity is challenged, she rouses a neurotic heat that cuts through her studied niceness. And Garfield really never makes a false move. Neither does Sam Jaffe, another occasional Group actor, who has a small part that is almost never remarked in accounts of the film, but which ought to be. He plays a Professor Lieberman, a freethinking Jew, a man challenging both Christian and Jewish pieties. Such figures at the time particularly troubled intellectual anti-Semites like T. S. Eliot because they threatened all forms of traditional religion. In a film that most basically wants to keep both Christians and Jews in their comfortably understood places, he's quite a remarkable—and novel—figure.

Some of the film's flaws were noted when it was released in November 1947. *Time* said, "With its crusading and its stout effort to present a serious social problem to mass audience, the film as a whole is better than the solution it offered." It wasn't enough, the magazine suggested, to say that the anti-Semitic weed could be stamped out solely by the middle class applying its decency and intelligence to it. Bosley Crowther, in the *New York Times,* was similarly inclined, but also spoke for what amounted to the majority critical opinion of the time. He found it "a fine and forceful film" that "should be profoundly effective in awakening millions to unsuspected cruelties." He compared it to a more violent study of anti-Semitism, *Crossfire* (with Robert Ryan's notably dark portrayal of a murderous bigot), which preceded it into the theaters, and thought that if these films only scratched the surface "of a complex social sore . . . this scratch may astonishingly reveal the basic principles of true democracy that any form of anti-Semitism enshrouds."

Rather surprisingly, Elliott E. Cohen, founding editor of the

Jewish intellectual journal *Commentary,* was similarly tolerant of the film. He was particularly sympathetic to Kathy. He wrote: "Kathy fights like a tiger because she is fighting for her Home—meaning all the great, desirable things like security, family, comfort, children with 'every advantage,' flowered chintz, lovely china, a garden. . . . Say no to that. Who could or would?" In other words, he added, *Gentleman's Agreement* correctly identified where this battle would be fought, "in the homes of America" and, while not blind to the movie's other defects, he thought this perhaps correct. Kathy's seemingly small gesture—permitting Dave and his family to rent her suburban cottage—was not, to Elliott Cohen, such a small gesture. He implies that if the Germans had been capable of taking such actions the Holocaust might not have happened.

Indeed, setting aside Siegfried Kracauer, the German-born film historian and theorist, who was entirely dismissive of *Gentleman's Agreement* ("a mountain of dialogue bringing forth a mouse"), it is impossible to find any criticial opinion of the film that does not take the film with full seriousness.

Permitted at least to do a few exterior sequences in New York, Kazan himself followed that line for a long time. He remained aware that it had required a certain amount of courage for Zanuck to produce the film at the time he did. At least the word "Jew" was spoken out loud on the screen and, as he said, "There were a hell of a lot of people who said to Zanuck, 'We're getting along all right. Why bring this up?' And in that sense it was a step forward at the time. . . . For the first time someone said that America is full of anti-Semitism, both conscious and unconscious and among the best and most liberal people. That was then a much bolder statement than it is now. In that sense, the picture broke some new ground, and Zanuck and Hart and I can take some credit. It was saying to the audience: 'You are an average American and you are anti-Semitic. Anti-Semitism is in you.' It is better than to say: 'It is a bunch of freaks that are anti-Semitic.'"

But, starting in the 1970s, he became more critical of the film. "Whenever I see it, it reminds me of those illustrations in 'Redbook' and 'Cosmopolitan' in those days. I mean, those people don't shit. They don't do any of the natural functions. They'd walk through, and their dress was always perfect."

Kazan was essentially right about the film—for the wrong reasons, I think. "I say it's too damn polite a film. It's too nice," he said. "It doesn't get into the parts of anti-Semitism that persist and hurt." But that's not strictly true. The kinds of slights and sneers and quotas and restrictions Jews were subjected to in the America of its time did hurt and did persist and did affect them. To the degree that *Gentleman's Agreement* brought all that to the surface, made people face up to it, it was, and remains, a historically important film, a not insignificant signpost on the road to our present situation, in which none of the behavior it shows is any longer acceptable in our public life—even, hopefully, in our secret selves.

But he ignored the film's signal failure, its silence about the Holocaust. By now it was a known tragedy. Moss Hart himself had staged Ben Hecht's pageant about the fate of European Jewry, *We Will Never Die,* during the war. We had all seen the newsreels showing what the liberating Allied armies had found in the death camps. Anne Frank's diary was published that very year in Europe (though, admittedly, it did not appear in America until 1952 and did not make its full impact until the play, starring Strasberg's daughter, Susan, opened in 1955). How could you make a movie about anti-Semitism and not at least mention this vast horror?

The excuses, of course, are many. One that Kazan alluded to was a theory of Zanuck's, "that every social problem and every human problem can be solved through the mechanics of a love story. You just get a love story in there and people differ on the theme of the movie and then you heal it up and they get together and everything is all right. Well, excuse me, bullshit. It doesn't work that way."

But it did in this movie. Once Peck and McGuire have their fight, and she is awakened to social responsibility by her conversation with Dave, we see Peck mounting the stairs to her apartment, the door opening and him disappearing behind it—which is, incidentally, the first very mild hint the movie offers that there just may be a sexual element to their relationship.

No matter. The film was a box office success, and it was named the year's best picture by the motion picture academy, with Kazan and Holm also winning Oscars in their categories. Kazan could never quite bring himself to disown it, but in his later years, he always seemed glad that people pretty much stopped seeing it, allowing it to fall into the *Going My Way* category of Oscar winners. The picture may have served his public liberalism, but it did not serve his secret radicalism.

In a curious way, his next theatrical project did serve that need. It was not in any overt sense a political play. It had nothing to say about social issues. But it examined, with fire and passion, a cut of life rarely explored in the theater—and never with the ferocity of this great work.

It was Audrey Wood, Tennessee Williams's agent, who brought *A Streetcar Named Desire* to Irene Mayer Selznick to produce. Louis B. Mayer's daughter and the (now estranged) wife of David O., she was a daring choice since so far she had succeeded only in closing one play—an early version of Arthur Laurents's *The Time of the Cuckoo* (which eventually became the basis of the David Lean–Katharine Hepburn movie hit *Summertime*). Selznick, in her autobiography, *A Private View*, was still wondering years later why Wood thought of her; it probably had something to do with Williams's unhappiness with other managements, like the Theatre Guild, which had not done right by a couple of his previous works.

Selznick, on first reading, had no doubt about the play's greatness, but initially rejected it; it seemed too big a project for her. She was eventually brought around after meeting with Wood and Williams on neutral ground—neither New York, which Selznick thought might expose her naïveté, nor New Orleans, where the playwright was then living, where she did not want to seem to be "swooping down" on him. They settled on a meeting in Charleston, South Carolina, where contracts were signed.

She claims that Kazan was always her first choice as director, though there is some evidence that she also flirted with Joshua Logan. Kazan certainly believed that was the case. But at some point in the spring, Williams saw *All My Sons*, was impressed with (and, he said, envious of) it and dropped Kazan a note saying he had asked Selznick to send him the script. "It may not be the sort of play that interests you, but I hope so," he said. Molly read it first, adored it and pressed it on her husband, who had certain unnamed reservations about it, but came passionately around after a meeting with "Tenn."

The elegant Selznick and the rumpled Kazan also hit it off. Whatever their differences in manner, they were well-matched in their energy and their taste for audacious enterprises. Not that they reached early or easy agreement on a contract. Kazan insisted that there must be no interference from the producer in his relationship with the author. He wanted formally to have what he had informally had with Miller on *All My Sons*—direct communication, unvexed by creative input from Selznick or anyone else—and he wanted billing that would reflect that arrangement. He almost lost the job and might have done so had not Williams been so steadfast in his support. Selznick finally conceded—giving Kazan twenty percent of the production. It was, Kazan claimed, an historic precedent, forcing Broadway's acknowledgment of the director's importance in its creative process.

Kazan had time only for a brief meeting with Williams, who was then living on Cape Cod, before leaving for his *Gentleman's Agreement* job. But Williams and Selznick would come westward to work on the play with Kazan over the course of the summer—mainly reworking the play's final scene—on the lanai next to Selznick's tennis court. She would claim that she rescued what may be the play's most famous line—"I have always depended on the kindness of strangers"—from Williams's wastebasket.

Her largest problem at this point was casting. They thought they had their Stanley Kowalski in the person of John Garfield, with whom, of course, Kazan was then working. In retrospect, he seems a strange choice. He had played many an outsider in the movies, but generally one who eventually reconciled whatever estrangements the script presented his character. More important, there was no menace in his sexuality, even in his recent (1946), self-consciously "hot" *The Postman Always Rings Twice*. The qualities that made him so effective in *Gentleman's Agreement* would not, one thinks, have worked particularly well for the Williams play. And, at thirty-three, he was a little old for the part.

But he was a star. And it was a star that Selznick needed at this point—someone who could help her secure backing and a good Broadway theater. But, alas, Garfield demanded certain starry perogatives—he would sign only for four months, not for the run of the play, because a movie deal might come up. He also wanted a guarantee that if *Streetcar* was made into a movie he would play Stanley in the film. Negotiations with him eventually broke down. As they did with Burt Lancaster, who wanted the role, but whose agent didn't want him to do it.

Kazan, Williams and Selznick were similarly at sea when it came to the two female leads. For Blanche they thought of Margaret Sullavan, of Pamela Brown, of Mary Martin (Kazan's idea). For Stella, they had no one firmly in mind.

At what point in their deliberations, the eventual—indeed, legendary—cast of *A Streetcar Named Desire* started to take shape is hard to say, but Jessica Tandy was the first one signed. English-born, raised in Canada, she had been a presence on Broadway for more than a decade, well-respected, but never quite a star (and certainly never a diva). Like her husband, Hume Cronyn, she was at this time playing character roles in the movies. Cronyn was a friend of Kazan's (which he remained until his death) and knew he was having casting difficulties with *Streetcar.* He also knew that Williams had written a sketch of Blanche in a one-act play called *Portrait of a Madonna.* He arranged a production of it at the Actor's Lab—it was a kind of West Coast offshoot of The Group and also something of a precursor of the Actors Studio, but, if anything, more overtly leftist, ideologically speaking, than either of them—and invited Kazan, Williams and Selznick to see it. Tandy won their instant approval.

It was Selznick who found their Stella. She had sat through a number of readings by young actresses, none of whom appealed to her. Then she noticed a short item in one of the trade papers reporting that Kim Hunter was touring in a summer production of *Claudia.* Selznick's former husband had once had Hunter under personal contract, making money off her—as he often did with actors—by lending her out to other movie producers. Mainly, she had worked in B pictures, but had recently, notably, appeared in Michael Powell's *A Matter of Life and Death* (known in the United States as *Stairway*

to Heaven). Irene Selznick thought she had a kind of forthright innocence (as well as a sort of implicit sexiness that Kazan would help
her to express on stage) that was right for Stella. So she dispatched
an associate to catch Hunter in performance, he reported back on
her favorably and she got the job.

But, as of September, with rehearsals just a month off, they still
did not have their Stanley. It was then that Kazan raised Brando's
name. Selznick was desperate enough, at this point, to agree to let
him read. If, that is, Brando could be located. He had no fixed address; he was crashing here and there with a variety of friends,
mostly female. But Kazan chased him down, sent him to see
Selznick ("He was wayward one moment, playful the next") and,
most important, Williams in Provincetown. Kazan gave Brando $20
for a bus ticket, which he instead spent on food. He hitchhiked to
the Cape, arriving two or three days later than expected. He found
Williams and a companion in chaos—their toilet clogged, their electricity not functioning. He went into handyman mode, fixed what
needed fixing, and charmed Williams both with his manner and with
his reading.

So Kazan had, at last, a Kazan cast (it also included Karl Malden as
Mitch, Blanche's less than steadfast suitor)—good actors who were not
stars, more responsive to him, to one another, than to their egos or
their images. He was pleased, he said, to have two young people,
Brando and Hunter, as the Kowalskis. He said later that he had always
felt they should be, almost parodistically, "young marrieds," a decade
or so younger than Blanche, among whose problems, as Kazan saw
them, was that she was feeling her age.

This is not to say that the production was entirely free of problems, which centered, finally, on Brando and, to a lesser extent, on
Tandy. The former, frankly, was frightened. He had never played a
role of this size. And Stanley was not a character he liked or could
easily identify with. "Why, he's the antithesis of me . . . a man without any sensitivity, without any kind of morality except his own
mewling, whimpering insistence on his own way," he would tell an
interviewer at the time. "Kowalski was always right, and never afraid.
He never wondered, he never doubted. . . . And he had the kind of
brutal aggressiveness I hate. I'm afraid of him. I detest the man."

This made him more than usually tentative in his approach to the part. Brando was always poor in rehearsals. He mumbled his lines (Selznick would say she never fully heard him until the opening night of the Philadelphia tryout) and very often he only approximated Williams's words. He was also often enough absent from rehearsals or late for them. But Selznick would remember Kazan casually draping his arm over the actor's shoulders and walking him away from the rest of the company in an attempt to steady him. The director would tell Selznick Brando was not being deliberately flaky, that he was honestly troubled by the role, struggling to find something in it that he could relate to his own experience—which may or may not have been true.

Brando's search for his character was one everyone in the company joined. "Jessica Cronin was very kind and very patient with him," Kazan would later recall, especially with his vocal problems, very annoying to this well-spoken, classically trained actress. "And soon she got to like him and admire him a lot. And Karl Malden was in it. Karl was one of his best friends [dating back to *Truckline Café*]. And Kim Hunter was in it and they were close friends. And all of a sudden I had a family of people that worked in the same way and had the same desire to reveal themselves. And to open up . . ."

Tennessee Williams was also helpful. He had, as Kazan would say, "a crush on Brando." This was not, Kazan hastened to add, a sexual attraction. He just liked the guy. "And he supported me in it. And in black moments and dark moments, he'd say, 'He's great, don't worry about him.'"

But finally Brando perhaps owed more to Kazan than to anyone— outside of himself, naturally—for his performance. Malden had the remarkable, but not entirely outrageous, idea that "Kazan would have loved to have played that part. . . . If he were acting he would have played the goddamn part. I don't know how, but he would have played it." This makes complete sense. There was a more than usual identification between the director, the actor and the role they were both working on. Brando manifested in this performance all of Kazan's hurt and anger and impatience with middle-class gentility, all his accumulated outsider's outrage.

There has never been any question in my mind that Kazan loved

Brando better than any actor he ever worked with. Brando was not an immigrant—he was a midwestern WASP—but he was profoundly a difficult, troublesome case like Kazan but without a temporizing Anatolian smile to mask his true feelings. Specifically he was a man whose deeply troubled relationship with his parents was something with which Kazan could identify. Finally he was, as the young Kazan had been, a theatrical rebel, obviously talented, but worrisome, irritating to his elders.

So, frankly, Kazan indulged him—pretty much playing older brother to the twenty-three-year-old actor. The way he worked with Brando was the way he wanted to work with every actor, and the generalizations he made about that experience were those he always tried to apply in his relationships with actors.

He said to me that he had never been able to storyboard a film or rigidly preplan a play's rehearsals. "If you have any respect for your own talent [for] stirring up an actor, or the actor's talent . . . you're not sure of what's going to happen. And a good director's not sure when he gets on the set what he's going to do. . . . I like directors who come on the set and create something that's a little dangerous, difficult or unusual. . . . I feel that the more ambivalent you are and the more uncertain you are in the morning, . . . then you get something that . . . you cannot anticipate and that no one else can anticipate."

Now, of course, he knew Brando from *Truckline*. And he also knew, or quite quickly came to know, about Brando's family. Both his parents were alcoholics, but more than that, there was something of Blanche in his mother, something of Stanley in his father. Dodie Brando was, like Blanche, a lost and dreamy soul, once a promising actress in her native Omaha (she had played opposite Henry Fonda in the once-famous Playhouse there), who had given up her career, but never her love of theater, for marriage and family. The father, on the other hand, was a hard, unforgiving and domineering man, rigid in his ways, strict in his sense of how his family should organize itself and present itself to the world.

All of this Kazan encouraged Brando to use in his performance: "The first thing you should do with an actor is not sign a contract with him . . . [it] is to take him to dinner. And take him for a walk afterwards. And speak to him. Or meet his wife or his girlfriend. Or whoever he just dropped or whoever he just took on. . . . Find out about him. See what he is as a human being. That's your material. His experience is your material."

This was, he said, pure Stanislavsky, pure Group Theatre, but "also me." "When you know what an actor has, you can reach in and arouse it, right? . . . But if you don't know what he has, you don't know what the hell is going on." Without this knowledge, a director is just blocking—telling the actor not to light a cigarette here, wait until you get over there—which is, he said, "all baloney." The important thing "is to get him going and see what he does and what you do in respect to what he does."

What he liked best about Brando was trying to keep up with him: "There's a hell of a lot of turmoil there. There's ambivalence there. He's uncertain of himself and he's passionate, both at the same time. And it's all there and available to a director. If he agrees with you. He has to agree with you."

Which, at that time, Brando did. He had come to acting after a life devoted mainly to goofing off. And, for the moment—a relatively brief one—it had become his salvation, his passion. "He was like a child," Kazan recalled, "but there was so much violence in him . . . the wonderful thing about him is the ambivalence again, between a soft, yearning girlish side to him and a dissatisfaction that is violent and can be dangerous. . . . He challenges not only the women . . . he challenges the whole system of politeness and good nature and ethics and everything else. . . . He did that in his life. He never knew where the hell he was going to sleep, you didn't know who he was angry with, or what he was angry about. Every day there was a drama that he brought on the set with him. I liked him so much."

Liked him, of course, because Brando was Kazan's great surrogate in intemperateness—maybe the only one of all his actors who could, when the occasion called for it, let his wild child's temper—with its sometimes crazy humor—rip and snort and tear. Kazan especially loved him in the "Napoleonic Code" scene, where he "pulled the drawers open and pulled the clothes out and messed up her [Blanche's] trunk. I did enjoy that. But he was ahead of me. He did what I enjoyed. And I don't know what the hell he was thinking."

But thinking Brando definitely was. "I made a study of guys like Kowalski," Brando would say later. "You know, guys who work hard and have lots of flesh, have nothing supple about them. They never open their fists, really. . . . They grip a cup of coffee like an animal would wrap a paw around it. They're heavily muscled in body and manner of speech. You see, Stanley Kowalski wasn't interested in how he said anything. He didn't give a damn how he said it. His purpose was to convey his idea. He had no awareness of himself at all . . ."

That's not quite the whole story of this performance, which we can, I think, fairly judge from its reproduction on the screen four years later. It leaves out, for example, the wild humor of it—especially when Stanley is in a rage. You can't help mingling laughter with fear when, criticized for his table manners, he threatens to "clear the table" by throwing his dishes against the wall. Similarly his sly shrewdness. He may not have the ability to articulate the threat Blanche poses to his marital hegemony, but, animalistically, he senses and responds to it. And then there's the pure sexiness of the work. He has awakened Stella from her gentility, made the "colored lights" blaze in her brain. And he knows that for all her airs, he can do the same to Blanche. There's an almost strutting sexual arrogance to the man that is also near to comic in its studliness—see the early scene where, daubed with axle grease from the car he's been working on, swigging a beer, he challenges Blanche's flutter and knows she can be his for the taking.

A decade later, Robert Brustein would trace Stanley's roots fairly far back into theatrical history—at least to O'Neill's *The Hairy Ape*—and find in him, by the late fifties, a figure, variously permutated, that was available almost everywhere in American popular culture—novels, movies, television programs and, of course, on the stage. "What he says is rarely important but he has mesmerized his auditor by the effort he takes to say it. He has communicated not information but feeling, he has revealed an inner life of unspecified anguish and torment." In the end, the critic found this "hero" wanting. He called for protagonists who, "without rejecting language, tradition, education, and art—without finding consolation in the impulsive anarchy of Stanley Kowalski—can express the nonconformism which stems from a long, hard, individualistic look at the world."

To which one has the impulse to reply, "Yeah, sure." What Williams has set up in *Streetcar* is a triangle in which, most basically, Stanley and Blanche are competing for Stella's soul. Blanche can, and does, articulate a vision of a coherent, comprehensible—and, alas, lost—world that has been crushed by the forces Stanley symbolizes. The reason the play goes on working, revival after revival, is that the conflict between Stanley and Blanche is primal: vulgarity versus tradition, brutality versus gentility, lust versus repression, immediate need vs. romantic loss. We are talking here about one of the most fundamental cultural conflicts of our times—possibly of all times.

We, in the audience, identify with both protagonists. Like him or not, Stanley *is* our surrogate. Maybe some of us are more articulate than he is, able to partially identify the sources of our misery, able to laugh at his puzzled pawings after some sort of meaning, but in the end we know what he's talking about. Or, rather, what he is not capable of talking about. Similarly Blanche. She is in some ways a ridiculous figure, a projection of a dying past lifted out of its historical moment and imposed on an ungracious, ungrateful one. Yet there is a bravery in her madness that is as touching as it is absurd.

I'll go a radical step further in analyzing this remarkable, to me almost perfect, play. I think we derive a perverse satisfaction from Stanley's rape of Blanche. She has been cock-teasing him—safely she thinks, because she is armored in her dream of the Old South, with its (shall we say?) impregnable code of correct behavior. But Stanley knows better, knows that after the loss of her homosexual lover she has resorted to young boys and lost her teaching job as a result. That is her reality, all airs and graces aside, and he will force her to acknowledge it at, as it were, cockpoint. Of course, we will allow the play its nominal tragic ending, Blanche's descent into madness. But vulgar modernism, brutally asserted, will triumph. The poker game will go on as she is led away to the mental asylum. And Stella will come when Stanley calls—in the play if not the movie.

Some part of us is, naturally, appalled by this outcome. But I think some part of us believes in Stanley's triumphant energy. We must remember that Williams was a devoted reader of D. H. Lawrence with his belief in the vitality, sexual and otherwise, of the lower classes, his belief that their—yes—thrusting energy contained the salvation of the enfeebled upper and middle classes. There is, I think, a hint of Lady Chatterley and her lover in this play—with the female figure bifurcated between Stella and Blanche, allowing Williams more ambivalence about his characters than Lawrence permitted himself.

The play worried Kazan; it has more layers of meaning, more interpretive choices, than anything he had previously attempted. His notes on it are more extensive than any he ever wrote. His very complete analyses of all its major characters (including Malden's Mitch, the mother-dominated man who represents salvation to Blanche, but who rejects her when Stanley reveals her past to him) are, broadly speaking, correct and they are (again, going by the film) presented very largely as he imagined them. For all his anarchism, Stanley is, when it comes to his home and woman, a conservative, defending the life he and Stella have built against the intruding Blanche. Interestingly, Kazan imagined a future life for Stanley, when his sexual prowess has waned, that predicts the life of the actor playing him—"He's going to get very fat later," he wrote. He also fully understood the sadism that is integral to Stanley's sexuality. He also understood that Stanley is turned on by Blanche's highfalutin manner, that essential to this turn-on is the act of bringing her down to his level.

Kazan is sympathetic to her. He is willing to contemplate the possibility that her attempt to keep the family plantation, Belle Reve is, "heroic," not an act of "absurd romanticism." He scribbles: "The thing about the 'tradition' in the nineteenth century was that *it worked then* [italics his]. It made a woman feel important, with her own secure positions and functions, her own special worth. It also made a woman at that time *one with her society.*" But today it is an anachronism. So, Blanche requires protection—"a haven, a *harbor.* She is a refugee, punch drunk and on the ropes, making her last stand, trying to keep up a gallant front, because she is a proud person." But still—she's also "a misfit, a liar, her 'airs' alienate people . . . She doesn't know how to make a living. She doesn't know how to work. . . . She's a last dying relic of the last century now adrift in our unfriendly day."

As for Stella, Kazan concretizes a point about her behavior that we notice only after reading him on the subject, namely that she is "narcotized" by Stanley. Kazan sees her as a creature dream-walking through her days, awaiting the night and Stanley's brutal, violently stirring attentions. He sees her as a woman saved from her sister's fate simply by the sexual awakening she owes to Stanley, sees her—perhaps more than he ever got Hunter to play—as being as resentful of Blanche in her way as Stanley is in his.

All of these notes were played, to one degree or another, in Kazan's production. What is somewhat more problematic is whether he achieved the style—or perhaps we should say the "stylization"—he wanted. *"This is a poetic tragedy,"* he wrote in italics in his notebook, *"not a realistic or a naturalistic one. So you must find a Don Quixote scheme of things for each."* He added, "Stylized acting and direction is to realistic acting and direction as poetry is to prose . . . you will fail unless you find this kind of poetic realization for the behavior of these people." Characteristically, he interpolated in these reflections, in parentheses, "(Say nothing about it to the producer and actors.)"

Jo Mielziner certainly achieved something poetic in his shadowy set, a suggestion of the apartment building and living quarters where the characters lived. It is a sketch for something more fully realized in *Death of a Salesman*—a mental landscape (mostly Blanche's) as much as it is a physical one. There was also a wispy, haunting incidental score by Alex North that helped the audience to detach the action from reality. And then there was Williams's perfect diction. Everyone sounds "real." But, of course, his words are heightened, carefully selected, highly intensified representations of reality, which means they are inherently poetic—though not in the high-flown manner of a Maxwell Anderson. It is probably because there is no obvious striving for the poetic that the play has contributed so many catchphrases to the language of literate Americans.

Still, Kazan had problems in achieving a properly balanced prodction. "I said to Tennessee," Kazan later recalled, "'This thing is becoming the Marlon Brando show.'" Visitors to rehearsals could not take their eyes off Brando, who had long since ceased muttering his lines, and was beginning to dominate the stage. "And I said, 'The play's not about Marlon Brando or that character, Stanley. It's about this woman, who's somehow a reflection of your own self.'" To which Williams replied, according to Kazan, both "bullshit" and "baloney."

Williams said that as the play went through rehearsals and out-of-town tryouts, "Jess will come up," meaning that she would start to be less of a victim, start asserting the bossy, annoying, side of Blanche, that really did need to be knocked down a peg or two. In any event, as Kazan would later ask, "What was I to say to Brando? 'Be less good.'" The point, more or less, became moot, for as Williams predicted, "Jess did come up. . . . By the time we opened it was all right. That problem didn't exist."

Tennessee Williams sent this telegram to Brando on opening night: "RIDE OUT BOY AND SEND IT SOLID. FROM THE GREASY POLACK YOU WILL SOMEDAY ARRIVE AT THE GLOOMY DANE. FOR YOU HAVE SOMETHING THAT MAKES THE THEATRE A WORLD OF GREAT POSSIBILITIES. EVER GRATEFULLY, TENNESSEE WILLIAMS."

He knew—as anyone with sound theatrical instincts knew—that Brando was The Man, the sensational soul of this production. But, in truth, and rather surprisingly, considering the legend that has accreted around Brando's performance, Tandy's work dominated the uniformly excellent reviews that greeted *Streetcar* the day after its December 3, 1947, opening at the Ethel Barrymore Theatre.

In part this was because she was, by Broadway's standards, the show's "star." In part, of course, it is because inevitably all the sympathy in the audience's response must flow to her; it has nowhere else to go. But it is curious that of seventeen daily and weekly reviews I consulted, only one reviewer particularly singled out Brando. He gets the kind of obligatory couple of sentences that supporting performers are generally awarded by reviewers, writing in haste. Often enough he is grouped with Hunter and/or Malden in the same not particularly discerning paragraph. Occasionally, he is said to be doing his best work so far on Broadway.

But the critics, men of limited, conventional and cautious minds, caught up in the routine of their jobs, which was basically to offer consumer guidance to the audience, simply failed to recognize the gift that lay before them. Of them all, only Wolcott Gibbs in the *New*

Yorker seemed to understand that this was a remarkable and perhaps even unprecedented performance.

It is astonishing—this initial neglect and incomprehension. This was one of those Broadway moments—the emergence out of nowhere of a remarkable actor—which we like to believe, from the perspective of some sixty years later, must have been widely and immediately recognized. Moreover, we are not talking here about an isolated performance; there were large cultural overtones in it. Brando was the controversial, larger-than-life presence that everyone in the acting tradition he represented, dating back to the earliest days of The Group Theatre, had been waiting for. This was not cynical, self-destructive Franchot Tone. Nor was it sweet, agreeable but insufficiently intense Julie Garfield. They had both had their chances to lead Stanislavskian acting out of the wilderness, and both had faltered. This guy was visibly, powerfully succeeding. That he would also, in time, reject the opportunity, fall into one of the worst disarrays any great actor has ever suffered is, for the moment, beside the point.

One also searches the reviews in vain for any acknowledgment of the uniqueness of the setting Williams explored, or the unusualness and intensity of the conflict he set forth. A few critics compared *Streetcar* to *The Glass Menagerie*, with the former being judged the somewhat more exciting work. They generally thought the struggle between Stanley's animalism and Blanche's anachronism quite arresting. Brooks Atkinson, at least, was more than usually sensitive to the particulars of Williams's poetic gift.

One or two reviewers, indeed, thought the play no more than dramatically fleshed out anecdote, others thought it static and somewhat repetitive in its development, several warned their readers that it might not be for the faint of heart. "Feverish," "squalid," "tumultuous" and "painful" were among the words applied to it. Some of the later reviews, in the intellectual journals, were even less admiring. George Jean Nathan did not care for it at all. And Mary McCarthy, in *Partisan Review*, was spectacularly wrongheaded about it. She thought Williams had missed the opportunity to do an in-law comedy, in which an unwanted relative arrives for a visit and overstays her welcome.

It was a long-forgotten reviewer, Robert Garland, from the long-defunct *Journal-American,* who accidentally—perhaps only partially—captured the essence of the play's immediate impact. "There were more encores—spontaneous encores—last night [opening night] at the Ethel Barrymore than your dutiful reporter could stay to count. The curtain rose, fell, then rose again until in response to 'Author! Author!' the Mississippian called Tennessee came on to take a beautifully bewildered bow."

The reviewer attributed this enthusiasm to Irene Selznick and her address book; the audience was full of knowing show folk, some from Hollywood, some from Broadway, all of whom had heard the buzz from out of town (Kim Hunter would later say that the company's biggest problem, in the run-up to Broadway, was overconfidence). And, in truth, the response of the insiders and the swells carried the day. It was the show business community that responded most fervently to the "work" of the players and the power of the play. It was their feverish excitement about *Streetcar,* that, to a degree, went forth to the nation at large. Somehow, even in the further, dimmer reaches of the Middle West, where I was restlessly enduring adolescence, we heard about this play. And about Marlon Brando. Somehow we understood that something was being said about the world we were going to inherit that was untraditional and devastating, something that spoke to the most basic psychological—possibly even existential—issues that we were beginning to wrestle with. How desperately we wanted to see it.

We would, in time, have that opportunity. The Broadway production would run 855 performances, something more than two years—but with cast changes. And there would be road companies before the movie opened, when, at last, we saw Brando's staggering performance. In that time, there was, naturally, much talk of Kazan's staging. People in New York knew that he, too, had achieved something new, not quite like anything he or anyone else had done before. But since direction is not an art one can fully analyze (or appreciate), much of that talk had to content itself with the sheer visceral impact of the show, the stunned quality that people walked out of the theater feeling. A month before the play opened, Murray Schumach, a veteran *New York Times* reporter, published a profile of Kazan in his paper's magazine. In it, Arthur Miller said that Kazan's purpose was always "to hit the audience in the belly because he knows all people are alike in the belly, no matter what their social position or education."

This became the standard line on Kazan—not unjustly so. Six years later, Eric Bentley would say simply that "Mr. Kazan's most commendable quality is a simple one: he is a showman." This attribute, he argued, was not as common as people thought, and besides, his dramatic efficiency, which is a part of showmanship, often entered the realm of legerdemain. "He is a wizard," Bentley said.

It was faith in his director that permitted Williams his serenity as *Streetcar* came together. He was a no less practical man of the theater than Kazan in those years. He understood that if an American play was to have any chance of a long afterlife it had first simply to be a hit—preferably one to the audience's belly. He had enough confidence in his play to believe that if the emphases in this production were wrong (or arguable), there would be plenty of opportunities in the future to correct them. That's why, after all, the works of Shakespeare and Chekhov are endlessly revived. We all know how they "come out," don't we? What we want from new productions are new shadings, new interpretations, discoveries of this or that aspect of the text that were previously ignored or handled differently. And *A Streetcar Named Desire* did become one of the few modern American plays to join the masterpieces of world theater that are constantly remounted, constantly handed to new generations of actors and directors to see what they make of it.

Whatever Kazan achieved with this play in the purely technical, mechanical sense, whatever nuances of performance he elicited are, of course, now lost in time. The contemporary critics being useless in conveying these matters and the memories of eyewitnesses now either faded or entirely lost, we had perhaps best confine ourselves to observing that Kazan achieved a kind of "grandeur"—a word Bentley would apply to some of Kazan's later work—in this first performance of *Streetcar.*

He was beginning, herewith, to push out beyond Odets's Bronx kitchens and living rooms, out beyond the political "problems" many of his earlier plays had explored. Tennessee Williams had offered

him a new country, grounded in reality, to be sure, but yet not entirely real, either—a place where poetics informed psychology and
vice versa, a place that seemed exotic, "un-American," if you will,
but yet offered Kazan, and his actors, primal American (and modernist) materials to play.

At thirty-eight years of age, Elia Kazan had begun to shake free
of the narrow social and political themes that had, until now, entrapped him. They would appear, of course, in his subsequent works,
but they would only occasionally dominate them. Not that he could,
at this moment, quite see any of that. All he knew, as 1947, his *annus
mirabilis,* drew to a close, was that he, no less than Williams and
Brando, had arrived. He was proud of the fact that he had two hits
running simultaneously on Broadway, that his latest film was being
talked up for Oscar nominations (in December *Gentleman's Agreement* was awarded the New York Film Critics best picture prize, and
he himself won its best director award for his work on both *Gentleman's Agreement* and *Boomerang*), that, as he told Schumach he had
earned $100,000 a year for the last three years.

The money probably meant as much to him as the prizes. There
was arrogance, of a sort, in his relentless work habits; he seems to
have been convinced that there was no film or play, no matter how
unpromising it appeared to be, that he could not make something of.
But there was need in them, too, an immigrant's need for the status
and security only a reassuring bank account could provide

Of course, his habit of moving heedlessly forward tended, sometimes, to leave people floundering in his wake—among them in the
early months of *Streetcar*'s run, its cast, dealing with the always erratic Brando. "If he felt bored or tired, he acted bored or tired,"
Tandy would recall. "If he felt gay it would go gay. I remember Karl
Malden smashing his fist against the wall because it was so frustrat-
ing. I can say I enjoyed acting with him sometimes and other times,
God knows, I could have wrung his little neck." Malden, in his later
years, affected a more sanguine view of his sometime friend, and
claimed to have found his own way of working with him. "I learned
to protect myself. I played off him. I let him do whatever he wanted
to do and I'd go from there." Something similar happened with Kim
Hunter. "It is," she admitted, "a tremendous experience to play in

relationship to him; he yanks you into his own sense of reality." Her example was the trunk scene, with Brando going through Blanche's clothes while Stella tries to protect them from his furious routings. "He had a different sort of attitude toward each of the belongings every night; sometimes he would lead me into quite a fight with him, and other times I'd be seeing him as a silly little boy. I got worn out after many months in the play, but I never got bored . . ."

Kazan, typically, did not often drop in at the Barrymore to see how his famous production was playing. He perhaps wanted it to have its own wayward life. In any case, he paused now, doing neither a play nor a film until the following fall, spending most of his time working at the Actors Studio—and, as the year wore on, starting to think about a new play, a first draft of which Arthur Miller had shown him in the early summer. Before they could turn to that, however, Kazan had a pair of less promising theatrical errands to run.

9

Attention Must Be Paid

For a director in possession of his first Academy Award—Kazan was awarded his *Gentleman's Agreement* Oscar on March 20, 1948—and two enormous hits running simultaneously on Broadway, the 1948–49 season began with a conspicuous lack of success. The Actors Studio was beginning its second year of operation and Kazan was beginning to use it, as Eli Wallach would later put it, "as a trout stream," fishing up the talent he needed for his work. He conceived the notion of putting on a play that would showcase the talents of the class he taught, which consisted of the younger, less experienced actors. What he found for them was a piece by Bessie Breuer, a novelist and short story writer, called *Sundown Beach*.

Set in 1945, it is about a group of air force flyers and their women, stationed on an island off the Florida coast, where the men are undergoing psychiatric treatment for their wartime traumas. The setting is a open-air restaurant where they gather in their off-hours—it reminded more than one reviewer of the setting for *Truckline Café*. It had a huge cast (twenty-eight speaking roles) and, by all accounts, no very powerful narrative line. Yet the company tried it out in August at the Westport Playhouse where it was quite respectfully received. One member of the company, Joan Copeland (who was Arthur Miller's sister), told Studio historian Foster Hirsch that they had been striving for something rough and unpolished, very lifelike, and felt they had succeeded in that aim at least.

Kazan himself played down the experiment. He observed in an

interview that he had never met any of his cast before he inter-viewed them for his class a year earlier, and that "We worked on the play for the fun of it. . . . When we liked what came to be, we de-cided to show it. Nothing else."

But, in the end, something else. When they determined to bring the play in, Kazan felt it needed more than casual work. Unfortunately, he was at the same time beginning to direct a more lavish and impor-tant Broadway production, Kurt Weill and Alan Jay Lerner's *Love Life*, which would open a little more than a month later. This meant that he was, from time to time, the absentee director of *Sundown Beach*, which had an effect on the show. The playwright, Breuer, noted in a letter to Cheryl Crawford: "When Gadge is away the performance falls to pieces and is like children reciting. . . . Yet the moment Gadge ap-pears, it's as if they were puppets and he held the strings, and he was their voice. In other words it is not an internal organism but an outer one that propels them. . . ."

She was raising a good question, possibly the most basic one, about directors as willful as Kazan. Others would bring it up in later years. He was always going for the jugular, for the production that would leave the audience drained, in no condition to consider alter-natives that might have been more thoughtful, more nuanced. And, of course, the more problematical the play, the more tentative his actors, the more he would assert himself.

That's what happened on *Sundown Beach*. Their final re-hearsals, at the Belasco, in the first week of September, took place in heat and in haste. Kazan, came in and, according to Crawford, "jazzed it up. It became frenetic." The critics noticed. They pretty much sympathized with the young and, as they saw them, ill-used actors, were dismissive of Breuer, but came down brutally hard on Kazan. Brooks Atkinson wrote. "In all conscience, Mr. Kazan's ag-gressive direction has not helped it much. The performance is man-nered and self-conscious. It is full of violent physical interludes that have no particular meaning. Sometimes it seems to be ignoring the play—so lost in its own inventiveness that it renders the lines unin-telligible. Most of the actors are tense and rigid and strain after ef-fects they do not wholly understand."

Crawford thought the play as written was better than the play as directed. But Arthur Penn, whose career as a stage and film director would soon rival Kazan's, but who was then a young man just out of college and heading for two years in Europe, thought the opposite. He was stunned by what he saw. He said to me that "with the exception of The Group, which was not enough appreciated, the American theater had been an adjunct of the British theater. It was all words, which they did expertly and we did not. But this company achieved a truly authentic emotional state. They weren't indicating those states. It was extraordinarily compelling." As he said to Foster Hirsch: "It was one of the illuminating experiences of my life. I was shaken to my very core. After seeing it, I walked the streets. It discarded everything that had come before. It completed the Group Theatre's attempt to shake the Theatre Guild gentility, which is as corrupt as it could be. *Sundown Beach* was Actors Studio grubbiness, which is what life is all about."

The play ran only seven performances, but the morning after it closed, Atkinson was on the attack again, openly blaming Kazan for the disaster: "The script was more exploited than acted. The actors played at such high speed, with so much conscious deliberation, that they seemed to be using each other for sounding boards. They rarely acted together as a company. They rushed at the lines as though panic-stricken. The general performance was occasionally interrupted by spurious diversions that would have been better suited to knockabout comedy than serious drama, and many of the scenes were mechanically contrived. . . . All this may be very useful for practice in a workshop production, but it was false and shallow on the professional stage."

A few years later Mary McCarthy would describe the typical character of "the so-called American realist school," as belonging "to the lower middle class sociologically, but biologically he is a member of some indeterminate lower order of primates" and call Kazan "the whip-cracking ringmaster of this school of brutes," staging plays full of "the sounds of furniture breaking, heavy-breathing and, eventually a sobbing confession of some sort of failure, possibly alcoholic or homosexual."

It is a cruel and less than half-truthful observation, but it can be made to apply to Kazan's work when it was less than its best, or when he was serving a play that was less than wonderful. Self-parody was the chance he always took.

Since he does not mention *Sundown Beach* in his autobiography, we must believe that Kazan agreed more with the reviewers than he did with the bedazzled Penn about this production. Certainly, we have to believe that, whatever idealism he brought to the Studio (he soon ceased to teach there on a regular basis), it was always tempered by his driving need to prove himself in more glamorous realms. He was, I think, a man whose attention required the profit motive in order to be fully engaged.

On the other hand, we must append an asterisk to this account. His *Sundown Beach* company included Nehemiah Persoff, Martin Balsam, Steven Hill, Edward Binns, Warren Stevens, Phyllis Thaxter, Julie Harris, Cloris Leachman and Lou Gilbert—not all of the good young actors who would align themselves with the Studio in the postwar years, but a very representative sampling of them. In that sense this largely forgotten work had a certain significance after all.

No historical significance attaches to the production, mounted by Crawford (who was serving the Actors Studio as a part-time administrator), that was competing for Kazan's attention. Despite the fact that *Love Life* was the work of Kurt Weill working with the young Alan Jay Lerner, whose *Brigadoon* had just been a huge hit, and had choreography by Michael Kidd, who had recently scored with *High Button Shoes*, it was an unhappy venture. Why, after *One Touch of Venus*, Weill chose to work with Kazan again is one of those unsolvable theater puzzles. Cheryl Crawford talked him into it; probably its structural resemblance to *The Skin of Our Teeth* was a factor.

For the musical play had a unique structure; it traced the decline and fall (and a hinted-at resurrection) of a typical American marriage, that of Sam and Susan Cooper (played by Ray Middleton, coming off a hit performance in *Annie Get Your Gun*, and Nanette Fabray, who left her star-making role in *High Button Shoes* to take this role). But Lerner's book placed that rather banal story against the background of 150 years of American history. It began in colonial America and ended at the present moment; Weill's songs caught the spirit of the changing times (and showed off his gift for satirical pastiches of popular music), though, generally speaking, these numbers do not directly affect Sam and Susan's fate. They do, however, support the show's much-discussed subtitle, "An American Vaudeville."

It was a "concept" musical—not unlike Weill's *Johnny Johnson* or *Lady in the Dark,* or for that matter Kazan's *Sing Out, Sweet Land* or Rodgers and Hammerstein's *Allegro,* which had been rather dubiously received the previous season. These shows are often beloved by musical theater professionals, because they expand the form's range of possibilities. They are equally often received skeptically by critics and audiences, because they tend toward abstraction, even a sort of emotional remoteness, that interferes with what audiences always like best in musicals—romance and fun, catchy songs and dances.

It isn't difficult to understand why Kazan, despite his lack of success with musicals, was drawn to this one. In his interview with Murray Schumach, he had said, "The essence of the stage is concentration and penetration. Of the screen action, movement, sweep." I think musicals offered him the "sweep" he hungered for and had not found in films.

Then, too, we must remember that he was still "Gadget," the young man with a talent for all the crafts that went into mounting a production—scenery, lighting, costumes, sound design. This had, over the years, translated into a gift, often remarked on by reviewers and colleagues, for flowing production, for smooth (and sometimes startling) transitions from place to place, scene to scene. Musicals had a need for that gift, and Kazan was more than willing to contribute it to them.

What he seems not to have fully grasped was that musicals, unlike straight plays, where he had only to serve the playwright, were much more collaborative enterprises—in this case, Weill, Lerner and Kidd all had power equal to, if not superior to, his. "I think there should be collaboration," he said to Michel Ciment, "but under my thumb." Moreover, he refused to see that what he did best—drawing performances out of actors who had some sort of psychological affinity for their roles—was not necessarily an asset when it came to musicals, which tended to be cast for the performer's ability to sing, not act, with audiences and critics genially forgiving failures in the latter realm.

As he did in his consideration of *One Touch of Venus,* Foster Hirsch, in *Kurt Weill on Stage,* found a number of people connected with the production who thought poorly of Kazan's work. A rehearsal pianist and general understudy named Lys Simonette, who eventually headed a foundation devoted to Weill's work, said simply, "He really messed it up—he didn't have any idea about how to stage the musical numbers." Fabray concurred: "He was not a man with a light touch, he was not a man of fun and magic. He directed with a heavy hand," though she conceded that he did well enough with the nonmusical scenes and with the more realistic musical numbers.

Eventually Kazan came to agree with these criticisms, confessing that he had no talent for musical theater. Indeed, he never did another after *Love Life* opened to mixed reviews. Some of the critics liked it enormously, responding warmly to its structural novelty; Richard Watts, Jr., in the *Post* called it "an imaginative and generally brilliant show." Others, like Howard Barnes, in the *Herald-Tribune*, found it "more of an approach than an accomplishment." Atkinson thought it "cute, complex and joyless—a general gripe masquerading as an entertainment."

A few of its songs aside, the show is impossible to judge retrospectively; Lerner refused all attempts to revive it, though it did achieve a respectable run—252 performances, something like two-thirds of a year, by no means an abject failure.

———

In April 1948 Arthur Miller said good-bye to his wife and children in Brooklyn and drove to a house they had recently purchased in Roxbury, Connecticut. It was the most visible symbol of the success of *All My Sons* and, indeed, Miller would live the rest of his life in Roxbury, though not always in this relatively modest place, situated on about forty acres of land.

According to John Lahr, who wrote a superb piece, "Making Willy Loman" for the *New Yorker* on the fiftieth anniversary of *Death of a Salesman*'s first production, Miller had two goals that spring. The first was to build a one room writing studio up a small hill in back of his house, the other was to put it to immediate use by writing a new play that he had been thinking about for a long time—perhaps longer than even he realized at the time.

The immediate inspiration for the play was an encounter Miller had in the lobby of the Colonial Theatre in Boston where *All My Sons* had its tryout run. There he had run into his uncle, Manny Newman, a dapper, slightly absurd, highly competitive figure who was—yes—a salesman working the New England territory. When Miller saw him, among the last members of a matinee audience straggling out of the play, his uncle had tears in his eyes. "Manny, how are you? It's great seeing you here," said Miller. Without missing a beat, his uncle replied, "Buddy is doing very well," referring to one of his two beloved sons.

The man was briefly embarrassed by the nakedness of his need to make a comparison between his boy, toiling away at some anonymous job, and the playwright, so obviously on the verge of a major success. The two men chatted a bit, then Manny merged into the dispersing crowd and disappeared. Miller did not immediately begin thinking he ought to write a play about a none-too-successful salesman. What struck him, as he reflected in *Timebends,* was how wonderful it would be to do an entire play that worked as Uncle Manny's mind appeared to do—without flashbacks between past and present, without elaborate mediations between disparate emotional topics. Hence his oft-repeated assertion that the setting of his play was the inside of his protagonist's mind.

But, of course, there's more to *Salesman* than the inside of Willy Loman's mind. It has a social context. Indeed, it is fair to say, I think, that Willy's inner life and his public life—the former grandiose, the latter paltry and demeaning—function reciprocally in this beautifully structured drama, generating its ineluctable power.

We need, perhaps, to look at the life of a salesman, before considering his death. Miller certainly did. "Selling was in the air through my boyhood," Miller told Lahr. His father had been a salesman before launching his own garment company, in which, as Miller said, "The whole idea of selling successfully was very important." Thus, his father, all the Millers, had known the bright side of the American dream—until his business failed, causing Isadore Miller to fall into a depression, from which he never recovered.

But he was not the model for Willy Loman. If anything, his father contributed some of his manner to the minor character of

Charley, Willy's sober and laconic next-door neighbor. As the writer phrased it, he "never raised his voice against my father"—not, that is, against the real, suffering man who so visibly failed himself and his family. But there was another, "metaphorical" father present in Miller's mind, whom he "resented because he did not know how to win out over the general collapse." This ghost father is, of course, the play's central presence.

So, too, is "the general collapse." The Depression was, in its way, as metaphorical for Miller as was the father who could not cope with it. The play is not set in the 1930s. And the "collapse" Miller speaks of is not just a temporary span of hard times. It is no less than a general collapse of values, from which we have yet to recover. For, as Charley says in his requiem for Willy, a salesman "don't put a nut to a bolt. He don't tell you the law or give you medicine." He sells you dreams, often as not symbolized by items you don't need or really want, items which are supposed to make you happy, but in the long run merely induce what we've since learned to call "buyer remorse." A salesman, as Charley also says, has "no bottom" to his life, no firm psychic ground in which to root himself. In what may be the play's most famous lines, he observes that a salesman is someone "riding on a smile and a shoeshine. And when they stop smiling back—that's an earthquake. And then you get yourself a couple of spots on your hat. And you're finished. Nobody dast blame this man. A salesman is got to dream, boy. It comes with the territory."

Underneath its rough poetic diction we are obliged to recognize that this is a very political play—a critique of American consumer capitalism and what it costs those who, like Willy, mindlessly serve it. Coming when it did, at the beginning of the great American postwar boom, Willy's goals are almost comically small and tentative, but he (and his son Biff) are no less ruined by his belief that being "well-liked" is at least as important as selling the (unnamed) product he hawks through New England. That motif is, of course, the source of the play's continuing relevance. The stakes are higher now, in the Age of Enron, but people still sell their souls to the god of sales, to the need to be big, bold, admired figures in the all-consuming consumer culture.

Miller had been making notes on his "salesman" play for some time, but had stopped a few months earlier. He sensed, he said, that at least part of the play would come forth in a rush. He had, in his mind, already, written its opening lines—"Willy!" says his wife, hearing him mount their porch, to which he replies "It's all right, I came back"—meaning that he's returned from an auto accident, psychosomatically caused by his inability to work his salesman's territory again. These words kept echoing in Miller's mind while he was building his studio. He also knew his play would end in the salesman's death, but that was all, consciously, he had.

Then one fine April morning, with some of his tools still stacked in the corner, he sat down at his desk, which he had fashioned from an old door, and began writing. By the wee hours of the next morning he had completed the first draft of the first act of his play. The second act required a little more time—something like six weeks—but considering that this play is almost every day, to this day, being performed somewhere in the world, considering that in book form it has sold more than eleven million copies, Miller has enjoyed an astounding return on a relatively modest investment of his time. And that says nothing, of course, about his psychic profits.

Miller recalled laughing quite a bit as he wrote his first act—at the absurdity of his protagonist's aspirations and values, so pathetically beyond his reach. It is, of course, in that disparity that some of the play's greatness lies. Everyone's dream life (of success, of glory) is beyond reach, and *Salesman* almost uniquely forces us to confront that bitter irony. Of course Miller must have laughed. How else could he have kept going?

Even his title was intended as a mild joke. He had originally toyed with the notion of calling his self-consciously expressionistic play *The Inside of His Head,* taking literally a sentence from a book by his college playwriting teacher, Kenneth Rowe: "Expressionism is an attempt to lift the skullcap and look inside at the brain and see how it works." But now he began toying with *Death* titles, "always austere and elevated" as he wrote in *Timebends—Death Comes for the Archbishop, Death and the Maiden,* that sort of thing. Now that word, perhaps the most resonant in the language, would be linked, in Miller's mind, with that common, and to him faintly contemptible little word "salesman."

Maybe that's all post facto rationalization on Miller's part, but no matter. "He didn't write *Death of a Salesman*," Kazan wrote in his autobiography, "he *released* it. It was there inside him, waiting to be turned loose. That's the measure of its merit." He was more right about this than he knew. Miller had more tentatively explored a somewhat similar father and sons relationship in his first Broadway production, the short-lived but very interesting *The Man Who Had All the Luck.* Later, his mother found among his papers an autobiographical fragment about the death of one of his father's salesmen, who, having borrowed subway fare from the young writer, killed himself by throwing himself in front of an onrushing elevated train. Later Miller turned up in his files some twenty pages of dialogue, written as early as 1937, involving embryonic sketches of Willy and his two sons, but lacking what Miller would call "the man's poetry, that is, the zig-zag shots of his mind." Both of these items he had totally forgotten when he sat down to write.

There is some dispute about how long it took Elia Kazan to read and respond to the manuscript "Art" Miller sent him in the early summer of 1948. Kazan recalls reading it instantly and deciding to do it before even sharing the script with Molly, which was his usual practice. Miller remembered that it was two days before he heard from his friend. But whenever the call came, Kazan's response predicted the response of audiences to come. There was something stunned, inarticulate in it. In the show's Philadelphia tryout, on opening night in New York, the audience did not burst into immediate applause when it ended; it sat in silence, a tearful one, before finally, thunderously, rewarding the production.

So it was with Kazan. He remembers telling Miller the play "killed" him. Miller remembers him saying, "My God, it's so sad." He also remembers him talking about his own failed father. There was no question about Kazan's directing the play the following fall or winter.

It was not, it would seem, a particularly difficult play to finance or to cast. Kazan and Miller offered it first to Cheryl Crawford, who hesitated too long over it, liking the play, but fearing audiences would resist it. So they casually dropped in on Kermit Bloomgarden, now among Broadway's most prestigious producers. He read Miller's manuscript that night, found that he could not sleep after doing so and early the next morning, well before most of show business was awake, he called to say that he (along with his partner, Walter Fried) would produce *Salesman*. As far as one can tell, his only immediate problem was with the grim title; he kept urging a change on Miller, which Kazan stoutly told him to resist. Shares or "units" in the $100,000 production, priced at $2,000 apiece, sold quickly. Many backers, believing in Miller's and Kazan's reputations, bought units without reading the script.

Casting, too, was relatively simple. Kazan first thought of his old friend Fredric March for Willy, an actor he knew would not embark on an ego trip, but March had just finished an epic production of *Christopher Columbus* in Europe, was tired and passed—though he would play Willy in the very poor movie version. Walter Huston also read for him, but Kazan did not particularly care for his approach. "Huston is not deeply anxious" Kazan wrote in his notes. "Cobb is."

He was, of course, referring to his old Group colleague, Lee J. Cobb, and he was, if anything, understating the depths of Cobb's prodigious neurotic needs. Trained as both an accountant and a concert violinist (an injured hand ended the latter career), Cobb was also a licensed pilot. But he had enjoyed no more than modest success as a character actor on stage and in film (he had a tendency to overact), though he had been effective for Kazan as a tough detective in *Boomerang*. The minute he read *Salesman*, he began telling both Miller and Kazan that he was born to play the role, that he understood Willy Loman in the very fiber of his being.

Perhaps it was true. Cobb was, in Kazan's description, a mass of contradictions: loving and hateful, smug and doubting, guilty and arrogant, fiercely competitive yet strangely withdrawn, suspicious but needing trust, boastful yet projecting a modest air. In short, there was a lot of Willy in him.

There was also, in his physical presence, a heaviness about him, as if he carried all the weight and sorrow of the world within his large frame. That physique bothered Miller. He had conceived Willy as a small, quick man, rather like his uncle Manny (when Dustin Hoffman played him in the Broadway revival of 1984 he finally got what he wanted, and there was an almost *spritzing* humor, a deal-making eagerness, in the performance that was quite unsettling to traditonalists). Cobb was also some twenty or twenty-five years younger than Willy was supposed to be. But Miller sensed the tragic power Cobb would bring to his play and agreed to his casting.

Mildred Dunnock was also cast physically against the type Miller had imagined. She was a slender, well-spoken woman (she had been an elocution teacher at one time), not quite the large, earth-mother sort Miller had conceived. But, again, she brought something to the play—some kind of vulnerability—that, as it were, outweighed her lack of weightiness. The other major roles were filled by Arthur Kennedy, brought over from *All My Sons* to play Biff, with Cameron Mitchell, an incisive actor whose career later swooned into B picture and television inconsequence, signed to play Hap.

Kazan would later say that *Death of a Salesman* was his favorite among all the plays he directed, though he thought *Streetcar* was better written. That was primarily because he could identify more closely with the implicit politics of the piece than he could with Williams's people and attitudes. I think he also perceived in it something of the American epic he had for so long wanted to do. *Salesman* is rather small in scale, but its tragic protagonist quite obviously contains within himself American multitudes. You could also argue that this was the play the Group Theatre had always sought. There are echoes of Odets in its people, in their setting, in their frustrated dreams, in its critique of capitalism.

Kazan was clearly aware of these elements in the play; his notebook is full of references to them. But in his staging he let them emerge almost inferentially. His stress was always on the personal drama. In his notes he insists that this is "a story of love," between Willy and his son Biff, a story that ends badly—tragically—for both of them.

In Kazan's view, Willy is good-natured and, before he is defeated by life, rather aggressive in his relationship with others, with the world at large. "His fatal error . . . is that he built his life and his *sense of worth* [italics his] on something completely false: the Opinion of Others." Kazan cannot resist broadening that indictment out beyond Willy. "This is the error of our whole capitalist system. We build our sense of worth not within ourselves, but thru our besting others. And at the same time having their constant perfect approval. A boy, Biff, must be both pre-eminent and still adored, conquering all and still loved by all. An impossibility."

As a result of this mixed message, Biff turns first into a petulant brat, then into a loser who cannot hold a job and, eventually, a petty criminal, yet one still emptily boasting and bragging. And, of course, he becomes a young man who turns violently against his father. One has to be careful in writing about *Salesman*; one can make it sound as if it were a one-dimensional indictment of society. But precisely because Willy is a complicated character, with odd sorts of integrity and cleverness—his resistance, for example, to his neighbor's offer of a steady job, based on his erroneous belief in his own importance to his firm; his lost, but formerly palpable, gift for deal making (his carefully plotted suicide, which brings in the insurance money that pays off their mortgage and renders his family debt-free, is his final nifty stroke)—the work does not play schematically.

Linda, his wife, puts this beautifully in her very moving final speech: ". . . Willy, dear, I can't cry. It seems to me you're just on another trip. I keep expecting you dear . . . Why did you do it? I search and search and I search and I can't understand it. Willy, I made the last payment on the house today. Today dear. And there'll be nobody home. *A sob rises in her throat.* We're free and clear . . . We're free . . . We're free . . . We're free."

Miller's writing in passages like these risks self-parody, certainly an excess of self-consciousness. And later he would become a slightly pompous figure, with an image of himself as a liberal humanist with important, uplifting messages to impart, but those qualities are not present here. We feel Linda Loman's puzzlement and passion just as we feel Charley's eulogy simply and strongly—especially in performance.

The play is, obviously, very aspiring, but it is grounded in a very Kazanian sense of reality—often enough, autobiographical reality. For example, he writes in his notebook: "*Another Similarity to You* [italics his]. He sees 'criticism' where none is intended. He sees imputation of guilt where none is intended. So he is constantly defending himself when there is no attack. He is 'swimming in guilt' and at the same time he attacks Linda. . . . He wants her absolute and uncritical love." To which thought he frankly appends this one: "In order to endure himself and his state of being he has to be continuously told he's great (*JUST LIKE YOU*)."

These highly personal readings—and the play may never have had a more passionate reader than Kazan—continue throughout his notes. He thinks, for example, that "The prototype of Willy in life was a very, very violent man—not a mouse at all." He was obviously thinking here of the moment when Willy, having been shabbily, dismissively treated by his employers, rounds on his son and cries: "I am not a dime a dozen. I am Willy Loman and you are Biff Loman"—not "low men" at all, but men who dreamed of excelling, of winning out over anonymity and meaninglessness, as Miller later put it.

Reflecting on this aspect of Willy, Kazan in his notes tells an anecdote about Miller, reading a newspaper account of his winning the Drama Critics' Circle Award for *All My Sons*. He threw the paper across the room angrily crying, "Everyone's son but mine!" By which he meant that the newspaper story made as much of the actors' and the director's contributions to its success as it did of the author's. Shrewd Elia Kazan saw the anger hiding under Miller's cloak of amiability.

Kazan also saw in Willy, in his oft-expressed desire to be "well-liked," something of his own father, " defeated . . . because he was shopped an ideal that was socially wrong, but also because it was not his virtue." But, in the end, that's not "proud, noble" Willy's ruling passion. There is, he writes, something "fierce, fanatic, compulsive" in his nature, which is "above compromise with his screwy ideals." Which brings Kazan back to the play's climactic incident, Willy's off-stage suicide. He understands that Willy does not see this as a defeat, but as a final, pulled-from-the-fire victory over capitalism. Yes, he dies. But he has wrested his reward from the system, the $20,000 payout from his life insurance. "At the end," Kazan writes, "he wins at all costs. He would and does sacrifice everything to his *ideal*," to the pot of gold capitalism has always promised him. "He really believes it as does *all our middle class* and he goes by it."

How bitter is this irony? At the time, I think, far deeper than it is now, when everyone in the specified class believes wealth—or at least a comfortable retirement—is an unquestioned entitlement. When we attend *Salesman* now we do not see it, I think, as quite the social indictment that Miller and Kazan did. We tend to see it as an individual rather than a social tragedy. And we tend to see Willy as more of a victim than the playwright may have intended him to be. But Miller remembered a friend coming up to him on opening night and saying his play was "a time bomb under American capitalism"— which, frankly, the playwright hoped it might be—"or at least under the bullshit of capitalism, this pseudo life that thought to touch the clouds by standing on top of the refrigerator, waving a paid-up mortgage at the moon, victorious at last."

The play reached its opening night apotheosis about as easily as any production can. Kazan, influenced by Molly, by Bloomgarden, by some of the investors who had bought into the play sight unseen, proposed at one point removing the flashbacks or, possibly, grouping them all in one place. Miller tried some rewrites along those lines, but they didn't work and were fairly quickly abandoned. Cobb, not unlike Brando, mumbled his way through the first weeks of rehearsal, causing considerable anxiety in Miller and Kazan before he unleashed the full power of his performance.

Kazan has generously acknowledged that the best thing that happened as the play found its feet was Jo Mielziner's set. Miller had intended a plain, unit set—three black platforms, playing areas picked out by lights, maybe a few simple props. But Mielziner thought it needed something more, and sketched in a skeletal house—a kitchen, a tiny bedroom for the boys, a porch, apartment blocks towering dimly over it. It is almost as ephemeral as a dream, but it is all the Lomans have, and it concretizes the play without dominating it. When Miller saw what it did for his work he wrote a description of it into the published version of the play, and in some variation or other, it persists to this day in most productions of it.

No need to quote the rave reviews that greeted *Salesman* the morning after its opening on February 10, 1949. They consisted of the usual superlatives largely unadorned by analysis, though a few reviewers approvingly noted the play's unique structure and one or two mentioned, in the blandest terms, its social criticism. Mostly they concentrated on Miller's writing, praised for its straightforward qualities, and on the performances. The weekly reviews were a little less fulsome—"the idea of the play is everywhere more moving than the play itself," *Time's* anonymous reviewer (Louis Kronenberger) wrote. He thought Miller was "relentlessly lugging" his story forward in a play "that has no fake poetry" but ". . . has no real poetry either," which is quite a wrongheaded judgment, considering the number of expressions, beginning with Charley's "smile and a shoeshine" trope, that the play has contributed to our common discourse.

It was later that some of the shine was rubbed off the play. That process perhaps began with Lee J. Cobb's increasingly indulgent performance. Visiting the play later in its run, Miller found him "enjoying rather than suffering the anguish of his character." Miller was not a Brechtian, but he did understand that the famous "distancing" effect that was at the center of the German playwright's theatrical theories— never a big item with Kazan—was being further foreshortened by Cobb's performance. He was, as well, often mean, even sadistic, with his fellow players and Kazan grew increasingly disenchanted with him as well—though he would use him again in *On the Waterfront*.

Kazan entirely agreed with Miller's judgment of the performance Cobb started giving; his hatred of indiscipline in performance is one of the stronger motifs in both his autobiography and his latter-day conversations. Cobb began agitating to leave *Salesman* early, claiming exhaustion. He even insisted that Kazan have a session with his shrink, in which the doctor claimed his client was near to a breakdown. "He began to masquerade as a martyr to an unappreciative theatre," and when he was not offered *Lear* or something similarly grand he sullenly withdrew to Los Angeles, to not-so-good movies and, finally a long-running role in *The Virginian* on television. As Kazan says, he is one of those not uncommon figures in theatrical history associated with a single great performance in a single great role. "What a waste," he concludes.

The criticism that accreted around *Death of a Salesman* over the years was more substantive—or anyway, more long-winded—than these thoughts about poor deluded Lee Cobb. There was, for instance, the matter of the Lomans' ethnicity. Everyone was convinced that they were—had to be—Jewish, if only because of some of their locutions ("attention must be paid," Linda's line about her husband's death, is the one most often cited). Miller always demurred from that interpretation. He thought it limited his play unnecessarily. He was after bigger, all-American themes and types. Speaking for the prosecution, Mary McCarthy thought him mistaken. Conceding that the strength of the play derived from the way it turned advertising art—mom, pop, the kids in their idealized home, the products being hawked prominently displayed—inside out, she still thought Willy "a capitalized Human Being, without being anyone . . . demanding a statistical attention and generalized, impersonal condolence, like that of the editorial page."

Beyond that, there was the relentlessly examined question of whether *Death of a Salesman* qualified as a true tragedy in the classic mold, with Eric Bentley early on laying out the lines of this argument, saying that social drama and tragedy are antithetical genres, with a tendency to cancel each other out when they are brought together in the same place.

There is some merit, I think, in the argument that the Lomans (their name, incidentally, is borrowed from a character in Fritz Lang's movie *The Testament of Dr. Marbuse,* "a terror stricken man calling into the void for help that will never come" as Miller described him) should be openly identified, particularized, as Jewish. But not, perhaps, as much as one might think. It is possible that had the play been written later, when Yiddishisms (thanks largely to show folks *spritzing* on the talk shows), entered the American language's mainstream, when thanks to Saul Bellow and all the other Jewish novelists and memoirists, the Jewish immigrant experience and sensibility entered our literary discourse, Miller's play might have been more openly Jewish in manner and substance. But in 1949 that was not yet the case. "Gentleman's agreement" anti-Semitism was obviously still rife in America, and in the arts Jews were almost universally portrayed comically and patronizingly. They were not yet—except, say, in the more rarefied circles where Mary McCarthy traveled—considered fit subjects for tragedy. Miller would have risked much had his work been more specifically ethnic.

Moreover, to insist that Willy and his family parade their ethnicity would be to vitiate the play's larger message, which is that we are all caught up in the falseness of American values. The play, if anything, stresses class issues over ethnic ones and it derives much of its power from the fact that most of us can still find something of our sad, impotently aspiring pasts in this story.

As for the notion that social criticism and elements of classic tragedy do not belong in the same play, it is, I think, one of those wet academic ideas that support a lot of anguished critical writing, but are close to useless in evaluating this play. When an artful, emotionally sound work reaches out beyond its ruling conventions, reaches out across the years, across all kinds of geographical divisions (and *Salesman* has been successfully performed everywhere from Communist China to beleaguered Israel), niggling questions about form tend to be obviated. Why should we care about the maintenance of, say, the classical unities or about the nobility of the protagonist or the nature of his fall from grace? Why, indeed, should we care if the vehicle taking up these matters is, technically, a tragedy at all—if we are moved by it to silence, tears or long, long thoughts? The thing simply is. We are free to make of it what we will when we encounter it, as surely all of us will at some time in our lives.

———————

Death of a Salesman went on to win all the prizes—the Pulitzer, the Tony, the Critics' Circle. It would run two years on Broadway, tour the country, enter the world's repertory. "Art" and "Gadge" were bound, for several more years, in best-friendship, a friendship that would be sundered—and never fully repaired—by political dispute. But not yet. For the moment they were both, to borrow a phrase, "free and clear." People would listen to their ideas for dream projects eagerly, with respect.

At this particular moment Miller, with Kazan's enthusiastic support, was writing a screenplay, drawn from a certain amount of personal experience, for a waterfront story, about a brave man fighting union corruption on the Brooklyn docks. It was called *The Hook*. At the same time a new Kazan friend, the novelist John Steinbeck, was working on a script, again with the director's enthusiastic backing, about the Mexican revolutionary Emiliano Zapata, which, as *Viva Zapata!* would contain a potent message about corruption of a different sort.

That some kind of a rightward shift was going on in the country seems, in retrospect, obvious. But it was not the least bit clear at the time in the cultural arena. One of the more interesting aspects of this shift struck close to Arthur Miller's home. This was the afore-mentioned *Amerasia* case, which began in 1945, when an OSS security analyst, browsing the magazine, which endorsed the idea that a Communist takeover of China was perhaps inevitable and probably desirable, found snippets of classified reports he had written in the publication. The FBI was called in and something like eight hundred purloined government documents were found in a State Department official's home, in *Amerasia*'s offices and in the possession of its proprietor, a greeting card manufacturer named Philip Jaffe. In time the leak was traced to several government officials, among them John Stewart Service, a left-leaning state department China hand. The case was, of course, controversial; were Service and his colleagues Soviet agents? Or were they far-seeing policy experts, warning America that its support of Chiang Kai-shek was misplaced, meanwhile urging that the Chinese Communists were in fact "democrats" of quite a familiar and unthreatening type? The right wing saw the *Amerasia* case as an early example of Soviet penetration of Washington policy circles; the left saw it as an attempt to smear the New Deal.

What is bound to interest us is the fact that Arthur Miller's wife, Mary, had for some years been a secretary at *Amerasia,* and that they bought their Roxbury house from Philip Jaffe, whose history as a patron of Popular Front causes has been well established. Indeed, Jaffe was, in these days, in contact with a Soviet spy, actively trying to recruit a U.S. naval officer as a Soviet agent. Eventually he decided that publishing information gleaned from classified documents in his magazine was a better way of getting that material to the Soviets.

In his memoir, Miller makes little of this connection, he's just a man happy to get early wind of a good real-estate deal, while calling *Amerasia* "a thin magazine . . . a vanity publication," without influence. He insisted that it was a victim of the then much-discussed "China lobby," the activities of which "blinded" the State Department "to Chinese reality," a position that vastly simplifies the matter.

We may judge the *Amerasia* case relatively mild in comparison to the cold war espionage cases soon to come. It led only to Service's dismissal from government, the tightening of security regulations by the Truman administration and a plea bargain; Jaffe and a state department official admitted guilt, paid fines, but served no jail terms. It was pretty much a whitewash, largely because the Truman administration, with the San Franscisco conference that established the United Nations looming large on its agenda, was in no mood to expose Soviet sympathizers in its state department. The case arose again in 1950, when the U.S. Senate's Tydings committee, investigating Senator Joseph McCarthy's many malfeasances, touched upon it. But, again, nothing much came of the matter.

On the other hand, Miller's bland explanation of his and his wife's closeness to one of the case's leading figures is quite remarkable. Writing more than forty years after the fact in *Timebends,* when candor would have had no cost, except to his image, he committed a large lie of omission. "Thin," "vanity" publications subsidized by rich patrons—witness the *New Republic,* among many others—can and do assert their influence on public affairs. We may also observe that the *Amerasia* case was not quite the minor matter Miller so lightly dismisses. Secret government documents were stolen and leaked to people of dubious loyalty, and a considerable furor in the press and among idealogues of both the left and right ensued. It, along with the almost simultaneous Gouzenko defection, was among the first major espionage cases of the cold war.

Which was growing hotter. In 1949–50 the contempt of Congress citations visited on the Hollywood Ten earlier were being tested in the courts. On June 1, 1949, Alger Hiss went on trial for perjury, having denied knowing Whittaker Chambers and thus, by implication, denying he had been a spy for the Soviet Union. That first trial ended in a hung jury, the second, later in the year, ended in Hiss's conviction. Between those trials, in August 1949 the Soviet Union exploded its first atomic bomb, several years before western experts had predicted it would. In June 1950 the Korean War began. These two events raised cold war anxiety to a flash point, although word that Russia's atomic capabilities were enhanced by information gleaned from its spies had not yet become public knowledge.

With the Hollywood Ten still, in effect, on trial, Hollywood was perhaps more anxious than anywhere. But that did not seem to affect the content of its more serious films, which remained liberal-minded, with Kazan happy to serve that spirit.

10

Movie-Making

It was Darryl Zanuck calling—less than a month after *Salesman* opened. He needed a favor. And he needed it in a hurry. John Ford had shot on a new picture for about ten days, but now, suddenly, he had, according to the official story, taken ill with shingles. Zanuck required an instant replacement. Would Kazan oblige? The studio would pay him his full salary, even though he had done no preparation—he didn't even read the script until he arrived in Los Angeles—and the minute he made his last shot he could leave, with no postproduction obligations. The film was not a particularly complicated one from a directorial point of view—small cast, studio-bound sets. Kazan could be in and out in a couple of months.

It was an offer Kazan couldn't refuse—particularly since the picture in question, *Pinky,* was a well-meaning soap opera about racial prejudice in a small southern town. He understood that Zanuck, who would again personally produce, consciously intended it as a sort of sequel to *Gentleman's Agreement,* which had brought him such agreeable profits and prestige. There was, so far as he could see, no downside, so he took a plane to Los Angeles on a Saturday, spent Sunday in conferences at the studio and began shooting on Monday. He shot the script as written, staging it as best he could while encouraging the best possible performances from his actors.

We cannot imagine him taking any satisfaction in replacing John Ford, since he admired him more than any other American director—perhaps in part because he was the anti-Kazan, a crude psychologist, but a great pictorialist, and a great celebrant not just of the American landscape, but of traditional American values. When, earlier, Kazan had sought out Ford, Ford had been flattered by the younger man's attention and free with his advice. Kazan, for example, had asked him where he got his ideas for his camera set-ups, which so often had an air of inevitability about them. "From the set," Ford had replied. "I go out on the set in the morning . . . way before anyone else, an hour before the crew, and I walk around and look . . . where they come in, where they go out." That is, Kazan explained, "the physical life of the scene is determined by whether the set squeezes people together or whether the set has an escape place in it" and so on. Kazan had already begun to follow this counsel, and would do so again on *Pinky*.

It was based on a novel, *Quality*, by a popular novelist named Cid Ricketts Sumner, first excerpted in the *Ladies' Home Journal* in December 1945, and sternly criticized by the NAACP on that occasion for Uncle Tomism. The studio, upon acquiring the novel, did what it could to make the script acceptable to the NAACP's leaders, including Walter White, its executive secretary, and Roy Wilkins, editor of its magazine, *The Crisis*. It went so far as to hire Jane White, Walter's daughter, to consult on the screenplay.

Its situation was this: The eponymous heroine (Jeanne Crain), a light-skinned Negro, has been sent north by her grandmother, Aunt Dicey (Ethel Waters), a washerwoman, to study nursing. There she has been able to "pass" and, indeed, has acquired a white fiancé, Dr. Thomas Adams (William Lundigan). Returning home on a visit, Pinky is recruited to nurse Miss Em (Ethel Barrymore) through her last illness. She's an impoverished old woman, proud and prickly, clinging to a fading mansion and her imperious ways. Aunt Dicey is devoted to her—Miss Em nursed her through a near-fatal illness—though her granddaughter believes she has been exploited by the white woman. Nevertheless, nurse and patient take a shine to each other, and when she dies the old lady leaves her house and land to Pinky, noting in her will that she believes the young woman will put the legacy to good, though unnamed, use. Unfortunately, Miss Em's only relative, a noxiously genteel and racist cousin, Melba (Evelyn Varden), contests the will, charging Pinky with exercising undue influence on her patient. A trial is held, the town's racist feelings come to a boil, but somehow—not entirely persuasively—Pinky wins the case and must now decide how best to use her inheritance.

It was on this topic that the NAACP focused its objections. The first draft screenplay was written by the impeccably liberal Dudley Nichols, author of many of Hollywood's most socially conscientious scripts of the 1930s and '40s and a longtime Ford collaborator (*The Informer, Stagecoach, The Long Voyage Home*). He had Pinky deciding to turn Miss Em's house into a clinic and day-care center, benefiting the local black population. This struck the NAACP as accommodationism. It thought she should sell the house and contribute the proceeds to black militancy. This, in turn, struck Zanuck as something less than dramatically stirring and he turned to one of his favorite writers, Philip Dunne, for a solution. Dunne was a highly civilized man, the son of the famous dialect humorist Peter Finley Dunne, and he knew Zanuck's tastes as well as Kazan did. He saw that the piece needed, at the end, to focus on the relationship between Pinky and her doctor-fiancé. He had the man reappear at the trial, and propose not merely marriage but a move to Denver, where he has been offered a share in a clinic. The advantage is obvious: In a place where they are not known Pinky can go on "passing." This offer she rejects and the last we see of her she is bustling about Miss Em's refurbished mansion, supervising an institution where both black and white doctors work amicably together, serving the black community.

This ending neatly elided the whole question of "mixed" marriages—remember, that even though Jeanne Crain never once looks like a black woman, that is what she is supposed to be and that is the way she is treated in this cracker community. Dunne would recall in his graceful memoir, *Take Two,* that only the Communist press made anything of this matter when the picture was released; it believed (not erroneously) in "mixed" marriages and wanted the film to endorse them.

This wrangle is certainly not why Jack Ford suddenly came down with "shingles." His fictitious ailment was attributable to Ethel Waters, a woman whose personality was at least as "difficult" as Ford's was. She had herself been, like Aunt Dicey, a washerwoman early in her life, and along her hard way to stardom, she had suffered much at the hands of white people. She basically hated them all, though this was covered, in public, by the warmth of the characters she generally played and by her passionate, fundamentalist religiosity. Ford, for his part, and despite his friendship with John Wayne, Ward Bond and the rest of the Hollywood right-wing community, was in those days a New Deal liberal and a man who had worked comfortably, and would continue doing so, with many black actors. On the other hand, he was, putting it mildly, a notoriously gruff, even occasionally abusive, director, especially when he was in drink. And drunk or sober, he was never a man who could patiently coax or cajole a performance out of anyone. Zanuck had said to Kazan, when he asked him to take over the picture, "They go on the set and they don't do a goddamned thing. They sit there and hate each other." Shrewd Darryl Zanuck understood that, whatever other attributes Kazan might bring to the project, his Anatolian smile was, perhaps, the most important of them.

"By the time I started to work on it," Kazan told Jeff Young, "the actors were all terrified. They all felt that they had a disaster. They had expected to work with Jack Ford, and he'd quit. He'd rejected them and they all felt very unworthy. You have no idea how fragile an actor's self-worth is. . . ."

Waters, as it happened, turned out to be the least of his worries. Kazan always identified, outsider to outsider as he saw it, with blacks, and soon she was responding to him with hugs and kisses and protestations of warm affection. He did not with her, with anyone, discuss "motivation." His technique, as always, was to help his actors find bits of business to focus on and let their feelings flow naturally from that activity. That was fine with Waters, and Kazan found Ethel Barrymore to be a delight. He said he loved hanging out with her, listening to her tales about her long life in show business, which was, of course, her family's business.

The heart of his concern was Jeanne Crain. She was an extraordinarily pretty young woman, California-born, a beauty contest winner and sometime model, who signed a long-term contract with Fox in 1943. She was a hard and earnest worker, and perfectly competent when she was cast, as she usually was, in musicals and light comedies. *Pinky,* however, was beyond her. There had, very briefly, been talk of casting Dorothy Dandridge, a light-skinned (and sexy) black woman in the part, which, at the time, would have given the film a scandalous energy (imagine, in 1948, a black woman kissing blond, bland William Lundigan), but Zanuck never seriously considered her. Instead, he went with Crain who was, as Kazan put it, "a sweet girl, but she was like a Sunday school teacher . . . she didn't have any fire." He shrewdly observed that the "only good thing about her face was that it went so far in the direction of no temperament that you felt Pinky was floating through her experiences without reacting to them, which is what 'passing' is."

It is true that Crain's makeup heightened her cheekbones, which fleetingly gave her a "Negro" look, and there are a couple of moments where the cameraman, Joe McDonald, seems to impart a slightly darker hue to her complexion, but these are mere hints of what might have been—in a different era. Even so, the Motion Picture Code censors were in a tizzy about miscegenation, and the love scenes between Crain and Lundigan were heatless; Lundigan, a handsome "leading man" of the old Hollywood school was, if anything, even stiffer than Crain. Kazan would correctly remember, "They sort of looked at each other, and posed attractively around a tree trunk, which was ridiculous."

There are some suggestions of what might have been in the subplotting. Jeff Young, for instance, correctly notes the work of Frederick O'Neal, who was at the time president of Actors' Equity, playing a slippery black man who exploits Aunt Dicey. He only has a few scenes, but they expose an almost comic malevolence that jerks the falseness of the picture briefly into reality. The man is all sly appetite—once literally so. There's a moment when he's giving bad advice to Aunt Dicey and he simply sits down at her table and begins gnawing on a chicken leg left over from her unfinished dinner. He has, as well, a lover, played by Nina Mae McKinney, one of those gifted black performers who never got the Hollywood jobs her talent entitled her to, but who here plays the only half-suppressed anger of the exploited with arresting force.

But such moments were few and far between in *Pinky*. And then at the wrap party, when both Kazan and Ethel Waters had a bit too much to drink, this exchange, as Kazan remembered it, took place:

"Ethel," I said, "we're good friends, aren't we?"

"Yes sir," she replied.

"But in your heart, deep down in your heart, something in you
hates me, doesn't it?"

"Yes, that's right. You're a white man."

But she was good in the film, playing a patient human sympathy
for the ruling whites that she never felt. Ultimately she (and Crain)
would both receive Academy Award nominations for their work. And
when it went into release, later that year, *Pinky* would, somewhat preposterously, be greeted by reviews comparable to those granted *Gentleman's Agreement*. Following two other films that dealt with prejudice
against blacks (a version of Arthur Laurents's *Home of the Brave,* in
which a racist officer bedevils a black soldier in World War II's South
Pacific theater and *Lost Boundaries,* also about blacks—this time a
family—"passing" in a northern community), it received no bad notices anywhere. *Time* even approved the stunned quality in Crain's performance that Kazan had grudgingly liked—"a morbid, almost marbleized Sleeping Beauty," which it said, Kazan underlined "by having
her walk with a dreamy gait, usually against the wind."

Perhaps the best thing about this emotionally detached film was
that it scored a breakthrough in the South; it actually broke house
records in cities like Atlanta, where, even a year or two earlier, it
would not have been booked. By such tiny increments did the mass
media begin to lay a very modest groundwork for the civil rights
movement soon to come.

Kazan left Hollywood both unhappy and determined. He told his
wife he was going to stop working in the theater for a while and con-
centrate on making better films than this one. He spent some time
working with Miller and with Steinbeck on their scripts in New York,
but then announced to Molly that he was going off alone for a while, as
he had done in the 1930s, looking for a better self, looking for a way to
make movies that expressed something he had yet to say in them.

"I said, 'Look, I'm only directing something like I would in the theater. I would get people together in a certain place, usually a room, and
move them about appropriately, and also come to some sort of visual
climax—all well and good.' But I said, 'You're not a film director, you

better go back to the theater.' And then I said to myself, 'I'm going to make a film where not one word is really important. I'm going to make it all action.' I'm still trying to make a film like Jack Ford. That sonuvabitch had a great influence on me. I kept thinking—'Jack Ford—that's what he does.' I don't remember anything anybody said in any Jack Ford picture. Nothing happens except action."

He was exaggerating, of course. There are actually a number of memorable dialogue scenes in Ford films—consider, for just one example, Tom Joad's poetic farewell to his mother in *The Grapes of Wrath*. But in the larger sense Kazan was right, for what we must vividly recall from Ford's best films is his sense of what directors sometimes call "panorama," a sweeping, often poeticized sense of the often towering, often lowering, landscapes that in some sense shape their characters' lives.

Leo Braudy put this matter in more abstract, but no less accurate, fashion when, in *The World in a Frame,* he made a distinction between the open and closed film, by which he meant far more than the difference between Fordian spaciousness and Kazan's cramped interiors. His is a complex and intriguing argument, but in essence he's saying that in an open film the characters have lives that extend beyond the confines of the on-screen narrative. We are implicitly encouraged to imagine those lives both before and after the story we are witnessing. Kazan, he suggests, was always ambivalent on this point. Method acting—and also acting by nonprofessionals—almost always suggests that sort of unscripted life. But Kazan's movies, especially at this time, offering, at best, variants on genre themes, were closed films, in which a problem was presented and then solved, with the actors' work circumscribed by the domineering plot.

I think that even though he could not formulate it in so intellectual a manner, this was the issue gnawing at Kazan during his hegira, spent wandering the American Southwest, where, predictably, he found himself drawn to its stark desert country and, rather oddly, to Galveston, the Texas seaport. There he absorbed the life of the docks—noting, for example, the play of the wind on the water, the sound of it in his ears, both notably absent in most films. He wanted particularly, he said, for Miller to capture those qualities in his waterfront script. He had previously visited Morelos, Emiliano Zapata's rocky native landscape in Mexico, but now he crossed the border again, looking for the visual nucleus he hoped would eventually inform the Steinbeck script about Zapata.

When he wrote about these travels in his autobiography, Kazan wrote romantically. He was not, he noted, a Hollywood big shot, and had never wanted to be one. Nor was he part of any narrow ideological group. Under the spacious western skies he felt himself to be just a plain, simple (and, most important, anonymous) American—free, independent, fearless. He raised a point that he would repeatedly bring up later—about the difference between ordinary American faces and Hollywood faces—"plump, soft-skinned, indoor faces." The features he would put in his films thereafter would be more weathered and worn. Put it simply: The man might have abandoned proletarian ideology, but he could not abandon his belief in the essential goodness of plain people.

He returned to New York refreshed, inspired. But found that neither Miller nor Steinbeck had a script ready for him. He began to think that sooner or later he would have to become a writer, too, capable of contributing something more than helpful suggestions to a screenwriter. That, however, was more than a decade off. For the moment, he found himself in luck.

Richard Murphy, who had written the screenplay for *Boomerang*, had now written another in a similar vein. There was no voice-over this time, and a lot more colorful action. The work was not purely Murphy's creation. It was based on a story Edward Anhalt (who would subsequently write many films, some banal, some aspiring) had originally published in *Dime Detective* magazine. He and his wife (and frequent collaborator), Edna, turned it into a screen story entitled "Quarantine." This became, in various versions, "Port of Entry" and "Outbreak," with Daniel Fuchs, a well-regarded realistic novelist turned screenwriter, earning an adaptation credit for his version of the story. Nevertheless, the script Murphy brought Kazan was sufficiently his so that he did not have to share his writing credit with any of the previous authors.

As this history suggests, there was nothing fancy about *Panic in the Streets*, as it was eventually called. It was, in essence, a genre film—a crime-chase movie in a noirish mood. But it suited Kazan's pressing need for a location shoot.

The story is this: A merchant sailor jumps ship in New Orleans. He has been unwittingly infected with pneumonic plague. His friends in the town are petty criminals—Blackie (Walter "Jack" Palance, as the billing would have him, making his movie debut), Raymond (Zero Mostel, returning to the screen after an eight-year absence) and Poldi (Guy Tomajan), the sailor's cousin. Already suffering the symptoms of the illness, the sailor scoops up the winnings of a poker game, in which the others believe he has been cheating. They murder him on the docks, and a police autopsy reveals his illness. Richard Widmark's Clint Reed, a uniformed public health officer, is called in and insists that a manhunt must be mounted to find and quarantine anyone the victim has been in touch with. A cranky, dubious detective (Paul Douglas) is his main ally. They have to proceed secretly; if the public knew that plague was loose in the city the movie's title condition, a panic in the streets, would ensue. But the criminals get wind of the manhunt and, naturally, think that perhaps the sailor was trying to smuggle something valuable into the city. Eventually Widmark and Douglas apprehend the criminals, who have, indeed, managed to infect a number of people, though a large-scale outbreak of the plague is avoided.

It is a trim little thriller, only ninety-six minutes long, and not exactly a cinematic landmark, either. In its star casting, it was very much a Kazan film: Widmark, late of *Dunnigan's Daughter*, more recently of *Kiss of Death* and a sensational movie debut; Paul Douglas, tough, burly but sometimes curiously sympathetic, had come even later to stardom, as the junk-dealer tycoon in the Broadway hit *Born Yesterday;* Barbara Bel Geddes, playing Widmark's wife, was of course a Kazan favorite. Here she has to keep soothing Widmark, who loves his work, but is ever worried about supporting his family on a tight government salary. Finally, there are Palance and Mostel to consider: The former had been, for a time, Brando's understudy and later his replacement in *Streetcar*; the latter had eked out a living as a painter and a comic until Kazan gave him this break, which, prior to his blacklisting, led to a nice little movie career as a secondary menace. He, of course, became a major Broadway star in his later years.

The movie had some incidentally interesting aspects. Widmark's character, struggling against a local officialdom in deep denial and eager to cover up the threat to their city is, in the Ibsenesque sense, "an enemy of the people." He also has a prescient, thrown-away speech in which he observes that, in the modern world, our sense of community must be expanded. The airplane, Widmark observes, can carry communicable disease to every corner of the world in a matter of hours. This is probably the first movie to make that point, however briefly.

But the movie's importance is, finally, as a signpost on the road Kazan wanted to take. Every minute of it was shot on location, and literally hundreds of its extras and small part players are locals, recruited on the spot. There are notable sequences in the city's morgue, city hall, police station, restaurants and laundromats, in a union hiring hall, on the ship from which the sailor absented himself. The lighting is effectively noirish, the blacks and whites sharp and contrasty.

"Whether I made a good film or not," Kazan would say later, "I kept getting as much action in it as I could. And I enjoyed the hell out of it because we were in New Orleans and my wife and I were on good terms then and my kids were with me [he had four by this time] . . . and we all lived together and all ate the damned food and got fat and all had a very good time. At the same time, we were winging it. . . . We weren't carrying the book around all the time. . . . And I found out this very important thing—not to pay very much [detailed] attention to the script. . . . So, anyway, I went all over that damned city and I shot everywhere—in all the streets and all the forbidden places, so to say, and I had a wonderful time. And it also gave me confidence in myself, [which] came out in *On the Waterfront*."

The film was shot between December 1949 and February 1950, and was released the following September, to generally excellent notices. The critics noted, with only mild interest, the location shooting, perhaps because the semidocumentary style had become, at the time, something of a cinematic commonplace. Some complained that the concluding chase was too long, others thought that it was just right (the problem is not so much one of length, but of occasional awkwardnesses caused by Kazan's inability to fully master the coffee warehouse where it largely takes place). Some complained about the domestic scenes between Widmark and Bel Geddes, though I think they add a texture of normalcy to the picture that it needs; they are nicely played, too, full of the affections and impatiences that accrue in good, long-term marriages. Palance and Mostel were often singled out, which was appropriate; they offer a kind of weirdness that sets them apart from the more usual movie heavies. The former drapes a kind of soft, silky, well-spoken menace over his character—you sometimes think he may be entertaining darker, more perverse thoughts than the role strictly calls for. The latter is tensely obliging; he would be funny were he not so pathetic.

Possibly the oddest review the picture got was from the *New Yorker*'s Philip Hamburger, who compared apples to oranges when he judged this film's story as definitely superior to that of *Sunset Boulevard,* which opened at the same time. Even Kazan, pleased as he was to have finally made something like a real genre movie, would not have judged his film superior to Billy Wilder's.

"If Jessica had played it," Karl Malden said, decades later, "I wouldn't have been in the movie, and neither would Kim Hunter. Because Jessica was no star, and neither was Brando. But Vivien, who after *Gone With the Wind* was the biggest thing you ever saw—she could carry us all."

The actor was talking about the film version of *A Streetcar Named Desire,* which went into production in the summer of 1950. Kazan had been reluctant to direct the film; it would be like marrying the same woman twice, he told Tennessee Williams, who desperately wanted Kazan's passion on board, for he, Charles Feldman (an agent turned producer who was packaging the project) and Warner Bros. (who would be distributing it) knew it would be hot, controversial stuff—sure to have its troubles with the industry's Production Code Administration. Williams believed he could not afford even a very good "Hollywood" director, used to compromising with the board.

So Kazan, who was paid the then princely sum of $175,000 for his services, came around—eventually making, though only after major struggles—a film version of the play that was only slightly compromised. He also acceded to Vivien Leigh's replacement of Jessica Tandy in the lead role, for precisely the reason Malden gave. Everyone felt bad about this; Tandy was the only Broadway principal not cast in the film. But not too bad. It occurred to Kazan, for example, that a fresh presence on the set, giving him fresh problems to face, might rekindle his interest in a way that Tandy would not. This proved to be so.

But first there was the matter of creating a shooting script that would preserve the integrity of Williams's work while satisfying the censors. In this niggling, absurd struggle Kazan fulfilled all of Williams's hopes. It was largely the director who carried the arguments over cuts and changes in the endless discussions with the so-called Breen office, informally named after its chief censor, Joe Breen. He was a Catholic layman who, as the production code's chief administrator, represented his church's moral interests in the movie world with a certain bonhomie; movie people liked his seeming good nature, his skill at trying to work out compromises that allowed sophisticated moviegoers to discern a film's true intent while protecting the innocent from whatever transgressions might offend their delicate sensibilities.

The censors immediately focused on three aspects of the script: the implication that Blanche had been fired from her small-town schoolteaching job because her marriage to a homosexual was a sham and she had started sleeping with her students; the fact that Stanley rapes her while his wife, Stella, is in the hospital having a baby; the implication, at the end of the play, that Stella remains in sexual thrall to Stanley and returns to him despite the rape.

In his preproduction discussions with Breen's chief censors, Geoffrey Shurlock and Jack Vizzard, Kazan said he could live with toning down the discussion of Blanche's past (though the finished film makes her young husband's sexual orientation quite clear). The rape was more difficult; it was central to the power of Williams's drama. He told Breen, according to Leonard Leff and Jerold L. Simons, who offer the best account of this fight, that without it "the play loses its meaning, which is the ravishment of the tender, the sensitive, the delicate by the savage and brutal forces of modern society."

The censors thought perhaps that incident could be rendered as something Blanche only imagined in her demented state. Another idea was to have Stanley merely contemplate raping her, but then back off. This Kazan could not agree to. Indeed, he threatened, with studio executives present, to withdraw from the project. This would have scuttled the film, since if he went, Williams and his play would go, too. A certain panic ensued, with the censors beginning to think Warner Bros. might be seriously contemplating what was still unthinkable in American filmmaking; taking the film out without a rating, as if it were a foreign art film.

Finally, everyone agreed that the rape could be presented if it were "done by suggestion and delicacy." As for Stella's temptation to return to Stanley, a line was inserted in which she promises her baby that they are never going to return to the now haunted apartment, but, in the end, Kazan shot ambiguously. One believes that Stella will eventually weaken and return to Stanley. In short, the film was made with careful, self-conscious ambiguity, with many people continuing to believe it one of the two or three finest movie adaptations of a play ever made.

When it came out most people "got" all its implications—in part because the play itself was by then so well known, in part because Kazan's direction was so shrewd. Yet it should be noted that the realist-idealist was quite capable of writing a memo to Jack Warner in which he observed that the play had superbly contradictory content; it had both fucking and class. "What made it a Pulitzer Prize winner—the poetry—must be kept in, untouched so that it will appeal to those who don't want to admit that they are interested in the moist seat department. (Everybody of course is!)"

What a figure he was! He had stood firm for the integrity of his friend's play. Yet he was perfectly capable of encouraging vulgar Jack Warner's crassest side. This talent for high-low poker is one reason people so distrust Kazan's political positions. It is difficult for most of us, eager to present ourselves to the world as reliably monolithic in character, to fully understand a man who could simultaneously appeal to the best and worst in us. But that was the man's essence. There was simply no piety, false or otherwise, about him—unless, of course, a protestation of piety might serve some ulterior purpose.

As script discussions proceeded, Kazan contemplated a return to New Orleans for another location shoot, which he thought might open up the play. In the end the film offered just a few second unit shots of the eponymous streetcar. In this period he also—

self-confessedly—came more and more to like the idea of casting
Vivien Leigh as Blanche, since she more than fulfilled his need for
some galvanizing contentiousness.

She had played Blanche on the London stage, under the direction
of her husband, Laurence Olivier, in a production that Tennessee
Williams disliked, but she had an instantly recognizable rightness for
the part. "Gadge told me something I've never forgotten about casting
for movies," Malden remembered. He said the first impression that
the public gets of the woman that's on the screen . . . is fifty percent
of the battle. If Jessica had played it, she would have had to work . . .
because she wasn't glamorous. Vivien was Hollywood glamour."

That glamour came at a price. She was a wildly ambitious actress, driving her modest talent into unfair competition with her pro-
tean husband. This was already taking a toll on her career and her
mental stability. She was just a few years from the breakdown that
would haunt—and shorten—her final years. She arrived on set—
Kazan had taken over a single Warner Bros. stage, on which was
erected the entire building, courtyard and streetfront housing the
Kowalski menage—with a desire to teach these Americans something about real acting, English acting.

Inevitably the confrontation with Kazan came. "When Larry and
I did the play in London . . ." she began, within earshot of the rest of
the cast. She then proceeded to give Kazan the details of that production. He responded gently ("I've only yelled at an actress twice,"
the actor Austin Pendleton recalled him saying once—perhaps forgetting the grand Bankhead battle—"and both times it was Jo Van
Fleet"): "But you're not making the film with Larry in London now,
Vivien. You're making it here with us."

She responded—slowly—to his direction. The theatricality of
her performance, often somewhat unfairly remarked on by critics,
came, Kazan later argued, in the scenes she completed before she
yielded to his sway. This judgment seems to me largely correct.
Kazan himself told me that the troubles she was beginning to have in
her off-screen life worked for him—the touch of authentic craziness
that she brought to the role as did her slightly fading beauty. At
thirty-seven, she was five years younger than Tandy, but she had

been a far greater, and more fragile, beauty, so its decline was more noticeable, perhaps more poignant.

Which does not mean she was ever uncomplicated for Kazan to direct. He grew close to her. He came to admire her. He had an affair with her, about which he later boasted in an ungentlemanly way. "She had a small talent," he later summed up, "but the greatest determination to excel of any actress I've known. She'd have crawled over broken glass if she thought it would help her performance."

Setting aside the contretemps with Leigh, the production went smoothly. Kazan would claim that he never discerned the slightest difference between Brando's screen and stage work. Malden's judgment about Brando was correct; he was not quite yet a movie star in the fullest sense of the term. He had one picture behind him, Fred Zinnemann's *The Men,* in which he had been well-received. But this was the performance everyone was awaiting, the replication for a mass audience of a legendary stage role, and he did not fail them. Or himself. It is a performance reduced just slightly in scale from his stage work for the intimacy of the screen, but lacking nothing in crazy humor, brutality or sexiness. Looked at now, from the wrong end of a career marked for much of its length by slovenly indifference to discipline, by contempt for the very business of acting, it perhaps seems more of a miracle than it did at the time.

When he finished shooting Kazan was entirely pleased with the results, though he did not abandon his loyalty to his stage production. "I liked it on the stage a little better," he would later recall. There were two reasons for this. The first of them was that it struck the theatrical audience with the force of revelation. "They hadn't really seen Brando before and they'd never seen Williams like this. Williams had written a tender, sort of nostalgic memory piece [*The Glass Menagerie*], but all of a sudden they saw [the] great dramatic strength that was in him and it overwhelmed people." Beyond that, there was the intense immediacy of the audience response that the theater can sometimes engender. "They [the characters] were trapped right in front of you and you watch this terrible thing going on and you aren't able to prevent it or do anything about it. That's one thing about the theater, right? It's happening then. It didn't happen some other time and you photographed it. . . . If there's some cruelty there you feel, 'Can I do anything about it? What should I do? Can I stop it? Will it stop? Will it ever stop?'"

He captured that immediacy in this film, precisely because he chose not to open up his production, but rather confined its intense actions and tense dialogue in his claustrophobic set. He further intensified this mood with a heavy reliance on tight close ups. Karl Malden feels that in some ways the movie reclaimed the work for Blanche. "Gadge could control it. He could cut it the way he wanted to cut it. So that . . . whenever it got too strong for Marlon, you cut to Vivien." As a result, he says, "the movie is more about Tennessee's Blanche DuBois than the play."

I think that's a good point. I also think that certain key scenes— where Brando is going through Blanche's trunk, imagining greater value for its pathetic contents than they have, the dinner table scene where Brando rages at the sisters' false gentility and starts throwing crockery around, even the rape scene—may work better on the screen. We are up close and personal with the raw power of Brando's work. More than that, the intimacy of film imparts to this adaptation a rutting feverishness that almost never penetrates the fourth wall of its theatrical productions.

Certainly I think that, almost alone of movie adaptations of stage plays, Kazan captured the reality of a setting—the sweaty heat of a New Orleans summer, the equally sweaty heat of these sexually stirred human beings—with intense vividness. It was the opposite of the epic-scale films Kazan aspired to make. But it was also the movie that drew most strongly on his greatest strength, his psychological acuity.

It is one of Kazan's three or four finest films. And unlike the vast majority of films, it requires no apology more than a half-century after its making. It remains as intense, as riveting, as vertiginous in its effect on us as it was the day it was released, which was, when Kazan wrapped in the fall of 1950, a year off.

11

Hooked

Between the completion of *Streetcar* and the start of production on *Viva Zapata!* the following spring, politics began decisively to intrude on Kazan. Every significant activity he undertook in this period was affected by the gathering tensions of domestic cold war politics.

A little background: On February 9, 1950, Senator Joseph R. McCarthy made his notorious speech in Wheeling, West Virginia, in which he brayed his fictitious charge that 205 Communists were "working and shaping policy" in the State Department. A month later, Klaus Fuchs, the German-born British subject, perhaps the most significant supplier of Los Alamos's secrets to the Soviet Union, was arrested, tried and sentenced for espionage in London. A few months later, the Korean War began, and in the summer of 1950 the Hollywood Ten, all appeals exhausted, began serving their jail terms. Kazan always said that he knew he could not for long evade official inquiry into his former Communist Party membership.

His first test came in the fall of 1950, when Cecil B. DeMille, a power in the Screen Directors Guild (latterly the Directors Guild of America) mounted an internal campaign to purge its ranks of leftists. The president of the guild at that time was Joseph L. Mankiewicz, nominally a Republican, but a man of liberal temperament and also a man well-known for not joining any heavily politicized groups. It may, indeed, have been his political quietism that caused DeMille and his clique, older directors of conservative beliefs, to endorse his presidency of the guild, which office he had taken the previous spring. They judged him not to be a troublemaker and were pleased to have as their leader a man then in the process of winning four Academy Awards back-to-back—for writing and directing *A Letter to Three Wives* in 1949 and *All About Eve* in 1950, an unprecedented feat.

The latter film, not yet in release, contained, incidentally, a portrait of a director that was, Mankiewicz admitted, at least partially inspired by his friend Kazan. This character, Bill Sampson (Gary Merrill), is a stage director who is heading for Hollywood to make his first movie. When Eve, the film's eponymous schemer, rather snootily chastises him for deserting Broadway, he snaps back: "Listen, junior. And learn. Want to know what the theatre is? A flea circus. Also opera. Also rodeos, carnivals, ballet . . . Wherever there's magic and an audience . . . Donald Duck, Ibsen and The Lone Ranger. Sarah Bernhardt, Poodles Hanneford, Lunt and Fontanne, Betty Grable—Rex the Wild Horse . . . It may not be your theatre, but it's theatre for someone, somewhere." Sampson is better dressed and better spoken than Kazan, who never directed a flea circus. But, yes, his tolerant taste matches Sampson's, as does his sense that theater can and must appeal to a less-than-grand audience in a multitude of forms.

But, at this point, having collected only half his academy hardware, Mankiewicz (who also made two other pictures between his winning titles) and, having finished postproduction on *Eve,* sailed for an extended European vacation. While he was away, DeMille and his allies struck. The recently passed Taft-Hartley labor relations bill included among its retrograde provisions one requiring all union officers (but not the rank and file membership) to sign loyalty oaths. As a union officer Mankiewicz had, in fact, signed the oath. But the DeMille faction now wanted to force the entire membership of the Directors Guild to sign it. This was an outrage. And many of the union's old conservatives joined their younger and more liberal colleagues in opposing this plan. Adding insult to injury, DeMille and his people insisted that the vote on whether to institute a loyalty oath be by open ballot; every director's name was printed on the ballots they were sent. Further, it was known that the names of those who refused to sign would be forwarded to the studios. The threat of blacklisting was clear, but almost everyone was afraid to oppose the loyalty oath, which was carried by an overwhelming majority (547 to 14 with 57 abstentions).

A large number of guild members, however, believed their approval had been coerced. They wished to debate the entire issue at an open meeting, which Mankiewicz decided to call. Whereupon DeMille and his crowd struck again. They began a movement to recall Mankiewicz before he could formally institute this meeting.

This time their ballot was even more outrageous. Its entire text was: "This is a ballot to recall Joe Mankiewicz. Sign here." There was a box marked "Yes," for recipients to check. There was no "No" box. It went out via a squadron of motorcycle messengers, some of whom, having been given erroneous addresses, did not complete their deliveries until three in the morning.

The next evening, before all these ballots were received at the guild offices, Mankiewicz and his allies mobilized. On the very night that *All About Eve* was premiering in New York, a group of Mankiewicz's supporters, Kazan among them, met in Chasen's restaurant, their idea being to call the open meeting before Mankiewicz could be recalled. They drafted a petition to that effect, which, under guild bylaws, required twenty-five signatures. Once again, motorcylists were dispatched, the signatures were collected and the meeting was scheduled for the Crystal Room of the Beverly Hills Hotel on the following Sunday, October 22, 1950.

This conclave went on until four the next morning, and has passed into Hollywood lore and legend. Everyone agrees that Mankiewicz's opening statement was a largely objective account of the events leading up to this moment. Everyone agrees that DeMille's response began in a conciliatory manner. He, indeed, offered to burn, uncounted, all the recall ballots. But he was not about to give up on the loyalty oath. And, in arguing for it, he made a horrendous tactical blunder. He began reading out the list of directors who had signed the petition calling for this meeting. As he did so, DeMille put a foreign—or should we say anti-Semitic?—spin on his pronunciation of some of the émigré names—William Wyler, for instance, became "Veely Vyler."

Boos and catcalls. And then member after member rising to denounce DeMille. Some, like Wyler and John Huston, who had served under fire in World War II, asked pointed questions about DeMille's whereabouts during the war. Some were in tears, more were spluttering in their outrage—and the more effective because of their obvious emotions. Through it all, John Ford, by common consent the greatest figure of his profession, remained silent, a baseball cap pulled low on his head, his sneakers untied, rubbing his glasses with a dirty handkerchief, occasionally chewing on it—a famous nervous mannerism of his.

Finally, Mankiewicz called on him. "I'm a maker of westerns," he began, with his equally famous false modesty. He launched into an attack on DeMille. "I don't agree with C. B. DeMille. I admire him. I don't like him," he said. He called both Mankiewicz and DeMille "the two blackest Republicans I know." Then he dropped his bomb. The Guild, of which he was a founding member, was in a life-threatening crisis. It needed to clean house completely. Therefore, he proposed that its entire board of directors, which included men of both the right and the left (there were, at the time only two women directors, Dorothy Arzner and Ida Lupino), resign, and an election for a replacement board be called. Ford concluded by saying that it was late and that many present needed to be on their sets, working, in a few hours. His proposal was a way out, and the weary membership quickly passed a motion endorsing it, added one praising the twenty-five members whose petition was responsible for this meeting and then, at last, adjourned. Many members were so stirred that they could not sleep; George Stevens hopped in his car and drove to and from Ventura, fifty miles distant, simply to discharge his exultant energy.

In truth, not a great deal was accomplished. The Screen Directors Guild did, indeed, begin requiring loyalty oaths of its members shortly thereafter. The next day Ford sent a conciliatory note to DeMille—they had both, after all, been in the movie industry virtually since its founding. The following spring Mankiewicz left the Guild's presidency after serving only a single one-year term.

Elia Kazan is entirely absent from this account. Despite his presence at the Chasen's meeting, he did not sign the petition to call the membership meeting. Despite working with John Huston and George Seaton to polish Mankiewicz's opening remarks, he hugged and kissed his friend, and then left the hotel.

Mankiewicz, at the time, could not understand this desertion, but, preoccupied by the larger issues at hand, made little of it. Kazan, however, knew that DeMille, who had contacts in right-wing government circles, where Kazan's past party membership was known, would probably cite him as a former Communist continuing to persist in his left-wing views. Kazan, in his autobiography, remembered Al Rogell, a minor director and guild board member who was one of DeMille's creatures, actively looking for him at the meeting. He says that Mankiewicz later recalled William Wyler approaching him to ask why Rogell was so determindedly seeking Kazan. As opposed, say, to the Writers Guild, the directors had few past or present Communists among their members (as far as one can tell, there were but two of them, Edward Dmytryk and Herbert Biberman, both then serving their Hollywood Ten jail terms), so Kazan would have been a prize for the DeMille faction had he been present. His absence certainly served himself, but it also served the guild, of which he was always a devoted and active member.

———————

With the circle drawing tighter around him, Kazan, aside from this one tactical withdrawal, did not shun controversy; he seemed to welcome it—and in a rather chipper, combative spirit. He left Hollywood sometime after the guild meeting, but returned in January 1951, with three pieces of business in hand. For one thing, he had learned that *Streetcar* was not yet free of problems. It hadn't played as well as it might in a sneak preview and he had to do some editorial tinkering on it. He was also beginning intensive preproduction on *Zapata* and, finally, he hoped to secure a contract to produce Arthur Miller's *The Hook*, which Kazan now believed was in presentable form.

Of these matters, *The Hook* was, in early 1951, the most pressing to Kazan, and Miller accompanied him to Los Angeles to help with his pitch. The script that they discussed in detail on the train ride west (Miller recalled Kazan wanting to do this picture in the Italian neo-realist vein) was destined for contention, but not production, but the story behind it, as well as the story of why it was not made, is an illuminating one.

It begins with the shared passion of two leftists, Miller and Kazan, for the waterfront and its workers. In *The Hook* (the title refers both to the Red Hook waterfront district in Brooklyn and to the bailing hook longshoremen always carried) a character says: "I'm gonna tell you a government fact. Longshore work is the second most dangerous job in America. The only job where more men get killed is out west where they cuts the big trees! It's even more dangerous than the coal mines!" These guys, in short, were the roughest proletarians handy to these New York radicals. To show audiences these crude, uneducated working stiffs, risking their lives for short money and no fringe benefits, yet coming to political consciousness, was irresistibly romantic to them. And, unbeknownst to them at the time, to another writer as well. That was Budd Schulberg, also a former Communist and the well-known author of a famous Hollywood novel, *What Makes Sammy Run?*

Schulberg had been impressed enough by a series of articles in the *New York Sun,* for which Malcolm Johnson, a drawling southerner, had been awarded the Pulitzer Prize in the spring of 1949 (the same year Miller won for *Death of a Salesman*), to acquire, with a partner who was Harry Cohn's nephew, the screen rights to the series and later to the book Johnson developed from it. Schulberg then spent considerable time on the docks (in Red Hook, but also on Manhattan's West Side and in Hoboken, which, of course, eventually became the film's location), becoming friendly with many of the longshoremen. He also attended all forty sessions of the commission set up to investigate waterfront crime. He was at least as well versed in this subject as Miller, who came to it in a more circuitous fashion.

As we've seen, after the success of *All My Sons*, the playwright became restless and dissatisfied and—his brief adventure in factory work finished—he began wandering the Brooklyn streets, seeking reconnection with what he thought of as his better self. Along his way, out of the corner of his eye, as it were, he claims he began observing graffiti chalked on sidewalks and walls near the waterfront. These scrawls asked, "Dove Pete Panto?"—Italian for "Where is Pete Panto?"

I suspect this is a pretty fiction, concocted after the fact by Miller. For Panto's story is not particularly mysterious. He was an idealistic young Italian immigrant, fighting mob penetration of the longshoremen's union, when one summer night, after a meeting with racketeers associated with Albert Anastasio, he was abducted and killed by two or three of his goons, his body dumped in New Jersey and covered in quicklime. This account of his demise was given by Abe "Kid Twist" Reles, when he turned state's evidence against the mob—and was murdered for so doing.

What's significant to our narrative is the fact that Pietro Panto (to give him his full, proper name) was murdered on the night of July 14, 1939, some eight years before Miller claimed to have seen the "Dove Pete Panto?" signs and graffiti, by which time, of course, people did know, because of Reles's testimony, what had become of him. Some attempt had been made, years earlier, to make a political martyr of him (though Panto was not a Communist), but those days were long gone. It is hard to believe that his death had any current relevance by the time Miller began wandering Red Hook or that current dockworkers would react—as Miller claims they did—with fearful silence when he mentioned Panto's name.

I think it more likely Miller heard of Panto (and the signage about him) from two new friends he made on the docks, liked their "Dove Pete Panto?" story and took it for his own. Such things are not unknown to imaginative writers. These friends, Vincent James Longhi and Mitch Berenson, have, however, a certain interest for us. The former had been a merchant sailor (he once shipped out with Woody Guthrie), who became a lawyer allied with the American Labor Party (ALP); the latter was a working stiff, but educated in Russian literature (and Marxisim) by an autodidact aunt. Miller would actually take a long trip to Europe with Longhi, during which he met, and was flattered by, many of its leading leftist intellectuals (and, by contrast, some Italian *Mafiosi*), before beginning work on *Death of a Salesman.*

We can, if we wish, imagine the thirty-two-year-old Miller romanticizing his association with these tough-talking worker-radicals. But in *Timebends,* published when he was seventy-two, he is less than forthright in his identifications of them. For example, he characterizes the American Labor Party (ALP) with a single neutral word: "young."

That's somewhat less than fully illuminating; the ALP was founded

in 1936 and by this time, it was a Communist front. That had not always been the case. In 1943, this party, an uneasy alliance between two
major elements among New York's garment workers—democratic socialists headed by David Dubinsky and a more radical group led by
Sidney Hillman—had split in two. The cause for the breach was Hillman's Communist-backed plan to align his union, the Amalgamated
Clothing Workers, with the CIO's Political Action Committee to back
Franklin Roosevelt's bid for a fourth presidential term. This infuriated
Dubinsky, head of the International Ladies' Garment Workers Union
(ILGWU), also an FDR supporter, but deeply suspicious of the CIO,
which had a substantial Communist presence among its leadership.
When the ALP formally joined with Hillman in May 1944, Dubinsky's
faction morphed into the Liberal Party, which became, and long remained, a significant third force in New York electoral politics. Over
the next decade the ALP became the home of Vito Marcantonio, the
radical New York congressman and Communist Party tool.

In any event, "Vinnie" Longhi (as Miller calls him, even though
he preferred to be called "Jimmy,") introduced Miller to Albert
Anastasio, the very man who had ordered Pete Panto's murder, and
his brother, "Tough Tony," who had, among other activities, led the
mob into its alliance with the Communists. For example, the murder
of Carlo Tresca, the noble Italian anarchist (and anti-Stalinist), was
accomplished by a Mafioso named Carmine "Lilo" Galante, probably because the mob and the Stalinists had made a deal: The Communists would stop attempting to organize the docks, leaving them
to the Mafia, while the mob would handle such "wet work" as the
party required. There is no other logical explanation for Galante
killing a total stranger on the corner of Fifth Avenue and Fifteenth
Street on the night of January 11, 1943.

It is hard to imagine Miller knowing much about that grim matter.
On the other hand, it is impossible to imagine Vincent James Longhi
not knowing something about it. For he was, at that time, one of a small
group of Stalinists inhabiting the far left of the Italian-speaking branch
of the labor movement. The majority of these leftists leaned toward anarchism and they all hated and feared the Stalinists.

Be that as it may, we know that Longhi was working at least part
of the time at an Italian-language Communist newspaper when

Tresca was murdered—its offices were near the place he was exe-
cuted—and his death would have been important news to the
paper's readers. Later, Longhi would be one of the attorneys defending the Communist Party leadership at the so-called Foley Square
trial, at which they were controversially convicted of violating the
Smith Act, which prohibited the advocacy of revolution.

All of this would eventually have serious consequences for
Miller, for *The Hook* and, to a lesser extent, for Kazan. Schulberg, it
should be noted, had also heard of Panto and, eventually, worked an
indirect reference to him into his script—the murder of young Joey
Doyle. But Schulberg's longshoremen were mainly Irish and exploited by a different branch of the mob.

That, for the moment, is of less consequence than the dates Miller
and Schulberg composed their screenplays, which were close to simultaneous. Miller began his dockyard wanderings in 1947, but appears
not have started turning this material into "A Play for the Screen," as
his subtitle would have it, until after *Salesman* opened in 1949. By that
time, Schulberg had already begun work on a script he called *Crime on
the Waterfront* (but which Kazan recalled being entitled *The Bottom of
the River*), which he says he finished a year before he met Kazan in
1952. By this time, he had begun to think of it as more appropriate for
a novel (which he eventually wrote, and which is substantially different
from his screenplay). He would also eventually write a play on this subject, which, like his novel, is less about Terry Malloy than about a waterfront priest. In any case, as Schulberg would write about his novel,
"The violent action line of Terry Malloy is now seen for what it is, one
of the many moral crises in the spiritual-social development of Father
Barry."

In any event, Schulberg has said that "not only have I never read
The Hook, but Kazan never discussed the Miller script with me. I
purposely didn't want to hear about it for fear my work might inad-
vertently overlap with his." It does not in any significant way. What
resemblance between the scripts exists is more generic than specific.
Both are about ignorant, decent men who move from accommodation
with corrupt union leaders into opposition to them. The scripts also, of
course, share the same mise-en-scène: the perpetual chill in the air,
the bleak surrounding slums, the bars where the men gather after

work. Both stress, too, the physical danger of the work, as well as the rough faces, forms and withdrawn manner of the men who do it.

Beyond this, the scripts have only two incidents in common. Both show the way the dockside shape-up boss determined the day's employment, by handing out metal checks to those he favored. Both scripts include a scene in which this figure tosses the last of these checks in the air, forcing the men to scramble for them as they hit the ground. It must be said, though, that this obvious and dramatically arresting feature of waterfront life could not have been ignored by any moderately observant writer. Both scripts also include a sequence in which a loading sling breaks, dumping cargo into the hold below and killing a worker. But in *The Hook* the incident is played purely as an industrial accident, the result of the union not assuring its members' safety; in *Waterfront* the spillage is malevolent, punishment for a worker who has opposed the racketeers.

Both scripts also feature a scene in which hero and heroine converse in a children's playground in sight of the docks. Doubtless Kazan remembered that setting from *The Hook* and used it in *Waterfront,* but the purport of each sequence is very different—in the former the protagonist is having an argument with his wife; in the latter it is the setting for the first shy love scene between Marlon Brando and Eva Marie Saint.

But there the similarities end. It is somewhat unfair to compare Miller's work with Schulberg's in that Miller did not have the chance to make the many additional production drafts that Schulberg did. But, frankly, Miller's script is not as powerfully worked out as Schulberg's. His story is of Marty Ferrarra, a 32-year-old longshoreman, trying to support his family on his erratic earnings, who quits when his friend is killed in the incident involving the overloaded cargo sling. He becomes a bookie, prospers, but is shamed by his daughter's disapproval of his petty criminal life and returns to the docks, where he attempts to organize his pier gang, who are being cheated out of their overtime pay. At a union meeting he prompts an almost successful protest, but a riot ensues. Thereafter, he is blackballed from work, but runs for president of his local. He loses the election, which appears at first to be rigged against him, but which he actually does lose because his friends, fearing for their jobs, vote against him.

Nevertheless, his campaign has heartened them and the script ends with a hint that Marty will continue his union work and that, through him, reform will eventually come to the docks.

It is a long script (173 pages) and nothing much really happens in it; the mob threat to Marty's life is never as real and menacing as it is to Terry Malloy. There are no murders, no dark-corner violence in this script—just a couple of brawls. The longshoremen, as a group, are colorful enough and Miller's dialogue is often pungent. But the script lacks the richness of character and incident that makes *On the Waterfront* so compelling. There is no priest character, and there is no figure comparable to Rod Steiger's Charlie, Terry's mobbed-up brother. Above all, there is no figure like Eva Marie Saint's Edie, no relationship in this screenplay that is remotely like the one that develops between her and Terry. Marty's wife, Theresa, is a good woman, patient, long-suffering, supportive, but she's not a fully developed—or sexy—character.

In short, *The Hook* is correct and dutiful, occasionally well-observed, but it is not moving. We cannot imagine it becoming a film as great as *On the Waterfront*. For Arthur Miller didn't write love stories and he didn't write muscular melodramas, and the suggestion of plagiarism on the part of Schulberg and Kazan, advanced by Miller's biographer, Martin Gottfried, is absurd.

But, for the moment, no matter. Whatever doubts Kazan still harbored about *The Hook,* he obviously deemed it good enough to present to the studios, where, given his recent track record, he was more eagerly received than Miller, who in his own account and Kazan's, is portrayed as an innocent being guided among thieves by his much more knowing friend.

It was on this trip that Miller encountered a substantial part of his personal destiny in the form of Marilyn Monroe. There is some dispute about where he and Kazan met her—were they introduced on the Fox lot by Cameron Mitchell or was she one of the many young women hanging around the perpetual party at Charles Feldman's house, where Miller and Kazan were bunking? It is of no consequence. Monroe's agent and lover, Johnny Hyde, had recently died and she was in mourning, but available. Kazan, as was his wont, cheerfully, inconsequentially, began fucking her. She was pretty (he

speaks of her luminous skin) and she was fun, just the sort of creature with whom he had relieved his perpetual horniness dozens of
times. For the sober-sided Miller, Monroe presented a more serious
temptation. He was unhappy in his marriage, looking without quite
being able to admit it, for a sexual adventure, but squeamish about
actually embarking on one. His wife, Mary, was a rather joyless creature. Kazan's eldest daughter, Judy, characterizes her as a skinny,
silent, disapproving figure, refusing to join in her husband's playfulness when the Millers and Kazans were together, as they often were
in those days (Miller's "public intellectual" sobriety came later). In
any event he thought Marilyn was bright, if untutored, and she presented herself to him as someone who would happily be mentored
by him. The three began hanging out together and when Kazan noticed "the lovely light of lechery" in Miller's eyes when they were
slow-dancing one night at Feldman's, he prepared to surrender
Monroe to his friend—though whether Miller and Monroe consummated their affair immediately or sometime later is hard to say.

Meantime, there was business to be done. Kazan's agent, Abe
Lastfogel, accompanied him to Fox where they received Zanuck's
rejection of *The Hook*, though he enthusiastically pressed Kazan for
a final script on *Viva Zapata!* Lastfogel alone heard Jack Warner's
rejection, also accompanied by strong protestations of his desire to
continue workng with Kazan. Finally, the agent set up a meeting between Miller, Kazan and Harry Cohn, head of production at Columbia. He was, to many, a fearsome figure, but he amused Kazan. The
trick to dealing with Cohn, as strong directors like Robert Rossen
and Fred Zinnemann also testified, was to stand up to him fearlessly.

Kazan and Miller brought Marilyn along to their first meeting.
She carried a steno pad and was introduced as their temporary assistant, Miss Baur. Cohn kept eyeing her—and not merely because she
was so pretty. He was convinced he had seen her before, which perhaps he had in one of the several small movie parts she had played.
But he never tumbled to the joke.

He did more or less tumble to *The Hook*. It was not that he particularly loved it, but he loved the idea of establishing a relationship
with Kazan and Miller. The former, of course, was hot in Hollywood.
And Cohn, at this moment, was releasing the screen version of

Death of a Salesman, produced by Stanley Kramer's independent company, which had a distribution deal at Columbia. Nevertheless, Cohn was determined to drive a hard bargain for *The Hook*—low budget, not much money up front for the writer and director. That was all right with them, and another meeting was scheduled.

Cohn was by no means a raving anti-Communist. But he was conscious of the growing anti-Communist fervor in the country, and he showed Miller's script to Roy Brewer, whom he invited to attend his next meeting with Kazan and Miller. Brewer was the "international representative"(i.e., president) of the International Alliance of Theatrical and Stage Employees (IATSE), a power in the Los Angeles trade unions council, which embraced all the area's organized labor, and chairman of something called the Motion Picture Industry Council, the only business of which was to keep movies free of Communist taint. Brewer had (possibly soluble) problems with Miller's work, and it was the purpose of this meeting to work them out.

There is a discrepancy between Kazan's and Miller's memories of it. Miller claims it took place after he had left for New York ahead of Kazan; he says it was merely reported to him by Kazan in a phone call. He also recalls the changes Brewer proposed as more radical than Kazan did. He has Brewer insisting that the whole idea of labor racketeering be thrown out and a Communist takeover being substituted for it. Conversely, Kazan has Miller present for the meeting and so does Brewer, who has recently written about it. Neither man suggests that anyone mentioned the idea of Communism being substituted wholesale for racketeering as the main threat to unionization. It was to have been a subtext—if one that Brewer eagerly desired.

Here some backstory is in order. IATSE had been, in the late thirties and early forties, a particularly corrupt force in show business, with mobsters conspiring with union officials and studio bosses in a system of payoffs that rendered the union essentially powerless to protect its members. It had been more or less cleaned up—jail terms and fines were meted out to gangsters and to Joe Schenck, the studio's bag man—but in 1945 and 1946 the IA (as it was generally referred to) became involved in a bitter jurisdictional dispute with another union, the Conference of Studio Unions, presided over by a man named Herbert

Sorrell. Basing his power in the studio painters union, of which he was president, he attempted to displace Brewer's IA as the lead labor organization among the industry's craft employees.

Sorrell was rumored to be a Communist, though this was never proved—except to Roy Brewer's satisfaction. But Sorrell was, indeed, a fiery and militant labor leader, and the 1945 strike he called, over which union, the CSU or the IA, should represent the studios' set decorators, was the most violent in Hollywood history. In a brutal confrontation at Warner Bros., heads were cracked and tear gas and fire hoses were used to break up picket lines. A second strike grew out of the first one. This time there was no violence, but the strike officially lasted until 1949, when it petered out in court cases, effectively ending CSU influence in Hollywood, but not Brewer's zealous commitment to anti-Communism, which these events inflamed.

Though he often championed New Deal causes, Brewer, along with the liberal attorney Martin Gang and the right-wing newspaper columnist George Skolsky, were the men suspected Communists went to in order to arrange clearances from studio blacklisting. His tone of voice was reasonable, his manner relaxed—Kazan observed that he was a formerly muscular man now running to fleshiness—but there was iron in his will. And, it must be admitted, a certain shrewdness in his intelligence.

He opened his meeting with Kazan, Cohn and Miller mildly by suggesting that *The Hook* really ought to make at least some reference to Communism. He thought perhaps a foreword to the film, mentioning the red threat to American unions, might be in order. Kazan quickly, shrewdly agreed; such forewords were often cut from the finished picture and when they did survive were generally unheeded by the audience. Brewer then went on to wonder if perhaps a reporter from the *People's World,* might approach Ferrarra with an offer of assistance that could be turned aside with some variant on the thought that honest American workers don't need help from the Commies. Miller muttered something about seeing what he might do along those lines, though his enthusiasm for the idea was obviously muted.

In Kazan's recollection Brewer at some point stated that surely Cohn did not want to make a picture that might be read as an implicit endorsement of Harry Bridges, latterly proved to be a Communist, but then a man with fearsome power over the West Coast docks, which he repeatedly tied up with vicious strikes. His career proved, at least to Brewer's satisfaction, that "The great problem in the unions is the Communist. The racketeers are much less a menace to labor than the Communists."

At best, that's a dubious statement. To be sure, racketeers were now a more omnipresent threat to dockworkers than the Communists. On the other hand, Communist-led unions represented about a quarter of all CIO members (1,370,000 workers) controlling about eighteen unions, among them the United Electrical Radio and Machine Workers and the Mine, Mill and Smelter's union (subject of the 1954 Communist-supported strike film, *Salt of the Earth,* which, on orders from Brewer, IA projectionists across the country refused to show).

But Brewer was only mildly interested in turning *The Hook* into anti-Communist propaganda. He was well connected to the FBI among others, probably knew of Miller's ALP friendships and may have been offering his ridiculous story suggestions as a way of testing Miller's current sentiments. And as a way of terrifying the playwright. In this, Brewer succeeded spectacularly.

There is nothing in Miller's script that could possibly be construed as supporting Communism, though we may infer that its antiracketeering stance alone would have been enough to alarm Brewer, heading a union lately rife with goons. But that's an all too innocent reading of this discussion, which broke up with Cohn still pressing Brewer for approval of *The Hook* and the union leader being evasive about it. He said he wanted to talk to AFL leadership about the script. But he added, menacingly, "If you plan to make the picture, make it," Kazan recalled. This no one at the meeting understood as encouragement; Brewer was reserving the right to attack the film later, possibly even mount a boycott against it.

As late as 2003, Roy Brewer, responding to an article in the *Los Angeles Times* about a television documentary tracing the Miller-Kazan relationship, wrote that the piece's implication that the FBI was responsible for stopping production on *The Hook* was untrue. He would take the credit for that, thank you. In his letter Brewer claimed "he wasn't against" exposing union corruption, but he was

"certain that the script's negative depiction of New York longshoremen would be exploited by the Communist Party." He recalled
Miller offering to have his hero be accused of being a Communist
and denying it. Not illogically, Brewer countered by saying that's just
what a Communist would do and he ended his letter this way:
"Miller has said that nothing in his life was ever written to follow a
line, but my experience with him in Hollywood more than 50 years
ago didn't make it seem that way."

Essentially, everyone is discussing not what was said at the meeting, but what was left unsaid—the implicit threat to expose Miller's
Communist connections. Which worked. Miller decamped for the
East the very next day, even though Cohn had not yet withdrawn from
the project and even though a budget meeting, for which Kazan prepared figures, remained on the schedule. Kazan knew what all movie
veterans know, that if you can get the studio to start spending real
money on a project it becomes infinitely more difficult to cancel. He
also knew that Harry Cohn was a genuinely tough guy. At the 1947
Waldorf conference of studio chieftains at which, after the Hollywood
Ten hearings, the studios agreed to blacklist known Communists, he
(along with the redoubtable Samuel Goldwyn) is said to have been the
most notable holdout against corporate cowardice; no outsider was
going to tell him how to run his studio.

A little later Kazan received some new pages from Miller, together
with a promise that he would soon write something that addressed
Brewer's concerns. Mostly, though, his cover letter concerned itself
with "Miss Baur" and his longing for her.

So Kazan forged ahead. He was actually in his budget meeting
when he received a phone call from Miller, telling him that he was
withdrawing the script, thereby collapsing the "huge edifice of
hope" Kazan had erected around their project (he had given up the
chance to direct Tennessee Williams's *The Rose Tattoo* to do this
film). He tried to keep *The Hook* alive at the studio, but he soon received a wire from the playwright telling him that Brewer (or someone) had informed the government about the script and Miller's
reluctance to revise it, and that official inquiries about his and
Kazan's political beliefs were being made. In this climate, "we'd have
no way of defending ourselves," he told Kazan.

Kazan didn't much care. He was convinced that it was only a matter of time before he would be testifying about his politics before some governmental body. I think he assumed that Miller, as a man of the left, was operating under the same threat.

Kazan had one last meeting with Cohn about the project and found the executive in full cry. "I knew it," he told Kazan. "Miller is a Communist." Kazan demurred. "Then tell me what other explanation there could be for what he did? First, he can't face any more questions. Second, he sees that the movie will not say what he hoped it would say. It all figures. I could tell just by looking at him, he's still one of them." Well then, asked Kazan, what about me? "You're just a good-hearted whore like me," Cohn laughed. "We'll find something else to do together." Which, soon enough, they would. Cohn, however, sent a telegram to Miller. It read: "ITS INTERESTING HOW THE MINUTE WE TRY TO MAKE THE SCRIPT PRO-AMERICAN YOU PULL OUT. HARRY COHN."

As late as 1988, when he published his autobiography, Kazan was still insisting that despite their closeness he and Miller had at this time never discussed politics, except in the most general terms. This seems to me improbable. But even if it is true, there is a strong possibility that Kazan had long since guessed that Miller was, or had been, a Communist, or at least a close sympathizer. The party often preferred that prominent artists and intellectuals avoid formal membership; it granted them a useful "objectivity" when they spoke out on the issues of the day.

I base this belief largely on circumstantial evidence. For one thing, despite his dismay at Kazan's "naming names" testimony, and the long breach it caused in their relationship, Miller never publicly criticized Kazan's behavior. He merely sorrowed over it. Gottfried speculates that a deal might have been struck between them; Kazan would not discuss Miller's CP past, Miller would not criticize his former friend for testifying. If that's so, the deal has held until this day.

There is, for example, an incident that Gottfried makes much of. According to Kazan's autobiography, when he returned to New York after *The Hook* collapse, Molly told him of at least three "frantic" phone calls from Miller. This is the passage from *A Life* in which Kazan discusses their purport: "'They will ask me,' he [Miller] told

Molly, 'if I was a member of—' Then he stopped short, Molly said, and there was a pause before he completed the sentence. 'A member of the Waldorf Peace Conference,' Art continued, 'and I would have to say, "Yes, I was," and that would finish me.'" According to Kazan his wife tried to buck up his spirits, while concurring with him that this was not, perhaps, the ideal time to produce *The Hook* (which, incidentally, she did not much care for).

Gottfried judges this "a dastardly bit of smearing" for it implied that Miller started to say, or perhaps did say, "a member of the Communist Party." He correctly adds that being a member of the Waldorf Peace Conference would not have "finished" anyone. The conference, held in 1949, briefly attempting to revive the Popular Front spirit, was aimed at dissipating the gathering cold war mentality. It was supported by the Communists, though it also attracted many nonparty leftists from all over the world. In and of itself attendance at the conference proved nothing about anyone—except, perhaps, irresistible innocence. But Gottfried is right to smell a lie in Kazan's account. I think it more likely that he was still protecting Miller with this rather lame fiction. This would further imply that Kazan knew that his friend had been either a CP member or a very close fellow traveler and that Miller admitted as much to Molly. If this is so—and it is a presumption every bit as reasonable as Gottfried's—it renders this passage from Kazan's book far from being a smear but rather payment on a debt to friendship.

Finally, we come to a provable fact. When in 1956 Miller was hauled before HUAC (he had been denied a passport on the grounds of his allegedly subversive beliefs and this hearing was intended to determine whether he had actually been a party member), committee counsel produced an unsigned application (number 23345) to join the Communist Party, dated in 1943, made out to "A. Miller" and listing an address at which Miller lived. Asked if he recognized the countersigning name on the application, that of Sue Warren, Miller refused to admit knowing her as, throughout his ordeal, he refused to recognize any of the names the committee threw at him.

Miller became something of a hero of the left at that point. He was indicted for contempt of Congress—one reason being his refusal to name Arnaud d'Usseau (of *Deep Are the Roots*) as chairman of a Communist writers meeting he once attended. The following winter the case went to trial, but by early 1957 the worst of the anti-Communist hysteria was over. HUAC was by now largely a joke—unless by some mischance you happened to be caught in its death throes. Miller was judged guilty, given a one-year suspended sentence (later reduced to a month suspended) and a $500 fine, which judgment was overturned on appeal.

We do not know if the lack of a signature on Miller's party application was an oversight or a deliberate attempt to avoid public proclamation of his beliefs, but it is a matter of indifference to me. I, of course, believe that by endorsing Stalinism one was endorsing tyranny. But, at the same time, I do not believe Communist artists and intellectuals did any concrete harm. They were not spies; they only favored a conspiratorial organization that also mounted a serious espionage threat. It is important to maintain that distinction. Arthur Miller was no Alger Hiss.

Yet I also cannot help but think there was something scuttling in Miller's behavior at this time. In supinely withdrawing *The Hook* without waging a fight for it he was denying his beliefs. Moreover, I think his accounts of the *Amerasia* matter and of his dockside friendships are self-serving lies of omission sustained well past the need for them. By 1987, when he published *Timebends,* full forthrightness on these matters was, I think, required of such a widely respected figure. I hold the admittedly peculiar opinion that we are often justified when we lie under oath, if that's what's needed to save ourselves from the law's mysterious toils, but that our obligation to history, exercised when we are not under oath, requires absolute integrity.

Miller and Kazan continued to correspond and Kazan continued to see "Miss Baur" from time to time. But his major preoccupations were elsewhere. There was, for instance, the business about *Streetcar* drawing laughter at a Santa Monica sneak preview. People had snickered at Blanche's desperation, and Charlie Feldman, who had a lot of his own money in the film, briefly panicked. Kazan, however, was unworried. Most of the problems centered on the little sequence where Blanche comes on to a young newsboy who rings the Kowalskis' bell to collect subscription money. In the sequence Blanche's neediness was too obvious. Kazan easily fixed that by eliminating most of the boy's discomfited (and discomfiting) reaction shots. In his final cut he is made to seem almost a figment of Blanche's feverish imagination.

Much more stirring to Kazan was the fact that *Viva Zapata!* was at last going to be made. This moment had been a long time coming. Kazan himself has said that he was drawn to Zapata's story as early as 1935, when he heard it on his first brief visit to Mexico, and that he had begun making notes on the project as early as 1943, drawn particularly to the notion of a successful revolutionary giving up power and attempting to return his revolution to its sources, the angry and exploited people. John Steinbeck, who had spent considerable time in Mexico, working on films—*The Forgotten Village* (a documentary) and *The Pearl,* a drama released in 1947—was also drawn to Zapata's story in the 1940s. In a letter written from Mexico in 1945 he talks about an offer from a small company to write a Zapata script and his interest in so doing. At that time his second wife, Gwyn, did research for him in the national library, and Steinbeck sketched a story outline. In the next few years Zapata remained on his mind, and in that period he and Kazan discovered this shared interest. Steinbeck began work on a speculative script for Kazan, who eventually obtained a development deal with Zanuck that paid Steinbeck $20,000 for the first draft and promised him another $75,000 for an acceptable final draft.

The film they eventually made is said, in some filmographies, to be based on a book, *Zapata the Unconquerable,* by one Edgecomb Pinchon, which had, in the 1930s, been acquired by MGM around the time it made its risible *Viva Villa!* Indeed, it was on an adaptation of this property that the Communist screenwriter Lester Cole was working when he was served his subpoena to testify before HUAC in 1947. The slightly loopy thought behind it was that agreeable Ricardo Montalban might be right for the lead in a heavily romanticized version of Zapata's life.

Rights to this book were at some point acquired by Fox, probably because the studio, as they often do, wanted, for legal reasons, an "underlying property" on which to base its film. There is, however, no evidence that Steinbeck or Kazan ever read the Pinchon book, and it is not accorded any credit on the finished film. According to his sympathetic biographer, Jay Parini, Steinbeck researched this project intensively once Zanuck's interest was secured; he spent weeks in the library while also pursuing interviews with old-timers who had either known Zapata or at least knew something about Mexico during his time. He also had before him a long memo from Kazan, summarizing his own views of Zapata, which included an analogy between him and Abraham Lincoln that seems rather strained. This material stirred Steinbeck to write a long essay summarizing his view of Zapata's psychology and of the tumultuous era in Mexican history that shaped him.

In this period Steinbeck's own life was tumultuous. He was engaged in a messy divorce, was in poor health, was concerned about his own career, which was in something of a trough—the distinguished early works behind him, the monumental and best-selling *East of Eden* a few years ahead—and beginning to court Elaine Scott, still married to the actor Zachary Scott. But he forged ahead, eventually delivering a first-draft screenplay, which was, at two hundred pages, more than one-third longer than the customary length. Zanuck assigned Jules Buck, a reliable screenwriting veteran, to assist Steinbeck on the next draft. The two men got along well and in a few weeks, with Steinbeck dictating into a machine and Buck rewriting his words, they created a draft both Zanuck and Kazan thought could be shaped into a shooting script.

It was this manuscript that Kazan, Steinbeck and Zanuck discussed at length during a long weekend largely devoted to croquet (at that time a passion of the producer) at his Palm Springs home in spring 1950. Kazan emerged from these confabulations guessing Zanuck saw the film as a sort of upscale Western—especially if whoever played Zapata could be induced to ride a totemic white horse, for which the studio boss had large symbolic plans. That horse, emblematic of Zapata's undying, unconquerable spirit, would survive the assassinated revolutionist and provide the movie an upbeat ending; they might kill the man, but they could not kill his spirit. The

horse is seen, in the film's last shots, roaming the mountains unteth-
ered. Kazan thought it unbearably corny—a Hollywood ending, if
ever there was one—but there it is, for all time, in his movie.

After the Palm Springs meeting, Kazan and Steinbeck returned
to New York, where they put in an intense two months on the script,
Kazan sitting at the typewriter, asking Steinbeck for new or revised
dialogue, giving his editorial comments, then typing what they
agreed on into a script that was eventually 128 pages long. This
close, almost daily collaboration was a kind of consummation for
Kazan. He was finally co-writing with a writer of high stature.

As they worked, the two men became more certain than ever
that their film had to be made in Mexico, and they resolved to revisit
that country—to scout locations in Morelos and to secure technical
personnel from the Mexican film industry. Thus it was, in May 1950,
that Kazan, Steinbeck and Elaine Scott found themselves in Cuer-
navaca at the Hotel Marik, awaiting a visit from Gabriel Figueroa,
Mexico's leading cinematographer, who was also president of the
Syndicate of Film Technicians and Workers—therefore vital to their
attempt to secure local cooperation with their film.

Figueroa had studied with Gregg Toland in Hollywood and then
achieved near-legendary status working with, among others, Luis
Bunuel and Emilio Fernandez (and, once, even with John Ford).
Kazan did not much like his work—too filtered, too dark, too sentimental in its views of peasant life. But with his sublime belief that he
could manipulate anyone and everyone into supporting his vision of
anything, Kazan was prepared to overlook what he saw as Figueroa's
artistic deficiencies.

But the minute he and Steinbeck mentioned Zapata, a cloud
passed over the cameraman's face. The man was as close to a saint as
anyone Mexican politics had ever produced, he said. It was shameful
that no film had ever been made about him in his native land. But . . .
for his story to be told by gringos, with, doubtless, an American actor
playing the role? This would require much thought. He requested a
copy of the screenplay. It was given to him, and he promised to read it
over the weekend and return.

Kazan thought they might be in trouble. He had heard that the
film workers union was Communist-dominated. He would later claim

that he spent some of the weekend telling Steinbeck anti-Communist tales. He said he spoke about his old Yale pal, Albert Maltz, who in 1946 had written an essay, famous in leftist circles, in *New Masses,* in which he decried the party's insistence that art must always be a class warfare weapon, that creative works must always be judged *"primarily* by their adherence to formal ideology." At a party meeting—held, incidentally, at the home of Kazan's old Group nemesis, Morris Carnovsky—he was so viciously criticized that he wrote a second article recanting his previous views in rather crawling terms. Kazan also claimed to have mentioned Budd Schulberg—whom he had not yet met—in these conversations. It is possible he had heard of the writer's run-in with his Communist colleagues when he refused to ask their permission to turn one of his short stories into his famous Hollywood novel, *What Makes Sammy Run?* Later, after it was published (and became a best-seller), he refused to apologize for it to the party (mostly, it seems, because he failed to mention class issues in Marxist terms or, indeed, to more than casually acknowledge the party's role in the prewar formation of the Writers Guild). The result was that he resigned from the party and later unapologetically named names to HUAC.

Steinbeck was more optimistic. He mentioned the word *"mordida"* (meaning bribes) and suggested that leftist objections to their *Zapata* script might be dissolved by a generous, judicious application of under-the-table money. About this, he was wrong. Figueroa returned on Monday, accompanied by a silent union functionary, to tell Steinbeck and Kazan that the script was unacceptable. It would have to be extensively reworked and then vetted by Mexican government censors to make sure it matched local hagiography.

Now Steinbeck said, "I smell the party line" and told Kazan that he'd be willing to write a fake script for the censors to approve. After that, they'd go ahead and make their film as originally intended. Kazan liked this idea, but back in Hollywood tough Darryl Zanuck, convinced the project was being victimized by Communists, ordered Kazan to scout locations in Texas, where no one would interfere with them politically.

The exchange with Figueroa and his friend was first publicly reported in a letter to the editor of the *Saturday Review of Literature,* in which Kazan responded to a particularly idiotic review of his film by the critic Hollis Alpert. This was Kazan's first public acknowledgment of his anti-Communism, and his comments on the incident are more detailed than they are in his autobiography. He and Steinbeck were attacked, he wrote, for including things they knew to be true about Zapata—that he "had a measure of Spanish blood and was proud of it," his acceptance of a very proper Spanish-style courtship and marriage, his vanity about dress and uniform, his indecision about taking up arms. Above all, Kazan wrote, the Mexicans "attacked with sarcastic fury our emphasis on his refusal to take power."

This was the crux of the matter, and it survived further tinkering with the script, which had a fairly straightforward three-act structure. In the first act, as Kazan indicated, Zapata comes slowly, out of increasing disgust with the cruelty of Porfirio Díaz's thirty-five-year regime, to his revolutionary stance, participates in Díaz's defeat, then lays down his arms; in the second act, he returns to battle when Díaz's successor, the weak-willed liberal Francisco Madero, proves almost equally indifferent to the needs of the peasants; in the final act he is named president of the republic, but then leaves office—in fact he and Pancho Villa were removed from power by the most successful of the revolutionists, Venustiano Carranza—after which he took up arms against Carranza, whose forces killed him in an ambush in 1919.

Insisting that alone of the world's great revolutionaries, Zapata refused formal power in a postrevolutionary government, the script also insists that only if the people themselves retain power can a revolution be regarded as successful; otherwise, it is just a matter of replacing one form of tyranny with another.

In his letter Kazan added: "By showing that Zapata did this, we spoiled a poster figure that the Communists have been at some pains to create." But, he went on to say, "Whenever the Communists stake a claim to any concept or person the people value, the overanxious Right plays into their hands . . . If they would treat the Communist claim to peace, to free speech—and to men like Zapata—with the same good sense that greets the Communist claim to the bicycle, it would make life easier for those of us who value those things."

Since there was, of course, "no such thing as a Communist Party at the time and place Zapata fought," Kazan said that he and Steinbeck imputed to their hero a purity of motive far beyond the ordinary understanding of the Left or the Right. "In his moment of decision, this taciturn, untaught leader must have felt, freshly and deeply, the impact of the ancient law: Power corrupts. And so he refused power." Kazan's letter may have been self-serving, since it was published just five days before his HUAC testimony. But it's also fair to say that Kazan had arrived at his principled anti-Communism years earlier. We can also say that at some point between their meeting with Figueroa in May 1950 and the beginning of production on *Viva Zapata!* in the spring of 1951, Steinbeck and Kazan either invented or more lengthily developed the character of Fernando, played (rather broadly) in the film by Joseph Wiseman, who is—no question about it—a premature Stalinist.

He first appears, a portable typewriter strapped to his belt, in the mountains where Zapata and his brother, Eufemio (Anthony Quinn), early in their revolutionary careers, are hiding out. Fernando has at this time attached himself to Madero (as he will subsequently attach himself to other revolutionary leaders, his eye always on the main chance). Eufemio, who instinctively wants to shoot Fernando, wonders why Madero is conducting his revolution from a safe haven on the other side of the American border. But Zapata instructs a friend to accompany Fernando northward, to gaze directly into Madero's face, to test the honorableness of his convictions. He returns, sometime later, with a favorable report. Thereafter Fernando is to be found lurking about Zapata's camps, amoral and bloodthirsty, urging Zapata to seize dictatorial power.

Indeed—and this is a point no critic seems to have made about *Viva Zapata!*—the Mexican revolution becomes in this film a rough analogue to the Russian revolution. Madero is the Kerensky figure, an impotent liberal who cannot master the rising revolutionary tide. Zapata himself becomes the Trotsky figure, not quite the intellectual he was, but assuredly the revolution's great military leader, as Trotsky was in Russia. The film lacks a fully-developed Lenin figure (probably the ruthless Carranza would qualify, but he is not a major character) and we don't see Fernando emerge, Stalin-like, from the shadows to take over. But still, it is hard to miss the film's historical analogies.

The location Kazan finally settled on was Roma, Texas, near the Rio Grande border with Mexico, with some additional shooting later at the Fox ranch near Malibu. It was the first time he shot in open country, Ford country, if you will, "with no sets and using the environment around me and I was very happy with that."

He liked his cast as well, a mixture of New York and Hollywood actors, with Marlon Brando in the title role. And a joy to Kazan, if not necessarily to Zanuck. Kazan had shot a test in which Brando partnered Julie Harris, whom Kazan wanted to use in the picture. He mumbled, naturally, as he always did when he was uncommitted to the role and Zanuck focused on him rather than Harris—to the point where he was insisting Kazan not use him in *Zapata*. The director calmed the producer down, Brando kept the role and was very good in it.

He wore fairly heavy makeup—besides a mustache, his skin color was darkened and invisible tape was applied to flare his nostrils and impart a slight slant to his eyes suggesting Zapata's Indian heritage. There were critics who felt he looked more Oriental than Indian, but he actually achieved quite a good resemblance to Zapata as he was later portrayed by the Mexican muralists. He was also, from time to time, a little mumbly, but mostly to good effect; Zapata was not, after all, an articulate man.

In the end Kazan judged him "remarkable" in the part; still, I think, the most authentic third-world revolutionist an American movie ever put on screen. "What I said to him," Kazan later recalled, "was, 'you have to think like a peasant.' I said, 'You're not impressed with anything. . . . You don't fall in love with anybody. You use women. You don't have any other interests in life except the hardships that have forced you to take this action—this series of actions. . . . It's not a romance . . . and you're not a hero. You're just a guy that's suppressed and you're talking back.'"

That's a good characterization of Brando's performance, although there are other elements in it that bear mentioning. There's a watchful shrewdness about him as he judges the many people seeking to use his growing status as a revolutionary legend for their own ends. There is also, sometimes, something sweetly yearning about him, especially when he is courting Josefa, played by Jean Peters (who was pretty and effective as Zapata's highborn wife, but more famous for keeping company with, and later marrying, Howard Hughes).

He is at first arrogant and cocksure with her (that's what she likes about him, though she pretends otherwise), and even brutal with her merchant father, who makes the mistake of sneering at his humble birth. But then he goes through a courtship ritual with her—they are obliged to exchange an endless series of aphorisms in front of his family in which his sobriety, earnestness and discomfort are played to moderate comic effect (the scene goes on too long). Much better is their wedding night, where after their first sexual encounter Zapata confesses his inability to read and begs her to teach him (which she immediately starts doing). Kazan later said he thought the scene too romantic, but I disagree. Brando is touching in it without loss either of soulfulness or of machismo.

But the most important coloration of his character is his hair-trigger temper. When a peasant is being led off to jail with a rope around his neck, when others break into a field that has been taken from them and are ridden down by horsemen from the hacienda, when a groom beats a child so hungry he is eating oats from a horse's stall, the sudden flare of Zapata's response is hot and commanding.

"The thing about Brando," Kazan later said, "was that I'd make these directions . . . and about halfway through he'd say to himself, 'Oh, shit, I know all that.' And he'd walk away. And I'd say to myself, 'Where's the bastard walking away to? Where's he going.' But that was something good. He'd heard enough. . . . The thing he wanted from a director, from me, was . . . to get the machine going. And once that machine was going he didn't need a hell of a lot more."

Brando was more measured in his appraisal of his work. A few years later he said, "Zapata was a hard characterization, which I don't think I fulfilled. It was a good workout." It was perhaps more than that for Anthony Quinn, playing his brother and eventually winning an Academy Award for his portrayal. At that point the actor, born of a Mexican mother and an Irish father, had been long in the movies, mostly as a sort of all-purpose exotic, generally of the roughneck subset, but he had not yet settled into the annoying testosterone-driven earthiness of his later years. He had spent some time at the Actors Studio and had, in fact, been one of Brando's replacements as Stanley Kowalski, so he was up for seriousness and a measure of restraint here, and both Kazan and Brando liked him.

According to Kazan, the two actors became buddies, going riding and swimming together, enjoying a relationship not untouched
by rivalry, but essentially good-natured. According to Brando, Kazan
drove a wedge between them, telling each that the other had been
saying unflattering things when his back was turned. Probably both
were right. Early in the film they were supposed to be mutually supportive; later Quinn's Eufemio succumbs to drink and corruption
and they turn bitterly against each other. That was just the kind of
situation in which Kazan liked to stir real-life acrimony to create the
fictional emotions he wanted.

But Kazan was voluble in his praise of Quinn's work, and of his
other contributions to the film's realism. He spoke particularly of a
sequence in which Zapata is arrested for his early revolutionary activities and is being led away with a noose around his neck. Watching,
the peasant women of his village begin clicking rocks together—
more and more of them, until it becomes a sub-verbal protest. That,
said Kazan, was Quinn's idea. "I'm not that good. I don't know Mexico that well. Tony got that and gave it to me and I've always been
grateful . . . I thought he was—I still think he is—a wonderful actor."

Quinn responded in kind. In a newspaper interview, given right
after the film wrapped, he spoke of his previous experiences in pictures, when he was given only a "cursory" knowledge of his characters
and, essentially, said the lines and moved through the scenes pretty
much as the director ordered. "They have no inner assurance. . . . They
are entirely objective . . . and therefore often superficial." With Kazan
it was different. "When Gadge directs a scene he is quite likely to say
to you, 'What would you do under these circumstances . . . ?' He wants
the actor to know and feel what he's doing, not just to be . . . a robot."

In short, *Viva Zapata!* was, for the actors, a typical Kazan love
fest. It is, as well, a handsome film, at least a partial fulfillment of his
ambition to make a picture on something like an epic scale. Yet, in
its immediate aftermath, the director was somewhat disappointed by
it. He would remember telling Arthur Miller that it was, for him,
"another 'almost'"—not quite the movie he had optimistically imagined and worked so hard, over so many years, to realize.

The thing we can imagine Kazan most unhappy about is the

somewhat truncated quality of its spectacle. Zanuck had cut the film's budget, and the result was that most of the battle sequences end too quickly. They lack build-up, detail and triumphant release. There were also sequences that showed Zapata being casually unfaithful to his wife that did not survive to the final cut, though possibly that was more a matter of morality than money. And Zapata's on-again, off-again relationship with armed rebellion, particularly at the film's end, feels rushed, not fully worked out.

Finally the films suffers the endemic problem of biopics; they are always, to some degree, anachronistic, imposing current ideas on past events. In his notes, Kazan shows how he visualized the point he most wanted to make, the one about using the revolution to empower the people, not using it to further exploit them. There are two matching scenes in the film, one early, the other late. In the first a delegation of peasants, Zapata among them, visits the Mexican president, Porfirio Díaz, to protest the land grabs of the *hidalgos*. They appear in his vast office, reluctant to speak, a sort of huddled mass, grouped tightly together for mutual support. Toward the end of the film, when Zapata is briefly in power, a similar group appears before him, voicing a similar complaint. This time, though, Kazan groups them more loosely. They are, as he wrote, "distinct, separate and proud individuals . . . They are younger, too . . . a young new race."

Do we fully believe this transformation? We want to. But we also know that Steinbeck and Kazan are making a point aimed at the 1950s audience, attuned to cold war politics and betrayed revolutions. *Viva Zapata!* is the only American film to advance a reasonably sophisticated anti-Communist argument; it bears not the slightest resemblance to other cold war films (*I Chose Freedom, I Was a Communist for the FBI*, etc.), which are to the movies what McCarthyism was to politics—crude, simple-minded, hysterical. But still, contemporary ideology is an imposition on this story and on the character of Emiliano Zapata. When, toward the end of the picture he tells his followers, "A strong people doesn't need a strong leader. Strong leaders make a weak people," we don't hear a peasant speaking; we hear well-meaning Yankee ventriloquism. Indeed, throughout the film there is often something overripe in Steinbeck's dialogue, something a little too self-conscious—"the people, *si!*"—in its diction.

Still, the film does contain some extraordinary moments. One thinks, for example, of the death of the liberal Madero, played with much anxious hand rubbing by Harold Gordon. He's a poseur, a temporizer, a man of words, not action. Placed under house arrest and stripped of his presidental powers by General Huerta (in Frank Silvera's portrayal a very menacing crypto-fascist, silent and brutally knowing behind his tinted glasses), he seeks a meeting with Huerta. One rainy night he gets his wish. He is driven to a blind alley, steps out of the car mystified by his surroundings. And confronts a squad of soldiers who, he realizes too late, are his assassins. It is an extremely powerful scene, among Kazan's best in its vein.

Then there is the moment Zapata renounces power. It comes after his meeting with the supplicant peasants. He and Fernando retreat to an inner office, where Zapata begins to empty his desk and don pistol and bandoleer. "In the name of all we've fought for, don't go," cries the professional revolutionary. "In the name of all we've fought for, I must," Zapata answers. Heading for the door—it's a very well-managed shot—Brando cries: "Now I know you . . . No fields, no farm, no wife, no woman, no friends, no love. You only destroy . . ." In other words, he is a rootless revolutionary, his passion ungrounded in all the things a true man of the people is willing to fight and die for. Zapata correctly predicts that he will go to other corrupt revolutionists—to anyone who seeks pure power, not pure reform.

Finally, there is the film's conclusion to consider. Zapata and his wife have literally taken to the hills with their little band of purists, continuing their fight against revolution's corrupters. They have been betrayed at least once. But now word is brought that the commander of a *federales* garrison is willing to join them—and turn over a rich cache of arms. A trap is suspected. Yet the man has passed every test of his intentions. Zapata is suspicious (and his wife is movingly convinced that he is doomed), but, by now a weary revolutionary, he is willing to surrender to his fate. He enters the fort alone, riding past a trove of stacked arms. His white stallion, long ago lost, awaits him. So does the officer who is about to betray him. Even

Fernando is glimpsed lurking in the shadows. Now a troop of soldiers arises from behind the battlements where they have been hiding. A fusillade of rifle shots tears into Zapata, ripping into his clothing. He is on his knees, twitching—by the standards of the time, it is quite a horrific end.

It is a sequence of great power. And the coda is good, too. Zapata's body is unceremoniously dumped on the well in his native town's square. Some of his loyalists gather around and begin whispering. Who are they trying to fool. This is not Zapata. He is alive, in the hills. He will return someday. Cut to the stallion, free and rearing in the mountain fastness.

In later years, Kazan came to feel that audiences learned to "respect it more—they feel more about it" than they did on its initial release. This, he said in 1990, is because they had grown more conscious of the failure of so many revolutions. "The notion that a revolution is not people just singing about it" had begun to dawn on them, he thought. His film, he came to think, did realize its largest ambition, which was "a rejection of a certain way of thinking . . . a rejection of over-facile, over-rigid, inhuman ways of saying the world must change."

The crucial elements of the Fernando character, in particular, Kazan came to feel very good about. "Everything about him was like the people I used to know in the Communist Party, where they had all the answers. We, including me, had the answers to everything and the answers didn't turn out to be valid or something we finally respected." At the same time he felt that the film's counterrevolutionary characters "also rejected . . . a kind of anti-Communism that McCarthy represented." Even as "the desire for change . . . went down, even as it died, [it] left behind a living desire for it. And that living desire is the film."

Viva Zapata! is, then, both a success and a failure. Shadowed by greatness—certainly in its ambitions, in some of its acting, some of its visual power—it does not quite achieve it. Yet it remains Kazan's most overtly ideological movie, the one in which he most openly stated the political ideas, and ideals, he would go on worrying for the rest of his life.

In the summer of 1951, when he wrapped the picture, Kazan learned that *Streetcar* was in further trouble with the censors; Darryl Zanuck had hinted much earlier that this might be so. During a preproduction meeting about *Zapata*, he asked Kazan if he was having problems with the picture. No, Kazan said, the Breen office had signed off on it. "We pay those guys," Zanuck said. "They're there to help us get pictures done, not prevent us." Another way of putting this was that the Breen office served as mediator between the studios and the Catholic Legion of Decency. Its rating was still to come and if it was C (for "condemned"), that would effectively kill the picture, because the majority of Catholics annually took a pledge in church not to attend movies the Legion so rated. In a couple of years the Legion would be revealed to be a paper tiger when the C-rated *The Moon Is Blue* became a box office hit, but even now Kazan professed himself unworried; it would be distinctly odd for the Legion to pursue a film once the Breen office had passed it. Besides, Jack Warner had promised him, with a handshake, that there would be no more cuts in *Streetcar*. But Kazan caught a skeptical look on Zanuck's face and began to fret.

Now, as Kazan was returning from the *Zapata* shoot, his concern increased when a scheduled booking of *Streetcar* at Radio City Music Hall was suddenly canceled. Then he learned that his editor, David Weisbart, was in New York, as was the producer, Charlie Feldman. He finally wormed from the former the news that he was trying to reedit the picture to conform to Legion demands. Soon enough Kazan himself was in the East—and meeting with Martin Quigley, Catholicism's most powerful voice in the movies. A publisher of motion picture trade journals, Quigley had invented the movie's production code—it had been written by a Catholic priest to his specifications—and he had appointed Joe Breen as its administrator. Mostly he kept his hands off Breen's day-to-day work. But not always. And not this time. He was, among other things, aware that Tennessee Williams was a lapsed Catholic and he apparently believed that *Streetcar* was a deliberate subversion of the writer's former faith and morals.

Or rather, as he put it to Kazan when they met, of "the long-prevailing standards of morality of the Western world . . ." Over and over at their meetings, according to Kazan, he insisted on "the pre-eminence of the moral order over artistic considerations." He was a fleshy, serenely self-confident man, not the least concerned, according to Kazan, with the fact that he was imposing the morality of a religious minority (many of whose adherents, incidentally, did not agree with him, either) on the American majority. Indeed, Quigley was convinced that he had "saved" the picture for Warner Bros., insisting he had intervened with the Legion's chief censor to protect it from still deeper cuts. Of course, Warner's had the option of taking the film out with a C rating. But then there were the Catholic War Veterans to consider; they might be induced to picket theaters. And there was the possibility of a boycott against all the studio's films.

Desperately, Kazan asked if his cut and the Legion's cut might not be played simultaneously, so the public could choose between them. He asked, too, that his uncensored version at least be allowed to play the Venice Film Festival, to which *Streetcar* had been invited. The answer of course, was no; if Kazan's version played anywhere in the world, even once, the C rating would be imposed.

No one stood up with him for the film. Feldman had washed his hands of it. Jack Warner was simply pleased that he had a releasable movie, no matter what form it took. So it went forth—about four minutes shorter than it had been. And received glowing notices. Even Bosley Crowther, himself a Catholic layman, though of a liberal stripe, liked it. He thought it perhaps "as fine, if not finer than the play." Like every other reviewer, he did not notice—or perhaps care about—the cuts imposed on the film. And, in an odd way, Crowther and the rest were right. It's perfectly true that the specific actions of the play that caught the alarmed eyes of the censors are truncated. But the implications of those actions—even if we do not see them in full detail—are so warped into the fabric of the piece that we understood them fully. Later, in 1993, the four cut minutes were found in a warehouse and restored to the film, but as Kazan said to me at the time, "they don't really make any difference, do they?" In the largest sense, he was right; the movie is better for their restoration, but they do not cause us to make a major revaluation of it.

In 1951, however, Kazan continued smarting (and brooding) over the treatment of his film. When Crowther asked him for a comment on the cuts, he asked, instead, to write a piece about them, Molly did some rewriting on it and it appeared in the Sunday *Times* about a month after *Streetcar*'s New York opening. Mostly he rehearsed the facts just stated, but he did record his puzzlement at some of the excisions. For example, the close shots of Stella coming back to Stanley after their first fight were eliminated as "too carnal" (and they are, indeed, very sexy as the restored version shows us), even though her intention remains clear in the longer shots. Then, too, one of Stanley's lines, delivered just before he assaults Blanche, was removed: "You know, you might not be so bad to interfere with." This Kazan, argued, made it clear that the thought of raping Blanche occurred to him in the moment, that it was not an idea he had long harbored. He comments, correctly: "This obviously changes the interpretation of the character, though how it serves the cause of morality is obscure to me . . ."

His piece demonstrated just how niggling and absurd the censor's interventions were, and it also gave him the opportunity to vent his frustrations. But Darryl Zanuck, whom Kazan had consulted about the wisdom of writing this piece, predicted that its only practical result might be a slight uptick in sales. Which, as it happened, was not required. The box office "is breaking records," Kazan wrote in his last line and so it was. Grossing $4,250,000, the film was the fifth highest earner of 1951. It also went on to receive eight Academy Award nominations, winning in four categories (for Leigh, Malden, Hunter and the art director), with Kazan, much to Tennessee Williams's amusement, sliding lower in his chair as most of the biggest prizes (best picture, best actor, best director) eluded the film. In particular, this was a typical Hollywood slap at a bad boy outsider—Brando—who of all the film's stars was the most deserving of recognition.

But by the time the Oscars were handed out, on March 20, 1952, Elia Kazan had more pressing matters on his mind. He was within three weeks of testifying, in open session, as a friendly witness, before the House Committee on Un-American Activities. He was about to enter the realm of the permanently "controversial."

12

Testimonies

On January 14, 1952, Elia Kazan appeared at an executive session of a subcommittee of the House Committee on Un-American Activities and testified about his membership in the Communist Party fifteen to seventeen years previously. He spoke fully about his own membership in, and disillusionment with, the party, but refused, as "a matter of conscience," to name the others in his "unit." Kazan knew his testimony had not satisfied HUAC's curiosity, and that sooner or later he would either have to give up some names, take the Fifth Amendment or flatly refuse to name names. He understood that if he took either of the last two courses his career as a movie director would be finished for the foreseeable future, although he might be able to continue directing in the theater.

Which, for the moment, after a hiatus of three years, he had resumed doing. At the time of his closed testimony he was rehearsing, again under Irene Selznick's management, a play by George Tabori, a Hungarian-born novelist, playwright and screenwriter, called *Flight into Egypt.* It was about a Viennese couple, Franz and Lili Engel (Paul Lukas and Gusti Huber, an Austrian actress making her American debut), trying to make their way to America. Accompanied by their twelve-year-old son, they are stuck, impoverished, in a Cairo hotel, awaiting a visa. Franz is ill—the result of an injury sustained in a concentration camp—and in what most reviewers thought was the play's best scene, he wills himself to rise from his wheelchair and walk across the room to prove his fitness for the visa to an American consular official. His ploy does not work. His wife gives herself to an evil, crippled doctor to get money and, at the end of the play, Franz kills himself, thus freeing his family to continue their journey "away from smallness and oldness and the guns."

One can see why the play attracted Kazan. The notion of America as a shining ideal, the great destination for would-be immigrants, would become one of his great themes, the subject of his novel and film, *America, America,* as well as a powerful motif in at least three of his other novels. The piece drew on Tabori's own experiences as an émigré and so had a certain heartfelt authenticity about it. On the other hand, it was dramatically quite conventional, no more than an exotically set problem play with predictable melodramatic beats. The critics, mindful that Selznick and Kazan had last given them *Streetcar,* were inclined to be kindly to *Flight into Egypt* when it opened on March 20. They were respectful of its intentions, paid tribute to its good acting—they particularly liked Huber—but thought the drama did not quite plunge them into the felt life of its characters. In general, their reviews might be characterized as "unmoved" and the play ran for only forty-six performances.

Selznick, in her memoirs, accuses Kazan of softening the play and attributes this to his HUAC problems. He had come to her in December, confessed his former Communist Party membership and said that he would soon be compelled to testify. He assured her he would not give up any names, and induced her to read the left-wing press (including the *Daily Worker*), which he said exactly represented his views on the committee. But Selznick also observed that he brought Molly along to their first meeting and that she accompanied him on the play's tryout run in Boston. He said to her that Molly would see to it that the play would be "politically safe." This, Selznick later wrote, puzzled her. She did not see anything controversial in Tabori's work. But Molly remained a presence throughout this production and Selznick implies, encouraged the weakening rewrites Kazan insisted upon. It is hard to know, absent variant drafts of the play, if this is so. It is possible that at some point *Flight* showed its protagonists as more left-leaning than the final version did. All we know for certain is that Molly Kazan, the dangerously unproduced playwright, was more fiercely ideological—and intellectual—than her husband was.

A person who was close to the elder Kazans thinks she was perhaps, by objective standards, more intelligent than her husband, "By which I mean, simply, if you had to take a test in terms of vocabulary or analytic ability, hers was superior to his. So he was always just slightly one down, which he didn't like." On the other hand, "she had a problem, because . . . the critical part of her brain was overdeveloped and the creative part of her brain was overwhelmed by the critical part." Several witnesses remember that when she was writing she would do a number of pages, hit a wall, and then feel she had to start again from the beginning. When that didn't work, she would play endless games of solitaire. There was one aspect of his intelligence that was clearly superior to hers, to almost anyone's: that was in the realm of "emotional intelligence." He had a gift for reading people—their needs, their hidden motives, their unspoken desires—and for manipulating them, often without their quite realizing what was going on, that amounted to a genius. One suspects that he was unable to deploy this gift on tough-minded Molly as easily as he did on, say, an aspiring actor.

Nonetheless, in these circumstances, she became, if anything, more abrupt in her opinions—particularly her political opinions. In this period, for example, Arthur Miller appeared at their door, excited about a book he had just read about the Salem witch hunts. He was convinced that the parallels between the search for people possessed by the devil in seventeenth-century New England and the search for secret Communists in twentieth-century America was clear and powerful and he would, indeed, write *The Crucible* to make that point. Molly observed to him that witches had not, in fact, ever existed, whereas Communists really did.

This portrait of a passionately critical intellectual must, however, be tempered by the portrait all her children offer, of a warm and caring mother. "She was always interruptible," her daughter, Judy, recalls. She remembers Molly getting up at five in the morning to pursue her writing, before the rest of the household awakened. She remembers, too, a "squirrel shelf," where she stashed little gifts for the kids which she would present to them when they were sick or discouraged about something. Beyond that, she presided serenely over a cheerful, even boisterous, household, with show folks constantly dropping in for meals and conversations—about the work they were doing, the ideas

they were entertaining—in which the children were unself-consciously
included. Molly and the children were often present on Kazan's movie
locations. Kate Kazan, for example, happily recalls riding a burro
around on the *Zapata* set in New Mexico. Kazan would later apologize
to Judy for being so frequently absent from the family's life, but she always remembered that when he was present she and her siblings received a great deal of undivided attention.

At this particular moment, Molly was by no means the only individual asserting influence on Kazan. The people at Fox weighed in
heavy-handedly. *Viva Zapata!* opened in early February, in the midst
of Kazan's personal-political turmoil, to a measured response. The
critics took it seriously, as they were obliged to, given the Kazan-
Steinbeck-Brando trifecta, but they did not write money reviews.
Many, like those in the *New Yorker* and *Time*, read it as a horse
opera gone pretentious. The latter also pointed out that the historic
Zapata had gone through twenty-six "bogus" marriages, a fact that
was inconvenient to the film's idealism. Even the sympathetic Bosley
Crowther could not entirely endorse it. He thought "the realities of
revolution got mixed with abstract ideas" to the disadvantage of
both; no other reviewer alluded even that glancingly to the film's
anti-Communist theme.

Even before the picture opened Fox was worried about it—not
quite a Western, not quite a hell-for-leather portrait of a dashing populist hero, certainly not a south-of-the-border romance, but it did well
initially, doubtless benefiting from the heat of Brando's performance in
Streetcar, before falling off sharply when the public became aware that
he was playing against what they thought of as his type.

At the same time, studio executives began worrying about Kazan's
political troubles. Spyros Skouras called Kazan into his New York office, urging him to sign a letter he had prepared in which the director
would publicly admit his past involvement with Communism and
grant the studio the right to drop his contract if his "confession" failed
to satisfy HUAC. Greek or not, Kazan had never much cared for the
oily Skouras, so he refused to sign while coolly rejecting the project
Skouras pressed upon him, an adaptation of Herbert Philbrick's account of his work as an anti-Communist mole, *I Led Three Lives.*

The following month Kazan found himself in Hollywood for the

Molly Kazan,
Elia Kazan's
first wife.

The Group Theatre. Elia Kazan is in the back row, far right.

Clifford Odets.

Elia Kazan and Frances Farmer in The Group Theatre's 1937
production of *Golden Boy*, by Clifford Odets.

Elia Kazan's first film, *People of the Cumberland,* 1937.
He was credited as an "assistant."

Elia Kazan directing Charles Bickford in The Group Theatre's
1938 production of *Casey Jones*.

Elia and Chris Kazan on the set of *Sea of Grass*, 1947.

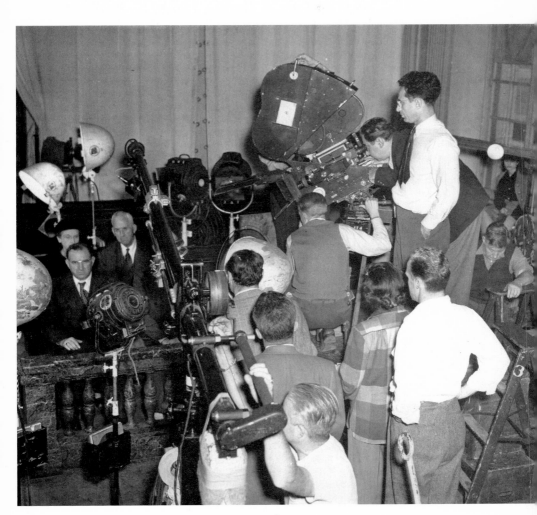

Boomerang! 1947.

Elia Kazan and
Tennessee Williams.

Vivien Leigh, Kim Hunter, and Elia Kazan on the set
of *A Streetcar Named Desire*, 1951.

Marlon Brando
and Elia Kazan
on the set of
Viva Zapata!
1952.

Marlon Brando and Elia Kazan on the set
of *On the Waterfront*, 1954.

Elia Kazan and James Dean on the set of *East of Eden*, 1955.

A Face in the Crowd, 1957.

On location for *Wild River*, 1960.

Natalie Wood, Elia Kazan, and William Inge on the set of
Splendor in the Grass, 1961.

A personal photo
of Arthur Miller
and Elia Kazan.

Arthur Miller, Barbara Loden, Jason Robards Jr., and Elia Kazan
on the opening night of *After the Fall*, 1964.

Elia Kazan and his novel, *The Arrangement*, 1967.

Frances and Elia Kazan at the Berlin Film Festival, 1996.

Oscar ceremonies, at which *Streetcar* fared so ambiguously. During this stay, Marilyn Monroe cheerfully slipped into Kazan's bed one night at the Bel Air Hotel to tell him that she was now engaged to Joe DiMaggio, whose "dignified" manner—she would soon learn that it masked a deep coldness—appealed to her.

Kazan's main business in Los Angeles turned out to be conversations at Fox about HUAC. The committee had slipped information about his earlier testimony to the rabidly anti-Communist *Hollywood Reporter,* which strongly hinted that he was about to be recalled. Zanuck and Skouras had also intervened with George Sokolsky, urging him not to run a piece about Kazan's politics, which he agreed to delay. But Zanuck was adamant: "Name the names for Chrissake," Kazan later quoted him as saying. "Who the hell are you going to jail for? You'll be sitting there and someone else will sure as hell name these people. Who are you saving?" Incidentally Zanuck wondered if it might be John Garfield, the major star the committee desperately wanted to nail and never did, whom Kazan was protecting. This he denied—he never believed the actor to be more than a naïve fellow traveler. The director also talked with Bud Lighton, who was brief with him. "There's nothing else you can do. Would you let someone go to jail for you?" he asked. But, Kazan protested, these people were once friends. "I don't care how good friends they were; there's nothing else you can do now."

These conversations caused Kazan to lean toward testifying, and I don't think that shift can be dismissed as purely opportunistic. It was always the Communist strategy to insist that anyone who surrendered the names of former party colleagues was betraying current friendships. But that is nonsense. This point needs always to be borne firmly in mind: Everyone who gave the committee names was a former Communist, not currently affiliated with the party. No one suddenly betrayed a current party colleague. All were, like Kazan, people who had fallen out with the party, and had, for many years, opposed its policies. All had just cause for their defections and brought to their task a bristling animus, born in dozens of meetings in which their dissent from the party line was shouted down. None had the slightest residual good feelings for their former comrades. They were as passionate (and as self-righteous) as their opponents. Their testimony made manifest a bitter internecine conflict that had previously been clandestine and of small consequence to the general public. This, too, needs to be said: HUAC never inquired very deeply into the content of the movies written by the Hollywood Reds. With good reason. They got next to nothing dangerous onto the screen—certainly nothing "un-American." Great, justifiable sport has been made—beginning with Murray Kempton in *Part of Our Time*—over their ludicrous efforts to propagandize the screen. But that was never their main goal. What they bent their best efforts toward was controlling the Hollywood unions. If they could gain a position in any of them where they could strike so highly visible an industry as the movies they would gain power and influence elsewhere denied them. This was the prize they energetically, secretly sought—and it was not nothing.

Finally, this also needs to be said, since it is always left out of accounts of the politics of this era: Sectarian enmity between the various, but always argumentative, partisans of the left—between, say, Stalinists and Trotskyites or between both of those groups and democratic socialists—was every bit as fierce as the enmity between the Communists and the troglodyte right. Speaking as reasonably as I can, I find it difficult to condemn Kazan, or anyone else who named names, for failing to protect people with whom they had no present contact and from whose ideological path they had long since diverged. Life does go on, whatever nostalgic affections may adhere to our recollections of old friends (very little in this case), and it is, as Zanuck said, difficult to face jail—or for that matter an interrupted career— on the behalf of former friends who are now ideological enemies. That is especially so, I think, if these former friends have the same opportunity, which they did, to testify to their past beliefs and acquaintances and get on with their lives. Kazan himself, in *A Life*, raised this point. With two exceptions, he had no way of knowing what the current beliefs of the people he named were, therefore had no way of knowing what effect his testimony might have on their present lives.

To testify as Kazan was obliged to do in 1952 is not a pleasant matter; it sticks in one's craw. But it should not have been, as it has become, the defining (and in the eyes of many, the indefensible) event of his life. Which, as he contemplated the possibility of testifying, Kazan almost certainly did not think it would be. HUAC was one of the ugly facts of American life at that time. It could not be evaded if you had a radically leftist past and any sort of current public life. In confronting it, the individual faced a stark choice and (to revert to a favorite Kazan theme) such a choice inevitably led to ugly consequences, no matter which option one chose. All along in this narrative we have seen that Kazan was, supremely, a realist in every aspect of his career. I think the choice he made in this instance, though informed by principle, was also dictated by his nature, which had its obviously opportunistic side, but did not include cowardice or a tendency toward right-wing beliefs.

He knew perfectly well that if he named names he would be excoriated by essentially liberal-minded show business. He was prepared for that. What he did not calculate was that this criticism would persist for decades, that his name would forever be associated with a betrayal of "friends" as well as of principles.

We need to do what few do: examine the alternative reality Kazan embraced. We need to see the world not as a Communist did, aiming to mobilize sentimental (and often infantile) liberal sentiment, but as a principled anti-Stalinist might. We may begin with Communism's insistence on the right to secrecy, on some imagined First Amendment guarantee that you need not openly state your membership in a political or quasi-political organization. Never mind that every court to which the party appealed on that basis rejected it; all had held that a congressional committee had the right to inquire into any citizen's membership in any organization. But this notion was, on its face, absurd. Most Americans casually and regularly state their political affiliations, not to mention their religious beliefs, their memberships in labor unions, trade associations, or for that matter the PTA. If the Communist Party was, as it claimed, just another electoral choice available to all, why would a member want to maintain secrecy? On the contrary, why would he or she not proudly proclaim its program and openly seek as many adherents to it as possible?

In 1971 Eric Bentley published his invaluable book *Thirty Years of Treason*. It is almost one thousand pages long and it consists largely of lengthy excerpts from the testimony of dozens of witnesses, friendly and unfriendly, before HUAC in the period 1938–68. There can be no doubt about Bentley's liberal credentials, and in his "afterword" he concedes that a Communist might well, given the American climate in the forties and fifties, choose to be discreet about his party affiliation, if only to protect his livelihood. But, he writes, the CP went much further: "Not only was it a Machiavellian scheme of life with widely spread nets, it was a veritable mystique, respected and adhered to beyond all rational plan. It was a way of life. And therein more than a revolution was betrayed. Marxism was betrayed. The whole tradition of radicalism was betrayed." Bentley cites the *Communist Manifesto* in this regard: "The Communists disdain to conceal their views and aims. They openly declare that their ends can be attained by the forcible overthrow of . . . existing social conditions . . ."

Bentley then contrasts that forthright radicalism with the behavior of the Stalinists who "lacked candor," which, he wrote, may be a common human failing, but "is an impossible lack for real radicals. For, to radicalism, candor is no adornment, it is of the essence. It is love of candor that makes men radical thinkers: a distaste for pretense, an awareness of the prevalence of false consciousness, a yearning for realities." Stalinism, he wrote, abandoned "that strenuous and joyful quest for reality which is the spiritual life of radicalism." The result, he said, was that "in the HUAC hearings, the rhetoric of John Howard Lawson (whose aggressive testimony turned many liberal supporters away from the Communists) merely counterbalances that of the committee. Bullshit equals bullshit."

Which was masking—what? Most basically two things: That the American Communist Party was the creature of the Soviet Union, almost wholly subsidized financially by a foreign power whose line it slavishly and instantly followed as it made its vertiginous switches; and that this party did contain a conspiratorial branch, the business of which was subversion and espionage. That there was very little crossover between the open party, ineptly attempting to sway public opinion on the great issues of the day, and the conspiratorial party, with its agents attempting to pilfer state secrets or to secretly influence public policy, is almost beside the point. Put simply, the Communist Party, in both its public and secret aspects, had one overriding aim, which was the destabilization of the democratic American consensus, by fair means or foul.

This was the central argument advanced by Sidney Hook, the New York University philosopher, in his book *Heresy Yes, Conspiracy No,* published in 1953, a year after Kazan's testimony. He was, like Kazan (whose lawyer put him in touch with Hook in this period), a liberal anti-Communist and he became, also like Kazan, one of the liberals—Arthur Schlesinger, Jr., was another of them—the Stalinists most loved to hate. Hook wrote:

> It is Communism as an international movement whose capital is Moscow which is the enemy of American democracy; and the American Communist Party, no matter what its size or influence (which is not entirely inconsiderable) is an integral part of that movement. Whoever overlooks this has overlooked the main point. For without this organic tie to the Soviet state apparatus with all its engines of war, espionage and terror, the American Communist Party would have only nuisance value, its members would be ineffectual, candidates for the political psychopathic ward now inhabited by various other Communist splinter groups like the Trotskyites. It is not the speech of members of the Communist Party that makes them dangerous but their organizational ties, for this in effect makes them a paramilitary fifth column of a powerful state, ready to strike whenever their foreign masters give the word.

Hook's rhetoric perhaps exceeds the dangers posed by the Communists—but not by much. Thomas Powers, who is the most reliable and thoughtful journalist writing about modern espionage, has this to say about Soviet spies in the thirties and forties: ". . . they were of the left generally, they supported liberal causes, they defended the Soviet Union in all circumstances, they were often secret members of the Communist Party, they were uniformly suspicious of American initiatives throughout the world, they tended to be contemptuous of American democracy, society, culture, and, above all, their offenses were too often minimized or explained away by apologists who felt that no man should be called traitor who did what he did for the cause of humanity."

Powers naturally notes that one result of these activities and attitudes was that "a pall of suspicion fell over the radical left generally and many hundreds of people who had never told the KGB so much as the time of day found themselves hounded by self-appointed watchdogs, blackballed from work in Hollywood or academia, hectored by congressional committees, and pressed under threat of contempt charges to reveal the names of friends, fellow travelers and chance acquaintances who had been members of the Communist Party . . ." Yet the fact remains that the CPUSA, precisely because it was double-tracking—openly advocating "ideas" and at the same time running spies—must be named as a coconspirator in creating that climate of suspicion that we loosely term "McCarthyism." The Communists, by their tactics, made it all too easy for the right wing to see fire where it smelled smoke—because there were real fires burning in "The Haunted Wood," to borrow the title of a book which reprints the so-called "Venona transcripts," secret exchanges between American Communist spies and their Soviet masters, which American intelligence had decrypted decades earlier, and which were declassified and published beginning in the mid-1990s.

As Powers, having studied the Venona papers, among other sources, all of which unexceptionably detail the extent of Soviet espionage in the United States, puts it:

> Once this new evidence is frankly faced no one can write the history of McCarthyism and the early cold war without taking into account that the hunt for spies was based on the fact that there were spies—lots of them; that those spies began with an idealism shared by a significant minority of the American people; and that the defensive response of many American liberals was not only wrong on the facts, but also exacerbated the suspicions of the right, making it easier for demogogues to argue that progressive causes and treason somehow went hand in hand.

In short, Kazan, as well as others who shared his liberal beliefs yet testified cooperatively before HUAC, were generally right about the Communists. Simply by reading the papers he had sufficient (though at that point incomplete) evidence that the party was heavily involved in espionage. He knew from firsthand experience of its desire to take over democratic institutions like The Group Theatre and Actors' Equity. He shared a general distaste for the relentless anti-Americanism of Communist opinion, not to mention the inhuman vulgarity of its rhetoric.

He was, I think, naïve only when he asked himself: What would the effect have been if the Communists had broken their silence, and openly admitted their allegiance, whether current or former? I think, as he obviously thought, that openness would have very largely disarmed Hollywood's blacklist. Certainly it would have rendered impotent the many freelance blacklisters, who were often, in fact, blackmailers, publishing their lists of people who had innocently contributed to this or that front organization and then agreeing to "clear" those names, often for a price. America is not merely a free country, it is a forgiving one—especially when it comes to youthful mistakes. It would have welcomed back former Communists as surely as today it welcomes back alcoholics and drug addicts once they have done their time in the Betty Ford Clinic.

But Communism loved martyrs. And it loved confrontations in which established political institutions could be painted as repressive, casually crushing "dissent" or "heresy." Above all, the hard-core Communist functionaries knew that the party could not withstand open scrutiny, precisely because of its secret espionage activities. Still, if you believed, or could be made to believe, that Communists were merely dissidents or heretics, then, curiously, HUAC was the party's perfect foil, an entity that could easily be made to look clownish, hysterical, incompetent to the non-Communist left.

Except that in a certain, limited sense this was not entirely true. For one thing, HUAC's staff work was expert. You cannot find, in Bentley's book, for example, any major instances where its information was wrong. The investigators were constantly laying before witnesses, both friendly and unfriendly, long-forgotten documents recording their former political passions—an article or a letter to the editor they had dashed off in the heat of some sectarian dispute, a petition or an advertisement they had casually signed in aid of some leftist cause. Often in their testimony we find a witness—Kazan was among them—agreeing that, well, yes, he must have lent his name to some cause or other, since there it was in black and white, but being unable to recall so doing. Memory is fallible and so are our personal filing systems.

Then, too, after a certain historical moment, the committee members do not come on as ogres. They are for the most part obvious provincials, small-town lawyers who got lucky in electoral politics, without, in the process, gaining a sophisticated understanding of conspiratorial politics. But the gavel-hammering shouting matches that marked the confrontation between J. Parnell Thomas in the Hollywood Ten hearings of 1947, especially the verbal brawl between him and John Howard Lawson, are notable by their absence later on. In public sessions, in the 1950s the committee members do not rant and rave. They give the impression of earnestly trying to understand what in the world it was that moved the witnesses to do whatever it was that they had done. Even when the latter invoke the Fifth Amendment, the congressmen are patient, almost weary, with them. There is something dully ritualistic in these occasions.

Finally, it must be said that the committee did not catch any innocent liberals in its net. All of its "friendly" witnesses had been Communists or very close fellow travelers. They all had firsthand knowledge of the way the party silenced opponents of the party line, so if you were a former Communist the temptation to tell what you knew of its operations and to name names was real, especially if your memory of past party conflicts still angrily gnawed at you.

Even Dalton Trumbo conceded that point. In 1970, upon receiving the Writers Guild Laurel Award for his lifetime achievements as a screenwriter, he turned his acceptance speech into a plea for reconciliation between old foes. In it he said, "we were *all* [italics his] victims because almost without exception each of us felt compelled to say things he did not want to say, to do things he did not want to do, to deliver and receive wounds he truly did not want to exchange. That is why none of us—right, left or center—emerged from that long nightmare without sin."

It was an astonishing statement, coming from one of the Hollywood Ten, graceful in expression and humane in its sentiments. But it did not go down well with another member of the Ten, Albert Maltz, whose career had not prospered as Trumbo's had in the postblacklist era and who was, in any case, much more of an ideologue, and a much less generous spirit. The two men engaged in a lengthy epistolary wrangle, quoted extensively in Victor Navasky's *Naming Names,* about Trumbo's speech. In the course of this dispute Trumbo forcefully argued that the Communist left was making a case against the wrong enemies. It was not, he said, the friendly witnesses who should be condemned. It was, he insisted, the craven studios which had surrendered to the government's hysteria about Communist "influence" in the movies and, by instituting a blacklist, forced their employees to make the ugly choice between testimony and silence, which could only cause terrible pain, no matter what option one chose.

But he went beyond that. He offered a long, sympathetic list of logical reasons why someone might feel obliged to friendly testimony. He conceded, of course, that one might do so from the motives generally imputed to them by the Communists—these were "the weak, the cunning, the ambitious and the greedy." But there were other, less venomous reasons to talk. He mentions, for example, deadly economic pressures, mental illness in a family that might endanger a spouse's life, fear of being exposed for a crime or behavior regarded at the time as worse than Communist Party membership (interestingly, he mentions homosexuality as one example of a secret in those days still in need of hiding). Significantly, he added these other possibilities: "A man who has left the CP to avoid constant attempts to meddle with the ideological content of his writing . . . a man who left the Party because he could not stomach its insistence that the early phases of World War II offered no choice between Hitler and the West . . . a person whose disagreement with the CP had turned to forthright hostility and who, when the crunch came, saw no reason to sacrifice his career in defense of the rights of people he now hated . . ."

What's striking about this passage is its seeming casualness. It has about it a "but, of course" quality. This, Trumbo implicitly says, is the way the world works and it is feckless to pretend otherwise. As far as I am concerned, this case closes with that argument (though it surely did not for Albert Maltz and his ilk).

But having said that, I must, in all conscience, add this: HUAC was, by this time, obviously among the most useless of the many useless inventions the Congress of the United States has foisted on the republic. If you read through Bentley's book, it soon becomes clear that all the actions it is investigating lie in the rapidly dimming past. There is not one instance in which anything amounting to a clear and *present* danger to the United States is uncovered. Essentially, HUAC and its hearings are a half-mad exercise in historicism, setting straight a record that no one gave—make that "should have given"—a hoot about at this late date—no matter whether they approved or disapproved its work. The committee rarely touched upon the only matter that counted, which was espionage.

Navasky calls the HUAC hearings "degradation ceremonies." They were not aimed at alerting us to current danger and they were not aimed at producing useful legislation. The idea, he argues, was to scapegoat a relative handful of people, isolate them from polite society, force them to take on guilt (and punishment) for some of its ills while making the majority feel smug and superior because it had avoided such deviance. That was, perhaps, the effect of HUAC's work, but I don't think it was a conscious goal of its members or supporters. They were, on the whole, too stupid to think in such sophisticated cultural-anthropological terms. Moreover, Navasky leaves out of his account the fact that the scapegoats were all eventually welcomed back, often enough as heroes, while the committee's informers are the ones now scapegoated by polite, liberal-minded society.

I think it may be useful to avoid such large historical theorizing and simply see HUAC for what it was at the time it exerted its greatest power. In the late forties and early fifties, it incontrovertibly appeared to be a harsh and permanent fact of American life. If you were unlucky enough to be caught in its sights, you had to deal with it as a reality, which, generally speaking, forced this choice on a witness: betrayal of long-lost colleagues who had, at one time, betrayed you; or abandonment of your present life and career for people you no longer respect, like or share the values of.

It is impossible to say when, exactly, Kazan decided to cooperate with the committee. We only know that in the late winter of 1952 he consulted a wide variety of friends about what he should do. Among them was Arthur Miller, and their accounts of this meeting vary. Both, however, agree that Kazan invited Miller to his Connecticut retreat, and that they went for a walk in the woods. Kazan told the playwright that he had been served a second HUAC subpoena and that he was thinking about cooperating with the committee. He rehearsed with Miller the fact that if he didn't cooperate he would be barred from motion picture production and his belief that he would never secure a passport so that he could make pictures abroad. Finally, he told Miller that his interest in Broadway had diminished and that the future he most wanted for himself was in the movies. He was prepared, he says, quoting from a diary entry he made immediately after this conversation, to give up movies for a "worthwhile" cause, but was not certain this was it. "What the hell am I giving all this up for? To defend a secrecy I didn't think right and to defend people who'd already been named or soon would be by someone else? I said I'd hated the Communists for many years and didn't feel right about giving up my career to defend them. . . ."

Here Kazan touched upon a crucial point—the redundancy of his testimony. The standard history of the blacklist is *The Inquisition in Hollywood,* by Larry Ceplair and Stephen Englund. It is written from a distinctly New Left point of view in a prose that is far from dispassionate. But even these writers, unforgiving as they are of the friendly witnesses, have to admit that

> Contrary to the victims' angry feelings, the informers did not *cause* [their italics] the destruction which overtook their uncompromising colleagues. By April 1951 it was eminently clear even to the most blithe Hollywood radical that HUAC did not need the exposes provided by the informers; that the Committee had sufficient wood, nails and bloodthirsty onlookers for all the crucifixions. Even if no one had "confessed" it is clear that [it] would have coldly, briskly and efficiently marched the entire list of Hollywood "Communists" through the witness box, listened to their recitals of the Fifth and waited for the studios to blacklist them.

In other words, the testimony of Kazan and the other friendly witnesses, both morally and practically speaking, harmed no one but themselves.

Which in some corner of his own very practical soul Elia Kazan surely recognized. He had no choice but to take his impending appearance seriously, if only because everyone else would. But having devoted so much of himself to his career, which had prospered in a way unmatched by any of his former cellmates, how could he abandon it to defend them and their corrupt ideals? All well and good, in the abstract, to demand the quixotic gesture, but as a practical matter—no, that was asking too much. Ask yourself: Could you, in similar circumstances, make that gesture? As one who has been as driven by ambition as Kazan was, I have to say I could not. And, apparently, even Arthur Miller could not bring himself to require this act of self-abnegation from his friend.

His conversation with Miller, according to Kazan, turned away from the immediate problem. Kazan offered an account of why he had left the party, and still later they entered into a discussion of current politics, with Miller stating his opposition to the Marshall Plan and to America's defense of South Korea—both, incidentally, congruent with the Communist Party position at the time. Still, at the end, Kazan has Miller giving him an awkward hug and saying, "Don't worry about what I think. Whatever you do will be okay with me. Because I know your heart is in the right place."

Miller, in *Timebends,* misstates one crucial fact about this encounter, insisting that it occurred after Kazan had given up the names of his former Group colleagues. But that cannot be true since it makes him seem to be crawling for forgiveness rather than seeking an answer to a problem still at least nominally open in his mind. I think that in speaking with the ideologically alert Miller he was looking for what he had not found, a compelling reason to maintain his silence.

Miller recalls saying (correctly as it turned out) that the committee would not for long hold sway over the American conscience, meaning that if he failed to name names Kazan's exile from filmmaking would probably be brief. He also records angry thoughts, allegedly on his friend's behalf—that "it was not his duty to be stronger than he was, that the government had no right to require anyone to be stronger than it was given him to be." He says also that he left the meeting with "a bitterness with the country I had never even imagined before, a hatred of its stupidity and its throwing away of its freedom." Unmentioned, of course, is the "deal" Gottfried speculates Miller and Kazan made. If it was struck, this is the moment when it would have occurred. All we know for certain is that neither man ever referred to Kazan's testimony in public in anything but rueful terms. No personal attacks were ever made.

For example, in *Timebends* Miller appends an incident unreported by Kazan, in which Molly comes flying out of the house to tell him that all the people living along their Connecticut road agreed with the committee and adding, somewhat irrelevantly, that the United Electrical Workers had been proved to be Communist-dominated. Finally, she repeated her idea that it was wrong to equate the Salem witch hunts (he was heading there to do more research for *The Crucible*) with the anti-Communist crusade. As he drove off, he says, he couldn't help but think that "Kazan might have sacrificed me had it been necessary."

That last remark is purely gratuitous. I also think his remarks about Kazan's "strength," or lack thereof, are pure hypocrisy. It is really not for Arthur Miller (or anyone else) to impute flaws of courage to anyone's choice of political action. We do what we think, at the time, is right. We can, of course, be wrong. But that does not necessarily betoken a flaw of spirit or character.

On the other hand, this incident is much more typical of their later, admittedly more distant, relationship. In 1955, Miller's play *A View from the Bridge* was produced. It is about a longshoreman in incestuous love with his niece, who in turn is in love with an illegal immigrant, sheltering in their home. In the end the longshoreman betrays the "submarine" to the authorities and is then killed for doing so. The play has its power, but it is not entirely successful, either. It is another high-flown metaphor about betrayal and its consequences and, despite its utter silence about politics, has been so understood by many—especially on the left—from the outset. The columnist Murray Kempton retailed a rumor that the playwright sent his work to Kazan, not as a project for him to direct, which Kempton has Kazan believing, but as a statement of his contempt for informers. In his account of the incident, Gottfried quotes Miller thus: "I will offer Kazan a play of mine to direct when I believe it would be best served by his kind of talent. I am sure he will accept or reject the job on the merits . . ." If, as Gottfried speculates, the two men had a "deal," this was its first major test and it held.

Kazan sought counsel from other friends. Among them was Lillian Hellman, with whom he spoke at the Oak Room of the Plaza. She heard him out, made a phone call to Kermit Bloomgarden, who shared her Stalinism, then took his advice and walked out on Kazan. He also talked with Clifford Odets. Kazan said that he would not name any names if the playwright—Kazan's only remaining close friend from The Group CP unit—wished to continue concealing his membership in it. Though Odets, after a long absence from Broadway (and a flop return), had scored a hit with *The Country Girl* the previous year, he was greatly diminished in comparison to his whirlwind younger self. What Kazan says he found in Odets was a man seeking the same permission Kazan was seeking from him—assent to respond truthfully to the committee's questions.

This he would do, five weeks after Kazan appeared, essentially naming the same Group Theatre people and adding a few others who had been part of a delegation of leftists he joined on a trip to Cuba in 1935, to investigate the harassment and deportation of dissidents by that country's dictatorship. In a way Odets lost more by his testimony than Kazan did. Or so the director believed. Odets had, less than two decades earlier, been the great proletarian playwright of the time, a colorful, exuberant rebel-hero to the left. Whatever his Hollywood misadventures, some on the left still awaited a return to his old form, and they were profoundly distressed by his testimony. "It choked off the voice he'd had," Kazan later wrote. "The ringing tone, the burst of passion, were no longer there. What in the end gave me strength drained him of his. I realize now that my action . . . had influenced him strongly. I wish it had not. I believe he should have remained defiant, maintained his treasured identity, and survived as his best self. He was to die before he died." On the other hand, Odets much more desperately needed his Hollywood paychecks than Kazan did.

Finally, Kazan went to Paula Strasberg, with her husband, Lee, joining the conversation. In his essentially apolitical way Lee thought Kazan had no choice but to testify. She was more dubious, saying that she could not herself name names. On the other hand, she raised no objection to his naming her. She was long gone from the party and her career as an acting coach—she would soon be Marilyn Monroe's on-set guru—would not be affected by anything Kazan said.

So the decision was made. Kazan appeared before HUAC on April 10, in room 330 of the Old House Office Building in Washington. He came armed with an affidavit that he read into the record. In it he named the following members of The Group Theatre's Communist Party Unit: Lewis Leverett and J. Edward Bromberg (now deceased), Phoebe Brand and Morris Carnovsky (who were married), Tony Kraber (who recruited Kazan), Paula Miller Strasberg, Clifford Odets and Art Smith. He named as well the somewhat mysterious Ted Wellman, also known as Sid Benson, who was not a Group member, and whom some thought was a journalist, others a sort of groupie. He also named V. J. Jerome and Andrew Overgaard, both well-known open party functionaries, and four others—Harry Elion, John Bonn, Alice Evans (who later married Jerome) and Anne Howe—all producers of a sort at the Theatre of Action, speaking for the party in its councils. Finally he named actor Robert Caille (also known as Robert Reed), now also deceased, who had, Kazan believed, represented the party's interests in the struggle within Actors' Equity to obtain rehearsal pay for performers. This fight was successful, but Kazan believed that as far as the CP was concerned, it was part of a larger attempt to gain control of the union, in which it failed.

The second portion of the affidavit is a slightly numbing recital of various Communist fronts to which Kazan contributed or didn't contribute his name or his money in the years after he left the party. The most interesting aspect of this portion of the document was his insistence that his friend Ralph Steiner of Frontier Films was an anti-Communist and that he knew nothing of the politics of the other principals in a company that had been named as a "subversive" organization and that almost certainly did harbor some CP members.

The last part of the affidavit is a full list of the plays and movies Kazan had directed, in which he offered ludicrously over-simplified

summaries of these works; you would think they might all be suitable entertainments for Republican fund-raisers.

And then it was—it seemed—over. The committee had no further questions for Kazan and merely indicated it might want to recall
him at some future date, which it never did. Its chairman, Francis
Walter, thanked him warmly for his contribution to public awareness
of "the machinations of this Communist conspiracy for world domination." Kazan returned to New York, and on April 12 the *Times*,
among other papers, reported his testimony. Odets was mentioned
in the lead and most, but not all, of the other names he mentioned
appeared later in the story, which on the whole stressed his tale of
disgust with party discipline in the 1930s.

But, of course, it was not over. Appended to the *Times* story was a
five-paragraph summary of the statement Kazan had placed as a paid
advertisement in its pages on the same day. This piece was a huge mistake, very possibly the largest of Kazan's public life, and it was largely
the creation of his wife. She felt, he later said, that he was being reviled
and that he must answer his critics. This is hard to believe. They were
talking a day after his testimony, "public opinion" (by which, of course,
she meant show business opinion; the public at large had only small interest in this matter) had not yet begun to form. But she was eager to
set the terms of the argument before others did.

Kazan, in his autobiography, represents himself as much less
certain about mounting a self-defense. "I said that was not my way,
that I didn't feel I owed anyone an explanation, my act explained itself." But she persisted. Molly's highly developed critical sense, described as "terrifying" by one observer, was at its height on this
occasion. "You always felt," this witness says, "that there was an objective standard, that she knew what it was and that you weren't
measuring up to it." Beyond that, she was his often-betrayed helpmate
to whom Elia Kazan owed a guilty debt he could never discharge.

She went into her study. He heard her typewriter keys clattering,
the carriage slamming back and forth. At the end of the afternoon she
emerged with her pages. She watched intently as Kazan read them.
He thought them "true and fair" in tone. And he could see how much
this statement meant to her. So the space in the *Times* was purchased.

"True and fair"? Well, yes and no. Much of the piece simply recounts Kazan's brief, unhappy experiences in The Group's Communist unit, and raises the point that the party's insistence on secrecy was in large measure responsible for the climate of fear and hysteria poisoning the political atmosphere of the moment. The piece also addresses Kazan's reluctance to name names because of the effect it might have on their "reputations and employment." It also makes the point that liberal reluctance to identify Communists on the grounds that they merely held "unpopular" opinions is an example of "specious reasoning." These opinions were, very often, something more than "unpopular"; they were often calculated, and outright, lies.

But the Kazans went too far. There is a logical disconnect between the long-ago and rather paltry doings of the Group Theatre Communists and the cosmic meanings "A Statement" imputed to them. I don't think Kazan really had a taste of the "police state," of "dictatorship and thought control" when he and The Group actors met with "the man from Detroit" in 1935. Yes, they were being encouraged to take over a fairly significant cultural institution in which large numbers of people had a sympathetic interest; had they succeeded it would have had some small effect on the spirit of the moment. And, yes, Kazan was increasingly miserable in this company and he was right, given his absolutism when it came to free speech and freedom of artistic expression, to quit the Communists in disgust. He even had a right to carry his personal grudge against the attempt "to control thought and to suppress personal opinion" across the years.

But that does not prove the case against "the dangerous and alien conspiracy" that he saw threatening the "free, open, healthy way of life that gives us self-respect." He could not, based on his own limited experience, so testify. He would have been better advised to keep his arguments against Communism on a purely personal level—the kind of arguments Trumbo later made. This is what Budd Schulberg had done a year earlier. Like Kazan, he testified primarily about his own arguments with the Communists while he was a party member, but thereafter resisted making world-historical generalizations about the party based on that experience. By this strategy he very largely managed to escape the calumny heaped on Kazan.

In his advertisement Kazan said, "I have no spy stories to tell, because I saw no spies," and that is a telling admission. He cannot persuasively equate naming a handful of show folks, at worst plotting the overthrow of Lee Strasberg, Harold Clurman and Cheryl Crawford, with Stalinism's plots to overthrow democratic governments everywhere. There is something ludicrously grandiose—or should we simply say "overheated"?—in this document that, however sympathetic I am to its ostensible author, I find difficult to accept.

For discreet silence very well served the people—there were at least seventy-three of them—who testified as Kazan did, among them Jerome Robbins, the choreographer; Abe Burrows, the comedy writer-performer; Burl Ives, the folksinger; Daniel Boorstin, the scholar (who testified a year later about Communist activities at Harvard). What you had to do was acknowledge, with a degree of shame, your testimony, then go about your business, trusting short-term memory loss, so characteristic of American public life, to do its healing work.

To be sure, those who named names earned the permanent enmity of the Communists, of the left in general. But on the whole people forgot about them as they hurried on about their lives. They required reminders of their apostasy, which as the years wore on, as the old Stalinists aged and died, became fewer and less impassioned. But Kazan's advertisement for himself made him a permanent target. By this one act he became the celebrity informer—the namer of names nearly everyone could name, the great symbolic stooge, rat fink of the era.

Never thereafter did he refer to "A Statement" until his brief remarks about it in his autobiography. Generally, he would in later life refuse to discuss his testimony, but when he did so he always argued from high principle, never referring to the tactical error the advertisement represented. Only once did he hint at the disastrous consequences of mixing the personal and the political in this instance. In his long discussion of his testimony with Michel Ciment, in 1974, he said, significantly in my view, "What's called 'a difficult decision' is a difficult decision because either way you go there are penalties. Right? . . . if you're marrying one woman, you're not marrying another woman." He may have been thinking—or half-thinking—that his ill-considered defense of his testimony was one of the "penalties" he paid for marrying Molly Day Thatcher instead of someone else.

13

To the Waterfront

Kazan kept to himself for a couple of days after his statement appeared. Then, characteristically, he resumed his New York rounds. Not for him the self-hatred of Jerome Robbins, calling himself "a Jewish, ex-commie fag who had to go into a mental hospital." He appeared at the Actors Studio. He submitted to the snubs of some old friends when he encountered them. He received a certain amount of hate mail.

The comment that rankled most came from Tony Kraber when he testified before HUAC a couple of years later. Asked whether any part of Kazan's testimony was erroneous, Kraber, who had recruited him to the party, replied, "Is this the Kazan who signed a contract for $500,000 the day after he gave names to this committee? Would you sell your brother for $500,000?" Aside from the fact that his feelings for Kraber could not be described as brotherly, Kazan resented his big lie. Nothing in Kazan's testimony was erroneous; more important, he had not signed any such contract and, in fact, his salary for the pictures remaining on his Fox contract was reduced as a result of his testimony.

But somehow, as he always said later, the experience put steel in his spine. "I think it made a man of me," he told Ciment. "Up to then, I was the blue-eyed boy, everybody's darling; I was both very successful and very left; the living demonstration of how you could be on the left and still be in the gossip columns and be envied for the money you made. I was essentially the other-directed man. I was really working for the praise of others, for notices in the papers. This thing made me say: well, not everybody likes me, I've lost many of my best friends . . . I said, okay, I'm going to satisfy myself now, not the critics, not even my friends."

This he did. A Stalinoid critical line about Kazan developed, holding that everything he did after his testimony was inferior to his previous work, which is ludicrous. It is true that in the theater he directed no more masterpieces on the level of *Streetcar* and *Salesman*. But that was pretty much the luck of the draw; he did direct a number of solid and successful plays in the next decade. More important, his movies in the 1950s were, in general, far better than those of the 1940s. This was not entirely—or largely—because of his politics. It had more to do with the decline of the old-fashioned studio system and the rise of independent production, which obliged directors to find, develop and bring to the studios projects that meant something to them.

In the aftermath of his testimony he met Budd Schulberg and encouraged him to begin work on a script they might do together. The writer showed Kazan his draft of his longshoremen screenplay and also mentioned another idea, something about some black youths known as the Camden Six, though Schulberg thought that material rather ambiguous—it was possible, he believed, that some of these defendants might actually be guilty. He settled on reworking his waterfront script.

Curiously, Kazan remained under suspicion with the lunatic right; it thought he might still be a secret subversive. Darryl Zanuck even wondered mildly about that point, but had what he thought was the perfect answer to such speculation—the true story, reported in *Life*, of the German Circus Brumbach, which escaped East Germany for the West by the simple expedient of mounting a circus parade that, at the last moment, veered toward the border and freedom.

Man on a Tightrope reset this story in Czechoslovakia and had the circus escaping to Austria, but would use some of the Brumbach people and their acts. Kazan scouted locations for the picture in Bavaria, flew over the pole for final conferences with Zanuck, then fully committed to the movie. It had a script by the impeccably liberal Robert E. Sherwood, who had given up playwriting during the war to serve as a speechwriter for Roosevelt, which Kazan did not fully like (though he always spoke warmly of Sherwood, who was ill at the time and would die three years later).

At least initially, Kazan found himself uncomfortable, even now, working on a project so explicitly critical of the Soviet Union. On the other hand, his old friend Fredric March was cast as Karil Cernik, the circus's owner, and Cameron Mitchell from *Salesman* also had a role. Best of all, the project would remove him from New York and his almost daily confrontations with his political opponents.

He quickly found his reluctance to criticize Communism fading. His notes for this comparatively minor film are quite extensive and, not surprisingly, very political. He understood, as many people in show business do, that the circus represents their last, best connection to the deepest historic roots of their profession. Its performers are a living link to the wandering players of the Middle Ages, singing their songs, doing their tricks, staging their simple little plays, in the courtyards of taverns, in the plazas in front of the cathedrals. Kazan somewhat romanticized this tradition as it lived on in this little one-ring show. But more to the point, he connected that tradition to the current political situation.

"The circus is a good image for democracy," he wrote in his notebook. "It has room for all kinds, it has need for all kinds. It must have humor, surprise, irreverence or it dies. Fantasy also; but based on realism: muscles, eyes, knowledge of danger. Also, of course, it has to have discipline, responsibility or it dies. Without these, anarchy."

He added: "There is another good element in the circus: as in any democracy, politics is secondary to these people. They just want to be a circus, but under certain conditions they can't be a circus— i.e. they can't live their normal lives—so they're prodded to a political step."

Now normalcy is a relative concept, and a circus is not, as most people understand the term, a "normal" environment. "The whole point of the circus," Kazan wrote, "is that these are the least uniform, the most individualistic, the oddest, the most eccentric, the most widely 'deviationist' (to use a Commie term) of any people." So, as he wrote in caps: "THIS IS AN ODE TO INDIVIDUALISM," about which he did not wish to be "mushy or gooey." The circus folks are not demonstrative about being "romantic anarchists," but they do have—more caps here—"PRIDE. IF THEY DON'T HAVE PRIDE, THEY WOULDN'T WANT TO BREAK OUT."

> THE THING THE COMMIES
> Must Attack & CRUSH
> IS THE PRIDE
> of the INDIVIDUAL

Having made that point to his own satisfaction, Kazan passes on to a calmer consideration of how Communism afflicts a society, by infecting it with "a distrust of each other and a fear of each other. . . . At the same time the profound fact [is] that the allegiance of each individual is not to the other, or to each's own self, but to an *authority*, which they accept because . . . there is no recourse. With them, as Molly points out, there is an inhibition of the natural human impulse," which, he observes, is compounded by the fact that Communism is administered, in places like Czechoslovakia, by the local population, not, as it was during the Nazi occupation, by a readily identifiable alien force.

It was, finally, the "impulsiveness" of the circus, the wayward humanity that drove its escape from Communism, that this film celebrated. You could use its escape to make an ideological point, as people did at the time, but that doesn't fully explain its act. Curiously, making one of those free associational leaps that often mark his notes, Kazan starts thinking of Arthur Miller. "The reason Art Miller speaks everywhere 'like a high school boy' is that he is anxious to put himself on record for 'clarity' & never allows himself to be caught in the true confusions of an act he cannot put together. The acceptance of conflict, complexity, confusion, the resistance of the impulse to clarify by over-simplifying is a mark of a maturing person. The artist is the depository of conflict . . . he knows both sides & all sides of all issues & the push and pull-away of all impulses and emotions. His certaintude [sic] is hard won."

This is obviously a variant on Kazan's standard justification for his own recent actions, but scribbled on the fly it has an unmediated authenticity that his more carefully worded public statements sometimes lack. "Everyone has his reasons," Jean Renoir famously said in *Rules of the Game* (a thought Kazan approvingly quoted in his autobiography) and that mixture of motives—some principled, some merely personal—is what Kazan would always and everywhere argue for. And I think it represents a fair criticism of Arthur Miller. Only once, in *Death of a Salesman,* did he sustain for the full length of a play the exquisite ambiguity, the sheer messiness of life. He was always an artist in search of, in need of, an organizing principle. When he imposed one (*The Crucible*) the work becomes sterile and schematic. When he failed to find one (*After the Fall*) it becomes strained and emptily rhetorical. Only in *Salesman* does he achieve a balance between social criticism and a lifelike confusion of motive ("Why did you do it? I search and search and I search, and I can't understand it") that is touching, riveting and plausible.

Kazan did not achieve anything of that high order with *Man on a Tightrope.* He had a good time on the shoot. March was his genial, joke-telling self. And Adolphe Menjou was a surprise. He was, of course, a famously dapper and worldly actor and, in his later years, an ultra-conservative Red-baiter. But, as Frank Capra noted in his autobiography, he was a man who could keep his politics to himself on a movie set. He was also, as everyone attested, a consummate professional. Here cast as a Communist policeman, increasingly suspicious of Cernik and his plan to escape, he is excellent, and even a little dowdy in appearance.

The largest problem remained Sherwood's script. He might invest March's character with some of what Kazan called his own "proud, unyielding" nature, but he invested the other figures with a certain amount of clichés. Thus we find Cernik's young wife (Gloria Grahame) lusting after a fatuous lion tamer (Alex D'Arcy), his daughter (Terry Moore, also eventually to be involved with Howard Hughes) having a secret love affair with Mitchell's roustabout and Richard Boone playing a rather-too-obvious police spy. Kazan's hoped-for waywardness is vitiated by these descents into standard movie tropes. What's best in the movie are the cat-and-mouse encounters between Menjou and March and, of course, the final escape, which was inherently novel and suspensefully staged.

Zanuck did not much like the film Kazan delivered. It was not quite art and not quite a genre piece. And by this time he probably sensed that, like every single film that took up cold war issues from a soberly anti-Communist view, it was bound to be a flop. Naturally he tried to "save" it by reediting Kazan's cut, but to no avail. When *Man on a Tightrope* came out in the spring of 1953, it received mixed reviews, perhaps a little more favorable than unfavorable, but it did no business.

———————

By the time the film appeared, Kazan had endured another Broadway flop, his production of Tennessee Williams's hugely ambitious and extraordinarily interesting *Camino Real*. In the playwright's canon it is an anomaly, his one major experiment with expressionism. Set in an unnamed South American country, it features a large cast, including such romantic refugees from literature and history as Don Quixote, Marguerite Gautier (Camille), Lord Byron, Jacques Casanova and the Baron De Charlus. Each of them is a variant on poor doomed Blanche DuBois, most of them are trying to escape on the "Fugitivo," an utterly unscheduled, indeed largely mythical, airliner that offers the only hope of exit from their bleak and menacing environment. Into their midst comes Kilroy (Eli Wallach) a classic American innocent, a sometime boxer (he wears little Golden Gloves around his neck), with a weak heart—it is eventually cut out of his body onstage—and, in his way, an admirable soul, deeply puzzled by life, but trying to come to grips with it.

This was a play Williams had worked on for at least six years, developing it from one act to full length with Kazan egging him on. He never intended anything like a conventional narrative. Mostly his doomed romantics do not escape their entrapment, except by death. Mainly they sing their little songs—sometimes poetically, sometimes comically, sometimes ruefully—and many in the audience, both on the pre-Broadway tour and on Broadway, purely hated what they saw, with many of them stumbling angrily from the theater before the final curtain.

It is, clearly, an imperfect and difficult play—with its meaning not so much difficult to pin down as diffusely stated. But it is, even on the printed page, an exciting one, not quite like anything Broadway then or now was used to—the major plays of that season were Miller's *The Crucible* and William Inge's *Picnic*, both metaphorically clear as bells.

In talking about his work at the time Williams kept using a metaphor involving caged birds. In a Sunday *New York Times* piece, reprinted as an introduction to the published text, he wrote: "A cage represents security as well as confinement to a bird that has grown used to being in it." He also thought that "when a theatrical work kicks over the traces with such apparent insouciance, security seems challenged and instead of participating in a sense of freedom . . . a certain number of playgoers will rush back out to the more accustomed implausibility of the street he lives on."

But birds, caged or otherwise, do not quite summarize this play. It had elements of the absurd about it—not, at that time, a huge factor in American playwriting. It was also, both in its early drafts and its later revisions, a more political play than the one that appeared on Broadway. Its nameless setting—skid row on one side of the stage, a luxury hotel on the other—is meant to be some sort of fascist state, though without a visible dictator. The street sweepers, whose job is mainly to clear away dead bodies, are also policemen, charged with keeping a fractious population in order. This element was toned down considerably as the play limped toward Broadway. Barbara Baxley, who won very good notices playing a Gypsy girl (whose virginity returns to her whenever the moon is full, which gives you some idea of the play's curious tenor), later said that Walter Winchell and Ed Sullivan both attacked the piece as un-American, a "leftist manifesto."

That was not so—even if, in his dreamy way, Williams was trying to say something about the dank mood of the nation, perhaps the world, at that moment. Talking about the play, Eli Wallach was recently reminded of something Maureen Stapleton said, when asked how she could tolerate doing Williams's plays when they involved such matters as cannibalism, homosexuality, incest. "Well," she said, quoting Williams, "'they're just folks.'" And this time, he was more explicit than usual in suggesting that his "folks" were entitled to sympathy not persecution. It was this love for the outsider—the very far outsider—that lay at the heart of Kazan's undying affection for

Williams. He always thought Williams spoke for him as well as for the cannibals.

Kazan gave *Camino Real* one of his sockaroo stagings, breaking down the theater's fourth wall with entrances down the aisles, exits into the stage boxes. He had a huge cast (thirty-nine speaking parts) and an expert one (among those present, besides those already named, were Jo Van Fleet, Frank Silvera, Martin Balsam, Nehemiah Persoff, Michael V. Gazzo, Joseph Anthony), all of them in constant, recklessly choreographed motion.

He was, as usual, up to his old tricks. "Go on stage and make friends," he instructed Wallach, playing the stranger trying to ingratiate himself. "Each person makes friends in a different way. I can't tell you how to do it." Then he'd gather the other actors around and say, "Don't go near him. He's got bad breath. He stinks." Wallach recalls one of them spitting at him as he approached.

Kazan and Williams both knew that *Camino Real,* an episodic play in sixteen scenes or "blocks," lacked a third act and a big finish. It just more or less peters out in a sweet, humanistic whisper (something about the violets breaking through the rocks in the desert just offstage). Kazan hoped to stir up enough sensation so the audience didn't notice this lack of a resounding conclusion.

According to some accounts, he almost pulled it off. Writing about the play in the *New Republic,* Eric Bentley said of Kazan that "it was no use knowing he's not a good director, unless you can also see that he's almost a great one." He praised his "efficiency," by which he meant his attention to detail, "the way everything is taken care of, second by second" (a quality, he noted, that was not as customary as it might be in professional theater, which he called "second only to international politics as a breeding ground for amatuerism, stupidity and sabotage"). Kazan, he said, was a "wizard," with his name in the program guaranteeing "Brilliant theatre work at a high emotional temperature." He particularly liked the choreography of the piece, worked out, he said, in terms of acting not of dance (though choreographer Anna Sokolow was credited as Kazan's assistant). But his main point was that he did not think *Camino Real* that much of a departure for Kazan. He was never quite the "realist" people said he was. The critic had found powerful elements of "phantasmagoria" in his stagings of *Streetcar* and *Sales-man,* and he thought Kazan was here bringing that element of his style more obviously to the surface.

I don't know if that's completely true, though certainly the physical productions of his stage works often hinted at the fantastic more than their acting manner did. What's important is that, dubious though he was about Williams's work, Bentley clearly thought this was a show people should see. In this, alas, he was almost alone. Most of the reviewers found the play too overtly "poetic," lacking that grounding in the real, which had made at least two of Williams's previous works so touching to them. They urged him to return quickly to his better self. And, some hinted, to his senses.

The one exception, and it was a major one, was Brooks Atkinson in the *Times*. He conceded, at the end of his review, that "Even the people who respect Mr. Williams' courage and recognize his talent are likely to be aghast at what he has to say." But, he added, "this is what Mr. Williams thinks and it has to be reckoned with. In the first place, he is honest about it. He does not hide behind the usual formalities. Some of it is explicit enough to be revolting. In the second place, Mr. Williams is an artist. Breaking with the realistic theatre entirely, he has now written a long incantation with a long cast of characters and a constant flow of mood and experience and the great mass of it is bold and pertinent."

Interestingly, Atkinson returned to *Camino Real* in an invaluable little book he wrote after his retirement from the *Times*. It was called *The Lively Years 1920–1973,* and it reconsidered the most significant—not necessarily the "best"—plays of that half century. In his essay on this work, he quoted a few of the play's summarizing lines. A Gypsy fortune-teller, for example, says, "We're all of us guinea pigs in the laboratory of God. Humanity is just a work in progress." A hotel manager asks: "Can this be all? Is there nothing more? Is this what the glittering wheels of the heavens turn for?" Atkinson's point is that audiences in the early fifties were, as they had been for decades, attuned to plays that presented limited issues that could be neatly settled within a theatrical evening's brief time frame. They were not ready for the cosmic despair Williams was offering. And no stagecraft could distract them from that discomfort. Very sensibly, Atkinson ends his little piece this way: "They could not imagine that Mr. Williams' dark view of life would seem less mythical twenty years [or we might add, fifty years] later. It is more like reality today."

Williams was a habitual rewriter. And he went to work on *Camino Real* while its brief Broadway run (sixty performances) was still proceeding. But to small avail. The play has too large a cast and is too complex to encourage many revivals. Then, too, it may nowadays seem the opposite of what it seemed in 1953—too simple a statement of despair. But one also has to say this: It is the most interesting play Kazan staged in the last decade of his theatrical career—dark, strange, curiously haunting.

If *Camino Real* had been a success on the order of *The Skin of Our Teeth,* Kazan's other obvious break with the theater's ruling conventions, it is possible that his career might have taken a different course. Or, indeed, that the theater as a whole might have proved more venturesome than it was in the fifties and sixties. On the other hand, it was always difficult to blend radical stagecraft with the Broadway audience's demand for a humane and uplifting viewpoint. And Kazan was never truly a modernist. He liked the stage pictures and the opportunities for crazy action the tradition sometimes offered. But he was never drawn to absurdity, indeterminacy, Pinteresque silences. He remained ever The Group's child. He liked explanations, political and psychological, for whatever issues he explored.

Kazan was worried. He had now endured two theatrical flops (*Flight into Egypt, Camino Real*) and three box-office failures in film (*Panic in the Streets, Viva Zapata!, Man on a Tightrope*) and the project he most cared about, now known simply as *Waterfront,* was suddenly in trouble.

It should not have been. Budd Schulberg's final first draft screenplay (which would go through many more rewrites) was excellent. "It's one of the three best I've ever had," Kazan told him. "And the other two were *Death of a Salesman* and *A Streetcar Named Desire.*" This opinion was converted into a litany by Kazan: Salesman . . . Streetcar . . . Waterfront . . .

Some of the more intriguing matters in Schulberg's many drafts were the things that he and Kazan decided to omit. For example, Terry Malloy, in the early drafts, was not a longshoreman at all; he was an investigative reporter—"kind of a cynical newspaper reporter" in Schulberg's description—whose growing emotional involvement with the exploited workers mirrored his own journey to commitment to their cause. He was also, at first, an older man, divorced, with a grown daughter.

At some point, however, Schulberg conceived the idea that Terry should be younger and that he should be involved with a woman. "With my Hollywood background, I felt that we were going to tell a pretty tough story and that we needed a love story in the middle of it."

What surprised Schulberg, when Kazan's autobiography was published, was the director's frank acknowledgment of the analogy between Terry's informing on the union racketeers and his own HUAC testimony. "I never denied it," Kazan said to me a little later. "People said that, and I said, 'Yeah, I guess so.' I did relate to it naturally and a lot of the emotion that's in the film, came out of the emotions Budd and I had." He added, however, that these feelings were not central to the passion he brought to the film. I believe him. The theme is there—no denying it. But it is not the picture's driving force. The first note Kazan wrote to himself was this: "Theme This motion picture is about one thing only: a young man who has let his dignity slip away, regains it." On the other hand, there are admittedly a couple of curious phrases in Kazan's notes. At one point he writes, "The biggest loyalty a man has is to all the people, which in a democracy is the state. The biggest obligation a man has is to be a citizen."

This is, for Kazan, a unique statement, unduplicated anywhere else. And some of his critics, most notably Peter Biskind, would read Waterfront not merely as an endorsement of informing, but as an endorsement of a sort of state-corporate liberalism, placing a new reliance on large institutions to defend individual rights, an unthinkable idea to thirties and forties radicals.

That this strain entered liberal thought in this period is, I think, true. That Waterfront is a hidden plea for this viewpoint is, I think, ludicrous. The constantly identified source of evil in it is an utterly corrupt labor union, which decent-minded people, whatever their political beliefs, must find abhorrent. If these two hastily jotted sentences do seem to align Kazan with this sort of revisionism, I think it is a sign of temporary weakness, a signal of what his HUAC testimony had cost him emotionally.

For it should be noted that he quite quickly righted himself; nothing like these sentiments are to be found in any of his other *Waterfront* jottings. And Schulberg swears that he and Kazan never discussed their testimony while working on this screenplay. "The odd thing," he said to me, "is that I do not remember ever talking to Gadge about that."

He also thinks—and Kazan agreed with him—that his friendship with a longshoreman named Tony Mike deVincenzo, to whom Schulberg introduced him, had a bracing effect on Kazan. The writer—who used his lifelong passion for boxing as a way of insinuating himself with the boxing-crazed dockers—was by now entirely accepted by his subjects, and he thought Tony Mike and Kazan might be soul mates. Which they proved to be. Tony Mike had once been a pier boss, and a beneficiary of mob favors. But eventually he turned against them. And testified against them in the government hearings Schulberg attended. "He would tell me about what he went through," Kazan recalled, "and the scorn thrown at him. I'd had a good deal of scorn thrown at me in those years, so I was hefty. I could take it. And he too—he was tough. He was ready to fight all the time. And that helped me a lot, seeing this man who had gone through the whole damn thing *On the Waterfront* was about and was in a fury about it. That was a great experience . . ."

What was not a great experience for Kazan and Schulberg was getting their picture financed. Kazan had believed, from the beginning, that Darryl Zanuck was their most logical backer. Indeed, he obtained development money from him for the film. More important, he thought this was Zanuck's kind of picture.

In this, he was not wrong. Early in his career, when he was head of production at Warner Bros., it was Zanuck, more than anyone else, who had created the studio's house style—gangster pictures, wisecracking, low-life comedies, working-stiff melodramas. Later, at Fox, his pictures, on the whole, became more upscale in setting, but he had made *The Grapes of Wrath* and *How Green Was My Valley,* and most of his personal productions had taken up serious social issues.

But the times were changing radically and Zanuck, like all the other studio chiefs, was confronting the worst crisis in their industry's history. This was television, which, as of 1953, had robbed the movies of close to half their audience. About a quarter of the nation's movie theaters had closed and box office receipts, though still substantial because of rising ticket prices, were also heading downward, as was the pace of production. All these figures would worsen in the years ahead, but the trend was clear and alarming and men like Zanuck were thrashing about, looking both to new technologies, like the wide-screen formats, and new sorts of content, to offset their losses.

Kazan did not seem to notice that the kind of pictures he had been making—intense, relatively small-scale realistic dramas, shot in black-and-white—were becoming outmoded. It was odd. He more than anyone else had been responsible for bringing a new, much talked about style of acting to the screen, but he was apparently unaware of the forces that would, in a short time, render him virtually obsolete as a movie director.

As far as he was concerned, Zanuck had in hand a long-nurtured, well-polished screenplay in which Kazan believed more deeply than any he had ever been involved with. As he and Schulberg entrained for Los Angeles in 1953 he was bristling with confidence. His collaborator, on the other hand, was less sure about the climate into which they were launching it. These doubts worsened when they arrived at the station and found no studio car waiting for them, deepened when there were no studio-sent floral arrangements in their rooms at the Beverly Hills Hotel. Schulberg, of course, was a Hollywood Prince—his father had once held a job similar to Zanuck's at Paramount—so he was more attuned to the signs and symbols of a studio's regard than Kazan, whose interest in polite gestures was nonexistent: He always dressed in a sloppy casual manner ("He sends his suits out to be rumpled," Vivien Leigh had said of him), had no taste for haute cuisine or delicate language and often directed, when he was on location, outdoors, stripped to the waist in an age when other directors still wore jackets and ties to work.

But Schulberg was right. Their accounts of their meeting with Zanuck vary slightly, but their essence is similar. The producer launched into a paean to the glories of movie technology and how it had driven progress in the business: the stabilization of the image when everyone agreed on the twenty-four-frames-per-second shooting and projection speed, the coming of sound, the rise of color—and now, yes, CinemaScope. The studio was enjoying huge success with *The Robe*, the first-ever production in the new wide screen process—it would eventually gross somewhere between $20 and $30 million—and Zanuck was now saying that every Fox production would henceforth be in CinemaScope. Both Kazan and Schulberg recalled Zanuck excitedly singing the potential of his next CinemaScope epic, *Prince Valiant*, an adaptation of the comic strip, nowadays a favorite pop movie subgenre, but, as it would turn out, not a 1950s success.

Eventually, Kazan got Zanuck back to the subject at hand. According to Schulberg, Zanuck said he hated everything about the script. Kazan responded by stressing a comparison with *The Grapes of Wrath*—downtrodden folks struggling for a better life—but the producer was not buying. "Who's going to care about a lot of sweaty longshoremen?" he asked. The meeting broke up with recriminations. Handshake deals were cited. And moral commitments. According to Schulberg, he and Kazan retreated to the office that had been assigned them and more or less trashed it, in the process liberating a typewriter and toting it back with them to the Beverly Hills Hotel, where they discouragedly began yet another revision of their script.

In Schulberg's account, Kazan began making calls to other studios, all of whom also passed on the project. "Goddam it," he remembers the director saying, "I'm going to stick with this thing if I have to get a 16 millimeter camera and shoot it myself." It is possible that the passing years may have added a certain dramatically potent melodrama to this tale. There were very likely two meetings with Zanuck, during which substantive discussions of the proffered script were undertaken. It is possible that Zanuck offered the suggestion that Terry Malloy might possibly be an undercover FBI agent (shades of *The Hook* meetings!). There exists, as well, a transcript of Zanuck's remarks, in the course of which he apparently said, "If you come to me with this story in its present state and you say, 'I have got

Marlon Brando for this picture' then it is a clear-cut and simple decision for me to make." But, of course, at this point, Brando was unin-
terested (Schulberg suspects he had not even read the script that
had been sent him). Later, after the picture was released, Schulberg
made some remarks in an article he wrote about the film, about a
certain producer's "cowardice" in backing off a "touchy" subject. He
did not mention Zanuck by name, but the producer fired off a letter
to Schulberg in which he wrote, "I cannot accept the idea that I lost
my courage or gave you a quick brush-off. I spent more time on your
project than I do on some of the pictures that we actually produce.
In addition to this I invested $40,000 in the property. If this is a
brush-off then I have a wrong interpretation of that phrase."

But it was a brush-off, however disputed the details. Indeed, I
think these encounters with Zanuck were watersheds in movie history. It was true that, throughout the 1950s, black-and-white movies
of considerable seriousness continued to be produced. In this very
year Columbia had a large, fully deserved success with *From Here to
Eternity*. But it is also true that CinemaScope (and competing wide-
screen processes like VistaVision) would very quickly become the
prevailing industry standard.

I'm not certain that, once the novelty had worn off, the audience
was primarily responding to the new aspect ratios. Content and stars
continued to be the largest factor in drawing people into the theaters. On the other hand, Hollywood soon learned that color and
wide screen did affect the stories the studios could effectively tell. It
was obviously bad for film noir as well as for all kinds of gritty, urban
dramas. It was a ponderous format, hard to cut quickly, and romantic comedies, for example, became slow and witless. That was true of
musicals as well. Wide screen was sometimes, though not always, advantageous for Westerns and for dull-witted spectacle, but put simply, the net effect of the new formats was to make American movies
slower, dumber, less artistically and intellectually stirring than they
had been.

And they did not in any way arrest the declining economic
power of the industry. By 1962, when they reached their all-time
low, the studios grossed only $903 million, down more than $700
million since that figure reached its modern height in 1946. By then

they produced only 121 films—a record low—roughly two-thirds fewer than they had immediately after World War II. Weekly attendance in that year was forty-four million, less than half what it had been in 1946. By the later date, the studios had essentially ceased offering long-term contracts of the kind Kazan had enjoyed. Projects were set up one at a time at whatever studio could be induced to take on the risk.

That this newly developing way of doing business did not kill *Waterfront* was something of a miracle—an oft-retold miracle. As it happened, Sam Spiegel was staying in a room down the hall from Kazan and Schulberg at the Beverly Hills. A sometime art director, he had produced mainly low-budget films—a notable exception had been John Huston's *The African Queen*—under the name S. P. Eagle, and was a legendary high roller who had just produced a resounding flop, *Melba,* about the opera singer who had lent her name to the toast and the peaches. But he was, of course, undaunted. Schulberg knew him and one night approached him about producing *Waterfront.* The producer asked Schulberg to come to his room the next morning and read him the script.

Schulberg found the producer's door open, with Spiegel reposing in his bed. Not entirely certain Spiegel was fully awake, the writer began his recitation. It was occasionally interrupted by mumbles, mutterings and the occasional groan. But, at the end of the reading, Spiegel agreed to produce it. Neither Kazan nor Schulberg entirely trusted his sleepy word, but Spiegel followed through. His best relationship was at Columbia, where Harry Cohn still reigned, and he was able to set the picture up there on a very low budget.

The film was an anomaly for Spiegel. He specialized in a different kind of picture—most famously David Lean's grand epics. Realism of a Kazanian sort was not at all his kind of thing. But he and Kazan somehow got along—tough, immigrant nuts that they were. Schulberg's relationship with him was much rockier, principally because Spiegel was obsessive about his scripts, demanding one niggling rewrite after another. There is a well-known story, which Schulberg insists is true, in which his wife awakened in the wee hours one morning at their Bucks County retreat, to find her husband getting dressed. Where in the world was he going? she asked. To New York, came the reply, to kill Sam Spiegel.

It appears that Spiegel's largest contribution to *On the Waterfront* was . . . Marlon Brando. The problem here was not the script he had not read, but his relationship with Kazan, which had deteriorated because of Kazan's HUAC testimony. In his autobiography, Brando represents himself as "conflicted" about the role. He said he knew some of the people "who had been deeply hurt. It was especially stupid because most of the people named were no longer Communists." Given these circumstances, a handshake deal to play Terry was instead struck with Frank Sinatra, a Hoboken native. His career as a movie crooner having faded, he had just scored a remarkable, ultimately Oscar-winning, comeback as Maggio, in *From Here to Eternity*, and was once again hot. Or at least hottish. But with him in the cast, Spiegel found that he could not get as big a budget for the film as he could with Brando starring. So the great *Schnorrer* (Brando's word) went to work on the actor. With, at first, indifferent results. In the meanwhile, it is said that Sinatra actually had a costume fitting for the role.

Enter now Kazan and his friend Karl Malden. Kazan had always had the notion that Malden should be a director, an opinion the actor did not share. But at this moment, in the summer of 1953, Kazan was hard-pressed. Not only was he preparing *Waterfront*, he was also beginning to rehearse Robert Anderson's play *Tea and Sympathy*. He needed help, and he asked Malden to cast the play, which—aside from Deborah Kerr—he did, keeping regular hours in an office next to John Steinbeck's at the Playwrights' Company.

This soon shaded over into assisting Kazan on *Waterfront* as well. At this point Sinatra still technically had the Terry role, but Spiegel (and doubtless Kazan) still harbored hopes for Brando. At which point, Kazan ordered Malden to direct a scene with Paul Newman—then still an Actors' Studio tyro, two years from making his first movie. The stated idea was to show this piece to Spiegel as another alternative. Malden spent a week rehearsing Newman and his wife, Joanne Woodward, in a scene from *Liliom* (the carousel barker in that play was a pretty fair emotional analog to Terry, and it must be said, the young Woodward would have been appropriate for Edie). Eventually they played the scene for Spiegel, but to no effect.

There was obviously a hidden agenda here; if Brando heard that a handsome young actor, cut from something like the same cloth, was in the running for a great role, it might move him to commitment. I don't know if this ploy influenced Brando. Malden recalls a late-night phone call from Brando's friend and agent, Jay Kantor, begging him to intercede with Brando to take the part. Malden says he refused to do so. He does, however, remember telling Kantor that this was the role of a lifetime and that the agent should do everything in his power to persuade Brando to do it. In the late summer or early fall Brando signed for the part.

Which, ironically, almost cost Malden his chance to play the waterfront priest, Father Barry. For when Sinatra heard that he had lost the lead he angrily demanded to play the priest. As it happened, Spiegel somehow settled with Sinatra (in his autobigraphy Malden suggests he gave the singer a museum-quality painting as heart balm) and Malden kept his role.

And made one other enormous contribution to the film. That was the casting of Edie. Typically, Kazan wanted a young, unknown actress for the part, but no one seemed quite right to him. Finally, Malden found himself equally drawn to two young actresses, Elizabeth Montgomery, a decade prior to her television stardom in *Bewitched,* and Eva Marie Saint, just beginning her career, working in live television and on the stage. It would, of course, be the latter who got the part—perhaps because, like the fictional Edie, she was convent educated and, as well, a beguiling combination of innocence and determination with just a hint of unacknowledged sexiness.

Whether casting for *Waterfront* (the words *On* and *the* were not added to the title until the movie was finished) was completed before Kazan diverted himself to Robert Anderson's *Tea and Sympathy* is impossible to say, but the likelihood is that it was not.

Anderson's wife, Phyllis, briefly moved into the Kazan household while her husband was in the Navy, and her good friend, Molly, began tracking *Tea and Sympathy* during the war years, when Anderson would send her drafts of it from his wartime postings. He was one of several young playwrights she was mentoring in those years—and a good thing, too, because his agent, Audrey Wood, had small faith in the play. Anderson would remember a lunch with her at which Wood presented him five tattered copies of his script—all rejected by various managements—and told him that she'd give back the sixth copy as soon as the Playwrights' Company returned it. Happily, they did not—Robert Sherwood had taken a liking to it, with Kazan contracting to do it soon after he returned from directing Sherwood's film script in Europe. Later, on the first night of its pre-Broadway out-of-town tryouts, when the play drew an enthusiastic audience response, Wood condescendingly said to Kazan, "So you've performed one of your miracles again."

He denied doing anything of the kind. This was a play for which he had more than customary fondness, despite the fact that it is a rather bourgeois work. A young man named Tom Lee (John Kerr) is disliked for his somewhat feminine ways by his New England prep school peers, by his uncomprehending parents and, most significantly, by his housemaster, Bill Reynolds (Leif Erikson, a Group veteran). The boy doubts his masculinity, especially after a failure with a prostitute and after he is cast in a female role in the all-male school's play. Laura, the housemaster's wife (Deborah Kerr), is the only one to whom the boy can pour out his heart and eventually, at the play's famous climax, she gives herself to the boy with these famous lines: "Years from now . . . when you talk about this . . . and you will . . . be kind."

The piece had a certain potential for the risible, which Kazan immediately recognized. It is essentially a long justification for a mercy fuck. Everyone feared the audience giggling and tittering at the end, when Laura begins unbuttoning her blouse, and, indeed, some unwanted laughter was heard early in the tryouts—before, as Kazan later said, the reviews insisted on the importance, seriousness and, above all, sensitivity of the piece. About this, they were not wrong, for the play does contain some good writing—slightly simple-minded, but also decently liberal-minded and occasionally even rather funny—about the rather odd permutations of middle-class sexuality in the 1950s. It is especially good in its assaults on traditional masculine posturing.

Indeed, it is fair to say that this—not the "sensational" ending—is what drew Kazan to the play. It is another in his studies of stern, repressive, sometimes excessively hearty fathers and father figures. But he cautioned himself not to overload the play with what he called "my characteristic heavy-handed dramatics."

It had to be neither a symphony nor a concerto, but rather a chamber piece (Kazan's metaphor)—quietly voiced, tactful, delicate—and starring an impeccably ladylike leading lady. It was Anderson who kept proposing Deborah Kerr for the part, and she won Kazan over on their first meeting, beginning a lifelong friendship.

But for all the delicacy he sought in its staging, Kazan saw a fierce conflict proceeding among the teacups. "The tension of the play," he scribbled, "consists in the contrast between the fatal event that is happening to Tom . . . and the quiet, cultured, 'intelligent,' tea and sympathy, soft-spoken, tradition seeped, golden-mean, good fellow, Harper's magazine, cork-floor, discreet and gentle atmosphere that keeps out the cruelty of the WRECKER: reality."

The "fatal event" Kazan was alluding to was a forced acknowledgment, on Tom's part, of his homosexual impulses. We have previously observed Kazan's close and unjudgmental relationship with Tennessee Williams, soon to be replicated by his relationship with William Inge. He always identified with gays as people, like himself, who were "different," outside the American mainstream. In Tom he sees a typical adolescent, unsure of his sexuality. Which means that his tragedy would be the imposition of a sexual choice upon him by this hearty, uncomprehending, male world, before he is ready to make up his own mind.

In this struggle for identity Laura is, at first, a rather fragile ally. When we discover her in the first act she has, as Kazan puts it, an excess of "good girl qualities," which mask the fact that she's been "denuded" of self-respect, largely as a result of her essentially loveless marriage to a man who has sublimated his sexual nature in his determination to get ahead in his job (he appears to be next in line for the headmaster's post at the school). Her "spine" is to "recover" her best self. "By involving herself she finds herself," Kazan writes.

Interestingly, Kazan spends the most time in his notes on her husband, Bill. The man married Laura, he thinks, partly because, with her breeding and good manners, she would help advance his career, which "is his life," but also because "vaguely he felt there was something wrong with him." He sensed something "dry, lonely, sterile, empty" in himself, which he hoped she would cure. But that didn't happen. Instead, she "confirmed him in his inner silence and his final reliance on his career."

In his notes Kazan suddenly remembers something Bud Lighton had once said to him about Melvyn Douglas, that he was "like a gelding mounting a mare"—and he imagines Bill as something like that, imagines him saying to himself about Laura, "When I fuck her she just lies there judging . . . she doesn't like a good clean fuck," the result being that he begins to avoid her sexually. At the same time, though, she's jealous of his career—her only real rival for his attentions—and he begins to read criticisms of himself into her "every little look." Kazan adds: "It's hard to fuck anyone who's critical of you."

Is he, one wonders, thinking about himself with Molly? We can't, of course, say, but in his notes, Kazan seems to imply that some of the housemaster's placatory behavior toward Laura is similar to his behavior toward Molly, especially in the way he let her into his professional life.

Be that as it may, he imputes to the housemaster a concern about his maleness that he thinks is akin to his creator Robert Anderson's worry "about his lack of superficially male qualities." Anderson was, in life, a gentlemanly and well-met man; his creation was much less so. Kazan imagines Bill characterizing Tom as a "sick, neurotic, weak, clinging, moon-struck little boy" who is "spoiling his wife with flattery and constant adulation. She laps it up and she is so gentle with him. With me, she is all criticism."

These notes suggest a savagery in the play that, if memory serves, did not manifest itself overtly on the stage. In his direction Kazan was as good as his word; he did create a kind of chamber piece, a trio of dissonances. You could not say that audiences were lulled into submitting to it; in the event Tom's neuroses were given an appealing spin and whatever disgust Laura felt for her husband was masked by an air of genteel sympathy for his needs.

The result was a hit, something a fifties audience could comfortably take to heart. The daily reviewers were generally knocked out by the piece, though Walter Kerr did note that it was "a sentimental play, almost a dream play in the goddess-like generosity of its warm, Titian-haired idealized heroine" but he, like all his colleagues, paid high tribute to the "sensitivity" of the actors and the director. The weekly reviewers were less kind. Wolcott Gibbs in the *New Yorker* thought the play "as tidily and trickily organized as a dance by the Rockettes," while Eric Bentley found it to be "folklore" in that everyone in it behaved with utter predictabily, receiving their rewards and comeuppances in ways that did not startle and left the audience in a state of glowing goodwill, sighing contentedly over a pretty fairy tale. But it was acted and staged "perfectly," even by Bentley's cranky standards, and so it ran for something like two years, went on a prosperous tour and was made into a successful movie in which the leading Broadway players repeated their roles. It was also the solid hit Kazan needed after his dry spell.

Throughout the late summer and early fall, the wrangles over *Waterfront* continued, though it appears Spiegel realized his (and Kazan's) heart's desire—Brando—fairly early in this period, with the rest of the players—almost all of them either Group Theatre or Actors Studio actors—falling fairly easily into place.

Discussions of the script proceeded on an almost daily basis in Spiegel's suite at the St. Regis Hotel. He was, in Schulberg's phrase, "A bear for structure." This was all right with the writer, but the discussions were excruciatingly detailed, repetitive and sometimes involved matters Kazan planned to address when he was actually shooting. The producer was also "maddeningly manipulative," and one day Schulberg returned from a trip to the bathroom to find Spiegel and Kazan whispering in what he took to be a conspiratorial manner. Whereupon he exploded: "I've been on this project for two years. I've taken practically nothing up front. I'm gambling, like you, on a percentage of the profits. It's beginning to break me. I've actually had to mortgage my farm. Sam hasn't even paid me the lousy

$5,000 he's owed me for months. I've written my heart out on this. So what the hell can you two bastards be whispering about?"

Kazan hustled his writer out for a cooling walk around the block. He conceded all of Schulberg's criticisms. But he urged his friend to remember, "with Sam, we were coming to bat with two outs at the bottom of the ninth. If we couldn't score with him, *Waterfront* was dead. 'Let's face it, Sam Spiegel has saved our butt.'"

So they soldiered on. Only to be assailed, not long before the cameras turned, from an astonishing source—Molly Kazan. One day, very late in the preproduction game, she said to Kazan and Schulberg (who was by this time living much of the time in the guest room of the Kazan brownstone), "Boys, you're making a big mistake. It's not ready. It's still not ready." Schulberg was infuriated—"I had gone through hell with that project"—and Kazan (who briefly confirms this incident in his autobiography) was apparently no less angry. Like so many other Kazan collaborators, Schulberg had observed him deferring to her—"the immigrant's attraction for the New England aristocracy, the Anglo-Saxon . . ." But she was also, in the writer's word, "like a judge. And she was a tough goddamn judge. While being fond of her, she could drive you bloody crazy."

The collaborators rejected her judgment, but, undeterred, she actually called up Spiegel, urging postponement. This was, even for Molly Kazan, an extraordinary intrusion on her husband's turf, and Spiegel rejected her advice. What Kazan may or may not have said to her we do not know. What we can say is that the wheels were turning, that this train was leaving the station. And that it finally had on board a leading lady.

Sometime shortly after *Tea and Sympathy* opened, Eva Marie Saint got her *Waterfront* role. Karl Malden takes only modest credit for her casting; he simply read and worked with her and Elizabeth Montgomery for a few days, until Kazan told him he had made his choice for the part, without telling Malden whom he had chosen. Saint, meantime, had gotten her first solid Broadway job, in Horton Foote's play *The Trip to Bountiful*, which starred Lillian Gish and which was due to premiere in early November.

Saint thinks Kazan must have seen her in it, but also vividly remembers an improvisation she and Brando did for him. The director's instructions to her, as she recalled, were these: "This is a young man who is coming to visit your sister, your older sister. She is not home. And your mother and your father do not want you alone in the house with the opposite sex. So your action is to get him out, in fact, not to let him in the door."

Brando's action was, naturally, the opposite—to somehow get flirtatiously in the room with the young woman, which he did. "The charm, the smile, he was beautiful then. He was just so attractive. And . . . we ended up dancing. I had an Ann Klein dress on, I remember. It had a belt and a full skirt and he took my skirt and he went like that [Saint made a whirling gesture and a whooshing noise]. All I know is that I ended up crying. Crying and laughing . . . I mean there was such an attraction there. . . . That smile of his. I mean, I can see it in my mind's eye to this day . . . I was not frightened. He didn't come in to rape the girl or anything. He wasn't mean. He was very tender and funny . . . And Kazan, in his genius, saw the chemistry there."

"Tender." That was the controlling impulse Kazan wanted for this movie, especially in Brando's performance. It characterizes Terry's relationships with everyone that matters to him in the film— Edie, his brother, even his beloved pigeons. It is the quality that allows the film to transcend the harsh reality of its setting, the murderous corruption of its mobsters, the cowed passivity of its worker-victims. Without tenderness the movie would have been no more than an "interesting" twist on quite a basic gangster trope. Instead, it is, of course, one of the few truly indispensable American movies.

The film would become, for Kazan, one of the three films that, late in life, he obsessively returned to (the others were *A Face in the Crowd* and *America, America*), running them again and again because he knew they were the ones on which rested what hopes of immortality he entertained. He said: "When I watch it . . . when he plays those scenes with her, I'm broken up. I break up. That one person should need so much from another person in the way of tenderness and all that. But we all do, don't we? We all marry or hopefully marry or hopefully hook up with some lady that's going to make us feel we're OK . . . We search for it and want it and crave it . . . And then sometimes it happens for a while. And something in that basic story is what stirs people. Not the social-political thing so much as the human element in it." Taking nothing away from Saint, Kazan attributes much of the film's heartbreaking power to Brando's work. "It seems to me however fine the script is and however fine . . . the look of the picture, there's something in that performance that just tears your heart out. And I'm not sure that's inherent in the script."

Talking to me about Brando's work, forty years later, Kazan was volubly generous. "Externally, he's very gritty. I mean, he liked the streets. He liked those people, he liked the longshoremen. He used to lie around on the roof and talk with them. But that wasn't it. The thing was with Brando there is . . . both a toughness, an exterior toughness, and a tremendous desire for gentleness and tenderness. And the best scenes in the movie, from my point of view, are the scenes with Eva Saint, where he's asking her to understand him, where they're sitting in the café. He's great in those scenes. Why? Because he's a tough guy revealing a side of himself you didn't expect . . . the side of himself you didn't know existed. . . . At the same time, he was a son of a bitch and a bad person. And a betrayer. Still, you wanted to help him. And she did, too. And that's what came off. He had that ambivalence to him . . . he's both hardy and indifferent and wants you to love him very much."

Interestingly, that scene—the first in which Edie calls gently to Terry's conscience—chimes with their tryout scene. It ends, after a certain amount of somewhat suppressed fractiousness, with the two of them dancing, just as they had at their first rehearsal-hall meeting. "He's like an enormous friendly dog," Kazan wrote in his production notes at the time, which was no more than superficially correct. There's so much more to Terry. And Kazan went on at much greater length, and with much greater subtlety, about Terry in a letter he wrote (but which we cannot be certain he sent) to Brando before he started shooting.

He says that he "really wants to be photographing the kid's insides as much as exterior events," within the context of his "regaining his dignity or self-esteem." This regeneration, he says, "happens inside the man and has to be done by you so I can photograph it."

He then passes on to a reconstruction of Terry's backstory, everything that made him what he is when we discover him in the film. He is an orphan, which, of course, makes his relationship to his only kin, his corrupt brother, so important to him. He owes something as well to Johnny Friendly, the pier union boss, who picked him up and made him into a prizefighter. But even so, he is "terribly and fundamentally lonely." Kazan even goes so far as to suggest that possibly the only women he has ever known are whores. If he has known other kinds of women, it has only been to conquer them, not to love them. (Kazan notes, in passing, that a lot of the prizefighters he has known are not very successful with women, possibly because that trade encourages them to remain arrested adolescents; he does not note some other possibilities—that it is an inherently violent trade encouraging a certain body-builder narcissism.)

He also suggests that in boxing Terry was able to find "revenge on a world that rejected him. He's like a rejected lover who after years still hasn't quite given up." But there is, Kazan says, "something of the ascetic about him. His best friends are pigeons." That's true, and his sweetness about his birds—he tells Edie they mate for life and brave skies that are full of hawks waiting to swoop on them—is in some way the first metaphor we have for his own redemptive potential.

Kazan then makes a helpful comparison between Terry and Brando's Kowalski. Superficially they are similar—half-educated, half-literate men with a taste for settling disputes with their fists. But, he writes, they are very different. "Stanley is undivided. He is confident. He is on top. He has no self-doubts. He has no sex problems. He is not conceivably lonely." Terry has a superficially similar swagger, "but his eyes betray him." He writes: "Marlon, this part is much closer to you and to myself, too." This was a shrewd stroke, for as we know, Brando detested Stanley. How much Kazan may have despised him is harder to say, since he hid his self-doubts—and his anger—much more cannily.

In any case, "I think his angers are deeper, and more animal-like, more superstitious, more unanswerable than Stanley's. Stanley flared and struck, Terry's angers are kept in, nursed, grow to a point where they can't be satisfied except by murder. Terry is truly dangerous, Stanley just fights a lot . . ."

There is more in this vein. Stanley is the "king of the dung heap. Terry is lonely, by himself, turned-in, mysterious . . . suspicious of all girls, all idealism. He doesn't want to be taken or fooled . . ." as opposed to Stanley who is beyond self-doubt. He has "complete confidence in his cock as the great leveller, the equalizer."

Terry, on the other hand, was "practically brought up not to trust the women in that world. They're either dogs or they're out to make a fool [of] you and cheat on you and talk about you behind your back and say you're a bust as a lay. It must have been far more pleasurable and comfortable when he was fighting to be wanted and desired and admired by a lot of men." This, however, according to Kazan, is "a complication he has always fought off. It's more secure and more pleasurable to be desired by 100 girls than to meet one on an equal basis. To be in love is traditionally a sign of weakness among adolescents. To lay girls is fine, because you are conquering and getting something for nothing."

Kazan is, I think, imputing too much to Terry, especially when he tries to delve into his sexuality. But it must also be said that there is a powerful shyness, amounting almost to ineptitude, when he meets and is mysteriously, inarticulately, moved by Edie. Kazan is right to attempt to get Brando thinking about these ambivalent subtexts. They are the keys to Terry's character and, therefore, the key to the entire movie.

"He is a primitive," Kazan summed up. "He really can only half-read. He thinks too much, it gets painful and then he shakes it off, like a fighter might shake off a right cross. This combination of primitiveness and gentleness, of false savagery and self doubt, of guilt and yet longing is the thing that makes the part fascinating to me." And, ultimately, to Brando.

———

From Kazan's point of view, this was a perfect shoot, a picture made in exactly the manner he had been aiming for since the beginning of his movie career. As he put it: "I was trained to work with people on location and I enjoyed it. I enjoyed the longshoremen. . . . I liked them a lot. It was a great experience for me because I was on my feet all the time in the city and I think from that point of view it's as close as I ever came to making a film exactly the way I wanted."

In particular, he relished the punishing weather. "It was a cold goddamn winter. As we went along, it was more and more into the winter and more and more cold and rain and we never stopped shooting. We had these great barrels there and people would break down boxes and throw them into the [barrels]. We had hot boxes all the time." But you could not, of course, act and try to keep yourself warm over these fires, and that, in the end, gave the performers a certain look that Kazan wanted. "They didn't have this lovely flush of success that actors in Hollywood have . . . their dimpled, pink beautiful complexion. They were miserable-looking human beings and that includes Brando."

Who was on his best behavior. It is true that he had a clause in his contract that permitted him to leave the set in the late afternoon to visit his psychiatrist in Manhattan, which caused a certain amount of permanent resentment in the case of Rod Steiger. But mostly he was the very model of good movie star manners. Saint would remember him frequently slipping his soon-to-be famous plaid jacket around her shivering shoulders. Kazan would remember having occasionally to drag him out of one of the rooms the production rented in a grim waterfront hotel to do his scenes, so reluctant was he to face the weather. But out he went—in good humor—with Schulberg remembering him saying, "You know, it's so fuckin' cold out here there's no way you c'n overact." And on the one occasion he began to do so—improvising with Steiger—Kazan put a quick stop to it: "Stop the shit, Buddy," was all he said.

That was pretty much what he did, directorially, on this picture—keep everyone underplaying in the naturalistic mode. Saint would recall that John Hamilton, the actor playing her father, went somewhat over the top in one highly emotional scene and she overheard Kazan whisper to him between takes, "just say the words, John," which quickly settled the actor. That sort of thing was pretty much his way on this film. He was always just sort of reassuringly *there* for his actors, as Saint recalled—"that great wonderful face of his right next to the camera . . . there was such empathy felt from this man."

He was particularly protective of this "thin, little, seemingly undernourished Catholic girl." Her first scene in the picture was one in which she comes up to the rooftop where Terry keeps his pigeons, to give him her dead brother's jacket, not yet knowing that it is Terry who betrayed him. The environment was, of course, strange to her, and Kazan told her to imagine that might be a ferocious animal in the pigeon coops—"it could be a bear, it could be a gorilla, it could be a lion." She remembers thinking, "My dear Gadge, you don't have to tell me to be frightened. I am so frightened—this is my first scene in the movie and all these people are watching."

But she soon settled into the rhythms of the location. Too much so, in Kazan's judgment. A friendly and rather uncomplicated person, Saint was soon genially chatting up the rest of the cast and crew. Until Kazan drew her aside and said: "Eva Marie, I want you to think of yourself as an hourglass. When you get up in the morning you've got so much energy and that's the sand going through. You have to learn how much sand there is and how it's going through, at what rate, so that you do not dissipate your energy. If I have a close-up of you, I can't put a card on the screen saying, 'Sorry, Eva Marie was just exhausted when she did this . . . close-up.'"

But still, she had a certain natural exuberance, which occasionally willed out. She often wore, when the camera couldn't see them, heavy red tights under her prim navy blue skirts and she would occasionally do a little can-can, flashing the tights, on the docks between takes. And she found herself very drawn to Brando. Were she not recently, happily married (to Jeffrey Hayden, a producer), she implies she might have fallen for her gently seductive costar.

That, of course, did not happen. And, indeed, toward the end of the shoot, when Brando invades her apartment, for the violent scene in which eventually he takes her virginity, she found herself suddenly embarrassed to have to play the scene in her slip. It was not a very revealing slip, but American movies were still in their buttoned-up phase and she was a nice girl. Kazan sensing her hesitation, sidled up to her and whispered one word in her ear—"Jeff." By which he meant that she would not be embarrassed to appear before him in a slip. It also reminded her of her own respectability, that this was just a few minutes of playacting. The scene is, as we all remember, one of the most powerful in the movie—the violent release of all the sexual tension that has been building between Terry and Edie.

There were other sorts of tensions on the location. There was some fear that the still potent mob might try to disrupt the production. Policemen were omnipresent and Kazan himself had a longshoreman bodyguard, whose active services were required only once; he had to shove a mob goon away from Kazan and up against a wall. But otherwise there was no need for strong-arm tactics, although Kazan, typically, resorted to them once himself. He had hired a group of fairly well-known former boxers to play some of the mobsters surrounding Lee J. Cobb's union boss, Johnny Friendly—Two-Ton Tony Galento, Abe Simon, Tami Mauriello and a middleweight named Roger Donohue, who had once actually killed an opponent in the ring. At one tense moment Kazan had Mauriello stationed close to the camera, needing a strong reaction from him. It didn't happen—the pug's attention kept wandering. So just before calling action, Kazan darted into frame, slapped Mauriello as hard as he could across the face, and leaped back out of retaliation's range. But he got the expression from him that he wanted.

Directorial heroics of that kind were, however, the exception rather than the rule. If anyone tested his directorial patience, it was his producer. Spiegel would occasionally arrive at the location in his limousine, accompanied by one of his interchangeable young lovelies, wearing his camel-hair overcoat and stepping daintily over cables and detritus in his bespoke alligator shoes, to complain to all and sundry about Kazan running over schedule, costing him money he didn't have. On one such occasion—it was the night scene in which Terry discovers his murdered brother hanging from a meat hook—the director entirely lost it, screaming threats at Spiegel, threatening to quit. Schulberg, who was at his side every day, had to take him for a little walk and replay the speech Kazan had given him when he had stormed out of their script conference—remember Sam came through for us when no one else would. Kazan, of course, had to laugh. And as the years went on both he and Schulberg began to concede a certain amount of the film's success to Spiegel's compulsive attention to the script. In his autobiography Kazan went so far as to say that without Spiegel's interventions the picture might have failed.

He was, indeed, more than usually modest about his contributions to the picture. I think he understood that there are certain—very rare—films that take on a life of their own, that seem, on the set, as they're being made, fated for greatness, and that wisdom consists of not intervening excessively in their progress. Later on, everyone can take credit for their foreordained success. Except, it must be said in this case, no one ever has. In retrospect, everyone simply defers modestly to the phenomenon *On the Waterfront* became.

Take, for instance, the scene in the playground where Terry and Edie meet and shyly begin to acknowledge mutual attraction. In a rehearsal Saint dropped one of her gloves and Brando picked it up and started wriggling his large fingers into the glove. It was wonderful. What else, we wondered, might he like to wriggle into some small, tight Catholic part of Edie? Kazan just stood there—"the stupid director" in his later words, asking only that the actors duplicate the moment with the camera turning.

Or take what became *On the Waterfront*'s signature scene, Brando and Steiger in the taxicab, with the former making his heartbreaking speech about his older brother not looking out for him, forcing him to take a dive in the bout which, had he won it, "coulda" made him a "contender." (That immortal line, now part of the common American language, was, incidentally, borrowed from Schulberg's father, like Budd himself, a boxing fanatic.) The scene kept bugging Brando, whose complaints went unheeded. Finally, Kazan and Schulberg settled down with him at lunch one day to get to the bottom of his problem. It seems the actor felt that his character would never have been so confessional with Charlie the Gent pointing a gun at him. He had a point—yet the gun was a necessary threat in the scene. So Kazan said, in effect, Well, what if it's not aimed at you? What if it's present but pointing downward. That would work, Brando said. And it was done. Indeed, he brushes the weapon lightly away as the brothers talk.

A larger problem was the setting for their encounter. What was needed and expected for the scene was a real taxi and a full-scale set. What they had was a cab with its side cut open to accommodate the camera and no more than a blank wall behind it, which the cinematographer, the great Boris Kaufman, somehow made work with artful, quite minimal, lighting.

There was worse to come. For Brando deserted the scene—as far as one can tell, the only one shot on a soundstage—before it was

finished. It was time for his sacred shrink appointment and he just
up and left. He was present, of course, for the two-shots and his
close-ups, but left when it was time for Steiger's singles. Kazan filled
in, reading Brando's words. The star's absence was a violation of
common movie protocol, and Steiger never forgot it. He would go
on about it the rest of his life, even though he eventually became a
lay analyst and thus possibly somewhat more attuned to the pressing
quality of doctor-patient relationships. And surely aware that in the
almost universal opinion of moviegoing mankind, the scene is regarded as unimprovable. Kazan always refused to take credit for the
scene. "I didn't do any directing with it. You can believe it. It's true.
I'm not a falsely modest man. . . . They did it. They made the scene,
those two men."

This sort of serendipity extended through the end of production,
early 1954. Nor does it seem that there were any great problems in
postproduction—though by this time Spiegel was increasingly nervous about the film and decided he needed a major composer to
score it—one more famous, insuring name to adorn the posters. At
the moment there was no bigger name than Leonard Bernstein,
with two hit musicals, *On the Town* and *Wonderful Town* (the latter
currently on Broadway) plus a number of more serious works, to his
credit, and Spiegel invited him to screen *Waterfront* with Kazan and
Brando also present. The former thought Spiegel too modest about
the picture, too obsequious about it to Bernstein, and after this running he told the producer that (a) the picture was "great" and (b)
Spiegel should stop hiding out behind that phony S. P. Eagle pseudonym (which he did). He was also disappointed that Brando left
the screening in silence, without a word. But Bernstein was swept
away by what he saw. "I heard music as I watched; that was enough,"
he later wrote.

He had never written a film score (and never would again) and
so did not know the highly technical tricks of the trade. Basically, he
sat down at a Moviola—no cue sheets, no tables that would allow
him to convert footage counts to minutes and seconds, no assistant
editor to run the machine. But he provided the perfect finishing
touch to the film, for Bernstein was himself a romantic and his
music plays to the film's most basic spirit, but without pandering to

it. It is quite spare, but it knows when dissonance is called for and it rises to sublimity at the climax when Brando, beaten to a point near death, must rise staggering to his feet and lead his men into work and away from Johnny Friendly's baleful influence.

When he had the music in, Kazan struck his answer print and showed it to Harry Cohn at his home, in his basement screening room. Cohn had reveled with some anonymous starlet before the screening and fell asleep, snoring, halfway through. The girl stayed awake, however, and told Kazan she liked what she saw. He decided not to risk a second running with Cohn and headed back to New York, choosing to read approval in those snores.

On the Waterfront opened in New York on July 28, 1954, and elsewhere around the same time. The vast majority of the first reviews were favorable. As is commonly the case with daily and weekly journalism, these notices simply accepted the movie on its own terms. They did not delve into its more controversial sociopolitical aspects. To these reviewers it was simply a more-than-usually realistic crime drama in which the protagonist comes to consciousness and overt opposition to the immediate evil oppressing him and his community. They could not help but observe the intensity of its acting, the power of its mise-en-scène. They did not anticipate the peculiarly intense public response to the movie. Or the ongoing controversy that would for decades thereafter attend it.

Kazan immediately guessed that his film was going to be a popular success. On the twenty-eighth he appeared at the Astor Theatre in Times Square to see if anyone was turning out for the first (11 A.M.) showing and was surprised to see something like one hundred customers in line at the box office. There had not been a lot of publicity for the opening, but here they were—a goodly bunch of ordinary filmgoers, a lot of them working class to judge from their garb, buying tickets.

Who knew what was drawing them—though we might guess it was Brando, seemingly very much back in the vein in which moviegoers liked him best. But it didn't matter what got them there. The word quickly spread and the picture became an immediate hit—not by any means the year's top grosser (Brando's ludicrous *Desiree,* appearing a little later, actually returned more money to the studio), but hugely profitable in relationship to its cost. In the long term, with its value in ancillary markets undreamed of at the time, and incalculable to us (because it is still earning money in those markets), it has to be one of the best investments Harry Cohn ever made.

This value was, of course, almost immediately enhanced by the awards it began winning. The New York Film Critics named it best picture, Kazan best director and Brando best actor. The Motion Picture Academy awarded it the same prizes, while also giving Saint; Schulberg; Boris Kaufman; the editor, Gene Milford; and the art director, Richard Day, Oscars in their categories. Additionally, Kazan won the DGA and Golden Globe awards as the year's best director.

This outpouring of plaques and statuary, largely from industry sources, indicates a general lack of concern over Kazan's HUAC testimony. As far as movie people were concerned, that was now in the past. As ever, they were only interested in the here and now. It must be said that Kazan, in the kinescopes of the Oscar ceremonies (he and the rest of his team, Brando aside, appeared on the broadcast from New York, which for a few years shared the ceremony with Los Angeles), appears uncommonly grim—no victor's geniality for him. Saint, who was by this time pregnant, made up for him by expressing a bubbly fear that she might have her baby on the spot. The New York contingent skipped the academy-sponsored party and repaired to a waterfront bar for their own celebration.

By now the intellectual community had begun closely to parse *On the Waterfront* for political correctness. And, typically, Kazan, to a degree, conceded a bit to them. Less than a month after the film opened, he gave an interview to Archer Winsten, movie reviewer for the New York *Post*. The paper was at the time a bastion of anti-Communist liberalism, and Winsten, in his piece, observed that the hard-line left was already trying to undermine the film through attacks on Kazan. "I'm not going to identify them because they are so demonstrably wrong that their attack discredits them to an extent I don't care to abet."

But, he says, he repeated the charges—essentially that the film justified "informing"—to Kazan, and received a response that was both blunt and subtle. The blunt part was this: "I was in the party for about a year and a half. I got out in 1936. They were trying to tell me how to run the Group Theatre. They stink." The subtle part was this: "As for the picture being an apology, of course we thought of that. Right from the beginning. But if we'd been trying for that, we wouldn't have had Brando's brother killed. Brando gave his evidence because he was angry. How's that an apology for us?" He conceded only that "any experience the artist goes through he uses in his work."

I think he raises a good point. After the early passages of the film, Brando's Terry is under constant pressure to tell what he knows about Johnny Friendly and his mob—from Edie, from Malden's Father Barry—and he constantly refuses to become "a cheese eater" (to use one of the many colloquialisms he employs for the word he never utters, which is "informer"). It is only when the mob murders his brother, because he cannot fully guarantee the volatile and obviously wavering Terry's silence, that he makes up his mind to testify. In short, it is for the most intensely personal reason that Terry acts. We may well imagine that absent this murder he might have maintained his silence,

This answer did not, of course, silence Kazan's critics. Out of the past, as it were, John Howard Lawson weighed in with a piece in the *Hollywood Quarterly*, calling the movie "anti-democratic, anti-labor and anti-human propaganda." He also contrasted it with the Communist-sponsored *Salt of the Earth*, about a Mine, Mill and Smelters Union strike that is, all politics aside, one of the most amateurish and inept movies ever made.

In the winter 1955 issue of *Sight and Sound*, the influential British film magazine, Lindsay Anderson launched what may remain the most influential attack on Kazan's film. Anderson was not yet the highly erratic feature film director he would become a decade later. He was a documentarian and the editor of a rather uneasy film journal called *Sequence*. But he was then, as ever, a political radical, of a uniquely British kind—not quite a Communist, but not merely a Fabian, either. There was something much more rough-hewn and slightly paranoid in his positions.

He called his piece "The Last Sequence of *On the Waterfront*," offering a detailed analysis of it as "implicitly (if unconsciously) Fas-

cist." Much of his argument is very woolly, and often, in fact, ig-
nores—as Robert Hughes pointed out in a rebuttal in the magazine's
next issue—much in the film that did not fit his argument. Which in
its essence is this: The longshoremen are sheep. They have no inherent social consciousness. They have passively accepted the corrupt
leadership of Johnny Friendly. Now, if Terry, having survived the
brutal beating administered by Friendly's goons, can rise to his feet
and lead them in to work, they will follow him with equal passivity.
Sure, he is now a "better" man than Friendly, a better man than he
was at the beginning of the picture. But—and this is surely true—he
is not a representative of awakened class consciousness. The implication is that sometime in the future he may become, because of his
lack of ideological grounding, as corruptible as Johnny Friendly.

Point taken. I suppose. We are obliged to depend on the goodness of Terry's converted heart should we care to contemplate his
life beyond the confines of this film. Kazan himself said to me that
after the investigators left the waterfront, and the media excitement
about its corruption died down, it did, historically, slip back into its
old shabby ways. But Kazan and Schulberg quite consciously wished
to make the very point Anderson criticizes them for making. It's a
variant on the one Kazan and Steinbeck had made in *Viva Zapata!*,
in which his hero's martyrdom serves as a continuing example to his
people. By now, though, Kazan's aims were more limited. He had
lost his faith in revolutionary posturings—and in the supposedly inherent, or at least awakenable—class consciousness of working stiffs.
He believed that if revolutions were going to be made, they would
be made the hard way, through one-by-one conversions. This was
the place he had come to, some distance from agitprop and strike
plays. It was, frankly, the place most of us have come to. And have
remained. Which is, of course, one reason that *Waterfront* has
grown in stature over the past half-century.

Except, of course, in the yearning hearts of New Leftists like Peter
Biskind. The movie obviously agitated him, for he wrote twice about it
at some length, first in a film journal (1975), which piece he extensively
revised for a chapter in *Seeing Is Believing* in 1983. His reading of the
film begins pretty much where Anderson's leaves off, with regret for
the fact that the class struggle is no more in America. He correctly

notes that the struggle in *Waterfront* is between two elements in labor itself—the crooked and the frightened. But essentially Biskind rejects the notion that there is any general validity in Terry's struggle with his "conscience." He insists that the movie is, instead, a heavily coded endorsement of, to borrow Arthur Schlesinger's phrase "The Vital Center."

By this the writer means that, in the 1950s, cold war, anti-Communist liberals began to perceive virtues in the "instruments of control" previously despised by the left—the state, primarily, but corporations and the church as well. Thus Terry's "informing" becomes not just a sign of "maturity," but a support of "pluralism," that is, a recognition that good may be found in institutions that were not so long before seen as the problem, not a part of the solution.

Biskind goes so far as to imagine a future for Terry and Edie in which, taking advantage of the tax breaks designed to encourage home ownership, they join the migration to the suburbs: "Their children will grow up breathing clean air far from the smell of the docks. By the sixties Edie will be teaching English at Forest Hills High and in her spare time will tidy up Terry's diction so he can become a professional commentator on working-class and urban problems." Biskind imagines him as a sort of Eric Hoffer figure—he was a self-educated dockworker who wrote slender volumes of philosophical reflections that became voguish in this period—"a regular on late-night talk shows."

The desire, indulged in by several commentators, to project the lives of *Waterfront* figures into the future, beyond the movie's confines, is perhaps a measure of the film's lasting power as an "open" movie, in Leo Braudy's term. But Biskind insisted that "Kazan, like his fellow pluralists, was a complexity monger. He regarded his transformation from a Red in the thirties to a cold-war liberal in the fifties . . . as a journey *away* from the infantile simplicities of the Left to the mature appreciation of the complexity characteristic of the center." This seems to me an extraordinarily simple-minded reading of both this man and this film. Yet it is also a truthful one, in its way.

For it is perfectly plausible to see Kazan's path as admirable. He surely had become a "complexity monger." But then, so have I. So have many of us. The substitution of a nuanced view of history and personality and their interaction is not necessarily a sign of "selling out." It may well be a sign of—well, yes—maturity. Is there, indeed, anything more tiresome than the public posturings of leftists, both old and new, prating their tired slogans and proudly accepting their hasty newspaper identifications as "activists," when the correct term for some of them might be "neo-Stalinist"?

More important to me, however, is the way narrowly political readings of *On the Waterfront* distort its essence. For they leave out of the discussion this simple fact: Johnny Friendly and his gang are thoroughly bad guys. They murder innocent people to obtain their ends. They cheat decent working men out of their livelihoods. They rule their admittedly petty fiefdom through terrorist tactics, not different in intent from those the CP visited, for example, on poor Albert Maltz, though the goons are, of course, infinitely more deadly. I have tried to understand how "informing" on them can be regarded as immoral in any sense and I cannot do so.

I think, finally, that the narrow emphasis placed on "informing" by *On the Waterfront*'s critics consitutes an ideologically blinkered reading of the work. Biskind, for example, approvingly quotes Victor Navasky thus: "Playing the informer runs against the American grain." Well, yes—but not always. Not, for example, when they are identified as "whistle-blowers." In the recent Enron cases, three of its employees who informed on the corporation's peculations were named "Persons of the Year" by *Time* magazine. The man who informed on his tobacco company's twisted research was heroically portrayed in a celebratory movie about him. We could multiply such instances endlessly. Indeed, we could say that very few inroads could have been made against organized crime without informers (and the witness protection program).

I would argue that what Terry Malloy eventually does, after much quite persuasive moral anguish, is in this vein. Johnny Friendly's "union" is, in fact, a highly visible extension of organized crime, which means that the act carries no abstract ideological weight; it is simply a response to systematized, economically motivated evil—different in scale from the Enron matter, but, if anything, more personally hurtful and hateful to its victims. These guys are not stealing from (and murdering) anonymous stockholders, but people they know on a day-to-day basis. To condemn Terry's act is to align yourself with Johnny Friendly and his mob, to say, in effect, "Aw, they're not so bad."

In other words, Biskind's view of *On the Waterfront* seems to me to make nonsense of ordinary morality as we practice it in life. It also travesties Kazan's and Schulberg's position. There is little in their statements on this film that would lead any reasonable observer to think that "informing," (as Biskind defines it) was their paramount concern. They were anti-Communist leftists. Their film is surely warmed by their regrets over the non-, even anti-, idealistic position American labor had arrived at by the early fifties. But their primary interest was in the way one lost, tortured young man comes, at great cost to himself and others, to self and social awareness over the course of a magnificent film.

The "romance of American Communism" is now inexplicable to the young. And, indeed, to the not-so-young. Seeing it as a twelve-year-old, the director Martin Scorsese found in *Waterfront* an utterly truthful representation of "people I knew." Yes, they were Irish and he was an Italian, but no matter; it was "just simply that they were street people and I got to tell you that that is what it was like. Those were people I was around. . . . It was like it was part of my blood." Especially, he felt, in the much-discussed ending, which he read in religious terms. "It takes on all the suffering, all the Catholic iconography, you know. I'd never seen anything like it." In this reading he was not entirely alone. There exists an early poster for the film, on which this line, the desperate concoction of an anonymous ad man, trying to warm the public to a harsh subject, appears: "A story as warm and moving as *Going My Way* . . . but with brass knuckles!"

In his lovely and informative book and television series, *A Personal Journey with Martin Scorsese Through American Movies,* the director called *On the Waterfront* a "breakthrough" of another kind. "Kazan was forging a new acting style. It had the appearance of realism. But actually it revealed something in the natural behavior of people that I hadn't see on the screen before: the truth behind the posture."

This view of the film is now, I think, the common one. If any film lives beyond its moment, it soon leaves behind the immediate controversies it engenders and takes on an aesthetic life of its own. Political readings of any work are always easier to make than purely artistic ones, because politics is the crude, blunt instrument preferred by observers who are themselves crude and blunt. It is a more subtle task—because the issues are more hidden, more gestural—to read art objects aesthetically. Or even, as Scorsese does, from the point of view of a highly sophisticated fellow filmmaker trying to learn what he can from a master.

We can adduce other examples of this. A few years ago the *New York Times* ran an occasional series in which a reporter sat with a leading modern director while he watched a classic film. Barry Levinson (director of *Diner* and *Rain Man* among other movies) chose to see *On the Waterfront*, which he had first seen as a twelve-year-old during its initial release. Levinson, whose liberalism is attested to by *Wag the Dog*, simply brushed aside the ideological issues raised by the film. They were at first glance, and upon mature consideration, irrelevant to him. When he first saw the picture, what blew him away was Brando's performance: "I was watching it and I thought, you know, I have never seen anything like this before." Looking at it anew he was struck by the complexity of the storytelling. "Look at how many characters there are at work in this story, and they're all so rich." He was also struck by Kazan's camera placements and editing. The film is not, for example, full of close-ups, but when they occur they really count. There was, he thought, a refusal by Kazan to show off his skills, but yet a subtle liveliness in his shot selection that identifies a fine director—this is by all odds Kazan's most assured (and yes, finally, panoramic) film—working at the top of his form.

This movie, like most movies, stand or falls on its details—in performance, in its visual variety, in, we might say, the way a man picks up a woman's glove and hands it back to her.

14

Country Roads

"Why do I have to pay for the fact that you were a bowlegged child?" Molly Kazan angrily asked her husband one day when he was working on his adaptation of John Steinbeck's *East of Eden.* It was not necessarily an unfair question.

For at this moment, Elia Kazan was a mass of contradictory ambitions, most of which stemmed from the overwhelming success of *On the Watefront.* Obviously, he had achieved great things in the past—*Salesman, Streetcar* in both its stage and screen incarnations. But he had never had such a major movie success, which by and large the reviewers attributed more to him than to any of his collaborators. Even Brando's great work was often traced back to his director.

This, coming so soon after his HUAC ordeal was, naturally, profoundly gratifying to him. He would not make a catastrophe of this success—he was too shrewd and self-aware for that to happen—and now, at least briefly, a number of possibilities opened to him.

In *A Life* he lists some of them. He might, for example, go on making big studio movies; maybe its capacities were diminished, but Hollywood still had the money, and the promotional organizations, to put over big projects with what remained of the old mass audience. On the other hand, independent production with its potential for making tight, tough little movies on relatively small budgets, but without maddening studio oversight, was an increasingly viable alternative. From this conflict others grew. More and more he wanted to write—the idea of writing his own and his family's history occurred to him at this time, but he also wanted to write his own screenplays, too. At the same time, he wanted access to writers he thought were more gifted in their craft than the average screenwriter.

In essence he wanted to move in the best circles, with the "big shots," as he put it. But he also wanted more time to himself, wanted a more contemplative life than he had previously known. He wanted to be rich, but he saw that the single-minded pursuit of wealth and comfort would destroy something essential in him. He wanted to remain a radical ("certainly a socialist—at least that"), but he also wanted to be a mainstream democrat. He still wanted Molly—"my smart, immaculate, completely honest and absolutely trustworthy wife"—but he also wanted his sexual adventures.

Molly, of course, wondered, selfishly, but not entirely inappropriately, why he wanted to add the burden of writing to his career as a director. We may safely imagine some sort of mid-life crisis brewing; Kazan was forty-five years old when these thoughts occurred to him, and he never resolved them. Over the next decade he would, in fact, be everything—or should one say, everyone?—he thought of being in 1954–55.

He would first be a big-time studio director. And he had the perfect property for that incarnation—John Steinbeck's *East of Eden,* which would be the first in a series of six movies, made over the next eight years, that would all deal with rural or small-town settings and figures, a definitive turning away from the largely urban environments and characters that had previously concerned him. One cannot believe this was entirely accidental. There was something in the earth—with one exception, the American earth—that he finally had to dig out.

He had stayed friends with Steinbeck after *Zapata,* with Steinbeck's wife saying they were like brothers, and they lived just a couple of doors apart on New York's east side. Miller might be gone, Kazan and Tennessee Williams would soon enter upon an edgy stretch in their relationship, but the novelist (and Schulberg) were there to fill the empty spaces. Moreover, Steinbeck had stood by him during the HUAC ordeal. "[A] good and honest man," he had written to his editor, Pascal Covici, adding that he hoped the "Communists and the second raters" would not "cut him to pieces."

Steinbeck's biographer, Jay Parini, cannot understand the novelist's support of Kazan—that the writer might also be a "complexity

monger" does not occur to him—though he does note that Steinbeck also defended Lillian Hellman's refusal to testify to HUAC.
"Each one is right in different ways," he said, and, curiously, his sentiments are correct; neither, given their natures, could have done
other than they did before the committee. In return, Kazan had
stood by his friend during the long run of poorish luck that had preceded *East of Eden*'s completion. He had not published a novel that
was fully successful critically or commercially since *The Grapes of
Wrath* in 1939, and though he remained a famous writer, he had become a distracted one.

East of Eden, which began as an attempt to fictionalize his own
family's history as pioneer Californians, was, for him, a great rallying
point. It was a long book (265,000 words) but one on which he toiled
obsessively, so that it took him just a little over a year to write.
Kazan, naturally, was one of its first readers, and he was enthusiastic
about it. While he was vacationing in Europe, after finishing revisions on the book, and after Kazan's testimony, Steinbeck heard
from the director that he wanted to make a movie based on his work.

Kazan claimed it was one of the easiest sales he ever made. Leaving his agent behind, he appeared in Jack Warner's office, listened to a
couple of the mogul's bad jokes, then told him he wanted to make a
film of *East of Eden.* Warner had not read the book and did not indicate that he was ever likely to do so. On the other hand, he had surely
heard of it, for despite a decidedly mixed reception from reviewers, it
had become an instant best-seller—its first printing was one hundred
thousand copies. In an age when the studios were placing particular
faith in what were then called "pre-sold properties" (hit novels and
plays) that was all Warner needed to know. He simply asked what
Kazan thought it would cost, was told $1.6 million, to which Warner
replied, "You've got it." Kazan told him that since it was largely about
young people, he might employ a cast of relative newcomers. Warner
said, "Come have lunch with me."

Kazan did not inform Warner that his movie was not an adaptation of Steinbeck's entire work. Apparently with the writer's approval
(there were many meetings between them, at which questions of
what to retain, what to omit from the movie were discussed) he jetti-
soned most of it, concentrating on the book's final section. And that

business about newcomers was not, at that point, strictly true. Kazan at least briefly entertained the hope that Brando might play the film's central role, that of Cal Trask, even though he was too old for the part. It is doubtful that Brando even read a script, which, as drafted by Paul Osborn, a successful minor playwright (*On Borrowed Time, Morning's at Seven*) with a gift for writing about small-town life and a talent for adaptations, shed about two-thirds of Steinbeck's novel. This strategy elided what had been one of the largest critical complaints about the book, that it was structurally misshapen. Steinbeck's attempt to tell his own family's story had been elbowed aside by the much more melodramatic Trask family, headed by the rectitudinous Adam (eventually played by the perfectly typecast Raymond Massey) and his two sons, Cain and Abel. Oh, sorry, Cal and Aron. The references to the Genesis myth were obvious, as was the notion of the Salinas Valley as a kind of Eden.

Kazan's most consistently sympathetic critic, Michel Ciment, places this film very firmly in the thin cinematic pastoral tradition, linking it especially with two later movies, *Giant* and *Days of Heaven*, each in its way a narrative of a virgin landscape's despoilment by modernism's dark, heavy machinery. In his long interview with Ciment, Kazan speaks lengthily about his love of the countryside, his habit of rising early to enjoy it in morning's first, dewy light. There is much in their discussion of *East of Eden*, about the greenish, sylvan glow Kazan imparted to his imagery (this was his first color picture, and his first in CinemaScope), and his determination not to let the balkiness of the wide screen format inhibit his editing. In his brief consideration of the film, Martin Scorsese observed Kazan showing that "CinemaScope could suit an intimate family drama as well as vast frescoes. You were not limited to landscapes or processions, horizontal lines or diagonal movements." He speaks approvingly (and correctly) of the way Kazan blocked out large sections of the wide screen by narrowing the frame with doorways and cramped corridors.

All of which is true enough and admirable enough. But that's only the way the film appears to cineastes and cinephiles. To most people, *East of Eden* is important mainly for its place in the enormously potent legend of its star, James Dean. It was Osborn who spotted him first, working as the homosexually tempting Arab boy in a stage adaptation of André Gide's *The Immoralist*. The writer saw in him something he thought Kazan could use as Cal, the troubled, rebellious Trask son—the one who finds his long-lost mother running a brothel in Monterey, the one who, moved by jealousy for his brother (stiffly played by Richard Davalos) falls in love with his girlfriend, Abra (Julie Harris), and drives his sibling to near-madness by revealing his mother's identity as a madam to him.

Kazan, when he met Dean, was ambivalent about him, if not downright hostile toward him. He found Dean slouched in his office, "a heap of twisted legs and denim rags, looking resentful for no particular reason." The director decided to keep him waiting, which cured the belligerence. But he was entirely inarticulate. Finally, he said to Kazan, "Do you want to ride on my bike?" Kazan said, "Yeah, I'll ride on your bike." "So I got on the back of his bike and we went around the city on the goddamned bike and I wish I'd never met him." But tongues were jounced loose on the ride, and Kazan called Steinbeck and said, "I'll tell you. I found a guy that may not be a great actor, but he is it." Was that important? the writer wondered, believing Kazan could charm what he needed out of anyone. Kazan assured him it was. "So I sent him up to John, like I sent Marlon up to Tennessee on *Streetcar* . . . and John said, 'I don't like the guy, but he's it.'"

Well, not quite. Not yet. There was still the matter of a screen test. Others were in contention, notably Paul Newman (and his wife, Joanne Woodward, up for the Abra role). But the intrigued Kazan loaded Dean on an airplane—his first—and they headed for Burbank, Dean packing his spare clothes in brown paper tied with string, and silently watching the country flow past below the plane. On their way to their hotel, Dean asked the driver to stop at an unprepossessing building, where, it turned out, his father lived. Kazan, watching their interaction, became more than ever convinced he had the right kid, so awkward and uncomprehending was this exchange. The test was, of course, a disaster, a succession of mumbles and unfocused gestures. Some of the crew, Kazan would later write, thought Dean some sort of stand-in, filling time until Kazan's real discovery showed up.

But none of that mattered. "You make your own luck in this business," Kazan would say to me. "You cast someone and you know it's there. You bring it out. He doesn't imitate you. You can't give him facial expressions or readings or anything else. You can't do a damned thing. You're stuck. You're stuck with him. And it's there. You know it because you've talked to him and you've gotten to know him. You've ridden on the back of his goddamned bike . . ."

It was, arguably, the biggest gamble Kazan had ever taken in a lifetime of risky casting. And one can't help but recall his wife's remark about paying for the fact that he was a bowlegged child, since, psychologically, that's what Dean was. And that says nothing about Kazan's difficult relationship with his own tyranically misunderstanding father. It is also perhaps correct to say that this is where his politics largely went—into the family microcosm, with fathers representing a sort of emotional totalitarianism, sons the rebels with a cause, which might be defined as a need to make their own destinies. Or mistakes.

We all know, because it has passed so firmly into the Dean legend, that the brutal tensions between Adam Trask and his son Cal reflected the on-set tensions between Raymond Massey and James Dean. Which were, naturally, encouraged by Kazan, playing one of his more dangerous directorial tricks.

Kazan: "Dean was impossible. He was always cutting in on his [Massey's] lines. Massey had learned the script exactly. He'd studied it with his wife. They'd gone over and over it. . . . His wife would read and then he'd respond and all of a sudden this little son of a bitch comes and he's saying the line wrong. . . . And he'd say to me, 'He's not saying the lines.' I said, 'All right, I'll get him to say the lines.' Then I'd let Jimmy—I was tricky—I'd let Jimmy do it the way he wanted because it irritated him. And I'd photograph it and photograph it. I'd say, don't trust directors . . . because they're going to get what they need for the film no matter what . . ."

It was not just a matter of screwing around with the text. Dean was constantly foul-mouthed on the set, offending Massey, who was a rich, rock-ribbed Republican (he was the scion of the Massey-Harris farm equipment manufacturing family) and, indeed, a McCarthyite. A couple of years after *East of Eden* was released, he was trouping the Midwest with Martin Gabel and Agnes Moorehead doing one-night stands of a staged reading of a play about the Lincoln-Douglass debates (Massey's acting specialty was playing the martyred president). As a young journalist, I joined this little troupe to do a story on the play and often sat with Massey and Gabel as they unwound over drinks after the show. Almost nightly, Massey would excoriate Dean, particularly for his offensive language. He claimed that when he blew up at the young actor, crew members came up to him to congratulate him on his stand. Talking to Kazan, I mentioned Massey's pride in his defense of decorum.

"Do you think I'd kill that?" Kazan asked me. "Do you think I would do anything to stop that antagonism? No, I increased it. I let it go. I let it go . . . because it was the central thing I photographed. . . . The absolute hatred that Ray Massey felt for Jimmy Dean and the hatred Jimmy Dean felt for Ray Massey. That's precious, man. You can't get that. I mean, you can pretend you have it, but you don't. You hopefully arouse it. You get me? Arouse it. You hopefully stimulate them and in that case I didn't have to. It was there."

Not that Kazan was having an easy time with Dean himself. A short while into the shoot, it came upon the actor that he was on the brink of stardom and he began behaving arrogantly to the crew members. Kazan put a stop to that. But he also began noticing that Dean was showing up for work in the morning looking wasted. He moved with him into one of the big-star dressing rooms with which movie lots in those day were dotted. They were really little fully equipped houses, and Kazan moved into one bedroom, Dean into the other—where through the night he alternately boffed and fought with his current amour, the actress Pier Angeli, keeping his boss awake and irritated.

In truth, however, Dean was at least as distracted by the palomino horse he purchased. Kazan let him keep it on the lot for a while, but he was too often absent, feeding it, grooming it, mooning over it—so Kazan banished the animal to the deeper reaches of the valley. He also forbade Dean, who had long since proved his reckless driving habits to the director, access to his motor scooter. Where-upon Dean acquired a camera and made everyone edgy by poking it in their faces. He also spent a lot of time shooting pictures of himself in the mirror. In short, Dean's capacity to drive people crazy extended in all directions, and Kazan was later voluble in his praise of Julie Harris, an actress he had long admired, who, besides playing the apex of the triangle with the Trask boys with ironic sharpness, had a steadying influence on Dean.

About Dean's performance, Kazan remained resolutely—what else?—ambivalent. He is hard on Dean in his autobiography. Yes, he concedes, most of the time he instinctively found the essence of a scene, but when he could not, he had no technique to rely on. Kazan contrasts him to Brando at that time, well-schooled by Stella Adler, disciplined and proficient in every aspect of his profession, including makeup and mimicry. He brought Brando to the set so he could enjoy Dean's worshipfulness—and perhaps act as an inspiration to the tyro. The star was gracious and accommodating to Dean, who in Kazan's description "seemed shrunken and twisted in misery" when they met. There were a couple of times when, desperate for what he needed and wasn't getting from Dean, Kazan got him drunk enough to get him in the right mood.

On the other hand, talking to me many years later, Kazan allowed that "gradually I got a terrific respect for Jimmy because of his talent. He . . . would do anything to be good. He was way open." Perhaps that retrospective revision was partly occasioned by the fact that the film turned out to be an inordinate success, the last major box office hit Kazan would enjoy for some six years.

In his notes on the film, Kazan warned himself, "Don't complicate it," underlining in red. "It is the story of a boy who kills his brother [which, in fact, he does not in the film] and that's all it is." But then, of course, he does complicate it: "The story is about rejection [that of Adam for Cal, who wants nothing but the respect of his almost inhumanly stern father] and the vicious circle of rejection. Rejection causes hate, causes vengeance, arouses guilt, which causes more feelings of rejection."

This theme comes to its climax in the famous confrontation between Cal and his father. The latter has sunk all his capital into a scheme to ship refrigerated vegetables east. It fails. But in the meantime Cal, having borrowed money from his mother (Jo Van Fleet, who won an Oscar for her performance) has speculated in bean futures, making enough to cover his father's losses. But this is wartime and Adam regards this money as tainted by immoral profiteering. He rejects his son's gift in quite a powerful scene that Kazan shot in slightly raked angles, which may or may not have been a good idea (it is uncommonly pretentious by his usual standards). Mewling and whining Dean tries to press the cash on Massey, eventually scattering it over a dining room table and exiting sobbing into the night.*

It is the film's turning point, but scarcely its climax. There's the whole business of dragging Aron to meet his madam/mother (a very powerfully made sequence, in which Aron ends up atop his mother in a sexually suggestive posture), Aron's subsequent exile (he is last seen on a troop train, bearing him off to the battlefields of World War I), and, finally, Adam's collapse with a stroke that renders him unable to move or to speak more than a few mumbled words.

But, as the film approaches its climax, man and boy do manage, belatedly, to forgive each other. It is quite an interesting climax in that, after all the film's Sturm und Drang they bond gently over their mutual dislike of the nurse tending Adam. The final image is of Cal pulling his chair up to Adam's bed, prepared to care for the stricken old man.

It is a very Kazanian moment—simple, even quotidian reality at the end of a very hot melodrama. But it was the point he was driving at all along. "A terribly important aspect of the theme of rejection," he had written, "is its positive side. That is to say, the healing of the rejection wound—the wound that causes all the trouble comes when and *only when* the child FORGIVES (understands) the parent. When Cal understands and forgives Adam he no longer feels the rejection, so he no longer needs to feel [his] own responsibility for evil."

Talking about *East of Eden* much later, Kazan elaborated more fully on this idea. "[W]hen I was making *East of Eden* I kept thinking, this is unfair to fathers. I had children . . . I said, 'No one realized how difficult it is to be a father, how demanding children are of you, and should be, I guess. But it's difficult. It's tough.'" He paused to reflect on his old friend Nick Ray's film also starring Dean, *Rebel*

---

* In the course of this scene Dean, without warning, kissed Massey, and the latter's bestartlement is entirely visible on screen.

Without a Cause. He was derisive about the way it so obviously loaded the picture in favor of the rebel boy, particularly by casting amiable Jim Backus as his weak-willed father and having him appear, in a crucial confrontation, wearing a woman's apron. He was proud of himself for insisting on making Massey's character so unyielding, so worthy of near-deadly opposition. Because the old man was so tough, it gave the Dean figure a more liberating triumph at the end.

"You can load the kid up with so much guilt that he struggles all his life against your image of him. But the father in *East of Eden* liberated the kid," he said to me. "You start at the bottom," he reflected, "and he [the father figure] doesn't approve of you and society doesn't approve of you and you're a rebel and a bad boy, but slowly, slowly you work back to . . . acceptance . . . if you watch it in action and especially if you see it in their faces . . . you respond to it." He thought, he said, that something similar had been at work in *Waterfront*. "That's what these kids want finally. They're rebellious and raise hell, but they really want to be liked, approved of, fit into society finally."

That, he said, was this movie's "reason for being. . . . If it doesn't, in the words of the old lefties, 'say something, say something' . . . it's not worth the trouble." By 1990 he was saying that he didn't want to see, let alone make, films that did not "stir you somewhere to believe something and want something. That's what art is. . . . And I think *East of Eden* has done that to a lot of people. It's the favorite film of mine to a lot of people, a lot of people."

To such a statement there is, really, no answer. But I think we ought to attempt one. It is, to begin with, more consciously, more schematically, psychological in its development than any of his other works, stark and unrelenting in its presentation of its Oedipal theme. It needs some diversions, some lightness of spirit, that Kazan did not impart to it. Beyond that, it seems to me that some of the criticisms Biskind and his kind made of *On the Waterfront* might more properly be applied to *East of Eden*. Intentionally or not, it drives its major characters toward a psychologically "centrist" position, that is, to mutually, mentally healthy forgiveness.

East of Eden seems to me perhaps the most problematical of all of Kazan's films. In large measure that's because the acting is so inconsistent. Massey, in particular, is as pious and as false as a Sunday-school teacher asserting his moralism. He's not really a hypocrite—he believes in the Bible, in the altruism of bringing fresh vegetables to the glum and vitamin-starved east, in the sunshine of nice California days—but it nonetheless feels fraudulent. I think the actor wanted to be liked, to appear to the audience as more curmudgeonly than truly dark. And Van Fleet, despite winning an Oscar, smirks too much as his radically estranged wife. We never believe that she was once a free and lively spirit being crushed by his sternness. And the hints that she has become some sort of addict (drugs? alcohol?) don't quite square with her take-no-prisoners business style. Which, in turn, does not quite support her place in the structure of the film, as the representative of the lusty alternative to Bible thumping. Julie Harris, caught between "good" Aron and "bad" Cal is sweet and communicates something of her inner conflict. But her ingenuous-ness sometimes cloys.

Which brings us to Dean (who had second billing to Harris). He has his moments, to be sure, especially at the end of the picture, where his mannerisms fall away and he engages forthrightly with the other characters. But too often his neediness is very crudely and an-noyingly expressed. He has two tricks: one is to look up at the cam-era wistfully, vulnerably, from beneath his hooded eyelids; the other is to turn away from the camera's gaze in a sulky teenage way, imply-ing that his thoughts are simply too inchoate to communicate. Under pressure—especially in the money scene with Massey—he howls, blubbers, mews and moans.

All right, he's embodying adolescent angst accurately enough. But he's annoying and tiresome much of the time in this film. There are, in my estimation, very few moments in it where he is uncomplicatedly lovable. He is all solipsism, all puling need. It is very hard to discern in him those hints of the decent grown-up that you want any fictional teenager, no matter how troubled, to become. You can only imagine him becoming one of those angst-ridden emotional cripples, con-vinced of his own uniqueness, but unable to demonstrate it, who make us want to run and hide when they appear in our own later lives.

The foregoing is, of course, a minority report. Most people re-gard Dean's work in this film as iconic. Partly, of course, that's because he died in his infamous auto wreck (Kazan was right to be anxious about his driving skills) not long after *East of Eden* was released, which caused everyone—especially his contemporary peers—to wildly overvalue the three movies that constitute his legacy.

But there's a little more to this matter than gross sentiment. Without Steinbeck or Kazan or anyone else connected with this production being aware of it, Dean's character plugged into the developing zeitgeist of the fifties. Since the end of World War II, juvenile delinquency had been a developing concept and concern, expressed especially in the popular culture by pop fictions about youthful urban gangs (*A Stone for Danny Fisher, The Amboy Dukes, The Blackboard Jungle*). There had, naturally, been fictions about "bad" boys (and occasionally girls) before. But now a teenage culture was in the process of developing. It was both an exploitable market, with its own music, mores, movies, clothing and patois, and a sociological worry. The sounds of rock and roll were abroad in the land. Brando himself had offered a pioneering portrayal of a kick-ass (though ultimately tamable) rebel motorcyclist in *The Wild One*. These "kids" seemed almost to be a race of aliens to concerned adults, and journalism of every sort was rife with anxious analysis. Dean's character fit right in with these fidgets. Indeed, because he appeared in a historical context, in a work based on a novel by a seriously regarded writer and directed by a man who had never made anything like a cheap exploitation picture, people felt obliged to take the film with great seriousness.

Except, perhaps, its first reviewers. On the whole—there were exceptions—they did not much care for *East of Eden*. Or its mannered acting, especially Dean's. "Sometimes he jumps up and down like a kangaroo," the *New Yorker*'s John McCarten wrote, fairly typically. "Sometimes he giggles like a lunatic, and sometimes he's surly and offended. He's a hard man to decipher." Lots of reviewers saw a Brando imitation here, and lots of them imagined Kazan directing Dean toward doing one, which is, as we've seen, not so.

But the reviews were meaningless. Rumors about the heat of Dean's performance had been widely retailed in the press. The world was primed for him—and didn't give a rap about whether he was imitating Brando or not. That was especially true of pubescent females. Kazan attended a preview of the film in Los Angeles, saw them swooning and heard them squealing and knew that he had his second hit in a row, one that actually outgrossed *Waterfront* at the domestic box office.

It was some years before he realized that it he had made not just a hit, but a cult phenomenon, which it has never ceased to be. Each new teenage generation rediscovers Dean, pins his posters on their walls, and sees in him the avatar of their sensitivity, their own misunderstanding by the unfeeling world. The phenomenon is doubtless harmless. But it is extremely tiresome. Especially when you observe that by the time of his last film, *Giant,* he had, if anything, regressed in technique—now either imitating himself or finding himself hopelessly out of his range when called upon to play, in that film's last half, an aging version of himself. Had he not died so young, with whatever promise he had unfulfilled, one has to believe he would have been no more than a momentary—and faintly risible—phenomenon of his very brief moment.

East of Eden premiered on Broadway (at a benefit for the Actors Studio) two weeks before the opening night of Kazan's production of *Cat on a Hot Tin Roof,* which must surely be numbered among Tennessee Williams's half-dozen best plays, and possibly the last of them to contain not one, but two theatrical figures of mythic dimensions—characters that almost every generation of actors have since lusted to reinterpret.

These are, of course, Maggie, the "Cat" of the title, and her father-in-law, "Big Daddy," a role Burl Ives permanently inhabits for everyone who ever saw him in it. Alas, he became, quite innocently, a source of contention between Kazan and Williams, one of several that surfaced during this production.

Kazan had professed himself "quite exhausted" in a letter to Williams, rejecting the possibility of taking on a revised version of his first play, *Battle of Angels.* "Out of gas. No gissum left. Also rather discouraged." He thought that he had repeated himself in *East of Eden.* He apparently told Audrey Wood, Williams's agent, that he'd rather wait for an entirely new play from him. Which, as it happened, Williams was ready to send him.

Kazan at first resisted *Cat*, with Williams thinking perhaps he feared failure more than the playwright did. It may be, however, that he didn't like its major characters in their early incarnations. It may also be that the play's rather radical manner challenged him at a moment when his creative energies were low. It does not proceed via intricate dialogue scenes. Rather, it primarily offers a series of arias for its principals, gathered at Big Daddy Pollitt's Mississippi Delta plantation ("20,000 acres of the richest land this side of the Valley Nile" as the proprietor describes it), to celebrate the *patron*'s sixty-fifth birthday. He is a huge, vigorous man who is nevertheless revealed to be dying of cancer—an inconvenient fact that has been kept from him and denied by his wife.

Questions of inheritance, naturally, hover in the air. They are complicated by the fact that his favorite son, Brick, a former football star (played by Ben Gazzara in the original production), continues to drink himself into a daily (and nightly) stupor and is thus unable to produce an heir with Maggie (Barbara Bel Geddes). That failure clouds their possibility of inheriting the plantation, since Big Daddy's other son, Gooper, a weak-willed realtor (Pat Hingle), has produced plenty of offspring ("no-neck monsters" as Maggie describes them) with his comically manipulative wife, Mae (Madeline Sherwood).

The unspoken subtext of the piece is Brick's homosexuality. He loved—whether purely platonically or physically, the play does not state—a professional football teammate named Skipper, who has since died, perhaps emotionally betrayed by Brick. He is crippled in other ways, as well. In addition to his alcoholism, he has a broken leg, which causes him to hobble about with a crutch throughout the play. Finally, he mourns the modern world's "mendacity," a topic on which Big Daddy spouts the most soaring (and wildly funny) of his arias, as he tries to inject a little steel into Brick's spine.

Since the play was far from realistic verbally, Kazan insisted on a stripped-down setting. Jo Mielziner provided him with a stage thrust diagonally out over the orchestra pit, most of the time adorned with only a single piece of furniture—a large bed. It is among the designer's most daring concepts. The costumes are similarly simple, with Bel Geddes, most notably, appearing in the first and last acts in a plain white slip. Within this space, Kazan staged the piece in a rather abstract way. His characters kept their distance, often appeared not to be speaking to one another, but rather directly to the audience.

Williams was at first dubious about casting Ives, whom he thought of as purely a folksinger. Big Daddy was a character to a degree based on Williams's own father, whom Ives did not resemble. Kazan, who had just employed him as the sheriff in *Eden,* thought this huge man, pushing a generous gut before him, physically perfect for Big Daddy as Williams had written him. Moreover, however often he had sweetly warbled "Blue Tail Fly," he was a permanently angry man. Kazan always recalled an evening when it required several strong men to prevent a drunken Ives from hurling himself out a window. In this performance Ives tended to speak quite softly, but that, combined with his contrasting bulk, tended only to make him seem more erratically menacing. He did not owe this role to the fact that he had been a friendly witnesss before HUAC—any more than Albert Dekker owed his casting in an *East of Eden* supporting role to the fact that he had stood up to the committee. Kazan remained politically color-blind when it came to casting.

Bel Geddes, too, was off-cast. She had been playing dewy innocence ever since she had first worked for Kazan in *Deep Are the Roots,* and people were, if anything, a little tired of her look of wide-eyed wonder. Kazan guessed she might have been a little overweight when she was younger, and thus might convey the sexual avidity of a woman who had not quite gotten over her earlier insecurities, which proved to be the case. In the end, she has to lie to Big Daddy, pretend that she is pregnant, which delights the old man (who by this time knows he's dying but hopes to live long enough to welcome his heir) and, also, at the final curtain, to start seducing Brick, in order to deliver on her promise.

This ending bothered Williams; he thought it might just possibly hint at the somewhat similar conclusion of *Tea and Sympathy.* He was also dubious about Kazan's insistence that Big Daddy needed to be brought back onstage in the third act, from which he was absent in Williams's earlier drafts. About this, I think, Kazan was right; Big Daddy was just too powerful a character to disappear abruptly from the play. I think he was right, too, about the show's finale. If memory serves, the scene was played ambiguously; we do not leave the theater certain that Brick and Maggie will consummate, only that they will give it a try. In his autobiography, Kazan records mild displeasure with Williams for making this dispute public, for publishing his play with two endings—his own and Kazan's.

The major argument against the play—some reviewers alluded to it—is that it does not quite come to grips with Brick's homosexuality. This is true enough. But it does not quite seem to me the full-scale evasion that Eric Bentley and Walter Kerr, among others, thought it was. The latter wrote: "When we do come to a fiery scene of open confession—between a belligerent father and his defiant son—the truth still dodges around verbal corners, slips somewhere between the veranda shutters, refuses to meet us on firm, clear terms."

It seems to me, however, that the question of whether Brick and Skipper actually "did it" is of small importance to the play. As a matter of fact, I rather think they did not. Theirs was a pure and idealized affection, of the kind that Williams had written about before and which, I think, he preferred—at least in his writing—to noisy, realistic consummations, entirely lacking the poetry of regret.

In any event, Brick's character had been fully debated long before the critics got into the act. With Kazan encouraging him, Williams made Maggie much more attractive in later drafts than she had been earlier. But he insisted on keeping the sources of Brick's alcoholism a mystery. There's a fascinating letter by Williams to Kazan in which he compares Brick to Marlon Brando, seeing them both as suppressed homosexuals. He says he likes the type—"Their innocence, their blindness makes them very, very touching, very beautiful and sad"—but he also says that if someone challenges their "adjustment" it knocks them off balance, forcing them either to own up to the truth about themselves or, as in Brick's case, drown themselves in liquor.

This, in any case, was Williams's explanation for Brick's behavior and he stuck with it, to good effect, I think. The man finally, almost wryly, respects his wife's tenacity. He has told her to jump off their hot tin roof and take a lover. But she won't. And damned if that doesn't make him admire her enough, perhaps, to sustain the sexual act with her.

To put it simply, I like this play's silences. Especially since they are contained within a work that is in other ways the most plainspoken of the playwright's more familiar works. It is, of course, a Broadway machine—that would be the main reason to hire Kazan to stage it—but it was also a work of the kind that is no longer done there, unless it is imported from abroad—a very vivid play of some seriousness and high theatrical skills. Among the theatrical productions he staged in the 1950s (all of which I saw), I think this one represented Kazan's clearest, cleanest and most powerful work.

Eventually it ran for almost two years, winning the Pulitzer Prize and narrowly beating out William Inge's *Bus Stop* for the Drama Critics' Circle Award.

In this period Kazan had been working with Nancy Franklin and Eli Wallach at the Actors Studio on a Tennessee Williams one-act play, *27 Wagons Full of Cotton,* in which he began to see the possibilities of a film, especially if it combined elements taken over from another short Williams work, *The Unsatisfactory Supper,* from which he borrowed a simple-minded aunt (played in the movie by Mildred Dunnock) whose inability to cook an acceptable dinner provides a goofy subplot for his movie. The director—"working as a writer in disguise"—cobbled together a rough, partial scenario, in which Carroll Baker was recruited, replacing Franklin. She, Wallach and Karl Malden played scenes from it for Williams, who expressed approval. He promised to work up a screenplay.

The film, *Baby Doll,* was to be produced independently by Kazan's recently formed Newtown Productions, named after the community where his country retreat was located, and largely financed by Warner Bros., with rights to the resultant film eventually reverting to Kazan's company. For the moment, things seemed to be running smoothly and professionally, with Baker—another in Kazan's panorama of blond actresses—thrilled to be cast by Kazan in her first starring, and weirdly sexy, screen role. Then things started to go slightly wrong. Williams was working hard on his next play, *Sweet Bird of Youth,* was distracted by the forthcoming release of the movie version of *The Rose Tattoo* and by a Florida production of *Streetcar* starring Tallulah Bankhead as Blanche, a part Williams had originally written for her. He was not focusing on the *Baby Doll* screenplay, which the director thought lacked a strong ending.

Kazan tried to isolate Williams from distractions by inviting him to work with him, near the film's eventual location, in Greenville, Mississippi. The playwright agreed to come—but only if a swimming pool was available. Kazan's faithful, longtime production manager and assistant director, Charles Maguire, located a disused municipal pool, then persuaded the locals of the high honor of letting the distinguished Mr. Williams dunk himself in it. The pool was refurbished, Williams came. And quickly went. He was ever a restless man, doing much of his writing in hotel rooms, and it was from them that Kazan would, from time to time, receive the odd couple of pages of material, some of which he used, some of which he didn't, as he continued crafting a more or less coherent whole out of the messy script.

It might be argued that this rather improvisatory method of composition served the picture well. Of all Kazan's films, this little black-and-white picture, again shot by Boris Kaufman, is the roughest in appearance, essentially a farce with an undercurrent of menace that never quite defines itself as a full-scale threat to anyone's well-being. Essentially, it is an impotent love triangle, opening with Archie Lee Meighan (Karl Malden), the proprietor of a tumbledown cotton gin, drilling a hole in the wall so he can spy on his wife, Baby Doll (Baker), as she sleeps in a child's crib, sucking her thumb, wearing what came to be called a "baby doll" nightie. They have not consummated their marriage, because Archie Lee has promised her daddy that he will not have carnal knowledge of her until she is twenty years old. She is nineteen, but, going on thirty—a whining, manipulative creature whose childishness is only skin deep.

The third side of the triangle is Eli Wallach's Silva Vacarro, a Sicilian smoothie (or so he thinks), whose more efficient cotton gin has stolen most of Archie Lee's business. The actor was making his film debut with a performance that funnily mixes misplaced confidence with unearned arrogance. Malden is no less good, unafraid to act entirely without amour propre. Eventually, desperately, Archie Lee burns down Silva's gin, and the latter determines to revenge himself by seducing Baby Doll. They have an extremely erotic, albeit utterly chaste, al fresco seduction scene on a swing and later madly chase through Archie Lee's house, with Wallach at one point sounding a bugle as doors slam and giggles mount.

It is never clear that Silva attains his goal—probably he doesn't—but he does end up curled, exhausted, in Baby Doll's crib. Malden always thought of the piece as commedia dell'arte and that's probably as good a description as any of the spirit in which it was played—as a romp, full of high, essentially innocent, spirits.

At the time, Kazan did not appear to see it that way. His notes for the production are quite sober. When we first meet Baby Doll, he writes, she "is almost defeated . . . she has lost her appetite for life and fun and sex." He thinks she has become little more than a dull, if not especially dutiful, wife. But, "Silva, driven by a bad motive—arrogance—brings her to life! She starts to put out sprouts! A bad initial motive brings on a miracle of living. Suddenly 2 starved people meet . . . and their last bit of sex play is sheer, wild, released exuberance, completely free and healthy . . . In fact, the most revolutionary, satisfying thing that has ever happened to them."

This is all well and good, as are Kazan's thoughts on Silva, whom he, typically, identifies with as a foreign-born outsider intruding on a community that seems to endorse the violence of Archie Lee's attack on his cotton gin.

Clearly, Kazan was thinking of something darker than he actually created, something in which the hidebound provincial community refuses to acknowledge: its own "cruelty, selfishness, boorishness." But he was in a good mood at the time. Paul Sylbert, working as an assistant art director to his twin brother, Richard, remembers a sketch of a set Richard rendered, which included all sorts of detritus. Kazan's eye fixed on a tube of medicine. "What is it?" he asked Sylbert, who didn't know. "It's a piles remedy," he chuckled. "See you in Mississippi."

Which is what completed his mood swing. The experience of shooting for some ten weeks in tiny (population: 341) Benoit, Missis-

sippi, was, Kazan declared, Chekhovian. He brought his whole family along for the shoot, and the town welcomed them as warmly as it
did his cast and crew. The younger Kazan kids were provided with
ponies, and for a decade later the family would receive Christmas
presents (mostly pecans from their own trees) from the townsfolk,
many of whom Kazan naturally cast as extras and small-part players.
He especially liked the black population, and he used them as a sort
of chorus in the film. "I like the way it starts with the blacks laughing
at the whites. I repeat that a lot of times . . . they just think the
whites are ridiculous."

Kazan was quite aware of the darker currents of provincial
southern life. He was taken on a deer hunt one day and witnessed
the slaughter of some forty animals, which utterly sickened him. But
that was not the story he was telling. In a *New York Times* piece,
written when the company moved back to New York to shoot interiors for a month, he was voluble in his affection for his new friends.
He talked about breaking down the natural suspicions the small
town folks harbored for the showbiz interlopers, how by letting them
hang around as he shot or using them as background, shyness was
replaced by a rooting interest in his production. "The man who plays
the deputy sheriff—he's a cotton grower—is typical. At first he was
curious. He got to accept us, got friendly, got devoted, then he'd do
anything. Why did we pick him? He has a tremendous sense of
humor, individualism, fearlessness." Kazan came away saying, "We
got more open-heartedness, more genuine hospitality there than in
any other location I've worked on."

He came out of the editing room a few months later with what
he thought was "a very cute movie . . . I don't know another word for
it . . . very adorable. Funny. . . . Their little lives are all messed up.
The absolute helplessness of everyone in it, wrestling with problems
that are impossible for them."

As it happened, the Motion Picture Code Administrators, the
Catholic Legion of Decency, a large number of critics and, most notably, Francis Cardinal Spellman, archbishop of New York, all violently disagreed with him. The Breen office was the most easily
placated—notably by the excision of a scene in which Carroll Baker
took a bath with Archie Lee watching. The Legion simply gave the

movie its C (for condemned) rating, calling it "an obvious violation" of the motion picture code. It was Spellman whose attack was the most virulent.

His Eminence was recently back from a Thanksgiving visit to American troops stationed in Korea, and made something out of the contrast between their dutiful patriotism and the "conscienceless, venal attitude" the film sponsors. Moreover, he launched his assault spectacularly. Celebrating a Mass in St. Patrick's Cathedral, he left his throne and mounted the pulpit, something he had not done since February 1949, when he had spoken out against the persecution of Joseph Cardinal Mindszenty by the Hungarian Communist regime. No one could remember a prince of the nation's largest Catholic diocese speaking out in this way against any film. Even when Spellman had condemned Roberto Rossellini's *The Miracle* in 1948 it had been in a written document read to congregations by their priests.

But he was in a fine, high dudgeon on the morning of December 16, 1956. "The revolting theme of this picture . . . and the brazen advertising promoting it constitute a contemptuous defiance of the natural law, the observance of which has been the source of strength in our national life. It is astonishing and deplorable that such an immoral motion picture should have received a certificate of approval under the so-called self-regulatory system of the Motion Picture Association . . ." There was much more in that thunderous vein, including, perhaps most curiously, the cardinal's assertion that he was speaking not merely as a church leader but as "a loyal citizen" defending his country from decay.

Kazan raised the standard defense. His film was "a personal story of four small pitiable people," which he and Williams had tried to tell "honestly and compassionately." He said that in our country "judgments on matters of thought and taste are not handed down ironclad from an unchallengeable authority. People see for themselves and finally judge for themselves." He'd take his chances, he said, in the court of public opinion. From Florida, Williams said, "I can't believe that an ancient and august branch of the Christian faith is not larger in heart and mind than those who set themselves up as censors. . . ."

Of course he did believe exactly that; it was doubtless one reason he had left Catholicism behind. And Kazan was right to suggest, in his statement, that very possibly the cardinal had not actually seen the film. It was, in fact, the "brazen advertising" that had popped his cork, specifically a block-long billboard in Times Square, showing Carroll Baker in her "baby doll" in her crib, sucking her thumb. The sign was so provocative—so much more so, indeed, than the film it advertised—that newpapers published pictures of it. But condemning the billboard—except perhaps as an invitation to traffic accidents—was not entirely to the point. Much later, Kazan was less politic in his comments: "That old priest was a fool. God Almighty, how foolish can you be? There's nothing in the movie except sweetness and humor."

That is not quite true; the picture did have an underlying Lolita-like erotic charge. Vladimir Nabokov's book had not yet been published in the United States, but it was out in Europe and already the subject of magazine articles here. Baby Doll was older by a few years than Nabokov's heroine, but her costuming and props, and Baker's playing, gave her a distinctly nymphet quality, subversive of the sexual status quo.

When I questioned him on this point in 1990, Kazan at first denied it. "There really wasn't much sex in it," he said. "You don't know whether she went down on him while the husband was away." But then I used the phrase "childish eroticism" and he owned up. "That's what it is. It's the childish eroticism. And that appeals to a lot of men, doesn't it? You're right. . . . I never thought of that, but that's what it is. . . . What could be more dangerous to conventional morality than childish eroticism. . . . Someone who's in a crib and thirsting for it and hungry for it and not ready for marriage. How are you going to beat that?"

I record this exchange not because my reading of the film is so brilliant—actually, it's pretty obvious—but because it seemed genuinely to surprise Kazan. I believe him when he says that the not-particularly-hidden sexual subtext of *Baby Doll* did not consciously occur to him when he was making the movie. His calculations on a project often revolved around plot and characters, with its larger implications only vaguely rattling around in his mind.

It must be said that the reviewers were not much sharper than

Kazan when they considered the film. Pokey Bosley Crowther was, for once, shrewder than most of his colleagues, when he noted the film's resemblance to *Tobacco Road,* a minor, if often hilarious, film by John Ford of Erskine Caldwell's famously hot novel. They have a similar, rather jaunty raunchiness about the low lives they record. But Crowther was, like the other reviewers, discomfited by the movie, without quite being able to say why. He called the major figures "morons" and concedes only that Williams wrote his "trashy, vicious people so that they are clinically interesting." He alludes to Baby Doll's sexual hysteria only in the most gingerly and uncomprehending way. Later, in a Sunday think piece, he pretentiously condemned Kazan for his failure to give us "some comprehension and compassion for the weaknesses and sadness of man." In the *Saturday Review* Arthur Knight rather liked Kazan's objectivity about his "mean, petty" and "corrupt" characters, an attitude he likened to that of Balzac and Zola. He also noted, intelligently, that the director's stance was not unlike that of his chorus of black people, shaking their heads over the mad goings on of these witless folks. But again, he barely mentioned the film's eroticism. *Time*'s lead was straightforward enough—"just possibly the dirtiest American made motion picture that has ever been exhibited." It got the eroticism of the film, all right, but it hated it: "The movie-goer can hardly help wondering if the sociological study has not degenerated into the prurient peep."

According to Kazan the accustomed scenario—moral condemnation creating good box office—did not work out in this case. Spellman's attack, he said, caused theaters all across the country not to book the film, while the uncomprehending reviews had the effect of puzzling those people who did have the opportunity to see the film. Not knowing whether it was soft-core porn or, perhaps, soft-core art, they just skipped the experience. It did better, at least critically, abroad, but remained unprofitable.

That's too bad, because in the Kazan canon *Baby Doll* is a unique film. For all the mysterious sociological prating it engentered, it is his only flat out comedy and his most overtly sexy movie. Given the perspective of a half-century, it is infinitely more droll— "cute," if you like—than most films of its era, which with a slight lib-

eration of the production code (it occurred just before this film's release) grew smirkier without becoming more authentically adult
about sex. *Baby Doll* may be a minor movie, but taking place as it
does, in a timeless, almost dreamy setting, it remains wonderfully
watchable.

———————

A Face in the Crowd is a major film that most people mistook at the
time as a minor—or at least noncontroversial—one. It was born in a
conversation Budd Schulberg had with Will Rogers, Jr., son of the
beloved homespun American philosopher. Rogers, if anything, was
more of a Hollywood prince than Schulberg, given his starry lineage,
and was at the time running—successfully, as it turned out—for a
congressional seat, largely on his father's name. One night, Schulberg remembered, "I was talking about my old man and he was talking about his father, and he said, 'My father was so full of shit,
because he pretends he's just one of the people, just one of the guys
. . . but in our house the only people that ever came as guests were
the richest people in town, the bankers and the power-brokers of
L.A. And those were his friends and that's where his heart is and he
[was] really a goddamned reactionary . . .' We were drinking a little
too much that night and I said, 'Jesus, Will, you'd better keep your
voice down because you can't knock Will Rogers. . . . You can't win
without Will Rogers.'"

Sometime later, Schulberg wrote a story, "Your Arkansas Traveler," about a Rogers-like character, a good-natured hillbilly with the
common touch, who, like Rogers, starts working sly political commentary into his corn-pone monologues, and when his wealth and
influence grows, becomes a menace to liberal-minded society. The
story was, perhaps, the most memorable one in Schulberg's 1953
collection, *Some Faces in the Crowd*. It appealed to Kazan, especially when, as he talked it over with Schulberg, they began to see
that a figure like Lonesome Rhodes (as Schulberg named him) could
have, in the new age of television, a power undreamed of by Rogers.
TV, in their view, changed all the old equations of mass communication. They could see it, for example, in the then hot career of Arthur

Godfrey, a ukelele-strumming hick with a popular music and talk radio show in Washington, who had come to a larger public's attention with his tearful coverage of Franklin D. Roosevelt's funeral on CBS. This he had parlayed into a national radio show, then TV talent scout and variety programs, growing increasingly tyrannical with his supporting cast, increasingly forward with his political opinions, until, a few years after this movie, his career flamed out.

For Kazan, at least, the manipulative power of television, nothing like as pervasive as it would shortly become, was an obvious social menace, and the film he and Schulberg crafted stressed that aspect of the Lonesome Rhodes story more heavily than the original story had. The two men took to hanging around Madison Avenue, soaking up ad agency ambiance, and that experience was also alarming to them. "We got the feeling," Kazan recalled, "that people were manipulating in the crudest way, with humor and whatever you want to call it, [other] people's thinking and I feel that still. I think people are . . . being made to think in a way they wouldn't ordinarily think."

This experience spoke to their traditional leftism. In their view the voice of the people was democracy's purest voice. They understood, of course, that it could be polluted, poisoned by easy, comforting lies. But in the past, it had been politicians, government organs, who had done the lying. There was something new and alarming about the way the mass media—seemingly apolitical, often, as Kazan said, rather humorous in its approach—undertook this task—especially in the age of television. It was prescient of Kazan and Schulberg to posit for this new medium a capacity for evil beyond what others imputed to it.

They were not entirely alone in this belief. There had been other fictions taking the same tack—from Fredrick Wakeman's *The Hucksters* and Herman Wouk's *Aurora Dawn,* assaulting the advertising game in the 1940s, to Al Morgan's Kane-like *The Great Man,* in which a suddenly deceased media figure not unlike Lonesome Rhodes (or Arthur Godfrey) is shown, by a man investigating his life for a tribute broadcast, to have feet of clay and a soul to match. In the very year *A Face in the Crowd* was released, an equally good film about viciously wielded media power, *The Sweet Smell of Success,* with a script half-written by none other than Clifford Odets, appeared.

This does not take anything away from *A Face in the Crowd,* which has a shrewdness and, above all, a satiric energy all its own. As it was finally developed, Lonesome Rhodes (Andy Griffith in an astonishing movie debut) is discovered in a small-town southern jail by a woman named Marcia Jeffries (Patricia Neal), a Sarah Lawrence graduate who is doing a sort of voice-of-the-people radio program for the local radio station, owned by her uncle. Lonesome is a hobo minstrel serving time on a drunk and disorderly charge. She gets him to sing a song and tell a tale—but only at a price, the lifting of his sentence. She senses an appeal in him—and she has the upper crust woman's sexual curiosity about proletarian males. She gets her uncle to give him a morning show, where his genial transgressiveness—his ability to voice the secret, subversive thoughts of his audience—makes him a hit. Soon he's off to Memphis, where kidding his sponsor (and getting the public to contribute money to needy, if not necessarily authentic, cases) makes him a regional success. New York, in the form of an unsuccessful patent medicine called Vita Jex, soon beckons. He becomes its spokesperson, the drug takes off, and so does Lonesome. He's soon advising Colonel Jeffries, Vita Jex's manufacturer, and his rich cronies on how to put over a senatorial nonentity. Senator Worthington Fuller (wonderfully played by Marshall Neilan, once a famous silent film director and protégé of D. W. Griffith, latterly an alcoholic chum of Schulberg's) as a presidential candidate.

The reference here is to Robert Montgomery, the actor-director (and a much smoother operative), who was engaged by the Eisenhower camp to warm up their man's image (though Kazan said he was also thinking of Robert A. Taft and Adlai Stevenson, as politicians in need of that service). Lonesome invests this character with a genial nickname ("Curley"), hound dogs, a passion for blood sports and a more relaxed public manner. He cannot, of course, invest him with a program—mostly the man believes in help-yourself conservatism as opposed to "socialist" programs like social security. By the end of the picture Lonesome has been promised a new cabinet position, as a sort of national minister for morale, and is bragging to the faithful, long-suffering Marcia about how he "owns" his lumpen proletarian audience. "This whole country jis like my flock of sheep," he tells her. "Rednecks, crackers, hillbillies, hausfraus, shut-ins, peapickers, everybody that's gotta jump when somebody else blows the whistle. . . . I'm an influence, a wielder of opinion, a force."

Marcia has already been betrayed by him sexually—he was married to a first wife he never divorced and never mentioned to Marcia, now he's married (overnight) to a drum majorette (played by Lee Remick in another marvelous film debut). We do occasionally wonder why a smart, attractive woman like Marcia remains so long in thrall to him (in his notes Kazan thinks of her as a Lady Chatterley type, enslaved by the uncomplicated sexual energy of her lower class stud). But her revolt and revenge is sweet. In the control room she overhears Lonesome speaking contemptuously of his audience as the closing credits of his *Cracker Barrel* program roll. She pulls some levers, and the audience hears that contempt—"Good night you stupid idiots, good night you miserable slobs"—and she ruins him—at least temporarily. The network switchboard lights up with calls from outraged Americans—this incident is obviously inspired by a famous incident, in which a radio kiddie show host, "Uncle Don" Carney spoke heedlessly into an open mike and destroyed his career—and the power elite suddenly absents itself from a banquet at Lonesome's lavish penthouse, at which he and "Curley" were going to endorse each other.

This outline of *A Face in the Crowd* makes it seem drier, more schematic than it actually was. For one thing, Kazan's filmmaking was never more propulsive; this movie just barrels along its tracks, and even when its satires on commercial television seem crude, they are also very broadly funny. And then there is Andy Griffith's hypnotic performance to consider. He had wanted, as a youth, to be a preacher, so he had the ability to easily command an audience's attention. Moreover, he had a drawling wit, manifested in a hit comedy record (about a rube who cannot understand football) and by his Broadway debut, as a wise-fool hillbilly, in the hit comedy *No Time for Sergeants*, which is where Kazan first noticed him. He's great in this film, dark and crudely scheming instead of being merely genial, as he was for the rest of his career, spent largely on television.

When we first meet Lonesome he's loud, intense, challenging, full of energy, his barely concealed hostility to the respectable world covered with only the thinnest layer of highly suspect good humor. But he's a natural radio and television personality. "Andy Griffith?" Kazan rhetorically asked me. "He's warm, he's human, funny, loving, cute, playful. Aren't those things great virtues? Come on. What do you want out of life?"

In other words, in Griffith's terrific portrayal, Lonesome had enough natural charm to disarm our fears of this character. Or if not that, to keep us rooting for the better angels of his nature to assert themselves. But he also had enough paranoia to fuel his contempt for his audience and enough poor-boy ambition to make us believe in his irresistible rise—and fall. "Whenever I get a character that's a hero," Kazan said, "I ask, 'What's wrong with him?' And whenever I have a character that's a villain, I say, 'But what's the good side?'" Of his many protagonists none was more nakedly poised on this fine line.

Working on the film, Kazan kept that conflict raw and open. In his production notebooks he didn't write much about the more abstract issue of democracy versus media manipulation. As always, his notes were mainly about his characters. He loved Neal's work in the film. At the time he thought of Gloria Vanderbilt, recently married to Sidney Lumet, late of the Yiddish theater, and saw Marcia as scarred "ABOVE ALL BY A PERSISTENT SENSE OF WORTH-LESSNESS," which he thought more or less endemic to certain types of ambitious, privileged women of this era.

He was not above playing a few typical Kazan tricks to get the responses he needed from Neal. Paul Sylbert recalls a scene in which she was required to go disgustedly through Lonesome's suitcase, supposedly filled with dirty socks and underwear. He wasn't getting quite the disdain he wanted from her and turned to a prop man, wondering if, perhaps, he had a condom on him. The man reluctantly produced a rubber, it was buried in the suitcase and got exactly the wide-eyed, nose-wrinkling expression he wanted from Neal. He was also flirtatiously attentive to her between shots—because he sensed that Griffith was smitten with her and wanted to stir some hostility in his onscreen relationship with her. Was there, perhaps, a touch of the young Molly in Marcia? In *A Life* Kazan says he always thought of himself as Molly's creation and suggests that Lonesome thought of himself as Marcia's creation, which is why emotionally both clung to them even as they cheated on them.

As for Remick, Kazan admired the way she had moved in with a family whose daughter was a baton twirler, learning enough about that curious art to give a persuasive imitation of it. He wondered, too, how such an obviously respectable young woman had learned the kind of sexuality her character represents, "where a young girl attracts and hold and bedevils an older man and then betrays him." He mused that perhaps nice young Lee Remick knew—or could imagine—more about the sexual transaction than she let on.

The whole film became for Kazan an exercise in ambiguity of this sort. He understood that for Lonesome to work as a character, he had to convey "a healthy, winning simplicity." At one point he toyed with the idea of him singing a hymn so beautifully that the audience (in the film, possibly of the film) is moved to tears. He felt he had to establish that "he really means something special to a lot of people. . . . He needs to be our champion. He needs to be our standard bearer." But after much back-and-forthing he finally wrote this simple (and I think accurate) summary of his volatile relationship with the public:

> HE IS ON THE MAKE FOR
> THEM SO HE CAN REVENGE
> HIMSELF BY
> ABANDONING THEM

In coming to this conclusion he set aside the temptation to go in what he guessed might be a deeper, more complex direction:

> This will be a tragedy and a deep one
> IF
> You fall in love with him just
> As <u>Marcia</u> does and just as the <u>Public Does</u>.

But Kazan finally shied away from anything that self-important. At one point he and Schulberg contemplated Lonesome committing suicide when the public turns against him—but they discarded that notion, possibly on the grounds that it might make the audience feel sorry for him. (Instead, Marcia fears that happening, but Walter Matthau, playing one of Lonesome's disaffected writers, says simply that he's not the suicidal type and that, indeed, after a certain lapse of time, he may well make a comeback.)

So Kazan chose the bold strokes and breakneck pace of the caricaturist. "This has to be Daumier," he wrote to himself. "It has to be drawn in acid, unsentimental cutting Acid. Sharp. Pitiless. This has to be directed in anger, anger at the Fraud, the general Fraud in our advertising-surrounded lives." He wanted, for example, Lonesome's on-camera pals to "look like L'il Abner versions of Hitler's gang." And he wanted Colonel Jeffries and his scheming power elitists to be "tough old men," like Toscanini, like the waiters in Barbetta's, looking down "at this crude hillbilly with all the snobbishness of poverty-bound European Aristocracy directed down at vulgar Americans."

Above all, he felt, that when Marcia pulls the plug on Lonesome "she <u>must recognize</u> that he's a menace, that he's a danger and that he finally should be destroyed. And here the audience should not be divided or pitying or anything like that. They must be <u>dead</u> against him. . . . They must feel his danger."

We did. Kazan always had a soft spot for this movie; he thought it was, "except for the last three minutes," one of his two or three best. I don't think there's anything wrong with the ending—if you are not going to push this plot toward full-scale tragedy what ending is possible but Lonesome alone in his penthouse, deserted by everyone, drunkenly raving, threatening the world, while his last pathetic henchman manipulates a machine that delivers recorded cheers and applause at the push of a button. I suspect Kazan disliked the scene because it was the one nice Andy Griffith couldn't quite cut. "So I loaded him up with Jack Daniels whiskey . . . we call it the 'Jack Daniels technique' . . . and that did it. He was open to everything."

Kazan was, in his way, as hard on himself as he was on Griffith. There's something tense and edgy in his notes on this film. The first day's shoot was in Memphis and he came home disappointed in himself, feeling that he was not as fully in command as he wanted to be. "Must face one thing," he scribbles. "I'm being careless and rushed too much . . . I'm not giving myself a chance to rehearse." He complained that cinematographer Harry Stradling was trying to move too fast, that Budd Schulberg was also urging him to unwonted speed. As a result he thought he was not getting the behavioral reality he wanted. So he writes:

> Don't let other people make the piece for you. Don't satisfy Budd
>   or Harry or the schedule. Satisfy yourself.
> Let them deal with you.
> Grow up and become a man!!

This last is, in its way, quite an amazing piece of self-advice. He was 46 years old at the time, as experienced and as honored as any director in America. He was as fully in control of his film as it was humanly possible to be. But he was demanding still more of himself as he addressed a film that in pace and purport was quite different from anything he had ever previously attempted.

In its way, *A Face in the Crowd* is the dark twin of *Baby Doll*. It, too, is in black and white and frugally produced. It, too, mixes Stanislavskian actors with nonprofessionals in real settings. But where the earlier film was, finally, warm and forgiving of its none-too-bright protagonists, this one is deeply suspicious of the peapickers. It clearly sees how easily they can be misled, manipulated, by a genial figurehead who is himself being used by an unscrupulous elite. When I spoke with Kazan about the film in 1990 he laughed: "It anticipates Ronald Reagan. And I can't say anything better than that . . ." We can. It also anticipates George W. Bush's manipulations of the crowd.

I think this film marks a significant passage in Kazan's development, for it openly acknowledges, as never before, his fear of the American mass, his sense that its fundamental good nature, its lack of historical sense, its feckless need for idle amusement, always leaves it open to some form of baronial (mis)leadership, to some form of benignly presented fascism. It was, for Kazan, the true end of his 1930s idealism, his implicit belief in the sturdy common sense of the American yeomanry.

That well-masked despair did not particularly come through to the reviewers of the time. In his autobiography Kazan reprints a long excerpt from a favorable review in the West Coast *People's World,* which identified him and Schulberg as "stool pigeon witnesses" before HUAC, but conceded "they must have learned something during their days in the progressive movement," for this film was "a hard-hitting exposé" that "will help educate the film audience into an understanding of how public opinion is manipulated in the U.S. and for what purpose." Kazan immediately contrasted that piece with one in the crazily right-wing *Counterattack,* which called *A Face in the Crowd* an example of "commercial liberalism," "raving about conformity and thought-control" because it has nothing else to stir people's fears.

The mainstream reviewers were, on the whole, unmoved by the film. They generally disliked Griffith's characterization. They wanted him to be either a snake or a charmer. They were dead set against ambiguity. Bosley Crowther, among others, thought that the film didn't pay due attention to the way Lonesome was entrapped, victimized as he saw it, by the communications machinery. Arthur Knight, also fretful about the two-faced quality of Griffith's work, wondered if such a figure could actually become the supernova portayed in the film. *Newsweek* pretty well summed up the immediate response: "Satire gone haywire."

In the decades since, some critics have seen the film in quite a different light, as a work entitled to the intensity of its tone as it tried to cut through the pervasive blandness of its moment. Post-Watergate, *New York Times* critic Nora Sayre wrote a piece praising the film, particularly noting how television had been employed, albeit not always successfully, to warm up chilly, chilling Richard Nixon. As late as the 2000 presidential election, the *Los Angeles Times's* expert television commentator, Howard Rosenberg, was writing: "It never got the credit it deserved for its commentary on media that in some ways was as visionary as 'Network' about what lay ahead for broadcasting." The film has never achieved wide popularity, but it has never disappeared, either. It keeps nagging away at us. At some of us, at least.

15

In Middle America

A Face in the Crowd was released in late May 1957, and it did not do particularly well at the box office. Kazan would not release another movie until 1960. Worse, his attempts to write his own screenplay for that film, eventually entitled *Wild River,* did not go well. Fox had two years earlier bought William Bradford Huie's novel *Mud on the Stars* for him as the basis for a movie, and it is possible that his attempts to blend that story about the creation of the Tennessee Valley Authority with his own ideas on the subject confused and stalled him. I think it likely, as well, that his demand on himself to "Grow up and be a man" was bound up with the notion of growing up and becoming a writer, which put further pressure on him. In any case, he decided to call in Paul Osborn for a read and a possible rewrite. Osborn did not care for what Kazan had written and begged off. But Kazan kept him in mind—and Osborn apparently kept thinking about the project—to which, after several other writers failed to please Kazan, he eventually returned, earning a sole screenplay credit on the finished film.

Kazan kept chipping away at the screenplay in such spare moments as he could find. But needing as always to keep busy, he took on three theatrical assignments that absorbed much of his time for the next two years. Meantime, Molly had finally finished a play and found a producer for it, a well-to-do Texas woman named Hope Abelson, who would make her theatrical debut with *The Egghead.* It became the central preoccupation of the Kazan household in the spring and summer of 1957.

It had a fairly straightforward plot. A slightly pompous, but essentially good-hearted liberal, Professor Hank Parson, wishes to bring back to his New England college campus his protégé and friend Perry Hall, a black man, to give a lecture. It is rumored that Hall is a Communist. Parson refuses to believe this and eagerly proceeds with this engagement, while the university falls into a controversial tizzy. At the end of the second act the Parsons' maid, Essie, whose family once lived next door to Hall and his family, reveals that he was indeed a secret Communist; he's for years been writing party propaganda under a pen name. The professor's second wife, Sally, heretofore seen only as a trophy bride, bravely confronts Perry (with a tape recorder hidden in the room) and he admits his sins without apologizing for him.

Does this sound schematic? It is. Does the dramaturgy sound old-fashioned, rather like one of those mystery plays that regularly used to regale theatergoers—clues carefully plotted and placed, revelations leading to a neat resolution? It is. It is rather didactic work, quite coldly spelling out Molly's unyielding political zeal. The work is all construction—joinery—but it has no waywardness. When he was approached to play the lead, Karl Malden turned it down—politely, because Molly was his good friend and supporter. He once said to her, "Molly, if we ever have to cross the country, any country, in covered wagons, I'm going to go with you." But still . . .

She tried to interest other actors in *The Egghead* with no more success. Then one day, Abe Lastfogel—Kazan's agent, Malden's agent, Molly's agent—called Malden and said, "Karl, I understand Molly gave you a play called *The Egghead*." So she had, Malden replied. "Listen, you're going to do the play," the agent said. Malden said he just didn't think he was right for it, hiding the fact that he thought the play itself was not much good. To which Lastfogel replied, "There are times you have to do things for a friend. And she is your friend." He remembers another of Molly's pals, Hume Cronyn, agreeing to direct the piece for the same reason. And Richard Sylbert came on to design his first Broadway set.

Everyone gave it his all. I'll never forget Malden's first act entrance—booming onto the stage, looking ruddy and energized from a workout, and staying on an eager, angry, principled pitch the entire evening. Lloyd Richards, who two years later would become the first black man to direct a Broadway show (Lorraine Hansberry's *A Raisin in the Sun*) and would still later become dean of the Yale Drama School, was scarcely less good as the Communist. He made you understand how a man of his color and background might just sacrifice his better self to this cause.

Kazan was all support and sympathy. He told one Broadway columnist that he had bought a share in the production, for rooting interest and as a show of husbandly support. To another journalist he said that his largest contribution to it was tending their children. On opening night, he said, he was Molly's to command. "If she wants to walk, I'll walk; if she wants to sit, I'll sit." He'd been there before. And she had loyally been there for him on many such occasions.

In his autobiography he says that the reviews in Cleveland, where the play tried out, were encouraging. But the play was long and talky and needed work. So Kazan volunteered to join Cronyn and Malden and the visiting Robert Anderson in Molly's hotel room, where he confidently believed he could reason her into making some cuts. As Cronyn recounts the meeting in his memoir, Kazan began with honeyed words, praising many aspects of the work. The others joined him, while Molly beamed. Then, however, Kazan got down to business, proposing a number of fixes. Molly made no reply. Soon enough Kazan was shouting at her. Hot, harsh words flowed from him. To which, she made no reply. She simply listened, serene yet adamant. Cronyn remembered thinking she looked a little like an odalisque, fully clothed, but with one leg drawn up, unmoved and unmoving. Kazan's fury was eventually spent, and Cronyn remembered being moved to giggles as the men withdrew from her presence. He knew she was wrong, but he couldn't help being amused by her certainty in the face of this massed, masculine—and largely correct—assault on her work.

It must be said that the Cleveland reviews were not entirely discouraging and that *The Egghead* received a couple of positive notices when it opened in New York on October 9. Even the negative reviews were for the most part polite, sympathetic to the actors, to the direction, to the playwright's good intentions and occasional felicities of language. No one, of course, noticed that Parson's wife, played by Phyllis Love, was, at least in the final act, a version of Molly as she saw herself—tougher-minded, more realistic than the man whose career she had so faithfully stood behind. But the notices damned with very faint praise. Brooks Atkinson wrote: "To arrange for the triumphant conclusion it has to manipulate people as if they were ideas. They have no life of their own." Walter Kerr said much the same thing: "It has not that independent existence, that assertion of created life quite apart from the editorial page, that gives a human-interest story the breath and the flesh of a work of art." The show closed after twenty-one performances, losing its entire, modest capitalization of $96,000.

Kazan essentially agreed with the critics. He thought Molly's didacticism, her own firm sense of right and wrong, closed her off from life. "The audience felt that she knew in advance the solution to everything happening on stage and that she'd uncover these solutions when she chose to. This produced the one unforgivable dramatic fault: The conclusion was predictable. The conflicts were not genuine because they did not exist in the author . . ."

Kazan felt a combination of sympathy and resentment for her. He knew how long and hard she had worked on this play, knew what hopes it carried for her. But the play objectively correlated all his dubious feelings for her, which revolved around her attempts to instill "order" in his life and thoughts. She seemed, more than ever "calcified" to him, and he more openly began to express the notion that "an artist needs an anarchist's heart and has to be pulled more than one way at a time." One manifestation of this feeling was his entrance into an affair—eventually he would both marry her and make her, briefly, a star—with Barbara Loden, who was in every way Molly's opposite. She was young, drop-dead gorgeous and basically from a poor-white-trash background—all passionate feeling, unmediated by any inkling of abstract ideas. She was, of course, blonde.

————

None of the plays Kazan directed between 1957 and 1959 was first-rate, though on the whole they were received as such and achieved substantial runs. They were, in order, a minor work by a playwright widely believed at the time to be a major writer but who turned out not to be; a pompous allegory by a famous writer creating a theatrical work for the first time; a sensational—make that hysterical—play that marked the beginnings of Tennessee Williams's long, sad decline. All of these Kazan staged with feverish energy and a conjurer's skill; he was never more nimble professionally. Yet one sometimes felt, attending them, that his emotions were not fully engaged by them, that try as he might he could not find in them those points of personal reference that had animated his work on *Salesman,* on *Streetcar,* even on something as modest as *Tea and Sympathy.*

Of the three plays the first, *The Dark at the Top of the Stairs,* was the best, because it was the least presuming. It's obvious that play agents had long since learned that Molly Kazan was the best back channel to her husband. If she read and liked a play you could be sure she would bring it to his attention. She knew William Inge, read *Dark* and urged it upon Kazan sometime in the spring of 1957, before she became entirely preoccupied with her own play. He did not at first care greatly for it—though he quickly came to like its insecure, depressive and sexually ambivalent author, whom he saw clinging to Molly as the similarly troubled Montgomery Clift once had. So he committed to the play for the following season.

Inge is one of the more curious, and perhaps tragic, figures of mid-twentieth century theatrical life. A midwesterner, he had been a schoolteacher and a drama critic in St. Louis before deciding to pursue playwriting full time. His first produced work, *Farther Off from Heaven,* was a failure when it was staged at the Margo Jones Theatre in Dallas in 1947. But in 1950 he had his first Broadway success, *Come Back, Little Sheba,* about the miserable marriage of an alcoholic and his dreamy, dominating wife. It was followed by two more hits, *Picnic* (1953) and *Bus Stop* (1955), in both of which posturing, studdish males are brought down to earth by women who are not quite the victims the audience is led at first to think they may be.

In this period it was thought by some in the theater that he might—or might soon—rank with Tennessee Williams (who was a friend and an admirer) and Arthur Miller as one of America's leading playwrights. This was not to be. In the 1960s he suffered as many failures as he had successes in the previous decade, and he succumbed to his long-standing suicidal impulse in 1973 (when Kazan worked with him he lived in a dark, first-floor apartment, as a higher floor, he said, might tempt him to leap).

Such confessions were rare with Inge, whom Kazan took under his protective wing. In his notes on this play, Kazan wrote, "His voice is almost a stylization of calm, as though he had been trained to speak that way, keeping down his real feelings, forcing himself to tread an even, level path." But he also recalled that Inge had once said he felt like "running at the late-comers in a theatre and attacking them, kicking them, pounding them, screaming at them." Naturally, a conflicted figure like that was someone Kazan, that connoisseur of conflict, had to protect and defend.

The Dark at the Top of the Stairs was a reworking of Inge's first play, and it was emotionally, though not literally, an autobiographical work, in which a young boy, overprotected by his mother, largely ignored by his traveling salesman father, observes life as his family lives it in a small Oklahoma town in the 1920s. There is only one dramatic incident in the play: A half-Jewish student at a nearby military academy, a pleasant and apparently stable youth, commits suicide (offstage) after an anti-Semitic incident at a dance. Kazan, interestingly, sees this, the most problematical of Inge's characters, as a version of the man who was then his only major rival as a film and theater director. "He plays up [to] and 'likes' everybody and asks that they like him like Josh Logan before he went to the 'home' [i.e., was institutionalized]. He offers himself to them, [as] a peace offering. A hostage of a kind."

Still, this figure stubbornly remains more dramatic device than fully fledged character. Most of the play is given over to the Flood family's squabbles over quotidian matters. The mother (played by Teresa Wright, then married to Robert Anderson) and Reuben, the father (hearty Pat Hingle), get into a fight over money and his wandering ways, which leads first to separation, then to reconciliation. An aunt (Eileen Heckart) confesses to emotionally castrating her husband. A sister—the painfully shy date of the military academy cadet—flutters aimlessly about. The little boy, much preoccupied with movie stars and the pictures of them he clips from magazines, grows up enough to confront, yes, the dark at the top of the stairs (symbolizing all his unnamed fears).

It doesn't sound like much, and it really wasn't much. But Inge did have a gift for sketching slightly troubled, if never truly threatening, characters and for dialogue that gently, yet persuasively, improved upon reality. Kazan's notes on this play are as full as any he ever wrote and for the first time the question of mortality enters them.

> THE DARK is the final, inescapable loneliness that is awaiting us all. We all die alone and lie in the grave alone and forgotten. But while we are alive we fend off, assuage, ease, put off make bearable the threat of this final loneliness thru love. Thru intercourse and connection with other people we fight to make some connection . . . to stay close and then . . . this DARK, this final threatening loneliness is not so threatening, not so imminent.

As Kazan admits, these glum reflections were not untoward for a man of his age. But, curiously, they were not particularly relevant to the work at hand. Yes, Sonny, the little boy in the play, fears the dark at the top of the stairs, but he's too young to see it as death; it represents the unknown in much more general terms (as Inge said at the time, when he was a lad he was certain that everyone he met was brave, that he was, in effect, the world's only coward). In other words, Kazan was imputing to the play deep, large questions the playwright himself did not particularly aspire to raise. On the other hand, by raising this ontological question he also raised the stakes in this game. It may account for the passionate staging—many critics would notice it—he gave this rather unassuming little play.

Still, in his notes, he quickly, and with a great deal more detail, passed on to other issues, most notably to the play's female characters. "Cora Cora Cora," he repeated the underlined name of the mother ten times. "This play and production is not going to mean a hell of a lot, is in fact going to be scattered and intermittent in its effects, unless you and your audience latch on to Cora . . . the emotional center of the play . . ." Her husband was—typical of Inge

males—a wild one when she met him, literally a man on horseback.
She yielded to him, became pregnant and entrapped him in a marriage he did not want. But Kazan uses words like "swamped" and
"bewildered" to describe her state of mind. In defense against these
feelings, he imagines her as a tidy, over-managing sort of person,
though "She is really a darling. She is . . . responsible, serious, feel-
ingful, with a sense of humor, ready and desirous to learn more. She
is not a committed prude . . . She is a person who wants to be generous and outgoing and at bottom there is a tremendous surge of feeling to change, to get out of herself . . ."

I'm not sure that even sweet-spirited Teresa Wright captured all
that in performance. I'm not sure any actress could. What one tends
to remember about her is the smothering quality of her love, which,
Kazan notes, does threaten to turn her son (according to then preva-
lent psychological theory) into a homosexual, which Kazan acknowledges more or less in passing. He also suggests, in not so casual a
way, that Cora's fatal flaw—it was a subtext much on his mind these
days, especially when he was working with Inge—was her overly respectable upbringing. It is what leads her to a lack of sympathy for
the cadet victimized by anti-Semitism, which, in turn, leads her to
blame herself for his death.

Generally speaking (there are exceptions, like *Streetcar*) Kazan's
notes became more voluble when he was insecure about a play or
film, and Kazan works himself up pretty intensely on the subject of
Cora. "Finally," he writes, "it is not Cora who is to blame. It is the
rigid, puritanical, prudish, narrow, self-defensive way she was
brought up by her father and mother. The villain is respectability.
The villainy is selfishness enshrined as ethics." I'm not sure the play
actually proves this point. He gives Cora much more of a backstory
than Inge did—and a larger measure of ambiguity. In his reading of
her character, he imbues her with a genuine liking for sex. The play
ends with her husband mounting the stairs to join her in bed, and in
Kazan's notes he imagines her welcoming him eagerly.

This would not have been true of her childless sister, Lottie, to
whom he devotes almost equal analytical space. She was very funny,
and Eileen Heckart commanded a lot of the reviewers' attention for
her showy performance. But she is also a motor-mouthed annoy-

ance, spewing anti-Catholic prejudice, and above all, henpecking her patient husband, Morris, into silent misery. She is Cora's opposite, a woman who, as Kazan puts it, "has missed it . . . life, fulfillment," but compensating for that with her quarrels, gossip, and general competitiveness about clothes, hairdos, what-have-you. She may be funny on the stage, but, as he capitalizes it, she is a "TRAGEDY A TRAGIC CASE."

In one of those leaps toward personal experience that so often make his notes so entertaining, he begins analogizing her to . . . Irene Selznick. "Hollywood is full of these types. She has nothing, so she is always pushing, squeezing and so on. Advising people, 'let me send you to my doctor' . . . the gossip, the phone calls, the frantic busyness and hustle to keep going and she will forget that she hasn't got the main thing"—some sort of loving fulfillment. He adds to these considerations this line, seemingly out of nowhere, but not really: "Many women who can't come in Hollywood are promiscuous."

Kazan is searching for something that is truly not present in the play—a sexiness, a feverishness, that calm, repressed Bill Inge could not bring to the surface. This Kazan supplied to his own satisfaction and that of most of the daily critics. A few days before the December 5 opening night he confessed to a theatrical reporter that, though he had occasionally known despair before some of his plays premiered, that was not the case now. He had invested in the show personally and, he said, "I've done everything I know how to do with the play. So let it open"—to raves, as it turned out.

Brooks Atkinson thought it Inge's best work. "Although the style is unassuming as usual, the sympathies are wider, the compassion deeper and the knowledge of adults and children more profound." Walter Kerr, among others, thought the offstage suicide too much for this fragile piece to comfortably bear. He also wrote that Kazan insists on "more terror than the dark stairwell really creates." But still, he felt that the thin thread of a play did not break under these impositions. It was, he concluded, "wonderfully evocative: warm, troubled and deeply moving."

The second thoughts came later. Kenneth Tynan, dropping in from London, found two other plays, *Look Homeward Angel* and *Blue Denim,* taking up a theme similar to Inge's—the failure of parents and their children to "communicate" across the generation gap. He conceded that these plays had poignant moments and opportunities for good acting, but "All of them are as intellectually flabby as they are emotionally redundant." He traced the problem, correctly I think, to the fact that in these waning years of the Eisenhower era, American theater, American culture in general, was so Freudianly fixated. The issues in all our fictions seemed to arise out of troubled—but not insolubly troubled—families. "All criticism, all protest is directed inwards, toward the parents: everything outside is accepted with nothing more rebellious than a shrug. The result is one-eyed drama with a squint induced by staring too long down domestic microscopes and never looking out the window."

Writing almost a year later, Robert Brustein observed that "Over the placid lake of this play, Elia Kazan hurled thunderbolts. His production was in a state of carefully controlled frenzy." He thought—again, I think, correctly—that Kazan's treatment demonstrated his "understandable impatience and bafflement with it. *Dark* drones on like a Midwestern cricket, making no powerful statement, displaying no moving action, uttering no memorable dialogue." It might be, he conceded, Inge's best play in that it generally refused forced melodramatics, but it also, in a somewhat more muted form, took up his only major theme, which was women mounting successful revolutions against male dominance, but then forgiving, comforting the befuddled males. This, he argued, was *contra* Williams (to whom Inge dedicated this play) and, perhaps, *contra* Kazan's natural impulses.

In his own recollections of the play Kazan, who at first thought of the piece as "not distinguished . . . the kind of story featured in women's magazines" felt it got "deeper and more poignant," tapping into a vein "of the most genuine emotion" as it proceeded. He also implicitly denied hurling any thunderbolts around the stage; "a quiet and affecting night in the theater," he mildly called it. But in one's own recollections, it is not quiet Cora or her repressed offspring that leap to mind. It is, rather, the characters that most naturally appeal to his own sensibility—the tense, half-crazed Lottie and Reuben that blustering American male, snorting and stomping through his genteel parlor, then coming to gently pawing rest at the end—that linger.

Frankly, not much of anything—aside from acute ennui—remains in mind from Kazan's next production, *J.B.* Boris Aronson, one of his two favorite scenic designers (the other being Jo Mielziner) recalled encountering Kazan on the street one day, not long after the Inge play opened. He apparently appeared mildly depressed, and Aronson undertook to give him some advice. "Look—for the rest of your life you can do that type of show. And it's very well done, well written, well acted, well designed, well lit, well directed. But you have to do something which is much less safe, but much more satisfying. Something which also has a very good chance of failing."

It must have seemed to Kazan that Archibald MacLeish's verse drama presented just such an opportunity. It undertook no less than a resetting of the story of Job in modern times, tormented by God, tempted by Satan, but somehow muddling through to acceptance of his lot—and something like a happy ending.

Why Kazan, or anyone else for that matter, might have thought this could be anything but the grand success it turned out to be is something of a mystery. To begin with, J.B. (or Job) is colorfully sore-pressed in the first act—his children are killed, his factory and fortune destroyed, his wife leaves him and he cannot understand why this should be happening to him, an optimistic, ambitious American who has lived by and prospered from the standard rules. In the second act he is offered false "comfort" by a Communist, a psychiatrist, a traditional preacher. In the end, he emerges as a sort of secular humanist, accepting the fact that we live in a world full of grief irrationally meted out, but determined to accept the doleful elements of his fate as part of the process of living, which is, on balance, A Good Thing. At the end of the 1950s, when American quietism was reaching its peak, when "acceptance" was a message being preached at every level of our public life, this was a conclusion "thoughtful people" everywhere were pleased to hear.

And it came most gratefully from MacLeish, a certified big thinker of many years standing, about as close to being an establishment figure as it is possible for a poet to be. A graduate of Yale and by now, at sixty-seven, Boylston Professor of Rhetoric at Harvard, he had been, as well, an expatriate in 1920s Paris, a writer for *Fortune*, when Henry Luce's business magazine aspired to literary merit, and, as well, the Librarian of Congress. His verse was rather dry and intellectual, though not unapproachable, and he was also a liberal-minded, New Dealish sort of public figure, constantly speaking out on the great issues of his times. He won a Pulitzer Prize in 1932 for a long narrative poem, *Conquistador*, and another one in 1952 for his collected poems and was, throughout his long career, affectionately regarded by the middle-brow community, rather suspiciously regarded by those with somewhat loftier brows. Edmund Wilson, for example, traced his development, poetically, from neo-Masefield to neo-Eliot, in which phase, that admirable critic thought, he utterly failed "to convince one of the moral necessity of his desperate invocation of the void." He added, devastatingly: "He writes admirable English verse: his instrument is of the very best make; but, emotionally and intellectually, I fear that a good deal of the time he is talking through his hat."

Wilson wrote that assessment as early as 1927, and thirty years later there was no reason to revise it. Still, nice Archie had written this obviously aspiring drama, had published it to some acclaim and rather good sales. It had been given a production at Yale, to which Brooks Atkinson (among other influential people), had journeyed to write a favorable impression. Another production at Salzburg in the summer of 1958 was also well received, and both Elia and Molly Kazan thought well of the piece. Aronson's spectacular setting was a version of the big top to which Pat Hingle was induced to bring his hearty American businessman over, intact, from the Inge play. Raymond Massey was engaged to play God disguised as a circus vendor, a rise in rank from Lincoln. The young Christopher Plummer did the Devil, also disguised as a vendor, and eventually he commanded most of the reviews with his memorably sinuous performance.

Again, Kazan's notes on this play were voluble and his correspondence with MacLeish was extensive—with much of this material being reprinted in *Esquire*, which is a measure of just how important this play seemed to the chattering classes in 1958–59. Possibly the most interesting revelation the magazine published was a note from MacLeish to Kazan which included Lillian Hellman's reaction to a run-through he had taken her to about three weeks into rehearsal. She was an old friend of the playwright, but it is surprising to find her present on an occasion at which her political enemy, Kazan, was also in the house. It is even more interesting to find her sympathetic to the director. Yes, she thought the performance "hypo-ed," but advised MacLeish not to worry: "Gadge, like other great directors, likes to begin high and work down." Ah, show business. To its denizens, its problems so often trump all the others that might temporarily distract them.

Gossipy tidbits aside, these notes and letters now seem almost as dull as the play they discuss. Mostly they have to do with thinning out some of MacLeish's most self-consciously "poetic" language as well as providing the play with a big finish—a manly acceptance of life's absurdities. This "recognition scene," as MacLeish called it, occurred to him during a walk with Kazan in Jackson Park, in front of the White House, when the Washington reviews of their tryout run were less than enthusiastic.

What is most interesting in this material now are some of Kazan's asides, remarks about matters not germane to his central concerns. For example, in his mind, J.B. was a version of Wendell Willkie, the liberal Republican businessman and presidential candidate in 1940. "Willkie was a whole era—liberal capitalism," he wrote to Lucinda Ballard, his costume designer, "a man who was forced to break out of his mold and learn and learn because history was moving so fast. A man with the natural, homely resilience and horse sense and outspokenness of the middle of this country."

Here, as in so many of his notes, he keeps thumbing through his own reality, looking for inspirations—ideas, memories, people—that will ground his production in reality. For example, he insisted on casting his Satan figure younger than MacLeish originally conceived him, more of a beat-generation type. But having made that decision he reminds himself that he must not be played as a pouting, sniveling "third rate James Dean."

Thinking about Zuss (God) he remembers how much he has always liked older actors and thinks old actor Massey should play that idealized type:

Not the phony manner of the old actor
But what you love about the old actor
The elegance
The politeness
The sly humor
The old actor, rather than be on T.V. and be made
A fool of, prefers to cover his face,
Cover his face and sell balloons.
A self-exiled king.

Even Molly, it seems, enters his thoughts when he considers
J.B.'s wife, Sarah—"all Yankee," he writes, "a Yankee mother."

Once MacLeish came up with his second act curtain speech
("We are—and that is all our answer. We are—and what we are can
suffer"), the die was cast. The show opened in the midst of a newspaper strike, but some the critics kept writing for radio and television, and the papers published their notices after the strike ended a
few weeks later. The vast majority were enthusiastic. Kerr thought
J.B. harmed by the formal limitations "elected by the author," but "If
they keep the evening at some remove from wholly touching drama,
they do nothing to rob it of its fascination as sheer theater." Atkinson
had no such reservations: "Mr. MacLeish has written a fresh and ex-
alting morality that has great stature . . . one of the memorable works
of the century as verse, as drama, as spiritual inquiry."

As ever, the magazines were more grudging. Especially Kenneth
Tynan. He noticed what no one else apparently did, which is that the
play is based on an essentially false premise. It rests "on the assumption . . . that we are judged by God. It then poses the question: why
are we judged so harshly? The answer, which destroys everything
that preceded it . . . is that He does not judge us at all. Having bothered us for more than two hours with an apparently insoluble problem, Mr. MacLeish blithely shrugs and confesses that it was the
wrong problem after all."

The critic could not have known about the Kazan/MacLeish
Washington walk, during which this contradictory scene was rather
desperately conceived to save the show, with no one thereafter
noticing the contradiction. But Tynan, was no fool; he was, in fact,

the great theatrical critic of his time. He knew what Kazan's strength and limits as a director were, and without quite coming out and saying so, he knew this material was wrong for him.

I think the physical production was spectacularly right. The very fluid staging was terrific as well. And Kazan clearly loved, was flattered by, the chance to serve a writer whose reputation in the literary world seemed to him so impeccable; he had not had such an opportunity since working with Thornton Wilder so long ago. But yet Tynan was right to notice the emptiness in much of the spectacle Kazan threw at the audience. His specialty, the critic noted, was plays that "rumble with passion, blaze into violence, and flower in a climate of frenzy"—all elements intrinsically lacking in this play. Thus, his direction seemed at odds with—almost pasted onto—*J.B.*, which stubbornly remained what it started out as, a play to be read rather than performed. "Long before the final curtain I was bored to exasperation by the lack of any recognizable human response to calamity," Tynan wrote. Another way of saying that for all his efforts, Kazan never quite turned MacLeish's drama into a Kazan play.

Which, latterly, he acknowledged. "*J.B.* is a play that won the Pulitzer Prize and all kinds of kudos but which I found terribly dull. Then why did I do it? Because it gave an opportunity to do a kind of production I'd never done before, one in which there is bold, unrealistic picturization and the kind of acting that amounts to choreographed movement. I directed the play as I might have a ballet . . ." He adds to this the observation that he had "little ear for poetry and little patience with it in the theatre unless it's Shakespeare's—and not all of his." In other words, he was seeking growth—by no means a dishonorable or oft-pursued goal for a man of his age—but he was, in this instance, looking for it in the wrong place; far from being one of its century's memorable works, *J.B.* now reads like a parody of its most highfalutin pretensions.

With this play, and with the one he began almost immediately to prepare, Tennessee Williams's *The Sweet Bird of Youth* (produced by Cheryl Crawford), some critics charged that Kazan was overpow-

ering his playwrights' more subtle intentions with staging that called
more attention to his direction than to their writing. In his autobiography he conceded the point. He says he was at the time compensating for the failure of his most recent films and feeling he had to "stop
forcing myself into another person's skin, but rather to look for my
own subjects and find . . . my own voice." So he was more than usually assertive as a director. On the other hand, these plays needed all
the help they could get from him.

That was, I think, particularly true of *Sweet Bird of Youth.* In 1954
or '55 Kazan had written a letter to Williams, who was then living in
Rome, chiding the playwright, then beginning to work on this play, for
his escapist ways. "It seems to me," he wrote, "that the things that
make a man want to write in the first place are those elements in his
environment, personal or social, that outrage him, hurt him, make him
bleed. Any artist is a misfit. Why the hell would he go to all the trouble
if he could make the 'adjustment' in a 'normal' way. In Rome, I'd say,
you feel a kind of suspension of discomfort. Things are distant but, in
so far as they impinge at all, not unpleasant."

This was shrewd of Kazan. The most basic problem with *Sweet
Bird* was its lack of felt reality. In all of Williams's best previous
work, his characters, if not drawn directly from his life, had been informed by it. That was not so in this case—they were purely fantasies, or phantasmagorias, fictions based on fictions. At its deepest
level—never plumbed persuasively—Williams wanted this to be a
meditation on mortality. In it, an aging movie star (Geraldine Page),
traveling under several names (Princess Paznezoglu and Ariadne
Del Lago among them), arrives in a small Gulf Coast town fleeing
what she's sure is a career-ending flop film. She's accompanied by
her gigolo, Chance Wayne (Paul Newman). He, too, feels old—at
least for his line of work. He also feels threatened. This is his home-
town, from which he fled hoping also to become a movie star. He
never got further than the chorus of *Oklahoma!* and, what's worse,
he soon discovers that he's a marked man here. It turns out that in
the course of a night's sport with the daughter of the local political
boss, he infected her with venereal disease, the cure for which rendered her unable to bear children. Boss Finley (played by Sidney

Blackmer, another old actor) decides that a just punishment for him would be castration. At the end of the play, Page's character learns that her movie is a hit after all, that more roles await her in Hollywood. She offers Chance a lift out of town, but he refuses and she blithely departs. As the play ends he is fatalistically awaiting the loss of his "sweet bird" and speaking to the audience, "I don't ask for your pity, but just for your understanding. Not even that, no—just for your recognition of the me in you and the enemy time in us all."

An unexceptional point. But one that might have been made by a man and a woman less melodramatically worrying about the loss of their looks while at the same time indulging habits designed to prematurely debilitate them. They are, at first, funny in a grotesque sort of way. But the laughter dies quickly. They may be "just folks" to Tennessee, but they aren't to us, no matter how much tolerance we bring to them. They have crossed a line, entered a country that is black and deeply unreal.

The same may be said of Chance's nemesis, Boss Finley. A number of reviewers thought he was a version of Big Daddy, but aside from their both being large, strong men, it is hard to see the resemblance. There was always something insinuating about Big Daddy: He wore his power quietly; he was not interested in politics except to advance and protect his own ends; he was not overtly a bigot; he was not, physically, a sadist. He was, as we have observed, an ambiguously envisioned version of Williams's own father. But for all the time (and drafts) Williams lavished on Finley, he was, like everyone else in this play, a poorly conceived and written caricature.

At this point in his biography of Williams, Donald Spoto quotes an interview he conducted with Kazan's friend Joe Mankiewicz: "Williams's drafts were so rough as submitted, they had to be turned into workable, playable dramas for the stage. . . . Kazan did this. Tennessee gave him the softness, the malleable material of the work and Kazan, like a truffle-dog, sniffed out the violence and brought it out into the open . . . sometimes, I think, over Tennessee's objections."

The two did not, in this case, fall into open quarrels. Williams was convinced, once again, that he was a dying man, that this was his last play. "But," Kazan laughed to Spoto, "he was always going to die the following week." In the meantime, he worked agreeably, generously with Kazan, faithfully bringing in the rewrites rehearsals seemed to demand, still the "adorable man to work with" that he had always been.

In his notes, Kazan saw him pretty much in full. "To Tennessee Williams the world is a hostile trap. 'You can't get out of it alive.'" Chance, as he saw it, was an honest, if exaggerated, projection of the playwright's feelings of helplessness, and he thought it was his job to dramatize Chance's entrapment: "Show Chance surrounded by his enemies, show them waiting like a *circle of wolves* to tear him apart, to castrate him."

Much of Williams's private behavior, Kazan thought, was an attempt to escape his own trap, and he listed his strategies:

—Drink
—Drugs
—Sex—the senses
—Memory of a better past
—Comradeship, tenderness, closeness to another
—An act of the Imagination
—By simply keeping moving!

He also created a none-too-persuasive rationalization for Chance's passivity in the face of castration:

Perhaps he knows he has sinned and feels he must pay for it to be
ACCEPTED BACK IN THE HUMAN RACE
He seems to want punishment
This must not be accidental
The thing is not a tragedy of size
Unless he chooses to stay in the TRAP
The Princess (in effect) opens the door for him and tries to pull it free
He does not go

Kazan also lists no less than fourteen sins committed by Chance and insists:

BUT HE IS STILL MORALLY ALIVE BECAUSE
HE FEELS GUILTY ABOUT THESE
THINGS AND FROM THE BEGINNING
HE ONLY WANTED TO "DO RIGHT"
AND SO THE ONLY WAY HE CAN GET BACK INTO THE
MORAL ORDER, THE MORAL COMMUNITY IS TO
ACCEPT HIS PUNISHMENT. AND HE'D REALLY RATHER
BE PUNISHED AND BE TAKEN BACK THAN TO BE
OUTSIDE IT . . .

In all of this, as more than one critic observed, Geraldine Page's movie star was pretty much a bystander. They all loved her performance because it was so grandly conceived and played. They had previously noticed her as shy, stammering Alma in a revival of Williams's *Summer and Smoke*. Now they were astounded by the sheer size, the blazing theatricality, of her work here. But really there was not much more than that to say about her. Everyone had seen divas narcissistically misbehaving in the past—*Sunset Boulevard, All About Eve*—and this was an expert variation on that theme. Kazan remembered stories he had heard about Marlene Dietrich acting with a mirror mounted near the camera's lens so she could study her effects on the spot. He also stressed the desperation with which she clung to her fast-fading youth. "The change in her skin, her hair, her body—these are all high, high drama to her. A white hair puts her in deep, deep depression." He adds:

WHEN YOU CONSIDER WHAT HER
YOUTH <u>WAS</u> NO WONDER SHE
DOESN'T WANT TO GIVE IT
UP. THE SPIRIT SHE HAD!!

But this is desperation talking. Alternately inhaling oxygen and hashish, Ariadne is not quite funny, not quite sympathetic. She's just a mess who doesn't quite belong in a play that, for better or worse, belongs to Chance. The play is riven along this fault line—and riven, as well, by the fact that its first act, dominated by Ariadne's self-absorption, does not prepare us for the darkness of the second and third acts, wherein Chance's impending doom takes over.

So Kazan came up with what he called "a trick." Or a diversion. Or a magician's act of misdirection. Or even, possibly, a coup de théâtre. He had Mielziner design an open set—no back wall—so he could bring in a huge television screen, on which he projected a vastly oversized image of Boss Finley making the vicious, racist speech Blackmer declaimed downstage, directly to the audience. Kazan sort of thought it implied that the power of the man was not merely local. Kenneth Tynan thought it was a way of giving the play spurious importance as an indictment of southern racism, in those days of the incipient civil rights movement very much on everyone's mind. We may simply regard it as a sign of Kazan's frenzied desire to make his friend's play "work."

But yet he got away with it—at least in part because the daily critics remained in thrall to Williams. They had made him a decade and a half earlier. And they were not yet ready to break him. They remained wistful for the wistfulness of *The Glass Menagerie*. They were conscious of the increasingly violent ends his males were coming to—torn to death by dogs in *Orpheus Descending*, cannibalized in *Suddenly, Last Summer*. But the man could still write! Which must mean that he still had something to say.

Brooks Atkinson, curiously, found Williams in "a relaxed mood as a writer. He seems to have made some sort of peace with himself." Walter Kerr responded to the sheer demonic energy of the piece. "This is the noise of passion, of creative energy, of exploration and adventure. It is enormously exciting."

Exciting enough to these first nighters that their enthusiasm made the play something of a succès de scandale. The dubiety of the weekly and monthly critics—their questions about the play's logical inconsistencies, their criticisms of Kazan's direction—"mannered," "hollow," "operatic," "hysterical" were just some of the adjectives applied to it—did not stem the tide.

Prior to the play's opening, Williams had complained of the pressures he felt to create a blockbuster every time he opened a show on Broadway. But with an advance sale of more than $400,000 and with $400,000 of MGM's money already in his pocket for the movie rights, the truth was that blockbusters were, and for some time had been, his business. What's curious about this moment is that it was Kazan who was getting out of the blockbuster business. He did not know it at the time—indeed, he and Williams the next year tried to collaborate on *Period of Adjustment* though they fell out—but *Sweet Bird of Youth* would turn out to be his last Broadway production. The commercial theater, he was beginning to recognize, was, for him, a fully realized dream. He had nothing left to prove there. But he had a lot to prove to himself in other arenas. Henceforth, the main—though not exclusive—line of his work would be much more personal in nature, direct expressions of his ideas and experiences. Beginning with *Wild River.*

By this time Ben Maddow, a very experienced sceenwriter whom Kazan had known since his Frontier Film days, and Calder Willingham, the novelist and occasional screenwriter, had done drafts of *Wild River* that didn't please Kazan any more than his own efforts had. Michel Ciment says that eight drafts were made (with six different titles) before Kazan went back to Paul Osborn, and between them they came up with the script that Kazan would start shooting in the summer of 1959. No script Kazan ever directed had been so agonizingly arrived at. But none had meant more to him.

As we've noted, he began thinking about the film—perhaps scratching a few notes about it—as early as 1943. In these earliest thoughts, an idealistic Department of Agriculture functionary, very like the man he had worked for on *It's Up to You,* was central to the plot. But this figure eventually disappeared, possibly because placing a younger, sexier character at the center of the story would give the film more commercial appeal, possibly because the debates he envisioned between this figure and his young hero struck him as long-winded and diversionary. Still, the essence of his story remained unwavering:

A youngish and idealistic New Dealer is sent out from Washington, charged with (a) buying the land that would be inundated when the TVA dams changed the course of the river and (b) resettling its occupants. It could be argued that on balance TVA would eventually change their lives for the better. Except for one factor: Many of the dispossessed were members of families that had lived and farmed this acreage for more than a century. They had a tradition—a culture—that was valuable, damageable and not easily transportable. The social engineering that would undoubtedly bring the greatest good to the greatest number would not necessarily include them.

In the film, this drama would be encapsulated in a confrontation between the idealistic New Dealer (Chuck Glover, played eventually by Montgomery Clift) and the Garth family, who farm an island in mid-river and who are led by a fierce, eighty-year-old matriarch, Ella Garth, memorably portrayed in the film by Jo Van Fleet. The story is complicated by the fact that Chuck falls in love with her widowed daughter-in-law, Carol, played with glowing beauty and shyly expressed strength of character by Lee Remick, in what may be her finest performance.

It must be clear, even from this very brief summary, that this idea offered Kazan his clearest opportunity yet to explore that favorite theme of his, the hidden ambiguity of idealistic enterprises. But it had other possibilities as well; it offered him a setting that had not been explored in a fictional movie, and one that could be examined (in color and CinemaScope) on a grand, highly cinematic, scale. Most important it offered him—less in the finished product than in his early drafts—a chance to explore his own younger self.

As we've seen, he meant his protagonist (initially called "Dave") to be a projection of himself and Clifford Odets, as they had been in the first flush of their early New York theatrical success in the mid-thirties—cocky know-it-alls, full of themselves, confident that there was nothing they could not accomplish in their own field, and perhaps a few others beside. Specifically, he thinks of himself and Ralph Steiner heading off to Tennessee to make *People of the Cumberland*: "YOU KNEW ALL ABOUT IT BEFORE YOU LEFT NEW YORK. Mighty dynamic you were . . . intense . . . full of a little knowledge (which is a dangerous thing), 100 times surer of everything than you are today." He was determined that *Wild River*'s protagonist have that self-confidence. He imagined him thinking of his life "as a series of contacts where he sows good deeds, wisdom, semen and then . . .

passes on." To him life was "a series of limited engagements" since he is "the instrument of history," confidently breaking eggs because he feels "it is good for them to be part of the omelet."

Reading these notes, one cannot help but think what a brutal and scarring movie *Wild River* might have been had Dave/Chuck turned out to be as Kazan had first envisioned him. Imagine it: A Jewish intellectual-activist, heedlessly driven by an ideal of social betterment, enters a primitive, instinctual culture determined to change it, and carelessly willing to destroy it as he pursues his abstraction. In the context of this film a man could get lynched for such behavior (and, indeed, even in the radically different finished product, Chuck is the victim of mob violence).

I think Kazan softened this initial vision for two reasons: One was that he could not make this tough, driven character sufficiently appealing to the audience; the other was that Kazan, at fifty, was obviously a very different man than he had been twenty-five years earlier, and try as he might, he could not make himself fully sympathize with his former self. Nor could he take the same slightly patronizing attitude toward the simple folks that Dave/Chuck needed to carry out his mission.

On research trips to Tennessee he could still be mistaken for a New York "kike" and menaced by people he was trying to ingratiate himself with. But, as he told Michel Ciment (among others), he had long since entered upon a "love affair with the people in the back parts of the country—how much I love and admire them. That's the first time I use the word, my *loving* [italics added] my material." He began to see these locals as not so very different from his own Greek family—very conservative, even defensive, in their manners, in their ways of relating to strangers, but also shyly welcoming, like the people he had met in Mississippi on *Baby Doll.*

So, inevitably, *Wild River* became a less brutally confrontational movie than he had originally conceived. But, one has to say, this evolution took place almost grudgingly. For example, Ella Garth and her family grew stronger and stronger as he and his collaborators worked on the script. He wrote:

AND ABOVE ALL KEEP THE PEOPLE TOUGH. Don't soften
Ella down into an articulate conversational stereotype. She should
never warm up to Dave [Chuck]. She should say, I guess he's all-
right, but I guess I ain't never going to like him. . . . What attracted
you and what will attract the audience is their unremitting, uncompromising toughness, their unrelenting meanness . . . the fact
that they are always themselves and not "nice."

This was a miscalculation on Kazan's part. The American movie
audience will tolerate unpleasantness only up to a point; eventually
hard cases have to soften, indicate that their crustiness is only skin
deep. Kazan would soften Glover, but he could not, would not, allow
Ella to melt down. "[Y]ou must realize, as she does, that the end of
the island is the end of her life. She's not fighting for the island, she's
fighting for her life." It is this, he says, that will give the film its size;
he even analogizes, not inappropriately, Ella's struggle for existence
with Willy Loman's.

It was Ben Maddow's failure fully to realize Ella's ferocity that led
Kazan to replace him. "It's the final fearless, uncompromising nature of
this personal emotion of hers which IS the piece. . . . Ben dissipates it
by making her become CASUAL and then friendly . . . as soon as you
become familiar and casual with an emotion it loses its size."

He never lost that dimension. She's the figure we carry away
from *Wild River*—those few who of us who have seen it—and carry
around with us forever. Curiously, Kazan was much more willing to
compromise with Chuck. At some point he lost his Jewishness,
partly because Kazan convinced himself that the WASP-Jewish conflict was stale, in part because he thought he might interest Brando
in the part. "In those days," he said to me, "I always wanted Brando."

It's unclear if Kazan ever made a serious approach to Brando on
this project. Probably he didn't, because in preproduction the script
remained so deeply in flux, particularly regarding Chuck Glover.
Kazan, who called Montgomery Clift "a dud" at one point, and the
studio were particularly concerned about his antiheroic qualities.
Buddy Adler, a reasonably civilized producer who had taken over as
Fox's head of production from Zanuck in 1956, while generally praising a draft script, wrote that it did not contain a compelling reason

that anyone would want to see the movie. He proposed strengthening the love story between Chuck and Carol, which was done. Later, according to Kazan, Adler would propose Marilyn Monroe as the love interest.

The problem they are implicity addressing was that TVA was old and irrelevant news to the mass audience. The film really needed a powerful romance if *Wild River* was going to succeed at the box office. The other issue worrying Kazan was the diffusion of focus that persisted through the various screenplay drafts. More and more powerfully he felt his film had to be about just one thing: "This unlikely Jew [Kazan clung long to that identification] meets these unlikely mountain people and conquers them, is not frightened and does the job, has his heart broken and leaves."

Desperate to make this figure relevant to a modern audience, Kazan began to think that his thirties idealism, so much like Kazan's own, could teach contemporaries a thing or two. "We actually can change things," he insisted to himself, "change the shape and spirit of the world we live in. It is futile and fruitless to bitch and complain all the time, to go through life clutching your grudge against your father like it was a life buoy." He went so far, now, as to hope that his hero could be a sort of answer to Brando and Dean—whose salient quality, their choked rebelliousness, he had himself done so much to create. He said he was tired of this younger generation "brought up to be takers."

That idea did not get developed more than inferentially in the finished film, in large measure because Montgomery Clift was cast as the New Dealer. It was Spyros Skouras who proposed him to Kazan, who at first resisted him. He had, of course, directed Clift in *The Skin of Our Teeth,* and there had been a time when he seemed to be always underfoot in the Kazan brownstone. Kazan liked him without quite achieving the kind of instinctive rapport with him that he had with Brando. "He was a dutiful kid, Monty," Kazan later said. "But he was still some way or other a cripple. Some way, some subtle way, he wasn't entirely healthy."

Kazan was, in fact, understating the case. Clift had always been sexually ambivalent, yet of course obliged to heterosexuality in his public persona. This led, when he was at his best, to a kind of ironic watchfulness in some of his work; it was almost as if he was judging just how successfully he was impersonating unambiguous masculinity. But by the time he reported to the *Wild River* location he was— no other word for it—a mess. An auto accident in 1956 permanently marred his truly beautiful countenance. He was also beginning to go bald, and Kazan says the makeup person was constantly blacking the bare patches on his scalp before the camera turned. All of this deepened his insecurities, and well before this shoot he had taken to dope and drink. Before starting on the picture Kazan said to him: "Monty, I don't want you to take one drink during this or else I can't work with you. I can't stand drunken actors." And—with Kazan admiring his will—he stayed sober until the day before the shoot ended. Then he showed up drunk on the set. But he had little to do that day, so Kazan simply said, "Congratulations, Monty, you've done it up to now fine. Lie down." Which Clift did, snoozing the day away.

This does not mean that working with Clift was ever without anxiety. He, for instance, had decided that he needed, à la Monroe, his own personal acting guru on the set, and on his first day, there she was, Mira Rostova, a New York acting teacher whose repute among suggestible actors was second only to Strasberg's at this time. She took up a position behind Kazan, nodding or shaking her head as Clift spoke his lines. She lasted one day. Kazan would have no codirector on this picture. But she did hang about, consulting with Clift in the evenings.

His more important consultations, in Kazan's view, were with his costars, Lee Remick and Jo Van Fleet. "They liked him. They supported him. They kept the thing going for his sake. Jo and Lee both were goddesses. They were great with him, but he was always trembling on the brink of collapse." At one crucial point in the film Kazan used Clift's dependency on Remick very effectively. They are strongly attracted to each other, even though Carol has a perfectly nice, rather dull boyfriend and both of them know that if they let matters go too far, each will, in effect, be consorting with the enemy. The scene where they transcend this hesitation was written with Chuck as the aggressor—a mode Clift simply could not manage. So Kazan turned it around, let Remick be the aggressor. It works persuasively, almost as an anti-cliché.

The same can be said of Chuck's relationship with Van Fleet's Ella.

She was still a notoriously difficult actress, whose "difficulty" eventually cost her her career. This naturally commended her to Kazan, who remembered coming upon her early in the morning, painstakingly painting liver spots on her hands (she was much younger than her character). He told her not to bother; the camera would not know if they were or were not present. "But I'll know," she said firmly.

Ella's relationship with Chuck is, of course, the fulcrum on which *Wild River* rests—and it is complicated in ways we do not often see in movies. He's the one making the long, idealistic speeches about the greatest good for the greatest number, about the power of the law to remove her and her family from Garth Island by force if necessary. But he cannot manage implacability, cannot evoke the requisite sureness of voice and manner these scenes require. On the other hand, he cannot, will not, give up, so he becomes an earnest puppy. Which seems to amuse her. She's a taciturn woman who speaks sparely and flatly. But something in her can't help being at least amused by an insecure man trying to bury that insecurity under his verbiage. Their duel takes on human shadings that Kazan probably did not imagine when he was struggling with the script.

In essence, what happened was that Montgomery Clift internalized all the conflicts Kazan had originally thought would be played out in dialogue and action. Those were still present, of course. Ella Garth and her sons and their extensive families are still in active opposition to the government man and his grandiose plans. So is much of the surrounding community. But Chuck Glover is no longer the cocksure outlander. He evolves into a sort of Kazan clone, a man who knows that the good he intends to do is not unambiguous. He persists because, by the narrowest of margins, he judges the engineering, both hydraulic and social, that he intends to do will likely be more useful than the harm he must also do.

As this drama played out on location—the picture was shot in and around Charleston, Tennessee, in October and November 1959—Kazan contented himself with making Clift's character even more insecure than the actor actually was. "I exaggerated it. I made him less strong. . . . It was a different version from what my script was, but he fitted it beautifully." There were other benefits as well. One was the intensification of the drama; as it became more narrowly focused on Chuck and Ella, some of Kazan's fears of his film sprawling too widely dissipated.

He also wanted to achieve what he called a "laconic, pictorial" style in the film, to "boil the words out of everything." He thought: "Art goes from peak to peak. Nature has valleys. Art should have none. Here in this picture you have a brilliant opportunity to do everything very, very pictorially and very much without words. . . . Just have a succession of meaningful events . . . Go from peak to peak."

He did not quite achieve that. There are plenty of words in *Wild River.* But they are rarely abstract words. And they are rarely pitched at the high melodramatic level of, say, *East of Eden* or *A Face in the Crowd.* These people are soft-spoken in their contrasting stubborn-nesses; their rages are more felt than openly expressed. And I think more effectively than he did in *East of Eden,* Kazan achieved the pastoral quality that Ciment imputed to that picture. Indeed, I think *Wild River* comes close to being a great film—in its—yes, laconic—humanization of a large conflict, in its evocation of a lost American landscape and spirit, in the simple beauty of its imagery (its largely unsung cinematographer was Ellsworth Fredericks), in the force of its acting, in its almost Chekhovian realization of little lives under pressures they do not entirely comprehend.

Indeed, in talking about the film with Kazan, I specifically mentioned the scene, late in the film, in which the Garths are being moved off the land, and workers are chopping down trees and preparing to torch buildings before the island is finally flooded. Knowing Chekhov was Kazan's favorite playwright, I mentioned the sound of the axes—reminiscent of the final moments of *The Cherry Orchard*—and once again my obvious little reference took him by surprise. "Never thought of it," he said. "Never thought of it." Then he paused and said, "Well, it's obvious I must have thought of it."

But if this is a near-great film, it has always been an unheralded one. When they saw it, Fox's executives had no confidence in it. They gave it what amounted to an art house release, hoping perhaps the critics would create an audience for it.

They were by no means unkind. Some carped a little about the Clift-Remick romance. One or two thought the piece lacked "poetry." But they did love the acting—especially Van Fleet's. Yet the first stringers, on the whole, did not turn out for the film, and the second stringers were more respectful than enthusiastic. The movie got only a very spotty release outside its brief runs in the major markets. And Kazan had to beg Skouras to release it in Europe, where the reviews were better, but the business was just as bad. Kazan told Ciment that he tried to buy the film back from Fox in order to release it himself, but they wanted more than he had, $300,000. The film has continued to languish for forty-five years, unavailable on tape, only recently released on DVD, rarely played on television—its stars are not "legendary" enough to carry it with the forgetful modern audience.

———————

"Bill Inge understood the inhibitions of Middle America better than anyone," Warren Beatty was to say more than forty years after he made his movie debut, in the starring role in *Splendor in the Grass*. Kazan always agreed with him. "He seems like a hack because you listen to the things and you think, 'Oh, shit. I hear that every day on TV. But he suddenly goes deeper and deeper . . .'"

Which is why a slightly odd trio—Kazan, Beatty and Natalie Wood, then enduring a palpable downturn in her star career—found themselves on a variety of locations around New York, trying (rather successfully, as it turned out) to duplicate Kansas as it had looked in the late twenties and early thirties. Kazan had been the prime mover in this enterprise. "I was very proud of my friendship with Bill Inge. I looked after him a lot and helped him a lot. I put that screenplay together from a novel he wrote . . . worked it over and made it good." Or, at the very least, made it a viable commercial proposition—the last hit movie Elia Kazan would ever make.

Inge's story was a novelty for him, in that it revolved around an intense adolescent love story that the two principals try to keep secret from their prying parents; he had never done such a narrative before. Beatty's character, Bud Stamper, is the scion of a self-made and (of course) vulgar rich man, Ace Stamper, played with his customary braying force by Pat Hingle. Bud's girlfriend, Wilma Loomis (Wood), is the daughter of a druggist and his narrow, repressive wife (Audrey Christie), convinced that her daughter is on the brink of ruination by

Bud. He, though, is far from being a wastrel, though the firestorm of teenage sexuality is surely sweeping through him. His problem is escaping his old man's ambitions for him; he wants his son to go to Yale and eventually to take over the family's rapidly growing business. Bud, however, wants to go to agriculture school and become a humble farmer (more pastoral yearnings). In a way everything works out badly for everyone. Wilma is driven to madness after she yields to Bud, and has to be institutionalized (though she does recover). Bud's father is destroyed by the Depression and commits suicide—which at least permits Bud to make some sort of decent, modest but not very interesting or intensly felt life for himself.

Of all Kazan's films, this is the one that most directly confronts American sexual hypocrisy. Early in 1960, on the day he originally committed to what he called in a note this "play," he wrote that the two parents, Ace and Mrs. Loomis, were "murderers" no less, killing "a rare and fine thing . . . romantic love. . . . And they do it . . . in the name of the Eisenhower virtues."

He goes on, frankly, in a vein of growing hysteria:

> They do it for their children's good. They do it with a sense of not being appreciated and understood. They do it also with a sense of self-righteousness, that they are holding the fort for what is right. They do it to SAVE their children. They do it without self-doubt, completely within their tradition. They are the great American middle class that is going down. . . . They are the killers. All their rules are business rules, what is practical, what will make the most money. They are the dominators and the castrators. AND YOU'D NEVER KNOW IT TO LOOK AT THEM . . . THEY ARE THE PERFECT IMAGE OF PATERNAL AND MATERNAL CONCERN AND LOVE.

Kazan sees these parents as emblematic of everything that is wrong with the country. And all his sympathies are again with rebellious, inarticulate youth. "The kids are kids," he writes. "They listen respectfully to their parents. And the advice and urging they get . . . which is counter to their own feelings. FILL THEM WITH A SENSE OF CONFUSION. THESE ARE GOOD KIDS WHO WANT to do what their parents tell them to do."

But can't quite manage that. All he can concede the youngsters is a conclusion that permits them to "go on loving each other to the end" and permits them, as well, a final "picking up the pieces and making a fair to middling life for themselves out of what is left."

To some degree, in the making of the film, Kazan betrayed his best instincts about it. For in his notes, he cautioned himself to present the parents with a certain subtlety. He wanted to disguise the "heavies," as he called them. "I would give them every VIRTUE: middle class wisdom, patience, self-sacrifice, real love, real tears, real concern . . ." There is even a fascinating aside in his notes in which Kazan toys with the idea of playing Mrs. Loomis as a version of Paula Strasberg: "Warm, seductive, feeding everyone, jolly, companionable, gossipy, intense, observant, political, into everything, consuming, lesbian, sexed but unsexed, expansive, embracing, babyish, making everyone else a baby."

It is possibly a great idea. Or possibly a very bad one, but it is, in any event, not one that went anywhere. In the film, as realized, Mrs. Loomis is, from the first moment we see her, the very emblem of pinch-souled small-town Protestantism. And Ace Stamper, as given, seems to have been taken over directly from a Sinclair Lewis novel. Or from Kazan's life, since Ace is a WASP version of his own money-mad father.

Each of these characters comes close to caricature. But, that said, this is the film in which Kazan most clearly assaults American Puritanism. It is also the one in which he most clearly confronts the bullying insensitivity with which our business life is conducted. Conceding its cartoonishness, one also has to concede that there is a real heat and feverish energy in Kazan's realization of *Splendor*. He is getting a lot off his chest here. Indeed, in its attitudes toward both sex and business it predicts—as Kazan at that point had no way of knowing—many of the attitudes that would be yet more screechingly stated by the rebellious youth culture of the sixties. This is rather curious, given the suspicion with which Kazan would come to view that culture, his contempt for its softness and self-indulgence. He surely did not intend to make a movie that could be read as a signature document for a false "revolution." On the other hand, he did intend to make a film that reflected something of the young man, confused, but striving for autonomy, that he had been in the late twenties and early thirties, the era in which it was set.

And, it must be said that, at heart, in the figures played by Beatty and Wood, *Splendor* is quite sound. The former would, of course, go on to become stud to the nation, in rumor at least, its most notorious womanizer (it was an unspoken point of reference between him and Kazan). But, at twenty-two, and a virtual unknown (he had appeared some on TV and had a good role in Inge's *A Loss of Roses* on Broadway), he had a natural skittishness, an insecurity that could seem mannered, but could also be quite appealing. His performance in *Splendor* is nicely poised between that quality and his insistent sexuality.

In a certain sense, Wood was everything Beatty was not. A child star since her debut in 1943, she was a veteran performer, but prior to this film, which includes a very discreet nude scene, her inherent sexiness, drawing on her great beauty, had never been allowed to flourish openly. Nor had she ever before been asked to draw on her deeply troubled relationship with her own controlling mother.

Kazan clearly wanted to bring that confusion to the surface and he succeeded. But around the time he was making this film he, for the second time in his life, entered psychiatric treatment, much more intensively than he previously had, and the film contains extensive passages, when Wilma is institutionalized, that are sympathetic both to her and to the treatment she is undergoing. Even so, Beatty thought Kazan more detailed, more fussy, in his direction of Wood than he was with himself. He had the impression, he said, that Kazan "didn't like good looking guys" and he remembered them getting off to a rocky start. Beatty pretty much had the job on the basis of his readings, but then made the mistake of letting Kazan see a quite awful silent screen test he had made with Jane Fonda. Kazan now told him he wasn't so sure about him after all. Another test was ordered. In its course, Beatty made a suggestion: He wondered if it would be better if he crossed to a piano instead of to a table. "I'm directing this picture," Kazan growled, but then relented and let Beatty do what he wanted.

Seeing something of his younger self in Beatty, Kazan took a shine to this bright, cheeky kid. Many years later he said to Frank

Rich of the *New York Times,* "I liked Warren right away. He was awkward in a way that was attractive. He was very, very ambitious. He had a lot of hunger, as all the stars do when they are young."

"He gave me a larger portion of respect than I deserved," Beatty later recalled. He had found that most directors and most of the acting gurus he had so far encountered "did not allow you the solitude you need as an actor." But Kazan "went against the rivers of emotional explanation" fifties directors constantly offered. And Kazan was protective of him—even to the point of barring Beatty from screenings of the dailies. He told him that what a leading actor (or a director) most needed while working on a film was plenty of rest, which meant to him clearing your mind of such "negatives" as might occur when studying dailies.

But what really sealed the deal between the two men was an incident that occurred on a New York soundstage. Kazan made some comment that Beatty didn't like. The actor cracked back, "Lemme ask you something—why did you name all those names." "What did you say?" a shocked Kazan asked. Beatty repeated himself. "It was my testosteronic desire to confront him." Kazan grabbed him by the arm and conducted him up three flights of stairs to a dressing room, where he sat Beatty down and, in careful detail, took him through the reasons for his testimony. These were not important to Beatty, but the time and the obvious earnestness Kazan expended on his explanation won him over.

That mood extended throughout the shoot. "He was anxious to teach me everything he could teach me." And Beatty was equally anxious to absorb everything he could. Kazan "could break down a script better than anyone I ever knew," he recalled, isolating its components—the actors' motivations, the camera's placement, all the myriad details of making a movie—clearly, unhesitatingly. In the end, Beatty thought, he learned more about being a producer (which Kazan also was on this picture) than about being a director. But whatever he learned, he became Kazan's lifelong friend.

In some respects, *Splendor in the Grass* was not an easy shoot. Beatty and Wood, for instance, began having an affair in the middle of it, with her husband of the time, Robert Wagner, present and certainly aware of it. Kazan knew that in some ways this was good for his picture. Yet he liked Wagner and felt a genuine compassion for him. Then there was the very difficult matter of the scene at a lovers' lane lake, where Wood attempts to drown herself. She came to Kazan and confessed her terror of dark water. He, of course, thought how perfect, just what he wanted for the scene. But he reassured her—the lake was shallow, her feet would never be far from the bottom. She still begged for a studio tank, where her feet could actually touch bottom. The compromise was to have Charlie Maguire in the water near her, just out of camera range, ready to rescue her. He didn't need to—she did the scene well—but collapsed in hysteria immediately thereafter. Twenty years later she was to die in the dark waters off Catalina, when she stepped off the boat she and Wagner (with whom she was by then reconciled) owned, apparently in the midst of a quarrel. The name of that boat was *Splendor.*

Kazan thought the dialogue he and Inge (who would win an Oscar for this screenplay) wrote worked smoothly. It would, he said, prove to be another encouragement to write his own screenplays (and novels). And there were some pieces of his own experience in the film. Beatty, for example, saw a bit of Molly Kazan in the character of Wilma's mother. "She withheld approval as only a WASP woman can," he said. At the same time Kazan was autobiographically helpful to Beatty in his scenes with Pat Hingle. He's very good in them—withering, dithering under the older man's bossy incomprehension. But the wimpishness these scenes called for was not necessarily good for a handsome young actor's image. So Kazan drew him aside and started talking about his tormented relationship with his own father: "I'm still afraid of that little, bent over man," he said, giving his actor permission to be weak.

To Kazan, the movie was about the smugness, the lack of awareness of the American bourgeoisie. "I think the whole middle class of America is spoiled," he would say. "I think they don't know what they've got here. . . . I think they don't appreciate their good fortune. I think they deserve a humbling lesson." Quite remarkably—he was speaking a decade before 9/11—he added, "They've never been bombed. I wish once they'd been bombed, so they'd know what Europe went through."

In this modest film Kazan allowed his protagonists to find some sort of escape and tentative peace. Wilma recovers her mental health. Bud buys a little farm and finds a sweet-seeming wife with whom he has children. "I do believe in honest effort in an honest cause," Kazan said. "I do feel that there's a dignity to honest labor. . . . I like work. I like workers. I like people that work. And I don't like the spoiled and I think almost everybody in the upper middle class—excuse me—is spoiled. I think our whole society is spoiled, so there you are. Make of it what you will. Maybe some [of that] is a hangover from the Communists." Short pause. "But I thought they were spoiled, too."

Kazan, however, did not end on that note. "I particularly love the last reel . . . when she goes out to visit him with her white hat and he's married to a rather plain but honest girl and they both remember . . .

"I don't know. We all have memories of what we might have had, might have known and didn't know and didn't have. Don't you? We're all still in love with somebody and we're glad we're not in love with them anymore, but still it means something. We're all full of memories and desires unfulfilled . . ."

He's right, and this very tender scene ends this movie on the right poignant note. The film, as a whole, is just a little slice of awkward American life, shaped by banal family pressures. But if you are caught up in them they can be, as they are here, life-shaping, even life-threatening.

Most of the reviews, when the picture was released in the fall of 1961, were favorable—though the negatives were particularly harsh—but they were not crucial to its box office success. For it very firmly touched a chord among the very people Kazan affected to despise—the spoiled children of the mildly privileged, a group just now beginning to coalesce into that market—the youth market—to which the American movie industry would eventually sell what passes for its soul. It was, if you will, *East of Eden* all over again though on a much smaller scale.

Kazan was not particularly aware of the power of this new audience. He was simply glad to have a success, whatever its sources, after his two previous box office failures. That was typical of him. One searches the records in vain for evidence that he ever consciously calculated the commercial appeal of any of his projects. He was very much of that generation that regarded conscious striving for popular acclaim as a form of "selling out."

Perhaps because of his psychoanalysis, which in his account was directing him toward a different kind of self-fulfillment, perhaps because he was finally fully fed up with serving the needs of his collaborators, perhaps because he was, even by his somewhat nervous standards, comfortably fixed financially, he obsessively devoted much of the year after he finished *Splendor* to a highly personal project, the end result of which he could only vaguely imagine.

16
Tragedy and Failures

"I made up my mind to do a film about my family coming here thirty years before I made it. I've got notes from way, way, way, way back . . . saying this, saying that."

As early as 1956 Kazan confessed to a journalist his desire to write and direct a movie about immigration, with specific reference to his own people. But it was not until his father died, in the fall of 1960, that, having previously journeyed back to Greece and Turkey, having gathered his notes and his thoughts, Elia Kazan sat down to write the film that was eventually called *America, America*. It was to become "my favorite film," he said, adding, "I don't think it's my best film. It's my favorite film."

The pleasure, for him, began as he sat at Budd Schulberg's desk (he had sublet his friend's apartment on Sixty-fifth Street) remembering—and creating. Alone. From scratch. No collaborators. This work—more than a treatment, but not a script in the formal sense of the word—drew on his deepest roots: "I used to sleep in bed with my grandmother when I was a boy of four, five and six and she used to tell me stories"—and on his most cherished current beliefs: "Gone back . . . to Turkey and looked at what my father came out of . . . And although I had initially great antagonism to my father, when I saw what he came out of and the courage it must have taken to say, 'I'm going to take my family to America' I can do nothing but revere him, which I do now." The same was true of his high-rolling uncle who made a small fortune in his newfound land, lost it in the Depression (and to gambling) but never lost his gusty spirit. Writing what was essentially his uncle's story became, for Kazan, the happiest time of his life to date.

On the whole, the work went smoothly. Most days, he emerged satisfied with his stint at the typewriter. In his notes, he recorded only one major difficulty: that was with the work's controlling theme. His initial impulse had been to celebrate America—not so much the reality of it, but the idea of it as the great shining place, goal and goad of millions of immigrants the world over.

On the other hand, as he wrote his uncle's story it began to take on a different cast. For the long, painful journey to America cost his uncle—called Stavros in the film—dearly. Sent forth by his Anatolian family, laden with what treasure they had, to find a better place for them to live—they did not initially imagine that it would necessarily be America; they thought Constantinople might serve their needs—his protagonist became a different man: harder, coarser, almost totally amoral.

In the course of Stavros's painful journey the family's small fortune is stolen from him, the much smaller fortune that he earns by his own sweat is also lost to a whore (who just happens to be a friend's daughter). He is literally obliged to eat garbage to survive. And to become a "hamal" (this was the first title of Kazan's treatment), the lowest of the low in Turkish society, a human beast of burden. He becomes a killer (of the man who stole his treasure). He becomes engaged to a woman he does not love and he undertakes an adulterous affair with another, richer woman, in order, finally, to secure his passage. About all that you can say for him is that he endures. At the end of the movie, Stavros is a shoeshine boy in New York. He catches a tip, grins broadly and cries out, "Next! Come on you, let's go you! People waiting!" And we know he's not talking solely about his next customers. The "people waiting" are his family in Anatolia, waiting for the money that will bring them to the Promised Land.

"I don't think there's another film in which the so-called central figure is less a hero," Kazan would say to me. "My uncle was no jewel. He got here some way or other. Somebody said they rolled him up in a rug, threw the rug on a boat—I don't know if that's true or exaggerated, but something like that happened. He got here. I believe in persistence a lot—if your screenplay isn't right, have another go at it. . . . And I don't think there's a song to persistence that can beat that film."

This emerging theme troubled him. After completing his screenplay's second draft he wrote these notes to himself: "Among the things he [Stavros] sacrifices is his innocence. Among the things he does are things which are ugly . . . If you raise this issue of ugliness to the *central position* and if it is to be discussed, commented upon and the emotions around it are dwelt upon—hardness, harshness, repentance—then it's a deeply different picture . . ."

So he wondered if his initial impulse, to make something celebratory of the American ideal, did not remain correct. "If that is the case, with everything else subsidiary—present, but subordinate . . . that seems to me to carry the meaning you most want."

What, finally, he decided to strive for was not so much a compromise between these two ideas, but a kind of objectivity. This one man's story might be unpleasant, but his goal was still a worthy one. He would try to present the hard facts and the redeeming dream straightforwardly—and attempt to mediate this contradiction stylistically. Kazan imagined his own directorial efforts

> should not be to bring out the theme or message, no matter how
>   indirectly
> RATHER
> Work to realize for the audience the POETRY
> Of the experience and the
> BEAUTY of the experience.

Kazan would not, in the end, create either a self-consciously beautiful or a poetic movie; *America, America* was more rough-hewn than that. But he did make a striking film, one that was not quite like anything a major American director had ever accomplished. More than any of his films it achieves that simple and rather artless realism that was at the heart of his aesthetic. Though it is rich in melodramatic incident, these passages are presented almost casually, without buildup and without obvious effect on Stavros. Neither he nor we are made aware of what is happening to him by any obvious dramatic devices, by any particularly underscored incident. In that sense the movie is very lifelike, for we are not generally aware, when an event in our lives is occurring, how it may reshape our lives. That happens later, when we view it retrospectively. For comparisons to this movie, I think you have to look to Europeans like the Tavianni brothers or, perhaps, going further back, to the Italian neo-realists.

For the moment, though, there was no movie. There was only this odd, arresting document, not at all a script, though it does contain much of the dialogue that was spoken from the screen three years later. In revised form it began circulating to the studios in 1961 where it found no takers. Whatever early-sixties Hollywood thought it might want—and its grosses were now reaching an all-time nadir—this was surely not it. This did not discourage Kazan. Somehow, some way, he was going to make this picture.

But not immediately. For if his passion to recall his deepest past was now at its height, one of the passions of his more recent professional past was also intruding on him. In 1959, after almost a decade of planning and fund-raising, ground had been broken for the new Lincoln Center for the Performing Arts. The idea was to house all the major New York arts entities—the Philharmonic, the Metropolitan Opera, the City Center Ballet—in a single complex. The only new enterprise in it would be a theatrical repertory company of the kind many New Yorkers had been dreaming of for most of the century—with a group of well-trained actors doing both the classics and new plays in a repertory that revolved every night. As early as 1909 a group of wealthy patrons had tried to establish such a theater on the Upper West Side. In the 1920s, as we've seen, Eva Le Gallienne's Civic Repertory Company had some success with Chekhov and Ibsen, but, like its predecessor, foundered for the lack of strong new American plays, as did a shorter-lived Le Gallienne enterprise, the American Repertory Company, which appeared briefly in the postwar years. Obviously, The Group Theatre had unrealized repertory ambitions. The same was true of the Actors Studio, which at this very moment was also discussing plans for a rep company.

The difference between the Lincoln Center company and all the others was that it had the backing of big New York money, both corporate and private (John D. Rockefeller III was the leading financial force behind Lincoln Center). From the late 1950s onward there was no doubt that theater would be prominently represented at Lincoln Center. The only real question was who would be placed in charge of this new enterprise. Not surprisingly, Lee Strasberg thought he would be ideal for the job.

But Robert Whitehead, an urbane and civilized Broadway producer, who had mounted many of its best plays of the postwar era, had been consulting with the Lincoln Center board and was rather obviously going to be the man in charge. He, in turn, brought Kazan in as a consultant. Many in the theatrical community, especially those who were committed to not-for-profit theater, were dubious about them. In a magazine article, Robert Brustein, long (and still) an envious scold of Broadway, wrote, "when it is commercialism that is debasing our theatre—the Lincoln Center project was handed over to two men who have shown no great interest in any other system."

But, of course, the men managing the Lincoln Center complex were not theater people—far from it. They were not about to hand their multimillion-dollar building, and its vague but ambitious hopes, over to academics or to provincials untried in New York. Whitehead and Kazan represented the best that Broadway had to offer. With them, Lincoln Center's leaders had a reasonable hope of producing a schedule of respectable works that would appeal to theater's core audience, middle-class middle-brow people who shied away from the avant-garde and the exotic. In principle, they had a better hope for building a solid institution quickly with them than with someone like Strasberg.

But thanks largely to Kazan, they heard Strasberg out. He felt the relatively small permanent company Whitehead and Kazan were advocating—perhaps twenty-five actors, plus some younger apprentices—was unnecessary. He proposed, instead, what he called a "floating" company, to be drawn from the ranks of the Actors Studio, as they were needed, but not kept on a permanent payroll. He believed, of course, that he and Cheryl Crawford should manage the company, drawing on Kazan, among others, to direct the plays they chose.

Kazan thought—or at least permitted himself to say—that Strasberg had developed into a fine teacher. But his record as a director was not a distinguished one, and there was nothing in his résumé to suggest any qualifications for managing a high-profile repertory company. Nonetheless, he arranged a meeting between Strasberg and some of the new theater's board. Kazan was not present at this encounter, but heard that it went badly, with Strasberg being his usual arrogant, lecturing self, particularly unattractive to the culturally timid establishment figures he was addressing.

In April 1961 a *New York Times* article announced that Kazan was turning his back on Broadway. Henceforth, he said, his theatrical direction would be confined to Lincoln Center. In the piece, he said he had become particularly "disgusted" with Broadway's short rehearsal periods—less than a month on each of his last two productions. Lincoln Center, where he said he would direct two plays during the first season and one each season thereafter, had promised him as many as six months' preparation.

Later that year Strasberg denounced Kazan at an Actors Studio meeting, saying, in effect, that he had betrayed the very organization he had founded. Kazan felt the hurt in his tone. This new company was precisely the sort of organization Strasberg had been, for decades, preparing himself to run, and now he had been ignored. There was, according to Kazan, who heard a tape of this meeting, much of the old "us against them" spirit of The Group Theatre in Strasberg's tone, a lot of what Kazan called the "tribal" suspicion of "outsiders."

By this time, it must be said, Strasberg's ego was totally out of control. There exists a tape of him "teaching" around this period (it was broadcast on a televised documentary about the The Group) in which, screaming hysterically, he reduces a young actress to tears (and a total inability to perform). You want to cry out: "Lee, it's only an acting lesson."

Later Kazan formally offered Lincoln Center's smaller theater to Strasberg and the studio for experimental productions, but Strasberg never replied to him. A year later, in May 1962, after Strasberg and Cheryl Crawford announced plans for a competing repertory company, based on Strasberg's "floating" concept, they asked Kazan to sign a letter of agreement obligating him to mount plays under the Studio's auspices. Kazan and his attorney, Bill Fitelson, formally resigned from the Studio's board citing the obvious conflict of interest between it and the Lincoln Center company.

Kazan, however, was not as certain about the wisdom of involving himself with Lincoln Center as his public statements indicated. To begin with, he was inherently a freelancer. He did not like institutions, even ones as free-form as The Group Theatre had been. Certainly one in which he would be reporting to men in suits was anathema to him. More important was his strong sense of his own limits as a director. Basically, he was a realist. And fundamentally his interests were contemporary. He could, if the occasion demanded it, break free of the box set, do something more expressionistic, but only if the characters in these works were recognizably figures of his own time. He had never done Ibsen or Chekhov, had never attempted Shakespeare or the classic Greeks and never had much interest in doing so.

Beyond that, I think Kazan by this time was feeling a more general disaffection with the theater. The movies, at least as he conceived them, were about "going into areas that you would not go into on the stage," he said to me many years later. "I wrote a note once. I said, 'I've never seen a breeze on stage. I've never seen a wind on stage. I've never seen a sound from a distance on stage that was any good.' I've seen 'em, but they're no damned good. I've never seen true difficulties on stage because, after all . . . the author's tamed them for you. The author's . . . a good fellow. He's on your side. But I think there'd be films, and there have been some, where you do feel challenged and you're not sure the author is on your side. You may dislike him. And it's stimulating to dislike someone, don't you think?"

These remarks deserve a gloss. I think what Kazan was saying was that the very thing most people treasure about the theater, the fact that they are in the presence of live actors, trying to bring a text to life, can also be a kind of betrayal of that text. All actors need to be loved and we must finally respond to their presence, acknowledge their effort, take them to our hearts. To oversimplify, we no longer hiss the villain, because playwrights have learned not to write completely hissable villains and actors have found ways to humanize them or, at the least, to make us respond to their technical skills as they play them. In the end, when it is time for the curtain calls, they are, indeed, tamed, and we welcome them back to the human race.

Movies, of course, are different. We can maintain our objectivity, our distance from performers, our fear and trembling if that's

what their work calls for. Yes, of course, "stardom," with all the dubious emotions it evokes, is redefined by the movies. But those emotions are, in fact, quite "untamed," even inchoate. Perhaps precisely
because we are not in the physical presence of a movie actor, we are
much freer to impute to them qualities they do not possess in reality.
That's much harder to do with a stage actor, yearning for the immediate approval of our applause.

As a movie director, Kazan was operating in a world very different from the one that has developed since, especially in the American film. It was then still possible to aspire to art in a mainstream
movie, still possible, whatever difficulties he was having with *America, America,* to imagine making an unforgiving, morally ambiguous
movie and imposing it on a substantial portion of the public.

These were issues he had to think over on his own. So in the
summer of 1962 he took off for Greece alone, cruising the islands on
a small boat with a crew of two, mulling his future. He knew that he
was approaching the point of no return as far as Lincoln Center was
concerned. If he was going to cut and run it had to be now. But he
returned from his holiday with his doubts buried. Who was he to
deny this long-cherished theatrical dream? Other civilized nations,
after all, had their national repertory companies, so why not America? Beyond that, Harold Clurman was going to come aboard as dramaturge and occasional director, and Bobby Lewis was to head the
acting school. It was not quite The Group Theatre redux, but it was
pretty close. Maybe this dream had to be tested, brought to life,
however inimical to it current reality seemed to be.

And besides, Molly believed in it. She liked Whitehead enormously
and thought he deserved her husband's support (indeed, they were
to become lifelong friends). Beyond that, she was a woman whose
sensibility had been formed in the old theater. Maybe the world had
moved on past the repertory dream, but she and her peers had not.

Here we enter, for the last time, the emotional minefield of this
marriage. For Elia Kazan was, for the first time since his affair with
Constance Dowling, fully committed to another woman—Barbara

Loden. She had, in effect, stalked him, appearing one day at a dubbing session for *A Face in the Crowd* to offer herself to him. He was so astonished by her determination (and her beauty) that they almost made love in the ladies' room lounge on this occasion. That did not happen, but they did not defer their consummation for long. He gave her small roles in *Wild River* and *Splendor in the Grass.* He was entirely smitten with her, in part because he saw in her something of his own younger self. She was not an immigrant, but had come out of a small midwestern town and a lower-class "outsider" background. Besides, she had beauty, a steely determination to make it in show business, and yet an odd lost quality—a visible vulnerability—that was inordinately appealing to him.

Did Molly know of her? Yes, she must have. But by now she was inured to her husband's wandering ways. She quite possibly did not discern the difference between Barbara Loden and a dozen—a hundred—women who had distracted Kazan. What she surely did not discern was the deeper alienation from her that had been growing in him since *The Egghead* fiasco. It was becoming harder and harder for him to keep up the appearances of their marriage.

Barbara openly accompanied him on a location scouting trip to Turkey where he knew the chances of their being photographed together were excellent. But he says he no longer cared. By now she was pregnant, and he didn't care about that either. They would be discreet about it, of course, but there was no question of an abortion. In his autobigraphy he would say that some of his friends thought Barbara had "trapped" him. But he was having none of that. She had encouraged him and stood by him, and he felt he owed her this child if that's what she wanted.

Indeed, he went beyond that. He would also give her the role of her (short) lifetime. All during this period, the Lincoln Center company had been coming together. Or, as Kazan would later come to think, compounding a series of mistakes. To begin with, it became clear that the Vivian Beaumont Theater, the structure in which it would be housed at Lincoln Center, would not be ready until 1965. Whitehead, in particular, thought a two-year delay in opening would be costly, such was the excitement the new company was stirring in New York. With the reluctant approval of Lincoln Center's management, he created a temporary theater just off Washington Square, on land leased from New York University. It was to be called the ANTA Washington Square Theatre (Whitehead was closely connected to the American National Theatre and Academy, which lent its name to the structure). It would be a geodesic dome, covering a theater whose ground plan, designed by Jo Mielziner, would imitate that of the Beaumont.

This was to be a thrust stage, not quite a theater-in-the-round, but still one that brought actors and audience into a proximity much closer than the traditional proscenium stage. It was not, as Kazan later admitted, an ideal playing space; there were certain kinds of theater that it would be difficult to do in it. For example, it had no wings or flies, which meant that traditional, realistic staging was impossible within its confines. That was all right with Kazan (and presumably Whitehead as well); this stage would be unique to their company's needs, a proclamation of its difference from everyone else.

It did, surely, suit what was announced as its first production— Arthur Miller's *After the Fall*. Whitehead had effected a reconciliation between the playwright and Kazan, based in part on Miller's enthusiasm for the repertory concept and perhaps in part on his desire to have the director he most respected stage his first play after nine years of silence and distraction. As with *Death of a Salesman,* this was to be a play taking place inside a man's mind, with characters appearing and disappearing not in logical sequence, but as they occurred in tangled memory. The thrust stage, with its several playing levels, with its inability to accommodate more than the merest suggestion of scenery and props, would work for it.

So, too, would the new company. Mainly, they were Stanislavskians, psychological realists who would be quite at home in Miller's play, which, despite his denials, was a thinly disguised account of his relationship with Marilyn Monroe. What few noticed, until it was too late, was that the range of these actors did not, could not, match the range of their theater's ambitions. As Kazan said later, they could not do poetic drama or epic drama or classic drama.

Alas, among their number there was no one who could play Maggie, as Miller called his Monroe figure. It was in the fall of 1962 that Kazan sent Loden, visibly pregnant and nursing a cold, to read for him. But decked out in a blond wig, she triumphed. For, as Kazan had observed, she naturally had that same blend of vulnerability and willfulness that had so characterized Monroe. And something like her sexual history, too. Like Brando and Dean before her, she entranced the man who had conceived her (or, in this case, journalistically reported her). She got the part, though it would be more than a year before she began to play it.

This was the last, and in some ways the greatest, service Kazan provided to the Lincoln Center rep in its early days. And there was yet time for him to make *America, America*. Kazan, greatly aided by the faithful Fitelson, had finally set it up with Seven Arts, a company presided over by Ray Stark, formerly an agent, latterly a producer with a taste for slick adaptations of largely fatuous Broadway hits, and Elliot Hyman, a onetime studio production executive. It was not at all the sort of thing Seven Arts normally undertook, especially since Kazan was determined, even more than usual, that no stars be employed in his film. But, as the saying goes, movies are "a relationship business," and for roughly a million and a half dollars Seven Arts might establish a relationship with a leading director.

Besides, *America, America,* in the fall of 1962, took on a public existence. Molly had read and liked Kazan's treatment and took it to her friend Sol Stein, who was setting up a new publishing house, Stein and Day. He decided that Kazan's work would be his company's first book. He and Molly undertook some minor revisions that turned the work into something that more or less resembled a novel (though it was narrated, as screen treatments always are, in the present tense). Many of the reviewers noticed this, but those who liked the book were unbothered by its origins. They responded to the book's obvious passion, to the intensity of its narrative drive, to its celebration of the immigrant heritage as Stavros embodied it.

It was not a "novelization" of a screenplay, nor was it simply a published screenplay. It was rawer, more immediate than that. In the introduction he wrote for the book, Sam Behrman made a good point: "The boy Stavros is rent by two homesicknesses; for the home he has abandoned, for the home he seeks. It is the pain at the heart of every migration." Readers recognized and responded to that pain. And going back to the book today, it still has the power to move one with the authenticity of emotions briefly and simply stated. It did not quite become a best-seller, but it did well enough (and was widely translated). Kazan must have flown off to his film's locations, in Turkey, with a certain confidence. He went by way of Stockholm (where he was doing promotional chores for *Splendor in the Grass*) and there he received a coded telegram from Barbara, telling him that he was the father of a son. This did nothing to dampen his mood. It was the phone call he received on his first day in Istanbul that cast him into panic.

Kazan was having drinks in the hotel bar with some of his cast and crew when he received that call. It was Fitelson, telling him that Stark and Hyman were pulling out—no explanations offered. In effect, the company was stranded. According to Kazan they collectively had just about enough cash to cover the bar bill. His lawyer advised Kazan to say and do nothing; he would handle the emergency. Which he immediately set about doing.

Why, exactly, Seven Arts reneged remains a mystery. But it is possible that casting had something to do with it. Stark and Hyman may have harbored hopes that Kazan would at least cast a young comer—as he had with Warren Beatty—in the lead. After all, whoever played Stavros would be the only actor visible in the picture from first to last; all the other characters would be quite briefly encountered figures. Kazan had tried to oblige this need. He held casting sessions in New York, Hollywood, France. Everyone he read seemed to him too good-looking, too professional. Eventually, in Athens, he noticed a young man named Stathis Giallelis sweeping the floor in a producer's office. He had almost no acting experience and almost no English. But there was something about him . . .

Kazan started talking to the boy in his typical way, learning about his history and his hopes. Some of what he discovered moved Kazan. "His father was a leftist, killed . . . ripped up by the rightists [in the Greek civil war following World War II]. He bled to death. And the boy held him in his arms while he bled to death. And I always thought that must have left a mark on the boy. And it did." He was—

the same words Kazan had used when he found James Dean—"the real thing." Unlike Dean, he was, as Kazan wrote in his autobiography, "A good boy."

But he was also, according to Kazan, what Greek mothers call sons they're proud of: a rooster. The only male in a family of four daughters, he'd been spoiled in every way; his women made him believe that all he had to do was speak and he'd be obeyed. They took care of his every need—food, clothing, above all, praise for virtues he possessed and some he did not possess.

Among his absent virtues was the ability to learn English. Kazan did not want perfection—only a certain clarity of expression. The director brought Giallelis to New York, found him a language teacher and a girlfriend with whom he could speak English all day, every day. But the rooster, in Kazan's estimation, was too lazy to crow effectively in a new tongue. He thought that, in the end, this hurt his picture.

I'm not so sure he's right. Giallelis was completely understandable and he played the dark, lying, cheating side of his character in a disarming way. There was always something shining in his face—an innocence, an eagerness, a hedgehog belief in the one big idea, America, America—that made us forgive Stavros. And not particularly care about his diction.

In any event, the casting of Giallelis was, at most, only one factor in the belated Seven Arts decision. Another may have been the long distance between Hollywood and Turkey; it's hard to maintain oversight of a production shooting so far from home. Stark and Hyman may have thought, too, that Kazan could not possibly finish the picture, on difficult locations, on the budget they had provided. Or maybe they just looked again at the script and thought there was no way they could make money on a film of such limited appeal. Whatever the case, it was doubtless the worst professional betrayal Kazan had ever endured.

Fitelson, however, was as good as his word. He went back to Warner Bros., which had never had a flop with a Kazan picture, and it came through—on terms, Kazan later grumbled, that were far more favorable to them than to him.

Kazan was not by nature a gambler—except, of course, on his own talent. To make this story Kazan had to replicate his uncle's journey in reverse—returning from the United States to the places where this odyssey had begun, more than a half-century ago, on a budget that was, in movie terms, roughly equivalent to the resources his uncle had when he set forth. Most of Kazan's more recent films had been shot on narrow margins, but *America, America* was guerrilla filmmaking of a new kind for him.

This financial pressure combined with his own passionate commitment to his subject combined to make him more than usually passionate—and more than usually cranky. Most Kazan sets and locations were fairly genial. Often he would use the difficulties encountered to set the mood of the company—us against the producer, us against the elements, us against the local authorities. That spirit was present here, but more grimly, more anxiously, than it had been in the past.

The first threat was from Turkish government censors. These functionaries questioned everything—including piles of garbage in the back of the frame. They did not want their country to appear to the world as anything but a smoothly functioning modern democracy—despite the fact that this film was set in the past, when it was no such thing. For a week the company was essentially sneaking shots, and getting some of them because cinematographer Haskell Wexler's small, hand-held camera looked, at first glance, like a tourist's camera. Even so, they were able to get very little in Turkey—mostly establishing shots of some of the environments Stavros passed through. It was the invaluable Charlie Maguire who insisted they leave Turkey. Up to a point he could bribe their minders, but he had noticed that their official watchers now had watchers watching them. He suggested a move to Greece.

Kazan resisted. The film they had shot in Turkey was precious to him. But Maguire had an answer for that problem, too. He put the exposed film in boxes marked "raw stock," the raw stock in containers marked "used." The censors confiscated unexposed film and let the exposed material through. There was a delay of no more than a week before they were shooting near Athens.

Even though the atmosphere was more welcoming, the shoot remained difficult. The central squabble was between Kazan and "Pete" Wexler, as he was then called. The latter is, of course, one of the legendary cameramen of the modern movie age. But he had not yet attained that status in 1962. Working out of his native Chicago, he had done second-unit work (and shot some stills) on *Wild River*, received praise for his work on Irvin Kershner's low-budget *The Hoodlum Priest*, but was not yet a member of the cameramen's union, which meant he could not command a union DP's fees. All that aside, his gritty style was perfect for this film, which Kazan always rather grudgingly acknowledged.

But from the first, he and Kazan did not see eye-to-eye. In his autobiography, Kazan complains that Wexler, who came from a wealthy family, refused to sign those dangerous bar bills, but instead charged his drinks to the production. More seriously, he would recall that Wexler criticized Kazan's eye, insisting that the angles he wanted were not as good as his. Working in the wide-screen 1:85 aspect ratio, Wexler wanted to frame the actors either a little left or a little right of center, while Kazan wanted them dead center. Wexler says he framed the shots his way, hoping to get away with it since dailies were not being shipped to Kazan. Test strips, however, were, and Kazan challenged Wexler about his camera placements when he saw them.

There was a political subtext to their disagreements. Wexler was one of those leftists appalled by Kazan's HUAC testimony, and though he does not recall discussing the matter with him, his opinion of Kazan's behavior added extra tension to their relationship. Occasionally he disliked Kazan's directorial manner as well. However fierce his political beliefs, Wexler is a man of soft voice and gentle demeanor, and he remembered an incident where Giallelis was obliged to strike one of his fellow players. He did so, at Kazan's suggestion, without warning and with uncommon force. A minor injury occurred, which Kazan shrugged off. "I just wanted your reaction," he innocently told the victim, who was, of course, visibly shocked. Wexler also thought Kazan was sometimes far too stinting with his praise. "Gadge was not overtly generous. He saw it as a sign of weakness. It was typical of him to put people in their places. If you knock 'em down a little, it makes you the director of life," he said, as opposed to being merely the director of a picture.

Yet, all of that aside, Wexler counted *America, America* "one of the higher points of my life," mainly because for eight or nine weeks he was in what he thought of as a near-demonic presence. "He was possessed," he said of Kazan. "Nothing would stop him. You say, 'Jesus Christ, the guy's over the top.' But he gave off a kind of electricity, an excitement, about the story. And when someone stays in that mood consistently you say, 'Well, he believes.'"

Kazan never yielded to Wexler's aesthetic or personality. Kazan talked often about Wexler's skills, particularly with a hand-held camera—he could, Kazan once said, drop from a standing position to his knees as smoothly as if he were a sort of human crane. Nevertheless, "I really didn't get along with him and didn't like him personally." Later, Kazan asked his editor, Dede Allen, why, given Wexler's political beliefs, he had taken the job in the first place. But Kazan did concede that their animosity, like Giallelis's amateurishness, contributed something that is hard to name, but important, to the film. It is one of those rare films—the works of John Cassavetes are like this—in which the difficulty of the production is warped into the very grain of the film and becomes an earnest of its authenticity. This palpable reality is so strikingly unlike what we expect from American films, generally so slick and easy in manner, that we begin unconsciously to root for the filmmakers struggling against their obvious difficulties.

When he finally saw the picture, Wexler thought it "too long and too boring," and he was not alone in that opinion. The movie—like many in the episodic form—runs close to three hours, and there is not quite enough conventional content—dialogue, dramatic incident, breathtaking imagery—to fully justify that length. Yet, oddly, if you surrender to its rhythms it is quite a hypnotic experience—not necessarily "poetic" or "beautiful," but still a film brutally determined to be truthful to one young man's harsh experience. It never justifies anything Stavros does to survive. It just flatly presents the facts. Best of all, it lets his obsession with America grow naturally, uncommented upon—from his first excited shouts and waves at officers on a U.S. ship in the harbor at Constantinople, to his contemplation of a transatlantic steamer in a travel agency's window, to his genial acceptance of a new American name (Joe Arness) at Ellis Island, to the moment when he steps onto American soil and falls to the ground in order to kiss it. (Kazan worried about that shot, which was, as he recognized, wildly over the top by modern standards, but which, trusting instinct and historical fact, he left in.)

Given the length of the movie, these scenes were not much. But somehow they were enough to convey Kazan's conflicting ideas about the film—his idealism about America and some sense that Stavros had so much coarsened himself in pursuit of his goal that he was (as it was for Kazan's uncle) beyond redemption. He was saying that the American Dream was once so powerful that men would destroy that which was best in them in order to attain it. And that it was up to the next generation to redeem their elders' sacrifice of their best selves.

Reflecting on another aspect of the film, the caution of the Anatolian Greeks, living fearfully under Turkish rule, "afraid all the time," he said to me, "that film tells more about me than I care to say." What, one wonders? Perhaps something about what motivated his HUAC testimony. I somehow could not ask that question and, of course, he did not volunteer anything, except this: "I essentially have the soul of an immigrant. I'm essentially an outsider. I still feel lucky to be here." And contemptuous of those who ignore or deny that good luck. And, perhaps, afraid that someone will take his good luck away.

During the week when *America, America* was transferring from Turkey to Greece, Kazan flew to Italy and the Spoleto Festival, where a play by Molly was being mounted as a companion piece to an Edward Albee one-acter. It was one of two such short works—*Rosemary* and *The Alligators*—that had been produced off-Broadway in 1960 by no less a figure than Roger Stevens, then perhaps the theater's leading producer. They had been well cast (Piper Laurie, Jo Van Fleet, William Daniels, Paul Richards) and well directed by Gerald Freedman, and they had been somewhat more respectably received than *The Egghead,* although their run at the York Theatre was brief. *Rosemary* was about two young vaudevillians trying to plan their act and their lives on the road encumbered by a new baby. *The Alligators* was about a movie producer trying to secure a release from the widow of a gangster so she

can be portrayed in a film he's planning. It comes to a trick ending—
the producer's girlfriend is mistaken for the widow by a hit man employed by a mobster determined to prevent the widow from revealing
gangland secrets. The plays are cleverly written, but they also put one
in mind of the innocuous minor dramas produced weekly in the 1950s
by the television anthology series.

This is a judgment in which, it is clear, Kazan concurred. He reports that the Albee play quite overshadowed Molly's at Spoleto. But
he was not about to say anything negative to her, though she asked
him many anxious questions. She was enjoying the beauty of Spoleto
and the high and affectionate regard of everyone at the festival.
They passed a pleasant three days together, before she left for New
York, he for Athens.

She did report that her attention was very scattered and drifting
these days—uncharacteristic of her—and wondered, half-humorously,
if she should try some of the exercises Strasberg had devised to cure
actors of that condition. Then, when she was planning to join Kazan for
a few weeks in Athens, she was hospitalized with phlebitis, a blood clot
in the leg. Rest and medication cured her condition, and she welcomed Kazan home to a new apartment, rather grander than the
brownstone they had inhabited for many years, which he did not like
nearly as well.

But he was there only to sleep. He had a film he regarded as
problematic to edit with Dede Allen, beginning her great career, and
he had Arthur Miller's play to get on its feet. And that says nothing
about his double personal life, for some attention had to be paid to
Barbara and their child. There are times in this life where one is
simply overawed by the energy it required—and the casualness with
which Kazan expended it. Allen is the only person I talked to who
observed that some of the unstoppable energy that all his life drove
him derived from a humble source—his ability to catnap. "He could
sleep anytime, anywhere. Everyone else was worn out and he'd be
bubbling."

So the film started coming together. Allen had been receiving
dailies from the Greek location, and had the makings of an assem-
blage, which included some sketchy music—temp scores were not at

all usual in those days—by the film's composer, Manos Hadjidakis, by the time Kazan returned from Greece. He pretty much left her alone to work with his material, telling her merely to be ruthless with it. She remembers him saying, "Only my enemies are careful with my feelings; my friends tell me the truth."

She was a young editor, with only two major films behind her—Robert Rossen's *The Hustler* and Robert Wise's *Odds Against Tomorrow*—and *Bonnie and Clyde* a few years ahead of her. But she was a strong-minded woman and she liked Kazan, despite having her own political differences with him. She remembers his bringing gifts of flowers to her when he sensed she was discouraged by the sheer weight of material he had provided her. For Kazan, the film made a great leap forward when Hadjidakis arrived from Greece to work more closely with the cut film. He was an adaptable artist, quick to sketch new material bridging narrative gaps. Suddenly, for Kazan, his episodic piece began to take on a certain coherence. He began to think that he just might get away with this film, after all.

———————

Manfully, he pretended the same thing about *After the Fall,* about which he and Miller had differing doubts. The latter had not written a play in almost a decade and was short of money; what he really needed, financially, was a long Broadway run, not intermittent inclusion of his new work in a repertory season. He also wondered if he could finish the play—which he had actually begun before Monroe's death—in time to open the new theater. But after meeting repeatedly with Whitehead, who had coproduced two of his plays, and with Kazan, he succumbed to his own idealism about the new venture. He would focus all his energies on *After the Fall*, which early in 1963 remained in messy condition. This was no *Salesman*, tumbling out of him in a rush. It was a much more agonized work, precisely because it was so rawly personal. It might never have worked—autobiography was not Miller's strongest suit—but surely it needed the one thing Kazan and Whitehead could not give him: time. Time to mull. Time to let passions cool—his own and his audience's. Monroe, after all, had been dead less than a year at this point. And even if he thought the play was not most significantly about her, Marilyn Monroe was still the most interesting person in this room.

It is possible to imagine now that Kazan was the wrong man to direct *After the Fall*. Miller wanted—thought he needed—him. But Kazan was also part of the story he was telling. Perhaps at some point in theatrical history a director had staged a production in which he was himself the model for a character, but not very often. Curiously, Miller was fairer to Kazan than Kazan was. Miller still believed, he later wrote in his autobiography, that Kazan had done the wrong thing in testifying, but now, a mere decade later, his position was softening. "In the intervening years, of course, the whole Communist issue had gone cold, and a new generation hardly understood what it had been all about . . . how many who knew by now that they had been supporting a paranoid and murderous Stalinist regime had really confronted their abetting of it?" It must be said that Miller wrote this figure—called Mickey in the play—honorably, providing him with a version of his own conversation with Kazan in the Connecticut woods. All he added to that encounter was a specific figure that the Kazan clone intended to betray, a saintly lawyer named Lou, beloved by both Mickey and Miller's theatrical alter ego, Quentin. Even then, he permits Mickey to charge Lou with revising a book he wrote about a visit to the Soviet Union in the 1930s, making it more in accord with the party line.

Kazan, on the other hand, finally cast Mickey, the character based on him, about as unsympathetically as he could, giving the role to Ralph Meeker. Technically, he was quite a good actor, and for a time—after taking over Brando's role in *Streetcar* and playing the lead in Inge's *Picnic*—the embodiment of some of the Stanislavskian's hopes for another leading man in the Brando mold. But there was something invulnerable in his persona, and his career quite quickly dwindled into villainous inconsequence. In any case, he was Kazan's antithesis in his lack of ingratiating qualities.

Kazan would later confess that he never much cared for Miller's first act, and essentially left it alone. To him, it was throat clearing; the play's moral weight and worth were concentrated in its second act, where Maggie, the Monroe figure, only briefly and rather comically introduced before the intermission, begins to dominate the play. It was on this act that Kazan focused all his energies, eventually dragging a complete rewrite of it out of Miller.

In his earliest notes (February 1963) he wryly tells Miller that just because something happened in real life it does not necessarily belong on stage. Less ironically, he says that in his first marriage (at least as presented on stage) Quentin/Miller needed a woman (she is called Louise) to "placate and look up to and rely upon." But then, Kazan observes, he tires of her "rigidity and coldness and lifelessness;" Quentin/Miller wants to be the moral exemplar—"an authoritarian figure of ethical monumentality." Maggie is introduced as a switchboard operator in Quentin's law office—yes, a "Miss Baur" figure. Later, when she has become a pop star, they meet again and marry and she at first concocts "a notion, inhuman and wishful, of what he was, a sort of Lincoln-Rabbi," a figure he enjoyed playing—for a while.

Early in the play, which Quentin narrates, "he was searching for a morality that had a breadth of humanity in it, not revenge or self-justification, or most plainly, *hatred*." Such a figure he finds in a third woman, Holga. She's a European who has witnessed the Holocaust firsthand, and she is clearly based on Miller's third wife, the photographer Inge Morath. In the play she refuses victimhood and radiates plainspoken spiritual health. Such action as the play has in the present tense revolves around Quentin trying uncomplicatedly to embrace her.

In a later note, Kazan records this exchange between himself and Miller, with the latter saying "Every person in this play, except Holga, makes an ethical God of the guy, a GOD, and he buys it and helps it along." To which Kazan replies, "What a terrible burden to place on a person." So far, so good. This is a valid, if not completely electrifying, dramatic situation—the humanizing of a smart, slightly priggish, but worthwhile human being.

But that largely leaves out of its equation Maggie, who simply took over the play. However interesting Miller was to the thinking classes, however "important" he was to their culture, he was no Marilyn. She was not just *a* celebrity. She was one of *the* celebrities of the twentieth century—one of those great empty vessels into which the multitudes could pour their longings and their wild surmises. If she or her simulacrum were present you could not take your eyes off her—and ethical questions be damned.

Here, I think, Kazan did not serve Arthur Miller as well as he might have. Remember that he, like Miller, had known her "before the fall," as a jolly sexual playmate. But he could not seem to remember her that way. He saw her now partly through Miller's eyes, partly through the lens the press and her friends, false and otherwise, had constructed both to view and project her after her mysterious and premature passing.

His take on her now was that she was a monster. Or, to use his word, a "heavy." As Miller wrote her, he noted, "Maggie is a barbarian. She can barely read. What she does know she's learned from the lash of living, from everything she's done (plenty!)." As a result, her arc in the play is quite simple—from victimhood, to a viciously commanding egotism, back to (suicidal) victimhood. And this imposes a complementary arc on Quentin. He adores the untutored, even quite funny, child-woman he meets on a park bench, he tries to serve the monstrous needs of the star she becomes (in the process betraying his own best self), then finds himself running madly from her: "No, no, anything but this, anything but her, anything but this new me."

Kazan: "I notice something about Art's voice when he was reading the part of Maggie. It was always 'pleading.' And the particular significance of this was not only that Maggie thinks of herself as worthless, or that she can only 'get by' by taking the stance of worthlessness.

"But also that Art enjoys being looked up to in that way . . . it is my feeling that it is the real 'real.' It's how she gets by. Also that in time Maggie, when she finds out that people are afraid of *her*, turns into a vengeful bully."

Vengeful for what, Kazan in effect asks. Well, naturally, for her ghastly childhood. She needs, quite simply, to be admired—"the opposite of what her asylumhood [in an orphanage] and her totally indifferent mother did for her. When she was a kid she found she could quiet the ache of worthlessness by getting men to fuck her. But it was the esteem she wanted, the being desired."

All of which is probably true enough. But not deep enough. Very early on, Kazan had urged Miller to be "ruthless" with his play, to discover what it was about in "concrete terms—what's in, what's out." In that regard, this pop psychologizing must only have been only moderately helpful to Miller. Much more interesting would have been an idea Kazan proposed, which was to bring none other than a Lee Strasberg figure on stage. For was it not to Lee and Paula that the real-life Marilyn turned as her relationship with Miller went rancid? And was not Lee Strasberg, in his arrogance, his utter sureness of his own infallibility, exactly what Miller in real life, Quentin in the play, had tried and failed to be. "I urged Art to show Strasberg taking his place, by offering Maggie an authority ever more absolute." Whether a Strasberg figure appeared in any of Miller's revisions I cannot say. In the final version of the play such a character is referred to, but is not brought onstage.*

I do not know how much that that would have helped, but it would, perhaps, have rounded off the play more effectively, by taking some of the focus off Maggie, whose increasingly crazy dominance of its last act makes her ever less sympathetic, more and more of a fame-addled showbiz horror.

Miller seems to have thought he was as hard on his simulacrum as he was on Marilyn's. But that's not so. The worst Quentin stands accused of in this play is being a cold fish, not able to love either of his first two wives. On the other hand, each of them, as presented, is unworthy of his—or possibly anyone's—love. One's a shrew, the other a drugged-out bitch. For the rest, Quentin drapes himself in shrouds of unearned guilt. He lived in the age of the death camps, so somehow he is complicit in their horror. He behaved by his lights honorably during the trials of American Stalinism, yet is frankly glad

---

*Interestingly, Miller finally did bring both Lee and Paula Strasberg onstage in *Finishing the Picture*, which premiered at Chicago's Goodman Theatre in fall 2004. It is about the movie he wrote for Marilyn, *The Misfits*, with Marilyn represented in this black comedy as a silent, often naked, always drugged out, almost ghostly presence, whose inability to work before the camera is threatening to close the production. The Strasbergs are monsters of ego, presented by the author with a great, comic malevolence that is obviously heartfelt. One couldn't help but think that the play's title, *Finishing the Picture*, was a pun. Yes, it is about trying to "finish" *The Misfits*, but it also finishes the picture presented in *After the Fall*—but with an irony, distance and wisdom the early play lacks.

when his Stalinist friend commits suicide and spares Quentin the necessity of defending him. When he reviewed the play, Robert Brustein asked this very valid question: "After all these terrible years, is Miller still defining Stalinism as if it were a sentiment without any reference to ideas, ideology, or power?"

This is a good question—and one that Kazan could not bring himself to ask his old-new friend. It is, as well, a question that could be extended to other aspects of the play. As written, Quentin never really comes to grips with the Holocaust. He keeps saying that he wants to locate his personal responsibility for it, for all horrors of his age. But as Brustein suggests, his identifications are all with vaguely generalized ideas—and, we may add, guilts. This is, of course, because none of us can actually take responsibility for anything but our own actions. And since he cannot make this case against himself stick, our attention focuses on the one thing he might, possibly, have done something about, his tormented relationship with Maggie. But since she's finally a hopeless head case he is reduced to rejecting her, which is possibly all anyone could have done, but which makes him seem emotionally impotent to the audience.

Kazan did what he could, in the summer of 1963, to help clarify these issues. He and Whitehead would at least weekly climb into a car and join Miller in Roxbury to hear him read his new pages and to discuss them. They were ever-encouraging. They could see their collaborator's pain. And all three of them knew that, to a larger degree than any of them initially imagined, the success or failure of their new theatrical company would be determined by the reception of *After the Fall*.

In his autobiography Kazan says he was distracted all the time he worked with Miller on rewrites. There was his movie to see through postproduction, there were his wife and mistress needing his attention, there were the myriad nondirectorial duties Lincoln Center imposed on him. Above all, he could not help but contrast his position as a sort of "enabler" of this production with the clear-cut pleasures *America, America* had offered him, where "all activity had started from a directive I gave, and each day's program based on my wishes. That was what I wanted to be, the unchallenged source."

All this leaves out of consideration the bind this particular play had placed Kazan in. For consider: He was reunited with a man who had once been his closest friend, who had chosen to write about the very events that had sundered their friendship and about the very woman they had once shared. Beyond that, Miller had based one of his characters on Kazan. Who, in turn, had cast his current mistress in the role of their formerly shared lover. It is, quite simply, mind-boggling—even for a man with Kazan's genius for compartmentalizing.

And his problems were not by any means over. For our schemes are ever subject to the accidents of history. A little less than a month after Kazan placed *After the Fall* into rehearsal in a hall above a kosher restaurant on the Lower East Side, history delivered a hard blow, the assassination of John F. Kennedy. With his glamour, élan, youth and sexuality, he was, of course, a showbiz favorite; its folks knew star quality when they saw it. Rehearsals were, naturally, called off, though Kazan noticed that many in the company hung about, clinging to one another for comfort.

The next day he found Molly, gritting her teeth, writing furiously, in unblocked concentration. By afternoon she had written a sort of prose poem, eulogizing Kennedy. A day or two later it was read at a memorial service for Broadway people at St. Clement's Church. A reporter from the *New York Herald-Tribune* was present, asked for a copy, took it back to his newsroom, where it moved his colleagues. She got a call from the paper, asking permission to print it. Prominently displayed on the front page of the *Trib*'s second section, it touched people inordinately.

It was not, in truth, much of a poem—if, indeed, it was a poem at all. But not much that was written in the immediate aftermath of Kennedy's death had any lasting value. What Molly Kazan accomplished, artlessly and with obvious sincerity, was to capture peoples' stunned inchoate feelings and her piece was widely reprinted. At last, in these unlikely circumstances, she had the writerly success she had yearned for all her life.

Less than three weeks later, Molly Kazan was dead.

Her husband came home from rehearsal one day, found a shaking maid telling him that his wife had been in the bathroom for hours, not responding to her calls. Kazan broke down the door and found her unconscious, her clothes in disarray. Doctors, ambulances were called. But she never revived. She had suffered an aneurysm, a burst blood vessel in her brain. The doctors told Kazan there was no hope of recovery; the seepage of blood had by this time destroyed mental capacity. Kazan naturally thought of her complaints of vagueness when he visited her in Spoleto, the previous summer's phlebitis. Was it possible they were warning signs? Worse, was it possible that his decades of bad domestic behavior had finally taken this terrible physical toll on his wife? These thoughts haunted him for weeks. But immediately there was nothing to be done. Around 3:00 A.M. the next morning, Molly Kazan died.

The next night *America, America* premiered at the Paris Theatre just off Fifth Avenue on Fifty-eighth Street. The scheduled party was canceled, but Kazan wandered near the theater, observed the crowds streaming in and then walked home. On the whole, the reviews were good. "If Mr. Kazan's picture weren't so overwhelming long, and, consequently, so often redundant it would be—what?" Bosley Crowther asked. And answered: "Even finer than it is." Judith Crist in the *Herald-Tribune* was less grudging: "A masterful motion picture," she wrote, "brilliant and powerful." She paid particular tribute to its lack of sentimentality. Others, like *Time,* fussed over its disbelief that someone as sweet-looking as Stavros could commit the many amoral acts his immigrant journey demanded of him. Walter Kerr told Kazan he hated the dubbing. Two months later, the Motion Picture Academy rewarded the film with best picture and best director nominations, though it won in neither category. Even so, Warner Bros. took a bath on the film.

Some of this was not yet known to Kazan, and what he did know about the immediate response to his film he did not care about. There was another memorial service at St. Clement's, this time for Molly. It was a standing-room-only occasion, which pleased Kazan on her behalf. She had offered tea, sympathy and mentoring to many, and they all turned out to pay her tribute. In his eulogy he called her—odd word—an "immaculate" woman. He also said she had no formal religion, that her religion was "truth," an observation he knew better than anyone. He read from a note he had found in her files, in which, acknowledging the imperfections of both American society and the human condition, she yet called on "our" writers not to cry "shame" over the misery and injustice, the cultural deserts that still existed, but to "esteem" what had been accomplished and not surrender to paralyzing shame.

Later family and friends gathered at the Kazan apartment for food, reminiscence, warmth. The next day Kazan, alone, with not even his children joining him, accompanied his wife's remains to their Connecticut home. He found Bill Fitelson and Karl Malden awaiting him. A great boulder was found at the site Kazan had chosen for Molly's grave. The man operating the backhoe prized it out and, accompanied only by Kazan's unknown, but doubtless ambiguous, thoughts, she was laid to rest. He had said at the memorial service that her monument was to be found only in the life she had lived.

Later, he received a note of condolence from Tony Kraber, one of the Communists he had named, and the one who had concocted the story that Kazan had signed a huge Hollywood contract immediately after his HUAC testimony. The note was warm and nostalgic and touched Kazan, who awkwardly replied in kind. Many years later, writing about this, he found himself dreaming of Kraber, his wife and child. It was a dream of mutual forgiveness, in the course of which Kazan found himself speaking the apologia quoted in this book's prologue—"I felt that no political cause was worth hurting any other human being for . . ."

Given this passage's placement in his autobiography, in the midst of Kazan's grappling with Miller's play, one can't help but think that at least on this issue—one in which his culpability was more direct and personal than any of those Miller was gaseously placing on stage—he did better than the playwright. I think he addressed his guilts more authentically, and more movingly, in a couple of paragraphs than Miller did in his endless play.

By late December, the ANTA Washington Square Theatre was ready for occupancy, and the Lincoln Center company began exploring its new playing space. Kazan, by all accounts, was at his best—cajoling, praising, reserving important criticisms of the actors for private meetings with them. There was no visible tension between Kazan and

Miller. Nick Kazan, then a teenager, and being encouraged by his father to hang around rehearsals, to absorb something of the family business (shades of the Kazan Carpet Company!), would recall being invited to spend the weekend with Inge and Arthur Miller and being warmly welcomed. Others would recall Kazan and Miller in close consultation over details, with occasionally cackling laughter arising from their confabulations. Kazan had said to a pair of journalists, on the very first day of rehearsal, "It's one of those things you meet in your life where you say, 'I hope I can live up to it,'" and his loyalty to Miller's work never wavered.

Even in his autobiography, twenty-four years later, Kazan was still insisting on the play's merits. Yes, he would concede, Quentin was never quite granted his full humanity, but that was, he thought, only a mild sin. He thought the portrayal of Monroe achieved, in its final scenes, "pitiable and tragic" dimensions.

Yet there was something not quite right about this company. Hal Holbrook was a member of it, playing a small role in *After the Fall,* the title role in its next production, Eugene O'Neill's *Marco Millions.* "It was a chilly company," he said. "Backstage in that tomb no one ever said hello to you." He said he always hungered for a personal moment with Kazan, of which he received only one, and that rather belatedly. On the other hand, he found Kazan to be attentively professional in rehearsals and attributed some of the company's coldness to a fundamental split between its method actors and the minority who, like himself, came from different acting traditions. For the moment, though, in the stir of getting on a play that ran for well over three hours, under the impress of the theatrical community's excitement about this new theater, these differences were largely papered over. The only performer who succumbed to the pressure was Jason Robards, Jr. Carrying the huge burden of Quentin (who was never offstage) and perhaps beginning to perceive that Loden, developing her extraordinary performance, was going to take the play away from him, he disappeared on a drunk of several days' duration. He returned in time to open on January 23 and, in fact, got very good notices, but not the more general publicity, the big *Life* photo spread, the admiring profiles, that went to Loden.

The initial reviews of *After the Fall* were mixed, but generally more favorable than not. Howard Taubman, who had replaced

Atkinson at the *Times,* was the least restrained. "Which to celebrate first?" he asked in his lead, the return of Arthur Miller or the inauguration of his new company. Both, he proclaimed. He did not find the play too painfully autobiographical. He saw Quentin as a twentieth-century everyman, hunting "for order in the painful and joyous chaos of living." For him the play was neither too long nor too gossipy. "For to sit in Mr. Miller's theater is to be in an adult world concerned with a search that cuts to the bone." The man from the *World-Telegraph and Sun* compared Miller's search for the truths in human relationships to Strindberg's and O'Neill's, and not invidiously so. The *Daily News* found the play "absolutely overpowering in its emotional impact."

Others thought it somewhat less compelling. Its length was often mentioned, and it appeared to the man from the *Post* "self-indulgent" and "lost in its own waywardness." The *Journal-American* thought Marilyn "might have been permitted to rest in peace." Walter Kerr in the *Herald-Tribune* was the most perceptive: "'After the Fall' resembles a confessional which Arthur Miller enters as a penitent and from which he emerges as the priest. It is a tricky quick change . . . but it constitutes neither an especially attractive nor especially persuasive performance.'"

The weeklies were more scathing. Robert Brustein in the *New Republic* called the play "a shameless piece of tabloid gossip, an act of exhibitionism which makes us all voyeurs." Gordon Rogoff in the *Nation* called it, "More a young author's autobiographical first novel than a mature artist's play. It is a dispiriting, unhappy, often infuriating beginning for a new company." Richard Gilman, in *Commonweal,* was the harshest of all: Miller, he wrote, "has engaged in a process of self-justification which at any time is repellent, but which becomes truly monstrous in the absence of any intelligence, craft or art." Worse, he found Miller's dialogue "unutterably pompous and flaccid . . . a rhetoric of . . . hopeless banality and adolescent mutterings."

A little later, in the quarterly *Hudson Review,* John Simon wrote: "Arthur Miller's mind has always loomed bulky on the stage—not like a genuine largeness, but like the elephantiasis of a flea." He, too, loathed the voyeuristic qualities of the piece, but made two points no one else did, which for me remain central to intelligent consideration of the play. The first of these is Miller's failure "to digest, transpose, transubstantiate the givens of his life . . . beyond the changing of a few names and professions," which leads to its voyeuristic qualities. The other is its telescoping of the Maggie/Marilyn character's development, in which she "hurtles from a paragon of healthy sexuality to a pathetic, abject, neurotic bitch," without any intervening explanation for this radical change of character.

Miller attempted to defend himself from these attacks in, of all places, *Life* magazine. The most popular of mass magazines could not resist the Maggie/Marilyn connection and, equally obviously, Miller could not resist having his say. To his side he summoned the shades of Tolstoy, Fitzgerald, Hemingway, even Goethe as authors whose personal histories readers had found in their works. But, he said, every work of art is in some sense autobiographical, and *After the Fall* was no different. He argued that Marilyn had been treated by him "not only with respect for her agony but with love." As for Quentin, he was not looking for exculpation when he wrote him, but for a precise sense of his "responsibility" for the terrors of his time. But—let's put this simply—if you take on "guilt" for the kind of world-historical crimes Quentin was agonizing over, you are really taking on no guilt at all—especially if the guilts you might take responsibility for (Maggie's self-destruction), you evade and blame on the victim, as Miller largely did. I think we can take it as axiomatic that any fiction that allows the Holocaust, that vastest of twentieth-century horrors, to shadow its path, but alludes to it only sentimentally, is striving for a sort of unearned importance. Which is why this play is such an unredeemed, and unredeemable, failure. And one that does not improve with age.

All of that said, however, most reviewers found at least a few things to admire in the production. And many spent space praising the idea of this new repertory company, qualifying whatever dispraise they had for *After the Fall* with the belief that a good and brave beginning was being made on West Fourth Street. No reviewer doubted that he had been present on a consequential occasion, one which they thought—quite erroneously as it turned out—would mark a significant historical turning point in the history of American theater.

About that, the general public cared considerably less. The production was an authentic succès de scandale. They simply had to see the thing and flocked to the dome in the village. It was, for all the wrong reasons, the hit both Miller and Lincoln Center needed.

It was not, however, quite the hit the theater's board wanted. *Scandale* had never been high on its agenda. The classics had been. "Poetic" modern dramas had been (how they would have loved *J.B.*). A half-naked actress imitating a movie star whose fate must have been, in their eyes, only dubiously tragic was . . . well, not quite what they had in mind. Some of the board, we may safely speculate, began eyeing the Whitehead-Kazan partnership suspiciously at this early point.

Marco Millions, which followed *After the Fall* into the repertory, was perhaps more to their liking. It was, to be sure, minor O'Neill, but José Quintero, who had mounted brilliant productions of *The Iceman Cometh* and *Long Day's Journey into Night*, gave it an elegant staging for which the new theater's playing space was well suited. The production was received with muted approval. This might not be a great play, but people were generally glad to see it again and certainly understood that mounting plays of this sort was precisely what repertory companies were meant to do. Again, it was the intellectual magazine critics who grumbled most about its relative unimportance.

In the meantime, the company did another thing that such organizations are supposed to do—it shared out one of its prizes, giving the role of Quentin to Hal Holbrook, first for the matinees, then for all the performances, allowing the unhappy Robards gracefully to withdraw from the company at the end of the season. I saw *After the Fall* with both actors, and I must say that I think Holbrook almost made the thing work. There had always been something harsh, aggressive, almost angry in Robards's interpretation. Holbrook made him gentler, less judgmental.

Holbrook recalled visting Miller in Roxbury, "freezing my ass off" in his stark workroom, but mentioning to the playwright the many uses of the word "innocence" in his dialogue. Miller seemed to Holbrook surprised by the remark, and maybe a trifle irritated by it. Well, Miller allowed, he meant innocence in the sense that a newborn babe is innocent. All well and good, the actor replied, but reasonably speaking, no audience could divine that meaning from the text they were hearing. For the repeated use of the word implied that the play's critics were right; that Miller was, in fact, trying to exculpate his alter ego.

Some of that innocence seeped into Holbrook's performance, and it humanized it. He was no longer a flawed hero. He was merely a flawed human being. Holbrook now says that he was, personally, in just such a condition. He was going through a messy divorce and beginning another relationship. He was raw. And when he performed a dress rehearsal, with that "chilly" company gathered in the front rows of the theater, in effect saying "show us" to him, he broke down sobbing and out of control at the end of the play. He was embarrassed. Until Kazan materialized out of the darkness, sat down next to him on the stage apron, patted him on the knee and asked, "What's the matter?" "I feel like an asshole," said Holbrook. Kazan, who was by this time having his own troubles with this company, simply said, "It's all right to cry, Hal."

It was also all right with him that Holbrook forged a powerful sympathy with his mistress. "She really got to me," said the actor. "She was such a sad girl. She never held anything back, she just ripped everything away. She was lost, that girl." Between them they made the play work in the only (limited) way it possibly could—not as a grand drama of ideas, but at some simpler, more approachable human level.

It was too late. Or almost too late. For with *After the Fall* and *Marco Millions* alternating, Kazan returned with a new production, *But for Whom, Charlie,* by his old friend Sam Behrman. It was not at all the sort of thing right-thinking people thought the Lincoln Center company should be doing. Behrman was over seventy, obviously a slick and expert Broadway veteran with many hits behind him, and this was a comedy of the kind people thought belonged in the old-fashioned commercial theater. Kazan disagreed. He thought it "wise and witty and beautifully written," with Behrman for the first time admitting his own Jewishness in his work and also writing about someone like himself, who as Kazan characterized him was "incapable"—by which he meant unable to cope with the world's practical demands.

That "incapable" figure was played by Robards, who runs a foundation, funded by money he inherited from his gross movie producer father. Its work, supervised by the Charlie of the title (Ralph

Meeker), is to distribute money to deserving, uncommercial writers. Charlie is wayward with his largesse, giving and withholding by mysterious standards of his own. Into their little world intrude a young man and woman (the latter played by the very young Faye Dunaway), children of a famous playwright. They seek a grant for the young man's book. Also appearing is Gillian, their hateful stepmother (Salome Jens), throwing passes at everyone, and a crotchety old writer (played by David Wayne, who commanded the reviews), living happily off the foundation and the high regard one of his novels still receives in literary circles. He is the author's spokesman on all sorts of current issues. He is sometimes witty, sometimes not, which could be said of all the other characters in the play, which concludes with Gillian making off with Charlie. Kazan always thought the play was about impotence versus potency, and, in this conclusion, the latter wins out, which he thought was, perhaps, a tragedy, albeit quite a muted one.

Kazan's notes on the production are more perfunctory—perhaps, understandably, given the year he had just lived, more weary—than usual. He thinks Charlie, who is essentially incompetent, but talks a good game, is a cross between Peter Viertel and Jed Harris—smart, energetic, but without depth, human consequence or real commitment to anything outside themselves. He also remarks, "Harold Clurman was once my Charlie. But it was my fault, not Harold's."

The main thing he observed about his text was that "Behrman's people entertain each other . . . they enjoy each other—even in conflict." But they did not entertain critics or audiences. The early reviews were inclined to indulge the play, with some looking back gratefully to occasions when Behrman had been more consistently amusing. One or two even said that of Lincoln Center Company's three initial productions this was the most enjoyable. The weeklies, however, came down hard on this frivolous enterprise. At the time, Kazan defended the play. "I think there are many cogent things said in that play," he told an interviewer. "And it's a charming play. It charms me. People ask what the hell did you do it for. I did it because I like it. You don't like it. That's not my problem."

But it was, of course. He later said it was the first "fatal" mistake of the new company. He also rued the fact that Behrman was so hurt by *Charlie*'s reception that he became a virtual recluse, shutting himself into a dark back room in his elegant apartment, seeing virtually no one.

As its first season ended, it is fair to say such successes as Lincoln Center enjoyed were highly qualified. It may be that its only unqualified one had been smart, charming Bobby Lewis's apprentice group—thirty young actors (among them Faye Dunaway, Martin Sheen, Frank Langella) vying for fifteen spots in the permanent company. They began their training a year before the theater opened, working daily in one of the small theaters in Carnegie Hall on a program not unlike those of The Group's summer camp. Of all his Lincoln Center duties this is the one Kazan enjoyed best. He was always dropping in, wearing a sweatshirt and chinos, sometimes sprawling on the floor. Always disarming the students with his unassuming ways, he never played, according to one of them, Austin Pendleton, the great man. More often he was the grateful man, glad to be free of the pressures mounting up on him elsewhere.

Publicly, of course, Kazan remained undaunted. He was, he said, eagerly looking forward to his first production of the next season. This was to be his first attempt to direct a not-quite-classic Jacobean melodrama, *The Changeling*, by Thomas Middleton and William Rowley, first staged in 1622.

Kazan saw it, possibly correctly, as a black comedy, not a tragedy, and his ideas about it were plausible enough. "It's an ironic, realistic, hard-headed view of the way humans behave. It deals with double-face. People present one face in order to get along [think the Anatolian smile here] and it's always a violation of their true face, their *spontaneous* and true feelings. The whole idea of *The Changeling* is that people wear masks in order to get by when their real feelings and real impulses are something else. And the 'something else' erupts every day on page four of the *Daily News* in violent and desperate actions."

All of this is true enough in reality, surely in Kazan's own view of the world. What was patently untrue was his belief that this minor and hard-to-stage work—kept alive mainly in the survey anthologies inflicted on drama students—was within the range of his young company. "We did not have the company for *The Changeling* . . . it was very method oriented," Holbrook remembered, though he does think that as the second season wore on, and new actors, representing different schools of acting, joined up, it might possibly have succeeded.

That, however, was too late for Kazan. He worked assiduously on *The Changeling.* He kept asking his designers for information on the realities of fifteenth-century life, wondering, among other things, what its toilet facilities were like. He wanted, he said, forbidding sets against which they would portray "the smashing human spirit of the Renaissance . . . breaking out of the dark." He toyed with the notion of having a huge crucifix looming over the stage. "Religion kills or cripples the human spirit," he noted, "because it is built on disapproval and fear and guilt."

He was trying to create a concept production, more of a commentary on the play than a pure presentation of it. And one can sympathize with him to a degree. Who can really care, today, about a play in which a woman, secretly loving one man, hires a killer to murder the other man her father has arranged for her to marry? Who then, faced with the killer's demand for her virginity as the price of his silence, substitutes her lady-in-waiting for herself? All of which is just a premise. There are infinitely more sorrows (and subplots), most of them blood-drenched, related in a language unelevated by poetry, to plod through before the play ends.

"Embarrassing," wrote Walter Kerr when he saw this production. And that opinion was universally echoed by the other reviewers. They were hard on all the actors, save perhaps Barry Primus as the hired assassin, and especially so on Barbara Loden, whose flat, thin voice could not, they thought, elevate this drama to its proper heights—if, indeed, it contained any heights. In her defense, one might ask, whose voice might have accomplished this transformative task? An English voice, came the answer; one reviewer actually suggested importing a company from London where the play has been more than once successfully revived in modern times.

In general, though, it was Kazan who bore the brunt of the critics' dismay. Kerr thought he did not have "the least notion" of how to stage the play, and caught on to the fact that his mixture of comic and melodramatic moments was careless and gimmicky. Richard Watts in the *Post* thought his "picturesque mystifications" only added to the confusion of the piece. In short, the production was "a clinker" as one headline had it.

Or, as Pendleton put it, "like a high school production in Kansas." Now, he said, the mood around the theater was "like that of an embattled fortress," with people constantly giving the company pep talks. To no avail. Less than two months after *The Changeling* opened, it was gone from the repertory and both Kazan and White-head were gone from Lincoln Center, though, curiously, in that in-terim, Arthur Miller (who would also resign) gave the company its second hit, *Incident at Vichy,* after which director Bill Ball was im-ported to stage a lively version of a true classic, Molière's *Tartuffe.*

As Kazan observed in a newspaper interview he gave while still entertaining hopes that Whitehead at least might retain his post, the new company's track record was not entirely shameful. They had had two hits in two seasons, and some of their other productions had been here and there respectfully received. He even defended *The Changeling* in typically ambiguous fashion. "I don't think 'The Changeling' is a failure," he told the *Times.* "It has considerable virtues. I'm proud of it." But, he added, "I have the right to fail."

As did this new theater. It needed some new actors, better new plays and a better selection of older works, all of which was possible. It was not as yet in need of radical reformation.

But that, somehow, is what it got. Kazan later wondered why the opinions of critics like Brustein and Gilman, writing in small, albeit in-fluential, publications had carried such weight with the board, why both men, apparently, had been consulted about finding a replacement for Whitehead before he was fired. The answer to that question is that Lincoln Center's culturally clueless board was dominated by improba-bly rich and "responsible" citizens used to uncomplicated gratitude for the gifts they laid before the public. When they didn't get that they turned, in something of a panic, to people who at least held plausible, coherent theories about how to rehabilitate their limping institution.

These drama-idealists naturally mistrusted Broadway types like Whitehead and Kazan, representatives of a theater they had for years deplored. The former was particularly vulnerable. For remem-ber, he had worked four years (without salary) before the theater opened, and he had probably used up more credit with the board than he realized. He did not have enough of it left to draw on when the pressures on his company reached critical mass.

The details and the recriminations of the Whitehead-Kazan-Miller dismissals (they took others with them) occupy many pages in Kazan's autobiography (and my files), but they are fundamentally uninteresting. Suffice it to say that their replacements did no better with the company,

Meantime Kazan, for the first time in his life, found himself lost in depression, idling about the little Greenwich Village apartment he had rented after Molly's death—it was convenient to his theater—briefly impotent, both sexually and professionally, mostly pursuing an increasingly quarrelsome relationship with Loden.

In this period, he would later say, he missed Molly more than ever; he had no one to discuss his dismissal with, no one whose counsel he could rely on. He says his disappearance from New York's theatrical life worried his friends; they had never known him to go to ground in this fashion. On the other hand, he came almost unconsciously to realize, a censoring hand had been lifted from his life. There was nothing external to himself to prevent him from writing—though what, exactly, that might be, he did not know.

As a man, needless to say, he quite quickly returned to himself. And he and Loden never fully sundered their relationship, though it was complicated by the fact that she, too, was a victim of the Lincoln Center fallout, which placed her career in a crisis from which it never recovered. Seeking relief from its fractiousness, Kazan took up another, more uncomplicated relationship with a newly widowed woman he met in Central Park. At some point, they took off for Europe, where his tensions began to melt away and where, at long last, he began to write.

17

Picking Up the Pieces

It was in Paris that Elia Kazan at last settled down to write—at first, letters to himself, about the events of his life. After some weeks of this soul-searching, none of it intended for publication, the shadow of a novel began to appear to him. It would preoccupy him for the next couple of years.

It was, in a certain sense, autobiographical. Its narrator and principal character is Eddie Anderson, eldest son of Seraphim Topouzoglou, better known to the customers of his failed Oriental carpet business as Sam Arness, just as Kazan's own father, George Kazanjoglou, was better known to his rug buyers as George Kazan. When we meet Eddie he is two name changes away from his heritage, but in all other respects his family is a pure projection of Kazan's family; the incidents of Kazan's early life quite neatly match those of his fictional alter ego. He even shares some of the details of Kazan's life. He loves Harold Clurman's theater reviews in the *Nation,* for example. He held a brief membership in the Communist Party, later than Kazan's and less consequential. And he loves his mother and loathes his father in the same way, learning from her that "the only way I could get the thing I wanted was to go after it tenaciously, yes, single-mindedly, yes, but in silence and secrecy. I learned from her how to live in the territory occupied by the enemy, gain my victory while I seemed to be bowing to his hegemony."

Eddie's wife is an altered version of Molly—though nowhere near as intelligent or as highly principled. Gwen, his mistress, is similarly a version of Barbara, maybe more ironic, maybe a little less ferocious (Kazan remembered Barbara pursuing a casting director down the street, beating on him with her fists), but also with a checkered sexual past. But the half-mad father, whose death is the chief subject of the novel's last half, is a portrait from life of Kazan's father, who had died—of arteriosclerosis of the brain (the same illness that afflicted his son in the last decade of his life)—in 1960.

Thus, we can say that most of the book's fictionalizations are as transparent as those Miller employed in *After the Fall*. Eddie is not in show business and he is not a congenital New Yorker the way Kazan was. He is an ad man living in Los Angeles. Nor did Kazan suffer the kind of crack-up Eddie endures, which includes a great deal of destructive behavior, directed at himself and others.

Yet, having said that, we can also say what Kazan did not say, which is that in the aftermath of the Lincoln Center fiasco, he did come as close as he ever did to a "nervous breakdown," close enough so that it was not difficult for him to imagine the full-scale meltdown that Eddie undergoes in the book. No, Kazan never accidentally-on-purpose tried to kill himself as Eddie does at the beginning of the book. He never burned down his father and mother's old house as Eddie does. And his wife never institutionalized him as Eddie's does.

But Eddie does lose a prestigious job just as Kazan did, and it is not hard to identify his smooth-talking agency boss, so perfectly turned out in dress and manner, so full of the conventional wisdom that prosperity and power impart to certain successful men. The founder-owner of Eddie's ad agency, "Mr. Finnegan," chimes perfectly with George Woods, chairman of the First Boston Corporation, who became Kazan's and Whitehead's great Lincoln Center tormentor. Both are men who have unquestioningly bought into "the arrangement" Kazan is criticizing, the one in which all the lies and hypocrisies of the ruling class are accepted in return for large sums of money. To quote a familiar distinction, such men become rich by smoothly anticipating the needs of truly wealthy men like John D. Rockefeller III (referred to as "Johnny Numbers" behind his back by his hirelings, among whom I myself once briefly served), unfailingly polite, intellectually vacuous, "lost in his cloud of global Baptist dollars" as he was once memorably described.

Kazan worked on his novel obssessively, seven days a week, from eight in the morning until two in the afternoon for about a year and a half. He told everyone, as he told a reporter from the *Saturday Review,* that "I had more pleasure writing it than anything else I've ever done," and there is no reason to doubt him.

We also cannot doubt that he had found in writing a perfect antidote to the Lincoln Center failure. Alone in his office, he was licking his wounds, restoring his strength, keeping his own counsel. And laying the groundwork for a comeback that would surprise both his friends and his enemies.

When he finished the novel in 1966, he triumphantly gave a manuscript copy of it to his analyst, saying that he could not have written it without his support, and to Barbara, whose response was a blend of hostility and resentment. She could see enough of herself in Gwen to feel that her privacy had been violated. He also left his manuscript with Sol Stein, who cabled him his acceptance while Kazan, Barbara, Hume Cronyn, and Jessica Tandy were on safari in Africa.

He was, of course, delighted, and later professed himself pleased with Stein's editorial ministrations; he cut upward of one hundred thousand words out of the book, over the course of five contentious months in which they worked on the manuscript almost every day. "Because he came out of the theater," Stein recalled, "we would work by reading things aloud . . . to each other. It's a very laborious way of doing it."

The publisher found in Kazan what he called "an actual storytelling gift," but also found quite a variable talent for language: "He has certain stylistic things that no writer who grew up as a writer would ever use. . . . At the other extreme, he writes beautifully, his imagery is sometimes extremely startling. He is a natural writer rather than a tutored writer. He is not a literary writer. At the same time he does not write like commercial writers. The truly commercial writers write with practically no attention to language; he has a great deal of interest in language and choice of precise words." Beyond that, the publisher said, "He cannot write about things that are not yanked up out of his throat. The things he writes best about are things that have been a very important part of his insides. He can't research a story."

This is a very fair characterization of the writer of *The Arrangement* and of the strengths and weaknesses of that book as it was published early in 1968. It is not a "good" book, or even an easily read-able one, and its social criticisms are crude if passionately felt. It may be that it is more interesting to me, finding clues in it to Kazan's mood and feelings at the time, than it would be to a reader uncom-mitted to such a project. But yet I do think it contains authentic, if rawly expressed, passions that somehow redeem it.

Even so, neither Stein nor Kazan was prepared for its vast com-mercial success. The reviews, though not overwhelmingly favorable, were respectable enough. Eliot Fremont-Smith in the daily *New York Times* saw traces of Mailer, Hemingway and Harold Robbins in it. "The best thing about the novel is its rollicking zest; Mr. Kazan never tires. The worst thing is that he doesn't." But he also conceded that "it does deal with feelings and fantasies that are serious, con-temporary and not uncommon," with the writer, "stirring up from the bottom of his cauldron tasty rewards—nice, subtle surprises of observation." Melvin Maddocks in the *Christian Science Monitor* got closer to the point. He saw in Eddie's experience the same be-trayal of the ideals that underlay *America, America* (and the desperate attempt to reclaim them, which was surely one of Kazan's inten-tions). And he was entirely correct when he wrote that once Eddie's father appears the book takes on a wayward and authentic life. "He is the real rebel of—and against—the novel. By his ornery presence he breaks up its overneat liberal patterns. He leaves it gasping with authentic passions—i.e., those that cannot be tidily verbalized."

But it was Eleanor Perry, the screenwriter, writing in *Life's* re-view section, who got to the heart of what made *The Arrangement* a surprise best-seller. Of Eddie, she wrote, "He totters, staggers, even-tually marches through a series of wild, crazy and oh-so-human ad-ventures toward that sensation he has never known—the feeling of being a man on his own. Independent of the judgment of others, se-cure in the knowledge of his own worth. . . . By the end of the book he has achieved what is most needed on this shaky planet—a new working model of a human being."

Or, to be specific about it, he surrenders all his money, all the glamour of his life-style and withdraws with Gwen and her child (not his, not anyone's that she can identify) to a small Connecticut town, where they eventually own a liquor store and a nice little house. In the mornings, before going in to clerk in the store, he writes—presumably the first person novel we have been reading. He is, in effect, an aging hippie, contentedly, presumably permanently, withdrawn from the high-pressure world of getting and spending.

This was 1967. The "sixties" were reaching their full flowering, and this book spoke to the contempt many people felt for their society, their government, their own materialism. Kazan had perhaps not planned to write anything that so squarely summarized the zeitgeist. On the other hand, he was in so many respects still a 1930s radical, still a man in contempt of bourgeois life and middle-class morality. The old leftist was giving voice to some of the criticisms of the still-forming New Left. Perhaps never in his life had his own experiences so perfectly matched what a lot of Americans were feeling. Neither before nor after its moment could this book have touched so many frayed American nerves. Indeed, in none of the novels Kazan subsequently wrote did he come close to achieving the immediate impact of this crude, powerful popular fiction.

It stayed on the *New York Times* best-seller list for thirty-seven weeks. Eventually it sold more than nine-hundred thousand copies in the hardback edition, upward of three million paperbacks. Kazan sold his book to Warner Bros. for a reputed million dollars, with himself set to produce, direct and—possibly—write. It was a comeback—and a reinvention—beyond any he had dreamed of. Contra Eddie's story, this was the kind of triumph over adversity that Americans most like to believe in.

Which, of course, was almost immediately blown by Kazan. The movie version of *The Arrangement* was the one film he refused to discuss with me twenty years later. "I think I goofed on the movie. So you goof. . . . I don't want to talk about it." Why not? I asked. The film was simply not as good as the novel, he said. "For various reasons, I guess. But one of them was that I shouldn't have made the screenplay myself. I should've got a real good screenwriter. And I now know whom I should have gotten. And I didn't get him."

Who he got instead was Arthur Laurents, the playwright and musical book writer (*West Side Story, Gypsy*), which was, indeed, a mistake. The two knew each other casually, but Laurents was a passionately committed leftist, totally unforgiving of Kazan's HUAC behavior. Still, as Laurents carefully put it, he "thought" he needed money at the time, thought Kazan's book "a pretentious potboiler," but also thought "a potboiler could make a good hot fudge sundae of a movie." If, as he said, Kazan could be "steered away from making an Important Film, always his Achilles heel."

But their collaboration got off to a poor start. Kazan, despite their fractious history, had started to "feel married" to Loden on their African safari and, indeed, did finally marry her in 1967. That summer they rented a house in Montauk on Long Island where Laurents also had a home. Kazan, Loden and their son came over to visit the writer, who sent Loden and her child to have lunch with his parents who lived nearby. In his account, "she just treated them like shit, like a servant." He found Kazan similarly "contemptuous." And worse. "He was very self-deluded at the time. He read me a letter he wrote Brando. It could go down as one of the love letters of all time. . . . But he absolutely expected Brando to do it [the film]. And then he read me Brando's response. I knew he wasn't going to do it . . . I think because he recognized what that novel was."

Laurents thought this, too, represented bad behavior on Kazan's part. "I didn't like him. I thought he was scary." Scary? "Yes, I didn't trust him. . . . I mean . . . I thought what kind of a man reads a very personal letter like that to someone he doesn't know very well. So I thought, just be careful. I didn't want him to know anything about me." The word "reptile" also came up in the course of this conversation.

If this was the long letter to Brando Kazan quotes in *A Life*, then Laurents possibly did not remember the exact exchange—if, indeed, there was an exchange. Kazan's letter is tough on Brando and shrewd about him. He tells him frankly that Warner Bros. thinks he's overweight, not trying and no longer the actor Kazan remembered. Kazan, however, had run *Reflections in a Golden Eye*, Brando's latest film, and (correctly) saw some of the old Brando in it. But, he recalled Brando saying he might "take a stab" at *The Arrangement*, which was much less of an emotional commitment than Kazan wanted. "I'm too old to pump up an actor I'm working with," he wrote. "I need all that energy for the real problems, which are enormous here." He cited his experiences at Lincoln Center, remembering "how corrosive the lack of genuine enthusiasm and devotion in the people with whom I'm working can be." And he said, "I don't want Eddie plump."

Not exactly a love letter, is it? And Kazan records no written reply from Brando. What he—what everyone—recalls was a tacit agreement that he would play the part. In any event, Laurents went ahead with the screenplay, taking, he said, full advantage of Kazan's encouragement to treat the material as freely as he wanted. He would remember writing a love scene between Eddie and his wife, which was to be staged on an X-ray machine, so only their bones— and their wedding rings—would be seen on screen.

This work he delivered to Kazan in chunks of thirty pages, each of which, he says, was received enthusiastically. Until he delivered the last batch of his work. At which point Kazan brought out another script, one that he had written and that, according to Laurents, was the script he eventually shot. He claims Kazan asked him to take it away on a ski holiday Laurents planned and to give Kazan whatever comments he had, even though Laurents would obviously be a bi- ased reader. Kazan also said, according to Laurents, that he'd be glad to give Laurents screenplay credit on the film—though within hours after making that offer, Laurents said, he got, by messenger, a release form from Kazan, waiving all rights to the credit, which he gratefully signed.

It is passing strange, this incident. Why would Kazan go to the expense and trouble of having Laurents write a script when, all along, he intended to use his own? Laurents thinks, perhaps, he was placating the studio's demand for a name screenwriter. All we know, for certain, is that many years later Laurents wrote a play about blacklisting (*Jolson Sings Again*) that contains an unflattering, yet in some respects quite understanding, portrait of Kazan. As D.H. Lawrence's saying goes, "Trust the tale, not the teller."

In the end, Brando betrayed Kazan. I don't believe he was ever wildly enthusiastic about the project, but his career was in the first of its two major troughs and he had come to be disgusted with acting, though he had not yet reached the levels of self-hatred he would later attain. Perhaps he thought reuniting with his old friend and best director would arouse him. In any case, Charlie Maguire would tell Brando biographer Peter Manso that expensive hairpieces were bought in Italy and would remember taking them to Brando's house for a fitting.

Whereupon Martin Luther King was assassinated. Brando summoned Kazan to his house to tell him, gently, that he could not, in light of this tragedy, go on with the picture. He walked Kazan to his car, helped him to settle in, even kissed him good-bye.

Kazan said later that he should have quit the picture at that point. Instead, he hired Kirk Douglas. There were other ramifications to this betrayal as well. Kazan had pretty well convinced Warners to cast Barbara Loden as Gwen—to, in effect, play herself, which despite her dubiety about the novel she was eager to do. For some reason the studio was prepared to accept this screen unknown opposite Brando, but not opposite Douglas. Instead, it insisted on casting Faye Dunaway, hot after her great success in *Bonnie and Clyde*. This was deeply galling to Loden; Dunaway had been her understudy in *After the Fall*.

I am not as certain as Kazan was that Douglas spoiled his movie. And not as certain that Brando would have been its salvation. Yes, as a young actor Brando had mustered the kind of angry studdishness (and underlying vulnerability) that Eddie required in the film's early passages. And he might have managed the nutsiness that his breakdown required. But, of late, he had been playing at martyrdom in the movies, taking all sorts of beatings, physical and moral He was not the actor—perhaps we should say, the presence—he had once been. Douglas, on the other hand, had always been at his best playing forceful heels; it was conventional leading man-ishness that he never quite mastered. And, besides, as Kazan knew and readers of his autobiography eventually came to know, Douglas had the right personal history for the part; his father had been an immigrant junk dealer, every bit as harsh to his son as Kazan's old man had been. He might just be able to pull off this role.

Indeed, I think he more or less did so. The failure of the film—and it was a failure—could not be blamed primarily on him. He worked hard on the movie. And Kazan "was his usual upbeat, positive, conniving self," said Carol Rossen, then a young actress, who played Gloria, Eddie's angrily simmering sister-in-law and his lead opponent in the family's councils. "He was a street guy who was smart and his guy-guyness was very comforting to me. He wasn't Scrooge walking down the hall, he was an effervescent guy." And "he didn't have to impress you" the way, she says, so many directors feel they must. She remembers Deborah Kerr, playing Eddie's wife, feeling the same way. "I just love working with Elia," she once said to Rossen. "I don't have to prepare. I just trust him."

Rossen thought Kazan might have been more "directive" on this film than he had been on others, "because he had written the novel and the screenplay and had 'heard' the dialogue in the actors' tones and rhythms before they spoke it." On the other hand, she recognized that "moment to moment he was very into being in control." She remembers having one argument with him about a scene in which he wanted her to be "really screaming and angry," when she had a different viewpoint—more quietly deadly. She gave Kazan what he wanted, but he later said to her that she might have been right about the scene.

About Douglas, though, he was much more duplicitous. One of the film's big scenes is a commitment hearing, with his wife and her lawyer trying to strip Eddie of what money and property he has and put him in a mental institution. When the master shot was completed, and the camera was being reset for isolation shots, Kazan turned to the room of actors with enthusiastic praise of Douglas. "This is one of the great actors. And so under-appreciated, so under-rated." And so on and on, stroking the massive, quavering ego.

He must have caught a dubious look in Rossen's eye—she was a well-studied performer in the New York style. "Did you see that piece of shit work Kirk just did?" he inquired quietly of her. She never knew if it was an unguarded comment he trusted her to keep to herself or if it was a ploy to get her into a competitive frame of mind for her scenes with Douglas.

The problem with Douglas's work—and you have to give him credit for being one of those rare actors who never sue their audiences for sympathy; he had the courage of his own mean spirits—was that simply by the nature of his screen presence, he more or less doubled the alienating effect of Eddie's personality. In his playing and in Kazan's adaptation one loses sight of what made the book a best-seller, its legitimate criticisms of mid-century America—its materialism, the crass vulgarity of its popular culture, the way people used one another while pretending to love one another. Yes, the picture offered a couple of nice satirical versions of TV commercials and billboards hawking cigarettes, but they did not have the passionate contempt that colored the pages of the book. And, yes, Kazan borrowed Arthur Miller's technique of avoiding formal flashbacks, so that characters from the past wander in and out of the present free-associationally, as they did in *Salesman* and *After the Fall.* But this manner remained no more than an incidental pleasure.

And there were other casting mistakes besides Douglas. Deborah Kerr, for example, was not quite what she should have been, as the soft monster clinging with sharpened nails to Eddie. We knew her too well as a nice woman from dozens of previous movies and she couldn't transcend that past. And then there was Dunaway—not at all the lusty hell-for-leather lover and street fighter that Gwen had been in the book. Her Gwen is too ironic, too plausible and respectable. Finally there was Richard Boone as Sam, Eddie's father. He was late of many television shows, but before that he'd been an Actors Studio guy and he was a good actor. The critics would come down hard on him, though I think now that he played Eddie's father rather well. But somehow what happened in the book—an increase in reader interest as he took over the last half of the book—was reversed in the film. One's attention began to wander when he was on the screen. This has something to do, I think, with our inherent expectations about film narratives. A movie hero cannot surrender to the character man, even if the former has to fight fiercely for our attention. And even if the writer and director shade the text in his direction, as happened here. The movie dwindled before our eyes. It never became Arthur Laurents's "hot fudge sundae." It seemed, instead, a failed reversion to the glamour-trash CinemaScope epics of the 1950s—something like *A Summer Place* or *Beloved Infidel* or *Two Weeks in Another Town,* with their pretensions to seriousness drowned in pretty clothes, handsome mise en scène and risible dialogue. Or, to put it briefly: You could see how Elia Kazan's experience and ideas led him to his novel; you could see little of that in the movie, which seemed to most reviewers a sort of cashing in. I was one of the harshest of them.

It was, I wrote in *Life,* "a curious spectacle: a movie about a man trying to recover from the effects of selling out that is itself a selling out on every conceivable level." Pauline Kael in the *New Yorker* said something similar: "How can Kazan be messianic about not selling out when he has coarsened and simplified whatever interest the novel—his *own* novel—had?" The movie died an ugly death at the box office. Where its source, in its brief moment, hit us where we lived, this movie, hit us where we no longer were.

And Kazan once again went to ground.

The Arrangement's failure pretty largely put an end to his mainstream movie career. He and Schulberg, for instance, had long been researching and trying to set up a combined adaptation of two books, Piri Thomas's *Down These Mean Streets* and Oscar Lewis's *In the Streets,* both nonfiction studies of Puerto Rican juvenile delinquents. At this point, Sam Spiegel had interested Warner Bros. in producing it, but this flop and the aging producer's increasing distaste for a return to *Waterfront*-like realism diminished interest in the project. The climate of dubiousness about Kazan killed interest in a sequel to *America, America* on which he had also toiled for some time.

Mostly, for the next decade, he would be a novelist, beginning with *The Assassins* (1972) and continuing with *The Understudy* (1974), *Acts of Love* (1978) and *The Anatolian* (1982). Much later, after publishing his autobiography, *A Life,* in 1988, there would be a final work of fiction, *Beyond the Aegean,* which came out in 1994. These were all extremely bulky works, particularly the last two, and all of them, save *The Assassins,* contained autobiographical elements. Some appeared briefly on the best-seller lists and all were reprinted as mass-market paperbacks. A few reviewers acknowledged Kazan's growing sureness as a realistic novelist, but most did not. His last book, which was in some ways the most interesting of them all, was scarcely noticed by the review media or the public. Kazan never quite became a brand-name popular author, yet he was never taken seriously as a novelist by the literary community.

But, and this was important to him, he made his principal living as a writer. Quite a good one, in fact. By the time he was working on *Acts of Love* he said he was getting a million-dollar advance, which he probably was, since his agent, by then, was the legendary Swifty Lazar. He was, however, frugal, not to say tight-fisted, about money. Stein told a reporter from *People*, "He's afraid of some cataclysm, so he's always got to have money squirreled away." Kazan would merely say, "The most important thing about being a writer is keeping expenses down." He would take his advances, estimate the years it would take to write a book and then live within the amount he had allotted for that period. "Once you begin to hurry [you] do things you don't want to do."

He thought perhaps his biggest problem was tenacity: "Sometimes I should give up things and I don't." Robert Gottlieb, his editor at Knopf, where he moved for *Acts of Love* and his later books, thought the issue with him, artistically (if that's the word we want), was keeping his concentration focused; his curiosity was constantly being aroused, leading him to follow tangents, which is one reason his books grew so fat.

But it was not the main reason for their bulk. For some reason he developed an almost Dreiserian taste for detail. His fictional people could not consume a meal without Kazan recording every aspect of its preparation and consumption. His books sagged under the weight of these irrelevancies. They were also dragged down by his research, by material he had merely observed, but not felt.

That was particularly true of *The Assassins*, the novel that followed *The Arrangement*. He wanted to write about "the kids," the inheritors of, or imitators of, the more serious revolutionary impulses that had shaped him. To that end he traveled to the Southwest and hung out with them in their crash pads and communes, partaking of their pot and hash (it had no more effect on him than a couple of martinis, he reported). He warped his reportage into a story about a dutiful Chicano air force sergeant who shoots the hippie drug dealer who deflowered his wayward daughter. He's a hero to the local Mexican-American community, a problem to the air force. It doesn't really want to punish one of its own, but it also doesn't want to look like it is protecting one of its own. The result is a truly awful and largely unreadable novel, all grimly maneuvered plot and no feeling—aside from an aging author's only slightly ambiguous contempt for the youth culture.

The next couple of books are marginally better. *The Understudy*, for example, is about an actor who idolizes an older star, then becomes responsible for him as he ages and his career falters while the younger man's prospers. Kazan a little bit based the old fellow—arrogant, roaring, irresponsible, yet unconquerable—on Clifford Odets as he had become in his late years (he died of cancer in 1963, still talking of the plays he was going to someday write and never did), and the book did contain some interesting showbiz lore and folk wisdom (as well as a Molly-like character). But the best writing in it—it might be the best Kazan ever did—had nothing to do with the theater. It was an extended passage about an African safari the younger actor takes. It is preoccupied with predation, with the stronger creatures of the plains endlessly feasting on the weaker ones. The actor comes to believe this to be the way life is everywhere organized. This was a topic—one might even call it a philosophy—much on Kazan's mind at the time; in the movie version of *The Arrangement* he included extensive passages from a nature film showing the gory deaths of animals in the wild, which his hero cannot tear his eyes from. What we don't know is whom Kazan was identifying with—the hunter or the hunted. One suspects that, in his wounded condition, it was the latter.

His next book, *Acts of Love*, was perhaps his most autobiographically daring. In a letter to his readers that he wrote for the paperback edition, he made much of his heroine's sexuality. "Ethel is a woman who, in her sex relations, actually does behave LIKE A MAN. She goes from lover to lover WITHOUT GUILT [caps his]," and he added that many women had told him, again and again, that they recognized Ethel as a "sister." How true that might have been it is hard to say, but we can surely recognize her as Barbara Loden's "sister," since, speaking of predators, that's how Kazan now saw her. But the truly daring aspect of the novel is that she, in turn, is sexually stalked—and eventually killed—by her husband's aged father, who is another version of Kazan's own father.

The final book in the group written when Kazan was proudly

identifying himself to everyone as a full-time professional novelist is the endless saga of his Uncle Joe's rise to wealth as a rug merchant in his new country. *The Anatolian* is, of course, the sequel to *America, America,* but with a cast of hundreds and an almost minute-by-minute accounting of Joe's life—and the lives of his sisters and his cousins and his aunts. It is a serious book—and not unilluminating if you have the patience for it.

But to look back on these fictions now is a duty for someone trying to make sense of this life, almost never a pleasure. With the exception of a scene here, a passage there, these novels all strike one as acts of will. Still, Kazan worked on them demonically, rising in the early hours of the morning, pounding away at his Royal typewriter until one or two in the afternoon, taking a break—often long enough to play some tennis, his lifelong recreational passion—then returning to his desk for revisions, which might entail ten, fifteen, twenty rewrites of something that didn't sit right for him.

He always professed himself happy in his work. And that seems to have been so. Some years earlier he was instrumental in getting a young actress named Patricia Bosworth accepted by the Actors Studio and they became friends. Their friendship deepened when she understudied the female roles in Molly's one-act plays ("She [Molly] was very cultivated and elegant and she wanted so much for him") and reached a new level when she found that she, too, wanted to make the transition from show business to writing, which Kazan encouraged. She would visit him in his office for long talks "about everything," laughingly fending off the occasional pass, which she thought he felt obliged to make. They talked often about her troubled parents and he would say, "You have so many stories to tell; get them out of your head." Which, eventually, she did in a memoir. She came to feel that he was not lying, to himself or to others, when he spoke of his pleasure in writing: "It seemed to me he felt he could really express himself—assert himself—in ways he couldn't when he was directing."

In a prepublication interview with a *Life* writer, as *The Assassins* was coming out, he enthused, "I hope I never adjust to success. I want to keep going and growing. And I think I can." Flipping a rolled-up paper napkin into a wastebasket ten feet away he exulted: "I feel organic. Full of life. Like a big bee loaded with honey."

This was always the best thing about Kazan, early and late—his un-daunted exuberance. We know he experienced self-pity and self-doubt, but he never let his critics, literary or otherwise, see it. If anything, he would preempt their criticism, by cheerfully, self-deprecatingly admit-ting his mistakes. It was not until much later, with the publication of his autobiography in 1988, that he let his deepest self-doubts swim to the surface. And even then he spoke of them gallantly.

But with all that said, one cannot help but see that writing was for him a kind of escape, a wonderful excuse for inattention, for not paying heed to anything—an unpaid bill, an unfulfilled wife, a tempting, problematical adventure. And for more than a decade he in every way made a profitable go of his new business.

But he could not quite manage a full withdrawal into authorship. For one thing, her acting career totally stalled, Barbara began writ-ing a movie script, suggested by a newspaper clipping she had read. For something like six years, according to Kazan, she was unable to interest anyone in producing the film. Then she met Nick Proferes, a man well versed in cinema verité filmmaking, and asked him to photograph and edit her 16mm film, *Wanda,* which was made on a budget of under $200,000. This was really guerrilla moviemaking—a small crew, grabbed locations, unknown actors other than Loden herself, straying improvisationally from a script about a young woman straying through lowerclass American life.

Kazan occasionally helped out, not with the direction, but toting gear, doing a little hasty set decoration. He didn't much care for the movie, which lacks a compelling dramatic structure or emotional dy-namics, but it had a kind of down-and-dirty reality about it. He had sometimes threatened to shoot in this manner when he was having trouble with his own financing and now had firsthand evidence that it could be done.

The film caused a certain stir in New York when it was released in 1971. There were not many female directors in those days—not that there are all that many today—and the reviews, while hesitant to highly praise the film, stressed Loden's gumption in making it. Domestic release outside New York was minimal, but it was acclaimed in Europe, even winning a prize at the Venice Film Festival. Based on that success, Loden began writing other, similar screenplays (to no avail) and Kazan began thinking of doing something along the same lines himself.

According to Proferes, Kazan was worried about his son Chris, then thirty-three. A Harvard graduate, he had worked as a newspaperman, written a couple of novels and was living on a farm near Kazan's in Connecticut, in Proferes's description, "depressed" and dropping out. But then Kazan asked a casual question of his son: "What happens after My Lai; suppose those boys come back to this country, what happens?" It energized the young man, who went off and quietly wrote his script. Kazan hired Proferes to shoot and edit *The Visitors*, as it was titled, on a budget of $135,000—less, he repeatedly said, than Faye Dunaway's salary on *The Arrangement*. Actors were hired at nonunion rates—among them James Woods, making his screen debut; Steve Railsback, and the veteran Patrick McVey—and Kazan took no salary for directing. The locations were his son's house and his own in Connecticut. Kazan took pleasure in the fact that some of the actors were actually sleeping in the rooms that, by day, were the sets.

The story is stark. A Vietnam veteran, Bill Schmidt (Woods) is living an alienated life, with a woman, Martha (Patricia Joyce) and their child in rural isolation. Her father, a drunken hack writer (McVey), lives in another house on the farm. One day two men Bill served with in the war, Sarge and Tony (Railsback and Chico Martinez), stop by for a visit. They seem friendly yet oddly menacing. With good reason. They were rapists and murderers in Vietnam, sent to jail (from which they have just been paroled) because of Bill's testimony against them. We quickly see that they mean to do him some sort of vengeful harm. Which eventually they do—Mike rapes Martha, beats Bill almost to death, and then the men leave. The picture ends with the battered couple staring numbly at each other.

Because the budget was so tight, Kazan was obliged to shoot the film on Super 16 stock, largely with a wide-angle lens at fairly low light levels, as he told Jeff Young in his book of interviews. The result is glum, grainy, emotionally distant—and, frankly, dull. It is also, I think, significantly miscast. Woods would go on to a good career as a sort of wild-card movie menace. He and Railsback should have switched roles, and Kazan, the casting master, should have noticed his mistake.

It is obvious that Kazan was again turning to the question of loyalty. Clearly, he was again saying that there are sometimes good reasons to speak hidden truths. But this exploration of this topic is too simple, too obvious. More interesting, potentially, is the old writer, hacking away at his pulp fiction. You can easily see him as a projection of Kazan at that moment, isolated with his slightly more aspiring novels, but surely wondering about his relevance in a radically, rapidly changing world. The old fellow in the movie is a right-wing crazy, which, of course, Kazan was not, and he was more violently angry than Kazan ever permitted himself to be. He is, in other words, more a projection of the director than a self-portrait, but he is never fully integrated into the film's main narrative line.

Finally, this is a painful movie to watch, lacking the energy and conviction Kazan had brought to his other films. He complained to Proferes that "there was a tenuous quality to being a director" and that he was beginning "to feel like a whore." *The Visitors* is not a particularly long movie (only ninety minutes), but it feels endless as it plods along on the same emotional level from start to finish. When Kazan previewed it at the Shubert Theatre (much too big a house for such a small film) the audience became volubly restive. "Why are they laughing?" Kazan kept asking Proferes, who had no gentle answer.

Most of the reviewers were soft-spoken in their condemnations, stressing the many past favors Kazan had granted his audiences. And one of them, the influential Vincent Canby of the *New York Times*, actually seemed to like the film, which he called "extremely moving," in part because "everything—from the physical production to the melodrama—is kept in small scale, as if not to get in the way of, or to confuse, its very legitimate expression of a major American sorrow."

What sorrow he did not specify. United Artists booked the movie sparingly in the United States, though it was received more enthusiastically in Europe. The critics there liked its emotionally flattening cinema verité manner; they thought it offered a rawer, therefore more truthful, style than conventional movies did. Kazan said at the time that he would like to do more films in this style, since it offered him more creative freedom than big-budget filmmaking did. But he did not pursue the idea. Beyond the bad reviews and grosses the film had one other unhappy result. Home Free Productions, the entity Kazan created to produce *The Visitors*, was placed on the Screen Actors Guild "unfair" list because its actors had signed nonunion contracts, and Kazan himself was fined by the Directors Guild, on the national board of which he devotedly served for many years, for not signing a DGA contract.

Indeed, aside from the commercial successes of his novels the rest of the 1970s were a miserable time for Kazan. He was only to make one more film, this time on a big budget, but with results no more happy than he achieved on a minuscule one. Far worse, his relationship with Barbara Loden disintegrated almost completely. They ceased sleeping together, and although they shared residences, they were estranged in other ways, as well. One area of contention remained his writing, which she continued to dislike.

Jeanine Basinger, the film scholar, who got to know Kazan at this time because he donated his papers to Wesleyan University Cinema Archives, where she supervised them, very shrewdly characterized Loden. "She was frightened and skittish and neurotic. But she focused very narrowly on what you said, and she had a natural intelligence without the apparatus to access it." Put these qualities together with her often thwarted ambition and you have the potential for a lot of anger, maybe even a degree of paranoia. Certainly, you have—especially given the reception her film got from women at a time when the feminist movement was defining itself—something of a handful, especially for a traditional male like Kazan.

He believed, without ever quite saying so, that she took up with Proferes, though the latter is silent on that subject. But they were assuredly close friends and partners in a number of filmmaking schemes that never resulted in a production. Oddly enough, though, Proferes and Kazan remained friends with Kazan recommending him to Milos Forman, then heading the Columbia University film department, for a teaching job he retains to this day. Proferes developed "a great love for the guy." And a shrewd understanding of him. He saw, for example, how his uncle Joe's fate, his sudden descent from riches to poverty, haunted Kazan, imposing on him an unncessary frugality. He thought, too, that he had a publicly unacknowledged need "to get back at the people who had looked down on him," whether it was Lee Strasberg or his political critics. Perhaps above all, Proferes thought, he was haunted by the absent Molly. Maybe she had thwarted some of his ambitions, and pushed him to places he didn't want to be, but her intelligent approval had validated him in ways that no one else could.

Some of that approval he started to receive, in the seventies, from his new association with Wesleyan. Nothing much had been done with his papers until Basinger took control of them. She was trying to make the Wesleyan archives into a major repository of Hollywood history—Frank Capra, Martin Scorsese, Clint Eastwood, among others, have since donated their papers—and she arranged a major retrospective of Kazan's films in 1973, to draw attention to the archives. It climaxed with a great speech by Kazan entitled "On What Makes a Director"—possibly the best thing of its kind ever written—smart, funny, down-to-earth. The Directors Guild keeps the speech in print to this day.

Encouraged by Basinger, Kazan became something of a familiar figure on campus. He even, for a time, had an office there, which he used when he was consulting his papers while writing his autobiography in the 1980s. He loved meeting with students in classrooms, at informal meals. "He was a performer," Basinger observed, "he'd take on the shape he needed for the occasion." But in class, he treated students as he had treated his actors, getting their histories, drawing out their opinions—and not belaboring them with his.

The film students neither knew nor cared much about his political past; they treated him as a film legend who was eager to share what he knew about the field they wanted to enter. Meantime, he and Basinger developed a warm relationship. They liked hitting the campus pizza parlors, in particular one owned by Greeks.

Like Proferes, Basinger found him wistful about Molly. He missed, she said, her capability and intelligence, and he was always "respectful, grateful and remorseful" when he spoke of her. Her papers, too, came to rest at Wesleyan, but he wanted them guarded more closely than he did his own. Perhaps to protect her memory—but also, Basinger guessed, his own.

Proferes had observed a certain resentment in Kazan, especially about the way his novels were received; "I'm tired of not getting credit for my writing," he told the filmmaker. As the years wore on, Basinger detected a more generalized bitterness in Kazan. "He felt he was young and energetic, but he couldn't act on it; he didn't feel he was any longer a part of the movie world. 'Tell your students,' she remembered him saying, 'they'll throw you away eventually.'"

———————

Sam Spiegel, however, remained in the mood to take a chance with Kazan. He had been for some time hoping to bring F. Scott Fitzgerald's unfinished novel, *The Last Tycoon,* to the screen. He was smitten by Harold Pinter, the gnomic playwright, who had, as well, written a number of more mainstream screenplays, and had put him together with Mike Nichols to work on this adaptation. After a while Nichols dropped out and Spiegel approached Kazan, who rather carelessly signed on. He later admitted that he had only glanced at Pinter's script. He also said his subsequent script conferences with the writer were disappointing; he claimed they discussed punctuation more thoroughly than they did structure.

In truth, the main thing Kazan wanted from this project was some time on the West Coast, where, perforce, this period piece—a fictionalized portrait of Irving Thalberg, the legendary Hollywood producer—had to be shot. Kazan's mother was mortally ill and increasingly distressed by the cold climate of the East. He thought an extended stay in Los Angeles would do her good.

It did not. Her condition worsened—eventually she died in Los Angeles—but her agony was, naturally, a major distraction for Kazan, who would rush back and forth between his sets and her hospital room, where he did his best to comfort the dying woman. He never claimed his inability to focus fully on the film was the cause of its failure, but he was not concentrating on its many inherent problems, which perhaps began with the fact that he was inherently the wrong man for the job.

Fitzgerald was, of course, a romantic, who as a failed screen-writer had idolized Thalberg's apparent mastery of the studio system. But Kazan was not a romantic—certainly not about the studio system. Yet, ironically, here he was, making a studio picture about a man running a studio and, indeed, working on Hollywood backlots and soundstages for the first time in twenty years. It is not surprising that his film had about it a distant, unfelt air.

There were, however, worse problems for him to deal with. They perhaps began with the fact that this was an *unfinished* novel. All the ideas of what Fitzgerald might have intended in its latter passages were guesses, with Kazan quite dubious about their accuracy. And he could see that Pinter—at the time thrown off-stride by an unpleasant divorce—had not addressed those issues. In particular Kazan felt Pinter had never successfully worked out the love story, which has Monroe Stahr (the Thalberg figure), being distracted from his obsessive concentration on his studio's management by a love affair with an actress named Kathleen Moore.

This problem was compounded by Kazan's casting. He settled on Robert De Niro as Stahr without meeting him—something he had never done before. And he had settled on a model named Ingrid Boulting (she was the stepdaughter of the well-known English producer Roy Boulting) largely because (Kazan said) Sam Spiegel had sexual designs on her. Now De Niro is, by common consent, a great actor; he and Kazan bonded and the emerging star (he had just finished Martin Scorsese's *Taxi Driver*) worked devotedly on the part. He lost thirty or forty pounds to achieve the willowy quality of the slender, sickly Thalberg, saw his old movies, studied biographies of him and other studio moguls. Boulting, too, tried her best; she, Kazan and De Niro worked weekends on exercises the director devised to loosen and warm her performance. Kazan grew fond of her and of Theresa Russell, playing Cecilia Brady, daughter of Stahr's boss and rival (the character is vaguely based on Louis B. Mayer), who is the novel's narrator and who also has a girlish crush on Stahr.

But this work was of small avail. So was the stunt casting in which fading actors (Tony Curtis, Ray Milland, Dana Andrews), young comers (notably Jack Nicholson) and the odd exotic (Jeanne Moreau) were brought in to play supporting roles. The film has some occasional visual felicities—particularly Boulting's introduction to the film and to Stahr, when he glimpses her floating down a flooded studio street clinging to a prop representation of Siva, the Hindu god of destruction—and Kazan, in his notes, had the right idea about Stahr's character.

He observed, for example, that Stahr had to be "awful tough," adding, "Perhaps it is necessary for a young man—Kubrick, for instance—to be ruthless when he comes to power so young. He has to command elders and he can't help thinking that they resent his authority over them. And that he also develops a taste for it since he is and has been right so often and they have been wrong so often. And it is inevitable that he soon gets trapped in this power, that he enjoys it, that it becomes habitual with him." It is shrewd and original, this idea of how talented youth responds to authority when it is granted them. All over America—especially in the entertainment field—this essential, Young Turk–Old Fud drama was constantly being played out.

So was an outcome that Kazan also envisaged. Because he has cut himself off from his best self, even from ordinary human congress, has also lost his wife, has endured a life of almost monastic loneliness, an encounter "with his feminine ideal of beauty, romance and goodness" unhinges Stahr. "Having realized how dried up and toughened and serene he has become, he reaches back to regain his humanity. When he does this he exposes what he has never exposed before, his vulnerability. His naked neck. When he exposes this, he is killed."

But Pauline Kael rather acutely noticed in her review that, though one doesn't quite believe the-world-well-lost-for-love theme, one also doesn't feel that Stahr's battles with the studio money men—he's producing a movie he (and they) are pretty sure won't make money—is sufficiently developed. Both of Fitzgerald's romantic ideals—about love and about the dream factory—emerge only in a shadowy and emotionally straitened way.

Spiegel had never thought De Niro quite right for the part and as he watched dailies tried constantly to undermine him with Kazan. He was, alas, correct, though, on the other hand, it is hard to imag-

ine any actor bringing out the deeply internalized passions of
Stahr/Thalberg. Kazan, in turn, though always supportive of Boulting once he got to know her, never got quite the performance out of
her that he sometimes thought she might be developing. So—a con-
strained script, polite direction, unrealized performances. And a
movie that was dead on arrival.

Kazan saw it coming, though he refused to admit it openly. For
the first time in his career, he was making shot lists, like a film school
tyro—and showing them to Spiegel for his approval. He wrote in his
notes, "the resilience has gone out of me. And the fun." And "it sure
as hell ain't good or original or startling or funny. Just routine."

When Kazan showed *The Last Tycoon* to cast and crew the response was dim. And a premiere at Lincoln Center's Alice Tully Hall in
New York, benefiting the Actors Studio, drew a restive response. The
reviews, though, were by no means disastrous. They were, in fact, quite
respectful on the whole. "We watch it as if at a far remove from what's
happening," Vincent Canby in the *New York Times* wrote, though for
some reason he felt that to be "appropriate." Almost all the reviewers
thought the movie "intelligent" and a conscientious adapatation of this
marginal and unfinished literary work. But they were not the sort of reviews that encouraged a large audience to attend the film.

There is some dispute as to whether it made or lost money, but
whatever it did at the box office, *The Last Tycoon* was, as they say, a
"disappointment"—especially considering the credentials of its creators. Neither Kazan nor Spiegel would ever make another film.

The former went back to writing novels. And, within two years, to
a preoccupying tragedy. For his wife discovered a lump in her breast in
1978. It was cancer, which she spent the next two years fighting, not always in the most effective ways. As the disease metastasized she went
from clinic to clinic, from doctor to doctor, some of them quite dubious, trying to find a cure, yet in the meantime continuing to teach her
acting classes and even directing a production, off-Broadway, of *Come
Back to the Five and Dime, Jimmy Dean, Jimmy Dean.* It was a brave
frenzy, and Kazan stayed with her every step of the way. "For the last
two years of her life," Proferes said, "he just stopped his life to take care
of her, to stay with her. He was like a saint."

Kazan, Proferes thought, had always had the idea that art would somehow "purify" Loden, grant her the controlling passion that she had never found elsewhere in her catch-as-catch-can life. It is impossible to say if she ever achieved that kind of focus. But it is possible that his devotion to her in her final days granted him some sort of purification, some lifting of the darkness that had descended on this marriage.

———

In *A Life* Kazan wrote that he and his collaborators had somehow neglected to create an ending for *The Last Tycoon.* So on the last day of shooting he improvised one—Stahr walking down the streets of the studio at night, entering a huge soundstage door and being swallowed up in the enveloping darkness. It is an ending that echoes that of *On the Waterfront,* with the pier door closing on Brando and the workers following him. For Kazan, it felt like the ending of his own career as a director—a final slow fade to black. He said that he came to that conclusion as he prepared the shot.

I don't think that's exhaustion talking, at the end of a wearying shoot. It was surely a decision subject to revision. The problem for Kazan was that in the years ahead plans and hopes fell through and it became more comfortable for Kazan to suggest that a conscious decision, rather than bad luck, dictated his professional silence.

For example, he gave an interview in Greece (to which he was constantly returning in these years) in which he confidently proclaimed that he was working on yet another sequel to *America, America,* but was, for the moment, casting it in the form of a novel. In these years he even talked about a return to the stage, and there were, indeed, serious discussions of his directing Richard Burton in *King Lear,* despite Kazan's oft-professed feeling that he and Shakespeare were not a good match. But that idea also eventually foundered—because Burton refused to play matinees and the Shubert organization declined to back a production in which the star denied them the performances that would have assured them profitability. The first time a young actress named Cathleen Leslie, later to become close friends with Kazan, met him was at a seder at Strasberg's home. She entered the music room to find Kazan, who had that day learned of the Shuberts' decision, prone on a couch, being consoled by Strasberg—lifelong enemy, lifelong friend.

He occupied the next few years by making a start on another novel and on his autobiography. In 1982 he married Frances Rudge, an attractive blond Englishwoman who entranced him, on their first meeting at a dinner party, by confessing that she had never heard of him. There were very few people in New York who could make such a claim. In that same year, Lee Strasberg died, and within a month Kazan was back at the Actors Studio, where with Arthur Penn and Joe Mankiewicz he helped organize a playwrights-directors unit.

There had been other, similar attempts at such a unit earlier in the Studio's history, but this one came out of a conversation Penn had one day with Norman Mailer, then attempting to write dramatically, and he brought Kazan and Mankiewicz in to help out with a group that had as many as forty members, among them at one time or another Don DeLillo and Harold Brodsky. Kazan, Penn recalled, was his usual energetic self—"pugnacious, confrontational" in his response to scenes the writers read out, but also showing "his very charming other side, a little frightened and seduced" by being in the room with all this literary talent. He stayed with the program for only a couple of years.

But he stayed with the Studio intermittently. It was out of an acting exercise he conducted there that Kazan's own first play since his experiments of the 1930s emerged. *The Chain* was a play-within-a-play blend of the Oresteia and reflections on the modern tragedy of Hiroshima and Nagasaki. Clearly, Kazan intended it as some sort of grand summing up of his beliefs. Two of its actresses, Cathleen Leslie and Frances Fisher, remember it as both "a glorious experience"(Leslie) and a total disaster. The glorious part was being directed by Kazan. Leslie recalled an early rehearsal in which, with his company assembled onstage, he simply cried: "Dawn. Early Greece. Hit it!" Fisher remembered being bent over in exhaustion and feeling his hands on her shoulders. "You're too young to be slumped over like that, young lady," he barked.

What Fisher liked was the way he would encourage the actors to work up whatever improvisations that came to them, bring them in and then see what worked and what didn't. The trouble with the play, she thought, was that it was old hat in construction and ideas. Full of freshness and energy in rehearsal, it went flat in performance. She remembered thinking that they should actually put the rehearsals on stage, with Kazan among the actors, working with his typical, galvanizing energy on the play.

Leslie's memories are somewhat different. Among the sixteen roles she was supposed to play was a horribly burned young Japanese boy, which Kazan insisted she imbue with perverse good cheer, almost as if he were an American cheerleader, a mysterious choice to her. She also felt Kazan was too concerned with the details of his writing.

Yet a third actress in the play, Corinne Chateau, thought the choice of a tryout venue—the Hartman Theatre in Connecticut, then being managed by the Edwin Sherin, the actor-director, was a mistake. It "was not the right place. It drew a white bread crowd." But she also concedes that the play needed to have been workshopped for many more months before being presented to an audience. It must be said, however, that the theatrical and literary friends Kazan invited to attend the production were scarcely more forgiving.

Leslie recalls looking out on an audience slumping miserably in their chairs, everyone trying to avoid everyone else's eyes. The next day, she says, Kazan bounded into rehearsal to reinterpret their body language. He thought they were all sick with envy. But the play died, unmentioned even in passing in *A Life*. Chateau thinks it was a more bitter blow to Kazan than he ever admitted.

Still, he kept looking into other film and theatrical ventures in this period. And, perhaps ironically, he enjoyed one last success—with a book, his lacerating—and self-lacerating—autobiography, *A Life*, which was published in 1988. In a letter to Leslie, then living in Paris, Kazan wrote: "So, OK, I did finish my book and all that remains now is fitting the photographs to it and standing up as the critics slam hell out of me, which I am used to by now. Since I wrote exactly what I wanted to, I won't mind negative opinions. Much."

Earlier, he had promised an interviewer full disclosure of his own life, but not "an effort to get even with people who have attacked me, I've had a very happy life, a very productive life. I have no desire to get even with anybody." But in the end he somewhat reneged on that promise. "There's no use doing an autobiography if you leave stuff out," he told the man from *U.S. News and World Report.* "I read John Huston's autobiography—a guy I liked—and there was very little of him in it. Why do all that work and not say anything? So I said what I thought of everything and everybody. I'm glad I did. I feel unburdened. I'm relieved at not having secret thoughts I'm trying to keep from others, my wife included. I let her know everything, including how bad it was when it came to women. I don't know any other biography that is as candid as mine, not any in the world."

Well, maybe Rousseau's. But essentially he was right. It is an astonishing book, narratively a little scattered, not completely reliable when it comes to dates, but full of raw, truthful and often contradictory feelings, which the author makes no attempt to smooth into neatly planed and polished arcs. It is a book almost without QEDs, very definitely a "concluding unscientific postscript," to borrow an apt phrase, since finally it was the work of an unselfconscious existentialist, defining himself in the moment, by the moment.

As it turned out, he needn't have worried about the critics. The sheer tumult of this 848-page book overwhelmed most of them. How, in their little essays, could they pretend to grasp the essence of its author? Mostly they fell back before the whirlwind, conceding a force that essentially blew away whatever reserve, whatever prissiness, they might muster.

This book was not a best-seller. But it was some kind of triumph, especially in that many of the reviewers conceded that Kazan at least had an argument when it came to his appearance before HUAC. They could not, on the whole, endorse his behavior, but they also could not condemn it as fully as once they might have. We might at this point risk this mild generalization: There were no Stalinists still reviewing for respectable literary journals and everyone else was inclined to have forgotten what, exactly, those old disputes entailed.

Publication of *A Life* was the last significant public act of Kazan's life—until the Oscar controversy a decade later. But he did not know that at the time. His new preoccupation was *Beyond the Aegean,* the idea for which he turned over to his son Chris, to make into a screenplay. With plenty of input from Kazan, it was ready to shoot in

1990. When I approached him with my plan to make a television documentary about his career, he cheerfully told me I might have to join him on location in Greece to shoot his interview. He assured me that I'd love it there.

He was authentically excited about this film's prospects. It would round off his trilogy about his uncle Joe, still called Stavros in this story. It would take him back to Anatolia at the moment, in the early 1920s, when Greece was fighting Turkey over this territory. His mission—the book was once again based on family legend—was to buy rugs for the family business (in wartime they were available at bargain rates) and perhaps to find a wife and resettle in his native land.

Kazan had set the project up with a well-regarded French producer, Anatole Dauman, who believed he could get a subsidy for it from the French government, whose ambitious minister of culture, Jack Lang, was pursuing a program of investing in foreign films. If they contained substantial numbers of French actors and technical people, it made no difference to him if the picture was shot on French soil or elsewhere.

This presented a not-insoluble problem to Kazan. He had thought of a number of American actors—Al Pacino and James Woods among them—but had finally settled on Nick Cage, a performer whose wildness in those days reminded Kazan of the other young men he had brought to stardom. Among the other Americans he intended to cast was Jo Van Fleet, now almost lost to sanity, but calling him almost daily to check on the film's progress. He was hoping to placate the French by casting Juliette Binoche, whom he had (correctly) loved in *The Unbearable Lightness of Being*, to play opposite Cage. According to Michael Wilson, who prepared a French translation of Kazan's script for the producers and was to be the project's American liaison, her lover, Leos Carax, a director, was wildly jealous of Kazan and determinedly opposed her signing for the film.

This was not necessarily fatal to the project, but another factor was. Kazan needed to obtain permission to shoot in Greece and to rent elements of its army and navy for his battle scenes. But Melina Mercouri, the politically passionate Greek actress who had been forced into exile by the reactionary junta that ruled her native land until 1974, was now minister of culture, youth and sports. She was also the wife of the blacklisted director Jules Dassin. And she refused the necessary permits. Or maybe she did not—in an interview her husband says she granted permission to shoot in Greece but left the question of military assistance open. Dassin claimed that the minister of defense called him, said the picture was anti-Greek, and told him he was going to refuse military cooperation. If we are to believe the novel, that anti-Greek charge is not true; it is quite evenhanded in its depiction of the struggle between the Greeks and Turks.

One suspects that, despising Kazan as he did (and misrepresenting both aspects of his own autobiography and his career in the same interview), Dassin and his wife probably sabotaged his plans without leaving any fingerprints. We certainly know that failure to make this film was a bitter blow to Kazan. In 1990 he was an ebullient, energetic, brilliantly articulate man. Despite the fact that he was more than eighty years old, he had the manner of a man in his fifties or sixties.

Four years later, that was not the case, and there were friends of his who attributed his decline to his bitter disappointment over bringing this one last film so close to fruition and then failing. I'm not sure that's completely the case. For one thing, his beloved son Chris died suddenly in 1993, and though he was articulate enough in expressing his grief, this was a blow more dreadful to him than the demise of their movie, which now reverted back to its original form, a novel, which Kazan worked on determinedly.

By this time according to his wife, they had been told by doctors that Kazan had the early symptoms of his father's disease, arteriosclerosis of the brain, and that though its progress was unpredictable, and certain ameliorative tactics could be employed, it would sooner or later render him incompetent. For the moment, however, it seemed to me that his deafness—he had a drawerful of hearing aids, none of which he would wear—was having a more isolating effect on him than the arteriosclerosis.

I encountered him at a mutual friend's wedding in 1994 and found him to be quite frail, in a panic about an imaginary incontinence problem, and unwilling to join the other guests in the banqueting tent. The actor Charles Grodin and I took turns keeping him company in an otherwise deserted living room, where the conversation, though coherent, was nothing like what I had been used to having with him.

When Knopf published *Beyond the Aegean* in a version that took full advantage of Chris's good work on the screenplay (which his father touchingly acknowledged), it was greeted by a deafening silence. I do not recall reading a single review of it anywhere, though I think it is his best novel—richly but not excessively detailed, well structured, with a good fluent balance between its romantic passages and its dramatic set pieces. This, too, was probably a blow to him; he was used to everything except being ignored.

But he continued to sit before his typewriter on the fourth floor of his brownstone, pretending to himself that he was still writing, though nothing tangible was produced. Because of his deafness he was unable to enjoy plays and movies anymore, and though his wife insisted they accept the many invitations to dinner that friends pressed on him, he was often silent and withdrawn on those occasions. He liked to run his old movies on videotape and invite friends and family to watch them with him. He was always enthusiastic about what he saw.

But still . . . the contrast between this Elia Kazan and the astoundingly energetic old man we had all so recently known was hard to take. I cannot help but think that one of Karl Malden's unspoken motives in proposing the honorary Oscar for him was the hope that it might reenergize his old friend. Or, perhaps at the least, make him realize that he had not been completely forgotten. If that was the case, Malden succeeded far beyond his dreams.

EPILOGUE

The Charm of It

On the morning of the seventy-first annual Academy Awards broadcast, the *Los Angeles Times* ran two articles about the Kazan award. One was a woozy piece by Neal Gabler analogizing Kazan's award to the honorary Oscar bestowed on Charles Chaplin twenty-seven years earlier in a bathetically bathed Oscar broadcast. "Anyone watching could see," Gabler wrote, "that Hollywood was less interested in saluting Chaplin than in staging a show of its bigheartedness," and he expected a similar performance tonight. He missed the point that Chaplin was being welcomed home from an exile caused, in part, by his leftist political beliefs, which the industry endorsed, while Kazan's beliefs were, it thought, the opposite—and, to a substantial portion of the Hollywood community, much less forgivable.

The article by historian Alan Wolfe was more substantive. A political scientist at Boston University and a contributing editor to the *New Republic,* he argued that certain crucial events in history do not necessarily end with their formal conclusions. The American Civil War, for example, ended not at Appomattox, but with the triumphs of the civil rights movement in the South more than one hundred years later. So it is with American Communism and the bitter controversy surrounding it.

He wrote that every element in the American Communist's victimized self-portrayal had by now been proved false. For example, Alger Hiss and at least one of the Rosenbergs had been spies; Paul Robeson had not been hounded into exile and destitution for his liberalism, but for his virulent anti-Americanism, which cost him the sympathy of public opinion. Most important, Wolfe wrote that the "progressives" (the code name Communists favored when referring to themselves) had always had dirty hands.

> Funded by the Soviet Union, the U.S. Communist Party put Soviet interests ahead of everything else, shifting positions a bewildering number of times to accommodate its subservient status. Determined to hide their real agenda, Communists practiced the art of insincerity and apology. Willing to hide behind the constitution, they supported repression of other left-wing parties with whom they disagreed. More power-hungry than idealistic, Communists took a chance on revolution—and lost. Who then are they, or their like-minded sympathizers today, to insist Kazan was vile, whereas their intentions were only pure?

Wolfe went on to speak the unspeakable. Acknowledging that a few industry Communists had been jailed, he noted that most blacklistees had found other work. He admitted, naturally, that McCarthy and his ilk had been demagogues "with no respect for civil liberties." But, he added, "politics is rough stuff. In the Soviet Union opponents of the regime lost their lives in massive purges. Here they had to make their movies under assumed names."

He was being a trifle unfair. Communist movie directors and actors could not work under assumed names. Only the writers could use pseudonyms. But still, many of their more visible colleagues did find work abroad or in the theater or in fields less avidly scrutinized than the movies or television. The blacklist was only occasionally a tragedy; mostly it was an inconvenience. And a fairly short-lived one, at that, essentially broken when Dalton Trumbo received credit on *Spartacus*, eight years after Kazan's testimony. Compared to the twenty million Soviet citizens killed by Stalin, the millions more imprisoned in the Gulag, their numbers were paltry, their punishment mild. American democracy had failed them as well as its highest ideals—it was, and is, strong enough to tolerate even revolutionary dissent—but their "martyrdom" to free speech, a principle with which they only selectively agreed, was mild and brief.

I agree with Wolfe; if you are going to play at revolutionary politics, you have got to at least consider the possibility that you may someday be called upon to pay a price for your opinions and actions. You may, as well, have an obligation to revisit them eventually. As Wolfe wrote, "it is time for U.S. Communists to admit their mistakes. They need not do so directly. Simply by welcoming Kazan's Oscar—indeed, even by ignoring the whole event—veterans of America's Communist movement can send the message that they now understand how morally complex the 1950s were."

––––––––––

Fat chance. By the time Wolfe's piece appeared, the two thousand people who would be attending the broadcast at the Dorothy Chandler Pavilion were beginning to primp and preen for the big event. The much larger number of Hollywood folks who would be watching at home were heading out for the dips, chips and deli that would fuel their Oscar parties. There would perhaps be time for the opinion section later.

Or not. For, in truth, few really cared about the politics of fifty years earlier. Even then, most people in Hollywood had not cared that much about them, either. They had been much more concerned with the steadily dwindling audience for movies, with the rise of television and the demise of the old-fashioned studio system, under which, until very recently, they had jobs that appeared to be guaranteed virtually for life. As for most Americans in 1998, they were much more interested in the increasingly tense best picture race between *Saving Private Ryan* and *Shakespeare in Love*.

With my companion, the journalist Barbara Isenberg, I set out for the Music Center around three-thirty in the afternoon. Because the TV broadcast begins promptly at six, you have to be in your seats well in advance of the appointed hour. We expected, correctly, that the traffic, despite the well-practiced efforts of the police, would be more difficult than usual; protesters and counterprotesters would be in the streets, shouting their slogans, waving their signs.

As we inched our way up the Temple Street hill, a couple of blocks from the Music Center, a senior-citizen van came to a stop in front of us. Its door opened and a skinny old lady, carrying a three-pronged metal cane, began a painful backward descent from its door. She was carrying a professionally lettered sign. It read: "Kazan Is a Rat." Gaining her footing on the sidewalk, she began her slow ascent of a long incline. It seemed to me doubtful that she would gain a place in whatever picket line she was heading for before the broadcast began.

It seemed to me, too, that she symbolized the whole darkly comic aspect of this occasion. She might just as well have been home, sipping her Ensure and watching the best part of the Oscar show, which is the entrance, down the red carpet, of the stars in designer finery. But no, here she was, drawing on such reserves of energy as she could muster, to make her dubious statement.

As we circled the Music Center, heading for the main entrance, progress was slow and not enlightened by knots of fervent demonstrators both pro- and anti-Kazan—more of the latter than the former. They were confined to the sidewalks and they were particularly noisy in front of the Dorothy Chandler Pavilion, where the limos were disgorging the swells. But we gained the auditorium in time, without incident.

I would say that the most curious—not to say grotesque—occurrences of the evening centered around the behavior of Roberto Benigni, the Italian actor-director, who won two prizes for his profoundly offensive comic-romantic take on the Holocaust, *Life Is Beautiful*. He affected a childlike excitement about his prizes, clambering over seats, nearly kicking Steven Spielberg in the head, as he leaped stageward to accept his awards in broken, babbling English. Nothing surrounding the Kazan award could possibly compete with this lunatic, yet clearly calculated, performance.

Indeed, after that hubbub, Kazan's appearance was distinctly anticlimactic. Scorsese and De Niro read my little introduction, my clip package played and Kazan, on the arm of his wife, appeared. Something like half the auditorium rose to greet him and something like another quarter of it applauded while remaining seated. The TV cameras noted a few prominent figures—Nick Nolte and Ed Harris among them—seated, not applauding, making their stony-faced statements.

Kazan appeared somewhat confused. "I really like to hear that," he said referring to the applause that greeted him, then added, haltingly: "I want to thank the Academy for its courage and generosity.

I'm pleased to say what's best about them—they're damned good to work with. Thank you all very much. I think I can just slip away." Whereupon he looked somewhat dazedly about, trying to find Scorsese and De Niro, who moved to his side, and escorted him offstage.

Several in the audience later grumbled to the press that it was a nonevent, a disappointment. But they, of course, had not known just how feeble Kazan now was. Walter Bernstein, the once blacklisted screenwriter, who knew Kazan personally and seemed, despite everything, to harbor a certain affection for him, had, of course, joined the protests, but he murmured, "I was more overwrought about Benigni getting the best actor award, because I didn't like the movie." (Amen to that.) He added, "The only good thing is that it may have made more people aware that there once was a blacklist." This may have been the understatement of the show business year.

As for me, I was drained. I thought perhaps that Kazan had intended a somewhat more coherent statement, but had been overwhelmed by the music, the lights, the huge stage and expectant audience. I had not, for a minute, anticipated anything like an apology, just something not quite so fumbling. On the other hand, it occurred to me that this stumbling, almost pathetic old man gave the lie to the braying ideologues who had beset him for two months. In the end, our passions must surrender to our humanity—to aging, to infirmity, to the passing years.

Later, at the Governors' Ball, I made my way to Kazan's table, placed my hands on his shoulders and told him I thought the evening had gone well, all things considered. "Well," he said, "at least they didn't boo." I think he genuinely expected such an occurrence. I thought then that he had shown more courage than his attackers. It takes a certain nerve, whatever your age or condition, to appear in public, expecting the worst, but yet refusing to deny your past, accepting whatever consequences it continued to carry.

Four days after the Oscar broadcast, a columnist for the *Los Angeles Times*, Shawn Hubler, stressed this point in a well-written piece. "In this town of stories and story-tellers Kazan's special Oscar became its own drama, acquired its own narrative. By Sunday night the world was expecting less a prize than a denouement. Then, in a twist, the evil snitch/misunderstood genius took the stage—and the camera revealed a befuddled 89-year-old man. . . . The story-tellers wanted justice on Sunday, but as Kazan could have told them, payback is a fiction. Panning the grim faces and crossed arms, the cameras found only the phoniness of stale disapproval—bullies picking on a senior citizen."

But yet a senior citizen capable of the unexpected snarl. Six years after the Oscar show, Haskell Wexler was to recall this incident. He was one of the academy's governors and, despite their differences, he had voted to bestow the honorary Oscar on Kazan. But then, as the controversy reached a peak, he wrote his old colleague, suggesting he make some sort of reconciliatory gesture to his enemies—maybe not a full-scale apology, but some acknowledgment, at least, that his critics might not be entirely wrong. Back came a one-line note. It read: "Fuck you, Pete."

Recounting the story, Wexler laughed. This was the old Kazan, the man he had served, fought with, learned from, in a faraway corner of the world thirty-five years earlier. He might be diminished, but in some corner of his addled mind, he was still himself—the fox who had known, or thought he had known, many, often contradictory, things, but was now a hedgehog knowing one big thing, which was that instinct was always to be trusted above ideology.

For all ideologies—even the most visibly perverse of them—pretend to speak for the betterment of humanity. But all of them, in the end, leave out the reality of human existence—its flaws, failures, disappointments, illnesses; its puzzled silences and its blaring surenesses. Generally speaking we are at our most mistaken when we embrace, give our lives to, some grand, abstract ideal. At the end of Kazan's last novel, his hero and occasional alter ego, Stavros Topouzoglou, remembered thinking, as the ocean liner brought him to the United States for the first time, "I believe that in America I will be washed clean." But now, returning to it from a vast adventure in the old country, his creator reflects on his behalf:

America America was not the country for that.
Nor was he a man capable of self-purification.

He, Kazan, all of us, are capable only of those improvisations we make in response to our circumstances—some of which work out, some of which do not, most of which end in ambiguity, in, as we might say, mixed reviews, with ignorant strangers imputing false motives and meanings to our efforts.

Elia Kazan lived on for five years after receiving his final Academy Award and making his last appearance on a national stage. He was always glad to see his friends, but his silences were impenetrable. He was lost in his own thoughts, the nature and quality of which no one could judge. When he spoke it was in fragments, a sentence or two about Darryl Zanuck, perhaps, or Marlon Brando. But it was, in my experience, at least, impossible to connect these dots, make a coherent conversation out of them. When he died, on Saturday, September 27, 2003, two weeks and three days after his ninety-fourth birthday, I embraced the cliché—it was a merciful end.

The obituaries somewhat surprised me; they mentioned his HUAC testimony, naturally, but did not, for the most part, excessively stress it. Film critics followed with appreciations that emphasized the "realism" of his manner and the immortal performances contained in his films. Most of them failed to mention that this largely psychological "realism" was deeply discounted in our times. It exists, in some American independent movies and in some foreign films, but the detailed examination of human behavior, out of which larger truths about the contemporary human condition can emerge—the legacy of The Group and the Actors Studio which he so significantly advanced—is in short supply in our films, on our stages, in our cultural consciousness. The mainstream of our movies is action-fantasy. The mainstream of our theater is musical and nostalgic. The day when a young director like Martin Scorsese would earnestly ask Kazan if he could work as an unpaid apprentice to him—as he did when The Arrangement was being planned—is long gone. If the Kazanian legacy exists at all it is in the work of individual actors, applying its principles in often inappropriate contexts.

Most of the critics, writing their obituary considerations, also insufficiently stressed the themes that emerged in Kazan's later works—the question of what constituted loyalty both to friends and ideas, obviously, but also the obsessive concentration on father-son relationships, the difference between America as an ideal and America as a reality.

But there was something else missing from these reflections, I thought. That was the joy of the man, the shrewd playfulness—yes, all right, his manipulativeness—as he strove to express what had generally been previously unexpressed in American plays and movies.

I found myself thumbing that Directors Guild pamphlet, reprinting his remarks to the Wesleyan students, "On What Makes a Director." In listing what a director needs to know he naturally mentioned the big, abstract things—a knowledge of literature, of comedy, painting, sculpture and dance; of cityscapes and country vistas; of topography and animals and the capabilities of the human voice; of actor psychology and the audience's, too. Of erotic life.

But then he passed on to the more personal attributes the craft demands. A director, he said, must have the qualities of a white hunter on safari, a construction-gang foreman, a psychoanalyst, a hypnotist, a poet, and "the cunning of a trader in a Baghdad bazaar," "the elusiveness of a jewel thief," "the firmness of an animal trainer," "the blarney of a PR man, not to mention good cheer, patience and the ability to say 'I am wrong' or 'I was wrong.'"

For, in the end, the director, whether we believe him to be the "auteur" of a movie or not, is always the senior officer present on any production, the man who gets most of the credit when it succeeds, most of the blame when it fails—even for the script (he should have demanded another rewrite) or the performances (an actor's failure is always the director's failure, since he's the man who called "print" when he should have gone for another take).

All of this requires courage, which as Kazan said, quoting Churchill, is the virtue that makes all the other virtues possible. All of which, with typical insouciance, he claimed to possess: "I've never stopped trying to educate myself and improve myself."

But still, that led him to this self-deprecating conclusion: "Ask me how, with all that knowledge and all that wisdom and all that training, and all those capabilities, including the strong legs of a major league outfielder, how did I manage to mess up some of the films I've directed so badly.

"Ah, but that's the charm of it."

This is as good a place as any to take leave of Elia Kazan—proud of what he had accomplished, yet also modest—and not falsely so—about those achievements. And still eager to ingratiate himself with his audience. We can imagine his Anatolian smile playing briefly about his lips.

Charm, like this hungry and passionate life, is finally a mystery. You succumb to it or you do not. You can explain some of it, but never all of it. This, one believes, would be just fine with Elia Kazan. A mystery solved is a mystery forgotten. A mystery unsolved, subject to endless reinterpretation, has the power to haunt us as long as memory lasts.

Notes

Prologue

page

xvi *"honor a friend"*: Karl Malden, interview with author.

xix *"in some ways, a direct"*: Bernard Weinraub, "Elia Kazan, Snubbed by Some, to Get an Honorary Oscar," *New York Times*, Jan. 13, 1999.

xix *"it's their achievement"*: Quoted in Patrick Goldstein, "Film Director Elia Kazan to Receive Oscar, Forgiveness," *Los Angeles Times*, Jan. 10, 1999.

xx *"We do not wish"*: quoted in Bernard Weinraub, "Kazan Award Is Stirring Protest by Blacklist Survivors," *New York Times*, Feb. 23, 1999.

xx *"alternately vigorous and frail"*: Quoted in Weinraub, Jan. 13, 1999.

xxi *"I'm flattered to death"*: Quoted in ibid.

xxi *"personally love the man"*: Allen Garfield, "Counterpunch: Despite Talent, Kazan Doesn't Deserve Honorary Oscar," *Los Angeles Times*, Jan. 25, 1999.

xxii *"I'll be watching"*: Quoted in Jeff Jensen, "Trophy Strife," *Entertainment Weekly*, Feb. 5, 1999.

xxii *"If a person's a good director"*: Quoted in Jeff Ressner, "Kazan (take) 1." Correspondent file to *Time* magazine, Feb. 4, 1999.

xxiv *rued their action*: See Army Archerd, "Just for Variety," *Variety*, Feb. 23, 1999.

xxiv *"elements of disgust and shame"*: Arthur Schlesinger, "Hollywood and Hypocrisy," *New York Times*, Feb. 28, 1999.

xxvi *"assert blind, retrospective loyalty"*: Richard Schickel, "An Oscar for Elia," *Time*, March 8, 1999.

xxvii *"I can only say"*: Quoted in Bernard Weinraub, "At the Movies," *New York Times*, March 12, 1999.

xxviii *"I thought what a terrible thing"*: Quoted in Allen Weinstein, "Regrets, He's Had a Few; Enough to Be Forgiven," *Los Angeles Times*, March 17, 1999.

xxix *"further his own career"*: "Don't Whitewash the Blacklist," *Variety* (advertisement), March 19, 1999.

Chapter 1: The Anatolian Smile

2 *"I used to spend"*: Kazan, *A Life*, p. 3.

3 *"It . . . made me rebellious"*: Elia Kazan, Interview with author.

6 *"I watched them all"*: Ibid.

6 *"How do you get a start"*: Ibid.

9 *"We have, on the American stage"*: Quoted in Smith, *Real Life Drama*, p. 5.

10 *"give their group feeling"*: Quoted in ibid., p. 7.

12 *"Mr. Sifton, we are not here"*: Quoted in Lewis, *Slings and Arrows*, p. 52.

13 *"Let's take Odets"*: Quoted in Smith, *Real Life Drama*, p. 6.

15 *"What I want"*: Quoted in Kazan, *A Life*, p. 6.

18 *"You may have talent"*: Quoted in ibid., p. 81.

20 *"The Group has put on"*: Quoted in Page, *Dawn Powell*, p. 130.

20 *"The play was one"*: Harold Clurman, *The Fervent Years*, p. 100.

20 *"one of the most painful"*: Ibid., p 105.

20 *"externally clear action"*: Kazan, *A Life*, p. 90.

21 *"what the Group directors"*: Ibid.

22 *"Lee and the actors"*: Ibid, p. 103.

23 *"I have not demonstrated"*: Quoted in Smith, *Real Life Drama*, p. 168.

27 *"Boys, I think"*: Quoted in ibid.

27 *"He was not a man"*: Kazan, *A Life*, p. 111.

27 *"transference"*: Arthur Penn, interview with author.

29 *"moved without the burden"*: Kazan, *A Life* , pp. 112–13.

30 *"proletariat thunderbolt"*: Quoted in ibid., p. 116.

30 *"a dollar buys"*: Quoted, ibid, p. 114.

31 *"HELLO AMERICA"*: "Waiting for Lefty" in Odets, *Waiting for Lefty and Other Plays*, p. 31.

Chapter 2: Awake and Sing

34   *"You don't seem to understand"*: Quoted in Kazan, *A Life*, p. 120. See also Smith, *Real Life Drama*, p. 196.

34   *"They began to doubt"*: Kazan in *Broadway Dreamers: the Legacy of The Group Theatre*, PBS documentary, 1984.

35   *"I'm twenty-two and kickin'"*: "Awake and Sing!" in Odets, *Waiting for Lefty and other Plays*, pp. 100–01.

38   *"were like top-speed basketball games"*: Norman Lloyd, interview with author.

38   *"professional theater worker"*: Quoted in Eisenschitz, *Nicholas Ray*, pp. 29–30.

39   *"too quiet an evening"*: L.N. [Lewis Nichols] "The Play," *New York Times*, May 29, 1935.

40   *"was not a collective person"*: Kazan, *A Life*, pp. 107–08.

40   *"Whereas up until so recently"*: Ibid., p. 116.

41   *"I was the hero"*: Kazan, *Wild River* notebook, Wesleyan Cinema Archives.

42   *"I AM DAVE"*: Ibid.

42   *"and planning to write"*: Ibid.

45   *"As it is practically impossible"*: Quoted in Clurman, *The Fervent Years*, p. 157.

45   Blankfort's troubles as a reviewer for Communist publications are recounted in Bentley, ed., *Thirty Years of Treason*. See especially pp. 464–66.

46   *"I was a good villain"*: Quoted in Eisenschitz, *Nicholas Ray*, p. 30.

47   *"It does not call for"*: Quoted in Smith, *Real Life Drama*, p. 255.

Chapter 3: The Drama of Ordinary Life

48   *"What the hell does Jerome know"*: Quoted in Kazan, *A Life*, p. 128.

49   *"Acting . . . was the biggest charge"*: Ibid., p. 147.

49   *"I wouldn't go up on a stage now"*: Maurice Zolotow, "Viewing the Kinetic Mr. Kazan," *New York Times*, March 9, 1952.

49   *"I was not what you'd call a first-class actor"*: Elia Kazan, interview with author.

50 Kazan's most complete account of his crisis of belief in the Communist Party is to be found in *A Life*, pp. 127–33.

51 *"that the Party had at heart"*: Quoted in Bentley, ed., *Thirty Years of Treason*, p. 486. This volume contains Kazan's complete public testimony before HUAC, together with other documents he submitted to the committee, pp. 484–95.

52 *"It was the Party"*: Gornick, *The Romance of American Communism*, p. 7.

52 *"the only one of a kind"*: Kazan, *Wild River* notebook, Wesleyan Cinema Archives.

52 *"for years after I resigned"*: Quoted in Ciment, *Kazan on Kazan*, p. 22.

55 *"How helpless Strasberg was"*: Quoted in Hirsch, *Kurt Weill on Stage*, p. 145.

56 *"part fantasy, part musical satire"*: Brooks Atkinson, "The Play," *New York Times*, Nov. 20, 1936.

57 *"We must set ourselves"*: Quoted in Smith, *Real Life Drama*, p. 292.

58 *"a possibility we have not discussed,"* Quoted in ibid., p. 293.

59 *"The Group Theatre of Motion Pictures"*: *Variety*, April 21, 1937. Quoted in Pauly, *An American Odyssey*, p. 42.

60 *"Group training gave him"*: Ibid.

60 *"great confidence in my ability"*: Quoted in Ciment, *Kazan on Kazan*, p. 23.

61 *"gravitation of left-wing aesthetics"* Quoted in Pauly, *An American Odyssey*, p. 43.

61 *"Realism is the artistic form"*: Terry Eagleton, "Porkchops and Pineapples," *London Review of Books*, Oct. 23, 2003.

61 *"with its heroic myths"*: Ibid.

62 *"Everybody in The Group"*: Elia Kazan, interview with author.

64 *"never got over"*: Sklar, *City Boys*, p. 82.

65 *"Broadway bug"*: Quoted in Brenman-Gibson, *Clifford Odets, American Playwright*, p. 483.

66 *"the simplest and most effective"*: Brooks Atkinson, "The Play," *New York Times*, Nov. 5, 1937.

67 *"on the slant"*: Karl Malden, interview with author.

67 *"His dominant mood"*: Brenman-Gibson, *Clifford Odets, American Playwright*, p. 469.

68 *"America is the most lonely"*: Kazan, *Casey Jones* notebook, Wesleyan Cinema Archives. His other reflections on the play are drawn from the same source.

70 *"hostile and invariably suspicious"*: Kazan, *A Life*, p. 168.

70 *"was a complete trial"*: Ibid.

Chapter 4: Quiet City, Restless Spirit

75 *"thin and inconsequential"*: Brooks Atkinson, "The Play," *New York Times*, Jan. 6, 1939.

75 *"That last syllable's too big"*: *Quiet City* manuscript, Wesleyan Cinema Archives.

76 *"There are times coming"*: Ibid.

76 *"one of the most exciting"*: Norman Lloyd, interview with author.

76 *"I think Irwin"*: Kazan, *Quiet City* notebook, Wesleyan Cinema Archives.

76 *"achieve failure"*: Quoted in Clurman, *The Fervent Years*, p. 226.

77 *"Very often The Group actor"*: Kazan, *Quiet City* notebook, Wesleyan Cinema Archives.

80 *"A man who fights"*: Robert Ardrey, *Thunder Rock*, p. 66.

80 *"America's not going to war"*: Quoted in Smith, *Real Life Drama*, p. 38.

81 *"vital belief"*: Kazan, *Thunder Rock* notebook, Wesleyan Cinema Archives.

81 *"This is not an old tired play"*: Ibid.

81 *"The cast of a play"*: Kazan, *A Life*, p. 182.

81 *"playing with a nervous tension"*: Brooks Atkinson, "The Play," *New York Times*, Nov. 15, 1939.

82 *"a song cycle"*: Quoted in Clurman, *The Fervent Years*, p. 244.

83 *"Harold, I think"*: Quoted in ibid, p. 246.

83 *"Now that Odets writes like Saroyan"*: Brooks Atkinson, "The Play," *New York Times*, Feb. 23, 1940.

84 *"one of the most exciting actors"*: Ibid.

84 *"He was oafish"*: Clurman, *The Fervent Years*, p. 248.

84 *"I'm not a good actor"*: Quoted in Eli Wallach, interview with author.

84 *"His arm's around her"*: Ibid.

84 *"I'd make sure"*: Kazan, *A Life,* p. 183.

86 *"What's pride when you have to beat"*: Kazan, *A Life,* p. 186.

87 *"many doubts in my mind"*: Ibid, p. 187.

87 *"I sure as hell"*: Ibid. p. 188.

87 *"The critics and the audience"*: Lewis, *Slings and Arrows,* p. 128.

87 *"he is getting to be"*: Brooks Atkinson, "The Play," *New York Times,* March 14, 1941.

89 *"The only thing about the production"*: Kazan, *A Life,* p. 189.

Chapter 5: "I'm Still Here"

91 *"had the thinnest talent"*: Kazan, *A Life,* p. 191.

91 *"the first art theater"*: Kazan, *Café Crown* notebook, Wesleyan Cinema Archives.

91 *"This theater is dying"*: *Café Crown* manuscript, Wesleyan Cinema Archives.

92 *"genial, comic and original"*: Brooks Atkinson, "The Play," *New York Times,* January 24, 1942.

92 *"The tension I had felt"*: Kazan, *A Life,* p. 192.

94 *"The people, yes!"*: Kazan, *The Strings My Lord, Are False* notebook; Wesleyan Cinema Archives.

94 *"played for the most part well"*: Lewis Nichols, "The Play," *New York Times,* May 20, 1942.

95 *"he needed a hit"*: Quoted in Norman Lloyd, interview with author.

100 *"I know you've been trying"*: Quoted in Kazan, *A Life,* p. 212.

100 *"The best play the Forties"*: Lewis Nichols, "The Play," *New York Times,* November 19, 1942.

101 *"Think of all the years"*: Quoted in Harrison, *The Enthusiast,* p. 232.

102 *"an adroit and amusing play"*: Wilson, "The Antrobuses and the Earwickers," in *Classics and Commercials,* p. 83.

102 *"In the first place, it is conservative"*: McCarthy, "The Skin of Our Teeth," in *Sights and Spectacles,* p. 53.

102 *"a lark"*: Ibid., p. 57.

103 *"The fact is"*: Kazan, *A Life,* p. 201.

103 *"Every fighter has"*: Quoted in Murray Schumach, "A Director Named Gadge," *New York Times* (magazine), Nov. 9, 1947.

103 *"Thanks for being right"*: Quoted in Bankhead, *Tallulah*, p. 256.

Chapter 6: Miracle Man

106 *"It is a portrait"*: Lewis Nichols, "The Play," *New York Times*, March 4, 1943.

106 *"a sweet, old-fashioned nosegay"*: Quoted in Lucius Beebe, "Stage Asides: The Happiness of Elia Kazan," *New York Herald-Tribune*, April 4, 1943.

107 *"The man behind the plow"*: *It's Up to You* manuscript, Wesleyan Cinema Archives

108 *"A silly thing, really"* Ciment, *Kazan on Kazan*, p. 31.

111 *"He didn't know what he was doing"*: This and the other negative comments about Kazan's direction of *One Touch of Venus* are quoted in Hirsch, *Kurt Weill on Stage*, pp. 217–21.

112 *"Kazan, Kazan"*: Quoted in Kazan, *A Life*, p. 223.

114 *"Werfel was delighted"*: Behrman, *People in a Diary*, p. 168. I have drawn extensively on this source for my account of *Jacobowsky's* pre-production trials.

115 *"A modern legend of rebirth"*: Quoted in Hermine Rich Isaacs, "First Rehearsals; Elia Kazan Directs a Modern Legend," *Theatre Arts*, March 1944.

118 *"nobility"* . . . *"is fulfilled"*: Kazan, *A Tree Grows in Brooklyn* notebook, Wesleyan Cinema Archives.

119 *"a new director"*: Elia Kazan, interview with author. All other direct quotes from Kazan about *A Tree Grows in Brooklyn* are from the same source.

124 *"It is my opinion"*: Elia Kazan, "The Director's Playbill," *New York Herald-Tribune*, Sept. 12, 1943.

Chapter 7: Eating Fire

127 *"the law of the least common denominator"*: Elia Kazan, "Audience Tomorrow: Preview in New Guinea," *Theatre Arts*, October 1945.

127   *"its accustomed toys"*: Quoted in Thomas H. Pauly, "Introduction," in Anderson, *Truckline Café*, p. 5.

128   *"a refugee"*: Quoted in ibid.

128   *"in its trappings and devices,"* Quoted in ibid., p. 6.

129   *"They'll return from Europe"*: Arnaud d'Usseau and James Gow, *Deep Are the Roots*, p. 88.

130   *"armed and awaiting the day"*: Ibid., p. 93.

130   *"falsely accused"*: Kazan, *A Life*, p. 294.

130   *he pointed out:* White's letter is extensively quoted in d'Usseau and Gow's preface to the published version of *Deep Are the Roots*, p. 10.

130   *"the whole marriage idea"*: Lewis Nichols, "Deep Are the Roots," *New York Times*, Oct. 7, 1945.

131   *"liked the orderly marshalling"*: Tennessee Williams to Elia Kazan, Feb. 24, 1950, Devlin and Tischler, eds., *The Selected Letters of Tennessee Williams*.

132   *"James Gow and I believe"*: Quoted in Kazan, *A Life*, p. 193.

132   *"I knew what the talk"*: Ibid., p. 295.

132   *"an endearing man"*: Ibid., p. 296.

133   *"she represented what he prized"*: Ibid., p. 297.

133   *"I was a virgin"*: Anne Jackson, interview with author. Subsequent quotes from the actress are drawn from the same source.

135   *"Our theater is strangled"*: Quoted in "The Theater: Café Brawl," *Time*, March 11, 1946. I have largely relied on this source for my account of the *Truckline Café* controversy.

138   *"I admired Jack Ford"*: Elia Kazan, interview with author.

138   *"I found that he did not like"*: Quoted in Ciment, *Kazan on Kazan*, p. 53.

139   *"[E]very time she went to the bathroom"*: Ibid.

139   *"She'd watch him shoot"*: Quoted in Young, *Kazan*, p. 31.

139   *"She cries too much"*: Quoted in Ciment, *Kazan on Kazan*, p. 54.

141   *"I question the value of stars"*: Elia Kazan, interview with author.

142   *"Boomerang meant this"*: Ibid.

143   *"Best fun I've ever had"*: Quoted in Mary Braggioti, "Names Don't Make a Hit," *New York Post*, Feb. 17, 1947.

143   *"my 'gang' of actors"*: Quoted in Ciment, ed., *Elia Kazan*, p. 66.

143   *"Just give me about twenty"*: Quoted in Karl Malden with Malden, *When Do I Start?*, p. 163.

144   *"the belief that the good"*: Ciment, *Kazan on Kazan*, p. 56.

147   *"Then what is this"*: Miller, *All My Sons*, p. 83.

147   *"Larry didn't kill himself"*: Ibid. p. 84.

148   *"The concept behind it"*: Quoted in Christopher Bigsly, "Introduction," *All My Sons*, p. xxii.

150   *"sensed that he wasn't"*: Karl Malden, interview with author.

150   *"Kazan was eating fire"*: Miller, *Timebends*, p. 273.

152   *"the theatre has acquired"*: Brooks Atkinson, "The Play in Review," *New York Times*, Jan. 30, 1947.

152   *"compact and sinewy prose"*: Brooks Atkinson, "Welcome, Stranger," *New York Times*, Feb. 9, 1947.

153   *"the ace of trumps"*: Bentley, *In Search of Theater*, p. 32. This book reprints, in slightly different form, pieces Bentley wrote for a variety of magazines.

Chapter 8: A Poetic Tragedy

156   *"Being what I was"*: Quoted in Ciment, ed., *Elia Kazan,* p. 68.

159   *"a naïve, pure-hearted"*: Quoted in Ciment, *Kazan on Kazan*, p. 57.

160   *Only it was not actually:* The story of Hobson's rewrite is in Steven Bach, *Dazzler*, pp. 279–80.

160   *"Greg's nature was very"*: Quoted in Young, *Kazan*, p. 47.

161   *"Gregory Peck"* . . . *"I could never"*: Quoted in Warren Beatty, interview with author

161   *"With its crusading"*: *Time*, "Cinema," Nov. 17, 1947.

161   *"a fine and forceful film"*: Bosley Crowther, "Something About It," *New York Times*, Nov. 11, 1947.

162   *"Kathy fights like a tiger"*: Elliott E. Cohen, "Mr. Zanuck's 'Gentleman's Agreement,'" *Commentary*, January 1948.

162   *"a mountain of dialogue"*: Siegfried Kracauer, "Three Movies with a Message," *Harper's*, June 1948.

162   *"There were a hell of a lot of people"*: Quoted in Stuart Byron and Martin L. Rubin, "Elia Kazan Interview," *Movie*, Winter, 1971-72. Reprinted in Baer, ed., *Elia Kazan Interviews*, pp. 130–31.

163 *theory of Zanuck's:* Elia Kazan, interview with author.

164 *"It may not be":* Quoted in Kazan, *A Life,* p. 327.

167 *"He was wayward":* Selznick, *A Private View,* p. 303.

167 *"Why, he's the antithesis of me":* Quoted in James Murray, "Marlon Brando, Take One," *Time* magazine archives, Sept. 17, 1954. This correspondent's "file" to the magazine was a principal source for the magazine's cover story about Brando, Oct. 11, 1954.

168 *"Jessica Cronin was very kind":* Elia Kazan, interview with author. All Kazan's comments on this production are from the same source.

168 *Kazan would have loved:* Karl Malden, interview with author.

171 *"I made a study":* James Murray, "Marlon Brando, Take One," *Time* magazine archives, Sept. 17, 1954.

171 *"What he says is":* Robert Brustein, "America's New Cultural Hero," *Commentary,* Fall 1958.

173 *"He's going to get very fat":* A *Streetcar Named Desire* notebook, Wesleyan Cinema Archives. Reprinted in Ciment, ed., *Elia Kazan,* p. 184. Kazan's other comments on this production are from the same source.

175 *"RIDE OUT BOY":* Quoted in Thomas, *The Films of Marlon Brando,* p. 2.

177 *There were more encores:* Robert Garland, "Williams New Play is Exciting Theatre," *New York Journal-American,* Dec. 4, 1947.

178 *"to hit the audience":* Quoted in Schumach, "A Director Named 'Gadge.' ".

178 *"Mr. Kazan's most commendable quality":* Eric Bentley, "Camino Unreal," reprinted in Bentley, *What Is Theatre?* p. 76.

179 *"If he felt bored or tired":* Quoted in "Interview with Jessica Tandy," *Time* archives, Sept. 29, 1954.

179 *"I learned to protect myself":* Karl Malden, interview with author.

179 *"a tremendous experience":* Quoted in Ross and Ross, *The Player,* p. 322.

Chapter 9: Attention Must Be Paid

182 *"We worked on the play":* Quoted in Hirsch, *A Method to Their Madness,* p. 249.

182 *"When Gadge is away"*: Ibid.

182 *"In all conscience"*: Brooks Atkinson, "At the Theatre," *New York Times*, Sept. 8, 1948.

183 *"with the exception of The Group"*: Arthur Penn, interview with author.

183 *"It was one of the illuminating experiences"*: Quoted in Hirsch, *A Method to Their Madness*, p. 250.

183 *"The script was more exploited"*: Brooks Atkinson, "New Season Opens," *New York Times*, Sept. 12, 1948.

183 *"the so-called American realist school"*: McCarthy, *Sights and Spectacles*, p. xiv.

185 *"The essence of the stage"*: Quoted in Schumach, "A Director Named 'Gadge.'"

185 *"I think there should be collaboration"*: Quoted in Ciment, *Kazan on Kazan*, p. 37.

186 *"He really messed it up"*: Quoted in Hirsch, *Kurt Weill on Stage*, p. 295.

186 *"He was not a man with a light touch"*: Ibid.

186 *"an imaginative and generally brilliant show"*: This and the other quotations from reviews are to be found in the newspapers cited in the text, Oct. 8, 1948.

187 *"Manny, how are you?"*: Quoted in Miller, *Timebends*, p. 130.

187 *"Selling was in the air"*: Quoted in John Lahr, "Making Willy Loman," *New Yorker*, Jan. 25, 1999.

188 *"never raised his voice"*: Quoted in ibid.

190 *"He didn't write"*: Kazan, *A Life*, p. 368.

190 *"the man's poetry"*: Lahr, "Making Willy Loman."

191 *"Huston is not deeply anxious"*: Kazan, *Death of a Salesman* notebook, Wesleyan Cinema Archives. For Kazan's full description of Cobb, see *A Life*, p. 362.

192 *"His fatal error"*: Kazan, *Death of a Salesman* notebook, Wesleyan Cinema Archives. Kazan's other comments on the play are drawn from the same source.

195 *"a time bomb"*: Quoted in Miller, *Timebends*, p. 184.

195 *Kazan, influenced by:* For a more detailed discussion of these rewrite proposals see Nicholas Kazan, "On Receiving 'Notes,'" *Written By: The Magazine of the Writers Guild of America, West*, January 2005.

195 *"the idea of the play"*: "The Theatre," *Time*, Feb. 21, 1949.

196   *"enjoying rather than suffering":* Miller, *Timebends,* p. 194.

196   *"He began to masquerade":* Kazan, *A Life,* p. 362.

197   *"a capitalized Human Being":* McCarthy, *Sights and Spectacles,* p. xvi.

199   *"a thin magazine":* Miller, *Timebends,* pp. 182–83.

Chapter 10: Movie-Making

202   *"From the set":* Quoted in Elia Kazan, interview with author.

204   *"They go on the set":* Ibid.

204   *"By the time I started":* Quoted in Young, *Kazan,* p. 57.

205   *"a sweet girl":* Quoted in ibid. p. 54.

205   *"They sort of looked":* Quoted in Ciment, *Kazan on Kazan,* p. 61.

206   *"Ethel," I said:* Elia Kazan, interview with author. Kazan also recounts the incident, using slightly different language, in *A Life,* p. 376.

206   *"a morbid, almost marbleized": Time,* "Cinema," Oct. 10, 1949.

206   *"I said 'Look'":* Elia Kazan, interview with author.

210   *"Whether I made a good film":* Ibid.

211   *"If Jessica had played it":* Karl Malden, interview with author.

212   *"the play loses its meaning":* Quoted in Leff and Simmons, *The Dame in the Kimono,* p. 174.

214   *"Gadge told me something":* Karl Malden, interview with author.

214   *"When Larry and I":* Quoted in Kazan, *A Life,* p. 386.

215   *"She had a small talent":* Ibid., p. 387.

215   *"I liked it on the stage":* Elia Kazan, interview with author.

216   *"Gadge could control it":* Karl Malden, interview with author.

Chapter 11: Hooked

218   *"Listen, junior. And learn":* "All About Eve" script in Carey and Mankiewicz, *More About All About Eve,* pp. 159–60.

219   *"This is a ballot":* Quoted in Geist, *People Will Talk,* p. 183. I have relied heavily on his account of the guild fight, pp. 173–206. Scott Eyman also offers a good account of it in *Print the Legend,* pp. 378–88.

220   *"I'm a maker of westerns":* Quoted in Eyman, *Print the Legend,* p. 384.

222 *"I'm gonna tell you a government fact":* Arthur Miller, *The Hook: A Play for the Screen,* manuscript, Arthur Miller Archive at the Henry Ransom Library, University of Texas, pp. 129–30.

222 *"Dove Pete Panto?":* Quoted in Miller, *Timebends,* p. 146. Miller's cautious account of his involvement with the dockers, their union representatives, their mob allies and his trip to Europe with Longhi is to be found in the same source, pp. 144–177. The story of Panto's murder is in Turkus and Feder, *Murder, Inc.,* pp. 470–73. Carlo Tresca's murder is recounted in Gallagher, *All the Right Enemies,* which is both a biography of Tresca and a kind of true crime story about his murder. Gallagher unhesitatingly identifies Galanti as the perpetrator (though he was never convicted of the crime). Other details about Longhi's rather ambiguous career—he was acquainted with both mobsters and Stalinists—are from Stephen Schwartz, "Arthur Miller's Proletariat: The True Stories of *On the Waterfront,* Pietro Panto and Vincenzo Longhi," an unpublished article.

225 *"The violent action line":* Quoted in Beck, *Budd Schulberg,* p. 52.

225 *"not only have I never read":* Budd Schulberg/Richard Schickel. Email, Aug. 13, 2004.

228 *"lovely light":* Kazan, *A Life,* p. 413.

231 *"If you plan to make the picture":* Quoted in *A Life,* p. 412

231 *"he wasn't against":* Roy Brewer, "Letters (Calendar)," *Los Angeles Times,* Sept. 14, 2003.

232 *"we'd have no way":* Quoted in Kazan, *A Life,* p. 426.

233 *"ITS INTERESTING":* Quoted in Miller, *Timebends,* p. 308.

233 *"'They will ask me'":* Quoted in Kazan, *A Life,* p. 426.

234 *"a dastardly bit of smearing":* Gottfried, *Arthur Miller,* p. 179.

239 *"primarily by their adherence":* Albert Maltz, "What Shall We Ask of Writers," *New Masses,* Feb. 12, 1946. His subsequent recantation, "Moving Forward," was published in *The Worker,* April 7, 1946.

239 *"I smell the party line":* Quoted in Elia Kazan, "Elia Kazan on 'Zapata,'" Letters to the Editor, *Saturday Review of Literature,* April 5, 1952. Subsequent quotations on the film's political stance are from the same source.

242 *"What I said to him":* Quoted, in Elia Kazan, interview with author.

243 *"The thing about Brando":* Ibid.

243 *"Zapata was a hard characterization":* Quoted in Murray, op. cit.

244 *"They have no inner assurance":* Quoted in "Hollywood in Review," *Los Angeles Times,* July 22, 1951.

247 *"The notion that a revolution":* Elia Kazan, interview with author.

248 *"the long-prevailing standards":* Quoted in Kazan, *A Life,* p. 435.

249 *"as fine, if not finer":* Bosley Crowther, "The Screen in Review," *New York Times,* Sept. 20, 1951.

250 *"This obviously changes":* Elia Kazan, "Pressure Problem," *New York Times,* Oct. 21, 1951.

Chapter 12: Testimonies

252 *"away from smallness":* *Flight into Egypt* manuscript, Wesleyan Cinema Archives.

252 *"politically safe":* Selznick, *A Private View,* p. 335.

253 *"By which I mean":* Anonymous, interview with author.

254 *"the realities of revolution":* Bosley Crowther, "Viva 'Viva Zapata,'" *New York Times,* Feb. 11, 1952.

255 *"Name the names":* Quoted in Kazan, *A Life,* p. 455.

255 *"There's nothing else":* Quoted in ibid.

258 *"Not only was it a Machiavellian":* Bentley, *Thirty Years of Treason,* pp. 945–46.

259 *"It is Communism":* Hook, *Heresy Yes, Conspiracy No,* pp. 105–06.

259 *"they were of the left":* Powers, *Intelligence Wars,* p. 105.

260 *"a pall of suspicion":* Ibid., p. 91.

260 *"Once this new evidence":* Ibid., p. 108.

262 *"we were all victims":* Dalton Trumbo, speech to the Writers Guild of America, March 13, 1970. Reprinted in Trumbo, *Additional Dialogue,* pp. 569–70.

263 *"the weak, the cunning":* Quoted in Navasky, *Naming Names,* p. 398. The entire, highly illuminating, exchange between Trumbo and Maltz is presented, with commentary by Navasky, on pp. 388–01.

264 *"degradation ceremonies":* Navasky, *Naming Names,* pp. 314–29. Navasky uses this phrase as the title of the chapter outlining this theory.

265 *"What the hell am I":* Kazan, *A Life,* p. 460.

265 *Contrary to the victims' angry feelings":* Ceplair and Englund, *The Inquisition in Hollywood,* p. 378.

266 *"Don't worry":* Quoted in Kazan, *A Life* , p. 461.

266 *"it was not his duty":* Miller, *Timebends,* p. 334.

268 *"I will offer Kazan":* Quoted in Gottfried, *Arthur Miller,* p. 264.

268 *"It choked off":* Kazan, *A Life,* p. 63.

270 *"I said that was not":* Ibid., p. 464.

270 *"very highly developed":* Anonymous, interview with author.

271 *"police state":* Elia Kazan, "A Statement," *New York Times* (advertisement), April 12, 1952. The quotations immediately following are from the same source.

272 *"What's called 'a difficult decision' ":* Quoted in Ciment, *Kazan on Kazan,* p. 86.

Chapter 13: To the Waterfront

273 *"a Jewish, ex-commie":* Quoted in Nicholas Fox Weber, "From Stravinsky to the Sharks," *New York Times Book Review,* May 1, 2004.

273 *"Is this the Kazan":* Quoted in Kazan, *A Life,* p. 469.

273 *"I think it made a man of me":* Ciment, *Kazan on Kazan,* pp. 87–88.

275 *"The circus is a good image":* Kazan, *Man on a Tightrope* notebook, Wesleyan Cinema Archives.

279 *"when a theatrical work":* Tennessee Williams, "Foreword," in Williams, *Camino Real,* p. 7.

279 *"leftist manifesto":* Quoted in Spoto, *The Kindness of Strangers,* p. 187.

279 *"'they're just folks'":* Quoted in Eli Wallach, interview with author.

280 *"Go on stage":* Quoted in ibid.

280 *"it was no use knowing":* Bentley, "Camino Unreal," in Bentley, *What Is Theatre?,* p. 76.

281 *"Even the people":* Brooks Atkinson, "The Theatre," *New York Times,* March 20, 1953.

281 *"We're all of us guinea pigs":* Quoted in Atkinson and Hirschfeld, *The Lively Years,* p. 230.

282 *"It's one of the three best":* Quoted in Budd Schulberg, "The Inside Story of 'Waterfront,'" *New York Times* (magazine), Jan. 6, 1980.

283 *"kind of a cynical newspaper reporter":* Budd Schulberg, interview with author.

283 *"With my Hollywood background":* Ibid.

283 *"I never denied it":* Elia Kazan, interview with author.

283 *"Theme: This motion picture":* Kazan, *On the Waterfront* notebook, Wesleyan Cinema Archives.

284 *"The odd thing":* Budd Schulberg, interview with author.

284 *"He would tell me about what he went through":* Elia Kazan, interview with author.

286 *"Who's going to care":* Quoted in Schulberg, "The Inside Story of 'Waterfront.'"

286 *"Goddam it":* Ibid.

286 *"if you come to me":* Quoted in Beck, *Budd Schulberg*, p. 48.

287 *"I cannot accept the idea":* Quoted in ibid.

289 *"who had been deeply hurt":* Brando with Lindsey, *Songs My Mother Taught Me*, p. 194.

291 *"So you've performed":* Quoted in Kazan, *A Life*, pp. 501–02.

292 *"my characteristic heavy-handed":* Ibid., p. 503.

292 *"The tension of the play":* *Tea and Sympathy* notebook, Wesleyan Cinema Archives. Subsequent comments by Kazan on the play are from the same source.

294 *"a sentimental play":* Walter Kerr, "The Theater," *New York Herald-Tribune*, Oct. 1. 1953.

294 *"as tidily and trickily organized":* Wolcott Gibbs, "The Theatre, Minority Report," *New Yorker*, Oct. 10, 1953.

294 *"A bear for structure":* Schulberg "The Inside Story of 'Waterfront.'"

294 *"maddeningly manipulative":* Ibid.

295 *"Boys, you're making a big mistake.":* Budd Schulberg, interview with author. His analysis of the Kazans' relationship is from the same source.

296 *"This is a young man":* Eva Marie Saint, interview with author. All other quotations attributed to her are from this source.

296 *"When I watch it':* Elia Kazan, interview with author.

297 *"Externally, he's very gritty":* Ibid.

297 *"He's like an enormous":* Kazan, *On the Waterfront* notebook, Wesleyan Cinema Archives.

297 *"really wants to be photographing":* Kazan to Brando, Nov. 2, 1953. Wesleyan Cinema Archive (included with production notebook). Subsequent analysis of Terry Malloy's character by Kazan is drawn from the same source.

299 *"I was trained to work":* Elia Kazan, interview with author.

300 *"You know, it's so fuckin' cold":* Quoted in Beck, *Budd Schulberg,* p. 56.

300 *"Stop the shit":* Ibid.

300 *"just say the words":* Quoted in Eva Marie Saint, interview with author.

304 *"I didn't do any directing":* Elia Kazan, interview with author.

304 *"I heard music":* Quoted in Jon Burlingame, "Leonard Bernstein and *On the Waterfront,"* in Joanna E. Rapf, ed., *On the Waterfront,* p. 127.

306 *"I'm not going to identify them":* Quoted in Archer Winsten, "Archer Winsten's Reviewing Stand: Elia Kazan Defends Himself," *New York Post,* Aug. 30, 1954.

307 *"anti-democratic, anti-labor":* John Howard Lawson, "Hollywood on the Waterfront: Union Leaders Are Gangsters, Workers Are Helpless," *Hollywood Review,* Nov./Dec. 1954.

307 *"implicitly (if unconsciously) Fascist":* Lindsay Anderson, "The Last Sequence of *On the Waterfront,"* *Sight and Sound* 24, January–March 1955.

309 *"Their children will grow up":* Biskind, *Seeing Is Believing,* p. 182.

309 *"Kazan, like his fellow pluralists":* Ibid., p. 179.

310 *"Playing the informer":* Ibid., p. 170.

311 *"people I knew":* Martin Scorsese, interview with author.

311 *"Kazan was forging":* Scorsese and Wilson, *A Personal Journey with Martin Scorsese Through American Movies,* p. 148.

312 *"I was watching":* Rick Lyman, "Watching Movies with Barry Levinson," *New York Times,* April 21, 2002.

Chapter 14: Country Roads

313 *"Why do I have to pay":* Quoted in Kazan, *East of Eden* notebook, Wesleyan Cinema Archives.

314 *"certainly a socialist":* Kazan, *A Life,* p. 533.

314 *"[A] good and honest man":* Quoted in Parini, *John Steinbeck,* p. 356.

315 *"You've got it":* Quoted in Kazan, *A Life,* p. 534.

316 *cinematic pastoral tradition:* For a longer discussion of this point, see Michel Ciment, "Terence Malick's Garden: Days of Heaven" in Ciment and Kardish, eds., *Positif 50 Years,* pp. 195–201.

316 *"CinemaScope could suit":* Scorsese and Wilson, *A Personal Journey with Martin Scorsese Through American Movies,* p. 89.

317 *"a heap of twisted legs":* Kazan, *A Life,* p. 534.

317 *"Do you want to ride":* Quoted in Elia Kazan, interview with author.

318 *"you make your own luck":* Quoted in Elia Kazan, interview with author.

318 *"Dean was impossible":* Ibid.

320 *"gradually I got":* Ibid.

320 *"Don't complicate it":* Kazan, *East of Eden* notebook, Wesleyan Cinema Archives.

321 *"A terribly important":* Ibid.

321 *"[W]hen I was making":* Elia Kazan, interview with author.

322 *"You can load the kid":* Ibid.

324 *"Sometimes he jumps":* John McCarten, "The Current Cinema," *New Yorker,* March 19, 1955.

325 *"Out of gas":* Quoted in Pauly, *An American Odyssey,* p. 202.

328 *"When we do come":* Walter Kerr, "Theater, Cat on a Hot Tin Roof," *New York Herald-Tribune,* March 25, 1955.

328 *"Their innocence, their blindness":* Tennessee Williams to Elia Kazan, Nov. 31, 1954, in Devlin and Tischles, eds., *The Selected Letters of Tennessee Williams,* p. 556.

329 *"working as a writer"* Quoted in Spoto, *The Kindness of Strangers,* p. 202.

331 *"is almost defeated":* Kazan, *Baby Doll* notebook, Wesleyan Cinema Archives.

331 *"What is it?"* Quoted in Paul Sylbert, interview with author.

332 *"I like the way":* Elia Kazan, interview with author.

332 *"a very cute movie":* Elia Kazan, interview with author.

333 *"The revolting theme":* Quoted in "Cardinal Scores 'Baby Doll' Film," *New York Times,* Dec. 17, 1956.

334 *"That old priest":* Elia Kazan, interview with author.

334 *"There really wasn't much sex"*: Ibid.

335 *"trashy, vicious people"*: Bosley Crowther, "Screen: Streetcar and Tobacco Road," *New York Times*, Dec. 18, 1956.

335 *"some comprehension and compassion"*: Bosley Crowther, "The Proper Drama of Mankind," *New York Times*, Jan. 6, 1957.

335 *"mean, petty"*: Arthur Knight, "SR Goes to the Movies: The Williams-Kazan Axis," *Saturday Review of Literature*, Dec. 29, 1956.

335 *"just possibly the dirtiest"*: "Cinema: New Picture," *Time*, Dec. 24, 1956.

336 *"I was talking"*: Budd Schulberg, interview with author.

337 *"We got the feeling"*: Elia Kazan, interview with author.

340 *"Andy Griffith?"*: Ibid.

340 *"ABOVE ALL"*: Elia Kazan, *A Face in the Crowd,* notebook.

342 *"This has to be Daumier"*: Ibid.

342 *"except for the last three minutes"*: Elia Kazan, interview with author.

344 *"stool pigeon witnesses"*: Quoted in Kazan, *A Life*, p. 566.

344 *"It never got the credit"*: Howard Rosenberg, "'Face in the Crowd' Saw the Danger," *Los Angeles Times*, Aug. 14, 2000.

Chapter 15: In Middle America

346 *"Molly, if we ever have to cross"*: Karl Malden, interview with author.

347 *"If she wants to walk"*: Quoted in Lewis Funke, "Rialto Gossip," *New York Times*, Oct. 6, 1957.

348 *"To arrange for the triumphant"*: Brooks Atkinson, "Theatre: 'The Egghead,'" *New York Times*, Oct. 10, 1957.

348 *"It has not that"*: Walter Kerr, "Theater: 'The Egghead,'" *New York Herald-Tribune*, Oct. 10, 1957.

348 *"The audience felt"*: Kazan, *A Life*, pp. 570–71.

350 *"His voice is almost a stylization"*: Kazan, *The Dark at the Top of the Stairs* notebook, Wesleyan Cinema Archives.

353 *"I've done everything"*: Quoted in Dean Ross, "Let It Open, Says Kazan, Its Director," *New York Herald-Tribune*, Dec. 1, 1957.

353 *"Although the style"*: Brooks Atkinson, "The Theatre: 'Illuminations by Inge,'" *New York Times*, Dec. 6, 1957.

353   *"more terror than the dark stairwell"*: Walter Kerr, "First Night Report: Walter Kerr's Review," *New York Herald-Tribune,* Dec. 6, 1957.

354   *"All of them are as intellectually"*: Kenneth Tynan, "In the Family" in Tynan, *Curtains,* pp. 274–76.

354   *"Over the placid lake"*: Robert Brustein, "The Man-taming Women of William Inge," *Harper's,* November 1958.

354   *"not distinguished"*: Elia Kazan, "The Plays I Directed" in Ciment, ed., *Elia Kazan,* pp. 167–68.

355   *"Look—for the rest of your life"*: Quoted in Pauly, *An American Odyssey,* p. 224.

356   *"to convince one of the moral necessity"*: Edmund Wilson, "The Muse Out of Work," in Wilson, *The Shores of Light,* p. 202.

357   *"Gadge, like other great directors"*: Quoted in Elia Kazan and Archibald MacLeish, "The Staging of a Play," *Esquire,* May 1959.

358   *"Not the phony manner"*: Kazan, *J.B.* notebook, Wesleyan Cinema Archives.

358   *"If they keep the evening"*: Walter Kerr, "Theater: MacLeish Drama Based on the Story of Job," *New York Herald-Tribune,* Dec. 30, 1958.

358   *"Mr. MacLeish has written"*: Brooks Atkinson, "Theatre: MacLeish's J.B.," *New York Times,* Dec. 12, 1958.

358   *"on the assumption"*: Kenneth Tynan, review of *The Cold Wind and the Warm* and *J.B.* in Tynan, *Curtains,* p. 294.

359   *"J.B. is a play"*: Ciment, ed., *Elia Kazan,* p. 169.

360   *"stop forcing myself"*: Elia Kazan, *A Life,* p. 546

360   *"It seems to me"*: Kazan to Tennessee Williams, reprinted in ibid., p. 190.

361   *"Williams's drafts were so rough"*: Quoted in Spoto, *The Kindness of Strangers,* p. 229.

361   *"he was always"*: Quoted in ibid., p. 230.

362   *"Show Chance surrounded"*: Kazan, *Sweet Bird of Youth* notebook, Wesleyan Cinema Archives.

364   *"a relaxed mood"*: Brooks Atkinson, "The Theatre: Portrait of Corruption," *New York Times,* March 11, 1959.

364   *"This is the noise"*: Walter Kerr, "First Night Report: 'Sweet Bird of Youth,'" *New York Herald-Tribune,* March 11, 1959.

366   *"YOU KNEW ALL ABOUT IT"*: Kazan, *Wild River* notebook, Wesleyan Cinema Archives.

367 *"love affair with the people":* Quoted in Ciment, *Kazan on Kazan,* p. 132.

367 *"AND ABOVE ALL":* Ibid.

369 *"He was a dutiful kid":* Elia Kazan, interview with author.

370 *"Monty, I don't want you":* Quoted in ibid.

370 *"They liked him.":* Ibid.

371 *"I exaggerated it":* Ibid.

371 *"laconic, pictorial":* *Wild River* notebook, Wesleyan Cinema Archives.

372 *"Never thought of it":* Elia Kazan, interview with author.

373 *"Bill Inge understood":* Warren Beatty, interview with author.

373 *"He seems like a hack":* Elia Kazan, interview with author.

373 *"I was very proud":* Ibid.

374 *"murderers," no less:* Kazan, *Splendor in the Grass* notebook, Wesleyan Cinema Archives.

376 *"I liked Warren right away.":* Quoted in Frank Rich, "Warren Beatty Strikes Again," *New York Times,* July 3, 1978.

376 *"He gave me a larger portion":* Warren Beatty, interview with author.

377 *"Lemme ask you something":* Ibid.

378 *"I'm still afraid":* Quoted in ibid.

378 *"I think the whole middle class":* Elia Kazan, interview with author.

Chapter 16: Tragedy and Failures

381 *"I made up my mind":* Elia Kazan, interview with author. Subsequent comments on *America, America*'s historical roots are from the same source.

383 *"Among the things":* Kazan, *America, America* notebook, Wesleyan Cinema Archives. Other comments on the structure of the film are from the same source.

385 *"when it is commercialism":* Robert Brustein, "Repertory Fever," *Harper's,* December 1960.

386 *"disgusted":* Quoted in Arthur Gelb, "Elia Kazan to End Relationship with the Theatre of Broadway," *New York Times,* April 7, 1961.

387 *"going into areas":* Elia Kazan, interview with author.

388 Kazan's account of the Strasberg/Lincoln Center discussions is in *A Life,* pp. 585–87, 607–09, 631–33.

391 *"The boy Stavros":* S. N. Behrman, "The Effrontery of a Director," introduction to Kazan, *America, America,* p. 15.

392 *"His father was a leftist":* Elia Kazan, interview with author.

395 *"I just wanted your reaction":* Haskell Wexler, interview with author. Other quotations from Wexler are from the same source.

398 *"He could sleep anytime, anywhere":* Dede Allen, interview with author.

400 *"In the intervening years":* Miller, *Timebends,* p. 529.

401 *"placate and look up to":* Kazan, *After the Fall* notebook, Wesleyan Cinema Archives.

401 *"Every person in this play":* Ibid.

402 *"Maggie is a barbarian":* Ibid.

402 *"I notice something":* Ibid.

404 *"After all these terrible years":* Robert Brustein, "Arthur Miller's Mea Culpa," *New Republic,* Feb. 8, 1964.

406 *"If Mr. Kazan's picture":* Bosley Crowther, "Screen: A Tribute to the Great Immigration," *New York Times,* Dec. 16, 1963.

406 *"A masterful motion picture":* Judith Crist, "Kazan's 'America America' Is Rich Tapestry of Truth," *New York Herald-Tribune,* Dec. 16, 1963.

407 *"I felt that no political cause":* Kazan, *A Life,* p. 685.

408 *"It was a chilly company":* Hal Holbrook, interview with author. Other quotations from Holbrook are from the same source.

409 *"Which to celebrate first?":* Howard Taubman, "Theater: 'After the Fall,'" *New York Times,* Jan. 24, 1964.

409 *"'After the Fall' resembles":* Walter Kerr, "Miller's 'After the Fall'— As Walter Kerr Sees It," *New York Herald-Tribune,* Jan. 24, 1964.

409 *"a shameless piece of tabloid":* Brustein, "Arthur Miller's Mea Culpa," op. cit.

409 *"More a young author's":* Gordon Rogoff, "Theatre, *Nation,* Feb. 10, 1964.

409 *"has engaged in a process":* Richard Gilman, "The Stage: Still Falling," *Commonweal,* Feb. 14, 1964.

409 *"Arthur Miller's mind":* John Simon, "The Theatre," *Hudson Review,* Summer, 1964.

413 *"Harold Clurman was once":* But for Whom, *Charlie* notebook, Wesleyan Cinema Archives.

413 *"Behrman's people entertain":* Ibid.

413 *"I think there are many cogent":* Quoted in Milton Esterow, "Kazan May Quit Lincoln Theater," *New York Times,* Dec. 10, 1964.

414 *"It's an ironic":* Kazan, *The Changeling* notebook, Wesleyan Cinema Archives.

416 *"like a high school production":* Austin Pendleton, interview with author.

416 *"I don't think 'The Changeling'":* Quoted in Esterow, op. cit.

Chapter 17: Picking Up the Pieces

418 *"the only way I could get":* Kazan, *The Arrangement,* p. 242.

420 *"I had more pleasure":* Quoted in Haskel Frankel, "Son of the Oven Maker," *Saturday Review,* March 4, 1967.

420 *"Because he came out of the theater":* Anonymous, interview with Sol Stein, *People* carbons, Time Inc. Edit Ref., Oct. 30, 1978. All other quotations from Stein are from the same source.

421 *"The best thing about the novel":* Eliot Fremont-Smith, "Books of the Times, All About Eddie," *New York Times,* Feb. 21, 1967.

421 *"He is the real rebel":* Melvin Maddocks, "Kazan's Balled Fist," *Christian Science Monitor,* March 2, 1967.

421 *"He totters, staggers, eventually marches":* Eleanor Perry, "A Phony's Fight to Get Human," *Life,* Feb. 17, 1967.

422 *"I think I goofed":* Elia Kazan, interview with author.

423 *"a pretentious potboiler":* Arthur Laurents, interview with author. All other quotations from Laurents are from the same source.

423 *"I'm too old to pump":* Elia Kazan to Marlon Brando, no date, quoted in Kazan, *A Life,* pp. 750–52.

425 *"was his usual upbeat":* Carol Rossen, interview with author. All other quotations from Rossen are from the same source.

428 *"a curious spectacle":* Richard Schickel, "A Worse Movie of a Bad Book," *Life,* Dec. 12, 1969.

428 *"How can Kazan be messianic":* Pauline Kael, "The Current Cinema, Kazan's Latest Arrangements," *New Yorker,* Nov. 22, 1969.

429 *"Sometimes I should give up":* Anonymous, interview with Kazan, *People* carbon files, Time Inc. Edit. Ref., Oct. 30, 1978.

431 *"She [Molly] was very cultivated":* Patricia Bosworth, interview with author. All other quotations from Bosworth are from the same source.

431 *"I hope I never adjust":* Quoted in Brad Darrach, "Parting Shots, *Life,* June 15, 1972.

434 *"there was a tenuous quality":* Nick Proferes, interview with author. All other quotations from Proferes are from the same source.

434 *"everything—from the physical production":* Vincent Canby, "'The Visitors' Portrays Ordeal of a Threatened G.I.," *New York Times,* Feb. 8, 1972.

435 *"She was frightened":* Jeanine Basinger, interview with author. All other quotations from Basinger are from the same source.

439 *"Perhaps it is necessary":* Kazan, *Last Tycoon* notebook, Wesleyan Cinema Archives.

440 *"We watch it as if at":* Vincent Canby, "'Tycoon' Echoes 30's Hollywood," *New York Times,* Nov. 18, 1976.

442 *"pugnacious, confrontational":* Arthur Penn, interview with author.

442 *"Dawn. Early Greece. Hit it!":* Quoted by Cathleen Leslie, interview with author.

443 *"was not the right place":* Corinne Chateau, interview with author.

443 *"So, OK, I did finish":* Elia Kazan to Cathleen Leslie, undated letter.

443 *"an effort to get even":* "Kazan on Greek Visit Relives Heritage and Charts Future," *New York Times,* April 29, 1978.

444 *"I read John Huston's autobiography":* Quoted in Alvin P. Sanoff, "I'm Not Afraid of Anything," *U.S. News and World Report,* June 6, 1988. Reprinted in Baer, ed., *Elia Kazan Interviews,* pp. 239–41.

445 *This was not necessarily fatal:* For an account of this incident, from Dassin's point of view, see McGilligan and Buhle, *Tender Comrades,* p. 215.

Epilogue: The Charm of It

448 *"Anyone watching could see":* Neal Gabler, "Why the Drama Never Ends," *Los Angeles Times,* March 21, 1999.

449 *"Funded by the Soviet Union":* Alan Wolfe, "Revising a False History," *Los Angeles Times,* March 21, 1999.

452 *"I was more overwrought":* Quoted in Patrick Goldstein, "Many Refuse to Clap as Kazan Receives Oscar," *Los Angeles Times,* March 22, 1999.

452 *"In this town of stories":* Shawn Hubler, "At Oscars, Poignancy Prevails Over Phoniness," *Los Angeles Times,* March 25, 1999.

453 *"Fuck you, Pete":* Quoted in Haskell Wexler, interview with author.

453 *"I believe that in America":* Kazan, *Beyond the Aegean,* p. 447.

455 *"the cunning of a trader":* Kazan, *On What Makes a Director,* p. 21. All subsequent quotations from Kazan on this topic are from the same source.

Bibliography

This bibliography confines itself to the books and articles that are directly quoted in this book or that significantly influenced its writing. A list of individuals interviewed by the author will be found in the "Author's Note" at the beginning of the volume. Elia Kazan's production notebooks, all held at the Wesleyan Cinema Archives, are cited, where appropriate, in the Notes, but are not bibliographed. It seemed superfluous to mention them again here. In order not to further burden this bibliography, many brief citations from the reviews of plays and films Kazan acted in or directed, included in the text to give a general sense of these works' critical reception, have not been cited here. Full citations for more lengthily quoted critical works are cited. The attentive reader will observe that the author has been drawn more toward the journalistic than the theoretical for sources. Most of the longer critical considerations of, for example, Arthur Miller's or Tennessee Williams's plays that Elia Kazan directed, seem to me not to have worn very well, and I have quoted from them sparingly. The purely journalistic articles—locating Kazan in the landscape of this or that historical moment—proved more useful and interesting to me.

Books

Anderson, Maxwell. *Truckline Café.* Proscenium Press, 1985.

Ardrey, Robert. *Casey Jones.* Ms. Wesleyan Cinema Archives.

———. *Thunder Rock.* Dramatists Play Service, n.d.

Arendt, Arthur. *It's Up to You.* Ms. Wesleyan Cinema Archives.

Atkinson, Brooks, and Al Hirschfeld. *The Lively Years, 1920-1973.* Da Capo Press, 1985.

Bach, Steven. *Dazzler: The Life and Times of Moss Hart.* Alfred A. Knopf, 2001.

Baer, William, ed. *Elia Kazan Interviews.* University Press of Mississippi, 2000.

Bankhead, Tallulah. *Tallulah: My Autobiography.* Harper & Brothers, 1952.

Basinger, Jeanine, John Frazer, and Joseph W. Reed, Jr., eds. *Working with Kazan.* Wesleyan University, 1973.

Beck, Nicholas. *Budd Schulberg: A Bio-Bibliography.* Scarecrow Press. 2001.

Behrman, S. N. *But for Whom Charlie.* Ms. Wesleyan Cinema Archives.

———. *Dunnigan's Daughter.* Ms. Wesleyan Cinema Archives.

———. *People in a Diary.* Little, Brown, 1972.

Bentley, Eric. *In Search of Theater.* Vintage Books, 1957.

———, ed. *Thirty Years of Treason.* Viking Press, 1971.

———. *What Is Theatre?* Limelight Editions, 1984.

Billingsley, Kenneth Lloyd. *Hollywood Party.* Forum (Rocklin, Ca.) 1998.

Biskind, Peter. *Seeing Is Believing: How Hollywood Taught Us to Stop Worrying and Love the Fifties.* Pantheon Books, 1983.

Brando, Marlon, with Robert Lindsey. *Songs My Mother Taught Me.* Random House, 1994.

Braudy, Leo. *The World in a Frame: What We See in Films.* Anchor Press/Doubleday, 1976.

Brenman-Gibson, Margaret. *Clifford Odets, American Playwright: The Years from 1906 to 1940.* Atheneum, 1981.

Carey, Gary and Joseph L. Mankiewicz. *More About All About Eve.* Random House, 1972

Carroll, Paul Vincent. *The Strings My Lord Are False.* Ms. Wesleyan Cinema Archives.

Ceplair, Larry, and Steven Englund. *The Inquisition in Hollywood.* Anchor Press/Doubleday, 1980.

Ciment, Michel, ed. *Elia Kazan: An American Odyssey.* Bloomsbury Publishing (London), 1988.

———. *Kazan on Kazan.* Viking Press, 1974.

Ciment, Michel, and Laurence Kardish, eds. *Positif 50 Years: Selections from the French Film Journal.* Museum of Modern Art, 2002.

Clurman, Harold. *The Fervent Years.* Hill and Wang, 1957.

Cronin, Hume. *A Terrible Liar.* William Morrow, 1991.

Devlin, Albert J., and Nancy M. Tischler, eds. *The Selected Letters of Tennessee Williams, Volume I, 1920–45.* New Directions, 2000.

Dunne, Philip. *Take Two,* McGraw-Hill, 1980.

d'Usseau, Arnaud and James Gow. *Deep Are the Roots.* Dramatists Play Service, n.d.

————. *The Selected Letters of Tennessee Williams, Vol II, 1948–1957.* New Directions, 2004.

Eisenschitz, Bernard. *Nicholas Ray: An American Journey.* Faber and Faber (London), 1993.

Eyman, Scott. *Print the Legend: The Life and Times of John Ford.* Simon and Schuster, 1999.

Gallagher, Dorothy. *All the Right Enemies: The Life and Murder of Carlo Tresca.* Penguin Books, 1989.

Geist, Kenneth L. *People Will Talk: The Life and Films of Joseph L. Mankiewicz.* Charles Scribner's Sons, 1978.

Gill, Brendan. *Tallulah.* Holt, Rinehart & Winston, 1972.

Gornick, Vivian. *The Romance of American Communism.* Basic Books, 1971.

Gottfried, Martin. *Arthur Miller: His Life and Work.* Da Capo Press, 2003.

Harrison, Gilbert A. *The Enthusiast: A Life of Thornton Wilder.* Ticknor & Fields, 1985.

Haynes, John Earl, and Harvey Klehr. *Venona: Decoding Soviet Espionage in America.* Yale Nota Bene, 2000.

Haynes, John Earl. *Red Scare or Red Menace?* Ivan R. Dee, 1996.

Hirsch, Foster. *Kurt Weill on Stage.* Alfred A. Knopf, 2002.

————. *A Method to Their Madness: The History of the Actors Studio.* W.W. Norton, 1984.

Hook, Sidney. *Heresy Yes, Conspiracy No.* John Day, 1953.

Inge, William. *The Dark at the Top of the Stairs.* Dramatists Play Service, n.d.

Kazan, Elia. *Acts of Love.* Alfred A. Knopf, 1978.

————. *America, America.* Popular Library, 1964.

————. *The Anatolian.* Alfred A. Knopf, 1982.

————. *The Arrangement.* Stein and Day, 1967.

————. *The Assassins.* Stein and Day, 1971.

————. *A Life.* Alfred A. Knopf, 1988.

————. *Beyond the Aegean.* Alfred A. Knopf, 1994.

————. *On What Makes a Director.* Directors Guild of America, 1973.

————. *The Understudy.* Stein and Day, 1974.

Kazan, Nicholas. "On Receiving 'Notes,'" *Written By: The Magazine of the Writers Guild of America, West,* January, 2005.

Kempton, Murray. *Part Of Our Time: Some Ruins and Monuments of the Thirties.* Simon & Schuster, 1955.

Klehr, Harvey, John Earl Haynes, and Fridrikh Igorevich Firsov. *The Secret World of American Communism.* Yale University Press, 1995.

Kraf, Hy S. *Café Crown.* Ms. Wesleyan Cinema Archive.

Laurents, Arthur. *Jolson Sings Again.* Ms. in possession of author.

Leff, Leonard J., and Jerold L. Simmons. *Dame in the Kimono: Hollywood, Censorship and the Production Code from the 1920s to the 1960s.* Grove Weidenfeld, 1990.

Lewis, Robert. *Slings and Arrows: Theater in My Life.* Stein and Day, 1984.

Loggia, Marjorie, and Glenn Young, eds. *The Collected Works of Harold Clurman.* Applause Books, 1994.

McCarthy, Mary. *Sights and Spectacles: Theatre Chronicles 1937–1956.* Meridian Books, 1957.

McGilligan, Pat, and Paul Buhle. *Tender Comrades: A Backstory of the Hollywood Blacklist.* St. Martin's Press, 1997.

MacLeish, Archibald. *J.B.* Samuel French, n.d.

Malden, Karl, with Carla Malden. *When Do I Start?* Simon & Schuster, 1997.

Miller, Arthur. *After the Fall.* Dramatists Play Service, n.d.

———. *All My Sons.* Penquin Books, 2000.

———. *Death of a Salesman.* Viking Press, 1960.

———. *The Hook: A Play for the Screen.* Ms. Arthur Miller Archive at the Henry Ransom Library, University of Texas.

———. *Timebends.* Grove Press, 1987.

Navasky, Victor S. *Naming Names.* Viking Press, 1980.

Odets, Clifford. *Waiting for Lefty and Other Plays.* Grove Press, n.d.

Page, Tim. *Dawn Powell: A Biography.* Henry Holt, 1998.

Parini, Jay. *John Steinbeck: A Biography.* Henry Holt, 1995.

Pauly, Thomas H. *An American Odyssey: Elia Kazan and American Culture.* Temple University Press, 1983.

Perelman, S.J., and Ogden Nash. *One Touch of Venus.* Ms. Wesleyan Cinema Archive.

Powers, Thomas. *Intelligence Wars: America's Secret History from Hitler to al-Qaeda.* New York Review of Books, 2002.

Rapf, Joanna E., ed. *On the Waterfront,* Cambridge University Press, 2003.

Ross, Lillian, and Helen Ross. *The Player: A Profile of an Art.* Limelight Editions, 1984.

Scorsese, Martin, and Henry Wilson. *A Personal Journey Through American Movies with Martin Scorsese.* Miramax, Hyperion, British Film Institute, 1997.

Selznick, Irene Mayer. *A Private View.* Alfred A. Knopf, 1983.

Shaw, Irwin. *Quiet City.* Ms. Wesleyan Cinema Archive.

Sklar, Robert. *City Boys: Cagney, Bogart, Garfield.* Princeton University Press, 1994.

Smith, Wendy. *Real Life Drama: The Group Theatre and America*. Alfred
    A. Knopf, 1990.
Spoto, Donald. *The Kindness of Strangers: The Life of Tennessee Williams*.
    Little, Brown, 1985.
Tabori, George. *Flight Into Egypt*. Ms. Wesleyan Cinema Archive.
Thomas, Tony. *The Films of Marlon Brando*. The Citadel Press, 1973.
Trumbo, Dalton. *Additional Dialogue: Letters of Dalton Trumbo, 1942–1962*.
    Edited by Helen Manfull. M. Evans, 1970.
Turkus, Burton B., and Sid Feder. *Murder, Inc.: The Story of the Syndicate*.
    Da Capo Press, 1992.
Tynan, Kenneth. *Curtains*. Atheneum, 1961.
Wilder, Thornton. *The Skin of Our Teeth*. Samuel French, n.d.
Williams, Tennessee. *Camino Real*. Dramatists Play Service, n.d.
————. *Cat on a Hot Tin Roof*. Signet, n.d.
————. *A Streetcar Named Desire*. Dramatists Play Service, n.d.
————. *Sweet Bird of Youth*. Dramatists Play Service, n.d.
Wilson, Edmund. *Classics and Commercials: A Literary Chronicle of the
    Forties*. Farrar Straus, 1950.
————. *The Shores of Light: A Literary Chronicle of the Twenties and
    Thirties*. Farrar, Straus and Young, 1952.
Young, Jeff. *Kazan: The Master Director Discusses His Films*. Newmarket
    Press, 1999.

Newspaper and Magazine Articles

Anonymous. "Cardinal Scores 'Baby Doll' Film." *New York Times*, Dec. 17,
    1956.
————. "The Group Theatre of Motion Pictures." *Variety*, April 21, 1937.
————. "Kazan on Greek Visit Relives Heritage and Charts Future." *New
    York Times*, April 29, 1978.
————. "'Sol' Stein, interview, *People* carbon files, Time Inc., Edit Refer-
    ence archive, Oct 30, 1978.
Archerd, Army. "Just for Variety," *Variety*, Feb. 23, 1999.
Beebe, Lucius. "Stage Asides: The Happiness of Elia Kazan." *New York
    Herald-Tribune*, April 4, 1943.
Braggiotti, Mary. "Names Don't Make a Hit." *New York Post*, Feb. 17,
    1947.
Brewer, Roy. "Letters (Calendar)." *The Los Angeles Times*, Sept. 14, 2003.
Brustein, Robert. "America's New Cultural Hero." *Commentary*, Fall,
    1958.

————. "Arthur Miller's Mea Culpa." *New Republic,* February 8, 1964.

————. "Repertory Fever." *Harper's*, December 1960.

————. "The Man-taming Women of William Inge." *Harper's*, November 1958.

Byron, Stuart, and Martin L. Rubin. "Elia Kazan Interview." *Movie,* Winter, 1971–72.

Cohen, Elliott E. "Mr. Zanuck's 'Gentleman's Agreement.'" *Commentary,* January 1948.

Darrach, Brad. "Parting Shots." *Life,* June 15, 1972.

Eagleton, Terry. "Porkchops and Pineapples." *London Review of Books,* Oct. 23, 2003.

Estrow, Milton. "Baby Doll in Brooklyn and Flatbush." *New York Times,* Feb. 26, 1956.

————. "Kazan May Quit Lincoln Center." *New York Times,* Dec. 10, 1964.

Gabler, Neal. "Why the Drama Never Ends." *Los Angeles Times,* March 21, 1999.

Garfield, Allen. "Counterpunch: Despite Talent, Kazan Doesn't Deserve Honorary Oscar." *Los Angeles Times,* Jan. 25, 1999.

Gelb, Arthur. "Elia Kazan to End Relationship with the Theatre of Broadway." *New York Times,* April 7, 1961.

Goldstein, Patrick. "Film Director Elia Kazan to Receive Oscar, Forgiveness." *Los Angeles Times,* Jan. 10, 1999.

————. "Many Refuse to Clap as Kazan Receives Oscar." *Los Angeles Times,* March 22, 1999.

Hubler, Shawn. "At Oscars, Poignancy Prevails Over Phoniness." *Los Angeles Times,* March 25, 1999.

Isaacs, Hermine Rich. "First Rehearsals; Elia Kazan Directs a Modern Legend." *Theatre Arts,* March, 1944.

Jensen, Jeff. "Trophy Strife." *Entertainment Weekly,* Feb. 5, 1999.

Kazan, Elia. "Audience Tomorrow: Preview in New Guinea." *Theatre Arts,* October 1945.

————. "A Statement." *New York Times* (advertisement), April 12, 1952.

Kazan, Elia, and Archibald MacLeish. "The Staging of a Play." *Esquire,* May 1959.

Kracauer, Siegfried. "Those Movies with a Message." *Harper's,* June 1948.

Lahr, John. "Making Willy Loman." *The New Yorker,* Jan. 25, 1999.

Larson, John Howard. "Hollywood on the Waterfront; Union Leaders Are Gangsters, Workers Are Helpless." *Hollywood Review,* Nov.–Dec. 1954.

Lyman, Rick. "Watching Movies with Barry Levinson." *New York Times,* April 21, 2002.

Maltz, Albert. "Moving Forward." *The Worker,* April 7, 1946.

———. "What Shall We Ask of Writers." *New Masses,* Feb 12, 1946.

Meyer, Richard D., and Nancy Meyer. "Setting the Stage for Lincoln Center." *Theatre Arts,* January 1964.

Miller, Arthur. "With Respect for Her Agony—But with Love." *Life,* Feb. 7, 1964.

Murray, James. "Brando, Take One." Interview, *Time* magazine Edit Ref. library (Brando file).

Rich, Frank. "Warren Beatty Strikes Again." *New York Times,* July 3, 1978.

Rosenberg, Howard. "'Face in the Crowd' Saw the Danger." *Los Angeles Times,* Aug. 14, 2000.

Sanoff, Alvin P. "I'm Not Afraid of Anything." *U.S. News and World Report,* June 6, 1988.

Schickel, Richard. "An Oscar for Elia." *Time,* March 8, 1999.

———. "A Worse Movie of a Bad Book." *Life,* Dec. 12, 1969.

Schlesinger, Arthur. "Hollywood and Hypocrisy." *New York Times,* Feb. 28, 1999.

Schoenwald, Jonathan M. "Rewriting Revolution: The Origins, Production and Reception of Viva Zapata." *Film History* 8, no. 2 (1996).

Schulberg, Budd. "The Inside Story of 'Waterfront.'" *New York Times* (magazine), June 6, 1980.

Schumach, Murray. "A Director Named 'Gadge.'" *New York Times* (magazine), Nov. 9, 1947.

Weinraub, Bernard. "At the Movies." *New York Times,* March 12, 1999.

———. "Kazan Award Is Stirring Protest by Blacklist Survivors." *New York Times,* Feb. 23, 1999.

———. "Snubbed by Some, Kazan to Get an Honorary Oscar." *New York Times,* Jan. 13, 1999.

Weinstein, Allen. "Regrets, He's Had a Few; Enough to Be Forgiven." *Los Angeles Times,* March 17, 1999.

Winsten, Archer. "Archer Winsten's Reviewing Stand: Elia Kazan Defends Himself." *New York Post,* Aug. 30, 1954.

Wolfe, Alan. "Reviving a False History." *Los Angeles Times,* March 21, 1999.

Zolotow, Maurice. "Viewing the Kinetic Mr. Kazan." *New York Times,* March 9, 1952.

Index